WINCHESTER

Martial Rose Library
Tel: 01962 827306

To be returned on or before the day marked above, subject to recall.

KA 0311970 X

UNIVERSITY OF MANCHESTER

0311970X

Lancelot and the Grail

A study of the Prose *Lancelot*

ELSPETH KENNEDY

CLARENDON PRESS · OXFORD

Oxford University Press, Walton Street, Oxford OX2 6DP

Oxford New York Toronto
Delhi Bombay Calcutta Madras Karachi
Petaling Jaya Singapore Hong Kong Tokyo
Nairobi Dar es Salaam Cape Town
Melbourne Auckland

and associated companies in
Berlin Ibadan

Oxford is a trade mark of Oxford University Press

Published in the United States
by Oxford University Press, New York

© Elspeth Kennedy 1986

First published 1986
First issued as a paperback 1990

All rights reserved. No part of this publication may be reproduced,
stored in a retrieval system, or transmitted, in any form or by any means,
electronic, mechanical, photocopying, recording, or otherwise, without
the prior permission of Oxford University Press

This book is sold subject to the condition that it shall not, by way
of trade or otherwise, be lent, re-sold, hired out or otherwise circulated
without the publisher's prior consent in any form of binding or cover
other than that in which it is published and without a similar condition
including this condition being imposed on the subsequent purchaser

British Library Cataloguing in Publication Data

Kennedy, Elspeth
Lancelot and the grail: a study of the prose
Lancelot.
1. French fiction—To 1500--History and
criticism
1. Title
843.1 PQ151

ISBN 0-19-815170-5

Library of Congress Cataloging in Publication Data

Data available

Printed in Great Britain by
Biddles Ltd, Guildford and King's Lynn

I should like to acknowledge with gratitude a generous loan towards the publishing costs from the Eugene Vinaver Fund.

CONTENTS

ABBREVIATIONS

ALMA	*Arthurian Literature in the Middle Ages*, ed. R. S. Loomis (Oxford, 1959).
BBSIA	*Bulletin Bibliographique de la Société Internationale Arthurienne* (Paris and Nottingham).
Brut	Wace, *Le Roman de Brut*, ed. I. Arnold, SATF (Paris, 1938–40), 2 vols.
CCM	*Cahiers de Civilisation Médiévale* (Poitiers).
Char.	Chrétien de Troyes, *Le Chevalier de la Charrette*, ed. M. Roques, CFMA (Paris, 1958).
Cligés	Chrétien de Troyes, *Cligés*, ed. A. Micha, CFMA (Paris, 1957).
1st Cont.	*The First Perceval Continuation*, vols. I–III of W. Roach's edition of the *Perceval Continuations* (Philadelphia, 1949–55).
2nd Cont.	*The Second Perceval Continuation*, vol. IV in the above edition (Philadelphia, 1971).
Erec	Chrétien de Troyes, *Erec et Enide*, ed. M. Roques, CFMA (Paris, 1953).
Euph.	*Euphorion* (Heidelberg).
Frappier, *Étude*	J. Frappier, *Étude sur la Mort le roi Artu*, 3rd edn. (Genève, 1972).
Jos. or *Joseph*	Robert de Boron, *Estoire dou Saint Graal*, ed. W. A. Nitze, CFMA (1927).
Lanz.	Ulrich von Zatzikhoven, *Lanzelet*, ed. K. A. Hahn (Frankfurt, 1845).
LBD	Renaut de Beaujeu, *Li Biaus Descouneüs*, ed. G. Perrie Williams, CFMA (1967).
LM	*Lancelot: roman en prose du XIIIᵉ siècle*, ed. A. Micha (Paris-Genève, 1978–83), 9 vols. The roman numerals refer to chapters, the arabic to paragraphs; references will be to the long version unless there is indication to the contrary.
Lot, *Étude*	F. Lot, *Étude sur le Lancelot en prose* (Paris, 1918).
MA	*La Mort le roi Artu*, ed. J. Frappier, 3rd edn., TLF (Genève-Paris, 1964). The arabic numerals refer to paragraph and line numbers.
Meraugis	Raoul de Houdenc, *Meraugis de Portlesguez*, ed. M. Friedwagner (Halle, 1897).
Merl. or *Merlin*	Robert de Boron, *Merlin*, ed. A. Micha (Paris–Genève, 1980).

MLR	Modern Language Review (Cambridge).
Pauphilet, Études	A. Pauphilet, Études sur la Queste del Saint Graal attribuée à Gautier Map (Paris, 1921).
P. Char.	Le Roman en Prose de Lancelot du Lac: le Conte de la Charrette, ed. G. Hutchings (Paris, 1938). Corresponds to S IV, pp. 155–226, and LM, Chapters XXXVI–XLII.
Perc.	Chrétien de Troyes, Le Roman de Perceval ou le Conte du Graal, ed. W. Roach, TLF (Genève–Lille, 1956).
Perl.	Le Haut Livre du Graal: Perlesvaus, ed. W. A. Nitze and T. Jenkins (Chicago, 1932–7), 2 vols.
PL	Lancelot do Lac: the non-cyclic Old French Prose Romance, ed. E. Kennedy (Oxford, 1980). The arabic numerals refer to page and line.
PMLA	Publications of the Modern Language Association of America (New York).
PQ	Philological Quarterly (Iowa).
Q or Queste	La Queste del Saint Graal, ed. A. Pauphilet, CFMA (Paris, 1923). The arabic numerals refer to page and line numbers.
RF	Romanische Forschungen (Frankfurt-am-Main).
Rom.	Romania (Paris).
Le Roman jusqu'à la fin du XIIIe siècle	Jean Frappier and Reinhold R. Grimm, ed., Le roman jusqu'à la fin du XIIIe siècle, vol. I (Partie historique) (Grundriss der romanischen Literaturen des Mittelalters IV/1) (Heidelberg, 1978).
Romans du Graal	Les Romans du Graal aux XIIe et XIIIe siècles, Colloques Internationaux du Centre National de la Recherche Scientifique, iii (Paris, 1956).
R.Ph.	Romance Philology (Berkeley).
RR	Romanic Review (Columbia University).
S	The Vulgate Version of the Arthurian Romances, ed. H. O. Sommer (Washington, 1909–13), 7 vols. The roman numerals refer to the volume, the arabic to page and line numbers.
TL	A. Tobler and E. Lommatzsch, Altfranzösisches Wörterbuch (Berlin, from 1925).
Trist.	Beroul, Le Roman de Tristan, ed. A. Ewert (Oxford, vol. I, 1958, vol. II, 1970).
V. Rag.	Raoul de Houdenc, La Vengeance Raguidel, ed. M. Friedwagner (Halle, 1909).
Yvain	Chrétien de Troyes, Le Chevalier au Lion (Yvain), ed. M. Roques, CFMA (Paris, 1960).

Z.f.d.A.   *Zeitschrift für deutsches Altertum* (Wiesbaden).
Z.f.fr.Spr.u.Lit.   *Zeitschrift für französische Sprache und Literatur* (Wiesbaden).
Z.f.rom.Phil.   *Zeitschrift für romanische Philologie* (Tübingen).

INTRODUCTION

Lancelot and the Grail would seem to represent opposite poles—the hero whose love for Arthur's Queen inspires him to become the greatest of all knights, and the holy vessel, from its first appearance (in Chrétien's *Conte del Graal*) described in a context of Christian ritual as 'sainte chose' and in the Vulgate *Queste* only to be approached by chaste or virgin knights. Yet these two themes and that of the Death of Arthur are combined in the *Lancelot-Grail* cycle. This vast work fills six volumes in Sommer's edition, starting with an early History of the Grail, followed by a *Merlin*, giving an account of the birth of Merlin, the early history of Arthur's reign (based on Robert de Boron), and a *suite* leading up to the three volumes of the *Lancelot propre* (volumes III, IV, and V), the last of which prepares the way for the *Queste*. The cycle ends with *la Mort Artu*. The contrasts and contradictions (including a reference to Perceval/Perlesvaus as Grailwinner and accomplisher of the adventure of the Perilous Seat) within a closely interlacing structure have puzzled and fascinated scholars for more than a hundred years. E. Brugger believed that the Vulgate Cycle was preceded by one combining a *Prose Lancelot* with a *Queste* of which Perceval or Perlesvaus was the hero, and had evolved through a series of major interpolations.[1] J. D. Bruce too emphasized what he saw as the disunity of the work and ascribed a major role to interpolators and *remanieurs*.[2] A. Pauphilet also denied the existence of a plan established in advance for the organization of the cycle.[3] F. Lot, on the other hand, in his pioneering and fundamental study of the *Lancelot*, emphasized the unity of the cycle and argued that a single author wrote the *Lancelot propre*, the *Queste*, the *Mort Artu*, even the *Estoire del Graal*; only the *Merlin* and its *suite* did he accept as a later addition.[4] J. Frappier in his great study of *la Mort Artu* advances most persuasively the theory of an architect who controlled a team of writers, rather than a single author, to explain what he termed the 'unity and diversity' of the *Lancelot-Grail* cycle.[5] However, he does not succeed in producing a satisfactory explanation for the puzzling change in Grailwinner, any more than does A. Micha who also writes eloquently on the unity of the work in other respects.[6] I will discuss this problem of the Grail reference in Chapter VI, 'Grail Allusions'.

Until comparatively recently, scholars, while aware of the existence of two versions of the episodes following Lancelot's installation as a Knight of the Round Table, that is the Journey to Sorelois and the False Guinevere episode, compared the two in terms of adventures designed to form part of a cycle

1

including the Grail, without realizing (because they had not been able to study all the manuscripts) that the shorter of the two versions forms the conclusion of a non-cyclic Prose *Lancelot*. In Part I of this book I propose to examine this 'Prose *Lancelot* without the Grail' to determine whether it has a sufficiently coherent structure of its own for it not to be dismissed as a lopping off of one section of an existing *Lancelot-Grail* cycle, without form or *sen*. In so doing I will see whether the Grail allusions within the account of Lancelot's early adventures, which conflict with later developments in the cycle, would fit in with a system of allusions outwards to Arthurian traditions already familiar to the readers. In Part II I will study the hypothesis of the bringing together of Lancelot and the Grail within the same work in terms of a 'rewriting' of an existing romance. 'Rewriting' can be taken in a literal sense as far as the Journey to Sorelois and the False Guinevere episode are concerned, where a new, longer version would seem to have replaced an existing one. It has the figurative sense of 'reinterpretation' in relation to the account of Lancelot's childhood and adventures up to his gaining of a seat at the Round Table (at the end of Sommer III); these events can now be seen in a different light within a new structure, whether through direct comments of characters such as hermits on the past or through a series of significant contrasts and parallels, brought out by the adventures themselves. At this stage and in this book I will be concerned with structures rather than authors (single or multiple) or 'architects' or 'planners', fascinating though it would be to speculate on the 'who' and the 'why'. However a study of the 'how' may itself suggest possible motives behind this remarkable literary transformation.

PART ONE

Lancelot without the Grail

I

A Description of the Non-Cyclic Romance

The non-cyclic Prose *Lancelot* is not the painstaking recreation of twentieth-century scholarship, but is to be found in its entirety in the Florence manuscript, Laurenziana 89 inf. 61, and the Rouen manuscript 1055 (O6). In BN fr. 768 it is almost complete (the last folio is missing from the manuscript); Pierpont Morgan 805–6 only leaves it after the death of the False Guinevere (*PL* 612.13) and joins the cyclic version; BN fr. 339 transfers in the middle of Lancelot's judicial duel against three knights (*PL* 605.18). Cyclic and non-cyclic versions only diverge after the installation of Lancelot as a Knight of the Round Table (at the end of Sommer III, *PL* 572.4); ten manuscripts[1] give the beginning of the non-cyclic version before transferring to one which prepares for the later branches of the cycle. This leads towards an abduction and rescue of Guinevere (the *Charrette* story), a Grail Quest in which Lancelot is surpassed by his son Galahad, and ultimately a *Mort Artu* in which Lancelot and Guinevere's love starts the dissension from which stems Arthur's death and the end of the Round Table.

The non-cylic romance contains an account of Lancelot's childhood and education, and the knightly adventures through which he gains a seat at the Round Table (a narrative common to both non-cyclic and cyclic versions). This is followed by a short version of his defence of Guinevere against the false charges of an impostor, and then by the death of his friend Galehot, the episode which concludes the story. The narrative can for the purpose of analysis be divided into the following interlinking phases. All references are to the *PL*.

Prologue (pp. 1–21)

Ban's wars with Claudas, his dispossession and death, his son's disappearance into a lake, his widow's founding of an abbey.

Phase I (pp. 21–166)

The childhood and education of Lancelot (and his cousins) by a fairy in a lake, leading up to his departure for Camelot, his first meeting with the Queen, and his knighting.

Phase II (pp. 166–95)

Lancelot's first adventures as White Knight, culminating in his conquest of the Dolorous Guard, a conquest in which he learns his own name.

Phase III (pp. 195–257)

(i) Arthur and his court hear of the conquest of the Dolorous Guard and go to the castle; the White Knight leaves it (p. 218).

(ii) Gauvain's first quest for the identity of the Unknown Knight (the White Knight, Lancelot) who achieved the conquest of the Dolorous Guard. This falls into two parts.

(*a*) (pp. 218–33)

Gauvain follows the traces of the Unknown Knight (Lancelot) up to the First Assembly of Logres, where Lancelot (under different arms) distinguishes himself above all other knights, in spite of a serious injury which causes him to travel in a litter and to be known as the Knight of the Litter. He departs before Gauvain has identified the Knight of the Litter with the object of his quest;

(*b*) (pp. 233–57)

Lancelot withdraws to recover from his injuries and so prepare for the Second Assembly, and then completes the adventure of the Dolorous Guard by putting an end to the castle's enchantments. Gauvain continues his quest up till the Second Assembly of Logres where Lancelot is again the best knight and where Gauvain learns that the unknown conqueror of the Dolorous Guard, the White Knight, and the Knight of the Litter, are all Lancelot, the son of Ban of Benoyc. Gauvain brings the news to court, Lancelot having eluded him by departing secretly.

Phase IV (pp. 257–358)

Arthur's battles against Galehot, son of la Jaiande (the Giantess) and lord of the Distant Isles, in which he is saved by an unknown knight (Lancelot), who then has his first secret meeting with Guinevere. This again falls into two parts:

(*a*) (pp. 257–304)

Lancelot's adventures up to his imprisonment by the Lady of Malohaut interlace with Galehot's challenge to Arthur and the King's dreams of disaster. Then Galehot fulfils his threat and invades Logres; this is followed by the first battle against Galehot (the Third Assembly of Logres) in which Arthur is only saved from defeat by the exploits of the mysterious Red Knight (Lancelot, temporarily emerging from prison). The dreams, interpreted in a confused and alarming way by the King's clerks before the battle, are given their true meaning by a *preudomme* (a wise man) after the battle. Gauvain sets out as leader of a quest (unsuccessful) by forty knights for the Red Knight who has disappeared back into prison.

(*b*) (pp. 304–58)

Gauvain returns in time for Arthur's second battle with Galehot in which the King is saved from defeat by a mysterious Black Knight who wins the friendship of Galehot by his exploits and persuades him to make peace with Arthur. This is followed by Lancelot's first secret meeting with Guinevere (arranged by Galehot who is hiding Lancelot in his camp) in which she learns that Lancelot is the Black Knight and that all his deeds as White Knight, Red Knight, and Black Knight were inspired by his love for her. She persuades him to confess to his name, and the first kiss is exchanged. Lancelot then departs secretly with Galehot for Sorelois.

Phase V (pp. 358–572)

Gauvain's quest, as leader of twenty companions, for the mysterious knight whom he with forty companions had failed to find. This successful quest ends with Lancelot's welcome at court and his installation at the Round Table. This again falls into two parts:

(*a*) (pp. 358–539)

Gauvain's adventures on his quest for Lancelot intertwine with those of Hector who is in search of Gauvain. They culminate in a battle between Gauvain (incognito) and Hector, on the one side, and Lancelot and the King of a Hundred Knights, on the other, a battle broken off when Lancelot learns that he is fighting Gauvain to whom the Queen had asked him to give every assistance. Lancelot finally confesses to his name in the presence of both Galehot and Gauvain.

(*b*) (pp. 539–72)

Arthur's kingdom is invaded by Saxons; during the war Lancelot, again fighting incognito, helps Arthur in the first battle. He is granted the physical consummation of his love by Guinevere, and once again saves Arthur who has been captured by the Saxons. He is finally presented under his own name to the King by Gauvain, is received at court, and he, Hector, and Galehot are all made Knights of the Round Table.

Phase VI (pp. 572–609)

The divergence between cyclic and non-cyclic versions starts here with

Galehot's journey with Lancelot to his own land and the False Guinevere episode.

(*a*) pp. 572–83

Galehot returns with Lancelot to his own lands and during the journey there are dreams and portents of disaster. These are interpreted by Arthur's clerks as signs of the coming death of Galehot through his love for Lancelot.

(*b*) (pp. 584–609)

An impostor, the False Guinevere, claims that she is the true Queen who brought the Round Table with her as part of her dowry. Lancelot fights single-handed in a judicial combat against three knights, confirms Guinevere's identity as the true Queen and in so doing also defends the integrity of the Round Table. He then makes peace between the King and the Queen and becomes a member of the King's *ostel*, thereby bringing to an end his companionship with Galehot who will have to return to his country as his duties as ruler demand.

Epilogue (pp. 609–613)

The knighting of Lyonel and the death of Galehot.

(*a*) pp. 609–12

The knighting of Lyonel (Lancelot's cousin and squire) and his fight with the Crowned Lion of Lybia, which confirms his right to his own name, are followed by his installation as a Knight of the Round Table.

(*b*) pp. 612–13

Galehot's death arises as a result of his separation from his friend through Lancelot's decision to remain with the King and Queen. Galehot hears a false rumour of Lancelot's death and dies of grief.

The earliest manuscript of the non-cyclic Prose *Lancelot* and indeed of any Prose *Lancelot* text is generally accepted to be BN fr. 768 which, on the style of its initials, has been assigned a probable date fairly early in the second quarter of the thirteenth century by the library's department of manuscripts. The exact date of the romance itself is uncertain, although we know that a Prose *Lancelot* existed before 1226 from external evidence,[2] and I have nothing to add to my discussion of the problem in the introduction to my edition of the text (*Lancelot do Lac*, II, pp. 41–4). I concluded there that it was written after Robert de Boron's *Joseph* and *Merlin* and the *First* and *Second Perceval Continuations*.[3] I also suggested that it was written before the *Perlesvaus* and was one of the earliest of the Arthurian prose romances, although probably later than the first prose versions of Robert de Boron's *Joseph* and *Merlin*. This would place it quite early in the thirteenth century, depending partly on the date given to the *Perlesvaus* (1206–13 according to Nitze, Carman, and Marx; 1220–5 according to Frappier; nearer 1250 than 1200 according to L. Foulet).[4] I will explore further in an appendix the relationship between the *Perlesvaus* and the non-cyclic Prose *Lancelot*, and the techniques used in both romances to place the individual texts within the Arthurian tradition as a whole.

The non-cyclic Prose *Lancelot* inherited from the twelfth century two main traditions concerning Lancelot. Firstly, there was the tale of the boy brought up in a lake, ignorant of his parentage, by a fairy, only learning his identity after performing a certain exploit. This variant of the Fair Unknown story survives in a Middle High German romance, Ulrich von Zatzikhoven's *Lanzelet*, based on a twelfth-century French romance, now lost. Secondly, there was the lover and rescuer of Guinevere as presented in *le Chevalier de la Charrette* of Chrétien de Troyes, who only alludes very briefly to Lancelot's upbringing in a lake by a fairy, but withholds the hero's name not only until he has raised a tomb slab identifying him as the knight destined to rescue the prisoners of Gorre, but also until named by Guinevere. The non-cyclic prose romance of *Lancelot* (or the independent Prose *Lancelot* as it might be called) is constructed around two interlacing main themes deriving from these traditions, the identity theme and that of Lancelot, the lover of Guinevere, but the author sets them within the context of the general Arthurian tradition by a web of cross-references to other well-known stories and familiar narrative patterns. It is this interplay between the prose romance and inherited tradition, especially as it is presented in the work of a master such as Chrétien de Troyes, which is one of the most interesting features of the work and one which will be investigated in the following chapters. I will be studying both the forms of coherence within the work and the way that the romance is presented as part of a wider Arthurian 'reality'. I will start by examining the identity theme—the making of a name—analysing each part of the story in turn.

II

The Making of a Name or Quest for Identity

One of the recurring themes in twelfth-century romance is the identity theme. A young man has to discover who he is, to make his name (sometimes in the most literal sense) through his exploits as a knight, or an older knight has to prove his right to a reputation won in the past, or recover a good name which he has lost. This theme, under its various aspects and in relation to a range of characters who provide a counterpoint to the development of Lancelot's quest for identity, runs right through the *PL*. It emerges clearly in terms of the narrative structure and the handling of the interlace (as will be examined further in Chapter VII) and is emphasized through interplay with the existing literary tradition by means of variations on familiar narrative patterns, subtle allusions to the heroes of earlier Arthurian romances.[1]

The childhood and education of Lancelot

This is the part of the romance which most closely resembles the *Lanzelet* of Ulrich von Zatzikhoven, and it seems likely that the author of the prose romance knew a work similar to the French source of Ulrich's poem.[2] But the *Conte del Graal* is an equally important influence in, as it were, a 'contrary' direction: the *PL*, as far as the preparation of a youth for knighthood is concerned, makes a deliberate contrast with the Perceval story, which the frequent echoes in the prose romance from Chrétien's poem and the *First* and *Second Continuations* only serve to emphasize. There may well already have been cross-influences between the Lancelot and Perceval stories in the twelfth century, but the situation is further complicated, as we shall see, by the influence of the well-known narrative pattern of the tale of the Fair Unknown.[3] All three romances, the *Conte del Graal*, *Lanzelet*, and the *PL* resemble this pattern of the Fair Unknown in that they each contain an account of a handsome youth arriving at Arthur's court, ignorant of his name and parentage, and only learning of his identity after performing a certain exploit. However, within this common framework there are also important differences between the three romances.

In the first place, the upbringing of a child in an isolated place, where he is kept out of contact with ordinary knightly society and given no indication of his own identity, is explained in different ways in the three romances. In the

Lanzelet the hero's father, Pant, King of Genewis, is a harsh tyrant who is driven
from his lands by his discontented barons, grown weary of his misrule.[4] He flees
wounded from his castle with his wife and baby son and dies beside a lake. A
lake fairy carries away the child and brings him up, in safe seclusion in a magic
land and in ignorance of his name and parentage, in order that he can become a
knight and conquer the man who has taken the land of the fairy's son. Lanzelet
learns his own name after he has defeated another knight, Iweret.[5]

In Chrétien's *Conte del Graal* Perceval is brought up by his widowed mother
in rustic isolation and in ignorance of his own identity and of everything to do
with knighthood, because his father had been maimed and eventually died
through the practice of chivalry, as had his two brothers, one of whom, perhaps
significantly from the point of view of twelfth-century cross-influences, was in
the service of King Ban de Gomeret.[6] His father, a noble knight, had, before his
death, lost his land through no fault of his own during the troubled times after
Uther's death.[7] The one desire of Perceval's mother is that he, as her sole surviving son, should not become a knight, lest she should lose him as she had lost
his father and his brothers. Perceval does not learn his name until a certain stage
in the story when he guesses it, but his mother tells him before he leaves for
Arthur's court that he is of noble lineage:

> N'ot chevalier de si haut pris,
> Tant redouté ne tant cremu,
> Biax fix, com vostre peres fu
> En toutes les illes de mer.
> Biax fix, bien vos poëz vanter
> Que vos ne dechaez de rien
> De son lignage ne del mien,
> Que je suis de chevaliers nee,
> Des meillors de ceste contree.
>
> (*Perc.* 416–24.)

In the *PL* the name of Lancelot's father, King Ban of Benoyc,[8] bears an obvious resemblance to that of Lanzelet, whereas in Chrétien, as we have seen, Ban
de Gomeret is just the lord of one of Perceval's brothers. In the prose romance
King Ban, like King Pant, is driven from his land, but here, leaving his one
remaining castle in the care of a seneschal, he sets forth with his wife and baby
son to seek help from Arthur. He dies beside a lake, not of wounds but of a
broken heart at the sight of his last castle going up in flames. Lancelot is carried
off by a fairy who lives in the semblance of a lake. She prepares him for
knighthood without any ulterior motive, bringing him up in ignorance of his
identity, which he only learns after achieving a marvellous adventure, the capture of an enchanted castle, the Dolorous Guard. However, Lancelot's father

Ban is quite different from Pant in that he is described as a noble and just ruler who (like Perceval's father and in somewhat similar circumstances) loses his lands through no fault of his own during the troubled times after Uther's death:

Quant li rois Aramonz fu morz, et Uter Pandragons, et la terre de Logres fu an la main lo roi Artur, si sordirent guerres an Bretaigne la Grant en pluseurs leus et guerroierent lo roi Artu li plus des barons. Et ce fu el comancement de son regnement, ne n'avoit encores la reigne Ganievre gaires tenue, si ot mout a faire de totes parz. Lors reprist Claudas sa guerre qui tant avoit esté entrelaissie, car il avoit sa terre tote recovree si tost comme li rois Aramonz fu morz. Lors recomança a guerroier lo roi Ban de Benoyc por ce que a lui marchissoit, et por ce que hom avoit esté Aramont par cui il avoit sa terre eüe perdue si longuement et que mout li avoit neü tant con il avoit esté au desouz. (*PL* 2.8–19.)

Yet the *Lanzelet* theme of the unjust ruler and the revolt of barons is also to be found in the *PL*, where the unjust ruler is not Lancelot's father, but the man who dispossesses him, Claudas de la Deserte, lord of Berri.[9] In the *PL* Claudas not only takes all the lands of Ban, but also those of his brother Bohort, King of Gaunes, who dies shortly after Ban. He captures Bohort's two young sons, Lyonel and Bohort, and keeps them for some time in captivity. The barons of Gaunes, who have paid homage to Claudas, now rise in defence of their old lord's sons, and the struggles between them and Claudas and the conflict of feudal loyalties are dealt with at considerable length.

It seems probable that the author of the *PL* modified the character of Ban and introduced the character of Claudas in order to adapt the Lancelot story to a conception of chivalry in which a noble heredity plays an important role in the making of a great knight.[10] When the Lady of the Lake explains the origin of chivalry to Lancelot, she says that at the beginning all men, as descendants from a common father, Adam, were equal. But after the Fall the strong and wicked began to oppress the weak, and God decreed that the noblest in mind and body should be chosen to be set above other men to defend the weak and see that justice be done:

'Et tant sachiez vos bien que chevaliers ne fu mie faiz a gas ne establiz, et non pas por ce qu'il fussient au commencement plus gentil home ne plus haut de lignage l'un des autres, car d'un pere et d'une mere descendirent totes les genz. Mais qant envie et coveitise commança a croistre el monde et force commança a vaintre droiture, a cele hore estoient encores paroil et un autre de lignage et de gentillece. Et qant li foible ne porent plus soffrir ne durer encontre les forz, si establirent desor aus garanz et desfandeors, por garantir les foibles et les paisibles et tenir selonc droiture, et por les forz boter arrieres des torz qu'il faisoient et des outraiges. A ceste garantie porter furent establi cil qui plus valoient a l'esgart del comun des genz. Ce furent li grant et li fort et li bel et li legier et li leial et li preu et li hardi, cil qui des bontez del cuer et del cors estoient plain.' (*PL* 142.16–30.)

However, when she is preparing the youth for his journey to Arthur's court to be knighted, she says:

'Et se vos saviez qui fu vostres peres ne de qex genz vostres lignages est estraiz de par la mere, vos n'avriez pas paor, si com ge cuit, d'estre prozdom, car nus qui de tel lignage fust ne devroit pas avoir corage de mauveitié.' (*PL* 147.17–20.)

When she has accompanied him to Camelot and is about to leave him, she tells him that he is the son of a *preudomme* and a beautiful lady, and of equal rank with the two younger boys, Lyonel and Bohort, who have been serving him and are his cousins and king's sons. As has been seen above, Perceval's mother makes similar and rather more explicit revelations to her son before he leaves for Arthur's court to be knighted (*Perc.* 416–76).

The young Lancelot's uncertainty concerning his parentage and his deep anxiety lest he be lacking in the necessary qualification to become a worthy knight are deliberately played upon by the Lady of the Lake and provide a recurring theme in the first part of the romance (*PL* 47–8, and 110–11). Indeed they play an important part in his education, as Jean Frappier has shown.[11] The author is able to explore more deeply this theme of uncertainty and the courageous way in which Lancelot faces the problem, thus revealing his natural nobility of character, because he has provided his hero with two young cousins, Lyonel and Bohort, who know their names and parentage. For example, Lancelot feels so instinctively that he is Lyonel's equal that he calls him 'cousin' when he tells him not to cry over his lost kingdom and gives him brave advice as to how he should win it back, unaware that he himself is in the same position (*PL* 109). When the Lady of the Lake asks him who he thinks is more noble, himself or Lyonel, he replies bravely:

'Ne ge ne sai combien ge sui gentis hom de par lignaige, mais par la foi que ge doi vos, ge ne me deigneroie pas esmaier de ce dont ge l'ai veü plorer. Et l'an me fait antandant que d'un home et d'une fame sont issues totes genz. Ce ne sai ge pas, par quel raison li un ont plus que li autre de gentillece, se l'an ne la conquiert par proesce autresin com l'an fait les terres et les onors. Mais tant sachiez vos bien de voir que, se li grant cuer faisoient les gentis homes, ge cuideroie encores estre des plus gentils.' (*PL* 110.34–111.3.)

The Lady of the Lake reassures him that 'vos ne perdroiz a estre uns des plus gentils homes do monde se par defaut de cuer non' (*PL* 111.4–6). He then replies proudly that he does not regret that he has been served by two king's sons, 'qant ge porrai ancor a els ataindre et a els valoir o a passer' (*PL* 111.14–15).

Throughout the romance Lyonel indeed provides a useful foil to Lancelot, as will be examined further in Chapter VIII in relation to the pairing of characters.

When Lancelot becomes a knight, the Lady of the Lake keeps Lyonel for a time and then sends him as a squire to Lancelot and Galehot (*PL* 358.7-18) who use him as a messenger to the Queen; he provides a useful link with Guinevere at Arthur's court (*PL* 473, 525, 542-3, 545-6) and on occasion with Gauvain (*PL* 493-501, 537). He also helps to provide a certain continuity between this first part of the romance, which concerns Lancelot's upbringing by the Lady of the Lake, and Lancelot's later adventures, after he has been knighted and met Guinevere for the first time. This is quite important, as Lancelot's arrival at court forms a natural break in the story (indeed it is with the arrival of the unknown youth at court that a romance such as *li Biaus Descouneüs* begins), and many of the characters (apart from the Lady of the Lake and her damsels) do not reappear in the story after his departure from the Lake. When the Lady of the Lake regretfully decides that it is her duty to send Lancelot to be a knight, she consoles herself with the thought that she can keep Lyonel for a time, and that when he reaches the age when he should leave her to train to become a knight, she will still have Bohort. Lyonel the squire is a foil to Lancelot, the unknown knight who is making his reputation and who, as we shall see, is in his turn measured in the way already traditional in Chrétien against Gauvain, the established knight, who has another foil in Hector, the promising young *bachelier* (knight bachelor). When the King makes Lancelot a member of his *ostel* (household), Lyonel has fulfilled his role and, as will be shown later in this chapter, his knighting, paralleling that of Lancelot at the beginning of his adventures, helps to round off the romance.

As we have seen, the motivation behind the bringing up of the child in an environment isolated from the knightly world of men is different for all three heroes, Perceval, Lanzelet, and Lancelot. The preparation which they receive for adult life is also very different. The Lady of the Lake's careful education of Lancelot for knighthood is in almost every respect, apart from the withholding of the name which is common to all three romances, in complete contrast to Perceval's mother's careful shielding of her son from all knowledge of chivalry—a contrast which is underlined by a series of oppositions and parallels which would have been recognized by an early thirteenth-century audience.

Perceval (*Perc.* 95-9) has, like Lanzelet (*Lanz.* 285-91) and Lancelot (*PL* 108.3-5), some skill in throwing (darts or sticks or stones); but, apart from some knowledge of swordsmanship, he is quite unversed in the use of arms (1530-4), in knightly pursuits and social graces, and departs for court without armour and clad in homespun, a ridiculous figure in the eyes of knightly society. Lanzelet is educated mainly by women, as he is carried off to a magic *Meidenland.* There he learns from them how to behave in the company of ladies, how to play an instrument, and how to sing; but, by the nature of the land in which he is brought up, the only tuition in arms which he receives is from 'mermen' who teach him the use of the sword and buckler, for, as there are no horses in the lake, he can gain no knowledge of horsemanship. As a result, although, unlike Perceval, he is sent off fully equipped with white armour, sword, and shield, he too is a somewhat ridiculous figure when he first sets out, as he has no idea how to manage his horse.

Lancelot's education, unlike that of Lanzelet, is not restricted by the strange and supernatural character of the land in which he is brought up, for the Lady of the Lake has to a considerable extent been rationalized: she has learned her magic from Merlin, she lives only in the semblance of a lake, has a perfectly ordinary *ami* (PL 148.23), and a retinue of knights and squires.[12] Lancelot, like Lanzelet, receives careful training in courtly behaviour, he sings well, is skilled at games such as chess, and knows how to carve meat correctly, but he does not have to rely on female tuition. Although he does not know whether he is a *gentil home*, he is taught by a master how to behave like one (PL 38), and indeed soon shows that he has a truer understanding of what this implies than has his master, who tries to punish him for showing *largece* (PL 45.16–26), one of the most important knightly qualities according to Claudas in his lament for his son (PL 71.29–37).[13] Lancelot is given a thorough training in horsemanship and leaves for Arthur's court fully equipped with white armour, rich robes, and knightly skills. The contrast between Lancelot's splendid retinue, with its string of horses bearing the hero's arms and magnificent wardrobe, and Perceval's departure, alone, in rustic homespun, is obvious, especially as it is preceded by scenes which have clear parallels in Chrétien's poem. Both Perceval's mother and the Lady of the Lake, when the young hero declares his determination to leave home to become a knight, are first overcome with grief, and then give him advice on the basic principles of chivalry and a little more information about his parentage, while still withholding his name (*Perc.* 510–94 and PL 141–7). But the Lady of the Lake recognizes fully, even before Lancelot says that he intends to go to Arthur's court to become a knight, that the time has come for this and that it would be wrong to delay it (PL 139.3–13); indeed, much earlier in the story (PL 111.16–34) she was already preparing herself regretfully for this moment; whereas Perceval's mother had hoped against hope that her son would never hear of chivalry:

> Biax dols fix, de chevalerie
> Vos quidoie si bien garder
> Que ja n'en oïssiez parler
> Ne que ja nul n'en veïssiez
> (*Perc.* 408–11.)

Perceval's mother's explanation of chivalry is much shorter and simpler than that of the Lady of the Lake, and is even then misinterpreted by Perceval. In contrast with this, Lancelot listens, apparently with great attention, to the Lady of the Lake's long and complicated disquisition on the origins and theory of chivalry, and on the symbolic significance of each piece of armour, an explanation which gives priority to the duty of the knight to defend the Church, but, like the explanation of Perceval's mother, also emphasizes the obligation to protect the helpless, the widows, and orphans. Unlike Perceval, Lancelot does not, in the later part of the romance, misinterpret the explanations of the Lady of the Lake, although it is true that the stress on the knight's duty to defend the Church is not particularly relevant to the tasks which he and other knights have to perform later, tasks which are concerned rather with the need to help King Arthur to see that justice is done and the rights of the weak protected within his feudal kingdom.[14] Whereas Perceval sets off alone, leaving his mother grieving so much that he sees her faint (and in fact she dies of sorrow), and, on his own initiative, asks to be knighted immediately after he has arrived at court, Lancelot is accompanied to Arthur's court by the Lady of the Lake. She continues to instruct him up till the moment of departure and insists that he must ask to be made a knight at once, a command which he is eager to obey. She also continues to emphasize the mystery of his origins and does not reveal her own name. The Lady of the Lake's request to Arthur that Lancelot should be made a knight in the armour which he has brought with him and Perceval's demand that he be made a knight in the arms of the Red Knight are both presented as deviations from the normal practice, but there is a contrast in the form of deviation: Perceval's lack of preparation and equipment is set against Lancelot's careful preparation and full equipment, although both are recognized by those who see them as showing in their handsome appearance and noble bearing the outward signs of a great destiny. In both romances there are scenes in which the young unknown youth behaves awkwardly. In Chrétien's poem there is splendid comedy in Perceval's arrival at court, when his horse unceremoniously knocks off the King's hat and he demands peremptorily to be knighted:

> Li vallés ne prise une chive
> Quanques li rois li dist et conte
> Ne de son dol ne de sa honte,
> De sa feme ne li chaut il.
> Faites moi chevalier, fait il,
> Sire rois, car aler m'en weil.'
>
> (*Perc.* 968–73.)

Arthur, angry at Kay for mocking the youth, suggests that his naïve behaviour may well come only from lack of proper instruction:

'Por che, se li vallés est niches,
S'est il, puet c'estre, gentix hom,
Que il li vient d'aprision,
Qu'il a esté a malvais mestre;
Encore puet preus vassax estre.'
(*Perc.* 1012–16.)

Lancelot too shows his awkwardness (albeit of a different kind) soon after his arrival at court. When he first sees the Queen, he is quite unable to answer her questions and murmurs uncertainly that he does not know. The Queen gives publicly the same explanation Arthur had suggested for Perceval's uncouth behaviour, when she says that the youth seems to have been ill taught (*PL* 158.9–10). But the text makes it clear that the origin of Lancelot's awkward behaviour lies not in *niceté* or lack of instruction, but in the overwhelming effect upon him of his first sight of Guinevere's beauty; it is in fact an outward symptom of love, and the Queen already suspects this and is trying to turn attention away from Lancelot's behaviour:

Maintenant aparçoit bien la reine qu'il est esbahiz et trespansez, mais ele n'osse pas cuidier que ce soit por li; et neporquant ele lo sospece un po, si an laisse la parole ester atant. Et por ce qu'ele nel velt en greignor folie metre, ele se lieve de la place et dit, por ce que ele ne velt que nus pant a vilenie et que nus ne s'aparçoive de ce que ele sospeçoit, que cil vallez ne li senble pas estre senez tres bien, et qui qu'il soit, sages o fox, il a esté enseigniez mauvaisement. (*PL* 158.3–10.)

As Lancelot is tongue-tied when the Queen asks him who he is and from whence he comes, this first glimpse of Lancelot in a lover's trance (a motif which recurs frequently in the romance) is linked with the theme of the hero's identity. Guinevere suspects that Lancelot cannot answer her questions because he is in love; Yvain suggests that perhaps the youth has been forbidden to say what he is called or whence he comes. Neither of them is aware that at this stage he himself does not know who he is. One reason for Lancelot's awkward silence links up, therefore, with the tradition of the unknown youth, common to the *Conte del Graal* and *Lanzelet*, but the other links up with the theme of Lancelot in love, inherited from Chrétien's *Chevalier de la Charrette* and to be discussed in Chapter III. There are, however, a few traces of the type of *niceté* so characteristic of the rustic young Perceval, and in general so uncharacteristic of the carefully educated young Lancelot, during his adventures on the way to his battle as champion of the Lady of Nohaut, as will emerge from the analysis of the next phase in the romance.

As we have seen, considerable emphasis is given to the effect on the young

Lancelot of his ignorance concerning his parentage and to the way that this uncertainty contributes towards the Lady of the Lake's careful preparation of the boy for knighthood; indeed, deliberate contrasts are made with the lack of preparation of the young Perceval through an interplay between the text and the well-known romance of Chrétien. In addition, the reactions of the people who meet Lancelot to the mystery of his birth also form an important element in the story, one which is used to place this tale firmly within an Arthurian world where feudal loyalties are as important as the traditional marvellous, as will be seen in Chapters IV and V.

There are two elements in this theme: firstly, anxiety over the unknown fate of Ban's only son (and, as with Lancelot's uncertainty over his own identity, extra emphasis is given through the introduction of the hero's young cousins and their widowed mother); secondly, curiosity as to who the noble youth can be. These two threads are brought together in certain episodes where someone who had known the father meets the unknown yet strangely familiar youth.

The disappearance of Lancelot through his withdrawal to some unknown or inaccessible place provides a recurring pattern within the romance.[15] In this early part of the story, Lancelot is withdrawn from the ordinary world when he is carried off by the Lady of the Lake to a land made inaccessible by its concealment beneath the semblance of a lake. Later in the story Lancelot is withdrawn for the healing of wounds or into prison or to Sorelois. These later disappearances are associated with a series of quests, led by Gauvain, for the mysterious knight; but in the first part of the story most people think that Lancelot is dead, and he, still only a child, is not yet in a position to establish a reputation as an unknown knight of such prowess that the finest knights of Arthur's court spend their time searching for him.

At the very beginning of the story the account of the death of Ban, the carrying-off of the unprotected child, and the grief of the distraught widow and mother, Helene, establishes a situation which will be important for the treatment of the Lancelot–Guinevere love theme within the romance. Arthur has failed in his duty to protect his vassal Ban, and Lancelot therefore owes him no loyalty as a vassal holding land from him; nor are there any blood-ties between them as there are between Mark and Tristan. Even greater emphasis is given to this failure of Arthur through the duplication of kings (Ban and Bohort), of widows (Helene and Evaine), and the multiplication of disinherited children (Lancelot, Lyonel, and Bohort). Claudas tells Ban that he has taken Ban's land only because Arthur is his lord:

'Ge ne la vos toli mie, fait Claudas, por chose que vos m'aiez faite, ne por haïne que j'aie a vos, mais por lo roi Artu que vos tenez a seignor, car ses peres, Uter Pandragon, me deserita' (*PL* 3.34-6.)

He offers Ban back his land if he will hold it from him instead of from Arthur, but Ban steadfastly refuses: 'Ce ne ferai ge mie . . . car ge me parjureroie envers lo roi Artu cui huem ge sui liges.' (*PL* 4.1–2.) Claudas offers him a truce of forty days so that he can send for help from Arthur. Ban goes off with his wife and child to appeal in person to his liege lord. In the mean time Claudas persuades Ban's seneschal to betray him, and captures his favourite fortified city, Trebe, which is swept by fire. When Ban sees from a distance the destruction of his only remaining stronghold, he dies of grief. This death-scene is dwelt on at some length: the king's thoughts concerning the fate of his wife and son, left to face their enemies unprotected, are described in some detail, he makes a moving and dignified dying speech and goes to his end as a good Christian, having said his *mea culpa,* prayed to the Trinity, and died with arms outstretched in the form of a cross, his head turned towards the east. Then the narrative lingers over the grief of the queen at the loss of her husband, and that of her son, carried off at the very moment when she lies prostrate over the body of her husband, and the scene is prolonged by the arrival of an abbess with her chapelain and three nuns. The queen takes the veil on the spot, an abbey is built where the king died, and the queen makes a custom of going every day, after mass has been sung in memory of her husband, to weep by the lake for her vanished son. This episode is followed immediately by an account of the capture of Lancelot's cousins, Lyonel and Bohort, after the death of Ban's brother Bohort, and of the meeting of the two sisters in the abbey, where they lament together over the loss of their husbands and children.

There are two more episodes in which the distress of the two queens over the loss of their sons is dwelt upon. In the first of these a *rendu* (former knight who has entered a religious order) finds Helene weeping by the Lake; from him she learns for the first time that her son is alive and well, but that she cannot know where he is. The *rendu* also tells Evaine that her children are alive. He then goes to Arthur's court to reproach the King before all his barons for being a bad king and for having failed to avenge the death of his vassal Ban and the widowhood and disinheritance of his wife, who has also lost her son, but he does not tell Arthur that this son is still alive and safe. This is followed by a parallel episode in which a damsel, sent by the Lady of the Lake, reproaches Claudas publicly for his treatment of Lyonel and Bohort; she then succeeds in carrying off the two boys to the safety of the Lake.

A similar pattern of grief and partial reassurance of the queens, followed by criticism of Arthur, is to be found later in the romance, just before the scenes leading up to Lancelot's departure from the Lake. The holy life of the two queens in the abbey is first described at length, then an account is given of the sufferings of Queen Evaine, who has heard that her sons have been taken away by a damsel and does not know whether they are alive or dead. She has a vision in which she sees three children in a beautiful garden, and when she awakens she finds in her left hand three names: Lyonel, Bohort, and Lancelot. This is followed immediately by another episode in which Arthur is reminded of his failure to avenge King Ban. Banyn, godson and faithful vassal of Ban, who had fought hard to defend his lord's castle and had refused to accept service with Claudas, comes to Arthur's court and, as victor in a tournament, is seated next to the King. When Arthur learns who he is, he falls into deep and brooding melancholy while still at table. When roused by his knights, he explains that he is brooding over his greatest dishonour since he became king—that his vassal Ban had died on the way to seek help from him and had never been avenged: 'Et ja en ai eü clamor, n'onques encor ne l'amandai, si ai si grant honte que ge ne puis greignor avoir.' (*PL* 138.12–13.) Gauvain admits that Arthur would have good reason to brood over this at the appropriate time and then to take action, but maintains that this great court (at the religious festival of Easter) is not the right time or season. Arthur then learns that Ban's widow has taken the veil, that no one knows where his son is, and that most people think that he is dead.

This is the first in a series of broodings by Arthur (another traditional Arthurian theme, here echoing scenes in the *Conte del Graal* and the *Perceval Continuations*).[16] In this episode, immediately preceding the account of Lancelot's departure from the Lake, Arthur is brooding over his own guilt concerning the loss of Ban and the disappearance of his son. Later in the romance, after Lancelot has been knighted and his exploits as an unknown knight have become famous, Arthur broods because his knights have failed to discover the identity of the mysterious knight or to bring him to court. Thus the theme is transformed as the narrative moves into the knightly, active phase of Lancelot's life, but a certain structure is given to the long romance by the repetition with variation of the brooding theme with its echoes of the Perceval romance of Chrétien and his continuators. All these episodes which dwell on the grief of the widowed queens and on the inadequacy of their feudal suserain, and which link up with the disappearance of the child Lancelot, emphasize Arthur's responsibilities as a monarch, a theme which will continue throughout the romance, helping to give a certain feudal coherence to the story.[17] The *rendu*'s visit to Arthur's court (and his stern reproof) is paralleled by the *preudomme*'s visit after the first battle against Galehot, when the King is lectured at length and sent back again to his priest to confess his sins with regard to Ban (*PL* 285). Elsewhere, as will be shown more fully in Chapter IV, the stress is on the role of Arthur's knights to see that the rights of the King's vassals are protected and that justice is done in all the lands over which he is suserain.

While some characters brood over the disappearance of Ban's son, others are speculating over the identity of an unknown, handsome youth. There are numerous episodes in the account of Lancelot's childhood in which those who meet the boy are so struck by his nobility of character and physical beauty that they are eager to learn who he is, and these also foreshadow a theme to be developed further, once he has become a knight. No one in the Lake, apart from the lady herself, knows who he is, not even his own cousins. As a child brought up without parents, he is called *Biaus Trovez* and *Riches Orphenins* (PL 24.14–18), while the Lady of the Lake usually calls him *filz de roi*, whereas Perceval's mother runs towards her son, calling him *biax fix* more than a hundred times (*Perc.* 373). If most of the characters (including the hero himself) do not know his identity, the author, unlike Chrétien, in relation to Perceval or Lancelot, reveals the name of his hero to the reader right at the beginning of the story (PL 1.8) and uses the name freely in the narrative up to his first journey to Arthur's court. From then on, the name is not used, apart from the passages which mark the various stages in the revelation of his identity, until after he has had his first secret meeting with Guinevere and she has told him that she knows who he is.[18]

The few people from outside the Lake whom Lancelot meets as a boy are all fascinated by his appearance and bearing, and are filled with an ardent desire to know who he is, especially those who see in him a resemblance to Ban whose son is presumed to be dead. For example, once, when hunting, he gets separated from his tutor and meets a vavasour to whom he gives a deer. After leaving him the vavasour feels certain that he reminds him of someone and eventually realizes that he resembles King Ban, who had been his lord. He urges the boy to tell him whether he is Ban's son, but of course Lancelot is unable to do so (PL 44). Lambegues, the young knight and tutor to Bohort, is allowed to visit the Lake so that he can take back the news of the safety of Lyonel and Bohort to the barons of Gaunes. When he sees Lancelot, his noble bearing and the honour which is shown to him, he is very impressed; he esteems him greatly, without knowing who he is, and is determined to try to discover his identity as soon as he can: 'Et mout lo prise, qant il ne set qui il est, mais il lo bee a savoir au plus tost que il porra.' (PL 107.22–3). Leonces, the baron who had come with Lambegues to the edge of the Lake and is eventually allowed to see all three children, is struck by the close resemblance of Lancelot to Ban, and although Lambegues tells him that Lancelot died with his father, Leonces still maintains that he must be Lancelot:

'Comment, fait Leonces, qu'il ait esté morz, tant sachiez vos bien que ce est il. Gel conois bien a son sanblant, et si lo me dit li cuers.' (PL 112.21–3.)

Such speculations serve, therefore, to link the lost Lancelot with the

unknown youth in the minds of a few characters, but these people do not succeed in resolving definitely the problem of the boy's identity and are left
wondering, just as Arthur is to be left wondering who the unknown knight is
until, late in the romance, Lancelot's identity is finally revealed to the King in
the episode leading up to the hero's installation as a Knight of the Round Table.

Lancelot's first adventures

The next stage in the development of the identity theme begins with Lancelot's
first adventures as a young knight and ends with the exploit through which he
learns his name: the conquest of the Dolorous Guard. His first adventures are in
some respects rather closer to the general pattern of the tale of the Fair
Unknown as it is to be found in a romance such as *li Biaus Descouneüs*[19] than to
those of Lanzelet or Chrétien's Perceval, but there are still scenes which seem to
make a conscious interplay between the Lancelot story and the *Conte del Graal*,
here through parallels rather than contrasts.

Lancelot's first action, after he has been dubbed a knight, is to undertake the
task of withdrawing the blades from the wounds of a knight who has come to
Arthur's court before Lancelot's arrival and whom he wanted to help while still
a squire. This entails swearing that he will avenge the knight against all those
who loved the man who did the wounding rather than the man who was
wounded.[20] King Arthur has advised his knights not to undertake the adventure,
for, as he tells the wounded knight, they would be undertaking an unlimited
commitment which could lead to a recurring series of battles (*PL* 150.17–20).
The oath sworn by Lancelot does indeed force him to kill most unwillingly a
number of knights, and the adventure is the only one he undertakes which
seems to have wholly destructive consequences; it finally leads to his imprisonment by the Lady of Malohaut.

The second task which he undertakes, and the first one he accomplishes, is
quite different in character and fits in much better with the role of the knight as
protector of the weak and defender of their just rights. Like le Bel Inconnu who,
when a messenger comes to seek a champion for his lady, asks to be allowed to
undertake this first adventure which presents itself after his knighting, Lancelot
offers himself as champion for the Lady of Nohaut (*LBD* 209–12, *PL* 162.35–7).
In both cases the King replies that the new knight is too young:

> 'Trop estes jovenes, biaus amis,
> Trop t'i esteveroit pener,
> Mius te vient ci en pais ester.'
> (*LBD* 214–16.)

'Vos ne savez que vos querez, car vos iestes si anfes et si juesnes que vos ne savez que monte granz fais de chevalerie.' (*PL* 162.38–163.1.)

In both romances the youth argues that his request is reasonable (*LBD* 220; *PL* 163.13–20), and it is granted. In *LBD* the messenger, a *pucele*, expresses with considerable force her opinion that the champion provided by Arthur is too young (*LBD* 229–40). In the *PL* the messenger only hints at his misgivings (*PL* 163.34–6). In both texts a series of adventures follow which test the quality of the young knight, tests which in the *PL* have been deliberately arranged, as the knight who came to get a champion at Arthur's court afterwards confesses (*PL* 178.3–23). The tests themselves do not correspond to the adventures in the tale of the Fair Unknown in the way that, as we shall see, do those undergone by Gauvain in his parallel adventures later in the *PL* (377–80); on the other hand they present echoes of the *niceté* so characteristic of the young hero in the *Conte del Graal* and to a lesser extent in the *Lanzelet*. The task undertaken is to defend the cause of the Lady of Nohaut in a judicial battle against the King of Northumberland. When the knight taking Lancelot to Nohaut turns on to a side path and explains that the road which they have been following is less safe, but refuses to say why, Lancelot advances upon him with his sword drawn and threatens to kill him, much to the amusement of the knight, who says that he is not as easy to kill as all that. Then follows an episode with a beautiful damsel in a tent, different from that in the *Conte del Graal* in that she is here protected by a tall and fierce knight and Lancelot does not kiss her against her will, but similar in that Lancelot insists, like a child responding to a dare, upon going into the tent to see her. This is an action very different from his usual behaviour, especially as, once he has set eyes on the Queen, he is not impressed by the beauty of any other woman. He was, for example, quite unmoved by the beauty of the Lady of Nohaut:

Quant il voit la dame, si ne s'esbaïst mie de sa grant biauté ne grant entandue n'i met; et si estoit ele une des tres beles. (*PL* 174.32–3.)

Throughout these adventures Lancelot's extreme youth and inexperience are emphasized. He does not address the people he meets with the courtesy characteristic of his own manners elsewhere in the text, whether before or after this particular series of incidents, the kind of courtesy which is also always shown by Gauvain, the knight against whom all other knights are measured in this romance, as is also often the case in Chrétien's work. Lancelot is so anxious to fight a battle to win a damsel, imprisoned on an island in a lake, that he forgets to take his shield (*PL* 171.6–7). Yet his achievements are such that the knight who has seen him fight is astonished to hear that he has only just been dubbed (*PL* 174.11).[21]

By the time that Lancelot arrives at Nohaut, his prowess has been so thoroughly tested that the Lady of Nohaut has no doubts about his suitability as champion. But Kay, still at Arthur's court, hearing that the battle has not yet been fought and unaware that it has been delayed because of the wounds Lancelot has received during the tests of his prowess, is characteristically scornful of the youth. He dismisses him as an unproved knight and says to the King:

'Sire, cuidiez vos que si juesnes hom com cil estoit poïst faire tele besoigne? Envoiez m'i, car preudomme doit l'on envoier en tel affaire.' (*PL* 175.18–20.)

He arrives at Nohaut, and only the diplomacy of the Lady of Nohaut prevents a battle taking place between Lancelot and Kay. In the *Conte del Graal* (1003–7) Kay starts treating the young hero with scorn as soon as he arrives at court, also in connection with his first exploit which is to be the killing of the knight in red armour. Much to the annoyance of the King, Kay mockingly tells Perceval to go and get the red armour, if that is what he wants, little dreaming that Perceval would go and do just that.

There are also parallels between *Yvain* and the *PL* in connection with Lancelot's defence of the Lady of Nohaut against the Duke of Northumberland who has invaded her land. Lancelot fights for her against the Duke's champion, wins the battle, and makes peace for her. Yvain fights a battle (not a judicial duel) for the lady of Norison whose land has been invaded by the Count Alier (*Yvain*, 2917–46) and makes peace for her (3138–309). The names have been transposed: Nohaut replaces Norison, but the Lady of Nohaut holds a tournament in the *Chevalier de la Charrette*; the King of Northumberland replaces Count Alier, but the name Alier is used elsewhere in the *PL* in connection with a war (*PL* 476.6, 481.11). As we shall see in the next chapter, the associations with the *PL* and *Yvain* at this and other points in the text may be not without significance.

Lancelot's next adventure (the fight with Alybon at the Gué la Reine) is mainly associated with the love theme, recalls an episode in the *Chevalier de la Charrette*, and will be examined more fully in the next chapter. There are nevertheless links with the identity theme in that Lancelot prefers to fight a battle with Alybon rather than reveal his name (*PL* 180.33–4); after the battle Alybon goes to Arthur's court to try to discover the identity of his opponent and by so doing helps to contribute towards the reputation which the nameless knight is already making for himself.

We then come to the adventure of the Dolorous Guard, which contains more magical elements than any other in the romance and is one of the key episodes in this tale of Lancelot. The hero achieves the first stage in the adventure, the conquest of the castle; he then enters the cemetery and raises the slab beneath which is inscribed the name of the conqueror of the Dolorous Guard. This scene in the cemetery, with the tombstones giving the names of those who are to lie there and the slab which can only be raised by the knight accomplishing a certain adventure, would have reverberations for an early thirteenth-century public. It would recall the similar scene in the *Chevalier de la Charrette* (1856–936), where Lancelot enters a marvellous cemetery in the company of a hermit who reads to him the inscriptions on the tombs, giving the names of those who will lie there. Lancelot then raises the slab which can only be raised by the knight who is destined to deliver the prisoners held in the land from which no one has yet returned. In Chrétien's poem Lancelot does not have to raise the slab to learn his own name, but refuses to reveal it to the hermit and the poet continues to withhold it from his audience. In the verse romance the adventure which will be accomplished by the knight who raises the slab still lies in the future; in the *PL* Lancelot is able to raise the slab after he has conquered the Dolorous Guard, but this represents just the first stage in the adventure, which he only completes when he puts an end to the enchantments of the castle (*PL* 248–50). Until then the castle and the cemetery continue to figure in the narrative, particularly in connection with the theme of identity. Sometimes the inscriptions on the tombs refer to the future, sometimes, when humans have intervened, to the past. But if this scene only represents the accomplishment of the first half of the adventure of the Dolorous Guard, it nevertheless forms a very important stage in the development of the identity theme, for at this point the hero learns his name and parentage. The inscription reads: 'Ci gerra Lanceloz del Lac, li filz au roi Ban de Benoyc' (*PL* 194.30–1). The solemn formula, with the name spelt out in full, followed by parentage, will be repeated at the end of each stage in the development of the identity theme. The significance is here underlined by the fact that he learns who he is in an episode in which the marvellous is emphasized in a way uncharacteristic of the work as a whole (see Chapter V) and in the presence of an emissary from the Lady of the Lake, namely the damsel sent by her to the castle who provided him with the magic shields which enabled him to conquer it; this damsel also learns Lancelot's name at this moment, much to his regret. Lanzelet learns his name and parentage after the episode of the *Jaemerlichen Urbor*, the Sorrowful Fief; after his battle with Iweret a priest comes out with a bier, expecting to bear away the body of the hero, but finds that it is Iweret who is dead. Then a damsel from the *Meidenland* comes to tell the young man that he is Lanzelet, son of Pant of Genewis (*Lanz.* 4706–10). Perceval, after his visit to the Grail Castle, guesses his name when he is talking to his cousin (*Perc.* 3573–7). Le Bel Inconnu learns his name from a mysterious voice after he has achieved the adventure of the *Fier Baissier* (*LBD* 3233). Thus, in both the *Conte del Graal* and *LBD*, as in the *PL*, the hero learns his name after an episode in which the supernatural plays an important part; in the *Lanzelet* too the episode has elements of mystery. The importance of the event is highlighted by the marvellous in all these works, but the effect is more marked in the *PL* because of the restrained use of the supernatural in the romance as a whole.

'Lancelot' is a *sorenon* (additional name), not a given name, conferred at baptism; he has won this name by a great exploit (both a noble heredity and the inspiration of love play a part in giving him the strength to fulfil his destiny in this way), but the name has not yet been established in the world at large. As has been seen, the name Lancelot has not been used in the narrative from the start of the Lady of the Lake's preparations to bring the youth to court. The young hero is designated by a series of titles used with some subtlety, not only to emphasize the continuing mystery of his identity for Arthur's court, and to draw attention to his succession of achievements under various disguises, but also to strengthen the interlacing technique, as will be shown in Chapter VII. News of the conquest of the Dolorous Guard by an unknown knight is soon to reach Arthur's court and will set in train the first of a series of quests led by Gauvain, the established knight who, by tradition, never hides his name if asked for it. The object of these quests is to resolve the mystery of this unknown knight, who knows his name but is determined to conceal it from others.

Gauvain's first quest for the identity of the Unknown Knight

One of the contrasts between this romance and most of the others in which an unknown knight plays a central role lies in the very active part played by Arthur's knights in trying to uncover the hero's identity, compared with their more passive role in, for example, *LBD*. As a result, in the *PL* the adventures of the individual hero are involved much more closely with Arthurian society as a whole, this involvement being strengthened by the nature of the tasks undertaken by the knights during their search, tasks which nearly all concern vassals of King Arthur, as will be seen in Chapter IV. It also means that the strands of individual adventures are woven into a much richer and firmer texture than would otherwise be the case. In the first phase of the work which has been analysed above (*PL* 1–166), the involvement of Arthur as King (and hence also that of his knights) with the fate of Lancelot is centred on Arthur's failure through inactivity to protect his vassal Ban—a sin of omission contrasted with the sins of commission by Claudas in his dispossession of the two kings, Ban and Bohort, and his imprisonment of the two children, Lyonel and Bohort. The narrative switches, therefore, from time to time from Lancelot's education in the Lake, in which his uncertainty over his own identity plays such an important part, to scenes at Arthur's court in which not only is the King's responsibility to avenge Ban's death emphasized, but also the fact that for the moment he can take no action, and to episodes concerning Claudas, who is shown to be destructively active and in dispute with his barons. The hopes and fears of those bound to Ban or Bohort, by blood relationship or feudal ties, concerning the safety of the vanished child and his two cousins provide a recurring subject for thought, but in Lancelot's case not for action. In the second phase, which leads up to Lancelot's discovery of his own name, attention is concentrated on the actions of the hero, although interest at Arthur's court is fostered by the periodic arrival of knights whom he has encountered. Once Lancelot has completed the first of his adventures which could be called spectacular, that is the conquest of the Dolorous Guard, and as a result has learned who he is, Arthur and his knights begin to participate more actively in the events of the story.

An expedition of the whole court to see at first-hand the marvels of which news has reached Arthur is to be found, for example, in *Yvain*, where the hero has to act quickly and depart secretly in order to reach the magic fountain before the arrival of Arthur (the expedition is planned, *Yvain*, 661–76 and executed, 2172–9). In the *PL* the news that the White Knight has captured the Dolorous Guard is brought to Arthur's court by the brother of Aiglyn des Vaus, one of Arthur's knights (*PL* 196). Most of the knights want to go to the Dolorous Guard to see if the news is true, and it is decided that a party of ten knights, led by Gauvain, will go. These reach the Dolorous Guard, but the White Knight is determined not to see them and orders the gates to be shut. This again is traditional: the hero will not want to be recognized until the time is ripe and he has completed his mission, whether it be to re-establish his reputation, as in *Erec* and *Yvain*, or to complete the establishment of one, as in the *PL*. Once again, the marvellous cemetery in the Dolorous Guard provides the focal point for this search for the name of the knight, but here, unlike the previous scene, the inscriptions are no longer all magical prophecies referring to the future. There has been human intervention on the part of the inhabitants of the castle, who believe that the coming of Arthur and his court may hasten the end of the enchantments. Inscriptions are made which give false information about events alleged to have taken place. Just as, during Lancelot's childhood, there are rumours of his death which have not yet been contradicted in the court, so here a false inscription declares that the conqueror (still unnamed) of the Dolorous Guard is dead, as well as many of Arthur's knights. This partial rationalization of the supernatural element in the cemetery is characteristic of the romance, as will be seen in Chapter V. One of the damsels from the Lake is also misled by this inscription (*PL* 199.20–2), which again limits the magical status of the emissaries from the Lake.

News of the reported death of the White Knight is sent to Arthur, who decides to come to see for himself, but, like Gauvain and his companions, he is plunged into confusion by the closing of the gates on the order of the White Knight and by more false inscriptions in the cemetery. The King's anxiety and frustration are increased by the imprisonment of Gauvain and his companions in another castle belonging to the Lord of the Dolorous Guard and by false reports of their deaths. They are eventually freed by Lancelot, still concealing his name. While they are still in prison, Kay tries to force Lancelot to come when summoned, a traditional theme, but with Gauvain in captivity there is no one to succeed by chivalrous courtesy where Kay's bad manners have failed, as happens in other texts.[22] The theme of the King's brooding (not here very fully developed) and that of Lancelot's love trances both recur and contribute to the confusion. Thus the first attempt of Arthur and his knights to discover the identity of the White Knight ends only in deeper bafflement.

The damsel from the Lake who was with Lancelot when he discovered his name is linked to the next attempt of Arthur's knights to uncover it. She is left imprisoned in the Dolorous Guard because she has, at the request of the White Knight, sworn an oath that she will stay there until he returns; he then becomes so preoccupied that he forgets her. The pleas for help from the damsel to Arthur lead up to Gauvain's first oath that he will not stay in any town more than one night, unless a prisoner or wounded, until he learns who the knight is, an oath which the King regrets as it means that Gauvain will leave court. The damsel tells Gauvain that he will hear news of the knight at the First Assembly of Logres, at the Second, and at the Third ((PL 219.38–9), a prophecy which gives some kind of structure to Gauvain's quest. This theme of an oath sworn by Gauvain as a prelude to a quest, followed by the grief of the King at the departure of his nephew, here only briefly sketched out, will recur in the romance in a much more developed form.[23] Such an oath, preceding a quest for a knight absent from court, is to be found in the *Conte del Graal* and the *Perceval Continuations*, but not in relation to an unknown knight, as will be seen below. Gauvain's quest is to be made more difficult by Lancelot's constant changes of shield (PL 224.23–6, 230.3–5, 250.35–6) and his withdrawals from circulation for long periods through injuries. Hence, more than once Gauvain meets Lancelot without recognizing him, realizing soon afterwards that he is the knight whom he is seeking, only to find that he is already too late. For example, he meets Lancelot in a litter, and learns soon afterwards that he is the knight who has sworn to avenge the wounded knight who came to Arthur's court, and is therefore the White Knight; by then the litter has disappeared (PL 226–7). The same thing happens in the First Assembly, where Lancelot, after distinguishing himself, collapses from his wounds; the Queen goes to see him, but then departs, apparently without having recognized him. Gauvain, learning that the wounded knight has an old wound as well as a new one, follows a chain of reasoning which links him with the knight of the litter, but is again frustrated in his intention of pressing the knight for his name by Lancelot's sudden departure. Thus Gauvain returns to court without achieving his quest and has to resume it after the First Assembly—a pattern which is repeated later in the romance.

During this first formal quest, which Gauvain has undertaken alone, he, as the established knight, is contrasted with the knight whose identity is the object of his quest by the fact, repeatedly stressed, that he is always willing to give his name.[24] Almost every time that he does so his opponents express regret at having fought him. At the same time, through no fault of his own, he has to endure some rather comic misadventures and is reproached by damsels from the Lake for having left a maiden in prison at the Dolorous Guard. His difficulties with a treacherous knight, Brehuz sanz Pitié, who has information about the unknown knight's whereabouts and is constantly leading Gauvain into slightly ridiculous situations, recall Gauvain's problems with Greoreas in the *Conte del Graal*.[25] The similarities are of particular interest as in the *PL* the position of the knight who has made his name (Gauvain) is contrasted with that of the knight who has yet to make it (Lancelot). Some scholars would explain the parallel adventures of Perceval and Gauvain in similar terms.[26] There is comedy in Perceval's appearance at court, but Gauvain, later in Chrétien's romance, is made to look somewhat ridiculous. In the *PL*, as we have seen, there are only a few traces of comedy in the presentation of Lancelot as a young knight, but this is not the only part of the romance in which Gauvain is put in a disadvantageous position, inappropriate for a knight of his reputation.[27]

Gauvain is helped in his quest by a damsel from the Lake who is anxious to deliver her colleague imprisoned in the Dolorous Guard. The first stage in their search is achieved when she recognizes the wounded Lancelot in the castle where he is being cared for by the Lady of Nohaut. She gives him secretly and without Gauvain's knowledge a letter addressed to 'Lancelot del Lac, lo fil lo roi Ban de Benoyc' (*PL* 239.5–6). This formula links up with that used at the end of Phase II of the making of Lancelot's name, when he raises the slab and discovers what he is called. The damsel then takes Gauvain to the Dolorous Guard, to the cemetery, where he is unable to raise the slab which hides Lancelot's name. But after Lancelot has recovered from his wound and won the Second Assembly, Gauvain, through the intervention of the damsel, learns that the name of the knight he is seeking is 'Lanceloz del Lac, li filz au roi Ban de Benoyc', the conqueror of the Dolorous Guard and the winner of two assemblies. He has therefore achieved his mission in' that he has brought back Lancelot's name to the court.

The author underlines the fact that this marks an important stage in the story by the formula he uses and by the threefold repetition: first Gauvain is told Lancelot's name (*PL* 255.32), then he tells Arthur the name of the knight who conquered the Dolorous Guard and won the two assemblies (256.33–6), and the information is repeated at the narrative switch (257.2–8), a technique which will be explored further in Chapter VII. Yet only the name is known at court, not the man himself, for the 'knight whose name has been brought to court' has departed. When Gauvain tells Arthur that the knight whom he has been seeking is Lancelot, son of Ban, he describes the young hero as 'uns des meillors qui ore i soit, et se il vit longuement, il sera toz li miaudres'. But Lancelot has still to make his name as the greatest knight of all, as indeed he strives to do in the next phase in the development of the identity theme, under yet another guise.

Arthur's wars with Galehot and the quest by forty knights

The mystery of the Unknown Knight (or rather Knights, with Lancelot's frequent changes of shields) continues to preoccupy Arthur, his Queen, and his knights, and to determine the narrative structure of alternating battles and quests. After an episode in which Lancelot, most regretfully, has to kill another knight because of his oath to avenge the wounded knight (one in a chain of such battles which will eventually land him in the prison of the Lady of Malohaut), the narrative switches to Arthur and to an account of the dreams which foretell that he will shortly be in peril of losing his throne. This is followed by the arrival of messengers who deliver Galehot's challenge to the King that he must become his vassal or have his land taken away from him by force. These are all episodes preparing the way for the Third Assembly at which, as the damsel has told the King and the court (*PL* 219.38–9), they will have more news of the knight who, after the Second Assembly, has been identified as Lancelot. But before the assembly there follows a comic interlude in which Lancelot, incognito, comes into contact with the Queen and some of Arthur's knights through a series of love trances. First, while contemplating the Queen, he lets his horse go deep into the river and is rescued by Yvain, who does not recognize him as he is carrying an ancient and battered shield. He then allows himself to be captured by a cowardly knight, called Daguenet, and to be brought as a prisoner to the Queen. She also shows no signs of recognizing him and tells Daguenet to let him go. After cutting such a ridiculous figure as a helpless, unnamed knight, he then proceeds in an abstracted way to kill two giants, an achievement witnessed by Yvain. Lancelot's only comment after the battle is to complain about 'ces vilains qui m'ont mort mon cheval' (*PL* 270.38–9). Just before he does so, a damsel passes and says: 'C'est la tierce' (270.35). Yvain reports to the Queen and some of the knights the victory over the giants and repeats the damsel's words.

These enable Gauvain to identify the knight with Lancelot of the Lake and to tell the Queen privately of this identification, thus providing a link between the two stages in the development of the theme. He reminds the Queen of what the damsel said:

'Ele nos dist, fait messire Gauvains, que nos orriens enseignes del chevalier qui nos fist entrer an la Doleruese Garde a la premiere asanblee qui seroit el reiaume de Logres, et a la seconde, et a la tierce. Et c'est la tierce, et li chevaliers qui les jaianz a morz si est Lanceloz del Lac, et de voir lo sachoiz.' (*PL* 272.14–18.)

Throughout this series of events the comic side is emphasized. There would seem to be an element of parody in this chain of episodes which brings together the love trance, with its inherent comic possibilities, and the theme of the Unknown Knight. Although the battle with giants is of course a common feature in Arthurian romance, it should nevertheless be noted that a giant-killing episode occurs in romances conforming to the narrative pattern of the Fair Unknown.[28] There may well be an ironic parallel and contrast intended here with the version found in *Erec* (4280–541). There the battle with giants occurs after Erec, who unlike Lancelot has been recognized, has been persuaded to make contact with Arthur's court; he does this reluctantly because he is still trying to prove something about his love and his reputation as a knight. After the battle the victory over the giants is reported to Arthur's court by the knight who has been rescued. But the episode in *Erec* does not end in a gale of laughter in Arthur's court, as it does in the *PL* where everyone, while glad that the giants are dead, is amused at the noise Daguenet is making about his capture of the knight who killed the giants:

Mais Daguenez fait tel noise que riens ne puet a lui durer, et dit a chascun que il avoit pris lo bon chevalier qui les jaianz ocist. 'Tel chevalier ne prenez vos mie.'

Ensin atandent jusque a vespres qe li rois revient. An li conte les novelles c'uns chevaliers avoit les jaianz morz. Mout an a li rois grant joie et si compaignon et totes les genz del païs. Et Daguenez vient a lui et si li dit:

'Sire, par la foi que vos doi, ge pris ce boen chevalier.'

Et li rois s'an rist mout volentiers et tuit li autre. (*PL* 272.20–8.)

It may also be significant that in the *PL* it is Yvain who brings the news back to court, just as it has been Yvain who rescues Lancelot from drowning while absorbed in thoughts of love, for Yvain himself, in Chrétien's poem, kills a giant during his process of redemption as a lover. This will be pursued further in the next chapter. The combination of humiliation and admiration of the hero also has resonances of *le Chevalier de la Charrette*.[29]

Lancelot is then again withdrawn from circulation, this time not by wounds but by imprisonment. The Lady of Malohaut imprisons him because, through his oath to the wounded knight, he has been forced to kill one of her knights. Throughout his imprisonment she makes vain efforts to discover his name. In this part of the romance he is often identified as the 'knight who is in prison'. As in a similar episode in *le Chevalier de la Charrette*, Lancelot is temporarily released from captivity to fight incognito in armour provided by the lady of the castle where he is held prisoner. In the *PL* he is freed on parole to take part not just in a tournament but in a battle where the fate of Arthur's kingdom is at stake. In Chrétien's poem Guinevere asks Lancelot, who is fighting incognito, to play the coward for a time in the tournament and as a result he is mocked by the others until the Queen reverses her command; he then performs great deeds of arms and wins honour and acclaim. In the prose romance the Unknown Knight, when he first appears with a red shield, is also mocked because he waits, deep in thought, on the edge of the battle and is suspected of being a coward; but the reason for his inactivity and apparent lack of knightly worth is not absolute obedience to his lady's commands but another characteristic of the true lover, that absorption in the thoughts of love which had already given a false impression of cowardly ineptitude earlier in the romance, in the near escape from drowning and the capture by Daguenet. When aroused by a wet clod of earth (the water treatment seems to be the standard remedy in the romance for lovers' trances), he confounds his mockers by plunging into battle and performing marvels, still unrecognized beneath the unfamilar red arms. Thus the promise of the damsel to Arthur and his knights, that they would see more of the Unknown Knight at the Third Assembly, is fulfilled, but no one realizes this, as they do not connect this new unknown knight in red armour with the knight in white armour whom they now know to have been Lancelot. The theme of a knight fighting incognito in different-coloured armour on different days in a tournament is a traditional one in romance, to be found in *Cligés* and in the *Lanzelet*;[30] but in the *PL* it is more integrated into the romance in that it forms part of a continuing theme. Lancelot makes a name for himself, not just once but several times, under different arms, and each time the admiring Arthur and his knights have to try to penetrate another disguise in order to learn the identity of a knight who has achieved great deeds.

The fighting ends for the day, the Unknown Knight withdraws, and the King is left deeply troubled. The visit to him by a *preudomme*, with its echoes of the earlier visit by a *rendu*, provides a final interpretation of his dreams, this time in religious terms: the need to seek help in God. The *preudomme* lectures him on the duties of kingship and reproaches him, as the *rendu* had done, for his failure to avenge his vassal Ban's death (*PL* 285.11–14). A link is thus made between the disappearance of Lancelot, the child, and the King's present troubles, and this serves to underline the dramatic irony of the situation, a dramatic irony which is central also to the love theme. Arthur, unknown to himself, because he, unlike the reader, is unaware of the identity of the Red Knight, can only be saved with the help of the man whom he has failed as a king and feudal lord, the same man whose exploits on Arthur's behalf are inspired by his love for Arthur's wife.

Galehot declares a truce after the second day of the assembly, but expresses his intention of returning to renew the battle a year hence, with the Red Knight (*le bon chevalier*) in his company. However, Lancelot has returned to his prison, and no one knows where he is. Thus Arthur and Guinevere and all their knights are again tormented by their desire to find out who an unknown knight is, but this time they do not need merely to discover his identity, but to have him with them in battle to save the kingdom. This, therefore, marks a further stage in the establishment of Lancelot's reputation, but a stage to which his identity as Lancelot of the Lake has not yet been attached.

Before the threat to himself as King, Arthur, understandably, falls into a deep, black brooding, which resembles very closely the episode earlier in the story when he was brooding over his failure to avenge the death of Ban and grieving over the reported death of his son (*PL* 137–8). Now he is brooding over the failure of his knights to bring him the knight he needs, whom he describes as the greatest of all knights, 'meillor chevalier de toz les prodomes' (*PL* 297.6–7). When roused, he accuses his men publicly of their failure, and this prompts Gauvain to start another quest for an unknown knight, this time as leader of forty knights. The brooding, followed by the forcible awakening, the accusations of Arthur against his knights, their recognition of the truth of what he says, the solemn declaration by Gauvain of his intention to find the knight, his appeal to his fellows which finds an immediate response, the lamentations of Arthur at the massive exodus from his court, the swearing of oaths that none will return until the knight is found, and the listing of the companions of the Quest, all provide yet another parallel with the *Conte del Graal* and with its *Continuations*, where the theme occurs several times.[31] The parallel with the Perceval romances is underlined by Gauvain's reference to the Grail Quest (which will be discussed further in Chapter VI):

'Seignor chevalier, qui ores voudra entrer an la plus haute queste qui onques fust aprés celi do Graal, si veigne aprés moi. Hui est toz li pris et tote l'enors do monde apareilliee a celui cui Dex fera aventureus de la haute troveüre, et por noiant se vantera ja mais d'anor conquerre qui ci la laisse.' (*PL* 297.20–4.)

But in the *Perceval Continuations* the quests are not for an unknown knight, but in the *First Continuation* for Girflet, imprisoned in Chastel Orguelleus, and in the *Second Continuation* for Perceval.

None of the adventures of the forty knights on their quest are given, not even those of Gauvain for, as the tale explains (*PL* 299.17–20) the quest is unsuccessful and the companions return to Arthur without the knight whom they are seeking. They break their oath because, as Gauvain says, it is better that they alone should lose their honour than that the King should lose his land and honour to Galehot through their absence, whereby they would also be dishonoured (*PL* 304.14–18). Instead, the narrative concentrates on the Lady of Malohaut's attempts to discover her captive's name. She is all the more anxious to do so because she can see from the state of his armour and from the marks on his face and arms that he has distinguished himself in battle. She goes to Arthur's court, expecting to get information there, only to discover that Gauvain and forty other knights are out looking for the Unknown Knight (on this occasion the Red Knight) who is safely concealed in her prison. She leaves Arthur's court without the name and without revealing the purpose of her visit. Her attempts to get the information from Lancelot are equally unsuccessful. She offers him three possible means of ransoming himself so that he can take part in the next assembly: to say who he is, to say whom he loves, or to say whether he ever expects to do as much at arms as he did in the first battle against Galehot. It should be noted that her captive's refusal to reveal either his name or that of the woman he loves links together the two main Lancelot themes. He reluctantly accepts the third ransom, says that he does expect to do as much again, and is therefore permitted to return, this time under black arms, to Arthur's second battle against Galehot.

Throughout the second of the battles with Galehot the preoccupation of those who are not so heavily involved in the fighting that they do not have time to think is the question of the identity of the Black Knight, who appears on the edge of the battle at exactly the same place as had appeared the Red Knight. The Lady of Malohaut knows that he is in fact the same person as the Red Knight and enjoys playing upon the knowledge which only she possesses by harping on the problem of his identity. 'Qui puet il estre?' she says, but she herself does not know his name. Gauvain is reminded of the Red Knight (*PL* 309.23–31) and wishes that this Black Knight might prove to be the one he is seeking, as earlier he had suspected during the Second Assembly of Logres that the 'bon Chevalier' (Lancelot) was the object of his quest (*PL* 255.1–2). Because of these hopes he is willing to collaborate with the Lady of Malohaut in sending the Black Knight lances and a message. The Queen is too troubled by the danger to the kingdom to turn her thoughts to such matters. Yet again, she does not recognize Lancelot, here in full armour, but is eventually persuaded to send him a message. The knight then performs such feats that Kay, even in the middle of the battle, spares a moment to ask who the Black Knight is. But once again, before Arthur or his knights can get hold of the knight, question him, and persuade him to stay with them, he leaves the battle, this time, to their horror, in the company of Galehot.[32] As before, Lancelot shows himself determined to conceal his identity and extracts from Galehot a promise that he will not ask his name. He agrees to fight the next day on the side of Galehot, on condition that when he asks him to do so, Galehot should submit to Arthur. Galehot fulfils his promise and Arthur is saved for the second time, but Lancelot is yet again withdrawn from circulation, this time to be concealed in Galehot's camp.

Once peace has been made between the two leaders, Galehot goes to Arthur's tent, and the conversation revolves around the identity of the Black Knight and the sacrifices which each person would be willing to make to have his company for ever. With Galehot and Guinevere's replies the love theme and the identity theme are once again brought together (see Chapter III). Throughout the subsequent visits of Galehot to Arthur's court, he, unlike the Lady of Malohaut after the first battle, does not revel in his secret knowledge of the whereabouts of the Unknown Knight, for he is afraid that he will lose his companion, still nameless, to Guinevere. Gauvain, once again, is the first to suspect that it was the Black Knight who persuaded Galehot to make peace; he tells Guinevere, and this time she believes him and herself guesses that the Black Knight is with Galehot. She persists in taking Galehot aside and pressing him to bring the Black Knight to see her, but he has difficulty in persuading his companion, who, in addition to his awe of the lady he loves, fears as always lest he should be recognized (*PL* 336.21–2, 338.36–8). Guinevere is even more anxious to meet him when she learns of this fear of recognition:

'Dex, fait ele, qui puet il estre?'
'Dame, fait Galehoz, si m'aïst Dex, ne sai, que onques ne me dist son non, ne qui il est.'
'Non? fait ele, Si m'aïst Dex, mervoilles oi. Or m'est assez plus tart que ge lo voie.' (*PL* 339.18–22.)

There is, therefore, a careful build-up to the scene central to the whole structure of the work in relation to both the love theme and the identity theme, namely Guinevere's first secret meeting with Lancelot. During her conversation with him, by persistent questioning, she finally makes him confess to all the exploits which he has achieved under his various arms, with his ever-changing succession of shields. She declares that she knows who he is:

'Ha! fait ele, donc sai ge bien qui vos iestes. Vos avez non Lanceloz do Lac.' (*PL* 344.11–12.)

She then forces him to admit that he has been inspired throughout by his love for her. The meeting ends with the Queen taking Lancelot by the right hand and giving him to Galehot as a companion, revealing his name as she does so:

'Et savez vos, fait ele a Galehot, que ge vos ai doné?'
'Dame, fait il, naie.'
'Ge vos ai doné Lancelot do Lac, lo fil au roi Ban de Benoyc.' (*PL* 349.13–15.)

The importance of this information is underlined by the author when he describes both the discomfort of Lancelot and the joy of Galehot:

Et ansi lo fait au chevalier conoistre, qui mout en a grant honte. Lors en a greignor joie Galehoz que il n'ot onques mais, car il avoit assez oï dire ansi com paroles vont que c'estoit Lanceloz do Lac et que ce estoit li miaudres chevaliers do monde, povres hom; et bien savoit que li rois Bans avoit esté mout jantils hom et mout puissanz d'amis et de terre. (*PL* 349.16–21.)

Thus Lancelot's name is attached to his achievements as both Black and Red Knight, and this, for those who know the secret, adds to the reputation he had already established as the White Knight when his name was made known in Arthur's court after the Second Assembly of Logres (*PL* 256–7). In this way the meeting in which Guinevere and Lancelot exchange their first kiss also marks a stage in the establishment of Lancelot's identity as a great knight in the eyes of the Queen and Galehot, the man and the woman who both desire his love. Indeed Lancelot finds himself through his love: his heredity as son of Ban of Benoyc, the name he wins at the Dolorous Guard, his winning of the love of Guinevere, all combine to create his identity as the hero Lancelot of the Lake. The author underlines the importance of the stage reached in the making of Lancelot's name and his love in the same way that he had given emphasis to the point in the story when Lancelot's name was first brought to Arthur's court, where he summed up the situation in a sentence beginning 'Et ci premierement fu . . .' (*PL* 257.2).

He uses a similar formula here:

Ansi fu li premiers acointemanz faiz de la reine et de Lancelot do Lac par Galehot. Et Galehoz ne l'avoit onques conneü que de veoir, et por ce li avoit fait Lanceloz creanter que il ne li demanderoit son non tant que il li deïst, ou autres por lui. (*PL* 349.21–5.)

This bestowal of Lancelot's companionship on Galehot by Guinevere leads up to the next secret departure of Lancelot, when he goes with Galehot to Sorelois, where he will be held out of circulation during Gauvain's last, and successful, quest for him. But before this happens, another person is added to the three (apart from the Lady of the Lake) who share the secret of the Black Knight's identity, namely the Lady of Malohaut in whose prison Lancelot spent his last period of retirement. There are therefore two pairs, the Queen and her companion, and Galehot and his companion, who can exchange secret messages and console one another. Without revealing her true motives, the Queen persuades the King to ask the Lady of Malohaut to stay with her. Galehot leaves for Sorelois, taking Lancelot secretly with him. There Lancelot will remain well hidden, as a long description of its inaccessibility emphasizes. At this stage in the story Lancelot has established his name and identity within a select circle, and above all in relation to the Queen. Descriptions such as Red or Black or White Knight are replaced in the narrative by the name Lancelot, for the Queen now knows that the renown won under all these different guises belongs to one knight, Lancelot of the Lake, son of King Ban of Benoyc, who is dedicated to her service. There is a parallel for this in *le Chevalier de la Charrette* where Lancelot's name is only used in the narrative and revealed to the reader after the Queen has told a damsel that the knight who is fighting Meleagant (after crossing the Sword Bridge) is Lancelot:

> 'Lanceloz del Lac a a non
> Li chevaliers mien esciant.'
> (*Char.* 3660–1.)

In *le Chevalier au Lion* (*Yvain*) the hero re-establishes his reputation under a new name (although his old one does not disappear entirely from the narrative), and his lady finally learns who he is; but the significance of the bringing together of the names is different. Laudine is eventually forced to accept that the Knight of the Lion, whose help she needs, is the same man as Yvain, who broke his promise to her. The resonance of the scene in the *PL* is increased by memories of other naming scenes in two of the great Arthurian romances of the twelfth century, and, as we shall see in Chapter III, this is part of a whole web of allusions to Chrétien's two great knightly lovers, Lancelot and Yvain.

Gauvain's renewed quest for the Unknown Knight, the war with the Saxons, and Lancelot's installation as Knight of the Round Table

This is the part of the romance in which the theme of a quest for the Unknown Knight by a company of Arthur's knights, led by Gauvain, is most fully developed and completely dominates the story. Lancelot plays a passive role, hidden away with Galehot in Sorelois, almost as if he were in prison, as he puts it:

'. . . nos somes ci an prison, et a mout grant piece, ne ne veïsmes pieç'a joster ne chevaleries, si perdons noz tans et noz aages.' (*PL* 531.21–3.)

The narrative switches to Lancelot occasionally, to show him pining, and Lyonel as messenger provides a contact not only between Lancelot and Guinevere, but also at times with Gauvain as he proceeds on his quest. The narrative pattern leading up to the quest is the same as that preceding the previous one, but the

King's brooding is treated at greater length, and of all the broodings in the text this one has the most details in common with the version of the motif in the *First Continuation*.[33] In both texts Arthur is holding a knife when he falls into his dark abstraction, Gauvain sends a message to him, and the King replies that he is thinking of their great shame. The knights then come and ask him what he means; when they have heard the reason for his melancholy, they agree that he has good cause and declare their intention of redeeming their honour. The knights taking part in the expedition are listed in both texts, with Gauvain taking the lead. In the *PL* Gauvain sends a female cupbearer, Lore de Carduel, to Arthur, in the *First Continuation* he sends a *vallet*; but the appearance of Lore in connection with a brooding episode has a parallel right at the end of *le Conte del Graal* (9216–32), where Lore, one of Guinevere's damsels, runs to tell the Queen that Arthur has fainted at table through grief at Gauvain's absence from court. The King's grief at the departure of Gauvain and so many knights and his vain efforts to dissuade them from leaving him, although also to be found in the earlier scene in the *PL* (297–8) before Gauvain's quest with the forty knights, are not found in the *First Continuation* version, where the King is himself involved in the expedition organized to redeem the honour of the Arthurian court. But there is a parallel in the episode in *le Conte del Graal*, mentioned above, with the Queen's role in trying to reassure the unhappy King about Gauvain's absence. The object of the expedition in the *First Continuation* is also different, namely the capture of the Chastel Orgueilleus, where Girflet is a prisoner, but in the *Second Continuation* Gauvain leads a quest for a knight absent from court, Perceval. Although the scenes leading up to this quest in the *Second Continuation* do not show the same close parallels with the *PL* as do those in the *First Continuation,* there are some names in common in the list of knights (although most seem to have been taken from *Erec*) and the passage following the listing in the *Second Continuation* (29190–208) shows close similarities with the corresponding one in the *PL* (365.35–366.3), as will be explored further in Chapter VI. Thus, just as before the Lancelot quest by forty knights we are reminded of the Perceval romances by Gauvain's description of the quest as the highest ever undertaken after that of the Grail (*PL* 297.20–1), so here there seems to be another deliberate echo of a quest for Perceval—yet another in the series of explicit or implicit cross-references in the text between the story of Lancelot and that of Perceval.

In the *Second Continuation* the knights are setting off in search of a named knight, Perceval; in the *PL* as far as Arthur and almost all the companions on the quest are concerned, they are seeking an unknown knight. For example, the Lord of the Estroite Marche reports that Yvain and Sagremor, both companions of the quest, have told him that 'il queroient lo meillor chevalier qui onques l'escu portast, et si ne savoient ou, ne il no conoissoient' (*PL* 447.30-3). But before the knights leave, Guinevere takes Gauvain aside and, on his promise to keep the secret from his companions, reveals to him that the knight he is seeking is with Galehot and that he is called Lancelot of the Lake. Guinevere has waited to tell Gauvain this until after Lancelot has gone, and the King's nephew speaks later of the *servise demi* (*PL* 401.39) that the Queen has done him; but at least he knows the name of the knight whom he is seeking and has some idea where to look, although he still has to find the elusive hero. On his journey, he tells a very few of the people whom he meets and from whom he gets directions that he is looking for Lancelot.

The twenty companions (the rest of the original forty are not free to come) all separate, and, as is explained later (*PL* 365.35-6), because Gauvain alone is successful in this quest, only his adventures are followed through in detail; we only learn what is happening to his companions when they happen to cross his path. His first series of adventures are of particular interest and play an important role in the structure of the work and in the development of the identity theme, because in them it is Gauvain the established knight, renowned throughout the world, and by tradition always willing to give his name, who here plays the part of the Unknown Knight. Thus we have here not only another element in the system of parallels and contrasts between Lancelot and Gauvain within the romance, but also another example of the complex interplay between this text and Arthurian literary tradition which would be recognized by the thirteenth-century reader.

In the *PL* five companions of the quest, having separated, meet again. They see a knight contemplating a shield and alternatively rejoicing and weeping. Gauvain's companions are determined to find out who the knight is and why he is behaving in this way, but are one after the other unhorsed by him. Just as Gauvain is about to take his turn, a dwarf appears, starts to beat the knight, and then leads him away. Gauvain decides to follow in order to find out the explanation for the strange behaviour of the knight.[34] He finds a beautiful damsel in a tent, who accuses him of being cowardly because he has not stopped a good knight from being beaten. He then undergoes further humiliation at the hands of the dwarf, who hits his horse and also accuses him of cowardice. He seizes the dwarf and threatens to kill him unless he explains why the knight behaved in the way he did. The dwarf agrees to do so, provided that Gauvain, whom he has not recognized, promises to fight a battle with justice on his side. Gauvain consents, and the dwarf then explains that his lady, the Lady of Roestoc, needs a champion in a judicial combat to defend her against a powerful neighbour, Segurades, who wants to marry her against her will. The knight who wept and rejoiced and was beaten is called Hector; he would like to undertake the battle,

but cannot because his *amie*, the damsel in the tent, who is the cousin of the
Lady of Roestoc, will not allow him to do so. While the dwarf is talking to
Gauvain, he receives a letter from his lady asking him to fetch Gauvain to be her
champion. The dwarf says that he has no hope of finding him as he is always
away from court, seeking adventures 'comme li plus prodom do monde' (*PL*
377.14). He declares, indicating Gauvain: 'Mais ge li manrai an eschange por monseignor Gauvain lo peior chevalier qui onqes portast escu: ce est cist chevaliers
qui ci est.' (*PL* 377.15–16.) Thus we have a variation on the theme of the
Unknown Knight who is unwillingly accepted as a champion for a judicial
combat to defend a lady by the messenger who has orders to get one of Arthur's
greatest knights. Here, ironically, the messenger believes that he has failed in his
mission when he has in fact succeeded. This should be compared with the situation at the beginning of Lancelot's career as a knight when he insists on being
chosen as champion and is accepted very doubtfully by the messenger (*PL* 163).
Both episodes echo the narrative pattern of the Tale of the Fair Unknown. The
more common situation is that the champion is reproached with his excessive
youth, as in the case of Lancelot and the hero of *li Biaus Descouneüs*, but here the
unrecognized Gauvain is reproached with his alleged cowardice. This is then
followed both here (*PL* 378–80) and for Lancelot earlier in the romance (*PL*
166–74) by a series of tests. As we have seen, the tests Lancelot undergoes after his
knighting do not follow quite the usual pattern, but here the series of battles on
the journey to Roestoc against numbers of attackers is more similar, except in
one important particular, to those to be found in the Fair Unknown tale. The
battles themselves are particularly close to the series in *Erec*, which, as scholars
such as Brugger, and more recently Luttrell, have pointed out, here shows
marked resemblances to the tale of the Fair Unknown.[35]

The usual pattern in the Fair Unknown tale as exemplified by *li Biaus Descouneüs* is that of the two messengers sent to fetch the champion, a damsel and a
dwarf, it is the damsel who continually pours scorn upon the Unknown Knight.
She is unwilling to be convinced by the ever mounting proofs of his valour, as
he successfully passes each test, whereas the dwarf is much more courteous and
sympathetic to the hero. In the *PL* there are a damsel and a dwarf who both
despise the knight they are bringing back, although it is the dwarf who plays the
main role as despiser; but there is an inversion of the usual situation in that,
although the series of proving battles is retained, they are not used to test the
champion's worthiness but that of Hector, the knight whom the champion
replaces. The dwarf continually reproaches Gauvain for his cowardliness, while
not allowing him to take part in any of the battles, as he says that the whole
party would be in danger if defended by so poor a knight. He therefore uses the
battles to prove Hector's chivalry at the expense of the anonymous Gauvain,

and, to underline the unfavourable comparison, Gauvain has to stand by and watch Hector bear the brunt of the attacks without being allowed to intervene. The unwillingly passive role of Gauvain here recalls the passive role which Erec attempted to force on Enide in Chrétien's poem, when he forbade her, under threat of punishment, to warn him of approaching danger; but unlike Gauvain, who cannot insist on fighting without appearing to cast doubts on Hector's chivalry, Enide, by refusing to obey orders, proves the quality of her love, while at the same time her husband is proving the quality of his chivalry. Thus we have here an inversion in the *PL* of the pattern in the Fair Unknown romances, an inversion by which the battles serve to reinforce the dwarf's conviction that he is bringing a useless champion, a conviction so deep that he does not trouble to find out the knight's name, almost as though he does not think him worthy of one. He sends word to the Lady of Roestoc that he is bringing her a knight whom he considers to be the worst in the world in place of Gauvain and that she should persuade Hector's *amie* to allow him to be champion instead. Hector's *amie* refuses once again. The Lady of Roestoc is understandably deeply dismayed and interprets every word and action of Gauvain as further proof of his inadequacy as a knight, while her seneschal, playing the role of the courteous dwarf in the Fair Unknown tale, urges her to take a more favourable view and at least receive the knight politely and give him tokens—a belt and a ring— as he is to fight for her. In the meantime the substitute Gauvain, here under the special circumstances acting against his usual practice, decides to conceal his true identity. He makes the lady and the seneschal promise not to ask his name, much to the regret of the seneschal who has just said privately to the lady that they should already have asked their champion who he is.

We have, therefore, throughout the episode an ironic play on the theme of the Fair Unknown. Gauvain wins his battle, and the Lady of Roestoc is so full of joy at her unexpected deliverance that she forgets the champion who has saved her and whose name she still does not know. He disappears after his victory, as Lancelot has always done after his, but in Gauvain's case for rather different reasons: Lancelot wants to escape the curiosity of all those who are only too anxious to discover his identity, whereas Gauvain leaves because no one is paying him enough attention to make any attempt to find out who he is. However, the parallel between Lancelot and Gauvain continues in that Gauvain's disappearance, like those of Lancelot, is followed by a quest for the vanished knight. The Lady of Roestoc goes to Arthur's court to try to get news of her unknown champion, and her cousin is eventually forced to consent to Hector's departure on a quest for him. He sets out to search for this unknown knight, and it is only after he has left court that definite evidence reaches the Lady of Roestoc that the champion she has so despised and neglected as an unworthy substitute for

Gauvain is none other than Gauvain himself. Thus, throughout the Roestoc episode the theme of the Unknown Knight is used in such a way as to make contrasts and parallels between the young, unknown knight, Lancelot, who has a reputation to establish, and the well-known and honoured Gauvain, who has made his reputation. The splendid touches of comedy here in the spectacle of Gauvain being scorned for not being Gauvain provide the humorous element in this study of the mature knight to balance the comedy in the behaviour of the immature knight, of which there were hints in Lancelot's early adventures. Similar parallels and contrasts are very characteristic of Chrétien's *Conte del Graal*. The theme of the Gauvain substitute is continued in the episode in which Gauvain knights a *vallet*, Helin, who has seen in a dream that he should be knighted by Gauvain, but has never succeeded in finding him at court. After seeing the battle fought on behalf of the Lady of Roestoc, Helin decides that her champion would be a worthy substitute for Gauvain. Gauvain has thus, as it were, proved himself worthy of his own name and, fighting incognito, has justified his own reputation, while Lancelot, the unproved knight, has had to prove himself before he could learn his name.

In the next adventure undertaken by Gauvain (again fighting anonymously) during his quest for Lancelot, he helps to establish the identity of the two greatest knights in the world. Agravain, his brother, is lying ill and can only be cured by the blood from the two best knights. The blood from the very best will cure his arm, the blood from the next best will cure his leg. Gauvain meets a damsel, who does not recognize him and tells him that if he will follow her into a certain chamber, she will reveal to him the names of the two greatest knights. He follows her, and a band of knights try to force him to give his blood; he resists valiantly, but eventually agrees because of his pity for the sick knight, whom he then discovers to be his own brother Agravain. His blood heals Agravain's leg, and the damsel then fulfils her promise to tell Gauvain the names of the best knights:

> 'Sire, fait ele, il i pert bien que vos an iestes li uns.'
> 'Et li autres, dist messires Gauvains, qui est?'
> Et ele dit que ce est cil qui vainqui l'asanblee do roi Artu et de Galehot.
> 'Mais ge no sai veraiement nomer.' (*PL* 420.9–13.)

Gauvain then tells her that the knight in question is called 'Lanceloz do Lac, li fiz au roi Ban de Benoyc.' (*PL* 420.37–8).

This episode represents, therefore, one more step in the establishment of the reputation of Lancelot; it indicates his position in the Arthurian hierarchy: he is an even greater knight than Gauvain, who here, as in the work of Chrétien, provides a measuring rod or point of comparison with the hero. The knight who can surpass Gauvain must be the greatest in the world. Yet, in spite of Gauvain's great reputation, frequently stressed in the romance, his own brother Agravain has not believed that Gauvain would be one of the two knights whose blood he needs in order to be healed (*PL* 419.25–31). This lack of faith probably reflects more on the quality of Agravain than on Gauvain.

Another character, Hector, is associated with these two *preudommes*, Lancelot and Gauvain, in this episode through a sword which is entrusted to Gauvain so that he can find a fitting recipient. Agravain explains that it is a sword suitable for a *bachelier* yet to be proved:

'Sire, se l'espee est tex com les letres tesmoignent, ele est bone a bacheler qui n'est mies esprovez. Mais ele ne seroit mies si boene a un prodome, car ce dient les letres que ele ne fera ja mais s'anpirier non, et cil sor cui ele sera amendera totevoies. Et qant ele me fu envoiee et ge soi que ele avoit tel costume, si me pansai que nus ne l'anploieroit miauz de vos, si la vos anveoié.' (*PL* 420.19–24.)

Gauvain sends it to Hector—in fact the arrival at Arthur's court of the messenger bearing it has already been described (*PL* 404). With Lancelot out of circulation in Sorelois, Hector, as has already been seen, plays an important role in the Roestoc episode in which Gauvain has the part of the Unknown Knight. Thus the traditional contrast between the young hero, yet to be proved, and Gauvain, the established knight, is made more complex by the introduction of Hector, who has still to make his reputation at Arthur's court and who is to have a seat at the Round Table at the same time as Lancelot. Sometimes his adventures have parallels with those of Gauvain, sometimes with those of Lancelot. The theme of Hector acting as a substitute for Gauvain, begun during the Roestoc Episode, when he fights instead of the anonymous Gauvain in the tests leading up to the judicial battle, is continued in episodes such as the delivery of Heliene sanz Per from Persides. As has already been seen, Hector does not just serve as a worthy substitute for Gauvain, but also as a contrast with him as the *bachelier* who is yet to be proved and, like Lancelot, as the faithful lover. The threefold comparison between Lancelot, Gauvain, and Hector will be examined in detail in my analysis of the technique of pairing in Chapter VII.

Hector achieves his quest for Gauvain and the two companions together challenge Galehot to send out champions at l'Isle Perdu, so that Hector too is involved in the final battle in which Gauvain, fighting incognito, obliges Lancelot to confess to his name. This is not, however, achieved through force of arms, for Gauvain is having to give way before Lancelot's furious onslaught, but through the revelation by Lyonel of Gauvain's identity. Previous battles in the romance have been stopped by such a revelation, as few knights wished to continue fighting Gauvain once they knew who he was, because of his great

UNIVERSITY OF WINCHESTER
LIBRARY

reputation;[36] but here it is the Queen's command which stops Lancelot in his tracks when Lyonel tells him that he is fighting Gauvain and that he must cease at once, for 'la reine li mande que il face qanque il [Gauvain] voudra.' (*PL* 537.4). Lancelot then flees from the battle. Gauvain leaps behind him on his horse, determined to learn his name, but Lancelot is still unwilling to give it. Gauvain tells Galehot that he already knows his companion's name and all his achievements:

'Ge sai, fait il, de voir que ce est Lanceloz do Lac, li filz lo roi Ban de Benoyc, cil qui fist la pais de monseignor lo roi Artu et de vos.' (*PL* 538.31-3.)

Once again an important point in the development of the theme is given emphasis by the use of a solemn formula. Then, at long last, with the help of Galehot, Gauvain fulfils his promise of making Lancelot pronounce his own name and acknowledge aloud who he is (*PL* 539.6-7), thus reaching another stage in the establishment of his identity and reputation.

However, Arthur is not to learn that it was Lancelot who saved him from Galehot or to welcome Lancelot openly at court until Lancelot has become Guinevere's lover in the full physical sense and has saved the King and his kingdom yet again, this time from his traditional enemies, the Saxons. Once again Lancelot fights incognito and in borrowed armour on the King's side, this time alongside his companions, Gauvain, Hector, and Galehot (also not in their own armour), but he wears a device so that he can be recognized by the Queen. Arthur is captured by the Saxons, but freed by Lancelot, and it is at this dramatic moment that Gauvain tells the King that he has succeeded in his quest:

'Sire, veez ci celui que nos avons tant quis. Ge l'ai trové, si m'an aquit.'
'Et Dex! fait li rois, qui est il?'
'C'est, fait messires Gauvains, Lanceloz do Lac, cil qui vainqui les deus asanblees de vos et de Galehot qui ci est.' (*PL* 566.17-21.)

Arthur then falls at Lancelot's feet and says:

'Biau sire, ge me met an vostre merci et moi et m'anor et ma terre, car vos m'avez randu et l'un et l'autre.' (*PL* 566.24-5.)

Thus it is only at the time that Arthur is freed by Lancelot that the King learns his name and how much he already owes him. But Guinevere had known Lancelot's name for very much longer and has to pretend that she does not know who he is. There is irony, as far as the King is concerned, in the terms which she uses:

'Sire chevaliers, ge ne sai qui vos iestes, ce poise moi; ne ge ne vos sai que offrir por l'annor mon seignor avant et por la moie aprés, que vos avez hui maintenue. Mais por lui avant et por moi aprés vos otroi ge moi et m'amor, si comme leiaus dame doit doner a leial chevalier.' (*PL* 569.11–15.)

But there is even more irony in the King's reaction: 'Et qant li rois l'ot, si l'am prise mout de ce que ele l'a fait sanz estre anseigniee?' (*PL* 569.16–17). He then proceeds to give the name which she already knows, with the phrase already used by Gauvain (*PL* 566.20–1):

'Or sachiez donc que ce est Lanceloz do Lac, cil qui vainqui les deus assenblees de moi et de Galehot.' (*PL* 569.29–30.)

The climax to all these revelations concerning the exploits of Lancelot is his installation, with Hector and Galehot, as a Knight of the Round Table, the crowning point in the career of a knight, followed by the recording of all the adventures by Arthur's learned clerks.

The Journey to Sorelois, the False Guinevere episode, and epilogue

The story does not, however, end with the establishment of Lancelot's identity and reputation at Arthur's court and the conferment of his seat at the Round Table. The celebrations are followed by the journey of Lancelot and Galehot to Sorelois, in the course of which Galehot is given signs and visions of his death through Lancelot, and by the False Guinevere episode. These events are closely concerned with the development of the love theme, but the False Guinevere episode is also related to the identity theme. Lancelot has established his name, but that of Guinevere is now questioned. Messengers arrive at Arthur's court to present a claim that the woman whom Arthur has up till now regarded as the Queen is an impostor, who was substituted for the true Guinevere on the wedding night.

Arthur is kidnapped and his judgement is clouded by a potion, so that he has already made up his mind that the Guinevere with whom he has been living is false before he, in company with the new Guinevere and the barons of Camelide, assemble with the knights from Logres and Lancelot and Galehot for the trial which will determine who is the true Guinevere. The streets of Camelide are decorated in honour of King Arthur and Queen Guinevere, but the inhabitants are not yet certain which is the true Queen: 'Et neporqant il ne savoient encores la quex estoit reine, mais li plus s'acorde a cele que li rois a en sa compaignie' (*PL* 599.36–7.)

Arthur, still influenced by the potion, decides that the Queen should be judged by a number of the barons of Camelide, and after they have deliberated he reports their verdict: the lady who has accused Guinevere is the true Queen. He pronounces the terrible sentence:

'Seignors, vos avez bien oï comment ceste damoiselle me manda que ge la repreïsse comme cele que j'avoie esposee. Et ge voil que vos sachiez que ge l'ai reconeüe et sai veraiement que ce est cele qui par la main Leodagan me fu donee. Or si avons, fait il, jugié que cele Guanievre qui la est doit avoir les treces colpees atot lo cuir, por ce qu'ele se fist reine et porta corone desus son chief qu'ele n'i deüst pas porter. Et après, fait il, si avra les mains escorchiees par dedanz, por ce que eles furent sacrees et enointes, que nules mains de fames ne doivent estre se rois ne l'a esposee bien et leiaument en Sainte Eglise. Et puis, fait il, si sera trainee parmi ceste vile, qui est li chiés del reiaume, por ce que par murtre et par traïson a esté en si grant honor. Et après tot ce, sera arse et la poudre vantee, si que la novelle corre par totes terres de la justise qui faite en sera, et que nule ja mais ne soit si hardie qui de si grant chose s'entremete.' (*PL* 602.15-29.)

The judgement decrees that each part of the Queen's body which has been associated specifically with the claim to a false identity, through contact with the crown or the oil in the coronation ceremony, should be flayed publicly, her body should be dragged through the streets where she has been falsely honoured, and her ashes scattered in the wind so that news of the punishment should reach all lands.[37] A public recognition of the falseness of a name is thus contrasted with the public recognition of the true making of a name, when Lancelot was installed at the Round Table, and his deeds and those of his companions were officially recorded for posterity by the King's clerks.

Lancelot, in a fight against three knights, proves the falseness of the judgement. It is the False Guinevere, therefore, who suffers the punishment for claiming a name which is not her own, and the Queen's identity is re-established. Lancelot's achievement in accomplishing this is described in similar terms to his achievement as the Black Knight in bringing to an end the war between Arthur and Galehot, the deed which set in motion Gauvain's last and greatest quest in search of the hero. We may compare 'Ensi est la paiz faite del roi et de la reine' (*PL* 608.25) with the terms in which Gauvain describes Lancelot, when, at the end of his quest, he finally tells Galehot that he knows who Lancelot is:

'Ge sai, fait il, de voir que ce est Lanceloz do Lac, li filz lo roi Ban de Benoyc, cil qui fist la pais de monseignor lo roi Artu et de vos.' (*PL* 538.31-3.)

It is not, however, only the identity of the Queen which is involved in this episode, but also the fate of the Round Table itself. The *PL* gives a different account of the origins of the Round Table from those given by Wace, according to whom it was founded by Arthur (*Brut*, 9747-60), and Robert de Boron, who says it was founded by Uther on the advice of Merlin (*Merlin*, paragraphs 48-50).[38] In the *PL* King Leodegan, father of Guinevere, gives Arthur the Round Table as part of his daughter's dowry (*PL* 585.40-586.7); hence the plot of the False Guinevere and Berthelais imperils not only the true Queen but the Round

Table itself. Thus Lancelot, in defeating the champions of the False Guinevere, saves both the Queen and the Round Table, as he has already saved Arthur and his Kingdom from both Galehot and the Saxons.

It is only fitting, therefore, now that Lancelot has been fully established as the greatest of all knights and the saviour of the Round Table, that Lyonel, whose role during the early part of the romance has to some extent doubled with that of Lancelot and provided a useful point of comparison and contrast, and who has then served as squire to his cousin while Lancelot is still in the process of making a name for himself, should now become a knight. The description of his knighting and his determination to undertake the first adventure which comes to Arthur's court parallels the account of Lancelot's first two days there. But for Lyonel, already known as Lancelot's cousin, the road to a seat at the Round Table is much shorter. He achieves this first adventure, the killing of the Crowned Lion of Lybia, an adventure closely associated with his own name and with his birthmark in the shape of a lion (a mark which, we have been told earlier, will disappear as soon as he kills the lion, *PL* 358.26–31), his deed is recorded by Arthur's clerks (*PL* 611.38–612.1), as had been those of Lancelot, and without more delay he wins his place as companion of the Round Table:

Et fu Lyoniaus aconpaigniez as conpaignons de la Table Reonde por la proesce qui en lui estoit et por l'amor de Lancelot, son coisin. (*PL* 612.1–3.)

Thus Lyonel's winning of a seat at the Round Table so soon after his knighting owes something to Lancelot's reputation as well as to his own personal achievement in accomplishing the adventure which proves his right to his own name. The whole episode provides a version in miniature of his cousin's progress towards the establishment of his name and reputation as a great knight. As Lancelot is now to remain permanently as a member of the King's *ostel*, the celebrations of a new Knight of the Round Table are not followed (as in the earlier parallel scene) by a journey to Sorelois by Galehot and Lancelot, but by a solitary journey by Galehot, followed by his death through a false rumour concerning that of Lancelot.

Conclusion

The identity theme runs right through the work. On the first page of the romance we are told that the hero's baptismal name is Galaaz (a matter to be discussed in Chapter VI), but that his *sorenon* was Lancelot: 'Et ce par quoi il fu apelez Lanceloz ce devisera bien li contes ça avant', a reference forward to the winning of that name at the Dolorous Guard. The subject of the romance is indeed the gaining of a name, 'Lanceloz do Lac, filz lo roi Ban de Benoyc', a name gained through personal effort by a youth without land (symbolized by *do Lac*) but taking his place proudly in a noble line (*filz do roi Ban de Benoyc*), and the winning of the title of the greatest knight under that name. Once he has left the Lake, Lancelot moves forward to this ultimate goal, with periodic withdrawals from the action through wounds or imprisonment. During the longest of these withdrawals (in Sorelois) continuity of the theme is preserved through Hector taking over the role of the young warrior and lover advancing towards fame as a knight. However Lancelot never experiences the kind of personal crisis characteristic of the structure of Chrétien's romances, except perhaps during his madness. He endures anguish and self-questioning in relation to his love (as will be seen in the next chapter), and has to struggle to find out who he is, not to regain a lost reputation but rather to bring together under his own name and as his father's son all the reputations which he has established under a series of different designations. Lyonel's name and his deeds are also closely connected. From his birth he has been known by the name Lyonel and his birthmark in the shape of a lion indicates its potential appropriateness; but he finally proves his right to such a name with his victory over the Crowned Lion of Lybia, and provides Yvain with a new explanation for his name (le Chevalier au Lion) with the gift of the lion-skin to be worn on Yvain's shield (*PL* 611.35–6). Other characters do indeed experience some form of identity crisis when at the summit of their careers. Gauvain has a great reputation, but, while incognito, he gives the appearance of cowardly behaviour and has to vindicate his right to his own great name. In the last part of the work Guinevere's identity is questioned, and her name and position as wife and Queen are challenged, as well as the integrity of the Round Table. All these problems are resolved within the framework of the making of Lancelot's name. Lyonel is Lancelot's cousin and his own progress a reflection of that of his more famous kinsman; Gauvain triumphantly demonstrates that he is worthy of his own name during a quest for Lancelot; Guinevere's identity is proved by Lancelot in judicial combat; only Galehot's inner conflict cannot be resolved and ends in death. The richness and complexity of the theme is enhanced by a series of literary allusions, of variations on known themes, evoking not only Lancelot, 'Chevalier de la Charrette', but also other familiar heroes and lovers who had to discover or rediscover who they were.

III

The Love Theme

Inextricably involved in the making of a name is the love theme, for it is made clear in the romance that it is Lancelot's love for Guinevere which provides the inspiration for the deeds of prowess by which he learns his own identity and establishes his reputation. This is done without the long monologues exploring the nature of love which are characteristic of Chrétien's Lancelot poem and with a minimum of comment from the author or the tale.

The idea, traditional to courtly romance, that love provides a spur to heroic exploits is first expressed in a somewhat unconventional form. Claudas, the king who was responsible for the dispossession and death of Lancelot's father, explains why he had only once loved *par amors* (*amer par amors* is the term used for *fin'amor* in the romance) and has now abandoned such love: he says that he wants to have a long life, and those who love should aim to surpass all other knights and are not likely to live long:

'... cuers de chevalier qui finement aimme ne doit baer qu'a une chose: c'est a tot lo monde passer; ne nus cors d'ome, tant fust preuz, ne porroit soffrir ce que li cuers oseroit emprandre, que ançois ne lo covenist fenir. Mais se la force del cors fust si granz que ele poïst aconplir les hardemenz del cuer, ge amasse par amors tote ma vie et passasse toz les prodomes de totes iceles proesces qui puent estre en cors de boen chevalier, car il ne puet estre tres preuz d'armes, se il n'aimme tres leialment, et ge conois tant mon cuer que ge amasse leiaument sor toz leiaus.' (PL 30.39–31.9.)

The first hint that love for Guinevere is to play an important role in Lancelot's development as a knight is given in the account of his childhood. In a long description of the young hero's physical and moral qualities in terms which foreshadow his achievements as a knight mention is made of the size of Lancelot's chest, which might seem disproportionately large to those who look at him:

Mais li piz fu tex qe en nul tel cors ne trovast an si gros ne si large ne si espés; ne an lui ne trova onques nus hom plus que reprandre, ainz disoient tuit cil qui lo devisoient que s'il fust un po mains garniz de piz, plus an fust atalantables et plaisanz. Mais puis avint que cele qui desor toz autres lo devisa, ce fu la vaillanz reine Guenievre, dist que Dex ne li avoit pas doné piz a outraige, de grant ne de gros ne d'espesseté qui i fust, car autresin estoit granz li cuers en son endroit, si covenist que il crevast par estovoir, s'il n'eüst tel estage o il se reposast a sa mesure. 'Ne se ge fusse, fist ele, Dex, ja an Lancelot ne meïsse ne plus ne mains.'¹ (*PL* 40.14–24.)

This refutation of a possible criticism of Lancelot, with its suggestion of a future intimate and tender relationship between Lancelot and Guinevere, a relationship which a thirteenth-century public, familiar with Chrétien's work, would expect to find, comes shortly before another refutation of a criticism of Lancelot, referring to his behaviour in his *grant joie*:

Et disoit maintes foiz, qant il estoit en sa grant joie, que rien nule ses cuers n'oseroit anprendre que ses cors ne poïst bien a chief mener, tant se fioit en la grant joie qui de maintes granz besoignes lou fist puis au desus venir. Et par ce que il en parloit si seürement, li fu il atorné a mal de maintes genz qui cuidoient qu'il lo deïst por bobanz et de vantance; mais nel faisoit, ainz lo disoit de la grant seürté qu'il avoit en ce dont tote sa joie venoit. (*PL* 40.34–41.2.)

The reference is veiled, but the *seürté* referred to here would appear to be that which derives from his love and should be compared with the phrase used to explain Lancelot's confident bearing when he goes out to fight three opponents single-handed to defend Guinevere from a charge of *traïson* in the False Guinevere episode:

Et qant Lanceloz les vit, si vint avant et se contint mout seürement comme cil cui force d'amors done cuer et seürté. (*PL* 604.1–3.)

Joie is of course, a term used in connection with love, as for example, at *PL* 373.38, 375.9, 557.20, and 596.21.²

There are no other references to love as an inspiration for chivalry until Lancelot's arrival as a young *vallet* at Arthur's court. The Lady of the Lake does not mention it in her discourse on chivalry which presents the knight as defender of the Church and of the people in ecclesiastical terms echoing those used in, for example, the forms of service for the blessing of arms and for the knighting ceremony.³ However, once Lancelot sees Guinevere for the first time, he is so overwhelmed by her beauty that he falls into the first of the series of love trances which occur at frequent intervals throughout the text and which serve to remind us that his every action from this moment onwards is dominated by his love for Guinevere:

Lors lo prant la reine par la main, si li demande don il est. Et qant il la sant, si tressaut toz autresin com s'il s'esveillast, et tant pense a li durement qu'il ne set qu'ele li a dit. (*PL* 157.37–9.)

It is true that even if he had heard the Queen's question, he would not have been able to answer, for, as we have already seen, the two themes of identity and love converge at this point. Those present wonder at the youth's apparent *naïveté*, but the Queen suspects the true reason for his confusion and she tries to turn away attention from what she suspects. She is also grieved to hear what Lancelot has undertaken to avenge the wounded knight:

Si l'an poise trop durement, car ele crient et dote qu'il ne l'amast de si grant amor qu'il eüst anpris por li a defferrer lo chevalier, si dit que mout est granz domages de lui et granz dolors. (*PL* 161.36–8.)

Thus at this very early stage Guinevere already divines Lancelot's love for her through his very silence and recognizes that in this love may lie the motivating power behind all his actions as a knight.

Lancelot too tries to see a hidden significance in Guinevere's behaviour, investing with meaning phrases which would normally only represent polite conventions. It is no empty formula of court ceremony when he asks her, as he takes leave of her before his departure for Nohaut, if he can hold himself to be her knight:

'Dame, fait il, se vos plaisoit, ge me tandroie en quel que leu que ge alasse por vostre chevalier.' (*PL* 165.19–20.)

And he interprets at the same deep level her reply: 'A Deu, fait ele, biax douz amis.' (*PL* 165.23.) He murmurs under his breath, 'Granz merciz, dame, qant il vos plaist que ge lo soie.' (*PL* 165.25.) As will be seen, the importance of these words as a source of inspiration for all his deeds of valour is made clear later, more than half-way through the romance, during Lancelot's first secret meeting with the Queen (*PL* 345–6); but already, at this early stage, we are given a hint of their significance.

Lancelot takes care that he will be truly the Queen's knight in another sense when he deliberately refrains from going back to the King to have his sword girded, which, as Yvain explains, is the final part of the knighting ceremony. Lancelot has no desire to receive his sword from the King:

Mais il n'a talant de retorner, car il n'atant pas a estre chevaliers de la main lo roi, mais *d'une autre dont il cuidera plus amander*. (*PL* 166.3–5.)

He carefully arranges for the Queen to send him his sword, and until the messenger comes back with the sword, Lancelot is always referred to in the text as *vallet*, because, as the tale explains, he is not yet a knight. In this way it is made clear, without any lengthy rhetorical procedures, that Lancelot ensures that he is made a knight by the person from whom he expects to draw inspiration and strength, namely the Queen. And again the importance of this gesture is underlined in the later scene, during the conversation which leads up to the first kiss (*PL* 341–2).

Lancelot falls into deep thought again on the way to the Lady of Nohaut; love is not directly mentioned, but the phrases used echo those to be found in episodes where the theme is explicitly related to love. He is roused from these thoughts to undertake his first adventures, the series of proving fights on the way to his battle at Nohaut, which have no particularly close connection with the Queen. Indeed, as suggested in Chapter II, his insistence on seeing a beautiful damsel in a tent, recalling as it does an episode in the *Conte del Graal* (667–772), is not compatible with his usual behaviour as a knight dedicated to the service of one particular lady and only concerned with others in so far as they need protection. However, there are discreet reminders at intervals that Lancelot's thoughts are directed only towards one object, the Queen, as for example when he refuses to use a sword in his battle against the big knight guarding the damsel in the tent:

'L'espee ne puis ge ceindre, ne ne doi, tant que ge n'avrai autre commandement.' (*PL* 172.34–5.)

Particularly striking in this respect is the contrast between his cool and detached attitude at his first sight of the Lady of Nohaut's beauty and the overwhelming effect upon his emotions of his first sight of Guinevere. He was struck dumb on meeting the Queen, but is calm and collected before the Lady of Nohaut:

Qant il voit la dame, si ne s'esbaïst mie de sa grant biauté, ne grant entandue n'i met; et si estoit ele une des tres beles. (*PL* 174.32–3.)

There is a contrast here with Gauvain, who is always stirred by female beauty, although he is not susceptible to trances.

Lancelot's adventures after he has defeated the King of Northumberland, as champion of the Lady of Nohaut, and made peace between them, open with another trance, this time significantly enough at the Queen's Ford, in an incident recalling an episode in the *Chevalier de la Charrette* (711–87), so that there is no need to spell out the subject of his thoughts or to mention the word 'love'. He is sitting on the bank, after drinking from the river, and he begins to think deeply. A knight rides into the ford and splashes him. He rises and protests angrily not only at being wetted, but also at being disturbed in his thoughts: 'Et autre anui m'avez vos fait, car mon pensé m'avez tolu.' (*PL* 179.17–18.) However, Lancelot does not want to fight, just to mount and ride away without a battle, 'por savoir s'il porroit son penser recovrer ausi doucement com il faisoit hore' (*PL* 179.21–2). But a mention of a command in the Queen's name that he should not cross the ford makes him stop instantly. A further command, allegedly in the Queen's name, to surrender his horse makes him start taking his foot out of the stirrup, preparatory to dismounting, but when he discovers on further enquiry that it is not really the Queen's command, his attitude changes, and he remains firmly in his saddle, although he still does not want to fight the knight until compelled to do so because he believes mistakenly that the knight has the Queen's protection: 'car vos avez trop bon conduit, puis que ma dame vos conduit' (*PL* 180.24). Thus the episode illustrates not only the lover's total absorption in thoughts of his beloved but also his desire to show instant obedience to her commands.

In the first part of Lancelot's great adventure, the conquest of the Dolorous Guard, it is the theme of identity which predominates, as it is after he has won his way into the castle and raised the slab on the tomb in the cemetery that he discovers his name. But here again the echoes of the episode in the *Chevalier de la Charrette*, in which Lancelot by raising the slab shows that he is the knight destined to achieve the adventure of freeing the Queen and all the prisoners in Gorre, would for a thirteenth-century public evoke memories of the famous poem of which Lancelot, lover of Guinevere, is the hero. It is after this that he receives the first message from the Lady of the Lake which stresses the importance of the right kind of love for his development as a knight, a point which she had not made when she gave him instruction on chivalry before leaving the Lake. A damsel is sent specially to tell him:

'que vos ne metoiz ja vostre cuer en amor qui vos face aparecir mais amander, car cuers qui por amor devient pareceus ne puet a haute chose ataindre, car il n'osse. Mais cil qui tozjorz bee a amender puet ataindre a hautes choses, autresin com il les ose anprandre.' (*PL* 205.38–206.2.)

The distinction between the right and the wrong kind of love, as we shall see, will be illustrated elsewhere in the romance in adventures which recall a similar distinction made in the romances of Chrétien de Troyes.

An important element in the kind of love which spurs on a knight to greater endeavour is fear. Chrétien de Troyes had developed this theme at considerable length in *Cligés*:

> Amors sanz criemme et sanz peor
> Est feus ardanz et sanz chalor,
> Jorz sanz soloil, cire sanz miel,
> Estez sanz flor, yvers sanz giel,
> Ciax sans lune, livres sanz letre.
> Et s'a neant le volez metre,
> Que la ou criemme se dessoivre,
> N'i fet Amors a ramantoivre.
> Qui amer vialt, crienbre l'estuet,
> Ou autrement amer ne puet;
> Mes seul celi qu'il aimme dot
> Et por li soit hardiz par tot.
> (*Cligés*, 3847–58.)

There is no such exposition of the theory in the *PL*, but it is clear from the text that Lancelot is haunted by the fear of incurring his lady's displeasure and that the fear associated with great love can be just as important a motive force towards great deeds as is the *grant seürté* which also stems from love. This is illustrated in the later part of the adventure of the Dolorous Guard in the consequences of Lancelot's two trances on the sight of Guinevere, during the period when the King and his court have come to the Dolorous Guard to try to find out the truth about the strange events there. Lancelot is on two occasions so absorbed in thought that he shuts the Queen out of the castle, having, as its unknown conqueror, just asked her if she would like to enter it (*PL* 207–8, 215–16). The Queen is understandably upset by such treatment, and Lancelot is rudely upbraided for it by Kay. His distress at having angered the Queen provides the motivation for his rescue of Gauvain and his companions from a castle, where they have been imprisoned by the former lord of the Dolorous Guard, and gives the tale another opportunity of underlining the love of Lancelot for the Queen and of indicating in a brief and dramatic way the feelings which underlie his actions:

Li contes dit que li Blans Chevaliers chevauche, maz et pansis por sa dame la reine qu'il a correcice, car il l'amoit de si grant amor des lo premier jor qu'il fu tenuz por chevaliers que il n'amoit tant ne soi ne autrui. Et por ce qu'il dotoit la haïne sa dame a tozjorz mais, si pense en son cuer tant a faire d'armes qu'il ravra monseignor Gauvain, ou il morra. Et par ce, s'il lo puet faire, bee a recovrer l'amor sa dame. (*PL* 209.5–11.)

Lancelot rescues the prisoners and tells them to thank the King and Queen for their deliverance, but there is a change of personal pronoun in mid-sentence: 'Si *les* me saluez *andeus*, et *les* merciez de ce que vos iestes hors de prison, car, bien sachiez, ce est *par li*.' (*PL* 218.13–14.) The next knight he saves, this time from a false accusation of having dishonoured another knight's wife, is a Queen's Knight, and this provides the main motive for the rescue, as he explains to the accuser: 'Par foi, fait li Blans Chevaliers, vous mesferés trop de li desfaire, puis qu'il est chevaliers madame la roine.' (*PL* 222.28–9.) The knight whom he has freed is also asked to thank the Queen for his deliverance, at the same time giving a description of the shield of his deliverer. This incident represents an interesting variation on the pattern to be found in the *Conte del Graal* (667–833, 3691–949), where Perceval, as a youth on his way to Arthur's court, forces his way into a tent and insists on kissing a damsel. Her *ami* does not believe the damsel's protestations that this was done against her will and punishes her by making her ride on a wretched horse, in such rags as to be almost naked. Perceval meets her in this unhappy state and has to fight her *ami*, the Orgueilleus de la Lande, to convince him of her innocence and to right the wrong he has done the damsel. In the *PL*, as we have seen, Lancelot un-characteristically forces his way into a damsel's tent but does not kiss her; the episode in which he fights to disprove a false accusation of dishonour to a damsel has no connection with the earlier incident, but is presented as yet another battle undertaken in the service of the Queen to save one of her knights. Hector, himself a Queen's Knight, avenges another knight who has been wounded because of a similar false accusation (*PL* 425–32).

It is at the Queen's command that Lancelot takes part in the assembly between the knights of King Arthur and those of the Roi d'Outre les Marches. He meets one of the Queen's damsels, who asks him to give a message to the knight who conquered the Dolorous Guard that he is to be there (*PL* 221.9–11). In order to obey this command Lancelot goes there in a litter, as he has been hurt in a fall and in a battle to avenge the wounded knight in fulfilment of the oath which he swore at Camelot. It is to rescue the Queen that he returns to the Dolorous Guard and undertakes the task of ending the enchantments. He is lured there by a false report that she is imprisoned there, is told that he is to be held in place of her, and, to obtain his release, agrees to attempt the adventure, richer in the supernatural than any other episode in the work. The people of the castle explain that they sent the false message, supposedly from the Queen, because they were sure that it would make him come: 'Car nos pansions que vostre granz proesce vos feroit por li antrer en prison.' (*PL* 250.26–7.) Thus, while in the first stage of the adventure of the Dolorous Guard the identity theme predominates, but with echoes of the cemetery scene in Chrétien's poem, Lancelot's achievement of the second stage is motivated by his resolve to rescue the Queen. The inhabitants of the Dolorous Guard are freed from the enchantments, just as the prisoners had been freed from Gorre, because Lancelot is determined to save the Queen, and in each case he, lover and predestined deliverer, overcomes strange and fearsome marvels.

It is therefore made clear, but without lengthy discourses or authorial comment, that in all Lancelot's exploits up to the Second Assembly (after which Gauvain brings Lancelot's name to court) he is acting under the inspiration of his love. Furthermore, he usually undertakes the adventures because of some specific link with his service to the Queen rather than on account of a more general desire to distinguish himself and thus gain honour in her eyes.

After the Second Assembly, which marks an important stage in the development of the identity theme, in the events leading up to the first battle against Galehot, the motif of the love trance is given a different twist within a pattern reminiscent in some ways of that of the unknown knight arriving at court and having to prove his worth. There is in fact an evocation, with an explicit reference back through Lancelot's memories, of Lancelot's own arrival at court in the explanation given for one of these trances. He comes towards Camelot, sees a lady (who, as we learn later, is Guinevere), and falls into a dream from which he is prodded by a knight who challenges him to follow him past the Queen if he dares. Lancelot replies:

'Certes, se vos alez en leu ou ge ne vos oserai sivre, passez avroiz toz les oseors qui onques fussient.' (*PL* 263.19–20.)

He follows the knight, who gives him lodging for the night and the next day leads him past Camelot, the sight of which stirs memories of his first visit:

Lors esgarde lo siege de la vile et la tor et les mostiers, tant que il se remenbre que ce est Chamahalot ou il fu chevaliers noviaus. Et il commence a penser mout durement, si an chevalcha plus soef, et ses ostes ala avant grant aleüre por savoir s'il demoreroit arrieres de coardise ou por pensé. (*PL* 265.11–15.)

The Queen sees him and tells him that the knight has gone towards the forest. At the sound of her voice he looks at her and falls so deeply into thought that he does not notice that his horse has plunged into the river and that he is in danger of drowning. The Queen calls to Yvain for help, and he pulls him out of the river (it was to Yvain that Arthur had entrusted Lancelot as a young unknown *vallet: PL* 155). Yvain looks at the old shield that he is carrying and is misled: 'et l'an prisa mains, car il cuide que il fust de mal affaire' (*PL* 267.16). Lancelot is then captured by the cowardly knight Daguenet, thereby increasing the impression that he is a knight of little worth, and is brought to Guinevere. This encounter has some features which recall Lancelot's first meeting with Guinevere. On both occasions Yvain is present and the unknown young man behaves awkwardly and does not dare to look at the Queen; here he behaves so clumsily that he lets his lance fall and cut the Queen's robe. However, on this occasion there is no suggestion that the Queen (who does not recognize Lancelot beneath his battered arms, but notices his well-made body) interprets his inability to answer her questions as a sign of his love for her. She is not therefore trying to create a diversion when she suggests to Yvain: 'Cist chevaliers ne semble mie estre sages.' (*PL* 268.18.) Hence the trance here leads to a doubting of the prowess of the Unknown Knight, a doubting followed by a testing, arranged by the host knight who has seen Lancelot in the trance. This testing (here a fight against giants) is, as we have seen in the last chapter, a common motif in Arthurian romance; it is a form of trial which does not occur in the first series, undergone by Lancelot as a young knight, but is to be found in *li Biaus Descouneus* and in *Yvain*. Thus, once again, the theme of love and that of identity are closely intertwined.

This motif of the love trance, brought on by the sight of the beloved, being

interpreted by those present as a sign of weakness in the Unknown Knight
recurs in the first of the two battles against Galehot (the Third Assembly of
Logres in the text). It is characteristic of Lancelot's trances that they precede
heroic activity, unlike those of Arthur which arise from inactivity and frustration and are linked to the mainly passive role of the King in the work.[4] Lancelot
is temporarily released from prison by the Lady of Malohaut to fight in the
assembly, in much the same way as he was released to fight in a tournament in
Chrétien's poem, except that in the *PL* the battle is a serious one in which
Arthur's crown is at stake. He stands on the edge of the battle, looking towards
the *loge* where the Queen and her ladies are gathered, he does not move when
called *neianz failliz* by the heralds, who are urging him to join the battle, and is
only roused when struck by a wet clod of earth. He then performs such deeds of
prowess that everyone is filled with admiration, and when he returns to prison,
his body, armour, and horse bear such marks that the Lady of Malohaut suspects
that it must be love which has inspired him to such great deeds:

Et bien pensoit en son cuer que il amoit par amors an mout haut leu, si vousist mout
savoir qui il estoit et an quel leu il avoit mis son cuer, et bien vousist que ce fust an lui.
*Mais ele santoit an lui si haute proece et si fier cuer qu'ele ne pooit mie penser que il amast se trop
haute chose non.* Mais ele se pense qu'ele lo savra se il puet estre. (*PL* 296.20–5.)

In the second battle against Galehot, Lancelot stands deep in thought in
exactly the same place, looking in exactly the same direction, but this time there
is no question of the knight being accused of cowardice and of having to prove
his worth; for now the Lady of Malohaut is with the Queen and is determined
to find out from where the knight draws the strength for his great deeds.
Lancelot is roused from his thoughts of love by a damsel bringing a message
from the Lady of Malohaut and all the ladies except Guinevere, and accompanied by a squire bearing two lances from Gauvain:

Si li mandent et prient que se il atant ja mais a avoir ne bien ne honor an leu o nules d'aus
ait ne force ne pooir, si face ancui d'armes por lor amor tant qe eles l'an doient gré savoir.
(*PL* 311.7–10.)

Lancelot performs great deeds, but, as soon as he has broken the two lances, he
returns to the place where he had first stood in thought and looks again towards
the *bretesche* where the Queen is, thus showing that he considers that he has fulfilled his obligation towards the ladies who sent the message. In the words of
the Lady of Malohaut: 'Il mostre bien a nos autres que por nos n'en fera il plus.'
(*PL* 312.13–14.) Gauvain then advises the Queen to send a message in the
following terms:

'Mandez a cestui saluz et que vos li criez merci dou reiaume de Logres et de l'onor mon seignor lo roi, qui hui ira a mal, se Dex et il n'i met consoil. Et se il ja mais atant a avoir ne honor ne joie en leu o vos aiez pooir, si face encui por vostre amor tant d'armes que vos l'an deiez gré savoir, et que il pere a ses uevres que il ait ses proesces mises en l'onor mon seignor lo roi et an la vostre.' (*PL* 312.22–8.)

She does so, and Gauvain sends with the damsel bearing the message squires with ten lances and three horses. Lancelot is again spurred into action, but this time his efforts extend beyond the ten lances and continue throughout the whole day; he performs such feats of arms that everyone wonders at him, and the following day he persuades Galehot to make peace. A clear contrast is therefore made between the limited duty which Lancelot considers that he as a knight owes to ladies in general and his unlimited commitment to Guinevere, a commitment which drives him on to superhuman achievement.

The peace prepares the way for the key episode in the structure of the romance, both in relation to the love theme and to the identity theme: the first secret meeting between Lancelot and Guinevere. It is then that the kiss is exchanged, and Guinevere by persistent questioning establishes both Lancelot's identity and the extent to which all his actions have been dominated by his love for her, Lancelot thereby admitting to both his name and his love.

The scene opens in a way which is reminiscent of Guinevere's first meeting with Lancelot (*PL* 157–8).[5] He is so overcome with awe that he cannot raise his eyes to her face (*PL* 341–2). As in the first meeting, she tries to find out who he is. She tells him that Galehot has assured her that he is the knight she wishes to see, but that she would like to hear from his own mouth who he is: 'Mais encorres voudroie ge bien savoir qui vos iestes par vostre boche se vostre plaisirs estoit.' (*PL* 341.1–2.) He replies, as in the first meeting, that he does not know (this time, unlike the earlier occasion, this is not true). She wonders at his reply, but suspects what is the matter: 'Et la reine se mervoille mout que il puet avoir, et tant que ele sopece une partie de ce que il a.' (*PL* 341.4–5). This should be compared with her suspicions at the first meeting concerning the cause of Lancelot's confusion (*PL* 158.4–6). She then succeeds in getting him to admit that he is the Black Knight, the knight whom she has asked to see. She also discovers that he was the youth, clad in white, who was brought to Camelot by a damsel, and he tells her that it was she, the Queen, who made him a knight, not the King. She makes him go over all that has happened to him since he left court and tells him that she knows that his name is Lancelot. She asks him why he performed such great deeds as the Black Knight, and persuades him to make a distinction between what he has done for the other ladies and what he has done for her: 'Dame, ge fis por aus ce que ge dui, et por vos ce que ge poi.' (*PL* 345.1–2.) She extracts from him the confession that he has performed all his deeds of chivalry for her:

'Or me dites, totes les chevaleries que vos avez faites, por cui les feïstes vos?'
'Dame, fait il, por vos.' (*PL* 345.3–5.)

She then asks him if he really loves her so much, and he finally declares his love
in words as he had already done in deeds; 'Dame, ge n'ain tant ne moi ne autrui.'
(*PL* 345.7.) She persuades him to tell her whence came that love, and he now
spells out in full the significance for him of the words which she said to him
before he left for Nohaut, 'A Deu, biax douz amis' (*PL* 165.23). For the first time
the tongue-tied Lancelot is moved to eloquence and speaks much as might a
poet in a love lyric:

'Ce fu li moz qui prodome me fera se gel suis. Ne onques puis ne vign an si grant meschief
que de cest mot ne me manbrast. Ciz moz m'a conforté an toz mes anuiz, cist moz m'a de
toz mes maus garantiz et m'a gari de toz periz; cist moz m'a saolé an totes mes fains, cist
moz m'a fait riche an totes mes granz povretez.' (*PL* 345.37–346.3.)

In this meeting, therefore, the author makes fully explicit the briefer indications given in the course of the narrative, namely that it is the love which has
made Lancelot the great knight that he is. In this way it is made clear that
Lancelot does not undertake adventure for adventure's sake, that the motivation
in each case comes from Guinevere, even though she is not always conscious of
it. The contrast between Lancelot's fearlessness in action on behalf of his lady and
his fearfulness and inarticulateness in his lady's presence brings out very clearly
the role of fear in this kind of love. Lancelot gives expression to his love in deeds,
not words, hence the almost total absence of love speeches in the romance, apart
from the one just quoted. His fear is also given physical rather than verbal
expression, as it makes him tremble and frequently reduces him to silence. Fear
and confidence are thus shown to be complementary aspects of love.

Guinevere's acceptance of Lancelot's love, sealed as it is by their first kiss (a
favourite subject for illustration in the manuscripts), marks an important stage
in the development of the love theme. At this point the lovers go no further.
Lancelot departs with Galehot for Sorelois, where he stays hidden, pining for
Guinevere, while the best knights of Arthur's court are searching for him. Continuity is, however, given to the theme through the shield sent to Guinevere by
the Lady of the Lake, which serves to chart the progress of the love. On this
shield are depicted a knight and a lady who are separated from one another by a
wide gap, except at the top where the lips of the couple have come close
together. The damsel from the Lake explains to the Queen the meaning of the
shield:

'Dame, cil est uns chevaliers, li miaudres qui orandroit soit, qui pria une dame d'amors, la
plus vaillant qui orandroit soit au mien cuidier. Tant fist li chevaliers, que par amor, que

par ovre, li dona sa dame s'amor, mais plus n'i a ancor aü que de baisier et d'acoler, si comme vos veez an cest escu. Et qant il avanra que l'amors sera anterine, si sachiez que cist escuz que vos veez si desjoint se rajoindra et tanront ansenble ces deus parties. Et sachiez que vos seroiz lors delivree do greignor duel qui onques vos avenist et seroiz an la greignor joie que vos aüssiez onques. Mais ce n'avandra devant que li miaudres chevaliers qui soit hors de la cort lo roi Artu soit devenuz de sa maisniee.' (*PL* 403.8–18.)

The Queen is glad at the news and thinks that she knows who this best knight, not yet a member of the King's *maisnie*, might be.

This explanation of the shield shows that the development of the love moves in step with the development of Lancelot's career as a knight and his progress towards establishing his name at Arthur's court and becoming a member of the King's household and a Knight of the Round Table. The gap in the shield closes after Lancelot returns secretly from Sorelois with Gauvain, Hector, and Galehot to help Arthur in his war against the Saxons. Lancelot and his companions join Arthur's army in disguise; but Lancelot wears the Queen's *enseigne* on his helmet so that she can recognize him. To fulfil her command that the fight should be brought beneath the tower from which she is watching the battle, he and his companions pretend to go over to the enemy, make Arthur's army retreat, and turn on the Saxons and slaughter them within the sight of Guinevere. This is a variation on the theme in the *Chevalier de la Charrette* (5635–56) that a lover should be so instantly obedient to his lady's command that he is prepared to play the coward at her request until told to do his best. Lancelot again saves Arthur by remounting him three times in the battle. That night, while Arthur has gone to see the Saxon maiden who uses his love to lure him into prison, Lancelot visits Guinevere secretly, they consummate their love, and the gap in the shield closes. However, it still continues to play a part in the next episode, in which Lancelot goes mad in the prison to which he, Galehot, Hector, and Gauvain have been lured by the Saxons. He is freed and finds his way, still raving, back to Guinevere's castle. An episode describing the madness of a lover who has failed to keep his promise to his lady is to be found in *Yvain*. Lancelot, however, has not committed the fault against love of which Yvain has been guilty. The author does not explain why Lancelot goes mad, beyond saying that it was the result of refusing to eat or drink in prison because of his grief, but he has both been separated from the Queen and failed to rescue the King, and while he is mad, he no longer knows who he is. The link with the love theme is made, firstly, because only Guinevere can make Lancelot keep quiet, and secondly, because only when the shield depicting the two lovers is hung on his neck does he recover his wits, only to lose them again as soon as the shield is removed at his request. The healing of Lancelot bears similarities to that of Yvain in that in both cases they are healed by the application of ointment to the forehead and the temples; in the *PL* it is also applied to the wrists, the pulse in the wrists, and the cranial suture (*PL* 555); in *Yvain* it is applied unnecessarily and against the lady's instructions to other parts of the body (2966, 2994–3003). The ointment in *Yvain* came from *Morgue la sage* (2949); in the *PL* it is brought by the Lady of the Lake who is a fairy, even if of a mainly rationalized kind. She had sent the shield, and she now brings the ointment in person and talks to Guinevere at length on her role in the development of Lancelot as a knight, an active role which will be discussed below.

Lancelot recovers from his illness, and the Queen tells him that he can be sure of her love, but this does not make him lapse into sloth (*peresce*). He returns to battle against the Saxons, bearing the pennon of the Queen, successfully replacing two hundred knights who have been sent away from the battle to guard the route by which the Saxons might attempt to take Arthur, their royal prisoner, out of the country. He performs even greater marvels than before, captures the castle, and releases Arthur. Thus the deeds he performs, bearing the Queen's pennon as an outward sign that he is fighting under the inspiration of his love for her, lead up to his welcome under his own name at Arthur's court, to his installation as a Knight of the Round Table and to his becoming a member of the King's *maisnie*, as the shield had foretold.

In the False Guinevere episode, the strength which Lancelot draws from his love is all the stronger in that it is the Queen who is in danger of death, and he is eager to accept the task of fighting three opponents single-handed:

> Et tant l'esprant ire et amors que bien li est avis orrandroit que bien porroit ses cors achever qancque ses cuers oseroit anprandre. (*PL* 603.2–4.)

This description of Lancelot's feelings should be compared with the remarks of Claudas on the effects of *fin' amor*, quoted at the beginning of this chapter. The hero confronts his enemies with confidence 'comme cil cui force d'amors done cuer et seürté' (*PL* 604.3). Thus his love for Guinevere gives him the power to prove her true identity, as it had given him the power to make his own name.

Love, therefore, spurs Lancelot on to action, as far as deeds of chivalry are concerned; and for this his fear of his lady's displeasure and of being unworthy of her has its positive side, and his love trances lead to action. However, as was seen above, when it comes to confessing his love to her, his fear makes him passive, unwilling to take the initiative; and here his love trances are associated with passivity. Others, therefore, have to act for him: Galehot, seeing his helpless grief, persuades him to meet Guinevere; Guinevere, seeing his helpless confusion in her presence has to take his chin, so that the first kiss can be exchanged.

Guinevere is not presented as the rather remote lady of Chrétien's poem,

seen mainly from Lancelot's point of view as an object of adoration, needing to
be given constant proof of the sincerity of his love, which she then accepts or
rejects. In the *PL* her feelings are explored as well as those of Lancelot, and she
plays a far more active role in the story. She is no longer suspicious and hard to
convince of the sincerity of Lancelot's love; in fact, from the very beginning it is
she who takes the initiative and asks Yvain to bring the newly arrived Lancelot
to her. She, like everyone else at court, is struck by his beauty: 'La reine dit que
preudome lo face Dex, car grant planté li a donee de biauté'. (*PL* 157.21–2) As
we have seen, she is the only one who senses the true cause of his confusion and
skilfully turns attention away from it. Yet this rapid awareness of his feelings
towards her is not presented in terms of the proud confidence of a very beautiful woman in the effect that her beauty will have on a young man, but much
more tentatively and as though she were afraid of assuming too much:

Maintenant aparçoit bien la reine qu'il est esbahiz et trespansez, mais ele n'osse pas cuidier
que ce soit por li; et neporquant ele lo sospece un po, si an laisse la parole atant. (*PL* 158.3–
6.)

Also significant is the fact that in this sense Lancelot's awestruck admiration of
her beauty is balanced by the general admiration of the whole court, including
the Queen, for his own handsome appearance and noble bearing.

   Whenever news of Lancelot's adventures as the White Knight reaches court
through the knights and damsels who have encountered him and who go to the
Queen (whether sent by Lancelot or of their own free will), Guinevere
welcomes the bearer of the news and asks eagerly about the White Knight's
welfare. A damsel from the Lake suspects at an early stage in the romance, after
the conquest of the Dolorous Guard but before the first assembly between the
knights of Arthur and of the Roi d'Outre les Marches, not only that Lancelot
loves the Queen, but that the love is returned.

Ele soupechonoit que li Blans Chevaliers amoit la roine; et quidoit bien que ele amast lui
autresi, por che qu'il ne se voloit partir del chastel devant qu'il l'eüst veüe, et que l'autre li
avoit conté comment ele l'avoit veü esbahi por li, le jor que li rois entra en la premiere
porte. (*PL* 218.37–219.2.)

The Queen takes active steps to get the White Knight to the First Assembly of
Logres, for she sends a damsel with a message:

'Ma dame li mande que s'il atent ja mais a avoir s'acointance ne sa compaignie, que il i
soit, car mout le verroit volentiers.' (*PL* 221.9–11.)

She shows even greater determination to see Lancelot, the Black Knight, after
the second battle against Galehot. It is she who forces Galehot to bring Lancelot
to meet her:

'Tant sai ge bien, fait ele, que se vos an faites vostre pooir, ge lo verrai. Et ge m'an atant a vos, et vos faites tant que ge an soie a tozjorz mais vostre, car c'est uns des homes o monde que ge verroie plus volentiers; et ne mie por esperance que g'i aie de lui conoistre, mais por ce que il n'et nus ne nule qui de prodome esgarder deüst estre anuiez.' (*PL* 335.10–15.)

As we shall see, the emphasis here on prowess is significant. Day after day she pesters him until he gives in. When she hears that the knight is to come that evening, she can scarcely wait until dusk falls:

Mout fait la reine grant joie do chevalier qui venuz est, et mout li tarde que la nuiz vaigne, si antant tant a parler et a ragier por lo jor oblier qui li annuie. (*PL* 339.33–6.)

Her impatience recalls that of Laudine in *Yvain*. In both cases the lady is impatient to have a first meeting with the knight, and the intermediary (Lunete/ Galehot) pretends that the knight is further away than he is (*PL* 334.32–340.38; *Yvain* 1882–905). Guinevere, however, seems to see through the subterfuge; indeed, as will be seen later, she realizes at an early stage that Galehot may have good reason to wish to postpone the meeting.

When Lancelot tells her of the effect the words *biaus douz amis* had upon him, she points out that the phrase should not normally be given such a deep significance, but nevertheless adds:

'Et vostre pansez ne fu mie vilains, ainz fu douz et debonaires; si vos en est bien venu, que prodome vos ai fait.' (*PL* 346.7–9.)

However, she goes on to express the traditional doubts about the sincerity of lovers:

'Et neporqant la costume est mais tele des chevaliers qui font granz sanblanz a maintes dames de tele chose do mout lor est petit au cuer.' (*PL* 346.9–11.)

She then proceeds to play the coquette and pretends to doubt Lancelot's sincerity by asking which of the ladies present he loves; but she does this only because she is enjoying his discomfort as a sign of his great love:

Et ce disoit ele bien por veoir coment ele lo porra metre a malaise, car ele cuide bien que il ne pansast d'amors s'a lui non, ja mar aüst il fait por li se la jornee non des noires armes. Mais ele se delitoit durement an sa messaise veoir et escouter. (*PL* 346.23–7.)

When Lancelot looks towards the Lady of Malohaut, the Queen charges him with loving another; but again the accusation is not serious. She requires little persuasion from Galehot to soften towards Lancelot, to accept his love and to seal the contract with a kiss. Indeed, it is she who takes the initiative by placing her hand under his chin and kissing him on the lips.[6]

It is true that before Lancelot is given the opportunity to go beyond *baisier et acoler* he gives further proof of the strength of his love by performing great feats against the Saxons; but Guinevere does not make Lancelot undergo humiliation to prove by his absolute submission to her commands that he is her true lover. If she sends him an order in battle, it is not that he should play the coward, but that he should bring the battle near where she is, presumably so that she can admire his prowess as he fights, with her *enseigne* on his helmet. He may pretend to go over to the enemy to do this, but not as a deliberate if temporary sacrifice of his individual honour, rather as a form of military strategy for which he enlists the aid of his companions (*PL* 543). After this battle it is Guinevere who sends for Lancelot to give full physical expression to their love, and there is as much emphasis on the joy which she receives from the love as there is on that of Lancelot. She does not encourage his fearfulness as a lover in order to compel him to make constant efforts to be worthy of her, for indeed she would have no need to do so; on the contrary, she constantly tries to reassure him. After their first night together, the gap in the shield closes, and the Lady of Malohaut says teasingly to Lancelot: 'Sire chevaliers, or n'i faut que la corone que vos ne soiez rois.' He is covered in shame, but the Queen immediately stresses their equality: 'Dame, se ge suis fille de roi, et il autresi; que se ge suis vaillanz et belle, et il plus.' (*PL* 547.18–19.)

She is now so determined that she should not be separated from him that she does not keep him on tenterhooks, but makes it clear that she wants him to stay at court:

La roine li commande que se messires Gauvains li prie, que il remaigne, que ele est si sorprise de s'amor que ele ne voit mies comment ele s'an puisse consirrer de lui veoir. (*PL* 547.25–8.)

She nurses him devotedly through his madness. When he recovers his reason and, ashamed of what he may have done in his delirium, fears that his illness may have lessened the Queen's love for him, the tale makes it clear that his fears are groundless: 'Mais il ne li estoit mie mestiers que il an aüst paor, car ele n'an avoit ne pooir ne volanté.' (*PL* 558.4–6.) She is quick to comfort him and does not hesitate to declare her undying love for him:

'N'an aiez ja garde, biaus dolz amis, que si voirement m'aïst Dex, vos iestes plus sires et plus seürs de moi que ge ne suis de vos. Et si ne l'ai pas ampris a or solement, mais a toz les jorz que l'ame me sera el cors.' (*PL* 558.8–11.)

During this period in which they are together, while Arthur is in the Saxon prison, she loves him so much that she dreads losing him through his very prowess, although she never tries to discourage him from performing valiant deeds:

Et la reine an ce sejor l'anama tant que ele ne voit mies comment ele se poïst consirrer de lui veoir. Et li poise de ce qu'ele lo set et lo voit a si volenteïf et a si corageus, car ele ne voit mies comment sa vie poïst durer sanz la soe, s'il s'an aloit ja mais de cort. Si voudroit bien que il aüst un po mains de hardement et de proece. (*PL* 558.16–21.)

At the King's request she asks Lancelot to become a member of the royal *maisnie* (*PL* 570), but she also encourages his journey to Sorelois with Galehot, on the understanding that he will soon return.

Up till this point (the journey to Sorelois) it is above all through the feats which Lancelot has performed for Guinevere to save Arthur and his kingdom that he has shown his love. In the False Guinevere episode, which is in a way a transposition of the theme of the rescue of Guinevere in the *Chevalier de la Charrette*, it is the Queen herself who is helpless and in danger, a danger which seems much more serious than anything which threatened her in the twelfth-century romance. It is true that in Chrétien's poem she showed great distress (*Char.* 208–21) as she was led away by Kay, but once she reached Gorre she was protected by Meleagant's father, the noble Bademaguz.[7] In the *PL* Guinevere seems to be much more in the position of Iseut under the threat of burning, except that the adultery theme is avoided and she is accused instead of *traïson* in pretending to be someone other than she is.[8] Just as Tristan and Iseut, under the spell of the love potion, were both threatened by death, so the honour of both Lancelot and Guinevere is equally involved, as the Queen's messenger makes clear when she comes to ask for help from Lancelot:

'Et vos, sire chevaliers, fait ele a Lancelot, i devriez metre poine et travail sor toz homes en l'anor madame la reine garantir; car se ele est deshonoree devant vos, por que vos l'en puissiez deffandre, dont avez vos par droit honor perdue.' (*PL* 596.9–12.)

She acknowledges the full extent of her debt in public, before Arthur and all his knights, after Lancelot has saved her, although the King and most of those present will be unaware of the full implications of the term *amer* here:

'Sire, l'ore soit beneoite que vos fustes nez, comme li plus prodom do monde. Et vos iestes li chevaliers el siegle que ge devroie plus amer, car vos m'avez randue honor et joie.' (*PL* 606.16–18.)

Nor will they grasp the full meaning of *soe*, when she says to Lancelot in the hearing of the King, 'que des ores en avant la puet il tenir por soe'. (*PL* 608.16).

Indeed her love is so great that she now has no doubts that Lancelot has so fully deserved this love that even if it were to become known, she would not be condemned for it:

Et se la reine aanma Lancelot ça an arrieres, or l'aimme plus que onques mais ne l'ama. Et dit que ele ne porra ja avoir honte des ores mais en chose que ele feïst por lui, car se toz li mondes savoit l'amor entr'aus deus, si li devroit l'an a bien jugier, tant l'a deservi en pluseurs leus. (*PL* 609.14–19.)

Guinevere's active response to Lancelot's deeds of prowess and her ready acceptance of the idea that it is her duty to encourage his chivalry by granting her love is in accordance with the teaching of the Lady of the Lake. The latter had urged Lancelot to play his part by only loving someone who could inspire him to great deeds (*PL* 205.38–206.2). When she comes to heal Lancelot from madness, she reminds Guinevere of her great role as *amie* of a knight such as Lancelot in a very important speech:

'Et ge vos pri que vos lo retenez et gardez, et amez sor totes riens celui qui sor tote rien vos aimme, et metez jus tot orgoil anvers lui, que rien ne valt: nulle rien ne prise anvers vos. Ne li pechié do siegle ne puent estre mené sanz folie, mais mout a grant raison de sa folie qui raison i trove et annor. Et se vos poez folie trover an voz amors, ceste folie est desor totes les autres annoree, car vos amez la seignorie et la flor de tot cest monde. Se vos poez de ce vanter que onques mais dame no pot faire, car vos iestes compaigne au plus preudome do monde et dame au meillor chevalier do monde. Et an la seignorie novelle que vos avez n'avez vos mies po gahaignié, car vos i avez gahaignié lui avant, qui est la flors de toz les chevaliers, et moi aprés, qanque ge porroie faire. Mais atant m'an covient aler, car ge ne puis plus demorer. Et sachiez que la greignor force qui soit m'an maine, c'est la force d'amors, car j'ain un chevalier qui ne set orandroit o ge suis. Mais uns suens freres est ci venuz aveques moi. Et neporqant ge n'ai mie garde qu'il se correçast a moi tant comme ge voldrai. Mais an doit autresin bien garder de corecier ce que l'an aimme comme soi meïsmes, car il n'est mies amez veraiement qui sor totes riens terrienes n'est amez. Et qui aimme par amor, il ne puet mies avoir joie se de ce non que il aimme; don doit an amer la rien dont totes joies vienent.' (*PL* 556.37–557.20.)

Thus the emphasis has shifted from the need to test the sincerity and to insist on proofs of a knight's love (an emphasis characteristic of the lyric and to some extent of Chrétien's *Chevalier de la Charrette*). A lover such as Lancelot should be encouraged, not made to suffer, for it is an honour as well as a *folie* for a lady to love a valiant knight. If a knight is full of prowess, a lady is in fact right to take active steps to win him, and any *folie* which she may commit on his behalf is amply justified.

In Chrétien's romances and in the *Perceval Continuations* there are indeed damsels sometimes only too anxious to encourage valiant knights. Nor is it only Guinevere in the *PL* who is willing to reward them. Thus the daughter of the King of Norgales, like the daughter of Norés de Lis,[9] is prepared to pay tribute to Gauvain's established reputation in chivalry by offering herself to him. Gauvain, also in keeping with his established reputation as eager to enjoy the charms of all beautiful women rather than dedicating his service to a single one, is very happy to accept the tribute. The daughter of the Lord of l'Estroite

Marche is not so fortunate when she comes to Hector's room at night to ask why he will not consider marrying her. Hector, who in his role of providing parallels with Lancelot is already in the service of an *amie* and draws his burning desire to perform deeds of prowess from that love, is not free to respond to the girl.[10]

The Lady of Malohaut is only with difficulty dissuaded by her damsel from kissing Lancelot, as he lies sleeping in her prison after distinguishing himself in the first battle against Galehot, for, as she says: 'L'an ne porroit pas avoir honte an chose q'an feïst por si preudome.' (*PL* 296.1–2.) She later confesses to Guinevere, without mentioning any name, that she has been in love, but only in thought:

'Et sachiez bien, fait ele, dame, que onques n'amai par amors que une foiz, ne de celi amor ne fis ge que lo penser.' Et ce dist ele de Lancelot que ele avoit tant amé comme nus cuers puet plus amer autre. Mais ele n'an avoit onques autre joie aüe, et neporqant ne dist mie que ce aüst il esté. (*PL* 352.20–4.)

She too has been unfortunate in that the knight whose prowess has inspired her with love is already committed heart and soul to a noble lady, capable of inspiring such great deeds, as she had already guessed while he was still in prison. (*PL* 296.20–5.)

Valour is, on occasion, shown to be a more important qualification than high social rank in a husband. Thus the wife of Synados of Windsor was right to follow the advice of her parents that she should take 'lo meillor bacheler que elle savoit d'armes, ne que ele porroit avoir, de que que povreté que il fust' (*PL* 440.20–2). It is also appropriate that it should be Hector, doubling with Lancelot in the role of faithful lover as well as young knight with a reputation still to make, who rescues husband and wife from the attacks of some of her relatives who consider that she has married beneath her.

Certain episodes in the story serve to contrast Guinevere's encouragement of Lancelot as a knight with the more negative attitude shown by some ladies who neglect their responsibilities towards *preudommes*. Some ladies may demand proofs of prowess which, unlike most of the adventures undertaken by Lancelot, Hector, or Gauvain, have little to do with the idea of a knight as a champion of the weak and oppressed and a righter of wrongs within Arthur's feudal kingdom. For example, Gauvain defeats a knight who has set up a series of lances at the Lande des Set Voies and insists on jousting with every knight who comes by. When Gauvain asks why he has done this, he replies that he loves a lady of high social rank who first refused him her love on the grounds that he was only a squire, 'car ele estoit dame, si seroit trop ampiriee' (*PL* 424.12). When he became a knight, she still refused, as she had not yet heard him spoken of as a knight; she said that 'quant ele en avroit oï parler de moi as chevaliers que ge fusse prisiez chevaliers, lors seroit bien droiz que ele m'amast' (*PL* 424.15-17). He then strove to do great deeds as a knight, so that he would please her; and he succeeded in doing so much that she became more gracious towards him. He then asked again for her love; but instead of rewarding him for having achieved so much, she said that she would grant her love only if he guarded the Lande des Set Voies and fought all the knights who passed there. When he had guarded it for a month without being defeated, she would be his. The task which she set him is not so destructive as that demanded by Mabonagrain's *amie* in the *Joie de la Cort* episode in *Erec*, but the jousts upon which he insists are presented as a somewhat pointless interruption in Gauvain's more important task of finding the Unknown Knight (Lancelot).

Then there are the ladies who doubt the prowess of their *ami* or champion. The romance contains several variants on this theme which plays an important part in the Fair Unknown story. Hector's *amie* has insufficient faith in his prowess and tries to overprotect him, to keep him to herself; she therefore forbids him to undertake the tasks which his love gives him the strength to achieve. Her fear for Hector therefore casts doubts on the quality of their love, much as Enide's enigmatic remark, *com mar i fu*, may question the value of the love she has inspired in Erec. She will not even allow Hector to undertake the battle against Segurades, although this time he has with her permission under-taken and surmounted a series of tests on the same pattern that Erec set himself in Chrétien's poem, and Gauvain, here playing the part of the Unknown Knight, has to fight as champion in Hector's place. She is eventually forced, appropriately enough by Guinevere, to allow Hector to go on the quest for Gauvain, but she does so most reluctantly:

Et qant ele voit que faire l'estuet, si dit que, se Deu plaist, par sa proiere ne par son commandement n'ira il ja an peril de mort. Mais s'il i velt aler, ele l'otroie bien sanz malevoillance. (*PL* 405.23-5.)

Until then she has withheld permission for Hector to undertake either the battle or the quest, even though this meant that Hector would not be allowed by her uncle to marry her, so that the two never had the opportunity to lapse into *peresce* like Erec and Enide. Hector, unlike his *amie*, has confidence in the power of his love and is eager to undertake adventures:

Qant cist chevaliers sot que il avroit s'amie a l'ore que Segurades seroit outrez, si li fu avis que tant se fioit an amor que, se il pooit venir an leu ou il fust, il l'outreroit bien d'armes. (*PL* 375.20-3.)

Hector, as the obedient lover, is therefore imprisoned by his love, for he would willingly go on the quest for the Lady of Roestoc's vanished champion (Gauvain), if he were allowed: 'Il i alast mout volentiers, se ele ne li aüst deffandu, mais il l'aime et dote sor tote rien.' (*PL* 401.13–14.) Thus a lover's fear, combined with the wrong attitude in the *amie*, can act as a brake, not as a spur. Hector's *amie* imprisons him with her love, just as surely as Mabonagrain in *Erec* had been imprisoned by his love, whereas Lancelot's love sends him out in the world to achieve greatness and do good. Guinevere, we have seen, recognizes that this must be so, although it may cause her sadness.

Another kind of doubter is the Lady of Roestoc, who before the battle fails to recognize her champion's prowess and after his victory neglects to reward it, only to fall in love when it is too late. The dwarf brings the unknown champion (Gauvain) to her as a wretched substitute for both Gauvain and Hector, and she takes him at his word instead of recognizing, as did her seneschal from Gauvain's bearing, that he is likely to be a worthy champion. When Gauvain has defeated Segurades, she is so joyful that she forgets to show her gratitude, and when Gauvain has disappeared, she laments: 'Ha lasse! com suis angigniee, qui lo plus prodome do monde avoie, ne onques honor ne li fis ne compaignie.' (*PL* 392.36–7.) Her inability to recognize prowess is underlined by the fact that the knight who was pressing an unwanted suit upon her and was defeated by Gauvain was himself a knight of great prowess, although older than her and of lower social rank (*PL* 374.5–6).

The third doubter of her knight's prowess has a better case, for her husband has refused to recognize the quality of her beauty. Heliene sanz Per, like Enide, is of a lower rank than her husband, but is very beautiful. Her sister explains:

'Ge ai une moie suer, la plus belle dame que ge onques veïsse, et totes les autres dient que eles ne virent onques si belle. Quant ele estoit pucelle, si l'anma uns chevaliers par amors qui cuidoit estre uns des miaudres chevaliers do monde, et li miaudres cuide il ancor estre. Et si est il assez plus hauz hom et plus jantis hom que ma suer.' (*PL* 519.10–15.)

The knight (Persides) marries her against his family's wishes and, like Erec, lapses into *peresce*:

'Un jor avint que li chevaliers et ma seror gisoient an un prael delez une fontaine, comme genz qui mout s'antramoient. Et li chevaliers estoit ja mout apereciz et antrelaisoit mout les armes.' (*PL* 519.18–20.)

An aged uncle of Persides comes and reproaches him for his shameful decline as a knight because of his love for his wife:

'Et dit que mout estoit honiz qui si estoit sorpris de sa fame qu'il ne pooit estre san li et que totes compaignies an avoit perdues et que toz li mondes s'en escharnisoit.' (*PL* 519.22–4.)

This recalls both Erec's situation and Gauvain's warnings to Yvain of the dangers of a knight being diminished through marriage (*Yvain*, 2486–540).

The reactions of Heliene sanz Per are different from those of Enide, when she hears similar reproaches. Heliene does not lament, but protests angrily against the assumption of the superiority of Persides and declares that her beauty is of greater significance than his chivalry in words which should be contrasted with Guinevere's protest to the Lady of Malohaut (quoted earlier) that Lancelot is her equal (*PL* 547.18–19). Heliene says:

'Por coi, sire, est il don si honiz por moi? S'il est jantis hom, ge ne suis mies de trop bas lignage. Et se il a perdue la compaignie des genz por moi, et ge autresi por lui, car maintes genz me venissent veoir chascun jor. Et certes, plus suis ge belle fame que il n'est biaus chevaliers ne bons, et plus a esté ma biautez loee que sa chevalerie.' (*PL* 519.26–31.)

When her husband hears this, he is enraged and swears that she will never leave his great tower before it is finally decided whether she is the most beautiful lady or he is the best knight:

'Et sachiez, fait il, biax oncles, se plus belle dame de li vient ci, que ja mais ne gerrai o li a mon pooir. Et se miaudres chevaliers de moi vient, si soit quite de sa prison.' (*PL* 519.35–7.)

This is an inversion of the Sparrowhawk episode in *Erec*, where both contestants by their prowess strive to prove the beauty of their ladies: here one of the contestants, Persides, is trying to disprove the beauty of his wife. For five years the lady remains imprisoned in the tower until Hector comes to vindicate her claims. He declares that he draws strength from her beauty and is in no hurry to begin the fight:

'Mout volentiers esgardasse la biauté de ceste dame, car ge an suis si amandez que ge an vail orrandroit tex deus com ge estoie qant ge vig çaianz.' (*PL* 521.14–17.)

He criticizes Persides for his unchivalrous behaviour:

'Mais il sont deus choses an bon chevalier que vos n'avez mies, car au mains ne puet estre tres bons chevaliers sanz cortoisie. Et la ne fustes vos mies cortois o vos vos correçastes de ce que ele se tint a plus belle.' (*PL* 521.34–7.)

He then demonstrates by his easy victory the falseness of Persides' position whereby he pits his prowess against beauty instead of putting it at the service of beauty.

The passage naming the three most beautiful women of the time as Guinevere, Heliene sanz Per, and the sister of Perceval (*PL* 33.4–15), with its reference forward to the episode which has just been discussed, helps to underline the contrast between the rich relationship which will develop between Lancelot and Guinevere and the sterile one between Persides and Heliene.[11]

Guinevere's worthiness to be a recipient of love is emphasized throughout, as well as Lancelot's appreciation of her qualities. When Lancelot is overwhelmed by her beauty and admires her above all other women, the tale explains that it was right to do so, and not for outward beauty alone:

Et il n'avoit mie tort s'il ne prisoit envers la reine nule autre dame, car ce fu la dame des dames et la fontaine de biauté; mais s'il saüst la grant valor qui en li estoit, encor l'esgardast il plus volentiers, car nule n'estoit, ne povre ne riche, de sa valor. (*PL* 157.27–31.)

Arthur, even when under the influence of the love potion given him by the False Guinevere and her supporters, cannot refrain from proclaiming the virtues of the woman whom he had up till then considered to be the true Queen:

'Mais bien sachiez, fait il, que ge ne cuidoie mie que nule dame del monde poïst valoir cele qui si m'a honi en terre par son engin et fait desleiauter vers mon Criator, dont j'ai au cuer grant angoisse. Car nule dame, fait il, ne fu onques de si grant sen com ele est, ne de si grant cortoisie, ne si douce, ne si deboennaire. Et a sa largesce estoient totes celes noienz qui onqes fussient, si ert si entechiee de boenes teches qe par sa grant valor a si gaaigniez les cuers des riches et des povres de par tot le reiaume de Bretaigne qu'il dient que c'est l'esmeraude de totes les dames qui soient. Mais ge cuit, fait il, que tot ce a ele fait por decevoir moi et les autres, si que nus n'aparceüst sa felenie ne sa desleiauté.' (*PL* 592.28–38.)

An important element in Guinevere's great worth is her positive attitude towards chivalric achievement, which means that love for her will not result in *peresce* or destructive activity. It is significant that it is she who obliges Hector's *amie* to allow him to go as one of the Queen's knights on the quest for Gauvain during which he performs exploits which help to demonstrate that love should provide a positive force. The quest for Gauvain itself has its origin in the failure of a lady (the Lady of Roestoc) to recognize prowess. His first adventure in this quest, a battle with Guinas de Blaqestan—a knight who has failed to recognize his own lady's fidelity—presents a different aspect of the theme, but the rescues of Synados and of Heliene are both concerned in varying ways with the relationship between love and prowess. Thus from the point of view of thematic structure, while Lancelot is pining for Guinevere in Sorelois, the adventures of Hector and Gauvain in their respective quests continue to develop the theme of love as well as that of identity.

If Guinevere's love for Lancelot is presented as a positive force for good in his development as a knight and as a model for the inspiration of chivalric achievement, what about Arthur's position as both Guinevere's husband and feudal suserain, head of the Round Table, the focal point for all chivalry? Care is taken to avoid a situation in which Lancelot could be accused of disloyalty and in which there would be, as in the Tristan story, a conflict between feudal or family loyalty and love. We have seen in the previous chapter that during the account of Lancelot's childhood and during the *preudomme*'s admonitions (*PL* 285.11–14) emphasis is laid on Arthur's failure to protect his vassal Ban. The dispossessed Lancelot holds no land from Arthur, he owes him no homage, it was the Queen rather than the King who performed the final act of the knighting ceremony, and as an unknown knight he is not a member of the court or of the King's household. Indeed, in winning his seat at the Round Table, he saves Arthur three times, once from Galehot before he receives his first kiss from Guinevere, a second time in the battle against the Saxons before the physical consummation of the love, and a third time when he rescues Arthur from a Saxon prison. On that first night which Lancelot spends with Guinevere, Arthur is trying to make love to a Saxon damsel, to some extent at least under the influence of magic (*PL* 540.26–9, 541.35–7). In the False Guinevere episode Arthur is induced through a potion to take the side of the False Guinevere against the true Queen, whose qualities are stressed throughout the episode and who receives the support of all Arthur's knights. In both these 'lapses' of Arthur it might be said that he himself cannot be held fully responsible as he is acting under the influence of spells and potions. Nevertheless the two episodes are used to make a contrast between Lancelot and Guinevere's love, stemming from their recognition in one another of moral and physical beauty and prowess, and presented as a positive force for good, and Arthur's love, artificially induced, which on the first occasion (his love for the Saxon damsel) threatens the defence of the Kingdom of Logres against the pagan Saxons, and on the second occasion (his love for the False Guinevere) threatens not only the true Queen's identity but the fate of the Round Table itself, the centre of chivalry. There are echoes of the Tristan story in the False Guinevere episode, but with a reversal in favour of Lancelot and Guinevere. It is Arthur who under the influence of the love potion is threatening society, although it is Guinevere who is on trial (but accused of claiming a false identity, not of adultery).

The structure of the *PL* does in fact require a delicate balance in the treatment of Arthur.[12] The King is at the centre of the story in the sense that knights set out from his court on adventures and return to it, and most of the tasks they perform (as we shall see in the next chapter) are concerned with the protection of the rights of his vassals, but his role is mainly a passive one. Unlike Lancelot's love trances, from which he draws strength, Arthur's broodings are not usually a prelude to his own great deeds, but represent his feelings of frustration at situations over which he seems to have no control, sometimes admittedly through no fault of his own. However, there are, as we shall see in Chapter IV, references in the text to his activities as King through allusions to events outside

the tale of Lancelot; furthermore, in the war against the Saxons he himself takes
an active part and shows great bravery. A series of contrasts and parallels with
other characters, according to a technique to be analysed further in Chapter
VIII, is also used to considerable effect to achieve the desired balance. As a ruler
he is contrasted favourably with Claudas, especially during the account of the
latter's visit to Britain. When Claudas, to test the opinion of the *serjant* who has
accompanied him, talks of trying to conquer Arthur, his companion declares
himself ready to renounce his homage and fight his lord:

'Ge vos gerpiroie tot vostre homage por garantir tot lo monde de dolor et de povreté et
por tote chevalerie tenir an haut, car se cist seus hom estoit morz, ge ne voi que ja mais
meïst chevalerie ne tenist gentillece la ou ele est.' (*PL* 35.19–23.)

Such passages make it more credible that Arthur has at his court 'la flor de tote
la terriene chevalerie' (*PL* 34.19–20) and help to ensure that the installation of
Lancelot as a Knight of the Round Table in recognition of his supreme achievements in chivalry does not come as an anti-climax. But it is equally important,
if this seat at the Round Table is to seem a fitting reward to the knight who is
after all the Queen's lover, that Arthur should not appear as the wronged
husband, but as the grateful King who would have lost his crown and even his
life without the help of a knight who owed him nothing, neither land nor even
knighthood.

This is where the role of Galehot is important. Firstly, he can be compared
favourably with Arthur. Indeed the terms used to praise Galehot, in particular
the listing of the qualities by which he wins the love of his men, recall both
those used by the *serjant* in his quarrel with Claudas and those used by the
preudomme in his description of what a king should do, as opposed to what
Arthur has actually been doing. This will be explored further in Chapter VIII,
where pairing is examined. The *preudomme* tells Arthur that he has failed in his
duty as king and that he must win back the hearts of his men by making sure
that all receive justice and by showing *largece* and *debonaireté* to the poor knight
as well as the powerful baron. Arthur is thus confronted by a noble and
formidable opponent who at the time of the battle knows better than Arthur
how to win the hearts of his men, so that Lancelot's achievement in persuading
Galehot to give up his heart's ambition of conquering the renowned Arthur is
all the greater and Arthur's debt all the more overwhelming. Galehot has had
built a castle in which he intends to be crowned when he has conquered Arthur
(*PL* 574.19–30). He is within reach of achieving this goal when he voluntarily
renounces it.

In the second place, Galehot's motives in renouncing his intention of
conquering Arthur are an important factor in the turning of attention away

from the adulterous aspect of Lancelot's love and thus from a Tristan-type situation in which the conflict between love and the respect due to Arthur as head of the Round Table, if not as liege lord, might detract from Lancelot's chivalric achievement under the influence of his feelings for Guinevere. The author has avoided as far as possible the triangle of royal husband, wife, and lover which might have threatened the integrity of the Round Table and the peace of the kingdom, a situation which will indeed be found, once the *Lancelot-Grail* cycle has been developed. The *PL* does not replace this conflict between husband and lover by the characteristic triangle of the love lyric in which the lover is opposed by the jealous rival who strives to cast doubts on the sincerity of his love for the lady, or by its adaptation in the *Chevalier de la Charrette*, where Lancelot has as an opponent Meleagant who has carried off Guinevere and also wants her love. There is a triangle in the *PL*, but not of two men struggling for one woman, but a man and a woman striving for the possession of one man. The struggle between Guinevere and Galehot is one of the main themes of the *PL*, and it emerges clearly from the discussion between Galehot and Arthur and his court over the Black Knight (Lancelot). Arthur says, with unconscious irony, that to win the companionship of the Black Knight he would offer half of all he has except his wife (*PL* 333.36–8). Gauvain declares:

'Se Dex, fait il, me doint la santé que ge desir, ge voudroie orendroit estre la plus bele damoisele do mont saine et haitiee, par covant que il m'amast sor tote rien, ausin bien com ge l'ameroie.' (*PL* 334.5–7.)

Guinevere laughingly says that she cannot offer more than this, and Galehot, when his turn comes, says:

'Et si m'aïst Dex, j'an voudroie avoir tornee ma grant honor a honte, par si que ge fusse a tozjorz ausi seürs de lui comme ge voudroie que il fust de moi.' (*PL* 334.17–19.)

Galehot's desire to have Lancelot's companionship is linked with Lancelot's prowess, and his love, like that of Guinevere, is a sign of his nobility and discernment, his ability to value a great knight such as Lancelot. He is capable of feeling love for a woman. The Queen brings him and the Lady of Malohaut together as lovers, and both he and Lancelot suffer the pain of separation from their *amies* when they leave for Sorelois (*PL* 355.39–356.1); but his love for the Lady of Malohaut comes after his love for Lancelot both chronologically and in intensity, although it is not shown to be in competition with it or in any sense incompatible with it. Indeed, in a way, the Lady of Malohaut is a particularly suitable object for his affection, as she too has loved Lancelot for his prowess, but has had to give way before his love for Guinevere.

Lancelot's love for Guinevere inspires him to great deeds, helps him to win his name, and brings him great honour before the world, however humble he may be before her. Galehot's love for Lancelot entails the sacrifice of his greatest moment of glory. He says at one point, in relation to Lancelot's request that he should surrender to Arthur, that nothing that he does for his companion can bring him shame: 'Ge ne porroie rien faire por vos o ge poïsse honte avoir' (*PL* 325.20–1; to be compared with *Char.* 4354–60). However, as quoted above, he later describes what he was prepared to offer for the companionship of the Black Knight as the turning of great honour into great shame (*PL* 334.17–19), an offer which Gauvain describes as a greater sacrifice than anything anyone else had proposed. Yet he is prepared to sacrifice even more for the man whose companionship he longs to have. To bring Lancelot happiness he is prepared to endanger his own chances of keeping him with him when he agrees to arrange a meeting between Lancelot and Guinevere. The Queen knows against whom she is competing. She recognizes Galehot's love for Lancelot and that he is a rival:

'Et si est totjorz la costume que la dessirree chose est totjorz la plus veé, et si i a de tex genz qui a autrui font a enviz aaise de la chose que il plus aimment.' (*PL* 337.37–9.)

Galehot realizes the danger, but sacrifices himself because he cannot bear to see his friend suffer; he brings Lancelot and Guinevere together, knowing that he is preparing his own ruin. Lancelot remains a more or less helpless figure, powerless to deny Guinevere but unwilling to bring grief to his friend. Galehot's only hope is that the Queen will not ask Lancelot to become a member of the King's *maisnie*. After his companion has freed the King from the Saxons and has been welcomed at court, Galehot discusses with him the possibility that the Queen will ask her lover to stay: 'Et que ferai ge qui tot ai mis an vos et cuer et cors?' (*PL* 568.34–5.) Lancelot promises that he will not stay with Arthur unless forced to do so, but explains that if the Queen commands he cannot refuse, and Galehot accepts this. Galehot says to Arthur: 'Ne ja ne m'aïst Dex, se ge savoie vivre sanz lui. Et comment me toudriez vos ma vie?' (*PL* 570.30–1.) He hopes that the Queen will not ask Lancelot to stay, but she does make the request. Galehot, a ruler with lands to govern, cannot leave his country indefinitely; Lancelot, still dispossessed, can remain a full member of Arthur's court, making it a centre from which he can depart to perform deeds of prowess, but to which he will always return. Indeed, to be without a kingdom, even though a king's son, is really a necessary qualification for the lover of Guinevere; hence in the *PL*, where considerable emphasis is laid on the need of kings to govern, Lancelot never does recover his lands. The Lady of Malohaut believes that the Queen has been much wiser than she has in choosing as her lover not a *riche home* like Galehot, but a poor knight like Lancelot, 'dont ele puet faire son plaisir sanz contredit' (*PL* 609.27).

Thus the Queen's request must inevitably bring about Galehot's death, as he cannot live without Lancelot. He himself saw this inevitable consequence: at the very time that he was arranging the first secret meeting between Lancelot and Guinevere, he realized that he was preparing his own doom. There is a temporary respite while the two go off to Sorelois, but even on the journey there Galehot broods deeply on the separation which is bound to come:

Et lors chaï Galehoz en un pensé dont ses cuers fu mout a malaise, si chevauche plus soef, et commança a penser a Lancelot, son conpaignon, qui remés est de la maisnie lo roi Artu. Si en a mout grant angoisse et dist a soi meïsmes que or a il perdu tote anor et tote joie par celui de cui il la cuidoit avoir recovree a toz les jorz de son vivant. (*PL* 572.19–24.)

He knows that the first time they go to court the Queen will ask Lancelot to stay, now that he is a member of the *maisnie*, and that that will be the end of the two friends' companionship. His sacrifice has therefore been in vain:

'S'ai ansi perdue l'amor que j'avoie en lui mise, et lo grant meschief que ge fis por sa conpaignie avoir, la ou g'estoie au desus de conquerre tot lo pris et tote l'anor del monde.' (*PL* 572.28–30.)

He is so overwhelmed by these thoughts that he falls from his horse in a faint. Lancelot himself is conscious that Galehot's love for him has brought his companion only misfortune:

'Et ge sai bien que puis que ge vos acointai premierement, ne vos avint chose que vos deüssiez tenir a mescheance qui par moi ne vos avenist.' (*PL* 573.12–14.)

When Galehot reaches Sorelois, he sees all his castles fall and has disturbing dreams. With the interpretation of the manifestations and visions Lancelot learns the full extent of the *mescheance* he will unwillingly bring upon his friend. Bademaguz tells Galehot that he will die through Lancelot:

'Car vos amez, fait il, Lancelot plus que nul home, et vos en verroiz tel chose avenir dont vos avroiz si grant duel qu'il covandra que vos en perdoiz la vie. Et lors morroiz par lui, que garantiz n'an poez estre.' (*PL* 582.39–583.2.)

There is a parallel here with the interpretation of Arthur's dreams (to be explored further in Chapter VIII), with Arthur's clerks in both cases asking three times for respite before giving the interpretation, and making a stipulation that the King should promise that no harm should come to them, whatever they say. However in Galehot's case the clerks do not need outside help, for Bademaguz, their leader, is capable of giving a full interpretation, thus filling the role of the *preudomme* who gives the true meaning of Arthur's dreams. As the King's dreams concerned the danger threatening his kingdom at the time of his war with Galehot and led up to the episode in which Galehot gives up his victory for Lancelot's sake, these parallels serve to underline the tragic consequences for Galehot himself of his love for Lancelot as well as the nobility of his sacrifice in bringing Lancelot and Guinevere together.[13]

In the False Guinevere episode Lancelot's love saves Guinevere, but the journey to Sorelois prepares us for a conclusion to the conflict between the two loves in which Galehot is lost through his love for Lancelot. The two friends are separated through Lancelot's inability to disobey the Queen's commands, and the fulfilment of the prophecy of the death of Galehot, arising from a false rumour of Lancelot's death, brings to an end the non-cyclic romance. The Lady of Malohaut cannot be comforted at the death of her lover, but Lancelot, deeply grieved as he is, can draw consolation from that love relationship with Guinevere which Galehot himself had helped him to achieve, thereby causing his own death:

Mais quant Lanceloz sot que por lui avoit mort receüe cil par cui il avoit toz les biens et totes les joies, si fist si grant duel qe totes genz qui lo veoient en ont grant pitié. Et se ne fust li cors la reine, ja mes par autre ne fust confortez; mes ce l'asoaje molt et done granz confort de totes ires et de totes angoisses oblier qu'il est en la compaignie de la plus vaillant dame dou monde et de la rien que il plus aime. (*PL* 612.34–613.3.)

The theme of love inspired by prowess and prowess inspired by love runs therefore throughout the work. Lancelot establishes his reputation as a knight greater even than Gauvain because he acts (although without the need of prompting) in accordance with the counsels of the Lady of the Lake: 'que vos ne metoiz ja vostre cuer en amor qui vos face aparecir mais amander' (*PL* 205.38–9). Guinevere's greatest achievement is to have inspired the love which made Lancelot the greatest of all knights and which made her (again in the words of the Lady of the Lake) 'compaigne au plus preudome do monde et dame au meillor chevalier' (*PL* 557.6–7).

There is little suggestion of a conflict between love and loyalty or of moral condemnation of adulterous love in the non-cyclic romance, which gives the short ('special' in the terminology of Micha) version of the journey to Sorelois and the False Guinevere episode and ends with the death of Galehot. There is apparently on the part of the lovers no great consciousness of sin, of retribution to come. It is true that the Lady of the Lake, when talking of the love between the Queen and Lancelot, says: 'Ne li pechié do siegle ne puent estre mené sanz folie', but she goes on to say: 'Mais mout a grant raison de sa folie qui raison i trove et annor.' (*PL* 557.1–3.) There is equally no suggestion that when the Queen is tried as an impostor, she is being punished for her relations with Lancelot, although the idea of retribution for some unspecified sin is mentioned in one passage. This describes how Guinevere, when standing trial, is overcome by grief, for she is very much afraid that for some sin which she had committed in the past—'por aucun pechié que ele ait fait ça en arrieres' (*PL* 595.22–3)—God wishes her to be shamed and dishonoured on earth. It would have been easy enough to point a moral here and to condemn adultery, but the author does not do so, and the allusion is left entirely vague. Nor is there any suggestion that Lancelot will be disqualified through his love from the highest achievement of chivalry. As we shall see in Chapter X, it is only in the cyclic version of the Journey to Sorelois and the False Guinevere episode that doubts concerning the morality of Lancelot and Guinevere's love are introduced.

In the *PL* the special quality of this love is underlined through comparison with that of other knights and ladies, and here again, as with the identity theme, use is made of an interplay between the text and literary traditions which would be known to the audience. There is a deliberate contrast with the Tristan situation in the False Guinevere episode through the reversal of a well-known pattern, as well as echoes of Lancelot's rescue of Guinevere in the *Chevalier de la Charrette*. Similarly, with the motif of the lady's doubting of prowess, the author presents a series of variations on the pattern of the love situation in *Erec*, just as there had been a series of variations on the pattern of the Fair Unknown tale, and here again we find a close connection between the themes of love and identity. The three knights whose adventures are followed through, Lancelot, Gauvain, and Hector, are used to present different aspects of the love and chivalry relationship, just as they had been used to present variations on the pattern of the young unknown knight in contrast with the well-known knight. It is also not without significance that it is to Yvain, hero of that well-known romance by Chrétien which (like *Erec*, but from a different angle) explores the relationship between love and chivalry, that Arthur entrusts Lancelot on his arrival at court. It is also Yvain, who in Chrétien's romance had killed a giant in the process of his redemption as knight and lover, who brings back news to Arthur's court of the victory over two giants by the Unknown Knight (Lancelot) whom he had pulled out of the river. It is Yvain too who supports the Queen while Lancelot is in the Saxon prison.[14]

Thus through this network of contrasts and parallels with well-known love romances of the twelfth century, not only is the Lancelot of the *Chevalier de la Charrette* evoked, but the story is also enriched with echoes of the other great knightly lovers, and the love theme is thereby given greater depth and resonance.

IV

Feudal Links and the Role of Arthur and His Court

The central role of Arthur and his court

There is thematic coherence throughout the work, as we have seen, but other means are also used to weave the individual threads of knights' adventures into a firm texture. At the centre of the web are Arthur and his court, as the examination of the thematic structure in Chapters II and III has already shown. No knight can truly be said to have made his name until he has won a reputation at Arthur's court and a seat at the Round Table; the inspiration which enables Lancelot to perform the feats which gain him this reputation is also to be found at Arthur's court in the person of the Queen. Lancelot has lost his father, his land, and his identity because of Arthur's failure to protect his vassal Ban, but he establishes his identity and re-establishes that of Guinevere through saving Arthur's person, his kingdom, his Queen, and his Round Table. It is Arthur's nephew Gauvain, acknowledged leader of the Knights of the Round Table, who sets out to uncover the identity of the Unknown Knight, who provides a measuring-rod for Lancelot's achievement, and who eventually presents him at court as the greatest knight of all. It is this unifying function of Arthur's court which we will examine further here.

There are two main aspects to the role of Arthur's court within the work. It performs its traditional function as the centre of chivalry throughout the whole of Christendom and even beyond, for in the *PL* the fame of the Round Table provides a focus for all the greatest knights of the world, as it had done in Wace, Chrétien de Troyes, and Robert de Boron. It is also the centre of Arthur's feudal kingdom within which it is his responsibility as suserain to protect his vassals. In the chronicles Arthur is presented as an active king, not simply presiding as the rather passive figure of most of Chrétien's romances over a court from which his knights set out on adventure, but with a land to govern, armies to lead, barons to control, enemies to be defeated.[1] In the *PL* particular emphasis is given to the King's responsibilities towards individual vassals who hold lands from him in return for providing knights for his wars. In relation to this the Knights of the Round Table serve not so much as champions of justice in a general sense, but as aids to the King to see that the rights of vassals within Arthur's kingdom are protected. As both an international focus and a more

closely defined feudal centre Arthur's court serves its traditional function as a
starting-point for adventures and as a rallying-point for joint enterprises, so that
the narrative threads start from the court, diverge, and then come together at
the court at intervals, for it is at the court of Arthur that any worthwhile
reputation must be established.

The story of Lancelot is integrated into the more general history of an
Arthurian feudal kingdom in two ways. Firstly, there are a series of references to
events lying outside the main narrative. Secondly, Lancelot's adventures are
directly involved with the fate of the Arthurian kingdom through the series of
assemblees and through the war with the Saxons in which Arthur performs the
traditional role attributed to him in the Chronicles—that of defender of Britain
against pagan Saxon invaders.

References to events in the past in relation to the main story and to events in Britain contemporary with Lancelot's childhood

The story does not begin at Arthur's court or even in Britain, but 'en la marche
de Gaule et de la Petite Bretaigne' (*PL* 1.1), in the lands of the two Kings, Ban
and Bohort. However, it is immediately made clear that the fate of these two is
closely bound up with that of Britain. In the 'historical' introduction which
opens the work and which describes the circumstances in which Lancelot's
father Ban lost his throne, great emphasis is given to the role of Ban's relationship as vassal to Arthur in the chain of events which causes both him and his
brother to lose their lands and their lives, a chain which stretches back to the
time of Uther, to events which happened before Lancelot was born and before
Arthur became king. Ban had a neighbour, King Claudas, lord of Berri, then
known as Terre Deserte. Claudas refused to acknowledge his allegiance to
Aramont (also known as Hoel), lord of Brittany, and took as his lord the King of
Gaule, a land then subject to Rome. Aramont made war on Claudas, but was
beginning to lose, as he had all the might of Rome against him. He then went to
Uther Pendragon, who was King of Britain, and agreed to become his vassal in
return for help in his wars. Uther came across the sea with his army, and he and
Aramont defeated Claudas and laid waste his land except for the city of
Bourges. Then Uther, after spending some time in Brittany, returned to Britain.
From that time on Brittany was 'desouz lo reiaume de Logres'. However, after
the death of Aramont and Uther Pendragon, when Arthur became King, many
wars broke out in Britain, and most of the barons fought the King. Therefore at
the beginning of his reign Arthur had many difficulties to contend with on
every side. It was then that Claudas resumed the war. He had recovered his land
on the death of Aramont. He now began to make war on Ban because they were

neighbours and because Ban had been a vassal of Aramont and therefore also a vassal of the King of Britain. In this renewal of war Claudas was helped by a consul from Rome. Ban sent many messengers to Arthur (*PL* 3.17–18) to ask for help, but Arthur could not respond to the appeals of his vassal because he was so busy with his own wars. Ban nevertheless still refused to renounce his allegiance, but eventually agreed to an offer from Claudas of a truce of forty days: if he had not received help from Arthur by the end of that time, he promised to become the vassal of Claudas. He set off to appeal for help in person; in the mean time Claudas captured Ban's one remaining castle through treachery, and Ban died of grief at seeing the castle go up in flames.

We have seen in Chapter II that this account of the disinheriting of Ban is different from that given in Ulrich, where Pant is presented as a cruel tyrant who loses his land because of a revolt of discontented barons. It may well be that the author of the *PL*, because of the importance given to heredity within the work, modified the existing Lancelot tradition by giving Claudas rather than Ban the role of greedy tyrant. Nevertheless, he takes care to fit the story into the general Arthurian 'historical' tradition, although the details do not correspond exactly to any surviving text. Claudas de la Deserte, for example, appears in the *Second Continuation*, where he and his brother Carras show arrogance ('trop grant posnee', 31304). Arthur, in punishment, lays waste the brothers' land and eventually makes peace with them.[2] In Wace, Hoel, King of *Bretainne la Menur*, is a contemporary of Arthur, not Uther, but at Arthur's command he conquers a region which is very similar to the one described as 'desouz Aramont', whose *sorenon* is Hoel, in the *PL*:

> Berri conquist et puis Toruigne,
> Ango et Alverne et Wascuine.
> (*Brut*, 10115–16.)

Cil Aramonz avoit desouz lui Gaunes et Benoyc et tote la terre jusque a la marche d'Auverne et de Gascoigne et devoit avoir desouz lui lo regne de Bohorges.[3] (*PL* 1.20–2.)

In the *PL* the relationship between Gaule and Rome is described as follows:

Et a cel tens estoit Gaule sougiete a Rome et li rendoit treü, et estoient tuit li roi par election. (*PL* 1.24–5.)

Wace explains that at the time of Arthur

> France aveit nun Galle a cel jur
> Si n'i aveit rei ne seinnur;
> Romain en demainne l'aveient
> Et en demainne la teneient.
> En guarde ert a Frolle livree

E il l'aveit lunges guardee;
Treüz e rentes receveit
Et par termes les trameteit
A Rome a Leu, l'empereür.
(*Brut*, 9905–13.)

At the beginning of the *PL* the reference to the troubled times after the death of Uther and to Arthur's wars with his barons during the first years of his reign and of his marriage with Guinevere places the story loosely within the general framework of the chronicle tradition as found in Geoffrey of Monmouth and Wace, but (as we have already seen) it also links up with the situation in which Perceval's father and other *gentil home* were disinherited. Perceval's mother tells her son:

Vostre peres, si nel savez,
Fu parmi la jambe navrez
Si que il mehaigna del cors.
Sa grant terre, ses grans tresors,
Que il avoit come preudom,
Ala tot a perdition,
Si chaï en grant povreté.
Apovri et deshireté
Et escillié furent a tort
Li gentil home aprés la mort
Uterpandragon qui rois fu
Et peres le bon roi Artu.
Les terres furent escillies,
Et les povres gens avillies,
Si s'en fuï qui fuïr pot.
(*Perc.* 435–49.)

During the account of the childhood of Lancelot and his cousins, there are a number of references both to Arthur's failure to avenge Ban and to the wars which prevented him from doing so. When Claudas visits Britain in disguise, there is another allusion to Arthur's wars with his barons after he first married Guinevere:

Tant chevaucha Claudas qu'il vint en la Grant Bretaigne et trova lo roi a Logres, sa cité; si avoit guerre a pluseurs de ses barons. Ne il n'avoit encores gaires esté rois, si avoit prise la reine Guenievre, n'avoit pas plus de set mois et demi. (*PL* 32.38–33.2.)

The author gives some more details of these wars:

En celui tans avoit li rois Artus guerre au roi Yon d'Irlande la Menor, et puis au roi

Aguisçant d'Escoce, son coisin meesmes, et aprés au Roi d'Outre les Marches de Galone, et a mainz autres de ses barons. (*PL* 33.20–3.)

According to Wace, Arthur's wars in the early part of his reign and of his marriage with Guinevere were with Saxons, Scots, Irish, and Icelanders, so that again there is only a very general rather than a precise correlation with surviving Arthurian texts. There is, however, through the person of the Roi d'Outre les Marches, a link within the *PL* itself with later wars in which Lancelot is to be directly involved, as the First and Second Assemblies, which Lancelot attends in disguise, arise from a challenge to King Arthur from the Roi d'Outre les Marches, who also later fights on the side of Galehot in his assembly against Arthur (*PL* 306.28–9).

When the *rendu* comes to Arthur's court on behalf of Queen Helene to reproach Arthur for not having avenged her husband Ban, it is explained that the King is able to hold court in London because of a truce in his wars, which again involves Aguisçant and the Roi d'Outre les Marches:

Et ce fu la premiere semainne de Septembre, ce dit li contes, que li rois Artus fu venuz d'Escoce de seur lou roi Aguisçant, son coisin meesmes, qui par trois feiees l'ot guerroié, si orent faite boenne pais et bien asseüree d'amedeux parz. Et ot li rois Artus trives prises devers lou Roi d'Outre les Marches jusq'a la Pasque, si s'en fu venuz por sejorner en son plus aesié païs et cil de son ostel avocques lui et d'autres chevaliers a grant planté. (*PL* 53.34–54.2.)

This repeated emphasis on the wars which Arthur has to wage serves to provide some justification for his failure to perform his duty as lord towards his vassal. As the *rendu* explained to the widowed queens before he went to Arthur's court:

'Et neporqant ge sai bien que tant a eü affeire ça en arrieres li rois Artus que n'est mie mervoille s'il a ceste chose mise an delai, car il n'a gaires baron qui ne li ait mené guerre tant que maintes genz ont quidié qu'il remainsist essilliez a la parclose.' (*PL* 53.25–9.)

Arthur excuses himself in similar terms for not having taken action over Ban's death:

'Il est voirs que ge l'ai pieç'a seü, et neporqant tex hore a esté que se g'en oïsse la conplainte, n'eüsse ge pas pooir de l'amender, car trop ai eü lons tens affeire tel hore que maintes janz ne baoient pas que ge en venisse au desus, ainz disoient par darrieres, si que maintes foiz l'oï, que en la fin me covendroit terre a guerpir. Mais ce que j'ai mauvaisement fait me covendra amender, qant Dex m'en donra lou pooir.' (*PL* 56.32–8.)

In addition to the reference to Arthur's difficulties there is also a link with the more distant past in this episode, for the *rendu*, before he left the world, had been a knight, Adragais li Bruns, at the court of Arthur's father Uther, and he

makes unfavourable comparisons between the discourteous reception accorded
to him by Beduier, the King's *bouteillier*, and the courtesy shown to all by
knights he had known at Uther's court:

'Et si ne cuit ge mie que vos seiez miauz vaillanz ne plus prisiez de tex deux preudomes vi
ge ja en maison lou roi Uter de Bretaigne, ce fu Hervis de Rivel et Kanez de Caerc. Cels vi
ge si preuz d'armes qu'il nes covenist a changier por nul cors de deus chevaliers; ne onques
par els ne fu povres hom besoigneux botez hors de cort, mais avenciez a lor poirs, et si
n'estoient pas mains seignor de la maison lou roi Uter, dont Dex ait l'ame, que vos iestes
de la maison lou roi Artu qui ses filz fu.' (PL 55.19–27.)

Hervis de Rivel then steps forward. He has been serving the King, and an
explanation is given of how King Arthur was always served by knights of all
ages which would seem designed to recall the enumeration in *Erec* of the counts
and kings summoned to Arthur's court, with its particular emphasis (in lines
1974–92 of Foerster's edition) on the very young, brought by Ban de Gomeret,
and the very old, brought by *Kerrins, li viauz rois de Riel*.[4] The link with the past is
further reinforced when the *rendu* is welcomed by King Urien, who, as father of
Yvain, is a representative of an older generation and has served as companion in
arms with Adragais at the time of Uther.

The third reference during the account of Lancelot's childhood to Arthur's
unfulfilled obligations towards Ban comes in the episode in which Banyn, Ban's
faithful knight and godson, sits next to Arthur at table and by his presence
reminds Arthur of his past failure and present guilt (*PL* 137), thereby plunging
him into the first of the three melancholy broodings at table which occur in the
text.

These references to Arthur's difficulties within his kingdom, which either
stretch back into the past or are contemporary with events in the Lancelot story,
occur in the part of the text which is mainly concerned with the struggles
between Claudas and his barons, and with the dilemma of Pharien, divided
between loyalty to his present lord, Claudas, and his duty towards the children
of his former lord, Ban. They serve to bring out a series of parallels and
contrasts between Claudas, who actively dispossesses a king, imprisons his
children, and as a result runs into trouble with his vassals, and Arthur, attacked
by unruly vassals, who is reproached not so much for what he has done, but for
what he has not done to protect his faithful vassals, a point which is taken up
later by the *preudomme* who visits Arthur after his first battle with Galehot.[5] The
emphasis on the importance of the relationship between lord and vassal is also
underlined in the long discussions between Lambegues and Pharien, and
between Pharien and Claudas, concerning the point at which a vassal is justified
in renouncing his homage to his lord.[6] Thus a kind of cohesion is given to the

romance from the beginning by the setting of the Lancelot story within a
network of feudal relations.

After Lancelot's first visit to Arthur's court and the start of his first
adventures as a knight, Arthur and his knights are brought into more direct
contact with the main line of the narrative. The author, however, continues to
introduce allusions to past events in the history of Arthur's kingdom which by
their very incompleteness present the Lancelot story as part of a wider
Arthurian 'reality' in terms of time and space. For example, in the middle of the
episode at the Gué la Reine, in which Lancelot defeats Alybon, who has been
guarding the ford in the Queen's name without her authority, an explanation is
given of the origin of the name. It was thus called because the Queen found it
within the first two years of her marriage to Arthur, during his war with the
seven kings. He and his army had been attacked in their tents where they were
encamped on the Humber. Arthur's men fled, and the King was left with Lot,
Gauvain, Urien, Yvain, who was then a young knight bachelor, and Kay, also
young, but who through his feats on that day won the reputation which earned
him the title of seneschal before he had actually been appointed as such. The
Queen passed over the ford, but Kay said that the six of them should halt their
flight and defend the ford against the seven kings who had ridden on alone,
having left their men looting the tents. The seven were then killed, Arthur and
his companions killing one each, except for Kay who killed two. The allusion is
mysterious in that the names of the seven kings are never given, nor is the
incident narrated in any of the surviving Arthurian texts, but the active roles of
both Arthur and Kay fit in with their roles in the chronicle tradition.[7] Thus,
once again, the kingdom of Arthur is given a depth in time through an allusion
to events outside the story. This helps to give the individual romance a greater
solidity by placing it within an established Arthurian setting which has a
'reality' beyond the Lancelot story. Such references may also well link up with
the social and political situation in the outside world of the early thirteenth
century, not in terms of precise historical events, but of contemporary
problems, aspirations, and tensions within society.[8]

References to past events are also used to give Galehot's position as a great
ruler and powerful rival of Arthur the same kind of depth in time. For example,
when Galehot takes Lancelot secretly to Sorelois, where he will remain hidden
while the best of Arthur's knights are encountering many adventures in their
quest for him, an explanation is given of the way Galehot acquired the land. He
has been introduced in the romance as 'li sires des Estranges Illes', not as the
lord of Sorelois, for he did not inherit Sorelois, which lies between Wales and
les Estranges Illes and is therefore not too far from Arthur's kingdom of Logres.
He had conquered it by force of arms from King Gloier, a nephew of the King

of Northumberland, who had been killed in the war and had left a small daughter whose mother had died in childbirth. Galehot was acting as her guardian until she grew up; she was to be married to a nephew of his, still only a child, who would also receive the land of Sorelois. The explanation does not refer to an episode in any existing text, but it serves to present Galehot as a ruler both successful in war and honourable in his treatment of orphans, hence fitting in with the portrait of the ideal ruler found elsewhere in the text.[9]

Sorelois is here described as a land acquired by ordinary earthly means and as particularly good for hunting. However, as the place in which Lancelot is hidden, although situated not too far from Arthur's kingdom, it must also be inaccessible, so another allusion to past events is introduced to account for its inaccessibility in both 'historical' and magical terms. The author explains that the land is surrounded by water and can only be reached by two *felons passages* which, at the time when Merlin prophesied the adventures to come, King Lohoz, father of Gloier, had had made because he feared the destruction of the land. Before the time of the *aventures* there were many ways of crossing the water, whether by wooden bridges or by ferries, but once the *aventures* started and for as long as they lasted there were only the two dangerous means of access:

Si n'i avoit au chevalier errant que deus passages, ne plus n'en i ot tant com les aventures durerent el reiaume de Logres et es illes d'anviron, qui durerent, ce dit la letre, mil et sis cenz semaines et nonnante. Cil dui passage estoient assez felon et orgoillos, car chascuns estoit d'une chauciee estroite et haute qui n'avoit mies plus de trois toises de lé, et si avoit plus de lonc de set mile et un, et desoz aive an avoit, an tex leus i avoit, plus de soisante dis. (PL 357.7–14.)

Ce dit la letre almost certainly represents only an imaginary written authority, but the reference to *les aventures* and *passage . . . assez felon et orgoillos* would evoke memories of the land of Gorre in Chrétien's *Chevalier de la Charrette*, which is associated with mysterious adventures and is difficult of access:

> Si puet l'en antrer totevoies
> Par deus mout perilleuses voies
> Et par deus mout felons passages.
> (*Char.* 653–5.)

In the PL however the bridges are less extraordinary than those in Chrétien; they are neither underwater nor knife-edged, but are long and narrow, guarded by a knight and ten *serjanz*.[10] Thus it is the reference to the time of Merlin and the *aventures* which suggests the marvellous rather than the description of the bridges themselves. This fits in well with the character of the lord of the land, Galehot, whose parentage hints at supernatural origin, *filz de la jaiande*,[11] and who is described as taller than ordinary men (*PL* 264.30-1), but who in the romance is presented very much in terms of a ruler fully of this world, with human subjects and earthly lands to govern.

There are also a series of allusions to the past, several of them somewhat mysterious, which concern less the 'historical' affairs of the kingdom than the past of individual Arthurian knights, but nevertheless help to integrate the adventures in the romance within the wider Arthurian tradition.

Most of the allusions to Arthur's past concern his wars at the beginning of his reign, soon after he had married Guinevere, but there is one which goes back to an earlier time. It occurs in the episode in which Gauvain and his companions, after being misled by false inscriptions in the cemetery of the Dolorous Guard, are lured into prison in the Doloreuse Chartre, a castle belonging to the former lord of the Dolorous Guard. There are already prisoners in the castle—some well known Arthurian knights who have been captured in unexplained circumstances:

Laianz estoit em prison li rois Yders et Guivrez de Lanbale et Yvains de Leonel et Kadoains de Qaermurzin, et Kehenins li Petiz et Kex d'Estraux et Girflez, li filz Dué, et Dodyniaus li Sauvages et li dux Taulas et Madoz de la Porte et Lohoz, li filz lo roi Artu, qui l'engendra en la bele damoisele qui avoit non Lisanor devant ce qu'il eüst la reine, et an cele prison prist il lo mal de la mort. Et avec aus estoit Gaheris de Caraheu. Tuit cist estoient an prison laianz. Et qant messires Gauvains et si compaignon les virent, si orent assez grant joie, car grant piece avoient esté perdu. Et cil refurent lié et dolant qant il les virent laianz amener: lié de ce que ja mais nes cuidoient veoir, et dolant de ce qu'il venoient en male prison. (*PL* 204.12-23.)

Most of these names are to be found on the list of Arthur's knights in *Erec*.[12] Girflet is traditionally a prisoner. An expedition is launched to rescue him in the *First Continuation* (*A* 3659-762), and later in the *PL* Gauvain, on hearing that Girflet has been in prison again, comments:

'Il ne fu onques, fait messires Gauvains, hom si sovant pris comme Guiflez. Et ce ne li vient mies de mauvaitié, car il est, si m'aïst Dex, et preuz et anprenanz et hardiz durement.' (*PL* 504.4-6.)

However it is the reference to Lohoz which is most interesting. It is continued further on (*PL* 209.31-2), where Lohoz is described as dangerously ill, but the allusion is not carried through as no account is given of his death in this text. Arthur's son is mentioned in two texts important for the *PL*. In *Erec*, in the list of knights which contains most of the names of the other prisoners mentioned here, 'Loholz, li filz le roi Artu' is described as 'un vassax de grant vertu' (*Erec*, 1699-700). In the *Lanzelet* (6882-951) *Lôût* (an emendation for manuscript readings *Lant* and *Lont*) is son of Arthur and Ginover, and comes with three thousand knights to help to rescue his mother. Ulrich writes that he won much renown and, according to the tale, in the end rode away with Arthur to a country from which the inhabitants of Britain still expect them both to return.[13] It is not surprising that, given the role of Guinevere in the *PL*, the author should have given Lohoz a different mother. In any case, the childlessness of Guinevere fits in with the chronicle tradition as exemplified by Wace, who writes of Arthur and Guinevere:

> Mais entre'els dous n'orent nul eir
> Ne ne porent emfant aveir.
> (*Brut*, 9657–8.)

Once again the incomplete allusion of the *PL* serves to present the Lancelot story as an element in a wider complex of events, with Arthur having a past (here a son by a woman other than Guinevere) outside the confines of the tale.

There are similar indications in the text in relation to Arthur's nephew Gauvain. The first of these is a reference to an event in the very recent past. On Gauvain's first appearance in the story we hear of a wound which he has received in battle with Gasoain d'Estrangot:

Messires Gauvains, ses niés, i fu, qui ancores avoit lo vis bandé d'une plaie que Gasoains d'Estrangot li avoit faite, ne n'avoit pas plus de trois semaines, car il s'estoient combatu devant lo roi ansanble entr'aus deus, et l'avoit apelé de desleiauté devant tote la cort lo roi. (*PL* 149.7–11.)

There is a Garravains d'Estrangot in some manuscripts of *Erec* (see Foerster's edition, line 1710). In the *First Continuation* (III, L 3568) Gasouains (variant: gassonains *P*) appears on a list of knights, but I know of no surviving text in which he fights Gauvain in such circumstances as are mentioned here. It would seem probable that the allusion was invented to provide Gauvain with a past outside the romance. It provides a distant echo of an episode in the *Conte del Graal* (4748–96) in which Guinganbresil comes to court to accuse Gauvain of treason, and Gauvain agrees to defend himself before the King of Escavalon.[14]

There is another even more mysterious allusion to an event in Gauvain's past later in the text. When Arthur's nephew refuses the Queen's pleas on the King's behalf that he should not leave the court on a quest for the Black Knight (Lancelot), he says:

'Dame, fait messires Gauvains, il me sovient bien d'un dun que vos me demandastes lo jor que messires li rois creanta a la damoisele chaitive a garantir un an et un jor, si me demandastes que ge remansisse de l'ost, et ge remex comme fox, si vi tel ore que ge vousise miauz estre morz et honiz.' (*PL* 362.26–30.)

I know of no text in which such an episode is to be found. In the *Conte del Graal*

(4706-20) there is a damsel besieged in Montesclaire whom Gauvain promises to deliver; there is also an episode in the later Long Version of the *First Continuation* (II, *E* 3970-4828) in which Gauvain carries out his promise; but in both cases the similarity with this allusion is very slight. However, the reference in the *PL* serves the same purpose as the earlier allusion in that it reminds us that Gauvain, as Arthur's nephew and best known of all his knights, has been involved in many adventures before Lancelot's arrival at court. This is important for the opposition between Gauvain, the mature knight with a past, and Lancelot, the unknown knight with a future, which, as we have seen, has a significant function in the structure of the text.

By means of these references the tale of Lancelot is therefore placed in relation to the past and present of the Arthurian kingdom, the King, his court, and his knights. The fact that the allusions are often incomplete and may refer to events which, although in Arthurian terms quite likely to happen, are not necessarily narrated in any text, makes a contrast with the Lancelot story, told in full. This helps to bring out the coherence of the *PL* within itself, while at the same time showing that it belongs to something larger.

The role of *assemblees*

Up till now we have been concerned with references to events in the Arthurian kingdom which lie outside the main narrative. There are, however, episodes in the romance in which Lancelot becomes directly involved in events concerning Arthur's court and kingdom as a whole—the great *assemblees* which bring Arthur's knights together in battle against the opponents of the kingdom of Logres. It is now time to examine the wars which happen within the romance rather than outside it.

These great assemblies, like the great courts held to celebrate the main religious feasts, serve an important function within the work in that they bring the knights together; hence, when the adventures of more than one knight are being followed in full, the different threads of narrative are drawn together and the knights brought back into contact with the King (and the Queen as she too is present as an observer at the assemblies). The battles provide a framework in that the date and place are usually known in advance to the knights of Arthur's court and Lancelot too in his wanderings receives news of them. Thus when Gauvain sets out on the first quest for Lancelot (which he undertakes single-handed), he already knows the date at which he will return, whether or not he has completed the quest; for there is already talk of an attack by the Roi d'Outre les Marches, and Arthur, on Gauvain's advice, sends a message to this king that he will meet him in battle in September, a month from then. Lancelot too receives early news of the First Assembly: a damsel tells him that the Queen commands that the White Knight should attend it. We also know that Gauvain has been told, before he sets out on his quest, that he will receive news of the knight he is seeking at the First, Second, and Third Assemblies of Logres. The first assembly which Lancelot attends in disguise is therefore explained in terms of a war with the Roi d'Outre les Marches who, as noted earlier, has already been mentioned in connection with Arthur's wars at the time of the journey of Claudas to Britain and also on the occasion of the *rendu*'s visit to Arthur's court, and will later in the story fight against Arthur in the war with Galehot. Through these explanations we are given periodic reminders that the wars with the Roi d'Outre les Marches form a background to most of the childhood and early adventures of Lancelot, and through these assemblies against that particular opponent of Arthur, Lancelot himself eventually becomes involved in general events in Britain. In the mean time, before either he or Gauvain actually come to the assembly, their individual adventures bring them into contact with the affairs of the kingdom. For example, Gauvain meets the party of the King of a Hundred Knights on the way to the assembly.[15] The King of a Hundred Knights is to fight on the side of the Roi d'Outre les Marches. We learn later that he is one of the chief vassals of Galehot, and he plays an important part in the war between Arthur and his lord. His knights here (*PL* 228-9) accost the Lady of Nohaut who, as vassal to Arthur, is also on the way to the First Assembly with her knights, and Gauvain rescues her.

The assembly itself, although presented earlier in the text as part of a real war to punish the Roi d'Outre les Marches for having attacked Arthur's land (*PL* 220.8-11), is organized much more on the lines of a tournament in that it takes place at a prescribed time and place and is stopped for the day, once the Red Knight (Lancelot) is wounded. It is true, however, that some of these tournaments in real life, although in theory friendly, were actually miniature wars.[16] On the second day, King Arthur and his men rout their opponents and force them to take refuge in their castle. The Roi d'Outre les Marches acknowledges defeat, but at his request and again on Gauvain's advice, another assembly between the knights of Arthur's *maisnie* and those of both the Roi d'Outre les Marches and the Roi des Cent Chevaliers is arranged for the Monday before Advent (*PL* 234). The armies separate, Arthur goes back to his country, and Gauvain sets out to complete his unfinished quest, once again knowing that he must return by a certain date to take part in the assembly. Thus the same pattern is repeated as that to be found at the beginning of his quest.

The Second Assembly, which, as was seen in Chapter II, marks an important stage in the establishment of Lancelot's identity, again brings together all Arthur's knights and Lancelot, but has no wider political implications for the

Arthurian kingdom. The King himself is not involved, only his *maisnie*, and the assembly is presented as a tournament, not a war. This time, the assembly is stopped because the Roi d'Outre les Marches is seriously wounded. With this battle or tournament Gauvain achieves his quest in that he discovers the identity of the White Knight and the unknown victorious knight of the two assemblies; but Lancelot himself departs secretly, although he does not go far. The main narrative thread remains with the court and the affairs of the kingdom, as the author prepares the way for the Third Assembly of Logres, the war against Galehot. Arthur has some mysterious and alarming dreams. The first time, he dreams that he loses his hair, the second time, his fingers, and the third time, his toes (*PL* 260). He sends for his wise clerks, as Vortigern did in Wace's *Brut* and Robert de Boron's *Merlin*, and they interpret his dreams as foretelling that he will lose 'tote honor terriene' unless he is saved by the Lion in the Water, the Doctor without Medicine, and the Flower Which Speaks. This leaves Arthur as baffled and as anxious as he was before.

The threat to Arthur's 'honor terriene', presaged by these dreams, soon manifests itself. Arthur receives an ultimatum from Galehot that unless he pays him homage for his kingdom, both it and the Queen will be taken from him. Arthur refuses, and Galehot's messenger warns him that his land will be invaded within a month. This prepares the way for the battle which will constitute the Third Assembly of Logres, at which, according to the prophecy originally given by the damsel from the Lake (*PL* 219), more will be learned concerning the White Knight. This prophecy is recalled in the Lancelot adventures which are interlaced with the theme of the threat to Arthur's kingdom. During these adventures Lancelot renews contact with Arthur's court, unintentionally and unrecognized but in a way which is a deliberate echo of his first arrival there (see Chapters II and III).

The familiar pattern is again made clear to the reader: the paths of Lancelot and those of the Arthurian knights are destined to come together in an assembly. On this occasion Lancelot is not summoned by the Queen to take part in the battle, but the convergence of the narrative threads of Lancelot and Gauvain at the place where Arthur, his Queen, and his knights have gathered is prepared for by the reiteration of the prophecy concerning the part to be played by the three assemblies of Logres in the uncovering of the identity of the White Knight. It is at this battle that Lancelot himself becomes directly involved in a war which threatens the whole Arthurian kingdom, the kind of war, between whole armies rather than rival teams of jousting knights, which is to be found in the chronicle tradition and in the *Mort Artu*.

For this Third Assembly Arthur summons his vassals from far and wide, telling them to bring as many men as they can (*PL* 276), although neither he nor Galehot fight themselves. Arthur does not wait until his vassals have arrived before moving against Galehot. The battle is not formalized to the extent that its predecessors in the romance have been, but is presented as a real war to the death. Galehot's men bring iron nets to protect their army from behind; as well as knights there are men on foot who have brought arrows tipped with poison. There is no listing of the battle order as in the *Chanson de Roland* or on the second day of the battle against Galehot (PL 309–10) because the fighting starts before there has been time to form up in battalions (PL 277). The description of the battle concentrates on fighting between armies rather than individual combats, but particular attention is given to the leadership, exploits, and endurance of Gauvain so that these can be surpassed by Lancelot on the second day. Even the traditional theme of the prison from which the hero has to obtain release to fight in disguise at an assembly is here brought into the feudal framework. Lancelot is imprisoned by the Lady of Malohaut because he has killed one of her men, but she holds her land from Arthur (PL 301.34) and sends her knights to serve in his army.

Although this assembly is mainly presented in terms of a war rather than a tournament, this is only true within limits. Arthur is genuinely afraid that he will lose, for his men have failed him and he has only been able to raise a small army in comparison with Galehot (PL 276). But Galehot seems to be more concerned with winning honour than with conquest of land and so adjourns the battle, as if it were a game, until the opponents can be more equally matched. He wishes to test himself against Arthur as the most famous king in Christendom. Earlier in the romance Claudas had wanted to do the same; but he had drawn back when his visit to Britain convinced him that Arthur lived up to his reputation. Galehot, on the contrary, draws back to give Arthur an opportunity to prove that he deserves his reputation and therefore offers a worthy challenge:

Mout a li rois grant peor de perdre sa terre et tote honor, et mout li sont failli si ome, einsi com li saige clerc li distrent, si an est mout espoantez. Et d'autre part reparole Galehoz a sa gent et dit que il n'a mie grant enor el roi Artus guerroier an ceste maniere, car trop a li rois petit de gent.

'Et se ge conqueroie, fait il, sa terre an cest point, ge n'i avroie pas enor, mais honte.'

'Sire, font si home, c'an volez vos faire?'

'Ge vos dirai, fait il, coi. Il ne me plest ore plus que ge lo guerroi an ceste maniere, ainz li donrai trives jusqu'a un an, par si que il amanra tot son pooir au chief de l'an. Et lors si avrai greignor enor an lui conquerre que ge n'avroie ja.' (PL 282.32–283.4.)

The reason for Arthur's failure to summon an army great enough to defeat Galehot is then explored at length in the episode with the mysterious *preudomme* who arrives at the end of the fighting on the second day. This is the second *preudomme* to come and lecture Arthur on his failings as a king: the episode here should be compared with the arrival of the *rendu* during the account of Lancelot's childhood which was examined in Chapter II in relation to the identity theme. On that occasion the *rendu* interrupted the court's banqueting with reproaches of the King for his failure to carry out his duty as monarch, but he concentrated his attack on the failure of Arthur to avenge his vassal Ban. This links up with a series of episodes in which Arthur, at ease with his barons, is suddenly shaken out of his complacency through a reminder either that he has failed to carry out his responsibilities as king or that his knights have failed to support him.[17] Here, however, the *preudomme* comes to Arthur not at table, when he is relaxed and at ease, but at the end of a day's fighting when he is deeply troubled and aware, because of his disturbing visions of the future and of the military situation, that he is in danger of losing his throne. On both occasions the *preudomme* fills part of the role of Merlin in the chronicle tradition of Geoffrey of Monmouth and Wace, and above all in Robert de Boron's *Merlin*, where his role as king's counsellor is so important. Indeed there are close parallels with Robert de Boron's *Merlin* as it has come down to us in the prose version. For example, the *preudomme*'s explanation in the *PL* of the clerks' error in seeing the lion in water as arising from their excessive worldliness should be compared with Merlin's explanation of the failure of the clerks of Vortigern:

'Itel estoient li clerc qui ton songe t'espelurent, et por ce cuiderent il avoir veü lo lion an l'eive qui est senefiez de pechié. Et neporqant, en l'eive n'estoit il mie, car Dex ne fu onques am pechié, ainz estoit en son glorioux siege. Mais l'espessetez de l'air estoit si granz antre lui et els que il ne lo porent veoir s'en autretel leu non com il estoient. Ce fu en l'eive, car li granz sans de la clergie qui en aus estoit lor fist veoir la figure del lion par force d'ancerchement. Mais por cele clergie qui n'estoit se terriene non, n'orent il del lion que la veüe, car nel conurent mie, ne ne sorent que ce poit estre, car il estoient terrien et li lions celestiene chose. Por ce ne veoient il mie la conoissance, si lo cuiderent il avoir veü en l'eve dom il furent deceü. Et por ce l'apelerent il evage.' (*PL* 290.8–20.)

'Molt sont fol vostre sen, quant vos cuidiez ouvrer d'art et vos ne voulez estre si bon ne si net ne si loial ne si prodome comme vos devez estre. Et por ce que vos estes fol et ort, failliez vos a ce que vos enquerez par la force de l'art des elemanz. Vos ne veistes onques rien de ce que l'en vos avoit demandé, car vos n'iestes pas tel que vos le deussiez veoir.' (*Merlin*, para. 29, lines 77–84.)

Arthur's clerks are more successful in interpreting Galehot's dreams than those of Arthur himself, but the episode in which Bademaguz, their leader, reveals to Galehot the significance of his crumbling castles and his dreams (*PL* 580–3) recalls both Robert de Boron's *Merlin* interpreting the dreams of Vortigern and the *preudomme* who explained Arthur's dreams.[18] In Robert de Boron (and

Geoffrey of Monmouth and Wace) Merlin combines the role of king's counsellor with that of prophet and possessor of magic powers; in the *PL* Merlin keeps his role as a source of magic powers (see Chapter V), but other characters, usually with unambiguous Christian connections, take over the role of king's adviser. The name Bademaguz keeps some trace of the magical,[19] but the man is just presented as a wise clerk who has the skill to interpret dreams:

Lors vient en la chanbre Galehot et fist figures del songe selonc ce que il entendoit. Et qant il ot ce fait, si lor mostra et dist que par ce lor feroit il savoir totes les senefiances del songe. Si lor devise ce qu'il l'an samble, tant qu'il sevent an la fin qu'il dit bien et raison. (*PL* 582.3–7.)

The *preudomme* has general advice to give to Arthur on how he should conduct himself as king.[20] He reminds him that God ordained that he should be king only in order to see that justice is done; he has failed in this and God will bring about his destruction:

'Si doiz savoir que nus hom mortex ne te baillast a garder la seignorie que tu tiens, mais Dex solement la te bailla por ce que tu l'an feïsses bone garde, et tu li as faite si mauvaisse que tu la destruiz qui garder la deüsses. Car li droiz do povre ne dou non puissant ne puet venir jusqu'a toi, ainz est li riches desleiaus oëz et henorez devant ta face por son avoir, et li povres droituriers n'i a loi por sa povreté. Li droit des veves et des orphelins est periz en ta seignorie. Et ce demandera Dex sor toi mout cruelment, car il meïsmes dit par la boiche Davi son prophete qu'il est garde des povres et sostient les orphenins et destruira les voies des pecheors. Tel garde fais tu a Deu de son pueple don il t'avoit baillié la terriene seignorie. Et par ce vandras tu a destruiement, car Dex destruira les pecheors.' (*PL* 283.21–33.)

He explains why Arthur has lost the hearts of his men and gives practical advice on how to win them back, emphasizing the virtues of *largece* and *debonaireté*. These are the qualities for which the squire of Claudas had praised Arthur so highly and for which Galehot too had been praised; they are also stressed as important chivalric virtues in the lament of Claudas for his son Dorin (*PL* 71–2) and in the description of Lancelot as a boy (*PL* 41). The significance of these parallels will be examined further in Chapter VIII. The *preudomme* also stresses the King's dependence in the exercise of his functions not just on his great barons but above all on his 'bas gentil home':

'Cil te faillent de lor gré cui tu deüsses faire les granz onors et porter les granz seignories et les granz compaignies: ce sont li bas gentil home de ta terre par cui tu doiz estre maintenuz, car li regnes ne puet estre tenuz se li comuns des genz ne s'i acorde.' (*PL* 285.36–9.)

Beaumanoir's explanation of the origin of kingship also stresses the importance of the role of the *gentil home* in helping the King to carry out his duties;[21] the explanation is based on the discourse on the origins of chivalry by the Lady of the Lake. It is also true that in the *PL* one of the main responsibilities of both knights and kings is presented as the upholding of justice and the defence of the right.

The King's forced reliance on others to defend his kingdom is here expressed by the *preudomme* in terms of a theory of kingship, but shortly after his up-braidings this dependence of Arthur on his knights is presented in a form more traditional to Arthurian romance in one of the King's broodings at table, of which, as has already been shown, a whole series are to be found in Chrétien and the *Perceval Continuations*. Twenty-three days after Arthur's return to Wales Gauvain rouses Arthur from his melancholy thoughts at dinner and reproaches him for his gloomy behaviour before his knights, as he had reproached him on the previous occasion, when Arthur had sat weeping after his conversation with Banyn had reminded him of his failure to avenge the death of his vassal Ban and the disappearance of his son Lancelot. Gauvain had then agreed that Arthur had good reason to be sad, but had said that it was not fitting that he should grieve publicly at one of his great courts—rather should he wait until the right time and then take action: 'Qant vos verroiz qu'il en sera et leu et tans, si i metez avoc lo pensé painne et travail.' (*PL* 138.16–17.) This time Arthur is not grieving over his own failure to take action in support of a vassal (he confessed to this failure and performed penance in public for it and other sins immediately after the battle with Galehot); he is brooding on the failure of his knights. Arthur must rely upon them to perform the task of bringing to him the help of the good knight (Lancelot) to save his kingdom at the next battle with Galehot. Yet his knights have done nothing to find the champion who has saved Arthur once, while Galehot has boasted (*PL* 293.17–19) that he will have him in his *maisnie*. The King says angrily to Gauvain:

'Gauvain, Gauvain, vos m'avez gité del plus cortois pensé que ge feïsse onques, ne nus ne m'an porroit a droit blasmer, car ge pensoie au meillor chevalier de toz les prodomes. Ce est li chevaliers qui vainquié l'asemblee de moi et de Galehot, dont Galehoz s'est vantez que il l'avra de sa maisnie. Si ai veü tele eure que, se li chevalier de ma maison et mi conpaignon seüssent une chose que ge desirasse, il la me queïssent, ja ne fust an si estrange terre. Et soloit l'an dire que tote la proece terriene estoit a mon ostel; mais ge di que ore n'i est ele mie, puis que li miaudres chevaliers do monde en est fors.' (*PL* 297.4–13.)

Gauvain acknowledges the justice of Arthur's reproaches and proceeds to call upon his fellow knights to help him in his quest; everyone prepares to leave, but after protests from the King at the emptying of the court, only forty are chosen. Then Gauvain, having persuaded his companions to pledge themselves in advance to whatever he swears, takes an oath which fills the King with dismay:

Aprés jura messires Gauvains que il verité diroit au revenir, et que il ne revanroit sanz lo chevalier que il aloit querre, o sanz veraies anseignes de lui, et que sanz nul des conpaignons ne revanroit se mort ne lo prenoit. (*PL* 298.27–30.)

What disturbs the King is that Gauvain has not mentioned the need to return for the battle with Galehot:

Mais li rois an fu esbahiz sor toz, car il li membra del jor de l'asemblee qui antre lui et Galehot devoit estre.

'Biaus niés, fait il, mal avez fait qant vos l'essoigne de m'asenblee n'avez mis fors de vostre sairement.'

'Sire, fait il, ne puet ore estre.' (*PL* 298.32–7.)

There is therefore a variation on the pattern which we have already seen of Gauvain setting out on a quest for the Unknown Knight (Lancelot) at the time when he also arranges that he and all Arthur's knights should return at a certain date to take part in an assembly. Here the object of the quest is to bring the knight back for the assembly, but no allowance is made by the companions for the possibility of failure in the quest, so there is no promise made that Gauvain and his companions will, whether successful or not, return for the battle. On the other hand, the tale makes it quite clear that the knights *will* return for the assembly and will perjure themselves by doing so because they are destined to fail in their task:

Mais onqes n'i ot si preu ne si hardi qui puis ne n'en tenist por fol, car puis en furent apelé tuit parjuré failli de la boche lo roi meesmes, car il errerent tot l'an jusque a l'asemblee, que onques ne troverent le chevalier, ne veraies enseignes n'en aporterent. (*PL* 299.13–17.)

Once again, therefore, the battle fixed for a certain date is used to provide a firm framework for the story. The motif of brooding, followed by oaths and a quest leading up to another assembly, is used here to emphasize the obligations of Arthur's knights to help him in his time of need, and the King's dependence, not only on them, but also on the Unknown Knight, who is neither a member of his *maisnie* nor a vassal. The author is using a pattern familiar to the thirteenth-century public of Arthurian romance, as was seen in Chapter II, but in the *PL* the recurring sequence is linked closely to the theme running right through the work of Arthur's problems as suserain and Lancelot's role in relation to these problems.

The term of Lancelot's imprisonment is also linked to the next assembly. The Lady of Malohaut tells her captive (Lancelot) that since he will not reveal his name, he will not be released before then:

'Certes, fait ele, mar lo m'avez celé, que par la foi que ge vos doi, vos n'istroiz ja mais de ma maison, ne par la rien que ge plus ain, devant l'asenblee qui doit estre de mon seignor lo roi Artus et Galehot. Et sachiez que vos avroiz des ore mais assez honte et messaise, car jusq'au jor de l'asanblee a encor pres d'un an.' (*PL* 300.6–10.)

Lancelot eventually achieves his release by admitting that he hopes to fight again as well as he had at the first battle with Galehot; he agrees to stay with the lady until the time of the next assembly. Thus the way is prepared both for the reappearance of Lancelot at the assembly and for the dishonourable return of Gauvain and his companions in time to take part in it. The Lady of Malohaut goes to see Arthur and is welcomed by him because she has helped him in his war: 'car mout li avoit aidié en sa guerre' (*PL* 301.4). The feudal link is emphasized too when she swears an oath on the faith she owes the King 'cui fame ge suis lige' (*PL* 301.34), and when Arthur thanks her again for the help she has given him (*PL* 302.9–10).

For the second battle against Galehot, Arthur, having followed the advice of the *preudomme*, succeeds in winning the hearts of his vassals and in bringing a greater army:

Et li rois est en sa terre et fait ensin come ses maistres li anseigna de ses genz honorer, tant que, ançois que la mitié de l'an fust passee, ot il lor cuers si recovrez que il orent plus de mil maisons faites an la place de terre ou l'asemblee devoit estre; et se hatissent bien tuit, que il voudront miauz morir a dolor an bataille que li rois perdist sa terre a lor vivant. Ansin atornent tuit lor cuers au roi par la grant debonaireté que il lor mostre, et vindrent avec lui au plus efforciement que il porent an place quinze jorz avant la faute de la trive. (*PL* 304.4–12.)

Gauvain and his companions, as has already been foretold, have been unsuccessful in their quest, but accept that the King's need is more important than their honour:

Et lors vint d'autre part messires Gauvains et si compaignon de lor queste, ne il n'avoient riens esploitié, si an furent tuit honteus. Mais l'angoisse de la bessoigne lo roi les ramena. Et messires Gauvains dit que miauz lor venoit estre honiz a l'enor de lor seignor lige, que il toz seus fust honiz et desheritez.

'Ne honiz, fait il, ne puet il estre sanz nos, mais nos porriens estre sanz lui, car nos poons terre perdre sanz sa honte, mais il ne la puet perdre sanz la nostre.' (*PL* 304.12–19.)

Yet again stress is laid on the obligations of the knights to their *seignor lige* and his dependence on their help. Galehot, however, has brought even more men than last time and even more iron nets, so that Arthur's army is still outnumbered.

The second battle at the start follows much the same pattern as the first. In neither battle does Arthur or Galehot take part in the fighting at the outset, but they direct operations and decide when reinforcements should be sent in. In both cases Arthur's men, led by Gauvain, do well against a larger force, but by the end of the first day's fighting Gauvain, who had performed marvels of prowess, is gravely wounded. In this second battle Lancelot again takes the place of Gauvain on the second day of fighting (which is to take place 'd'ui en tierz jor', more like a tournament than a real battle) and turns the tables on Galehot's men. But unlike the first battle, Lancelot does not just disappear at the end of the second day's fighting nor is a truce then declared. Galehot partially carries out his threat to have Lancelot as a member of his *maisnie* (PL 293.18); he persuades the Black Knight to go with him to his tents and to spend the night there, but only after making a promise to do whatever Lancelot asks him, a promise which means that the *preudomme*'s prediction that Lancelot will not be 'devers lui [Galehot] au chief de l'an' (PL 294.1) is also fulfilled. However, Arthur and his knights, unlike the reader, are unaware of the promise, and when they see the one knight who on the second day had saved them from defeat appear to go over to the enemy, they are filled with despair. Gauvain links the loss of the knight with the prophecy of the clerks and reproaches Arthur for being less of a *preudomme* than Galehot, who has retained the services of the good knight:

'Sire, or est venuz li termes que li clerc vos distrent. Esgardez quel tressor vos avez perdu. Cil vos toudra terre qui hui tote jor la vos a garantie par son cors. Et se vos fussiez prodon, vos l'aüssiez retenu autresi com a fait li plus prodom qui vive, qui devant vos l'an moine, ne ne li fist onques se nuire non. Et vos l'avez laissié qui vos a rendue honor et terre. Ensi se mostrent bien li preudome, la ou il sont.' (PL 322.14–20.)

Predictions concerning the role to be played by the Unknown Knight in relation to the first three Assemblies of Logres (the two against the Roi d'Outre les Marches and the first battle against Galehot) help to provide a coherent framework to events from the beginning of Gauvain's first quest for Lancelot to the beginning of the war against Galehot. The dreams of Arthur and their interpretation, first by his clerks and then by the *preudomme*, serve the same purpose in relation to the wars with Galehot and help to underline the connection between the fate of Arthur's kingdom and the adventures which Lancelot is destined to achieve; but the author, compared with Chrétien in, for example, *le Chevalier de la Charrette* or *le Conte del Graal*, takes care to give his public a clearer idea of what is happening or will happen than is granted to Arthur and his knights. Thus, for instance, the reader is given an account of the promise made by Galehot to Lancelot to grant the following request, a promise unknown either to Arthur's army or to that of Galehot:

'Sire, ge vos demant que si tost com vos seroiz au desseure do roi Artu, que devers lui n'avra mais nul recovrier, si tost comme ge vos en semondrai, que vos li ailliez crier merci et vos metez outreement en sa menaie.' (PL 325.9–12.)

The fulfilment of promises and predictions forms, therefore, an important part of the author's narrative technique. The mysterious, unexpected adventure remains an important element in this Arthurian romance, and the author employs the traditional marvellous test to reveal the identity of the predestined hero, but he also uses a whole network of predictions or promises by characters in the romance or interventions with reference to the tale rather than the author, so that much of the suspense lies in wondering how the expectation is to be fulfilled rather than what will be the outcome. This also means that attention can be concentrated on the relationship of the events to the main themes and on the reactions of the characters to them. The fulfilment of Galehot's promise to Lancelot is to dominate both the relationship between these two companions and that between Lancelot and Arthur and his court. Perhaps Lancelot's greatest achievement is to have brought to an end (for the sake of Guinevere) the war between Galehot and Arthur, and it is as peacemaker as well as victor in the last war in the romance, against the Saxons, that he is received as a Companion of the Round Table. It may be significant in relation to the way in which chivalry is presented in the work that the act of bringing peace receives as much acclaim as the act of bringing death to many pagan Saxons, but, as we shall see, this may also be linked to a difference in nature between the two wars.

To return to the last day of fighting in Arthur's war against Galehot, it is again made clear that this is no ordinary tournament for the glory of individual knights, but that Arthur's life and his kingdom are at stake. The King himself is bearing arms, fighting to defend his own standard, and has entrusted the Queen to four knights to be taken to safety. At the moment when Galehot rides towards the standard to put himself at Arthur's mercy, all seems to the King to be lost, and he is overcome with grief at seeing his men thus defeated:

Donc hurte des esperons droit a l'estandart o li roi estoit, qui par un po ne crevoit de duel de ses genz que il veoit desconfites. Si estoit ja la reine montee, si l'an menoient li quatre chevalier au ferir des esperons, car il n'avoient mais nul recovrier, et monseignor Gauvain en voloient il porter en litiere. Mais il dist que il voloit miauz morir en cel leu que ensi veoir tote joie morte et tote enor honie. Si se pasmoit si menuement que chascuns qui lo voit quidoit bien que il morist maintenant. (*PL* 327.4–11.)

Lancelot too is overcome with emotion at the thought of the sacrifice Galehot is about to make:

Et quant li bons chevaliers an voit aler Galehot et faire si grant meschief por lui, si cuide bien et dit que nus si bons amis ne si veritable compaignon n'ot onques mais. Si an a si grant pitié que il an sospire do cuer aval et plore des iauz de sa teste soz le hiaume, et dit entre ses danz:

'Biaus sire Dex, qui porra ce deservir?' (*PL* 327.11–16.)

Then Galehot rides up to Arthur and puts himself at the King's mercy[22] with the gestures which a vassal makes when paying homage to his lord:

Et des si loin com Galehoz lo voit, si descent do cheval a terre, si s'agenoille et joint ses mains, et dit:

'Sire, ge vos vain faire droit de ce que ge vos ai meffait, si m'an repant et m'an met an vostre merci outreement.' (*PL* 327.22-6.)

Arthur's wonder and his joy are then dwelt on at some length.

The author brings out with great skill the dramatic nature of the scene and describes in vivid terms the emotions aroused by this reversal of the situation, when the conqueror kneels to the conquered. The importance of the event is underlined by references in later episodes to the knight who made the peace between Arthur and Galehot (*PL* 334.22-4, 582.23) or to the time at which the peace was made (*PL* 418.18-19, 528.29). References to the sacrifice Galehot made for Lancelot also recur (*PL* 349.7-8, 572.28-30). The peacemaking is represented in the visions of Galehot during his journey back to his lands (*PL* 577-8) and in their interpretation (*PL* 580-2).

Thus the theme of the war with Galehot is important for the structure of the work. Links with the earlier wars of Arthur which take place outside the main narrative are created through the appearance of the Roi d'Outre les Marches and to a lesser extent the Roi des Cent Chevaliers in these earlier wars and in the Galehot battles. The conflict with Galehot is prepared for by prophecies of what Lancelot will do in the Third Assembly, even before Lancelot has put an end to the enchantments of the Dolorous Guard, and through this it is related to the development of the identity theme. It is linked to the idea of kingship and to Arthur's failure in relation to Lancelot's father, Ban of Benoyc, through the King's visions and their interpretation by his wise clerks and by the *preudomme*. It provides an opportunity for Lancelot to show the magnitude of his love for Guinevere, and the wonder which he inspires through his great exploits and through the mysterious and unexpected end to the war serves to motivate their first secret meeting. This wonder at the Unknown Knight also gives rise to a brooding by Arthur, very similar to the one which occurred after the first battle with Galehot, and to another quest for Lancelot by Gauvain and his companions. The wonder at Lancelot's feats in both the assemblies against Galehot is also an important element in the struggle between Galehot and Guinevere for Lancelot which comes to a tragic conclusion with the death of Galehot at the end of the romance. Through the network of references forwards and backwards to the battle and to the peace which ends it, the episode makes an important contribution towards the provision of a framework for the romance.

The war between Arthur and the Saxons does not receive the same long and careful preparation, although, as we have seen, there is a reference to a war with Saxons in one of the allusions to events taking place in the past in relation to the Lancelot story (*PL* 506.11–15). It therefore occupies a rather different position within the structure of the work, even if it too, like the earlier wars, brings together again the knights who had scattered in search of Lancelot. In a way, this war links up more directly than do the first four assemblies with Arthur's traditional role in the chronicles, where one of his main claims to fame is his successful defence of Britain against Saxon invaders. It is perhaps for this reason that there is not the same need for careful preparation, as a war against the Saxons might be considered to be always hovering in the background in any work in which 'Arthur's active role as king receives some emphasis. This particular war is located within the chronicle tradition by relating the time of the fortifying of the castle at Restel, where the siege is taking place, to the time when Vortigern married the daughter of Hengist the Saxon (*PL* 540.22–3).

The war with the Saxons is presented in very different terms from that with Galehot. He is portrayed as a great Christian ruler who can be compared favourably with Arthur and who is admired and respected by his barons; the Saxons have barbaric-sounding names (Hargadabranz, for example), magic connections (the Saxon maiden, sister of Hargadabranz, has a knowledge of spells which, unlike the Lady of the Lake, she uses for evil purposes), and no chivalrous ideals. There can be no question of making peace with such an enemy. Arthur fights in the battle from the beginning, his bravery balanced by his weakness over the Saxon maiden. Once again the battle brings threads together and everyone back to Arthur. The knights return from their quest for the Unknown Knight, but secretly, in twos and threes, for Gauvain does not intend to announce the successful conclusion of his search until the battle is over. Once again, Lancelot helps Arthur, disguised by yet another change of arms, this time supported by Hector, Galehot, and Gauvain, all fighting incognito. Once again, Lancelot resumes an active part in events to repel Arthur's enemies, only to be withdrawn through imprisonment and illness. The causes of his absence from the battle combine elements from the first pair of assemblies, where he disappears from the one to heal his wounds, only to re-emerge to win the Second Assembly, with elements from the next pair, where he emerges from prison to fight. Once again, Lancelot saves Arthur's kingdom, and the extent of the King's debt is further increased because not only does Lancelot defeat and slaughter his heathen enemies, but he also saves the person of the King from Saxon captivity.

We have therefore a repeated pattern of quests, providing a chain of adventures involving individual knights, and assemblies, which bring all the knights together and engage Lancelot and Arthur's men in communal endeavours. The first two assemblies are interlinked and also closely connected with the quest for Lancelot's identity, but it is the war against Galehot which occupies a central position within the work. For the first time the fate of the kingdom is involved, for Arthur risks the loss of his throne and his wife. Lancelot's dazzling achievements in this battle provide motivation for the first secret meeting between Lancelot and Guinevere, the rivalry between Galehot and the Queen for the love of Lancelot, and the last, long quest for the Unknown Knight before he as Lancelot becomes a member of the Round Table. However, it is only in the last and the bloodiest of the great battles between the armies in the romance that Lancelot becomes involved in the struggle between Arthur, as the great Christian leader, and the pagan Saxon invaders which is central to the Arthurian tradition of the chronicles. This war assembles as allies not only Lancelot, Arthur and all his knights, but also the King's former opponents, and in addition provides the occasion for the physical consummation of Lancelot's love for Guinevere. In this way, many strands of narrative are brought together at this point, the defeat of the Saxons leading naturally into the great peaceful and festive assembly at court in which Lancelot, Galehot, and Hector are all given seats at the Round Table.

The individual knight as champion of justice within Arthur's kingdom

It is not only in terms of general battles that Lancelot and the other knights are involved in helping Arthur with the affairs of the kingdom. Many of the tasks undertaken by the knights are concerned with the protection of Arthur's vassals; therefore, in a way, the very adventures themselves are dependent upon Arthur as suserain. Thus one of the first duties of Lancelot as a young knight is to champion the cause of the Lady of Nohaut in her dispute with the King of Northumberland, and this is given an explicitly feudal motivation. The Lady of Nohaut's messenger says that his lady has sent him to Arthur to ask for help 'com a celui qui ses sires liges ies et ele ta fame lige' (*PL* 162.20–1). Arthur acknowledges that it is his duty to give assistance to his vassal: 'Ge la secorrai mout volentiers. Et ge conois bien que gel doi faire, car ele est ma fame lige et tient de moi tote sa terre.' But he also gives the traditional courtly motive: 'Et se ele n'en tenoit rien, s'est ele tant vaillanz dame et tant debonaire et tant bele et tant gentils fame que bien la devroie secorre.' (*PL* 162.25–9.)

Apart from this first adventure, it is mainly through the assemblies that Lancelot is directly involved in the affairs of the kingdom until his judicial battle for Guinevere (and indirectly for the Round Table) in the False Guinevere episode. But during his long period of withdrawal in Sorelois the connection between the affairs of Arthur's kingdom and the numerous adventures of Gauvain's quest for Lancelot and Hector's quest for Gauvain is maintained through the involvement of Arthur's vassals in many of the episodes. Each adventure seems to present itself by chance, but the explanation then given for the events in nearly every case links up in some way either with a war which is going on between the Duke of Cambenic, a vassal of Arthur (*PL* 477.16–17), and the King of Norgales, through whose lands both Gauvain and Hector travel, or with disputes related to the struggle between Segurades and his neighbours. For example, in the first adventure in which Gauvain becomes involved during his journey from the Severn through Wales to Sorelois, he has to fight as unknown champion for the Lady of Roestoc to defend her against the unwelcome suit of Segurades; she herself had sent a dwarf to Arthur's court to ask for a champion, as did the Lady of Nohaut when Lancelot first arrived at Camelot, and, as has been seen in Chapters II and III, there are deliberate contrasts and parallels between the two sets of adventures. Gauvain, having been forgotten by the Lady of Roestoc, slips off quietly and knights a squire who is one of her vassals ('cui home ge suis', 'ses hom liges', *PL* 394.6, 409.15–16) and who, unlike his lady, recognizes true prowess and accepts the anonymous Gauvain as a worthy substitute. In the mean time, the Lady of Roestoc goes to Arthur's court as the natural place in which to seek for information and help in her search for her neglected and vanished champion.

Gauvain proceeds on his way. In the forest of Brequehan, on the border between the Duchy of Cambenic and the kingdom of Norgales, he meets a damsel sent out by Agravain to find the two best knights, whose blood will heal him in his illness. Gauvain learns from Agravain that his brother's *amie* is the daughter of the King of Norgales, who tried to give her hand in marriage to a knight she did not want as husband (*PL* 418.24–6). Agravain also explains that the castle in which he is living has been given to him by the Duke of Cambenic; the Duke had won it from the King of Norgales who had had it fortified (*PL* 419.33–5).

In the next adventure in the forest of Brequehan, in the Lande des Set Voies, when Gauvain defeats a knight and sends him back to the Lady of Roestoc, there is no direct link with either of the wars, although the incident plays its part in the development of the love theme (see Chapter III). But in Hector's first adventure on his quest for Gauvain, when he avenges the unjustified wounding of a knight, even if the episode is not directly connected with the war between the Duke of Cambenic and the King of Norgales, a reference to the conflict is introduced to explain why the knight's opponent, Guinas de Blaqestan, went fully armed into the wood:

'Cist chevaliers que ge vos di, qui si est fel, estoit alez o bois toz armez, car il n'i osoit autrement aler, car il estoit de la guerre au roi de Norvales et au duc de Cambenic.' (*PL* 427.18–20.)

Immediately after this adventure Hector meets fourteen knights and *serjants* armed for war. The leader of these is identified as the Lord of Palerne, a castle on the border between Norgales and Cambenic. This lord's castle is in the land of the Duke and held as a fief from him, but he holds all his other land from the King of Norgales, so that his situation as a man with two lords at war with one another is very complicated: 'Et il estoit hom liges au duc de Canbenic, et por ce estoit il ses cors devers lo duc et une partie de ses chevaliers devers lo roi de Norvales.' (*PL* 433.16–19.)

Hector next helps Synados de Windessores in his war against his wife's relations, who are angry at her marriage with him, and here there is no reference to Cambenic or Norgales. However, the next episode, based on an adventure of Perceval in the *Conte del Graal*,[23] is carefully fitted into the network of feudal relationships in the *PL*. Hector arrives at the Castle of the Estroite Marche, where he is immediately involved in the defence of the castle, whose lord holds it and all his land from Arthur: 'Ge sui hom liges lo roi Artu de cest chastel et de qanque il li apant.' (*PL* 445.17–18.) The lord then explains the origin of the siege of the castle and once again makes a link with the war between Norgales and Cambenic, but he also provides a connection through the person of the Roi des Cent Chevaliers with both Arthur's past wars and with Galehot, at present with Lancelot in Sorelois. The lord tells Hector that his castle is coveted by three barons:[24]

'Li uns est li rois Benianz de Norgales, et li autres Malauguins, li Rois des Cent Chevaliers, uns rois mout fiers et mout puissanz et mout bons chevaliers et coisins Galehot, lo fil a la Jaiande. Et li tierz est li dus Esçauz de Cambenic. Cist troi ont tozjorz cest chastel encovi et tozjorz m'ont guerroié, mais, Deu merci, ancor n'en ont il mies. Et neporqant ai perdu tant que ores est montee une tançons et une guerre antre lo roi de Norgales et lo duc de Cambenic, si ne me guerroierent passé a trois anz. Ne ge n'ai orandroit guerre fors dou Roi des Cent Chevaliers, et non mies de lui, car il est grant pieç'a en la terre Galehot, son cosin. Mais uns suens seneschauz me fait mout mal, qui est mout preuz et mout guerroianz, si a non Marcanors.' (*PL* 445.38–446.12.)

We have here another vassal to whom Arthur has been unable to send any assistance:

'Et a mon seignor lo roi Artu an ai envoié maintes foiz por ce que il i meïst consoil, mais il a tant a faire de ses granz anuiz que il a au cuer que il n'i puet consoil metre.' (*PL* 446.28–31.)

This echoes the words of the *rendu* when he explains Arthur's difficulties to the widowed queens (*PL* 53.25-9). The lord then tells Hector that two of Arthur's knights, who happened to be passing that way on their quest for the Unknown Knight, spent the night at the Estroite Marche and were compelled by the custom of the castle to fight in its defence. Yvain, who was one of these knights, accepted that it was right that they should defend the castle because the lord was a vassal of Arthur. The two were later captured by the besiegers. Therefore Hector, when he defeats Marganor, leader of the attackers, does not just defend one of Arthur's vassals but also frees two of Arthur's knights.

In the next adventure of Hector there is a rather distant link with the war between Norgales and Cambenic. He meets the bier of a knight whom he killed when defending Synados and is then imprisoned by the dead knight's father, the sire des Marés; but his life is saved because the wounded knight whom he avenged against Guinas de Blaqestan and who, as we have seen, was involved in the war between Norgales and Cambenic, was the lord's other son.

The narrative then switches to Gauvain who passes through territory devastated by the war between Norgales and Cambenic (*PL* 474.34-8). He spends a night in a hermitage and hears first about the war between Segurades and Marez, son of Alier (*PL* 475-6). He is then told of the origins of the Cambenic and Norgales war:

> Et lors commance li clers a parler de la guerre lo duc de Canbenic et do roi de Norgales, si dit a l'ermite que au chastel de Leverzep devoit lo matin venir les genz lo roi. Et li dus i estoit atot son effort. Mais mout a, ce dient, de la plus chevaliers. Et lors demande messires Gauvains li quex a tort de ceste guerre. Et li hermites dit: 'Li rois, car il ferma, ce dit, an la terre lo duc un chastel mout fort, tant con messires li dus fu ou servise lo roi Artu, tant que il l'a perdu. Et messires li dus l'a doné a un mout bon chevalier por ce que il avoit tolue au roi sa fille.' (*PL* 477.10-18.)

Gauvain realizes that the hermit is talking of the castle given to Agravain (*PL* 419.33-5). He is then told of the progress of the war. The Duke is gaining the upper hand except that he has lost his son (*PL* 477.21-6). Gauvain then asks to be shown the way to the castle of Leverzep, where the Duke of Cambenic is fighting the forces of Norgales, and thus becomes for the first time directly involved in the war. As is fitting for one of Arthur's knights, he supports the side of the Duke, a vassal of Arthur. Another knight, Girflet, is also there; through him a link is made with the other war between Marez, son of Alier, and the nephew of Segurades, when the author explains that Gauvain did not recognize him because he had lost his arms when taken prisoner in that war (*PL* 481.6-13). Gauvain and Girflet win the battle for the Duke, who avenges the death of his son by killing the nephew of the King of Norgales.

Gauvain then slips away and in the next adventure meets a damsel. She takes

him to a mysterious mistress who turns out to be the daughter of the King of
Norgales. This encounter has already been prepared for by the allusion to the
girl's admiration for Gauvain, made by her sister during Gauvain's visit to the
castle held by Agravain from the Duke of Cambenic (*PL* 419.39–420.6). On the
way to the girl, Gauvain has another adventure which is linked to the
Cambenic–Norgales war when he defends a vavasour, vassal of the Duke of
Cambenic, who has been falsely accused by a treacherous seneschal of having
caused the death of the Duke's son, a loss which has already been mentioned
twice in the text. The Duke thanks Gauvain both for defending the vavasour
and for helping him at Leverzep, and they talk of Agravain and of his illness.
The Duke says that he would not have been in such difficulties in his war if it
had not been for the illness of Agravain who had fought so well for him (*PL*
501.27–31).

   The adventures of Gauvain and Hector on their quests are not, therefore, just
strung together like a series of beads on two different and mainly parallel
threads, but the whole narrative is given a much closer texture through these
periodic references to episodes connected with the war, although the war itself
is kept very much in the background. No full account of it is ever given: various
characters whom the questers meet mention it, but we are only given a direct
account of the incidents in which Gauvain himself happens to participate. The
periodic intertwining of the threads of narrative which are followed right
through (here the adventures of Gauvain and those of Hector) with the interrupted pattern of events only partially narrated achieves a similar effect to that
achieved earlier in the romance through the use of periodic references to wars
of Arthur which lie outside the main narrative. The adventures told in full in
the romance are thus shown to be part of a whole web of events which concern
the kingdom of Arthur as a whole and in which feudal connections play an
important part. The adventures of Lancelot, Gauvain, and Hector are linked
closely to the development of the themes of love and identity, as has been
shown in Chapters II and III, but they also have another kind of motivation in
that they are associated, through the emphasis on the feudal tie, with Arthur as
suserain of most of the persons involved. The stress on the element of chance,
characteristic of the adventures of a knight errant whose duty is to seek
adventure and to help all those in distress, is still present in the narrative
technique. For example, Gauvain sets off on his quest for Lancelot, 'si chevauche
deus jorz antiers que il ne trova avanture dom a parler face' (*PL* 366.5–6). The
third day he meets four knights and is just preparing to joust when he
recognizes that they are four of his companions on the quest. They explain that
they had met by chance at some crossroads: 'La desus a un carefor de ces voies, si
nos i amena orandroit avanture toz quatre ansanble.' (*PL* 367.1–2.) Hector comes

to the castle of the Estroite Marche by chance and becomes involved with the rescue of Yvain and Sagremor. They leave the castle together, but as they are riding along, they see a knight carrying off a damsel by force and at a little distance two knights fighting a single one:

Et an ce qu'il regardent ces deus choses, si dist Sagremors li Desreez:

'Ha! Dex, por qoi n'est ores ci la tierce avanture, que chascuns aüst la soe?'

Et com il ot ce dit, si ot dariés aus les greignors criz do monde, et sanble bien que il i aüst plus de cent gent.

'An non Deu, fait Hestors, Sagremor, Deu vos a oï, que la tierce avanture n'est mies loign. Or praigne chascuns la soe, que nos n'avons que demorer.' (*PL* 465.32–466.5.)

This traditional pattern of adventures and meetings presenting themselves at the right moment by some mysterious process is also combined with a series of allusions which suggest another kind of motivation and a more closely knit structure in which Arthur's knights help the King to perform his royal duty. The holding of Arthur's great courts is as important an element in this structure as are the great warlike assemblies.

Arthur's great courts

The greatest courts, at which the King wears his crown, are held at the main religious festivals,[25] as the author explains in some detail:

En celui tans avoit costume li rois Artus que plus richement se demenoit a Pasques tozjorz que a nule autre feste, et si vos dirai raison por qoi. Il ne tenoit cort esforciee de porter corone que cinq foiz l'an: ce estoit a Pasques, a l'Encension, a Pantecoste, a la feste Toz Sainz et a Noel. Et a maintes autres festes tenoit il corz, mais n'estoient pas apelees corz esforciees, si com a la Chandelor, a la Miaost, ou au jor de la feste de la vile ou il estoit, et a mainz autres jors, qant il li sorvenoient genz cui il voloit honorer et festoier. (*PL* 134.23–31.)

He then goes on to underline the religious significance of the particular festivals. These courts link the events in the romance to the high days in the religious calendar, they provide stable points in time, and they naturally tend to bring all the knights together. But, unlike the great fighting assemblies, also often fixed in advance on known dates, they do not provide either an interruption in a quest (the First Assembly against the Roi d'Outre les Marches, the Fourth Assembly against Galehot) or a culminating point in it (the Second Assembly against the Roi d'Outre les Marches, the battle against the Saxons). These great courts tend to serve rather as starting-points for new adventures, as occasions on which unexpected or sometimes disturbing visitors appear, as indeed they had done traditionally in Chrétien de Troyes.[26] This role of initiating a new phase in the action is often given visible form by an extra large decorated initial or in some manuscripts a historiated initial portraying Arthur sitting at court. Kay complains bitterly that Arthur has held his court for a long time at Carduel without any notable event occurring and suggests that they should move to Camelot:

'Certes, fait il, ge loeroie que nos alissiens a Camahalot, car la cité est plus belle et la plus delitable et la plus aventureuse que vos aiez, si orrons sovent et verrons qe nos ne veons mie ci, ne n'oons; car vos avez sejornez ci plus a de deus mois, n'onques ne veïmes avenir qi a gaires de chose montast.' (*PL* 260.26–30.)

It is to court that new adventures come, often in the form of people asking for help. Thus it is to the court which Arthur holds on the eve of the Feast of St John that the Lady of the Lake brings Lancelot to be knighted, the wounded knight comes to seek vengeance against all the friends of the man who wounded him, and the messenger of the Lady of Nohaut comes to ask for a champion. It is at the court held at Whitsun that Lyonel is knighted and the lady with the Crowned Lion of Lybia appears. It is at Arthur's court, held at the beginning of September with great state, many strangers being present, that a disturbing visitor arrives, the *rendu* who praises Arthur as the king who does the most to maintain chivalry with honour, but blames him as slow to avenge shame and dishonour suffered by his vassals. Claudas, in the next episode, holding a court on the anniversary of his coronation, receives an even more disconcerting visitor in the person of a damsel from the Lake who reproaches him for damaging his reputation as a noble king by his treatment of the sons of King Bohort. At the great court held by Arthur to celebrate Easter, the presence of Banyn, a stranger knight, again disturbs the occasion by drawing attention to Arthur's failure to avenge a vassal, although he does not come specifically for that purpose. These first two disturbing visits (by the *rendu* and Banyn) do not set off an immediate train of adventure, although they certainly jolt the court out of its festive frame of mind. Disturbing thoughts without a visitor can break up a great court even more effectively, as for example Arthur's two broodings about the Unknown Knight which clear the court when they set in motion the quests for Lancelot. Some bearers of alarming or disruptive tidings do not arrive when the court is sitting in state for a great feast. Arthur is only at supper, with no great formality, when the ultimatum from Galehot arrives. The most disturbing visitors of all, the messengers from the False Guinevere, come when Arthur is at dinner at Carduel, not actually on the eve of a great religious festival but with many of his barons gathered round him because Christmas is approaching. Christmas itself is reserved for the trial of Guinevere and the crowning of her rival. Guinevere tells Lancelot and Galehot that the King has sent word to Gauvain and all his barons that they should go to him at Camelide:

'Car il velt a cest Noel tenir cort en Camelide et coroner la damoiselle qui ensin l'a deceü par son savoir. Et a commandé que ge soie prise et amenee a cele grant feste por estre destruite devant totes les genz par lo jugement as traïtors qui ceste chose ont porchaciee.' (*PL* 596.34-8.)

This brings us to another important function of Arthur's court, its role as a centre for justice, a court of law. Guinevere, like Ganelon, is tried before a court consisting of the King and his barons, although Arthur elects to try her before the barons of Camelide rather than his own barons of Logres. The *preudomme*, in his advice to Arthur after the first battle against Galehot on how to win back the hearts of his people, stresses the importance of the role of the King in maintaining justice and urges him to travel around and continue to hold his court in all the good cities, in order to distribute *largece* (a necessary virtue in both kings and knights) but above all to defend the right and to see that all receive justice:

'Tu t'an iras an ton païs, si venras sejorner an totes les boenes viles, an l'une plus, en l'autre moins, selonc ce que l'une vaudra miauz de l'autre. Si garde que tu i soies tant que tu aies oïz et les droiz et les torz, et les granz et les petiz, car li povres hom sera assez plus liez, se droiz li done sa querele devant toi, que se il an avoit plus devant un autre, et dira par tot que tu meïsmes li as sa droiture desraisniee.' (*PL* 286.32-8.)

This links up with what the Lady of the Lake has said about the duty of the knight to defend justice. The knight should be 'droiz jugierres sanz amor et sanz haïne, et sanz amor d'aidier au tort por lo droit grever, et sanz haïne de nuire au droit por traire lo tort avant' (*PL* 142.37-40). The Lady of the Lake expresses this duty in general terms, but in the *PL* the adventures undertaken by the knights mainly concern the maintenance of justice within Arthur's kingdom. Vassals who need champions in judicial battles come to Arthur's court to find them, as for example the Lady of Nohaut.

Thus the theory concerning the obligations of a knight to protect the weak and maintain the law is presented in universal terms, but in practice the knights fulfil these obligations with particular reference to a specific kingdom and feudal relationship.[27]

In the same way, Arthur's court provides both a centre of government for his kingdom and an international centre for the maintenance of chivalry as a more general ideal. There is frequent emphasis on the number of foreign knights who come there from all over Christendom and even from Muslim lands. Men come from all parts to help him in his wars:

Et de toz vint au desus par l'aide Nostre Seignor qui en mainz leus li fu apareilliez, et par les preudomes qui de totes les terres de crestienté li venoient aidier par la grant vaillance de lui; et neïs de maintes terres de paiennime lo vindrent servir li Tur, et se crestienerent por sa valor de tes qui puis furent de hautes proeces en son ostel. (*PL* 33.23-8.)

At his court is 'la flor de tote la terriene chevalerie' (PL 34.19–20). He is surrounded by 'genz de maintes manieres et de mainz estranges païs' (PL 54.4–5). Knights come to his court from all these lands because recognition by Arthur and the Round Table was necessary before a knight could establish his worth:

Car a celui tans n'estoit nus por preuz tenuz, de quel terre que il fust, s'il n'eüst avant esté en la maison lo roi Artu et s'il ne conust de cels de la Table Reonde et de l'Eschargaite. Lors estoit tenuz en son païs por bien erranz. (PL 135.40–136.4.)

To Arthur's court come all those who want to learn about chivalry or about marvels. Indeed it is an important centre for information within the work, as messengers speed to and fro. Messengers come to Arthur's court with news of marvellous deeds. For example, the young brother of Aiglyn des Vaus comes to court with news of the conquest of the Dolorous Guard, and the court is kept in touch with the progress of events through the constant arrival of knights and damsels rescued or conquered by Lancelot or Gauvain. Both the Lady of Malohaut and the Lady of Roestoc go to Arthur's court to find out the identity of unknown knights. While the Lady of Roestoc is at court, she does in fact learn from a squire who arrives with a shield that it is Gauvain himself whom she has scorned and rejected (PL 408). It is also at Arthur's court that all the adventures of the knights are recorded, as will be seen in Chapter VII.

Thus Arthur's court remains at the centre of the web of the events both told and left untold in the romance, and it helps not only to give some kind of cohesion to the individual work, but also to link it to a wider Arthurian world, partly through the interplay with the tradition to be found in other well-known texts. It is at the centre of a realm which is presented as more of a real kingdom than is perhaps usual in most Arthurian romances, particularly verse romance. When the knights leave court, they may well ride through the forest, but the dangers lurking there are not so much from strange forces as from warring hostile barons who are quarrelling over a particular piece of land. There is, however, a more mysterious domain which plays an important role in the work, as we shall see in the next chapter.

V

The Lake and Arthurian magic

A certain marvellous element, suggesting a world in which events occur mysteriously, is a necessary part of Arthurian romance even in a work like the *PL* which, as we have seen, gives particular emphasis to a feudal framework characteristic of human society and tends to keep magic in its place.[1] As one might well expect in a romance in which Lancelot of the Lake is the main hero, this marvellous element is centred in the Lake, and, although by definition it implies mysterious happenings rather than a natural sequence of events, it nevertheless helps to give a certain cohesion to the work.

In the *PL* it is not only during the childhood of the hero that the Lake plays an important part; periodic contacts with it continue until Lancelot is eventually made a Knight of the Round Table. Through the Lady of the Lake there is a link with the most famous representative of the magical element in Arthurian romance, Merlin, and references to him in connection with the mysterious adventures of the Arthurian past are also used at intervals to remind the reader of the marvellous aspect of the kingdom of Logres.

A long account is given of Lancelot's upbringing and education in the Lake and of the expedition to bring his two cousins to safety there, so that a good deal of the action in the first part of the story takes place in and around the Lake and at some distance from Britain and Arthur's kingdom. The author succeeds in preserving the tradition of the child brought up by a fairy in a lake, while at the same time introducing a considerable degree of rationalization, so that the story presents a tantalizing mixture of the natural and the supernatural.

The Lake has to be inaccessible to ordinary humans without special guidance, for it must provide a safe refuge for Lancelot; but it must also be near the theatre of human events in Ban's kingdom, for it is from a hill near the Lake that the King sees his fortified city going up in flames and dies of grief. From the context it is evident therefore that it is on the borders of Brittany and Gaul. When it is first mentioned, there is no suggestion that it is not a real lake. The author gives it a name, 'li lais Dyanez', which has associations with magic and the old religion, but at the same time he gives a rationalizing explanation of Diana:

Li lais estoit apelez, des lo tens as paiens, li lais Dianez. Diane fu reine de Sezile et regna au

UNIVERSITY OF WINCHESTER LIBRARY

tans Virgile, lou bon autor, si la tenoient la fole genz mescreanz qui lors estoient por deesse. Et c'estoit la dame del monde qui plus amoit deduit de bois et tote jor aloit chacier, et por ce l'apeloient li mescreant la deesse del bois. (*PL* 7.1–6.)

When the queen sees her infant son being carried into the Lake by a lady, there is no mention of fairies or of a magic lake. It is only after a detailed account of how an abbess meets the grieving queen, who decides to take the veil, that it is explained that the lady who took Lancelot was a fairy. The author defines a fairy as someone who knows how to make spells and enchantments: 'A celui tens estoient apelees fees totes iceles qui savoient d'anchantement et de charaies.' (*PL* 21.12–13.) He says that there were more fairies in Great Britain at that time than in any other country. They knew the power of the words, herbs, and stones, a knowledge which kept them young, beautiful, and powerful. All this was established at the time of Merlin 'la prophete as Anglois', who had all the wisdom which can derive from devils. As a result he was feared and honoured by the Britons:

Por ce fu il tant redotez de Bretons et tant honorez que tuit l'apeloient la sainte prophete, et tote la menue gent lor deu. (*PL* 21.19–21.)

It was from Merlin that the Lady of the Lake learned all her knowledge of necromancy (*nigromence*).

The author thus makes it clear at an early stage that the Lady of the Lake is a fairy by education, not by nature or heredity. The source of her learning in magic is shown to be Merlin, whose knowledge is diabolical in origin. His father was an incubus, one of the fallen angels, according to the author:

Voirs fu que Merlins fu anjandrez an fame par deiable et de deiable meesmes, car por ce fu il apelez li anfes sanz pere. Et cele maniere de daiable converse mout au siegle, mais n'ont force ne pooir d'aconplir lor volenté ne sor creant ne sor mescreant, car il sont chaut et luxurieus. Et trovons que qant il furent fait angle si bel et si plaisant, que il se delitoient en esgarder li uns en l'autre jusq'a eschaufement de luxure. Et qant il furent chaü avecques lor maleureus maistre, il retindrent la luxure en terre qu'il avoient es hauz sieges commanciee. De ceste maniere de deiable fu estraiz Merlins, ce dit li contes des estoires, et si vos dirai comment. (*PL* 21.24–34.)

There are similarities here with the description in Wace, where Magant, a learned clerk, explains:

> 'Trové avum, dist il, escrit,
> Qu'une manere d'esperit
> Est entre la lune e la terre.
> Ki vult de lur nature enquerre,
> En partie unt nature humaine

> E en partie suveraine.
> Incubi demones unt nun;
> Par tut l'eir unt lur regiun,
> E en la terre unt lur repaire.
> Ne püent mie grant mal faire;
> Ne püent mie mult noisir
> Fors de gaber e d'escharnir.
> Bien prenent humaine figure
> E ço cunsent bien lur nature.
> Mainte meschine unt deceüe
> E en tel guise purgeüe;
> Issi puet Merlin estre nez
> E issi puet estre engendrez.'
>
> (*Brut*, 7439-56.)

To ascribe Merlin's knowledge to his inheritance from a diabolical father is a form of rationalization in that the magic is fitted into the Christian system in which supernatural powers come either from God or the Devil. In Geoffrey of Monmouth and in Wace Merlin uses the powers derived from his father mainly for good, but it is never made clear whether he has been completely purified and redeemed through baptism. Robert de Boron, who links together the three tables, that of the Last Supper, the Grail Table, and the Round Table, needs a virtuous Christian Merlin to advise the founding of the Round Table and to prophesy the coming of the knight who will achieve the adventure of the Perilous Seat. In his work Merlin's birth stems from a failed plot to create an Antichrist, he is baptized and completely redeemed; there is therefore little ambiguity about his character and little suggestion of a magic which comes from a world not only different from the ordinary human world but also belonging neither to Heaven nor to Hell. In the *PL* the magic is again rationalized in that it is ultimately derived from a devil, but this time Merlin's diabolical origin is not redeemed through baptism; there is no thwarting of a plot of the council of Hell, but he is the child of a casual love affair between a girl and an incubus, so that there are none of the wider theological implications of Robert de Boron's version. His mother was born 'en la maresche de la terre d'Escoce et d'Irlande' (*PL* 21.35). Brugger suggests that *Escoce* is here the Pictish kingdom of the North-East, and a Scottish association fits in with the traditions connecting Merlin with the North and with Scotland.[2] She was the daughter of a vavasour of no very great wealth, and her only peculiarity was that she could not bear to marry a husband she could see. Eventually an incubus comes to her in the night. She feels him and falls in love with him.[3] The author explains carefully how it could come about that she could touch a devil with no earthly body:

La damoisele lo tasta, si senti que il avoit lo cors mout gent et mout bien fait. Et neporqant deiables n'a ne cors ne autres menbres que l'an puisse manoier, car esperitex chose ne puet estre manoiee, et tuit deiables sont choses esperitex. Mais deiable antrepranent a la foiee cors de l'air, si qu'il senble a cels qui les voient qu'il soient formé de char et d'os. (*PL* 22.27–32.)

The girl yields herself to the devil, and eventually a child is born who, at the request of his father, is called Merlin and is never baptized:

Cil anfes fu uns vallez, si ot non Mellins, car issi lo commanda li deiables a la damoisele ainz qu'il nasquist; mais il ne fu onques bauptiziez. (*PL* 22.40–23.2.)

He receives his name, therefore, from his father, a devil, not at the font. The author then gives a brief account of Merlin's activities as a child, how he went to Uther Pendragon at twelve years old, 'si com l'estoire de ses ovres lo tesmoigne et devise' (*PL* 23.3–4), and how he helped Uther to get the Duke of Tintagel's wife Ygerne. He then retreated into the 'forez parfondes et enciennes'. This allusion to his early activities fits in with the accounts in Geoffrey of Monmouth and Wace, and in Robert de Boron, particularly with that of the latter,[4] so that once again the author can be seen to be placing his story within the known Arthurian tradition. But he does not hesitate to make radical modifications to the familiar versions as presented in the well-known texts for the purposes of his own romance, for these references are then followed by a description of Merlin's character which is in conflict with the chronicles, where, even if there is a certain ambiguity about his origins and some of his powers, he is clearly a force for good. The *PL* is here above all in flagrant contradiction with Robert de Boron's *Merlin*, where his Christianization is emphasized. Not only is Merlin unbaptized in the *PL*, but the author states plainly that his character is bad: 'Il fu de la nature son pere, decevanz et desleiaus, et sot qanque cuers porroit savoir de tote parverse science.' (*PL* 23.7–9.)[5]

All Merlin's knowledge of magic is given a devilish origin, because this fits in with the way in which the author explains away the tradition, potentially uncomfortable for the *PL* with its emphasis on an Arthurian 'reality' having some affinity with the contemporary world, that Lancelot was brought up by a fairy. He achieves this without losing the particular element of mystery which distinguished Lancelot from other knights in both the *Lanzelet* and the *Chevalier de la Charrette*. The magic is preserved and, through being ascribed ultimately to the devil, it is given its place in a Christian conception of the world; but the Lady of the Lake is able to acquire her knowledge of it without incurring any blame and without having any dubious ancestors. She is *sage et cortoise*, rightly resists this unredeemed Merlin's amorous advances, but tricks him into giving her all his knowledge, while preserving her own virginity, and finally seals him up asleep in a cave. Throughout the whole episode the diabolical side of his nature is emphasized in a way which is not found in other texts, and because Merlin, as the representative of the diabolical element in magic, is imprisoned and his pupil is virtuous, the Lady of the Lake's gifts are not dangerous.

Thus the origins of the magic connected with Lancelot's childhood in the Lake are linked with the Arthurian past through the reference to Merlin, just as the origins of the conflict in which Lancelot lost both his father and his land are linked to another kind of Arthurian past through references to Uther's wars and to the early years of Arthur's reign. Merlin and Arthur, natives of Britain and the Kingdom of Logres, are linked with the Lady of the Lake, a damsel of Brittany, with Lancelot, son of the King of Benoyc, and with the Lake, which is from the strictly geographical point of view first presented in the text as near Brittany and Benoyc and not far from the land of Claudas. Its physical presence seems very real to those who do not live in it. Lancelot's mother founds the Mostier Reial on the spot where her husband died and goes every day to the place on the shore of the Lake where she lost her son, reads her psalter, and weeps (*PL* 17.34–8). Evaine, the widow of Bohort and mother of Lyonel and Bohort, in order to escape from the treachery of Claudas, joins her sister there as a nun. Thus the two queens seek refuge from Claudas in a convent on the shores of the lake in which first Lancelot and then his two cousins are hidden to protect them from Claudas. The Christian foundation and the magic Lake are side by side; but the queens do not realize that their sons are safe close by, for they regard the Lake as real. However, Helene is told by the *rendu* who finds her weeping on the edge of the Lake that Lancelot is safe, although he does not reveal where he is. The man of God has some contact with the people in the Lake, because he has learned where Lancelot is from someone who sees the boy every day, 'celui qui lo vit main et soir'. This man of religion, as was seen in the last chapter, acts as king's counsellor, thus filling part of the traditional role of Merlin jointly with the *preudomme* who visits Arthur after his first battle with Galehot and interprets his visions for him. It is therefore interesting that the *rendu* should have knowledge of Lancelot's presence in the Lake, a secret not shared with anyone else outside it.

Some kind of contact between the religious world and the Lake is also to be found in the episode in which Evaine, while praying, has a vision and is carried away in spirit to another place, where she sees three children in a beautiful garden near a forest:

La ou ele estoit en ses oreisons et en ces proieres vers Damedeu, li avint une avisions. Et ele fu autresins com endormie, et lors fu raviz ses esperiz et s'an ala en petit d'eure auques loig. Si li fu avis que ele estoit el chief d'un mout tres biau jardin en l'oroille d'une forest grant et espesse. En la close de cel jardin avoit maisons mout beles et mout granz. Et ele esgardoit, si veoit hors de ces maisons issir anfanz assez, mais trois en i avoit qui sanbloient estre seignors de toz les autres. (*PL* 133.23–30.)

With the children are two men whom she recognizes as Pharien and his nephew Lambegues. A man she does not know then seizes her by the hand and brings her back to the abbey. When she awakens from her vision, she finds the three names of the children written in her right hand.

The physical proximity of abbey and land beneath the Lake, unrecognized by the inhabitants of the abbey and unknown to the children in the Lake, and those further contacts through a man of God and the vision of a devout nun between a Christian refuge and a magic refuge help to 'tame' the magic.[6] They make the Lake a place which is at once inaccessible and near, mysterious and yet not so alien as to be an unsuitable land for Lancelot's protectress and educator. The inaccessibility is suggested through an illusion, a false appearance, for the Lake in the Prose *Lancelot* is only a lake by enchantment; in reality, there is no lake at all, but a land with houses, a small river, and forests:

La dame qui lo norrissoit ne conversoit nule foiee s'an forelz non granz et parfondes, ne li lais ou ele sailli atot lui, qant ele l'am porta, n'estoit se d'anchantement non, si estoit el plain d'un tertre plus bas assez de celui o li rois Banz avoit esté morz. En cel leu ou il sanbloit que li lais fust granz et parfonz avoit la dame mout beles maisons et mout riches, et el plain desouz corrut une riviere petite, mout planteüreuse de poissons. Si estoit cil herbergemenz si celez que nus nel poïst trover, car la sanblance do lac lo covroit si que veüz ne pooit estre. (*PL* 24.22–31.)

This should be compared with the description of the fairy's land in *Lanzelet* (193–301), where the supernatural element is much more strongly emphasized: the land is a crystal mountain inhabited only by ladies, Lanzelet is taught the use of sword and buckler by mermen, but cannot learn from them how to fight as a knight on horseback.

The closeness of this 'lake' in the French romance to the land of Benoyc is brought out in the episode in which Lancelot, when out hunting, meets a vavasour who had been a vassal of his father and who asks the unknown boy where he comes from. Lancelot replies that he is from 'cel autre païs' (*PL* 43.9–10). The vavasour tells him that the land around them used to belong to Ban of Benoyc: 'Si fu toz cist païs suens.' (*PL* 44.13–14.) Lancelot is therefore in the land which should be his, without realizing it because he does not know who he is. We can compare the treatment of the mysterious land of Gorre in the *Chevalier de la Charrette*, of which the boundaries, in spite of the perilous bridges which have to be crossed by the rescuer of Guinevere to reach it, seem strangely ill defined, as some of the prisoners of Gorre are on this side of the bridges.[7] The Grail Castle in the *Conte del Graal* also seems to appear in a mysterious way, but there is a certain ambiguity over the suddenness of its appearance. Was it just a curious lie of the land which had kept it hidden or was it something more? What happened to it the next morning?[8] The author of the *PL* does not leave us in suspense: he makes it clear that the Lake in which Lancelot is hidden is produced by enchantment, an enchantment which, as is so characteristic of spells, affects the appearance only; but he also underlines the 'reality' of the land beneath the appearances. The semblance of water is, however, so convincing that the children are safe there, even though they are not far from Gaunes, once the city of Bohort but now owing allegiance to Claudas. Lambegues and one companion, Leonces, are taken by a damsel to a castle near the Lake, and their journey is described in such terms that it sounds as if it has been a comparatively short one (*PL* 103.10-16). The damsel leaves Leonces at this point because she has sworn not to reveal the secret of the Lake to anyone but Lambegues or Pharien, the tutors of Bohort and Lyonel. She then rides on with Lambegues until they come in the evening to the Lake, which looks so real that Lambegues is astonished that the damsel dares to ride into such a great expanse of water at that hour:

Et antre la damoisele et Lanbegue chevauchant tant qu'il sont venu au lac. Il antrent anz; si estoit ja nuiz qant il i vindrent, et mout se merveilla Lambegues comment la damoisele osoit a cele hore entrer dedanz cele eive qui si estoit granz. Mais il n'en sot onques mot tant qu'il se vit tres devant unes granz portes a l'antree d'une haute maison. Il regarda entor soi, mais il ne vit mie del lac qu'il avoit ores si grant veü, si s'an mervoille trop durement. (*PL* 103.34–104.2.)

Next morning the children are taken out under escort to see Leonces and then return to the Lake.

What distinguishes the land lying beneath this appearance of a lake from other lands in the *PL* is not anything strange about the land itself or its inhabitants, but the fact that it lies outside the network of feudal relationships and is free from the conflict between rival lords. No feudal terms are used in connection with it; the Lady of the Lake is one of the few visitors to Arthur's court who claims no allegiance either to anyone or from anyone. Therefore the Lake represents a safe refuge, beneath the mirage of water, from the wars to which Arthur and his vassals are subject. However, its magical associations are not reduced to the level of a magnificent example of successful camouflage. The Lady of the Lake's knowledge of the magic arts is shown in other ways, again with a particular emphasis on the ability to change the appearance of things. Thus the damsel of the Lady of the Lake is able to cast a spell on Lyonel and Bohort which transforms them outwardly to greyhounds:

Si giete son anchantement et fait resenbler les deus anfanz as deus levriers; et li dui levrier orent la sanblance as deus anfanz, ce fu avis a toz ceus qui les veoient. (*PL* 67.32–5.)

Claudas looks at the children and thinks they are greyhounds, and looks at the greyhounds and thinks they are children (*PL* 68.7-11). All the people, when they see the damsel and one of her squires carrying off the children, believe them to be greyhounds, as does the squire himself: 'Si quide chascuns qui les voit que ce soient dui levrier que il en portent, et li escuiers meesmes qui Bohort en porte lo cuide bien.' (*PL* 69.2-4.) It is only when night has fallen and it is time for the children to have something to eat that the damsel uncovers the reality beneath the outward semblance and reveals them to her companions: 'Lors descovri la damoisele son anchantement et mostra as chevaliers les deus anfanz.' (*PL* 69.12-13.) They are astonished and ask where she has found them, but she refuses to tell them: 'mais ele ne lor en dist mie la verité, ançois dit que tant a fait qu'ele les a' (*PL* 69.19-20). At the very same moment that the damsel revealed the children to those who were with her, the greyhounds were revealed as dogs to those who thought they were children:

Et d'autre part resont en la tor Phariens et les soes genz, et font grant joie de ce que lor seignors cuident avoir. Mais si tost com vint a l'anuitier, tot droitement a cele hore que la damoiselle del lac descovri les anfanz a cels qui avec li estoient, qant ele lor dona a mengier, a cele hore meesmes furent descovert et coneü li dui levrier en la tor de Gaunes. Et furent tuit si esbahi c'onques mais nules genz ne furent plus esbahi. (*PL* 80.15-21.)

It appears to be only in the eyes of the beholders that these changes take place, not in the eyes of the children themselves, nor, presumably, in the eyes of the dogs, and the secret of the spell is kept from the damsel's companions who are also from the Lake. Lancelot questions his own identity, but never the nature of the land in which he lives, so that it would seem that the element of magic is kept very much in the background both for him and for the other inhabitants of the Lake. There is however one marvel in the Lake which does arouse his curiosity—the wreath of red roses which he finds on his pillow every morning, winter and summer, except for Fridays, the eves of the great religious feast days, and Lent. The Lake's magic is in harmony with the religious calendar. There is no suggestion in the text that the roses have a divine source, but just as there is no hint of any clash between Lancelot finding refuge in the Lake and his mother in an abbey, so here the marvel does not offend Christian decorum. Not only do the roses appear at seasons of the year when it is not natural for them to do so, but they also arrive mysteriously. Lancelot tries in vain to catch someone bringing them: 'ne ja ne s'en preïst garde qu'il onques poïst aparcevoir qui li aportoit illuec, et maintes foiees i gaita por lo savoir' (*PL* 106.39-107.2). This would seem to suggest that he does not take magic happenings as a matter of course but assumes that someone must bring the flowers. It is also significant that the appearance of the wreath provides not only a visible sign that Lancelot is a hero predestined for great deeds—a use of the supernatural characteristic of

Arthurian romance—but also evidence of his noble qualities, for he carefully divides the roses into three so that he can give wreaths to Lyonel and Bohort: 'si li fu atorné a grant gentillece de cuer de toz cels qui lo veoient' (*PL* 107.5-6).

The magic element is therefore still present in the Lake in the *PL*, but it is kept under careful control, as typified by the account given of the Lady of the Lake's imprisonment of Merlin. This is important for the whole structure of the romance; for the Lady of the Lake not only keeps Lancelot safe but plays a considerable role in his education. Unlike the fairy in *Lanzelet*, her motives appear wholly disinterested.[9] She arranges for him to be taught the arts of courtly society, hunting, and the use of arms (*PL* 38-9), but she is also concerned with his education in chivalry at a deeper level. We have seen that she makes use of the mystery of his identity to spur him on to greater individual effort.[10] She also gives him an explanation of chivalry which stresses the knight's responsibilities towards the Church and has much in common with the religious rituals for knighting and the blessing of arms.[11]

It is of interest that it is in the Lake, which is outside the structure of relations between lord and vassal, that Lancelot receives an exposition of the theory of chivalry which, while stressing the knight's role as champion of justice and defender of the weak and defenceless, does not mention the relationship between the knight and his lord, a relationship which receives great emphasis in the actual adventures the knights in the romance undertake. The Lady of the Lake's account of the origin of chivalry as a consequence of the Fall and of its main purpose as defence of the Church does not take in another aspect, important for later events, namely the role of love in the inspiration of a knight; however she herself plays a part in relation to the love theme after Lancelot has left the Lake through the messages she sends to him and through her own visit to Lancelot and Guinevere, as will be seen when the role of the Lake in the romance after Lancelot has left for Camelot is examined.

The role of the Lake and of its Lady in Lancelot's preparation for knighthood is therefore extremely important. The Lake remains a significant influence even after he has gone to Arthur's court, but the centre of action has moved away from it and from Benoyc and Gaunes to Britain, and we never enter the Lake again, just as in the non-cyclic romance we hear nothing more of the two widowed queens or of the Mostier Reial. However, contact is kept with the Lake, as the Lady and her damsels continue to play a part in the action through leaving the Lake at intervals and entering the Arthurian kingdom.

The Lady had already briefly emerged from the Lake to take the baby Lancelot to safety; she had also ridden out with the children from her own land to meet one of the lords of Gaunes and had sent one of her own damsels to the court of Claudas. These are only brief excursions into the outside world. The first time in the romance that she leaves the Lake for any length of time and comes into direct contact with Arthur's court is when she journeys across the sea with Lancelot to appear in person at Camelot. On this occasion the details of the sea route used and the enquiries made concerning the whereabouts of Arthur present the journey as an ordinary one within this world. She leaves the Lake on a Tuesday with a splendid train of knights, squires, and damsels, all dressed in white, and arrives in Camelot on a Friday evening (of the following week apparently):

Tant ont chevauchié qu'a la mer vienent, si entrent anz, et sont arivé en la Grant Bretaigne a un diemenche assoir au port de Floudehueg. D'iluec chevauchierent par droites anseignes del roi Artu, si lor fu enseignié que li rois seroit a Chamahalot a cele feste. Et il acoillent lor chemin tant qu'il vindrent lo juesdi assoir a un chastel qui a non Lawenor, si est a vint deus liues anglesches de Chamahalot. (*PL* 148.28–34.)

In spite of all these details there is still a hint of mystery about the Lady of the Lake's arrival. King Arthur had never heard of her before, whereas most of the lords and ladies in the romance who send messengers or come to court in person are known to him at least by reputation, and hold lands which fit into the network of feudal relationships which link Arthur and his allies, or Arthur's enemies and their allies. The lady tells Arthur that she is known as the Lady of the Lake, and he wonders at this: 'De cest non se mervoile mout li rois, car onques mais de li n'avoit oï parler.' (*PL* 153.36–7.) The direct link with magic in the episode is to be found in the ring given to Lancelot by the Lady of the Lake which has the power to uncover enchantments:

Lors traist la dame de son doi un anelet, sel met a l'anfant en son doi, et li dit qu'il a tel force qu'il descuevre toz anchantemanz et fait veoir. (*PL* 154.29–31.)

In the *Chevalier de la Charrette* Lancelot received a ring with similar properties from the fairy who brought him up in the Lake:

> Mes cil don plus dire vos doi
> avoit un anel an son doi
> don la pierre tel force avoit
> qu'anchantemanz ne le pooit
> tenir puis qu'il l'avoit veüe.
> (*Char.* 2335–9.)

As is characteristic in Arthurian romance, much of the supernatural is concentrated in objects rather than in the characters themselves.[12] There is, however, already a hint that the Lady of the Lake has some knowledge of the future in the advice she gives to Lancelot before she leaves him:

'Biax filz de roi, itant vos anseignerai au partir, qant plus avroiz achevees aventures felonesses et perilleusses, plus seürement anprenez les aventures a achever, car la ou vos lairoiz a achever les aventures par proesce que Dex ait mise en chevalier, il n'est pas encores nez qui maint a chief celes que vos avroiz laissiees. Assez vos deïsse, mais ge ne puis, car trop m'est li cuers serrez et la parole me faut. Mais or vos en alez, et bons et biax et gracieus et dessirrez de totes genz et amez sor toz chevaliers de totes dames; itex seroiz vos, car bien lo sai.'[13] (*PL* 154.33–155.2.)

This suggestion of more than human knowledge both of the future and of events taking place at a distance from her would fit in both with what she has learned from Merlin, who himself has this power in Geoffrey of Monmouth, Wace, and Robert de Boron, and with the twelfth-century tradition concerning Lancelot's lake fairy as expressed by Chrétien de Troyes:

> L'anel met devant sa veüe,
> s'esgarde la pierre, et si dit:
> 'Dame, dame, se Dex m'aït,
> or avroie je grant mestier
> que vos me poïssiez eidier!'
> Cele dame une fee estoit,
> qui l'anel doné li avoit,
> et si le norri an s'anfance;
> s'avoit an li molt grant fïance
> que ele, an quel leu que il fust,
> secorre et eidier li deüst;
> mes il voit bien a son apel
> et a la pierre de l'anel
> qu'il n'i a point d'anchantemant.
> (*Char.* 2340–53.)

Both the Lady of the Lake's special knowledge of events and her store of magic objects play a part in the development of the themes of identity and of love and help to provide links between the different episodes in the text.

During Lancelot's first adventures, leading up to the time when Gauvain first brings his name back to court as the victor of the Dolorous Guard, the messengers from the Lake are above all concerned with the quest for Lancelot's identity. This is to be expected, for it was the mystery surrounding his name which was given the greatest emphasis in the episodes connected with the Lake in the early part of the work. Damsels from the Lake play a particularly important role in the episode of the conquest of the Dolorous Guard, during which Lancelot learns his own name and in which so much of the supernatural in the work is concentrated. They have already had a part in the childhood of Lancelot and his cousins. Lyonel and Bohort are rescued by a damsel from the Lake called Saraide, who received a wound on her face during the escape and who was able to carry out a magic transformation on her lady's instructions. She reappears in the story during Lambegues' visit to the Lake (*PL* 104–6), when she shows Lyonel her wound, and, as we shall see, this is picked up again much later in the romance (*PL* 495–6). There is also another damsel from the Lake, unnamed, who goes to Gaunes to bring Lambegues to the children who are pining for their tutors. It is stated explicitly in the text that she is not the one who brought the children to the Lake (*PL* 99.33–5).

The damsels the Lady of the Lake sends with messages to Lancelot after he has left the Lake are also unnamed; they may be given magic objects to deliver but use no spells and have no more than human knowledge of events. Indeed, their limited knowledge of what is happening is often in contrast with the Lady of the Lake's omniscience. Hence the damsels who play a part in the revealing of Lancelot's identity, first to himself and then later to Gauvain, have themselves to discover it, as they have not been given prior knowledge by the Lady of the Lake.

The first damsel from the Lake to have contact with Lancelot after he has left to become a knight is waiting for him at the Dolorous Guard, which suggests that the Lady of the Lake knew that his adventures would bring him to that particular castle where he would perform the feat by which he would learn his name. When Lancelot comes to the castle, the tale gives an account of the peculiar customs which govern it, customs already mentioned briefly when he meets a weeping damsel whose explanation of her grief—that her knight has been killed in the castle because of its *mauvaisses costumes*—directs him towards the Dolorous Guard. He approaches the castle, and we learn more about its customs. These consist mainly in the forcing of a knight errant who enters it to fight his way through the gates in the outer and inner walls, each defended by ten knights who attack in turn, being replaced by another knight as each one tires. However, there are also certain supernatural elements: in particular, a metal figure of a knight on a horse, to be seen high above the gate in the inner wall, set up there by enchantment, which will only fall when the knight destined to conquer the castle comes through the first gate. The conquest of the castle will bring its enchantments to an end in that they will be uncovered, seen openly, but to achieve their cessation the knight must remain in the castle for forty days:

Mais si tost com cil entroit dedanz la premiere porte qui lo chastel devroit conquerre, et il porroit lo chevalier de cuivre veoir, tant tost fondroit a terre. Et lors charroient tuit li anchentement del chastel dom il estoit toz plains, en tel maniere qu'il seroient veü apertement. Mais del tot ne remaindroient il mie devant que cil qui lo chastel conquerroit i demorast quarante jorz sanz gesir hors nule nuit. Tele estoit la force des anchantemenz del chastel. (*PL* 183.34–184.2.)

It is significant that the expression *seroient veü apertement* is used of the uncovering of the enchantments. The castle has, therefore, important elements of
magic, but its setting is described in everyday terms. Below it there is a com-
fortable town (*bourg*) where a knight errant can find anything he needs; the
name of the town is Chaneviere and it is situated on the river Humber.

This description of the castle is immediately followed by a meeting with the
damsel from the Lake; although she is not revealed as such immediately, the tale
makes it clear that she has links with Lancelot's past, for it explains that if she
had uncovered her face, Lancelot would have recognized her immediately: 'La
damoisele fu envelopee mout bien, car s'ele fust descoverte, il l'eüst bien
conneüe.' (*PL* 184.11–12.) She then explains to Lancelot the customs of the castle,
an account of which has just been given to the reader. After Lancelot has fought
for some time, it becomes too dark to continue, and the damsel reappears, still
veiled, to take him to a good lodging for the night. She then comes before him
richly apparelled and unveiled, and from his reactions it becomes clear that she
comes from the Lake:

Lors la regarde; et qant il la voit a descovert, si la conoist mout bien. Et il li saut les braz
estanduz, et si li dit:

'Ha! bele douce damoisele, vos seiez la bienvenue sor totes les autres damoiseles. Mais,
por Deu, me dites que fait ma boene dame?' (*PL* 187.37–188.2.)

Thus, through the presence of this damsel, a link is made between the
adventure of the Dolorous Guard and Lancelot's childhood in the Lake, and
once again an emissary from the Lake is associated with supernatural events,
even if, this time, she is not directly responsible for them. The damsel is
Lancelot's guide throughout his conquest of the castle, and she acts on instructions from the Lady of the Lake which provide evidence of the two main aspects
of that lady's special powers, namely her knowledge of the future (only shown
in relation to Lancelot) and her possession of objects endowed with magic
properties. The damsel first explains that she has been sent by the Lady of the
Lake and that the next day Lancelot will learn his name and conquer the castle:

Lors lo trait a une part, si li dit que sa Dame del Lac l'anvoie a lui. 'Et demain, fait ele,
savroiz vostre non et lo non vostre pere. Et ce sera laïssus en cel chastel dont vos seroiz
sires ainz que vespres soient sonees, car gel sai de voir par la boche ma dame meesmes.' (*PL*
188.3–7.)

Then she produces three marvellous shields which will enable Lancelot to
capture the castle and which he will use throughout his adventures until just
before the First Assembly against the Roi d'Outre les Marches (*PL* 230.4–5), so
that they provide a continuing link with the Lake. She describes these shields as
assez merveilleus. The first has a single red band, 'une bande vermoille de bellic',

and will give Lancelot the strength added to his own of another knight; the
second, with two such bands, will give him the additional strength of two other
knights; the third, with three bands, will give him the additional strength of
three others. He is not to rely on his own youth and vigour, but to use the
shields as he feels his own strength diminish or when he wants to make all the
world marvel at his deeds.

The damsel also gives Lancelot instructions from the Lady of the Lake
concerning his behaviour—he must not settle at Arthur's court or anywhere else
until he is known throughout many lands for his deeds of prowess:

'Mais bien gardez que vos ne remeigniez n'au roi Artu n'a autrui devant que vos seiez
quencüz par vos proesces en pluseurs terres, car ensin velt ma dame que vos lo faciez por
vos essaucier et amender.' (*PL* 188.20–3.)

Thus the damsel who had received Lancelot at the castle continues to give
him encouragement and support throughout his battle to conquer the Dolorous
Guard with the help of the shields. After *prime* Lancelot takes up the shield with
one band and find his strength doubled (*PL* 191.26). After *tierce* the damsel from
the Lake and the squire bring him the shield with two bands, and the damsel
herself substitutes it for the one with one band (*PL* 191.36). Lancelot defeats the
ten knights guarding the first gate, passes through it, and is given the shield
with three bands which he accepts rather unwillingly (*PL* 193.4–9). The damsel
tells him to look above the gate, and he sees the marvellous statue of the knight,
which immediately falls down. Thus is fulfilled the prediction that the figure
will crash to the ground as soon as the knight destined to conquer the castle sees
it. Lancelot defeats the remaining knights and a damsel gives him the keys of
the castle.

The damsel from the Lake plays a more active part in the events leading up
to the conquest than does the lord of the castle, who is not allowed to intervene
until all the other knights have been conquered, and indeed the customs of the
castle seem to function more or less independently of him:

Mais sor toz les autres en est esbahiz li sires del chastel, qui les esgarde desor lo mur o il
est, si a tel duel que par un po que il n'anrage de ce qu'il n'est a la meslee. Mais il n'i puet
estre, ne ne doit, selonc les costumes do chastel, devant que tuit li autre fussient conquis. Si
a mout grant paor de veoir sa grant dolor, a coi il n'avoit onques quidié que nus cors d'un
seul chevalier poïst atandre. (*PL* 192.14–20.)

However, he does not stay to fight Lancelot, but flees. Indeed, he remains a very
elusive character throughout the text, his appearances and disappearances
serving to prolong the mysteries and enchantments of the Dolorous Guard. If
he does not play an active part in the defence of the castle and seems to be
bound by its customs rather than in control of them, he continues plotting to

prevent either the conqueror of the castle or Arthur from ending the enchantments, and his flights and plots (*PL* 194–5, 200, 202–6, 209–14) provide a
recurring motif up till his final flight after Lancelot has captured and released
him in return for the freeing of Gauvain and his companions. The hermit who
has told Lancelot where to find the lord protests at this release of Brandin,
whose only power appears to have been that of ending the spells:

'Comment, sire? Lairoiz en vos aler Brandin? Dons avez vos tot perdu, qe ja mais li
anchantement de la Doloreuse Garde ne remaindront se par lui non.' (*PL* 214.33–5.)

The shields which help Lancelot to conquer the Dolorous Guard also provide
an element of continuity, providing both a reference back to the great
adventure in which he learnt his name and a continuing link with the Lady of
the Lake. After the fight to capture the castle, during which their magic power
is emphasized, there is no direct allusion to any increase in strength deriving
from the bearing of the shields, although there may be an implication of this
increase in the damsel's insistence that Lancelot should take the shield with
three bands when he goes to ambush the lord of the Dolorous Guard (*PL*
206.15–16). On this occasion, just the sight of him bearing the shield makes all
the enemy flee, and indeed the main role of the shields after the fall of the castle
is to provide a means of identifying its conqueror when he performs other
exploits, in much the same way as the colour of arms in other parts of the
romance. All Lancelot's changes of shield are carefully listed. When, in an
abstraction caused by love, he closes the gate in the Queen's face, he is carrying
the shield with one band (*PL* 207.12), and this is referred to again during his
first secret meeting with Guinevere (*PL* 342.39–40). When he gives orders that
Kay and the King and Queen should be allowed to pass through the gate, and
they finally penetrate right inside the castle, he is bearing the shield with two
bands (*PL* 215.27), as is also mentioned later (*PL* 342.40). When he leaves the
castle to tell Gauvain that he can return to the Dolorous Guard and to his uncle,
he has the shield with three bands (*PL* 216.30), again referred to later on (*PL*
343.5). He is still using this shield when he rescues the Queen's knight who is
being dragged along behind a horse. The knight whom he has saved then goes
back to court, describes his rescuer's shield, and thus enables him to be identified as the conqueror of the Dolorous Guard. Before the First Assembly against
the Roi d'Outre les Marches, Lancelot finally abandons the shield with three
bands and has another made so that he shall not be recognized (*PL* 230.3–4).
Much later, during Lancelot's first secret meeting with Guinevere, when she is
trying to extract from him an account of his past activities (*PL* 341–4), it is
through the carrying of these three shields, as well as the different-coloured
arms, that she is able to confirm the truth of what he has been telling her. The

shields, therefore, serve two main functions within the structure of the romance. Firstly, they contribute to Lancelot's status as predestined hero who receives help from objects with marvellous properties, sent by a beneficent source of magic power (the Lady of the Lake), in his defeat of a maleficent magic power (residing in the evil customs of the castle, to which the lord himself is to a considerable extent subject). Secondly, they provide a means of identifying the hero as he makes his name under varying disguises and thus help to pull the threads together in the key episode in the middle of the romance, that conversation with Guinevere which leads up to the first kiss.

When Lancelot has conquered the castle, he is taken to a 'cimetire mout merveilleus' (*PL* 194–5). Its marvellous quality is to be seen most clearly in two of its features, both of which involve predictions concerning the future. There are a number of tombs which bear inscriptions giving the names of the Arthurian knights who will lie there.[14] There is also the marvellous tomb with a slab which can only be raised by the knight who conquers the castle and whose name is written beneath it. This tomb, which recalls in some ways the one in the *Chevalier de la Charrette* (1888–909), not only predicts the future but also presents a test that, like the metal figure of the knight above the castle gate, can only be passed by the predestined achiever of the adventure. The slab is so large that it would require the strength of more than four men to raise it. The feat, achieved by Lancelot, is, as has been seen, central to the development of the identity theme in that it is through passing this test that the hero learns his own name. The completion of this stage in the quest for Lancelot's identity is connected with the Lake in that it fulfils the prediction which the damsel from the Lake had made to Lancelot on her lady's instructions near the beginning of the episode (see above). The Lady of the Lake knew that Lancelot would come to the Dolorous Guard, that he would raise the slab and learn his name. Not only that: a damsel from the Lake is present when he does so, and herself discovers his name (*PL* 194.32–4).

Lancelot has conquered the castle and raised the slab, but the lord has escaped, so that the marvels and enchantments which happen by day and by night will continue; the disturbing nature of these phenomena, which are connected with the customs of the castle, and the desire of the inhabitants to be rid of them are stressed. If the lord had been captured and held, these strange mysteries would have been laid bare by him; the townspeople fear that now they will never be discovered and thus brought to an end, for they feel that it will be impossible to keep the conqueror there for forty days:

Mais trop sont cil del chastel dolant del seignor qui eschapez est, car s'il fust pris, si fust descovrez par lui toz li covines de laianz. Or ne sera ja mais seüz, ce dotent, car il ont paor qu'il ne puissent mie retenir ce chevalier quarante jorz; car s'il i demorast, lors chaïssent tuit li anchantement et les merveilles qui par jor et par nuit venoient, car nus n'i bevoit, ne ne menjoit asseür, ne n'i couchoit, ne ne levoit. (*PL* 195.10–17.)

This use of *descovrir* should be compared with that in connection with the uncovering by the damsel from the Lake of the spell which outwardly transformed children into greyhounds and vice versa (*PL* 69.12), and that in relation to the ring, given to Lancelot by the Lady of the Lake, which uncovers enchantments (*PL* 154.29–31).

The Lady of the Lake continues, therefore, to watch over Lancelot and to send him help and guidance after he has left the Lake. Her guiding hand (through her damsels) is particularly evident during the episode of the Dolorous Guard in which he learns his name. However, the influence from the Lake does not just dominate this particular episode in the *PL*, but provides a recurring motif which is particularly important in relation to the whole identity theme. The paths of the damsels are constantly crossing those of both Lancelot and Gauvain right up until the moment when Gauvain discovers Lancelot's name and brings it back to court after the Second Assembly with the Roi d'Outre les Marches, just as the adventures of the two knights bring them back at intervals to the Dolorous Guard during this part of the story.[15]

After Lancelot's initial visit, the narrative returns to the cemetery for the second time when Gauvain and his companions first come to the castle. For their visit, some of the predictions concerning the future of Arthur's knights have been changed the night before by human means to false statements about the present, in order to persuade Arthur to come to the castle and to put an end to its evil customs (*PL* 198.18–22):

Li clers commence a lire sor les tombes, et trueve sor une des tombes escrit: 'Ci gist cil, et veez la sa teste.' Et an pluseurs des tombes dit ensin et nome chevaliers assez de la maison lo roi Artu et de sa terre. Et qant messires Gauvains ot qu'il sont ensin mort, si am plore mout durement, car il cuide bien et tuit li autre que ce soit voirs. Et si estoit il de tex i avoit, et si estoit mençonge de toz cels dont les letres avoient esté faites la nuit devant. (*PL* 198.32–8.)

The greatest lie of all concerns the fate of the good knight, conqueror of the castle (Lancelot), who, according to the inscription, already lies in the tomb (*PL* 199.6–8). Gauvain and his companions, weeping over the alleged death of the knight, are inveigled into spending the night in a castle and fall into the hands of the lord of the Dolorous Guard. By the time of the third visit to the cemetery, this time by Arthur, the lying inscriptions have been extended to include the names of Gauvain and all his companions (*PL* 208.24–33).

In the enchanted cemetery there is a mixture of misleading appearance and reality, of supernatural and natural, similar to that to be found in the Lake and in the castle of the Dolorous Guard itself. There is also a certain blurring of the division between the magical and the human mystifications. There is no deception about the predictions, which play an important part in the conquest of the Dolorous Guard as well as in the cemetery; they help to prepare for later events and to give some cohesion to a narrative where a logical sequence of cause and effect in human terms or in those of divine providence is not always apparent.

The fourth visit to the cemetery (Gauvain's second visit) occurs some time afterwards (*PL* 240). He is taken there by one of the damsels from the Lake after the First Assembly of Logres, during his quest for the identity of Lancelot. He tries unsuccessfully to lift the slab beneath which is hidden Lancelot's name. The damsel makes an explicit reference back to his earlier visit: 'Ci avez vos esté, fait ele, autrefoiz.' She also refers to the false inscriptions there which had been made after Gauvain's visit:

'Sor ceste tombe, fait ele, ot ja escrit: "Ci gist Gauvains, li niés lo roi Artu, et veez la sa teste." Et de toz voz compaignons autresi. Ne onques rien de tot ce n'i trovastes com vos i venistes.' (*PL* 240.17–19.)

Gauvain asks how this could be, and she interprets it not in terms of purely human intervention, in spite of the explanation given earlier for the lying inscriptions which Gauvain himself had seen, but as part of the enchantments: 'Ce sont, fait ele, li enchantement de ceianz.' She therefore uses the term *enchantement* to cover both the inscriptions of which the origin remains mysterious and those which have presumably the same origin (in the inhabitants of the Dolorous Guard) as did the lying inscription concerning the death of the White Knight, although the making of the inscriptions may possibly have been achieved by the use of magic arts.

Lancelot too returns to the Dolorous Guard. For his first return visit (to the castle, not to the cemetery), he comes in a litter with the Lady of Nohaut who intends to lodge for the night in the town below the castle. Lancelot refuses and weeps when he sees the gate of the castle which he had inadvertently shut in the Queen's face. This brief return to the Dolorous Guard is linked with the development of the love theme and makes an explicit link with earlier events. Lancelot looks at the door and says:

'Ha! porte, porte, por quoi ne fustes vos a tans overte?' Et ce disoit il de la porte o il fist muser la reine, com il fu esbahiz sor les murs. Si cuidoit que la reine lo saüst autresin com il savoit, et que ele l'an haïst a tozjorz mais. (*PL* 237.1–4.)

Lancelot, at last cured of his wounds, is lured back to the cemetery by the inhabitants of the Dolorous Guard to put an end to the enchantments. These enchantments turn out to be a characteristic mixture of the mechanical and the diabolical. Lancelot is taken to a chapel in the cemetery and told to go through an opening into a cellar beneath the ground. He makes the sign of the cross and enters, his sword drawn and his shield before him. He hears a great noise, and it seems to him that the earth is moving and that the walls will collapse. He then comes upon a door guarded by automata, metal figures of knights who rain blows upon him. He succeeds in passing them, smells a great stench, and comes to another door. To get through it he sees that he has to pass between a dark and dreadful well from which strange noises come and a man with a head as black as pitch, breathing flame and brandishing an axe. Lancelot fells the man with the axe and comes to a metal statue of a damsel holding the keys of the enchantment in her right hand. He takes the keys, opens a metal pillar in the middle of the room with one key, and then finds the *coffre perilleus*. The chest seems to resemble a strange and frightening organ; from it come thirty tubes which emit terrible voices, and it is these voices that are the source of the enchantments and marvels: 'De cels voiz venoient li anchantement et les mervoilles de laianz.' (*PL* 250.8–9). Lancelot opens the chest, and a great whirlwind bursts forth with such a roar that he thinks all the devils of hell must be in it—and indeed there are devils there: 'Si an sailli uns granz estorbeillons et une si granz noisse que il li fu avis que tuit li deiable d'anfer i fuissient; et por voir si estoient il, que deiable estoient ce.' (*PL* 250.10–12.) He then draws the key from the chest, looks around, and sees that the well has disappeared and that the pillar and all the metal figures have fallen to the ground. He comes out into the cemetery and finds that all the tombs with the helmeted heads above them have also vanished. He places the keys on the altar, having brought peace to the Dolorous Guard, which is henceforth called the Joyous Guard. Here, therefore, we have a variation on the changing or remaking of a name: Lancelot discovers his name at the Dolorous Guard, and through him the castle gains a new and joyful name.

Lancelot, by fetching the keys and opening the perilous chest, has therefore laid bare the enchantments, revealed them for what they are, and so they cease to exist, just as the damsel had shown that the transformation of the children into greyhounds was only an illusion. The writer talks about devils in relation to these enchantments; but the devils are located in the tubes, and there seems to be no diabolical intelligence directing all these strange events. The lord of the castle, who had fled, could have brought the marvels to an end, but, apart from this, they seem to function independently of him. The enchantments of the Dolorous Guard have the autonomy characteristic of many of the marvels in Arthurian romance.[16]

This adventure is therefore completed in two stages, the first stage linked to Lancelot's discovery of his own identity and the second to his love for the

Queen (through a false message concerning her capture which lures him to the castle). The Dolorous Guard thus plays a key role in this part of the work, a role in which, as has already been suggested, the messengers from the Lake are also deeply involved. It is the part played by these messengers which it is now proposed to examine further.

The damsel from the Lake who acts as a guide to Lancelot throughout the conquest of the Dolorous Guard and provides him with the magic shields does not disappear from the scene once he has conquered the castle and learned his name. Bound by a promise to Lancelot that she will not leave a tower in the Dolorous Guard until he returns (*PL* 205.15–19), she remains a prisoner to her word. Her plight helps to motivate Gauvain's quest for Lancelot; during this quest he is reproached by a second damsel from the Lake for leaving the first one in prison (*PL* 226.10–11), and when he meets the damsel again, he recalls the reproach (*PL* 235.12–13). These reproaches, the first damsel's pleas for release (*PL* 215.9, 219.23, 239.4–8), and her predictions of where Lancelot will be found (*PL* 219.38–9), all help to provide a thread of continuity for the narrative up till the first battle against Galehot, a thread which links both the world of the Lake and the Arthurian kingdom and associates them in the quest for Lancelot's identity. Thus the damsel's prediction that Lancelot will be at the First Assembly of Logres is immediately followed by the announcement of the First Assembly between Arthur's knights and the Roi d'Outre les Marches (*PL* 220.8–15, 221.2–11). After her release from prison, when Lancelot's ring is brought to her by the second damsel from the Lake, she takes Gauvain to the slab in the cemetery beneath which Lancelot had found his name, and when Gauvain fails to raise it, promises to take him to the unknown knight so that he can learn who he is. When she hears of the Second Assembly, she immediately declares that the knight will be there, but with a proviso—if he is not physically prevented from coming: 'La sera il, se del cors n'a essoigne.' (*PL* 242.17.) She then accompanies Gauvain on his search, except for a brief period when she is treacherously taken from him (*PL* 244–52). She goes with the other damsel from the Lake to a castle near this Second Assembly. After it Gauvain goes to the castle to ask her to keep her promise (*PL* 255). She tells him that she thinks that the knight who won the assembly is the one whom Gauvain is seeking. They both ride after Lancelot, who refuses to give his name, but the damsel reveals it to keep her promise to Gauvain, much to Lancelot's disgust. She continues to help Gauvain to learn more about Lancelot, even after she has left him and ridden off with Lancelot as the latter had promised when he left her in prison (*PL* 215.12). When Lancelot has killed the giants, a mysterious damsel, not explicitly identified at this point in the narrative, rides by, saying: 'C'est la tierce.' (*PL* 270.35.) Yvain does not understand why she says this, but Gauvain remembers the earlier prediction, repeats it to Guinevere, and is thus able to share with the Queen his knowledge that it is Lancelot who killed the giants. Soon after this the tale confirms Gauvain's interpretation of the words by identifying the damsel who said 'C'est la tierce' with the one who has been riding with Lancelot since the assembly—that is, the one who promised to stay in the tower and had originally made the predictions. She continues to accompany Lancelot until he is surrounded by the men of the Lady of Malohaut and taken off by them to the Lady's castle. She is shut out of the castle and, believing that Lancelot is dead, does not dare to return to the Lake but becomes a nun—once again no incongruity is perceived between the inhabitants of the Lake and the religious life. The part this damsel played in Lancelot's adventures is recalled by Lancelot and Guinevere during their first secret meeting, when they go over together all the important moments in his development as both knight and lover (*PL* 343.15–28, 344.17–18).

This particular damsel from the Lake has, therefore, an important role in helping Lancelot to discover his own identity as a knight and in bringing him and Gauvain together. She is enabled to do this partly through the instructions and the magic objects which she receives from the Lady of the Lake, who evidently has foreknowledge of events. Thus the damsel has been sent to the Dolorous Guard and can assure Lancelot that he is destined to conquer the castle because she has heard this from the lips of the Lady of the Lake, and she can give Lancelot the magic shields which will give him the strength to defeat his enemies, and can tell him when to use them. She shows little sign of possessing special powers of her own, and her own knowledge is limited. She learns of Lancelot's identity at the same time that he does. She is by no means always in control of events and does not come and go at will, as does her lady. She has to wait in the tower until Lancelot agrees to release her from her oath; she is dependent on Gauvain for protection when she leaves with him, so that one of the links provided by her adventures arises from her very dependence upon others. But in another way she makes a more positive contribution to the structure of the narrative by her predictions concerning Lancelot's appearance at the three assemblies, foreknowledge which is not specifically attributed to her mistress rather than herself. Lancelot attends the First Assembly because the Queen sends a message to the White Knight asking him to do so; the damsel makes the prediction *before* the Queen sends her message, but there is no suggestion in the narrative that the Queen has been influenced in her action by the predictions. When Lancelot decides to go to the assemblies, he both obeys the command of the Queen and fulfils his own destiny. The nature of the damsel's foreknowledge is never explored, and the force of her prediction is somewhat weakened at one point by the addition of a qualification (*se del cors n'a essoigne*), which suggests that she was sure of Lancelot's intentions but unsure whether it would be physically possible for him to fulfil them. The limitations of the damsel's knowledge are shown very clearly when she retires to the convent, erroneously believing that Lancelot is dead.

The second damsel from the Lake, who also helps to bind together this part of the story and to remind us of the links between Lancelot and the Lake, suffers from the same limitations to her knowledge. She has been sent by the Lady of the Lake to give Lancelot the instructions concerning the importance of the role of love in the development of a knight (*PL* 205.38–206.2). This second damsel appears in the story as an unidentified maiden, weeping because she has been told that the White Knight is dead; she tells Gauvain and his companions what she has heard (*PL* 199). Later, when Lancelot, hearing from a *vallet* of a damsel who has news that Gauvain and his companions have been captured, rides after the damsel, is recognized by her, and in his turn recognizes her as 'une damoisele qui est a sa Dame del Lac' (*PL* 205.30–1), we learn that the weeping damsel had come from the Lake. She says:

'Mais l'an me dist, fait ele, la ou messires Gauvains est pris, que vos gissiez morz en la Garde Doleruese, et por ce n'i vos ge onques antrer, car ge ne la pooie neïs veoir.' (*PL* 205.34–6.)

She then delivers the message from her mistress.

This damsel is sent by her imprisoned colleague in search of Lancelot and serves as a link between her and Gauvain, away from court on his quest for the White Knight (Lancelot), by reminding him of the damsel he has left in prison. It is as an unidentified damsel that she first abuses Gauvain roundly, echoing a traditional theme of the person met in the forest who reproaches a knight for his behaviour;[17] but here both the meeting and the damsel are soon explained:

Et la pucele qui a lui avoit parlé estoit cele qui darreainnement avoit esté anveiee au chevalier que messires Gauvains queroit de par sa Dame del Lac. Et ele meesmes lo queroit, car l'autre pucele li enveioit. (*PL* 226.18–21.)

On their second meeting, where there is an explicit reference back to the first encounter (*PL* 235), she helps Gauvain to follow Lancelot's traces, although they are nearly always one step behind. She is as easily misled by false rumours of Lancelot's death (*PL* 199, 205) as is the damsel in the tower, but, unlike her, shows no signs of any special foreknowledge of where to find Lancelot; indeed, she and Gauvain are dependent on the treacherous Brehuz for information. However, she knows that the White Knight's identity lies hidden beneath the tomb in the Dolorous Guard and she is able to persuade Lancelot to send his ring. When her companion from the Lake is released, they both ride with

Gauvain. She intervenes to stop knights from continuing to fight Gauvain by revealing his identity, but with the other damsel is captured by Brehuz to be rescued again later. She is left at the castle near the Second Assembly by Gauvain and is not mentioned again.

She serves on more than one occasion in this part of the narrative to give a temporary appearance of mystery which each time is soon dispelled. By withholding her identity at the beginning of an episode, the author can imply that his narrative is following the traditional pattern of unknown damsels with mysterious knowledge suddenly appearing by a preordained but unexplained 'chance' so characteristic of Arthurian romance.[18] The author's subsequent explanations identify the damsel, fit her into a logical sequence of events, and bring out clearly that she has no special knowledge of what is happening, although she comes from the Lake.

After the two assemblies against Galehot and the first secret meeting between Lancelot and Guinevere, periodic contacts with the marvellous continue during Lancelot's retirement to Sorelois. This land is given an aura of mystery as well as inaccessibility by the explanation which the author gives, after he has accounted for Galehot's possession of the land in terms of earthly wars and conquests, concerning the two *felons passages* (PL 357) which provide the only means of access to knights errant as long as the adventures last in the kingdom of Logres. The tale places the building of the two causeways to the island at the time when Merlin prophesied the adventures to come:[19]

Et se dit li contes que, au tans que Merlins profecia les aventures qui devoient avenir, fist faire ces deus chauciees li rois Lohoz, li peres au roi Glohier, qui a cel tans estoit sires de Sorolois, por ce que il dotoit la destrucion de sa terre. Et neporqant, ançois que les avantures commançassent a avenir, avoit sor cele aigue assez autres passages de fust et de nes passanz. Mais si tost com eles commancerent, furent tuit abatu, qe onques puis chevaliers estranges ne passa se par ces deus chauciees non. (PL 357.25–32.)

When Gauvain and his companions set off on another quest for Lancelot (hidden in Sorelois), the author again links the adventures to a mysterious Arthurian past by making Gauvain pause to give his companions advice at 'une pierre qui a non li Perrons Merlin, la ou Merlins ocist les deus anchanteors' (PL 365.9–11). I know of no text in which such a killing is described (although such a tale may once have existed), but the allusion, left hanging as it were, serves to remind us that this is a quest in an Arthurian world in which strange things happen, without the author being obliged to scatter enchanted castles everywhere. Thus he can reserve the supernatural episodes in his work for marking particularly important moments in the life of his hero and in the development of the main themes of the romance. The references to a marvellous Arthurian past are usually linked to Merlin, just as the marvels, contemporary with events in the narrative and indeed forming part of the narrative, also have for the most part their ultimate origin in Merlin, in so far as he is the source of the Lady of the Lake's magic and hence of her qualifications for the title of *fee*.

To suggest the Arthurian marvels of the present during the quests of Gauvain and Hector and the war against the Saxons, the author relies mainly on damsels coming from the Lake. In this part of the romance the activities of the damsels and the Lady of the Lake herself are no longer mainly associated with identity, but with the love theme. This is exemplified by the shield with the gap in it which closes as the love progresses and is therefore itself an object with magic properties.[20] Like the shields which helped Lancelot to conquer the Dolorous Guard, this shield is brought by a damsel from the Lake (*PL* 401). She appears mysteriously at Arthur's court in the company of a knight with a broken arm. We do not learn now why she arrives with this knight, as the episode of the battle in which he received his wound is only told later (see Chapter VII). The damsel first suggests that the shield has marvellous properties and then reveals that she has been sent by 'la Pucele del Lac'. What is interesting about this episode and the whole of the shield theme is that the Lady of the Lake makes contact with Guinevere for the first time through the present of the shield, and eventually the two women who are important in Lancelot's life actually meet.

The greetings which the Lady of the Lake sends to Guinevere might at first sight seem disconcertingly ambiguous. She declares that she knows the thoughts of Guinevere and loves what she loves:

'Dame, saluz vos mande la plus sage pucele qui orendroit vive et la plus belle que ge saiche au mien escient. Et si vos mande que vos gardez cest escu por amor de li et d'autrui que vos plus amez. Et si vos mande que ele est la pucele o monde qui plus set de voz pensez et plus s'i acorde, que ele aimme ce que vos amez. Et bien sachiez, se vos cest escu gardez, il vos getera de la greignor dolor o vos fussiez onques et metra an la greignor joie que vos onques aüssiez.' (*PL* 402.13-20.)

Indeed, the Lady of the Lake declares later that she regrets having sent part of the message:

'Et si vos mandai par li une chose don ge fui mout dolante aprés, et si dotai que vos fussiez a malaise; car ge vos mandai que ge estoie la dame o monde qui plus savoit de voz pensees et qui miauz s'i acordoit, car ge amoie ce que vos amez. Et sachiez que ge ne l'ain fors por pitié de norreture, et por lui vos ain ge.' (*PL* 556.31-6.)

In the message the Lady of the Lake shows her mysterious knowledge not only of the hidden thoughts of Guinevere and the secret love between her and Lancelot, but also of future events. In the further explanation given by her damsel concerning the shield, emphasis is again given to prophecies concerning the future, prophecies which help to prepare the way for the physical consummation of Lancelot and Guinevere's love, for the Queen's distress at the madness of Lancelot, and for Lancelot's entry into the *maisnie* of the King;

'Et qant il avanra que l'amors sera anterine, si sachiez que cist escuz que vos veez si desjoint se rajoindra et tanront ansenble ces deus parties. Et sachiez que vos seroiz lors delivree do greignor duel qui onques vos avenist et seroiz an la greignor joie que vos aüssiez onques. Mais ce n'avandra devant que li miaudres chevaliers qui soit hors de la cort lo roi Artu soit devenuz de sa maisniee.' (*PL* 403.12–18.)

The fact that these rather general prophecies concerning joy and grief are eventually fulfilled is underlined by the references back to this message during the episode in which the Lady of the Lake cures Lancelot and talks to Guinevere.

Once again therefore, here through her damsel's visit to court, the Lady of the Lake gives us a supernatural glimpse into future events, and, through the shield which she leaves behind, provides a physical reminder of the love between Lancelot and Guinevere during his period of withdrawal in Sorelois. The shield brought by the maiden is hung in the Queen's room so that she can see it:

Et l'escu que la pucele avoit aporté fist pandre an sa chambre, si que ele lo veoit totjorz, car mout se delitoit an lui veoir. Ne onques puis n'ala nul leu que il ne fust aportez devant li et panduz an sa chanbre totjorz jusque a cele ore que il fu rejoinz par avanture que cist contes devisera ça avant. (*PL* 407.15–19.)

A framework for future events is thus provided through the shield, just as the prophecy of the damsel from the Lake that more would be heard of the Unknown Knight at the three assemblies helps to give a framework to the adventurous wanderings of Lancelot and Gauvain up to the Third Assembly, that is the first battle against Galehot.

The damsel who brought the shield then leaves the court, and we hear no more explicit account of her subsequent adventures, although two other damsels, one definitely identified as coming from the Lake, appear later. However, we are told of the events leading up to her visit to court when the narrative switches back to Gauvain and back in time to relate the episodes which give an explanation of the mysterious arrival of knights and damsel at court. Gauvain meets the damsel from the Lake on her way to Guinevere. He asks in vain questions concerning the meaning of the shield, questions to which the reader already has the answers (a narrative technique to be examined in Chapter VII).

The shield itself figures again in the story during the episode in which Lancelot and Guinevere spend their first night together (*PL* 547). When the Queen looks at the shield 'que la damoisele del lac avoit aporté' and finds the gap between the knight and the lady closed from the top of the shield to the bottom, she explains to Galehot that it has been sent by 'Cele do Lac'. During Lancelot's madness he seizes the shield 'que la Pucelle do Lac avoit anvoié la reine' (*PL* 553.27) and temporarily recovers his wits. When the Lady of the Lake comes herself, clad in snow-white silk and with a train of damsels, knights, and *vallets* (we can compare the description of her first arrival at Arthur's court, *PL* 151–2), she uses the shield and ointment to heal him and then gives instructions that while there is anything left of this shield, he must take no other into battle. During the battle against the Saxons, Lancelot is able, through the shield, to uncover a door closed by enchantment:

Et Lanceloz s'an fu venuz par la porte desus l'aive ou li enchantemenz estoit, qui estoit close de l'air. Et ses escuz avoit tel force que nuns anchantemenz no pooit tenir. (*PL* 564.15–18.)

Almost every time that the shield is mentioned, there is a reference back to the episode in which the damsel from the Lake brought it to the Queen. Its magic properties are not restricted to the closing of the gap as a symbol of the progress of the love: it also has healing powers which help to quieten Lancelot when he, like another well-known lover, Yvain, goes mad; and it uncovers magic, like the ring already associated with Lancelot in Chrétien (*Char.* 2335–9) and given to him by the Lady of the Lake when she takes leave of him as a young squire at Camelot. The appearance of the shield in the story usually brings with it associations with the Lady of the Lake. Through it she plays an important part in the development of the love between Lancelot and Guinevere. She has given the ring to Lancelot, in addition to advice on how he should conduct himself as a knight, to which she later adds, through a message brought by a damsel, counsel on the importance of the right kind of love in a knight's development; she gives the shield to Guinevere with advice on how she should conduct herself as Lancelot's *amie* and on her great responsibilities as the person whom the flower of chivalry loves above all others.

During this episode, when the Lady of the Lake, for only the second time since she carried off Lancelot, leaves her land beneath the semblance of a lake and comes to Arthur's court, both her supernatural powers and her more human qualities are shown. She has the ability to send help or appear herself at the moment when she is needed without being summoned.[21] Her arrival is mysterious and unannounced, although there is no suggestion that she has used unnatural means of transport to get there. On the occasion of her first visit,

which produced a similar impression (there are obvious parallels in the description, with a stress on white in both), she travelled by boat and by horse; she
herself recalls this first visit (*PL* 556.3–4). She calls Lancelot by the name she
used to call him in the Lake—li Biaus Trovez—thus taking him back to his
childhood, and he is immediately quietened. In fact, the whole episode contains
frequent references back to Lancelot's childhood in the Lake. The Lady of the
Lake has a marvellous ointment which can cure him, like the ointment used to
cure Yvain. In *Yvain* there is a reference to the ointment having come from
'Morgue la sage' (*Yvain*, 2949), but in the *PL* there is no need to bring in another
fairy. The lady's predictions concerning the future, made when the shield was
brought, have been fulfilled, as the Queen says: 'Vos m'envoiastes cel escu la que
j'ai si bien esprové que onques ne m'an mandastes rien de l'escu que ge n'aie
trové.' (*PL* 556.14–16.) The Lady of the Lake foretells even greater marvels
concerning the shield: 'Dame, dame, fait cele do Lac, bien sachiez que vos
verroiz ancor greignors mervoilles de l'escu que n'en avez veües.' (*PL* 556.17–18.)
She also makes a prophecy concerning the freeing of Arthur which is fulfilled
in due course: 'Et il an sera gitiez hors dedanz nuef jorz, et sachiez que cist
[Lancelot] lo gitera.' (*PL* 556.28–9.) Lancelot will succeed in these battles
provided that he uses the shield sent by the Lady of the Lake.

   She is therefore associated here with magic powers in that she can foretell the
future (like Merlin), she can heal, and possesses magic objects. However, her
motives and her feelings are explained in more human terms. It is true that she
brought Lancelot up because she was aware of his great destiny, of the prowess
which he would later give proof of:

'Et sachiez bien que, por la grant proece que an lui devoit estre, lo norri ge tant que il fust
si granz et si biaus comme vos lo veïstes a cort.' (*PL* 556.21–3.)

But the love which she feels for him is the human love that a mother might feel
for a child, a love which is not in any sense a rival to that of Guinevere: 'Et
sachiez que ge ne l'ain fors por pitié de norreture, et por lui vos ain ge.' (*PL*
556.35–6.) Her motive for keeping his identity secret she links with the very
human one of love for a knight, an ordinary earthly lover in whom she is very
anxious to avoid arousing feelings of jealousy:

'Ne onques ne sot qui il estoit, ainz lo celoie ge por un chevalier que ge amoie par amors
plus que nul home qui vive, car ge dotoie que se il lo saüst, que il i pansast autre chose. Si
faisoie dire que il fust mes niés. Et ancor dirai ge, qant ge serai arrieres, que ge suis venue
do roi Artu giter de prison.' (*PL* 556.23–8.)

Because of her own experience of love, she is able to give advice to Guinevere
on the importance of not angering or grieving one's beloved (*PL* 557.11–20).

By the end of the conversation, Guinevere and the Lady of the Lake have become firm allies in their mission of giving encouragement to the greatest of all knights, Lancelot, so that he can realize to the full his magnificent potential. In this way, the Lake (with its mixture of the natural and supernatural) and the court are brought together in the persons of these two women in an episode which has been prepared for by the series of damsels who have, since the Lady of the Lake's first visit to Camelot, kept the two worlds in touch and given periodic reminders of Lancelot's association with the marvellous through his childhood in the Lake.

The role of the damsels from the Lake stops at this point, but before this second and final visit of the Lady of the Lake there has been another intervention (unconnected with the shield) by a damsel from the Lake. It provides a very direct link with the childhood of Lancelot and his cousin Lyonel, and recalls those interventions of emissaries from the Lake in the quest by Gauvain for Lancelot which are so characteristic of the narrative before the assemblies with Galehot. A mysterious, veiled damsel appears during a battle between the treacherous seneschal of the Duke of Cambenic and Gauvain, which is being watched by Lyonel on his way to court, to give Guinevere a message from Lancelot and Galehot. She tells Lyonel that she is the person whom he should love most and finally reveals herself as the damsel who was wounded in saving him, as a small boy, from the sword of Claudas. Her conversation with Lyonel provides a clear reference back to the events of the childhood, as is underlined in the text, a linking technique to be explored further in Chapter VIII. The damsel, having revealed herself, calls out to Gauvain:

'Gauvain, Gauvain, voi toi ci celui qui te puet asener de ce que tu quierz. Et se il eschape, s'esloigne ta queste.' (*PL* 496.12–13.)

She does this because she wants Lyonel to leave. Gauvain rapidly ends his fight, pursues Lyonel, and extracts from him the information that Lancelot is in Sorelois (*PL* 501). Thus through this damsel the earlier pattern of Gauvain being assisted in his quest for Lancelot by maidens associated with his childhood in the Lake is repeated.

There are other mysterious damsels in the work who are unconnected with the Lake, but who appear in an unexplained way at strategic moments in the story to give information, or who have objects with remarkable properties. There is, for example, the damsel who arrives in the traditional way at Arthur's court on the occasion of a great feast to offer an adventure. She brings a strange beast, the lion of Lybia which has a crown growing on its head:

Et qant il orent lo tierz mes eü, si antra laianz une damoiselle de mout grant biauté et tint en sa main destre un lion qui mout estoit de grant fierté, lié par lo col en une chaainne, mais tant cremoit la damoisele que ja ne fust si hardiz qu'il se meüst tant com ele fust an sa compaignie. Cil lieons fu esgardez a grant mervoille par laianz, car il avoit une corone desus son chief qui de meïsmes la teste li est creüe. Si s'an merveillierent mout tuit li chevalier qui en la sale estoient, por ce que onques mais lyeon coroné n'avoient veü. (*PL* 610.12-20.)

This strange beast is linked with the making of Lyonel's name and the disappearance of the strange birthmark on his chest, as the strange tomb in the enchanted cemetery is linked with Lancelot's discovery of his name; in each case, a damsel plays a part in the adventure.

There is also the damsel with the sword who meets Gauvain without recognizing him, tells him that she can reveal the names of the two greatest knights, and brings him to his brother Agravain in an episode which involves several supernatural elements (*PL* 410-22). Agravain is suffering from an illness which is a punishment for bad conduct towards two damsels. The illness was produced by an ointment put on by two mysterious damsels who used a magic pillow to keep him asleep; they set a limit to the illness: Agravain will be cured by the blood of the two best knights in the world. These two damsels, therefore, share certain characteristics with the Lady of the Lake: they have objects with special properties—a pillow, an ointment—and a power to forecast or determine the effect of these properties in relation to the future. Unlike the Lady of the Lake, they inflict pain and suffering, but they do not do so in an arbitrary way, as Agravain has deserved his punishment and they have set a limit on it.

Within the structure of the romance the episode provides an adventure for Gauvain which begins mysteriously, continues to have some suggestion of the marvellous, even when the strange events are explained, and helps to establish Lancelot's reputation as a great knight, even greater than Gauvain. It is followed up later in the romance in that, when Gauvain finally catches up with Lancelot, he persuades the latter to send his blood as that of the greatest knight to complete the healing of Agravain. The sword carried by the damsel who takes Gauvain to Agravain also has some strange properties, although these are much less spectacular than the shields given to Lancelot or Guinevere. Agravain says of it:

'Sire, se l'espee est tex com les letres tesmoignent, ele est bone a bacheler qui n'est mies esprovez. Mais ele ne seroit mies si boene a un prodome, car ce dient les letres que ele ne fera ja mais s'anpirier non, et cil sor cui ele sera amendera totevoies.' (*PL* 420.19-22.)

Like the magic shields, it helps to provide both an element of mystery and a thread of continuity. The sword is brought to Arthur's court and given to Hector before we know its origin (*PL* 404.17-27). Hector takes it with him on his quest for Gauvain, and it is through the sword that Gauvain recognizes his opponent during their battle at the *pont de la chauciee* and stops the fight (*PL* 530.15–16).

There is also a mysterious damsel who appears at the right moment to tell two damsels seeking Gauvain and Girflet where to find them and how to identify them by their shields. They all wonder who the damsel can be, but they never find out (*PL* 487.6–20). Nor is her identity revealed to the reader, and she does not, as far as we know, appear again. Another damsel who gives directions and seems to have mysterious knowledge appears more than once, and later intervenes directly in events. Gauvain and Hector meet her first on the quest for Lancelot. She says that she will tell Gauvain where Lancelot is, if he promises to grant her the first boon which she asks (*PL* 532.28–533.4).[22] Galehot, Lancelot, Gauvain, and Hector later meet the same damsel, as is made clear in the text (*PL* 540.1–3); they make a similar promise in return for information concerning Arthur's whereabouts. These promises have to be fulfilled when the damsel summons the four knights by their *fiances* (again with an explicit reference back by the narrator, *PL* 548.5–6) to go with her to rescue Arthur. She then betrays them and lures them into a Saxon prison.

This betrayal suggests a link between this mysterious damsel and the Saxon maiden (Gartissiee/Canile)[23] to whom a knowledge of magic is expressly attributed:

Si savoit plus d'anchantement que damoiselle do païs et mout estoit belle et estoit do linage as Saisnes. Et ele amoit tant lo roi Artu com ele pooit plus rien amer, et li rois n'em savoit rien. (*PL* 540.26–9.)

She later manages to make Arthur love her:

Et li rois Artus toz les jorz parloit a la damoiselle do chastel et la prioit d'amors. Et ele n'an avoit cure, et si l'avoit tel conreé que il l'amoit outre messure. (*PL* 541.35–7.)

But no details are given as to how she achieves this. She is presented as a hostile figure who keeps in chains a female rival, foolish enough to be the *amie* of a knight, Gadraselain, whom Canile herself loves. The Saxon fortress has a door magically closed by air (*PL* 552.4–9, 564.16–18) for which she may be responsible, but we are never told. With the help of her books, her powers are considerable, as Kay is warned:

'Sire, fait ele, se ele amporte ses livres et ses boites, tot avez perdu, car, par les livres que ele a, feroit ele corre une aive ci contramont.' (*PL* 568.1–3.)

Once the books, which are in a big chest, are burnt and reduced to ashes, she is helpless and throws herself from the rock in despair. Like the Lady of the Lake, therefore, she learns her art, but she remains dependent on her books, whereas the Lady of the Lake, once she has learnt her spells from Merlin, can stay independent of him and shut him up for ever. In other ways they remain opposing figures, however beautiful they both may be. The Lady of the Lake comes from a land of peace, exercises a beneficent influence, and is friendly towards Arthur's court. Gartissiee/Canile is of Saxon lineage, hence from an alien race, traditionally hostile towards Arthur and Christianity; she throws people into prison, including innocent damsels, and finally tries to commit suicide, itself a sin. She also helps to point the contrast between Arthur's struggle with Galehot, a noble opponent, and his war against the Saxons, portrayed as a barbarous people (rather like the pagans in a *chanson de geste*) who do not fight according to the noble rules of war but are prepared to use black arts to trap their enemy.

After Lancelot becomes a Companion of the Round Table and he and Galehot go back to Sorelois, there is no more mention of the Lake, and the role of the marvellous is still more restricted. There is a limited kind of magical herbalism in the False Guinevere episode where the impostor and Berthelais brew a potion which makes Arthur fall in love with the false Queen, thus echoing a Tristan situation in reverse, and near the end of the work there is the adventure of Lyonel with the Crowned Lion of Lybia, already discussed. The crumbling of Galehot's castles, his dreams, and their interpretation and ful- filment introduce a supernatural element which, as has been seen in the previous chapter, recalls some of Merlin's activities as counsellor of kings and prophet of the future in both the chronicles and Robert de Boron's *Merlin*. In Arthur's dreams and their interpretation, the religious element is emphasized: the *preudomme* makes Arthur confess his sins and do penance, and his interpreta- tion of the dreams is like a miniature sermon with the allegorical figures, the *Lion Evage*, the *Mire sanz Mecine*, the *Flor qui parle*, being given a religious significance as Christ and the Virgin Mary. Galehot's dreams in the non-cyclic version of the Journey to Sorelois and the False Guinevere episode are not given such a strongly religious colour, but, as has been noted in Chapter IV, only a few hints of magical associations are to be found: for example, in the resonances of the name Bademaguz rather than in the figure of the man himself.

The *PL*, therefore, contains enough elements of the type of marvellous characteristic of Arthurian romance to give the appropriate aura of mystery to the work, while retaining its emphasis on the 'reality' of the Arthurian kingdom, where events which may at first appear mysterious are often later given a motivation in feudal relationships, war between kings and barons, conflicts between neighbours or members of a family. The supernatural associated with the Lake is the most pervasive, but is presented in such a way as to avoid conflict with Christian society and with another level of motivation belonging to the human, natural world. While damsels whose special arts, properties, or knowledge seem to derive almost entirely from their mistress, the Lady of the Lake, tend to appear mysteriously, without any explanation—at least at that point—their main function is not just to disrupt the ordinary sequence of cause and effect. They also help to weave together the various adventures both through the links which they provide with Lancelot's childhood and through the predictions which they are able to make concerning future events. The magic objects they bring, which continue to play a part in what happens, also serve to provide a certain continuity. As the damsels have only a limited knowledge of events, and the Lady of the Lake does not often intervene directly herself, this element of foreknowledge does not dominate the whole work. The lady's powers have, however, their ultimate origin in *Merlin la prophete as Anglois*, whose ability to see into the future was perhaps his most notable characteristic in twelfth- and thirteenth-century literary and 'historical' tradition. This serves both to 'rationalize' the Lake fairy's arts by explaining her knowledge of magic and at the same time to set the story of Lancelot in the context of events which lie outside the individual romance and to give a depth in time through the references to the strange adventures which used to happen at the time of Merlin. The Lake and the magic associated with it are not explained away through this medieval type of rationalization; a direct clash with the Christian system may be avoided, but they continue to provide a motivation on a different plane and of a different kind from that given in feudal, 'historical' terms, as discussed in Chapter IV, and thereby contribute to the rich complexity of the Arthurian world to be found in this particular romance.

VI

The Grail Allusions

There is another kind of Arthurian supernatural, more directly associated with Christianity, namely that of the Grail theme. The relationship between the Grail story and the tale of Lancelot as presented in the *PL* is of crucial importance in any examination of the position of the non-cyclic romance in the development of the *Lancelot-Grail* cycle. We have seen that there are many passages in the text which serve to set the story within a wider Arthurian tradition and to link it with the past history of the Arthurian kingdom and with the magic and marvels associated with the time of the Prophet Merlin, son of a devil, whose activities are placed in the past in relation to the events in the life of Lancelot. There are also a number of passages which refer to the Christian marvels associated with the Grail and with Joseph of Arimathea which form another main thread in the texture of Arthurian romance early in the thirteenth century.

Some scholars have interpreted a series of references (with biblical echoes, but with no specific mention of the Grail) concerning the ancestry of Lancelot and his cousins as a preparation for the coming of a Grailwinner, Galahad, son of Lancelot, whose genealogy is taken back, like that of Christ, to David:

(*a*) Ban, as he lies dying, recalls that his wife 'est descendue de la haute ligniee Davi lo roi' (*PL* 13.12). He prays that God may have pity upon her:

'Biax Peres piteus, preigne vos pitiez de ma fame Helene, qui est descendue del haut lignage que vos establites el Regne Aventureus a essaucier vostre non et la hautesce de vostre foi, et a avoir voz granz repostailles, qui devant les estranges puepules lor avez victoire donee.'[1] (*PL* 13.39–14.5.)

(*b*) Queen Helene describes Lancelot's lineage as follows:

'estraiz de haut lignage cui Dex eslut a veoir ses granz merveilles et a honorer les estranches terres de sa venue et a honorer son haut non et a essaucier et sa creance.' (*PL* 49.39–50.2.)

(*c*) Leonces de Paerne says of the lineage of Lancelot's aunt, Queen Evaine:

'Nos savons par lo tesmoign des Escriptures que ele et si encessor sont descendu del haut lignage au haut roi Davi. Ne nos ne savons a com grant chose il porroient encores monter, car ce savons nos bien que an la Grant Bretaine atandent tuit a estre delivré des mervoilles

et des aventures qui i avienent par un qui sera del lignage a la mere a ces anfanz.' (*PL*
108.37–109.2.)

These references, in which the Grail is not mentioned, have a role within the
structure of the *PL* in that they emphasize the illustrious ancestry of the hero in
a romance in which the making of a name, as was shown in Chapter II, is one of
the main themes. Lancelot, during his childhood, is spurred on by his ignorance
of his parentage to great individual effort in order to prove himself worthy to be
a knight. When he finally achieves the exploit through which he discovers his
identity, he learns not just his own name but his parentage—*Lanceloz del Lac, filz
au roi Ban de Benoyc* (*PL* 194.30–1). The allusions to his mother's family, which
all occur during his childhood and outside his presence, show that he has a great
heredity on his mother's side as well as on his father's.[2] He knows nothing of
this until the Lady of the Lake tells him, as she takes leave of him at Camelot:

'Biaus filz de roi, vos en iroiz; et ge voil que vos sachiez que vos n'iestes pas mes filz, ainz
fustes fiz a un des plus prodomes do monde et des meillors chevaliers, et a une des plus
beles dames et des meillors qui onques fust; mais vos ne savroiz ores pas ne del pere ne de
la mere la verité et si lo savroiz vos prochainement.' (*PL* 153.39–154.3.)

It is fitting that Lancelot's ancestry should be traced back to one of the first
great knights, David, the slayer of Goliath, whose name often occurs in prayers
connected with the knighting ceremony,[3] and who figures on the Lady of the
Lake's list of great knights of the past, alongside John the Ircanian, Judas
Maccabees, and his brother Symon (*PL* 146.10–14).

A link with the Old Testament is also suggested in the somewhat mysterious
reference, quoted above (*a*), to the *Regne Aventureus* and the *granz repostailles*
which gave the ancestors of Lancelot's mother victory over the *estranges pueples*.
In the Bible, the Ark of the Covenant, containing the Testimony of God, the
tokens representing the mysteries of God, was carried before the Children of
Israel into battle:

Cumque elevaretur arca, dicebat Moyses: 'Surge, Domine, et dissipentur inimici tui, et
fugiant qui oderunt te a facie tua.' (Num. 10:35.)[4]

The allusions, therefore, set off echoes of the Old Testament, but also, perhaps,
of the *Joseph* of Robert de Boron, where the Grail represents the Ark of the New
Covenant and is also associated with the secrets of God (*Jos.*, line 3335 and pp.
XII–XIII). The reference by the dying Ban to his wife's lineage is directed
towards past events, not towards adventures in the future, although the *Regne
Aventureus* has an Arthurian ring to it rather than a purely biblical one. The
same is true of Queen Helene's allusion to the noble lineage from which her son
is descended. In (*c*) above, Leonces refers both to a biblical past in the descent

from David and also to the possibility of a deliverance in the future from marvels happening in Great Britain by someone of the lineage of Lyonel and Bohort's mother. However, in this reference there is no mention of *repostailles*, and it seems likely that the allusion to marvels here prepares the way for Lancelot's adventures at the Dolorous Guard, where he puts an end to the enchantments discussed in the previous chapter.

The Lady of the Lake too refers to the great adventures which Lancelot is destined to achieve, as she takes leave of him in Camelot:

'Biax filz de roi, itant vos anseignerai au partir, qant plus avroiz achevees aventures felonesses et perilleusses, plus seürement anprenez les aventures a achever, car la ou vos lairoiz a achever les aventures par proesce que Dex ait mise en chevalier, il n'est pas encores nez qui maint a chief celes que vos avroiz laissiees.' (*PL* 154.33–8.)

Some scholars, such as F. Lot and A. Micha,[5] interpret these lines as a reference to the Grail adventures which Galahad, not Lancelot, is destined to achieve. However, *il n'est pas encores nez* is an expression used elsewhere in the text as a strong negative, 'no one in the world' without any suggestion of an as yet unborn hero (*PL* 375.32, 522.26).[6] It would seem that the Lady of the Lake is encouraging Lancelot to undertake adventures by expressing her confidence in his power to succeed in them, with an emphasis on the fact that there is no knight alive who can surpass him rather than on the idea that someone in the future will do so.

It is quite true that there are some clear references in the text to figures connected with the Grail tradition. Joseph of Arimathea is mentioned by name three times. The Lady of the Lake lists him after Maccabees and his brother as one of the great knights of the past, the first after the Crucifixion:

'Si en fu Joseph d'Arimathie, li gentils chevaliers, qui Jhesu Crist despendié de la Sainte Croiz a ses deus mains et coucha dedanz lo sepulcre.' (*PL* 146.17–19.)

This recalls Robert de Boron's description of Joseph of Arimathea as a good knight (*Jos.* 1351–8), and the passage in the *First Continuation* (long version) where he is described as a good knight who carries a sword which had belonged to Judas Maccabees (*First Cont.* II, *E* 4688–96).[7]

Lancelot, after defeating Alybon, stays the night in a religious house in which is to be found the tomb of Leucain, a nephew of Joseph of Arimathea, and here the Grail is mentioned:

En cele maison avoit une sepulture que l'an apeloit Leucain. Cil Leucanz fu niés Joseph de Darimathie, cel dont li granz lignages descendié par cui la Granz Bretaigne fu puis enluminee, car il i porterent lo Graal et conquistrent la terre mescreant a Nostre Seignor.[8] (*PL* 179.1–5.)

This again should be compared with a passage in Robert de Boron's *Joseph*, where Joseph of Arimathea, after handing over the Grail to the Riche Pescheor (Hebron or Bron), remains behind, while Bron and his company go to the West:

> Ausi cum li monz va avant
> Et touz jours en amenuisant,
> Couvient que toute ceste gent
> Se treie devers Occident.
> Si tost com il seisiz sera
> De ten veissel et il l'ara,
> Il li couvient que il s'en voit
> Par devers Occident tout droit,
> En quelque liu que il vourra
> Et lau li cuers plus le treira.
> Et quant il sera arrestez,
> La ou il voura demourez,
> Il atendra le fil sen fil
> Seürement et sanz peril.
>
> (*Jos.* 3351–64.)

There is another significant passage later in the poem:

> Ainsi Joseph se demoura,
> Li boens Pescherres s'en ala,
> Dont furent puis meintes paroles
> Contees ki ne sunt pas foles,
> En la terre lau il fu nez,
> Et Joseph si est demourez.
>
> (*Jos.* 3455–60.)

There is no mention of battle or conquest in Robert de Boron, but in the *First Continuation*, in both short and long versions, Joseph himself goes to England, and he and his company fight their enemies there before Joseph hands over the Grail to the Riche Pescheor and his descendants; he then dies:

> Einz ne finerent de nagier
> Tant qu'il troverent le païs
> Que Dex ot a Josep promis.
> L'Isle Blanche ot non la contree,
> Einsi sai bien qu'el fu nomee;
> Une partie est d'Eingleterre
> Cui la mers clot antor et serre.
> La pristrent port, la ariverent,
> Herberjages i estorerent
> Et ice qui lor fu mestiers.

Deus anz i furent toz antiers,
C'onques nus hom ne lor fist guerre
Ne ne toli plain pié de terre,
Mes ou tierz an, ce m'est avis,
S'asanblerent cil del païs,
Ses guerroierent duremant
Et domagierent malemant;
Sovant a ax se conbatirent
Et gaaignierent et perdirent.
                    (*First Cont. A* 7586–604.)

Et par ce maintint le païs
Josep contre ses enemis
Tant com il ot vie et santé.
Et en la fin de son ahé
Deprïa Deu molt dolcemant
Que il par son comandemant
Li consantist que sa ligniee
Fust par le Graal essauciee,
Et il si fu, c'est vertez fine;
Que puis sa mort n'en ot seisine
Nus hom del mont, de nul aage,
Se il ne fu de lor linage.
                    (*First Cont. A* 7619–30.)

The third reference to Joseph of Arimathea comes in the interpretation of Arthur's dreams by the *preudomme* who, as has been seen, fills part of the role of king's counsellor and interpreter of dreams which belongs to Merlin in Robert de Boron's work. He is explaining the meaning of the *Flor qui Parle*, which, together with the *Lion Evage* and the *Mire sanz Mecine* (Christ) can save Arthur from disaster. He tells Arthur that the flower is the Virgin Mary from whom came the fruit which nourishes all things:

'C'est li fruiz don li cors est sostenuz et l'ame paüe. C'est li fruiz qui saola les cinc mile homes en la praerie qant les doze corboilles furent anplies del reillié. Ce est li fruiz par coi li pueples Israel fu sostenuz quinze anz es desserz, la ou li om, ce dit l'Escripture, manja lo pain as angles. Ce est li fruiz par coi Josep de Barimathia et si compaignon furent sostenu qant il s'an venoient de la terre de promission an ceste estrange païs par lo comendement Jhesu Crist et par son conduit. Ce est li fruiz don Sainte Eglise est repaüe chascun jor. Ce est Jhesu Criz, li Filz Deu.' (*PL* 292.1–9.)

The Old Testament parallels with the Children of Israel being fed by manna (*panes de coelo*) in the wilderness (Exodus 16:4) fit in with the way in which Joseph of Arimathea's journeying with the Grail is presented in Robert de

Boron's *Joseph*, where the parallels between the Ark of the Old Covenant and the Grail, representing the New Covenant, are brought out and the Elect receive sustenance at the Grail Table:

> ... et cil qui au mengier
> Sistrent, si eurent sanz targier
> La douceur, l'acomplissement
> De leurs cuers tout entierement.
>
> (*Jos.* 2563–6.)

The nourishing of Joseph of Arimathea and his companions by the 'fruit' (*PL* 292.5–8) should also be compared with the *First Continuation*, where the Grail provides food for Joseph and his companions:

> Et li Graax menois venoit,
> Pain et vin par trestot metoit,
> Et autres mes a grant planté,
> Ce qu'a chascun venoit a gre.
>
> (*First Cont. A* 7615–18.)

However, in the *First Continuation* (*A* 7587–8) *le païs que Dex ot a Josep promis* is identified with Isle Blanche, which is part of England, whereas this passage in the *PL* suggests that Joseph has left *la terre de promission* (the Holy Land) which had eventually been reached by the Children of Israel after their wanderings in the wilderness.

These periodic references to Joseph of Arimathea, usually in association with Old Testament allusions, serve therefore both to remind us of the religious aspect of chivalry as a defence of Church and people against the strong and wicked, and to set the tale of Lancelot within the tradition of the Grail, another aspect of the marvellous past of the Arthurian kingdom. The allusions to Joseph of Arimathea, connected as he was with the early history of the Grail, are of course to past events, but references to other names, already associated with the Grail or later to be linked with it, are also turned to the past rather than to the future.

Let us look first at the name Galaaz which occurs twice in the text. Near the beginning of the romance the author explains that Lancelot is only a *sorenon* and that his hero's baptismal name was Galaaz:

Et avoit non Lanceloz en sorenon, mais il avoit non an baptaisme Galaaz. Et ce par quoi il fu apelez Lanceloz ce devisera bien li contes ça avant, car li leus n'i est ores mies ne la raisons. (*PL* 1.7–10.)

The promise to explain why he is called Lancelot is fulfilled in one way in the *PL*, in the episode in which Lancelot *discovers* his own *sorenon*, inscribed beneath the slab in the marvellous cemetery of the Dolorous Guard, and thereby earns the right to be called by it. As we shall see in Part II, this promise is fulfilled in a different way and given a new meaning in the *Lancelot-Grail* cycle. The name Galaaz is also given to Joseph of Arimathea's son, who, like his father, is listed by the Lady of the Lake as one of the good knights of the past: 'Si an fu ses filz Galahaz, li hauz rois de Hosselice, qui puis fu apelee Gales en l'anor de lui.' (*PL* 146.19–21.) In Robert de Boron Joseph has no son, and the lineage of the Grail Guardians descends from his sister Enygeus and his brother-in-law, Bron. F. Lot has drawn attention to the fact that in the Vulgate Bible (Num. 26: 28–9 and I Par. 7: 14) Galaad is named as the grandson of Joseph, son of Jacob.[9] The use of the name Galaaz in the list of great knights serves therefore to prolong the biblical reverberations of the names by giving Joseph of Arimathea a son whose name echoes an Old Testament genealogical descent from the first famous Joseph, but can also be used as an explanation of a place-name, Gales. Galaaz is linked to the Grail tradition through being the son of Joseph of Arimathea, but there is no suggestion in the text of the non-cyclic romance of a Grailwinner to come called Galaaz, and the name, in spite of its possible biblical connections, does not bear overtones of a mystical equivalent of Christ, which some scholars have attributed to it in their interpretation of its significance in the Vulgate *Queste*.[10]

This list of great knights contains other names linked with the Grail tradition:

'Si an fu li rois Perlés de Listenois, qui encor estoit de celui lignage li plus hauz qant il vivoit, et ses freres Helais li Gros.' (*PL* 146.22–4.)

In Robert de Boron's *Joseph* Helain/Alain, as son of Bron, was of the lineage of Joseph of Arimathea. The epithet *gros* is not applied to him there, but is to be found in the Prose *Joseph* (and in the *Didot Perceval*), in *Perlesvaus* (under Alain and the variant Julain), and in the *Chevalier as deus espees*.[11] Of these texts the Prose *Joseph* is usually dated early in the thirteenth century, before the great prose romances; the others may well be later than the *PL*.[12] Perlés or Pellés de Listenois[13] is here described as the brother of Helain, and the phrase 'qui encor estoit . . . qant il vivoit' indicates that he was already dead when the Lady of the Lake was talking. This would conflict with the role which Pellés has yet to play in the Vulgate *Queste*; one group of manuscripts, which gives the whole cycle, removes the contradiction by modifying the reading through the introduction of the present tense: 'qui encor est de celui lignage li plus haus et ses freres'.[14] However, a study of the manuscript tradition shows that this is a later correction to the original reading in which Pellés is spoken of as though he were already dead.

The other reference to Pellés in the *PL* occurs in a passage which displays several blatant contradictions with the later branches of the cycle, and again a study of the manuscript tradition provides overwhelming evidence for the authenticity of the reading of BN fr. 768 given here.[15] The author explains that there were only two other women whose beauty could be compared with that of Guinevere. The first is Heliene sanz Per, and there is a reference forward to an adventure later in the story in which she appears. The second is the daughter of Pellés:

> Et l'autre fu fille au roi mehaignië, ce fu li rois Pellés qui fu peres Perlesvax, a celui qui vit apertement les granz mervoilles del Graal et acompli lo Siege Perilleus de la Table Reonde et mena a fin les aventures del Reiaume Perilleus Aventureus, ce fu li regnes de Logres. Cele fu sa suer, si fu de si grant biauté que nus des contes ne dit que nule qui a son tens fust se poïst de biauté a li apareillier, si avoit non Amide en sornon et an son droit non Heliabel. (*PL* 33.8–15.)

This passage provides no preparation for events in the Vulgate *Queste*, where Perceval does not accomplish the adventure of the Siege Perilous, nor is he the son of Pellés or of the Roi Mehaignié, who are two different characters; once again a number of manuscripts (including those mentioned above) correct the inconsistencies, this time in varying ways.[16] The allusion would seem to refer not to what is to come, but to what has already taken place. Although the form Perlesvaus is used in several manuscripts,[17] the reference is in conflict with the *Perlesvaus* since in the romance Perlesvaus is the son of Alain, Pellés is his uncle, and there is no adventure of the Perilous Seat. The allusion would fit in general terms into the context of the Grail tradition as presented by Robert de Boron and Chrétien's *Conte del Graal* (as we have seen, an important text in relation to the *PL*). In Chrétien, Perceval seems clearly destined to be the Grailwinner and has a maimed, unnamed father (wounded in the legs before he died and no longer living at the beginning of the poem):

> 'Vostre peres, si nel savez,
> Fu parmi la jambe navrez
> Si que il mehaigna del cors.'
> (*Perc.* 435–7.)

The *Joseph* and the Prose *Merlin* (based on Robert de Boron) contain the prophecy that the Grailwinner will accomplish the adventure of the Perilous Seat at both the Grail Table and the Round Table and will be the grandson of Bron (Hebron), guardian of the Grail. Joseph is told by a voice from Heaven:

> Meis le te di pour ton confort,
> Que cist lius empliz ne sera
> Devant que li tierz hons venra

Qui descendra de ten lignage
Et istera de ten parage,
Et Hebruns le doit engenrer
Et Enygeus ta suer porter;
Et cil qui de sen fil istra
Cest liu meïsmes emplira.

(*Jos.* 2788–96.)

De lui [Moysés] plus ne pallera on
Ne en fable ne en chançon
Devant ce que cil revenra
Qui le liu vuit raemplira:
Cil meïsmes le doit trouver;
Meis de lui plus n'estuet paller.

(*Jos.* 2815–20.)

Merlin tells Uther (in relation to the Perilous Seat at the Round Table):

Et Merlins respont: 'Tant te puis je bien dire que il ne sera ja acompliz a ton tens ne cil qui engenderra celui qui acomplir le doit n'a encor point de feme prise ne ne set pas que il le doie engendrer; et covendra a celui qui doit acomplir cest leu acomplir avant celui dou vaissel dou graal: car cil qui le gardent nou virent onques acomplir, ne ce n'avendra mie a ton tens, mais ce sera au tens le roi qui aprés toi venra.' (*Merlin*, para. 49, lines 75–83.)[18]

Bron had a son, Alain. Perceval's father, according to the passage in the *PL* quoted earlier, was Pellés, now dead, who was Alain's brother and of the lineage of Joseph of Arimathea. Although there is no mention of a sister of Perceval in Chrétien, one plays a part in the *Second Continuation*, but is not given a name. The passage, therefore, seems to have a composite origin in Robert de Boron and in Chrétien and the *Second Continuation*. The allusion to Heliene sanz Per, to the adventure, yet to be told, concerning a lady whose beauty was a cause for conflict with her knight, not for chivalric inspiration, links up with the love theme to be developed in the work. The allusion to Perceval's sister sets the Lancelot story in the context of existing tradition and relates it to one of the great themes of the Arthurian past, the quest for the Grail.[19]

Similarly, when Gauvain sets out on the quest by forty knights for Lancelot, in order to emphasize the great significance of the quest and to suggest the appropriate background of Arthurian mystery, he declares:

'Seignor chevalier, qui ores voudra entrer an la plus haute queste qui onques fust aprés celi do Graal, si veigne aprés moi.' (*PL* 297.20–1.)

Once again, the words used suggest that the Grail quest has already taken place or, at the very least, been initiated, and the same group of manuscripts which had corrected the two readings concerning Pellés remove the inconsistency with later branches of the cycle, here by omitting the allusion to the Grail quest, which would be out of place in a version in which the Grail adventures form a branch yet to come.[20]

There is one more very important reference to the Grail in the *PL*, just before the departure of Lancelot and Galehot for Sorelois. We are told how four learned clerks of Arthur's court wrote down the adventures of the various knights:

Cil quatre mestoient en escrit qanque li compaignon lo roi faisoient d'armes, si mistrent en escrit les avantures monseignor Gauvain tot avant, por ce que c'estoit li commancemenz de la queste, et puis les Estor, por ce que do conte meïsmes estoient branche, et puis les avantures a toz les dis huit compaignons. Et tot ce fu del conte Lancelot, et tuit cist autre furent branches de cestui. Et li contes Lancelot fu meïsmes branche del Greal, si qu'il i fu ajostez. (*PL* 571.24–31.)

Si que in the text usually means 'with the result that', and I would translate the last sentence of the passage just quoted: 'And the tale of Lancelot was itself a branch of the Grail, so that it was set beside it.'

Two manuscripts (BN fr. 751 and BL Lansdowne 757) give an interesting reading:

Et le grant conte de Lancelot couvient repairier an la fin a Perceval qui est chiés en la fin de toz les contes as autres chevaliers. Et tuit sont branches de lui por ce qu'il acheva la grant queste. Et li contes Perceval meismes est une branche del haut conte del Graal qui est chiez de tous les contes, car por le Graal se traveillent tuit li bon chevalier dont l'an parole de celui tans.

Jessie Weston saw in this proof of the existence of a Perceval Quest within a Lancelot romance.[21] I would, however, interpret both readings in a different way and would link them with formulae used in other passages in the romance.

At the outset of Gauvain's renewed quest for Lancelot, the knights separate and there occurs the following explanation:

Si se taist d'aus toz li contes et parole de monseignor Gauvain por ce que il aquesta de ceste queste. Et neporqant chascuns de ces vint chevaliers a son conte tot antier, qui sont branches de monseignor Gauvain, car ce est li chiés et a cestui les covient an la fin toz ahurter, por ce que il issent de cestui. (*PL* 365.35–366.3.)

Similarly, there is a reference to some *conte* in which all the adventures of Arthur's knights are written down when Banyn, the godson of Lancelot's father, is dismissed from the story thus:

Mais de lui ne parole ores li contes plus, mais li contes del comun devise et les huevres et les proesces de lui. Et cist contes retorne a parler de Lancelot et de sa Dame del Lac et de lor companie. (*PL* 138.33–6.)

There are other references to *estoires* or *contes* in which are related the adventures of individual knights which may not necessarily be told in this particular romance of Lancelot. The author explains that Lyonel gave the skin of the Crowned Lion of Lybia, which he had killed, to Yvain to wear on his shield:

Et de celui lion porta messire Yvains la pel en son escu, car Lioneaus li dona quant il l'ot mort, einsi comme l'estoire de ses fez le devise. (*PL* 358.28–30.)

The episode of the killing of the lion is related later in the romance and is concluded with another reference to the giving of the skin to Yvain:

Et de celui lyeon porta messires Yvains, li filz au roi Urien, la pel en son escu, et por ce fu il apelez li Chevaliers au Lyeon. (*PL* 611.35–6.)

This is followed by another reference to the setting down in writing of the adventures of Arthur's knights:

Et lors furent mandé li clerc qui les proesces as chevaliers de la maison lo roi Artu metoient en escrit, si com li contes l'a autrefoiz conté. (*PL* 611.38–612.1.)

Then Lyonel is dismissed from the story with a reference to his own tale:

Ensi remest Lyoniaus avoc sa dame, ne plus ne parole cist contes de lui ne d'aventure qui li avenist, car il a son conte tot entier. (*PL* 612.12–14.)

The *Second Continuation* also offers an interesting parallel in a passage describing how Gauvain and forty companions set out on a quest for Perceval, which is similar to the account in the *PL* of the departure of Gauvain, in the renewed search for Lancelot (with twenty of the original forty knights). In the *Second Continuation* the companions separate, and the poet explains that he is only going to tell of Gauvain's adventures:

> An l'estoire n'ai pas trové
> Que messires Yvains devint;
> Ne de Lancelot, qui bien tint
> Lou grant chemin o il antra,
> Ne des autres ne dirai ja
> Quiex avantures lor avindrent.
> Des voies, des chemins qu'il tindrent,
> Ne m'orroiz vos avant conter;
> Mais de Gauvain vos voil parler
> Ce que l'estoire nos an conte.
> Or escoutez avant le conte,
> Qui molt fait bien a escouster;

> Que por l'estoire consomer
> Fait l'an lou conte durer tant.
> Assez i avroit plus que tant,
> Qui tot vorroit an rime metre;
> Mais li miaudres est an la letre,
> Et miaudres vient adés avant,
> Que li contes vet amandant.
> (*Second Cont.* 29190–208.)

In the *PL*, in the passage already quoted, we are told that only Gauvain's adventures will be related 'por ce que il aquesta de ceste queste', but it is stressed that each knight has his own tale, for each knight promises, when he sets out on a quest, to tell the truth about his adventures when he returns (*PL* 298.10–15, 406.14–19), and all these adventures are then recorded by Arthur's clerks. This subject will be explored further in Chapter VII. 'Authenticity' is thus given to the tale of Lancelot as narrated in this romance through reference to a written source, compiled by Arthur's wisest clerks. Neither Gauvain's adventures on his unsuccessful quest for Lancelot nor those of his companions are recounted, because they all failed. However, the tale of Gauvain's adventures when he renews this quest, unlike those of his companions, forms part of the Lancelot story, because the finding of Lancelot by Gauvain is an important episode in Lancelot's own progress as a knight, and Hector's adventures, linking as they do with those of Gauvain and Lancelot, are also part of this tale. Yet Lancelot's own tale also forms part of a larger whole, for it is a strand in the web of all the tales written about Arthur's court, of which the most illustrious of all is the story of the Grail. Robert de Boron in his *Merlin* has prepared the readers of the *PL* for this. Merlin tells Blaise:

'Et tes livres, par ce que tu en as ja fait et par ce que tu en feras, quant il seront parti de cest siecle et alé au plaisir Jhesu Crist—de que je ne te doi retraire—et tu seras alez de cest siecle et morz, si avra non toz jorz mais, tant com li mondes durera, tes livres li LIVRES DOU GRAAL et sera molt volentiers oïz, qu'il avra poi chose faite et dite en nul leu qui bonne soit ne profitable dont il n'i ait aucune partie.' (*Merlin*, para. 23, lines 58–66.)

The Grail references in the *PL* do not, therefore, lead up to a Grail quest—rather they lead away from one. They enhance the importance of the Lancelot story by placing it in relation to the greatest tale of all to form one more element in the interplay between the Lancelot and Perceval stories and the work of Robert de Boron so evident throughout the romance.

These references to events lying outside the Lancelot tale, discussed in this chapter and in Chapters IV and V, serve to relate the story to the three main strands of Arthurian tradition which would have been familiar to an early thirteenth-century audience: the 'historical', represented by the allusions to Uther and Arthur's wars and those of their vassals; the magical, represented mainly by Merlin; and the Christian supernatural, represented by the Grail, with its biblical associations and overtones of Arthurian marvellous adventures. The method used is in contrast with that of later writers, *remanieurs*, and scribes, who will increasingly try to contain all the Arthurian world within one great cyclic work, as will be seen in Part II. In the *PL* the tale of Lancelot is thus given an Arthurian 'authenticity' by being shown to be part of a wider Arthurian reality existing outside the individual work.[22] The relationship between the tale of Lancelot and other tales will be explored in the next chapter, which examines in greater detail the formulae referring to *le conte* and the working of the interlace.

VII

The Tale and the Interlace

Allusions to *le conte* and other formulae

Le Conte is the basis of the work, as the recurring references to it make clear. The author does not intervene frequently in the first person singular;[1] the source of almost all comments or explanations is *le conte*, and it is cited as the authority for the relevance and accurate reporting of all the adventures related.[2] We have already seen in earlier chapters that the tale of Lancelot is presented as part of a larger whole, and it is in this context that the references to the *conte* are particularly important. Two passages already quoted in Chapter VI explain that Arthur's clerks recorded in a great book all the adventures of the knights (*PL* 571.24–31, 611.38–612.1). This recording is linked with the oath sworn by knights leaving court on a quest that on their return they will give a truthful account of all that happens to them while they are away. This is explained in relation to the quest by the forty knights for Lancelot:

Et li saint furent aporté, si com il estoit a costume, que nus chevaliers ne movoit de la maison lo roi por aventure querre qui avant ne jurast sor sainz que il verité diroit au revenir de totes les choses qui li avandroient a son escient. Et se il au movoir nel juroit, il lo jureroit au revenir, ainz que il fust creüz de nule rien. (*PL* 298.10–15.)

Gauvain then swears:

Aprés jura messires Gauvains que il verité diroit au revenir, et que il ne revanroit sanz lo chevalier que il aloit querre, o sanz veraies anseignes de lui, et que sanz nul des conpaignons ne revanroit se mort ne lo prenoit. (*PL* 298.27–30.)

Hector too swears an oath before he goes on a quest for the Lady of Roestoc's champion (Gauvain):

Si jure ce que li rois li devise, si con a cel tans estoit costume: que il querroit lo chevalier a son pooir tant comme queste devoit durer—c'estoit un an—et que il ne vanroit sanz lui o sanz veraies enseignes por coi an savroit de voir que il l'avroit trové; et que de chose qui li avenist an sa queste ne mantiroit a son pooir, ne por sa honte covrir, ne por s'anor avancier. (*PL* 406.10–16.)

This is followed by the same explanation given earlier, that all knights who set out on a quest swore such an oath.[3]

Of all these accounts of adventures told under oath and recorded by the clerks only those which have some connection with the story of Lancelot are to be recounted here, for the subject of this romance is the tale of Lancelot; the references to *le conte* apply to this tale and distinguish it quite clearly from other *contes*,[1] and are often used to justify the inclusion of material as relevant to Lancelot's story or its exclusion as irrelevant. For example, as was seen in Chapter VI, the tale will only relate Gauvain's adventures on the renewed quest for Lancelot, although each knight has his own tale, because Gauvain was the only one who achieved his quest (*PL* 365.35–366.3). Hector's adventures are also relevant to the narrative because through his successful achievement of his quest for Gauvain he becomes Gauvain's companion in the last stages of the quest for Lancelot.[5] Therefore Hector's tale is a branch of Gauvain's, and that of Gauvain a branch of Lancelot's. Here I repeat the quotation concerning the recording of the adventures by Arthur's clerks, already discussed in relation to the Grail, because it is essential to the analysis of the concept of the *conte*:

Cil quatre mestoient en escrit qanque li compaignon lo roi faisoient d'armes, si mistrent en escrit les avantures monseignor Gauvain tot avant, por ce que c'estoit li commancemenz de la queste, et puis les Estor, por ce que do conte meïsmes estoient branche, et puis les avantures a toz les dis huit compaignons. Et tot ce fu del conte Lancelot, et tuit cist autre furent branches de cestuit. Et li contes Lancelot fu meïsmes branche del Greal, si qu'il i fu ajostez. (*PL* 571.24–31.)

Not all these tales are relevant to the tale of Lancelot, even if they are subordinate to it and form part of the same larger whole, any more than can be contained within *le conte* the story of the Grail, the greatest tale of all, which dominates all others. Nor is all of Gauvain's tale relevant to the *conte meïsmes* as told in this romance. For example, his adventures on the quest for Lancelot by the forty companions are not related because, like those of his companions, they did not lead him to Lancelot: 'Ne de nule aventure qui lor avenist en la qeste ne parole li contes ci, por ce que il faillirent tuit a lor qeste.' (*PL* 299.17–18.)

There are other shorter formulae used to dismiss incidents as irrelevant or unimportant to the tale: the standard phrase 'sanz avanture trover dom a parler face' is applied to Gauvain (*PL* 409.21–2, 526.4–5.) and to Hector (*PL* 425.19–20). A phrase may be used to introduce a rapid summary of events: 'Ne plus n'en devise cist contes, fors tant que . . .' (*PL* 250.34 in relation to Lancelot; 256.20 in relation to Gauvain). Occasionally an expression in the first person is found. For example, the author avoids giving details of the hospitality offered to Hector with the following phrase: 'Q'en vos deviseroie gié totes les choses?' (*PL* 435.18.)

Short formulae are also used to justify the inclusion of extra details or explanations, introduced into a narrative which usually presents events taking place away from court and from the great assemblies (where people meet together in war or in peace) in terms of the experience of the particular knight whose adventures are being followed during this part of the romance and whose account of what has happened to him will form the basis of the tale recorded by Arthur's clerks. *Voirs fu*, sometimes in combination with *si orroiz comment* or *si vos dirai comment*, is used to introduce explanations related to the past.[6] For example, the episode in which Queen Evaine's children are taken in charge by a knight called Pharien, who had once held land from her husband, is presented in the following terms:

Illuec avint la reine une de ses mescheances, et orroiz comment. Voirs fu que li rois Bohorz avoit en sa vie desherité un chevalier por un autre que il avoit ocis, car ce fu uns des homes do monde . . . (*PL* 18.28–31.)

The return to the point of time contemporary with the narrative line is marked by a reference to a particular day:

Celui jor que la reine s'en aloit de Monlair au mostier sa seror, avint que en cele forest ou ele passoit estoit li rois Claudas. (*PL* 18.39–40.)[7]

En celui tans avoit costume or *Itex estoit la costume* may also be used to introduce explanations (*PL* 134.23–135.15, 406.31–8). There are a number of formulae used to signal the end of such digressions from the main narrative line. For example, after the passage on Arthur's custom of holding great courts to celebrate the principal religious feast days, the main thread of the narrative is picked up again with the phrase 'Au jor de cele Pasque que ge vos di' (*PL* 135.16), which refers back to the opening of this particular section of the story: 'Li contes dit ci endroit que a l'antree d'avri, au jor d'une Pasque estoit li rois Artus a Karahais' (*PL* 134.20–1). A variation of this is to be found at the end of an explanation of the origin of the name Gué la Reine which interrupts the account of Lancelot's encounter with Alybon at this ford: 'Itex fu l'aventure del gué, mais or dirons des deus chevaliers qui se combatent.' (*PL* 181.20–1.)

There are a number of phrases used to introduce an explanation in terms of recent past events for a situation which is present in relation to the point in time reached in the main narrative line. For example, when Claudas sends a seneschal to fetch Lyonel and Bohort, at the time the seneschal arrives the children and their two *maistres* are very disturbed, and we are given an explanation of this distress in terms of Lyonel's character and of the events of the preceding day which had led up to the particular situation:

Li seneschax fait lo comandement son seignor, si prant chevaliers et sergenz et escuiers a grant planté, et vait a la tor as deus anfanz, qui n'estoient pas a eise, ne il, ne cil qui les gardoient, car il avoient a grant leisir ploré et fait lor duel et lor complainte, car Lyoniaus les avoit troblez *et la nuit devant et lo jor.* Et ce fu li plus desfrenez cuers d'anfant qui onques fust que le Lyonel, ne nus ne retraist onques si naturelment a Lancelot com il faisoit. Et Galehoz li proz, li preuzdom, li sires des Estranges Illes, li filz a la Bele Jaiande, l'apela une foiz Cuer sanz Frain, por ce qu'il nel pooit vaintre por chastier, celui jor meïsmes que li rois Artus lo fist chevalier ensi com li contes devisera ça avant. *Mais or oez que li contes dira por quoi* Lyoniaus les avoit troblez, dont il avoient plaint et ploré *et la voille et lo jor meesmes.*

Il avint chose que qant vint la voille et lor mengiers fu atornez a soper, si assistrent li dui anfant . . . (*PL* 60.29–61.5.)

In the description of Lyonel's character there is a reference forward to a comment said to have been made years later. The knighting of Lyonel is indeed recounted near the end of the romance (*PL* 609–11), but without reference to Galehot's words. These references forward will be discussed in the next chapter. When the account of the incident which upset the children is completed, the narrative line comes back to the time of the seneschal's arrival to collect them, that is at the point reached before the switch back to events of the previous day, with repeated emphasis on temporal expressions both at the beginning and end of the explanation. The return is marked thus: '*Qant vint l'andemain* que li seneschaux Claudas ala querre les anfanz . . .' (*PL* 63.36–7). This is followed by a description of the state of Lyonel and Bohort that morning, which is then linked to the time of the seneschal's arrival by the phrases *A cele hore . . . Et lors vint*:

A cele hore seoit Phariens delez Lyonel et ploroit des iauz mout durement. Et lors vint avant li seneschauz, et quant il vit Lyonel, il s'agenoille devant lui, comme cil qui mout estoit preuz et vaillanz. (*PL* 64.1–4.)

The same type of formula is used to move from a general description to a point in time at which a particular event occurs:

Mout estoit granz la corz et efforciee que Claudas tenoit et por lou jor de son coronnement et por la hautesce de son fil qui chevaliers noviaus estoit. Si avoit plus esté larges entre la voille de la feste et lou jor qu'il n'avoit onques mais esté a son vivant, et ancores donast il mout plus ançois que la corz departist, car mout l'avoit amendé la granz largesce qu'il avoit veüe el roi Artu. *Mais la corz fu troblee et ampiriee par une aventure merveilleuse qu'il i avint, et si orroiz quex ele fu.*

La ou Claudas seoit au mengier en tel joie et en tel feste con vos oez, si avint chose que la danmoisele qui del lach venoit entra en la sale, ne n'avoit ancores Claudas que lou premier mes eü. (*PL* 58.20–31.)

Ce dit li contes is the phrase used first to introduce and then to mark the conclusion of an explanation for Arthur's presence in London when the *rendu* travels to see him (*PL* 53.35, 54.3).[8] *Et dit li contes* is sometimes inserted into a passage in order to incorporate precise details about the day and time into the story line in preparation for the narration of a particular incident:

Ce dit li contes que or s'an va messires Gauvains seus et pensis, si chevauche deus jorz antiers que il ne trova avanture dom a parler face. Et tant a alé que li langaiges li change si et anforce que a poines puet les genz antandre. *Et dit li contes que* au tierz jor fu mout main levez et chevauche tote la matinee tant que il vint a ore de prime. Et ce fu an esté, o mois de juin, et si faisoit mout bele matinee, si estoient li aubre vert et foillié et li pré covert d'erbe et de flors, et li chanp de plusors oisiaus retantissent de plusors chanz. *Et dit li contes que* messires Gauvains vint esperonant fors d'une forest et antra . . . (PL 366.4–13.)

'Et ce fu, ce dit li contes, li plus biax anfes do monde . . .' is the opening phrase of a long formal portrait of Lancelot (*PL* 39.15). The formal portrait of Claudas is integrated into the narrative in a slightly different way. No opening formula is used, but the transition from description to narrative is marked by a variation on the phrase which opens the section, here followed by a precise indication of time. The section begins: 'Ensin tint Claudas lo regne de Gaunes et celui de Benoyc sanz contredit' (*PL* 30.3). This is picked up after the description: 'Qant il ot tenuz les deus reiaumes qu'il avoit conquis deus anz et plus' (*PL* 31.18–19). A longer phrase is used to explain why the particular incidents in Lancelot's childhood which led to his rejection of his tutor's criticism are chosen to illustrate the qualities and development of the hero:

Ensin conforte la Dame del Lac Lancelot et asseüre, si com li contes trait avant ceste aventure por seulement la haute parole que il avoit dite. (*PL* 48.4–6.)

A frequently recurring type of reference to the *conte* concerns what the tale has told or will tell. This serves to draw threads together and will be examined in greater detail in the next chapter in relation to other forms of repetition and linkage. It is combined with other formulae to assert the authenticity of the tale of Lancelot as told in this particular romance as being the truth, the whole truth, and nothing but the truth in terms of medieval story-telling. In the conclusion of the non-cyclic *Lancelot* the allusion to the tale is used to stress that care has been taken to include all the adventures which belong to the story of Lancelot and to exclude all those which lie outside it:

Ensi est remés avoc lo roi. Si tast atant li contes de lui, que plus n'en parole, car bien a a chief menees totes les avantures qi li avindrent puis qe la reine Helaine, qui sa mere fu, lo perdié par l'aventure que cist livres conta el comencement. Ne li contes ne viaut amentevoir dont il corronpist la matire. Por ce si a racontees totes les avantures q'il mena a fin jusq'a ceste ore ensi com eles furent contees en l'ostel lo roi Artu et l'estoire de ses faiz lo nos tesmoigne. (*PL* 613.4–11.)

Such a declaration would be familiar to the medieval public and should be compared with that at the end of *Yvain*, the romance of the Knight of the Lion which has just been evoked in the *PL* by the reference to Lyonel's gift of the

lion-skin to Yvain, hence the name Chevalier au Lion (*PL* 611.35–6). Chrétien's
romance concludes thus:

> Del *Chevalier au lyeon* fine
> Crestïens son romans ensi;
> n'onques plus conter n'an oï,
> ne ja plus n'en orroiz conter,
> s'an n'i vialt mançonge ajoster.
>
> (*Yvain*, 6804–8.)

Formal switches to another narrative thread

The longer formulae justifying inclusion or exclusion of material from the *conte*
are often placed just before one of the formal switches of direction in the tale
which serve to articulate the various parts and to interweave the different
strands of adventures, thus giving a close texture to the whole, while high-
lighting the main points in the narrative structure.[9] These formal switches are
usually found in the same place in all manuscripts, although the phrases used
and the precise form of the links made through repetition may vary from one
manuscript to another.

There are usually three elements in the formal switch. (*a*) A declaration that
at this point no more will be said about a character or set of characters. (*b*) An
indication of the new direction which the tale will take, sometimes repeating
information about the circumstances in which the character to whom the tale is
returning found himself at the point when it last left him. (*c*) A new sentence
beginning the next stage in the action, almost always marked by a coloured
initial, usually introducing the name of the character whose adventures are now
to be followed, often with a *qant* clause to place this resumption of a particular
narrative thread in relation to events already told, and quite frequently containing a reference to the *conte*. Typical forms used in the different parts are as
follows: (*a*) 'Mais atant se taist ores li contes de', followed by the name or
other designation of a character (*PL* 18.3, 166.19, 220.21–2, 294.5–6); 'mais d'aus
lo laisse atant ester li contes ici endroit, que plus n'en parole' (*PL* 30.1, 272.28–
30); 'si se taist ore atant li contes une piece d'aus' (*PL* 70.17). (*b*) 'et retorne a',
followed by name of the character (*PL* 18.4, 70.17, 148.40); 'ainz retorne a parler
del chevalier qui l'asemblee avoit vaincue, la ou il se herberja chiés lo chevalier
qu'il devoit sivre' (*PL* 265.2–4). (*c*) 'Li contes dit que qant li chevaliers qui toli a la
reine de Gaunes ses deus anfanz si fu alez an son païs que li rois Claudas' (*PL*
24.36); 'Messires Gauvains, ce dit li contes, puis qu'il fu antrez an la queste' (*PL*
226.3–4); 'Messires Gauvains, qant il se parti de' (*PL* 242.9); 'Or chevauche
Phariens entre lui et sa compaignie' (*PL* 130.18).

There are variations to this pattern. For example, (*b*) may be extended if there is not to be a straightforward switch to the main character whose adventures are to be followed in the next section:

Mais ci endroit laisse li contes une piece a parler de lui et des deux reines qui sont ansamble en Roial Mostier, et retorne au roi Claudas de la Deserte; mais avant parole un petit de la Danmoisele del Lach, et si orroiz por coi.

Cant la Danmoisele del Lac sot de Lyonel et de Bohort, les deus filz au roi Bohort de Gaunes, qu'il estoient en la tor de Gaunes en prison . . . (*PL* 57.9–16.)

Here the thread of the Lady of the Lake's messenger is followed to the court of Claudas where the dramatic events in this section will take place. In long quests, where switches are not frequent, more information may be repeated in (*b*) or (*c*) to give greater cohesion to the text, and this will be studied below in relation to the interweaving of the quests of Gauvain and Hector.

The formulae justifying the inclusion or exclusion of material, which were examined earlier, may be included within the framework of the switch and thus given greater emphasis. An example of this is the explanation why Gauvain's adventures on a quest for Lancelot are related while those of his companions are not (*PL* 365.35–366.3, quoted above). A formula for exclusion, followed by a rapid summary of events, leading directly into a switch, may be found:

Issi s'an part li chevaliers, si oirre tant a petites jornees qu'a l'asemblee vient. Ne de chose qui entredeus li aveigne ne parole li contes ci, fors tant que a la cité ou il avoit fait l'escu vermoil, fist un escu blanc a une bande noire, et celui porta il a l'asenblee. Or retorne li contes a monseignor Gauvain.

Or s'an va messires Gauvains, antre lui et lo chevalier del port et la damoisele qui son ami avoit laissié navré . . . (*PL* 250.32–9.)

The switch away from a character who will not reappear in the story may be given a special form, with a reference to the character's own tale or to the *conte del commun*, as, for example, in the dismissal of Banyn from the non-cyclic romance, quoted in the previous chapter (*PL* 138.33–7).[10] However, this is not always the case. For instance, the normal forms are used in relation to the Queen of Benoyc and her sister, even if the events preceding the final re-assurance of the queens over the safety of their children, and the death of one sister, suggest that the remaining widowed queen has little part left to play in the story, and indeed the tale does not return to her:[11]

Mais a ceste foiz ne parole ores plus li contes d'eles ne de lor compaignie, ançois retorne a parler del roi Artu.

Li contes dit ci endroit que . . . (*PL* 134.17–20.)

Knights have their own tales as recorded by Arthur's clerks, but women, even queens, suffer misadventures or receive homage and inspire deeds rather than actively seeking adventure, so they would have no part to play in the *conte del commun*.

Sometimes a part of the normal pattern may be omitted or considerably modified: for instance (*b*) may be curtailed or omitted if the switch is in the first place to an eyewitness who will carry the news and the narrative line to court:

> Mais plus ne parole li contes ci endroit de lui, ainz retorne en une autre voie, si com vos orroiz.
>
> Quant li Blans Chevaliers ot la Dolereuse Garde conquise et la lame levee, si avoit en la place un vallet gentil home, mout preu et mout viste, qui estoit freres a un chevalier de la maison lo roi Artu, si avoit non li chevaliers Aiglyns des Vaus. Li vallez sot bien que se ces noveles estoient saües a cort, trop seroient volentiers oïes . . . (*PL* 195.18–26.)

> Mais or laisse li contes atant d'aus toz que plus n'en parole, ne del chastel ne de cels qi i sont, tant que leus resoit del parler.
>
> A l'ore que messires Gauvains ot fait lire les letres qui disoient que morz estoit li chevaliers as blanches armes, si renveia Ayglins des Vaux son frere au roi Artu por ces noveles dire. (*PL* 199.33–7.)

Sometimes (*a*) may be omitted:

> Lo soir se retraist li rois en ses loges et sa compaignie. Et la nuit ot si grant doleur entre ses genz que onques n'i ot ne beü ne mengié. Mais or reparole un po li contes del Blanc Chevalier si com il se parti del chastel, la ou la porte fu vee a la reine.
>
> Li contes dit que li Blans Chevaliers chevauche maz et pansis . . . (*PL* 209.1–5.)[12]

Or (*a*) may be omitted and (*b*) incorporated in (*c*):

> Mais au roi poise sor toz homes que messires Gauvains n'a achevee sa queste, por sa grant bessoigne que il avoit a faire, car il ne savoit rien sanz lui tozjorz.
>
> Or revient li contes a Lancelot, qui estoit an la tor de l'Ile Perdue, mout angoiseus et mout pansis . . . (*PL* 532.19–23.)[13]

In the following example there is no (*a*) or (*b*), but the beginning of (*c*) suggests a switch in time:

> Or est Hestors mout annorez laianz. Et messires Gauvains fait de lui mout grant joie. Et il li conte comment il l'avoit anpris a querre et mout le mercia de l'espee que il li avoit anvoiee.
>
> Or dit li contes que a l'ore que messires Gauvains se combatié au chevalier de la chauciee que il avoit navré, et il se tint por outré, et il avoit les serjanz par sa proece si conquis que plus ne s'oserent movoir, si s'an ala droit uns vallez en Sorhaut, ou Galehoz estoit antre lui et son compaignon . . . (*PL* 531.5–13.)

On one occasion (*a*) incorporates a justification for the omission of adventures, and (*c*) is not marked by the beginning of a fresh sentence, but is linked to (*b*):

Ensi remest Lyoniaus avoc sa dame, ne plus ne parole cist contes de lui ne d'aventure qui li avenist, car il a son conte tot entier. Ençois retorne a parler del roi et de sa compaignie, et dit que qant vint l'amdemain de la feste . . . (*PL* 612.12–15.)

It will be noted that the essential characteristic of what I have termed the formal switch is the emphasis given to a change in direction, even if this, as we shall see, may not be a move from one strand of narrative to a completely different one but a dividing of threads, a concentration on the adventures of one character out of a group whose threads had up till then run together. Very occasionally, although the development of the plot suggests that an important new phase in the action has begun, neither (*a*) nor (*b*) is to be found, and no change in direction is underlined by any form of words.

One instance where a formal switch might at first sight have been expected concerns the beginning of the episode of Lancelot's madness. A description is given of Arthur's army surrounding the castle in which Lancelot, Arthur, and several of his leading knights are imprisoned. Then the narrative line moves to Lancelot: 'Or si dit li contes que Lanceloz est laianz tex conreez' (*PL* 551.26). *Ce or Et dit li contes* is used in places where there is no formal switch to another thread; nevertheless, such phrases usually only occur where there is some change in emphasis, such as a move from a general description to a particular point in time, and this is often picked out with a small decorated initial, as is the case here in BN fr. 768 and other manuscripts.[14] It is also characteristic of situations in the romance where two groups are opposed that the narrative line can pass from one to the other without a formal change in direction, as will be shown later in the chapter. It is therefore not so surprising that a full formal switch should not be made here.

The second case is both more unexpected and more complex. After Lancelot, having saved Arthur from the Saxons, has been made a Knight of the Round Table, Arthur and Galehot separate and return to their lands. One would expect a formal switch at the beginning of the journey of Lancelot and Galehot, but this is not found in BN fr. 768, the base text used in my *Lancelot* edition. The situation is complicated here by the fact that it is at this point that the division between the cyclic and non-cyclic versions begins. In almost all manuscripts, whichever version they give, the conclusion of one stage in the story and the beginning of the new one are clearly marked, but for the study of the non-cyclic Prose *Lancelot* only those manuscripts which give that version concern us here. BN fr. 768, 339, Rouen 1055, and Laurenziana 89 inf. 61 end the section thus: 'Si s'an partent atant antre Galehot et Lancelot, si s'an vont an lor païs, et li rois et sa compaignie s'en vont en Bretaigne.' (*PL* 572.2–4.) BN fr. 768 opens the next section with what appears to be a scribal error: 'quil s'en vont entre Galehot et Lancelot qui'. BN fr. 339, Rouen 1055, and Laurenziana 89 inf. 61 read: 'Or s'en vont entre Galehot et Lancelot qui'. *Or* has a small decorated initial, a capital within the line in 339, a large decorated initial in Rouen 1055. Pierpont Morgan 805-6 reads: 'Or sen ua Galeh' entre lui et lanc' and uses a small decorated initial. The other nine manuscripts giving the non-cyclic version at this point[15] mark the new beginning much more clearly, both verbally and with a large decorated initial: 'En ceste partie dist li contes que Galehot s'en part de la maison lo roi artu et retorne an son païs o Lancelot son compaignon qui'. BN fr. 112, 113-16, Bonn 526, and Bodmer 105 also precede this with (*a*) and (*b*) forms. For full details see the notes and variants to 572.4-5 in *PL* II. The majority of manuscripts giving the non-cyclic version, therefore, use a formal switch here; the four which do not, even if they do not contain any of the usual set formulae indicating a change in direction, have some of the repetitions characteristic of the switching pattern. Apart from this one example, BN fr. 768, like the other manuscripts, gives firm emphasis through clearly recognizable formulae to these key points in the interlacing narrative structure.

These moves from one strand to another are skilfully placed in the narrative in order to achieve various effects. They may be used to give emphasis to the start of some new course of action or to underline the completion of a particular stage in the development of the plot or the thematic structure, and in this context the passage leading up to the switching formula can be particularly important.

Departure on a journey or a quest is frequently underlined by a switch and will often be led up to by an account of the preparations for the journey and the motives for it, or the ceremonies to be gone through before starting on a quest. An example is Hector's departure on his quest for Gauvain (*PL* 406-7), with its account of the oath to be sworn, the farewells to be said, the retaining of Hector as Queen's knight, the directions given concerning the location of the object of the quest. The departure on this important mission is picked up again with Hector's thread.

Mais or ne parole ci androit plus li contes de monseignor Gauvain ne d'els, ançois retorne a Hector qui est antrez an la qeste por monseignor Gauvain.
Ce dit li contes que Hectors . . . (*PL* 425.15-19.)

The switch may come at a brief pause in a journey, and this is particularly characteristic of the narrative strand of knights travelling in search of adventure or on a quest, because they have often sworn not to spend more than one night anywhere, unless physically compelled to do so, before they have achieved the object of their journey.[16] For example, the story leaves Lancelot when he spends the night with a vavasour and sets out again the next morning (*PL* 218.20-3, picked up again 220.21-5).

An example of the marking of the conclusion of an important stage in the thematic development and of the narrative structure, both by the placing of the switch and by the form which it takes, can be seen in the way that Gauvain's discovery of the identity of the White Knight (and hence completion of his quest) is presented. The episode in which Gauvain persuades the damsel to reveal the identity of the conqueror of the Dolorous Guard in Lancelot's presence ends with Gauvain's departure for court and Lancelot's rapid disappearance from the assembly:

Messires Gauvains s'an vient atant, et s'an torne au chastel arrieres, si fait liees maintes genz de sa qeste qu'il a achevee. Et d'autre part s'an va li chevaliers, et la damoisele lo siust, et il fait mout laide chiere. Et dui de ses escuiers, qui tote jor avoient esté avoc lui el tornoiement, s'en furent alé avant a l'ostel.

Ensi fu li chevaliers conéüz de monseignor Gauvain, et por ce n'osa il l'andemain venir a l'asemblee, car il cremoit estre delaiez. Si se taist orendroit li contes de lui et de sa compaignie, et retorne a monseignor Gauvain, qui mout est liez de sa queste qu'il a a fin menee. (*PL* 256.9–18.)

The next very short section opens with a rapid summary of the end of the assembly and then moves to the really significant event as far as the identity theme is concerned: Gauvain gives Lancelot's name to Arthur and the news spreads:

Tant est espandue la novelle que tuit lo sevent, et chevalier et dames, par laianz. Et ci premierement fu seüz a cort li nons Lanceloz del Lac, li filz au roi Ban de Benoyc, et qu'il estoit vis et sains, dont maintes genz orent grant joie qui longuement avoient cuidié que il fust morz des s'anfance. Et messires Gauvains aporta son non a cort en tel maniere. Mais ci endroit ne parole plus li contes de monseignor Gauvain ne del roi, ainz retorne au chevalier dont li nons est aportez a cort.

Qant li chevaliers fu queneüz de monseignor Gauvain, si jut . . . (*PL* 257.1–10.)

The two switches made in rapid succession, the sentences immediately preceding these, the information given in the switching formulae, and the phrase used to designate Lancelot, all serve to give emphasis to the end of this stage in the making of Lancelot's name.

The beginning of a new phase in the story at the separation of a group of knights is sometimes given particular emphasis with phrases marking the concentration on the adventures of one character to the exclusion of his companions. The most elaborately developed example of this is the passage discussed in the previous chapter in which the twenty companions all go their different ways on their quest for Lancelot and only Gauvain's adventures are recounted (*PL* 365.35–366.4). However, the parting of Gauvain from his fellows is usually presented in simpler terms, as in the following instance:

Et maintenant les comande a Deu et lor dit que plus tost que il porront, lo sivent. Et il dient que si feront il. Ansi remanent tuit quatre, mais or se taist atant li contes d'aus et parole de monseignor Gauvain.

Or dit li contes que messires Gauvains s'en va . . . (*PL* 371.32–6.)

The move from one narrative line to another may take place in the middle of the action, but this happens less frequently and is used either to achieve special effects of suspense or emotional tension in relation to a particular event or to mark a significant convergence of the paths of two characters. A striking example of this technique of dramatic interruption is to be found in the breaking-off of the account of Ban's journey to seek help from Arthur at the point when he has climbed the hill by the lake to take a farewell look at his beloved castle and city, Trebe:

Li rois apuie lo tertre, car mout viaut lo chastel veoir que tant amoit. Mais or laisse li contes un po a parler de lui et parole de son seneschal. (*PL* 7.10–12.)

The narrative then recounts how the seneschal betrayed his lord and handed over the castle to Claudas and how the city was burnt:

Mais d'une chose fu Claudas mout corrociez, que ne sai li qex de ses homes mist an la vile lo feu, si fu la richesce des beles maisons arse et fondue. (*PL* 9.14–16.)

The story continues with the siege of the great tower of Trebe, the surrender of Banyn the godson of Ban, his revenge on the treacherous seneschal, and departure from the court of Claudas. At that point it turns back to Ban climbing the hill:

Mais ci endroit ne parole plus li contes ne de Banyn ne Claudas ne de sa compaignie, ançois retorne au roi Ban dont il s'est longuement teüz.

Li rois Bans, ce dit li contes, apoie lo tertre por son chastel veoir que tant amoit de grant chierté. Et li jorz commança a esclarcir durement, et il esgarde, si voit les murs blancheier et la tor haute et lo baille environ. Mais ne l'ot gaires esgardé qant il vit el chastel grant fumee, et un po après vit par tot lo chastel flanbe saillir, si voit an po d'uere les riches sales verser a terre, et fondre les eglises et les mostiers, et lo feu voler de leu en autre, et la flambe hideuse et espoentable qui envers lo ciel se lance, si en est li airs roges et anbrassez, et antor en reluist tote la terre. (*PL* 12.32–13.4.)

The sight of his one remaining and much-loved walled city in flames causes Ban's death, and the placing of the switch at this particular point means that no explanations are required which might lessen the dramatic impact of the scene, as we already know that these flames link up with the entry of the army of Claudas into Trebes and that eventually the great tower itself will have to surrender. The link between the account of Ban's journey and events in Trebe is made through the King's visual perception of the disaster from a distance and his tragic reaction to it.[17] A sudden change of direction in the middle of a description of a battle may be connected with the arrival of another character, as occurs, for example, during Gauvain's fight against the seneschal of Cambenic:

> Or si se destorne li contes une piece de la bataille por conter une avanture de Lyonel, lo cosin Lancelot, qui a la cort s'an aloit. Si lo porta aventure par la ou messires Gauvains se conbatoit, si voit les genz qui aloient a la bataille. (*PL* 493.25–8.)

A different type of transfer in mid-action occurs during the confusion which follows the killing of Dorin, the son of Claudas, by Lyonel. The damsel from the Lake, trying to escape with the children, transforms them into hounds as Claudas approaches, sword in hand, and is herself wounded; the king turns from the children who now look like hounds to the hounds who now look like children, his sword breaks as he tries to strike them, and he suddenly realizes that he is trying to kill two children:

> Lors giete jus de l'espee lo remanant et saut aprés, si les saisist; et en cuide por voir mener les deus anfanz, si les baille a garder a cels en cui il plus se fie jusque tant que il se soit conseilliez comment il en esploitera.
> Mais se li rois a duel de son fil qu'il voit a terre gesir mort, li maistre as deus anfanz ne sont pas mains dolant de lui, car bien cuident q'a mort soient livré lor dui seignor. Mais d'els ne del roi Claudas ne parole plus li contes ci endroit, ençois retorne a la damoisele del lac qui les anfanz en mainne et les a de mort garantiz, si orroiz comment ele les an porte la dont ele estoit venue.
> Qant la damoisele del lac, cele qui les anfanz ot garantiz si com vos avez oï, vit que tote fu la corz troblee et que ele ot fait grant partie de ce que ele baoit affaire, si fu mout liee et petit prisa lo cop que ele avoit receü enmi lo vis. Ele en mainne hors de la porte les deus anfanz. (*PL* 68.21–35.)

The story returns to Claudas shortly afterwards, with a much more precise indication of time than is usual in relation to him, as will be seen when the pattern of interlace characteristic of kings is examined:

> Si se taist ore atant li contes une piece d'aus et retorne au roi Claudas.
> Or dit li contes que a l'ore que li rois Claudas ot pris les deus levriers en leu des deus anfanz, si retorna a son fil que il vit mort . . . (*PL* 70.17–20.)

This move from Claudas to the damsel from the Lake represents a particularly dramatic version of a parting of the ways in the middle of turmoil as opposed to the usual formal leave-taking of knights or maidens whose paths are to diverge.

A different kind of effect is achieved through an unusual placing of the switch when emphasis is given to Lancelot's grief at being forced to kill his host by the oath he made shortly after his arrival at Camelot as an unknown youth:

> Et qant il lo vit neié, si an commance a plorer mout durement. Mais or laisse li contes ci

endroit a parler de lui et des aventures qui li avindrent, et retorne a parler del roi Artu, la ou il lo laissa. (*PL* 260.15–17.)

This painful victory over a knight who had shown Lancelot hospitality is again alluded to when the hero's story is resumed:

Si se taist ores li contes atant de lui et de sa compaignie et retorne au chevalier dont messires Gauvains ot aporté lo non a cort, la ou il s'est partiz de la place ou il se combati a son oste.

   Quant li chevaliers qui l'asemblee avoit vencue se parti de la o il se combatié a son oste, si erra tote jor sanz plus d'aventures trover. (*PL* 262.22–8.)

Another unusual break leaving Gauvain and his companions in the enchanted cemetery, perplexed and grieving, waiting to see what will happen (*PL* 199.30–4), raises complex questions concerning the interlacing of episodes and of timing and will be studied in relation to the handling of Gauvain's strand of adventures. One notes also the section ending with the horn being sounded from the tower for daybreak and Arthur entering the courtyard (*PL* 218.3–7, picked up again 218.22–8). The suspension at this point helps to highlight both Arthur's bafflement at the mystery surrounding him and the damsel's predicament, forced by her oath to stay in the tower until Lancelot's return. His failure to release her from her promise serves to motivate Gauvain's first solitary quest for Lancelot.

   In contrast to the kind of examples so far examined, the formal switch may be made, not at a specific point in time, where it serves to initiate or conclude or provide a dramatic interruption, but during a period representing continuity. Where characters are left travelling when the formal change in narrative direction occurs (as for example Lancelot in his litter, *PL* 225.38, or Gauvain with Brehuz, 241.9–11), this might be regarded as just a variation on the motif of a knight setting out on a journey or continuing it after accepting hospitality for the night. The real contrast lies rather in transfers where the emphasis is on a continuing situation, as for example during Lancelot's childhood in the Lake or his periods of captivity or withdrawal, which will be studied in detail later in relation to the handling of Lancelot's adventures.

   The moves to and from the widowed queens in Mostier Reial provide particularly interesting examples of the presentation within an interlacing structure of continuing situations where either the beginning or the end or both may not be clearly defined. The founding of the Mostier Reial and its development are described at the end of the section which begins at a precise moment in time with Ban's ascent of the hill and his death and goes on to describe the disappearance of Lancelot into the Lake. The abbey is built on the place where Ban died and the Queen became a nun, and her life there is described:

Toz les jorz qui ajornoient avoit la dame une costume que si tost com ele avoit oïe la messe que l'an chantoit por le roi, si venoit sor lo lac, et illuec endroit o ele avoit son fil perdu, si lisoit son sautier tex hore estoit, et ce disoit qu' ele savoit de bien et ploroit mout durement. Et la chose fu seüe par lo païs que la reine Helene de Benoyc estoit none, et cil leus fu apelez Mostiers Reiaus. Durement crut li leus et essauça, et les gentis fames do païs s'i rendirent espessement, et por Deu, et por amor de la roine. Mais atant se taist ores li contes de la reine et de sa conpaignie et retorne au roi Claudas de la Deserte. (*PL* 17.34–18.4.)

The story line returns to Mostier Reial with the arrival there of Evaine, widow of Bohort of Gaunes. The two sisters talk to one another about the loss first of their husbands and then of their children. The passage leading up to the conclusion of this particular segment recalls the events which have led up to the founding of the abbey, but also prepares the way for the switch to the damsel who has carried Lancelot into the Lake; hence it provides a link with the beginning of the next part of the romance which takes us into the Lake:

Et lors li comence a conter comment ses sires avoit esté morz, et comment ele avoit perdu Lancelot, son fil, qant la damoisele se lança otot lui dedanz lo lac. Granz fu li diaus as deus serors de la grant perte que faite avoient, et s'eles ne fussient ansemble, ancores fust graindre lor angoisse. Mais de ce qe eles estoient ensemble estoient maindres lor dolors.

   Maintenant que l'abaesse fu illocques venue, si se fist la reine de Gaunes reoignier et veler, car mout avoient grant paor de la desleiauté Claudas. Et puis que eles estoient velees et rooigniees, n'avoient eles garde de lui. Mais d'eles ne parole li contes plus a ceste foiz, ançois retorne a Lancelot, la o il en est portez le lac. (*PL* 20.39–21.10.)

The following account of Lancelot's early years in the Lake ends with a description of his progress, including the phrase 'si croist et amande' (*PL* 24.32) which recalls the words used to describe the progress of Mostier Reial ('crut li leus et essauça', *PL* 18.1). The end of a later series of episodes dealing with his life in the Lake provides the next lead into Mostier Reial in a passage which picks up the one just quoted with the allusion to the two queens grieving together in the abbey, but also links up with the earlier passage with its references to increase in strength (*PL* 18.1–3, 24.32) and to the Queen's custom of going to pray by the Lake where her son disappeared (*PL* 17.34):

Ensi conforte la Dame del Lac Lancelot et asseüre, si com li contes trait avant ceste aventure par seulement la haute parole que il avoit dite. Mais ci endroit ne parole plus li contes de lui a ceste foiee, ançois retorne a sa mere et a sa tantain, la reine de Gaunes, la ou eles sont en Mostier Reial dolentes et desconseilliees.

   Li contes dit que la reine Helainne de Benoyc et sa suer, la reine de Gaunes, sont ansenble en Reial Mostier. La reine de Benoyc menoit mout bele vie et mout sainte, et si faisoit la reine, sa suer; *et mout amanda li leus et crut,* tant que dedanz les set anz que la reine s'i fu randue, i ot bien trante nonains, totes gentis fames del païs. Et puis fist ele tant que a celui leu vint li chiés de l'abaïe.

La reine de Benoyc avoit an cutume que toz les jorz, aprés la grant messe, aloit sor lo tertre o ses sires avoit esté morz et sor lo lac ou ele avoit perdu son fil, et disoit tant de bien come Dex li avoit enseignié, por l'ame de son seignor, que Dex en eüst pitié, et por son fil dont ele cuidoit que il fust morz certainement. (*PL* 48.4–20.)

The move from the general situation as described here and in the earlier passages to the meeting with a *rendu* at a particular point in time is made with the kind of phrase studied at the beginning of this chapter, but in this case without a reference to the *conte*: 'A un lundi matin avint que . . .' (*PL* 48.20–1). The story line travels with the *rendu* from Mostier Reial to Arthur's court and back again; he then departs and this segment ends as it had opened with the two queens together at the abbey (*PL* 57.9–13). The last time the tale moves back from the Lake to the queens in Mostier Reial there is once more no precise link in time, but the reference to their holy life links up with the *beginning* of the last section on the abbey (*PL* 48.9–15) and there are also allusions to Lyonel and Bohort's escape from Claudas:

Mais ci endroit laisse li contes une piece a parler d'els et des trois coisins et de lor conpaignie, et retorne a parler des deus reines qui serors estoient et qui ensemble conversoient en Reial Mostier.

Li contes dit que tant furent les deus reines serors en Roial Mostier que mout furent brisiees del veillier et del geüner et del panser et del plorer et nuit et jor. La reine de Gaunes avoit bien la novelle oïe que perdu estoient li dui anfant, et comment Claudas les vost ocirre, et comment une damoisele les anbla par grant savoir. (*PL* 132.5–14.)

The tale goes on to give a long description of the *boene vie* led by the queens: 'Et se ele estoit de boene vie et de grant religion, ce ne monta rien a la sainte vie que sa suers menoit . . .' (*PL* 132.20–1.) Duration is again emphasized: 'En iceste vie dura mout longuement.' (*PL* 133.8.) The whole segment develops the themes contained in its opening and in the earlier passages on the life of the queens in the abbey: a holy life of austerity and self-denial and a continuing anxiety over the fate of the children. By its conclusion the anxiety is resolved: one queen dies peacefully and thankfully, but Lancelot's mother gains in strength and beauty through her religious faith and practices (*PL* 133.4–8) and continues her peaceful and holy life in the Mostier Reial.

The absence of precise points in time as links for the interlacing of the strand of the queens' story in Mostier Reial means therefore that particular emphasis is given to a different kind of binding together of all four passages through the repetition of certain elements within them. They are also integrated into the main structure of the romance through certain repeated themes or sequences. The growth of the Queen's abbey and its increasing reputation as a place of holy life runs parallel to the growth and development of Lancelot, as is shown by the use of similar phrases in relation to both. There is also a repeated pattern of an episode in which the grieving queens are reassured concerning the safety of their children followed by one in which Arthur and his knights are reminded of the King's failure to avenge the death of his vassal Ban, a type of repetition which will be studied further in the next chapter.

The integrating of activities of kings into the interlace involves the handling of a different kind of duration and raises other interesting questions in relation to characters who may have a major role to play in certain parts of the romance but whose narrative threads are not followed through continuously, as many of their actions as rulers are not directly relevant to *le conte*.

Claudas plays a more active part in events in the first part of the story than does Arthur in the romance as a whole. The tale may take up his tale at a precise point in time (for example, *PL* 68.21–8, picked up at 70.19), but in some places, especially where his role as a ruler (even if usurper) is emphasized, the opening after a switch and the close before one are treated in a different way. For instance, after a section dealing with Queen Helene and Mostier Reial, the narrative moves to Claudas and opens after the formal change in direction with a rapid summary of his conquest of the lands of Benoyc and of Gaunes, and then transfers to Lyonel and Bohort, whose fate is the real subject of the following series of episodes:

Mais atant se taist ores li contes de la reine et de sa conpaignie et retorne au roi Claudas de la Deserte.

Ici androit dit li contes que tant esploita Claudas li rois qu'il ot tote la terre del reiaume de Benoyc et tote la terre de Gaunes, que, puis qe la morz au roi Ban fu seüe, ne vesqui li rois Bohorz que deus jorz, si quide l'an miauz qu'il soit morz de diau de son frere que de la soe maladie. Il avoit deus filz . . . (*PL* 18.3–9.)

The narrative moves back to Claudas and his seizure of the castle of Monlair towards the end of the section, which closes with a sentence implying duration:

Mais qant il ne trova ne la reine ne les anfanz, si an fu mout iriez; et neporqant do chastel se saisi. Et tint endeus les reiaumes an tel maniere. Mais atant se taist ores li contes que plus n'an parole, ançois . . . (*PL* 20.8–11.)

A similar sentence is used to open a new segment, after one dealing with the early stage of Pharien's conflict with Claudas over Lyonel and Bohort:

Ensin tint Claudas lo regne de Gaunes et celui de Benoyc sanz contredit que nus i meïst, et mout fu dotez de ses veisins et d'autres genz. (*PL* 30.3–5.)

After the descriptive passage which follows this the opening is picked up again: 'Qant il ot tenuz les deus reiaumes qu'il avoit conquis deus anz et plus . . .' (*PL* 31.18–19). This leads into the decision of Claudas to go to Arthur's court. The section has a type of ending often used in relation to Arthur—the return of the king to his land: 'Ensin est li rois Claudas repairiez en sa terre.' (*PL* 38.25.) Such an ending makes it easy to bring Claudas back into the story line in the middle of his normal activities as ruler with no need to bridge the gap in between. Thus he reappears in the tale as he holds a great court (*PL* 58.14) and then is personally involved in the dramatic events which follow, so that this is succeeded by a series of switches made at clearly defined points in time. The role of Claudas ends with peace made between him and the barons before the narrative switches to Pharien's final journey to the Lake, where he stays until his death and has no further part to play in the story. Claudas is dismissed thus:

Ensin est la pais faite des barons del regne de Gaunes et de Claudas. Mais or se taist atant li contes d'aus toz et retorne a Pharien et as anfanz lo roi Bohort de Gaunes qui sont el lac. (*PL* 130.14–17.)

The role of Arthur and his court has already been examined as part of the feudal structure forming an element of cohesion within the romance. His importance as suserain in relation to all the adventures of the tale of Lancelot does not mean that his thread is followed without a break: indeed, as we have seen, the very fact that we only have glimpses of Arthur's activities as King of Britain contributes towards the presentation of the Lancelot story as part of a wider 'reality'. This has an effect on the interlacing technique.

During most of the time that Lancelot is in the Lake the narrative line only moves to Arthur (and even then, without a formal change in direction) when someone travels to his court. Claudas goes to Britain and finds Arthur at Logres (*PL* 32.39). This leads into an account of Arthur's wars and a description of his court. Then the story leaves Logres with the departure of Claudas and follows him on his journey back to his own kingdom. Similarly, the narrative next returns to Arthur's court with the visit of the *rendu* who finds Arthur in London. This again leads into a description of Arthur's present situation and activities, prefaced by an indication of the time of year and the phrase 'ce dit li contes' (*PL* 53.34–6). The phrase is repeated with further precision about the date as the story moves from description back to the account of the arrival of the *rendu* (*PL* 54.3–7). When the *rendu* has delivered his message, he and the narrative leave Arthur's court and return to Mostier Reial (*PL* 57.4).

The first formal narrative switch directly to Arthur occurs when the narrative passes from the Queen of Benoyc at Mostier Reial to Arthur's court:

Mais a ceste foiz ne parole ores plus li contes d'eles ne de lor compaignie, ançois retorne a
parler del roi Artu.

Li contes dit ci endroit que a l'antree d'avri, au jor d'une Pasque, estoit li rois Artus a
Karahais, une soe cité mout boenne et bien seant de maintes choses. (*PL* 134.17–22.)

As usual, details concerning the date and the city where he is holding his court
are given. Although this time we do not follow the journey of a traveller to
Arthur, nevertheless it is the presence of a knight from Benoyc, Banyn, godson
of Ban, which motivates this episode of the first royal brooding; it ends with a
description of Banyn's stay at court, and it is Banyn who figures in the concluding formulae, not Arthur (*PL* 138.31–6). The return of the story to Arthur
on the next occasion is motivated by a journey, or rather two journeys: that of
the Lady of the Lake and Lancelot, and that of the wounded knight who wants
to be avenged. There is a formal move to Arthur away from Lancelot and the
Lady of the Lake, who, having spent the Thursday night near Camelot, are on
Friday on the way to court, so that the King's first meeting with the wounded
knight can be narrated before their arrival. The tale leaves the Lady of the Lake
weeping at the thought of her approaching separation from Lancelot:

car mout li faisoit mal li cuers del vallet qui de li se devoit partir, si an sospire del cuer et
plore des iauz mout tanrement. Mais atant laisse ores li contes a parler de li un petit et
retorne au roi Artu.

A cel jor, ce dit li contes, estoit a Chamahalot li rois Artus, car il i sejornoit, et avocques
lui grant planté de chevaliers, et i devoit sa cort tenir au jor de feste Saint Jehan. Au
vendredi matin se leva li rois si main com il pot lo jor aparcevoir, car il voloit en bois aler
por archoier, si oï messe au plus matin que il onques pot. (*PL* 148.37–149.5.)

Again the opening provides details of place and date, and the narrative stays at
the court, where the Lady of the Lake and Lancelot are soon to arrive, for a
considerable length of time. The court is eventually left speculating about the
reasons for the unknown youth's sudden departure for Nohaut without having
gone through the last stage of the knighting ceremonies. These speculations are
linked with both the love theme (the true motive for Lancelot's failure to have
his sword girded by the King) and the identity theme, and are highlighted by
their position just before the narrative switch (*PL* 166.19–21).

Now that Lancelot has left the Lake and started on his adventures as a knight,
the main types of interlace in relation to Arthur are linked with the holding of
great courts and assemblies in battle and with the bringing of news to court.
The formal change of direction to Arthur, often about to hold a great court or
to receive a message or request for help, is used, but does not usually occur
when Gauvain is absent from court. There is often no direct link with the last
appearance of Arthur in the story: the court is presented as part of the recurrent

pattern of Arthur's life as ruler and of his custom of holding courts in various parts of his kingdom rather than as part of a continuous narrative strand.[18]

However, closer links may be made, as for example in switches placed after an *assemblee* when the armies disperse and Arthur returns to his own land:

> Et li rois Artus redepart les soes et prant congié de son maistre, si s'en retorne an son païs et an fet porter en litiere monseignor Gauvain qui mout estoit malades durement. Mais or se taist atant li contes del roi Artus et de Galehot et de sa maisniee, et torne sor la dame des Puis de Malohaut qui lo boen chevalier tient em prison. (*PL* 294.3–8.)

This is picked up by a later point in the interlace which links up both with Arthur's return to his land and with the advice given him by the *maistre*:

> . . . ainz retorne au roi Artus qui est repairiez an sa terre.
>
> Ce dit li contes que il vint premierement sejorner a Carduel an Gales, qui plus estoit pres et mout estoit aesiez chastiaus de totes choses. Si sejorna li rois en la vile vint trois jorz et tint toz les jorz cort efforciee, et mout fist bien les comandemenz son maistre de totes choses. Dedanz les quinze jorz fu messires Gauvains toz gariz de ses bleceüres, si an fu tote la corz mout liee. (*PL* 296.28–35.)[19]

The bringing of news to Arthur's court also supplies a recurring pattern in the interlace and is one of the principal means by which the King and court are integrated into the narrative structure while the adventures of Gauvain and Lancelot take them away from court. A section may open with the beginning of the journey of an eyewitness to court: for example, the youth who witnessed Lancelot's conquest of Dolorous Guard (*PL* 195), who also reports the false inscriptions in the magic cemetery (*PL* 199).[20] Or it may end with news brought to court, when the narrative line leaves the knight errant and follows the messenger: for example, Alybon brings news of his battle with the White Knight at the ford (*PL* 182), and a knight brings the Queen news of Hector's achievement of his quest (*PL* 532). The placing of important news near a formal switch, not only gives it greater emphasis but also highlights the court's reaction to the information, a very important element in a romance in which the making of a name at Arthur's court is one of the main themes.

When Arthur, together with his knights, is personally involved in the adventures, the link-up in time can be much more precise. For example, one segment ends with the King at the Dolorous Guard rising in the morning and going into the courtyard (*PL* 218.4–7). The break at this particular point, as was seen above, serves to underline Arthur's frustrated perplexity over the mysteries of the castle. This is picked up:

> Ne de lui ne sera ores plus parole, ainz retorne li contes a parler de monseignor Gauvain et del roi, son oncle.

Quant li rois se fu au matin levez et venuz en la cort devant son ostel, si ne sot que faire. (*PL* 218.22–5.)

The King's departures on hunting expeditions in the morning and his returns later in the day, both before the switch (*PL* 262, picked up 263.32; 264–5, picked up 272), also help to provide clear points of reference in chronological terms for the interlace.

However, in relation to Arthur the general pattern of interlace and, in particular, of narrative formal changes in direction is characterized by an absence of links involving precise points of time. The moves to the King's court fit into a cyclic pattern linked to the great religious festivals and his royal duty to hold great courts in the important centres of his kingdom, hence the emphasis on time of year and place. The moves away from the King's court are often related to the dispersal of armies and the return of the opposing rulers to their lands. Apart from this, the beginning or ending of a section at Arthur's court usually arises through the arrival of people bringing news or asking for help or information. There is therefore a contrast between communal activity, necessarily associated with Arthur's role, and individual activity and solitary journeys, which knights can undertake (although they too have to return to the King to play their part in great courts and battles), a contrast which is brought out by the type of interlace. It is precisely because Arthur as King has a major role outside the limits of Lancelot's tale, as is shown by the periodic references to his wars, that his strand (and that of his court) is not followed through with the consistency and continuity characteristic of the presentation of the adventures of Lancelot, of Gauvain, once Lancelot has left the Lake, and of Hector, once he makes his first appearance.

If formal moves away from court are not usually picked up at the beginning of a later segment with a reference back to a precise moment in time, a very characteristic pattern is for the narrative to be taken up again at the point when the knight whose adventures are being recounted continues his journey and the messenger departs for court (for example, *PL* 181.36, picked up at the next formal switch, 182.27). Another recurring pattern is that of the departure of a knight from court; the tale does not follow him immediately, but remains a little longer at court and transfers back to the departure of the knight at the beginning of either the next or a later section (for example, *PL* 166.3, picked up on 166.22; 271.10, picked up 272.30). We have the reverse process when the formal switch at *PL* 407.8–12 is away from Hector, as he leaves on his quest, back to the Queen and the wounded knight (*PL* 407.12 links up with 407.1). A return to a character at a precise point in the narrative of his adventures does not therefore necessarily link up with an earlier formal switch away from this character, but may take up the account in the middle or towards the end of a segment, usually at a separation or departure. It is also true that a formal change in direction away from a character may be picked up in the middle of a following section; for example, the last stage of the Lady of the Lake's journey to Arthur's court, with which one train of events ends (*PL* 148.34–40), is picked up at 151.20, when Arthur meets her as he returns from hunting, part way through the next section. These variations in the interlacing pattern give greater suppleness and flexibility to the narrative technique, and make it possible to highlight stages in the development of the two main themes, especially that of the quest for identity.

While it can be illuminating to analyse the effects achieved by the skilful placing of formal switches, it is also important to see where they are not made. We have seen some examples of a departure or separation not occurring just before a formal change in the story line, but being linked with a later one, but there are also crossings of threads and separations which are not marked in a formal way. For example, in a segment which begins and ends with the queens at Mostier Reial, the departure of the *rendu* from there and his journey to Arthur's court to reproach the King receives no special emphasis because he returns to Mostier Reial before the section ends. The great assemblies, as would be expected, bring the paths of the knights errant together. In great battles no more emphasis is given to moves from one side to the other than the occasional use of phrases such as 'd'autre part' (*PL* 79.33, 80.15) and 'Et autretant an refist' (*PL* 310.5). There are, therefore, stretches in the text where there are very few formal changes in direction and others where they occur in quite rapid succession. Apart from a fairly long segment devoted to the struggles between Claudas and the barons of Gaunes, there are a good many in the first part of the romance, where there are three important and geographically distinct narrative centres: Gaunes, Mostier Reial, and the Lake, with occasional journeys to Britain. There are also quite frequent moves during Lancelot's adventures at the Dolorous Guard and during Gauvain's first quest for Lancelot, where they serve to underline Arthur and Gauvain's frantic efforts to find out more about the Unknown Knight. There is a long and important central section without a formal switch, dealing with the last battle against Galehot, the making of the peace, and Lancelot's long meeting with Guinevere in which by her questions she recalls his earlier adventures. As we shall see, in Gauvain's last and successful quest for Lancelot, and in Hector's quest for Gauvain, the number of switches between the questing knights and Lancelot, far away in Sorelois, are less frequent than between Lancelot and Gauvain in the first quest, but, as will be shown, the strands of the two questers are none the less interwoven through a special kind of interlace, as Hector and Gauvain each achieve their quests and all the questers and the quested travel back to help Arthur in the war against the Saxons. The last part of the romance, the Journey to Sorelois and the False Guinevere episode, also has comparatively few formal changes in direction because of the type of narrative: there is no quest by individual knights, and after the opening the journeys, in general, bring the characters together rather than separating them.

Apart from the linking mechanism to be found in the switch formula itself, there are other patterns in the sequence of moves from one narrative line to another, as has already been seen in relation to the moves between Mostier Reial and Arthur's court. Openings relating to different characters may echo the same phrases, or the passage leading up to the change in direction may well contain elements which ease the transition. I now hope to shed further light on these processes by examining in greater detail how the strands of three important characters, Lancelot, Gauvain, and Hector, are followed through and intertwined. I will examine first Lancelot's thread, for this tale is the subject of the romance; therefore, if all his adventures worthy to be related are to be told here, one would expect his strand never to be broken, however much it may be interwoven with those of other knights.

The interlacing of Lancelot's thread

In the first part of the text Lancelot, as a small baby, does not play an active role. He is carried in a basket on Ban's journey to seek help from Arthur; when Ban dies, he is left alone for a short time by his mother who goes to weep over her husband's body, and he is carried off by a damsel into the Lake. The first section in which he plays a slightly less passive role, although still limited by his extreme youth, is preceded by a switching formula, 'ançois retorne a Lancelot, la o il en est portez el lac' (*PL* 21), which picks up the moment in the story when he is taken into the Lake (*PL* 15.28–30). However, the formula (*c*) which opens the new section gives emphasis to the damsel who bore him away: 'Or dit li contes que la damoisele qui Lancelot am porta el lac estoit une fee.' (*PL* 21.11– 12.) The major part of the section is indeed devoted to the Lady of the Lake rather than to Lancelot; it begins with a general description of fairies and then moves into an explanation of how she acquired her supernatural knowledge which takes us into the past as it traces her magic back through Merlin to his father, a devil. The way is prepared for this explanation by one of the transitional formulae referring to the *conte* which were discussed earlier in this chapter:

Cele damoisele dont li contes parole savoit par Merlin qancq'ele savoit de nigromence, et lo sot par mout grant voisdie. (*PL* 21.21–3.)

This is followed by the formula 'voirs fu', which, as has been seen, is often used in the romance to introduce 'historical' information:

Voirs fu que Merlins fu anjandrez an fame par deiable et de deiable meesmes, car por ce fu il apelez li anfes sanz pere. (*PL* 21.24–5.)

The formula 'voirs fu' is also used in the second stage in the explanation, which concerns Merlin's mother:

Il fu voirs que en la maresche de la terre d'Escoce et d'Irlande ot jadis une damoisele, gentil fame de grant biauté, et fu fille a un vavasor qui n'estoit pas de grant richece. (*PL* 21.35–7.)

The return to a time contemporary with the main narrative line and to the account of Lancelot's childhood is marked by the picking up of the opening phrase in the section:

Cele qui l'andormi et seela, si fu la damoisele qui Lancelot en porta dedanz lo lac. Et qant ele l'an ot porté, il ne fait pas a demander se ele lo tint chier . . . (*PL* 24.7–8.)

This is followed by a description of Lancelot's early upbringing in the Lake. There is a reference to a definite period of time: 'Ensi fu trois anz Lanceloz an la garde a la damoisele a trop grant aise' (*PL* 24.19–20), and more descriptive details of the land hidden beneath the semblance of a lake are given. The section ends with a sentence preparing the way for the next description of Lancelot's development, followed by a switching formula:

Ensi est Lanceloz en la garde a la dame remés, si croist et amande si com vos poez oïr. Mais de lui ne parole plus li contes ci endroit, ençois retorne a parler de Lionel, son coisin, et de Bohort, lo fil au roi Bohort de Gaunes. (*PL* 24.32–5.)

The period of three years is picked up again in the following segment in relation to Pharien hiding Lyonel and Bohort:

Ensins les tint plus de trois anz an sa maison si celeement que nus ne savoit qui il estoient fors sa fame seulement. (*PL* 25.4–5.)

The link in time made with Claudas is less precise in a section following the one which relates how he discovered the children after Pharien had hidden them for three years: 'Qant il ot tenuz les deus reiaumes qu'il avoit conquis deus anz et plus' (*PL* 31.18). The narrative thread dealing with Lancelot's childhood in the Lake is continued in a section introduced with a reference back to the period of three years given earlier:

Qant Lancelot ot esté an la garde a la damoisele les trois anz que vos avez oï, si fu tant biaus que nus nel veïst qui ne cuidast q'il fust de greignor aage la tierce part. (*PL* 38.28–30.)

It goes on to expand the theme of the nameless Lancelot's unusually rapid growth and progress, already explored in the earlier section (*PL* 24.7–34), and in particular the reference forwards, 'si croist et amande si com vos poez oïr', and the variety of titles given to the unknown youth (*PL* 24.16–18). These names are picked up again, with a reference back:

Et neporqant de toz cels qui laianz estoient, ne savoit nus qui il estoit fors seulement la damoisele et une soe pucele, si apeloient l'anfant par laianz si com l'estoire a ça arrieres devisé. (*PL* 38.34–7.)

Within this segment a formal portrait of Lancelot is introduced by a formula justifying its inclusion within the *conte*:

Et ce fu, ce dit li contes, li plus biax anfes do monde et li miauz tailliez et de cors et de toz manbres, ne sa façons ne fait pas a oblier en conte, mais a retraire oiant totes genz qui de grant biauté d'anfant voudroient oïr parole. (*PL* 39.15–18.)

The static portrait ends with a comment on the boy's clear ideas as to what he should and should not do:

Et il estoit de si cler san et de si droite antencion que puis qu'il ot dis anz passez ne faisoit il gaires choses qui n'apartenissent a boenne anfance; et s'il avoit an talant a faire aucune chose qui li semblast an son cuer estre boenne et raisnable, n'en estoit pas legiere a remuer, ne ja son maistre ne creüst de nule rien. (*PL* 41.15–19.)

The movement from the static portrait into an incident which illustrates the qualities described is made through another formula: 'Il avint un jor que' (*PL* 41.20). The inclusion of this particular incident as representative of an important stage in his development towards maturity and therefore worthy to be told in the tale is explained in the sentence leading up to the switching formula. This takes us to the widowed queens and to Mostier Reial, which is also, as we have seen earlier, developing in a remarkable way:

Ensi conforte la Dame del Lac Lancelot et asseüre, si com li contes trait avant ceste aventure por seulement la haute parole que il avoit dite. Mais ci endroit ne parole plus li contes de lui a ceste foiee, ançois retorne a sa mere et a sa tantain, la reine de Gaunes, la ou eles sont en Mostier Reial dolentes et desconseilliees. (*PL* 48.4–8.)

The whole section provides a good example of the skilful way in which these passages describing Lancelot's childhood are integrated into the general structure and shown to be relevant to the tale.

Lancelot figures briefly but by no means insignificantly at the end of a segment devoted mainly to Lyonel and Bohort's arrival at the Lake. His instinctive reaction to treat them as equals is recorded just before the switch and is thus thrown into relief, so that the story of the cousins is related to his development as the main hero (*PL* 70.3–16). He also makes a notable appearance in the episode in which Lambegues and Leonces come to see the children (*PL* 106–11), and takes over the main line of the *conte* so that the story of Lyonel and Bohort is again shown to be subordinate to his own in a passage leading up to a formal switch:

En tel penser chevauche la dame jusq'au lac. Et se ele a les anfanz amez et chiers tenuz, or se paine assez plus que il aient lor volenté tote; et ce fait ele por amor de Lancelot. Si se pense que tant les tandra entor li com ele les porra tenir; et qant Lanceloz sera chevaliers, si li remenra Lyoniaus et Bohorz en sa baillie; et qant Lyoniax revenra a chevalerie, au mains li remanra Bohorz en sa baillie. Ensin se bee a conforter de l'un por l'autre. Mais atant lo lait ores li contes ci endroit ester et de li et des anfanz et de sa compaignie tote, si retorne au seignor de Paerne et a Lanbegue qui s'an vont. (*PL* 111.28–37.)

This appearance of Lancelot continues to dominate the thoughts of Lambegues and Leonces de Paerne at the beginning of the next section when the tale turns to the account of their journey back to Gaunes, so that a change in direction is combined with the continuation of a theme explored in the part just ended, namely the admiration inspired by the appearance and conduct of the unknown youth. The next segment that deals with the Lake begins with the journey of Pharien and Lambegues towards it, but again includes the appearance of Lancelot on his return from hunting. The *haute parole* of Lancelot which Lambegues had heard on his first visit to the Lake is recalled and Pharien's admiration for the youth is dwelt upon just before the section ends with a brief summary of Pharien's stay in the Lake until his death (*PL* 131.29–132.5). This is followed by another move from the Lake to the queens in the abbey on its shores (*PL* 132.5–10).

The third part of the story devoted entirely to Lancelot in the Lake opens with a formula recalling the earlier account of his childhood there which began 'Qant Lancelot ot esté an la garde a la damoisele les trois anz que vos avez oï' (*PL* 38.28–9). This one begins:

Or dit li contes que tant a esté Lanceloz en la garde a la Dame del Lac que bien est en l'aage de dishuit anz. (*PL* 138.37–8.)

There is one sentence of general description, then his age is repeated: 'Qant il fu an l'aage de dishuit anz'. This leads into a passage which picks up the theme of the Lady of the Lake's reluctant acceptance of her obligation to send Lancelot to be a knight as soon as the right time comes—a sad resignation to the inevitable which was foreshadowed at the end of the section dealing with the visit of Leonces and Lambegues to the Lake (*PL* 111.28–37); this theme is taken up again before the narrative transfers to Arthur:

Si estoit mervoilles pensive et esbahie, car mout li faisoit mal li cuers del vallet qui de li se
devoit partir, si an sospire del cuer et plore des iauz mout tanrement. Mais atant laisse ores
li contes a parler de li un petit et retorne au roi Artu. (*PL* 148.36–40.)

To return to the earlier part of the section: there follows the pattern seen
earlier of the move from a description of the general situation to the particular
day, with yet another reference to the age of eighteen, 'Qant vint au chief de
dishuit anz', this time followed by a reference to a date, Whitsun. We have
therefore a series of echoes or references back linking up all the parts of the text
dealing with Lancelot's life in the Lake. These represent various stages in his
development over a long period in time, and by their very nature description
plays an important part in them. The technique for weaving into the interlace
these passages giving an account of a period in Lancelot's life of withdrawal
from the outside world is similar to that used in relation to the queens' life at
Mostier Reial, and, as we have seen, parallels are brought out between life in the
abbey and childhood in the Lake. But in the later part of this section, with
Lancelot's departure from the Lake, we move into a different type of narrative
structure and hence of interlacing technique, in which the kind of switch made
will be very different, in spite of the echoes from earlier passages. It has already
been pointed out that the change in direction is made towards the end of a
journey, with precise details concerning the date. The party spends Thursday
night at a place near Camelot, and the tale then leaves them as they start on the
next day to ride to Camelot. The date and the place are picked up in the
opening to the next section to underline the fact that the thread of the party
from the Lake and that of Arthur and his court are drawing together (*PL* 149.1–
4). The two threads finally converge, not at the beginning of a section but in the
middle of one, as Arthur's party, returning from a hunt, meets the Lady of the
Lake and her company as they approach Camelot (*PL* 151.20). This scene takes
up and expands the description of the procession, all clad in white, already
given in the preceding segment, a repetition which is part of an interweaving
process. Once Lancelot has reached Arthur's court, his adventures follow the
familiar pattern of those of a hero of Arthurian romance who journeys to seek
adventure, and we move into a new phase of the interlace.

The first stage in Lancelot's career as a knight (or almost a knight, as he has
not yet gone through the girding of the sword which comes at the end of the
knighting ritual) is underlined by the use of a formal switch. This follows the
pattern described earlier in the chapter of sending the knight away from court
with a brief phrase and ending the section with a short discussion between the
King and Queen and their company on the unknown youth's motive for not
returning to have his sword girded. The story line returns to Lancelot with a
transitional passage looking forward to the task undertaken, 'retorne au vallet

qui la dame de Nohauz vait delivrer', and backwards to the departure of the knight from Nohaut who had already left, 'Or s'an vait li vallez aprés lo chevalier qui vint querre lo secors et aprés son hernois qui avant vait' (*PL* 166.20–3, picking up the knight's departure earlier, 164.23). There is therefore no move from one knight at the end of one section to another at the beginning of the next, but the narrative line stays temporarily with Arthur and the court to dwell briefly on their reactions to the mystery of this nameless youth and his sudden departure before the final stage in the knighting ceremony, thus linking up with the two main themes of the romance.

During Lancelot's first adventures various messengers or newsbearers go to and fro between him and the court without any formal switch of the narrative line (*PL* 174.14–19, 175.15–22, 177.30–2). A digression on the origin of a place-name in a past event is introduced as follows: 'Et cil guez avoit ensin non por ce que la reine . . .' (*PL* 180.37). The return to the main thread is marked by the formulaic phrase 'Itex fu l'aventure del gué, mais or dirons des deus chevaliers . . .' (*PL* 181.20). The section ends again with the reactions of the court, for the story line follows Alybon, the knight of the ford, conquered by the White Knight (Lancelot), to the court, where he tries to find out who has defeated him (*PL* 182.26). Again the formal switch back to Lancelot, picking up his thread at the point where Alybon left him, serves to underline the beginning of an important stage in his development as a knight: the adventure of the Dolorous Guard in which the hero is to learn his name. The phrase 'si erra tote jor sanz aventure trover dont a parler face', a recurring one in the *PL*,[21] is used to make it clear that only the significant events, that is those relevant to Lancelot's progress as a knight, are to be told in this romance. The segment ends with a passage which underlines the fact that he has only achieved the first part of the adventure (*PL* 195.10–19); several other episodes are interposed between the conquest of the castle and the ending of the enchantments (*PL* 250). Lancelot is left resting in the castle, and the departure of a messenger to Arthur's court here initiates a new series of events. The arrival of this messenger starts Gauvain off on his adventures, which, like those of Lancelot, are followed through with no real gaps in continuity until Lancelot's installation as a member of the Round Table. I will discuss later the interlacing of Gauvain's adventures, and, like the tale, now leave Gauvain to study the different kinds of interlace used in connection with Lancelot.

As Lancelot was left resting in the Dolorous Guard, when the narrative returns to him it does not pick up the precise point in time when it moved away from him; instead an undefined period is mentioned, and the relative chronology between the thread of Gauvain and that of Lancelot is provided by the opening:

Mais ci endroit lait ores li contes a parler d'aus et retorne au chevalier qui lo chastel avoit conquise.

Aprés ce que messires Gauvains et si compaignon furent pris, demora grant piece que li chevaliers qui la Dolereuse Garde avoit conquise n'an sot mot. Et qant il lo sot, si an fu tant dolanz que plus ne pot estre. (*PL* 204.23-9.)

The *grant piece* comes to an end with the next sentence starting *Un jor avint*:

Un jor avint qu'il seoit au mengier en une haute tornelle el chief do palais et menjoit si richement que mout se merveillast qui veïst et les serveors et la vaiselemente. La o il menjoit ensin, entra laianz uns vallez et ploroit mout durement. (*PL* 204.29-33.)

It is characteristic of the use of interlace in the work that the story line usually moves between characters without any formal switches when they are in the same place. Thus while Arthur and Lancelot are both in the Dolorous Guard, even though Arthur has still not got beyond the first door, the narrative moves between them without any emphasis on change of direction. A formal switch is made at *PL* 209.3-4, after a description of Arthur's feelings of grief and frustration when he has penetrated the magic cemetery and seen false inscriptions about his knights and has still not been allowed through the inner gate. The next section begins by picking up Lancelot's departure from the Dolorous Guard (*PL* 208.16-20). This repeats, therefore, the kind of pattern seen on his first departure from court. The Unknown Knight leaves, while the story line remains with the King and his company and describes their bewilderment before mysterious events. The formal switch back to Lancelot is used to give emphasis to the start of a new effort by the hero (here the rescue of Gauvain) and the motive which inspires him to undertake it, that is his desire, above all, to win the Queen's forgiveness for the shutting of the great door of the castle in her face (*PL* 209.5-11).

This pattern is repeated again with the next formal change in direction. Lancelot departs, and the story line remains with Arthur, who has at last got right inside the castle but has failed to stop Lancelot and is still mystified by the strange events (*PL* 217-18). There is then a formal switch away from the King with Lancelot's departure to tell Gauvain and his companions that they are free to return to the Dolorous Guard the next day. This time Lancelot does not return to the castle, and the story leaves him setting off on another journey to rejoin his squire, thus marking the end of his first contact with the Dolorous Guard (*PL* 218.18-22).

This departure from the castle is picked up again with repetition when Lancelot's thread is resumed (*PL* 220.24) in a new series of adventures which end in the injured hero being carried in a litter. The adventures are linked to what has gone before through the description of Lancelot as 'li chevaliers qui conquist la Dolerouse Garde'. This type of designation is particularly character-istic of the Lancelot thread and arises from one of the main themes of the work, the making of a name and a reputation. The name Lancelot is not used in the narrative until after Guinevere has identified him: instead a variety of titles are to be found, corresponding to the variety of identities which Gauvain tries to disentangle in his quest for the Unknown Knight. These various titles provide references back to earlier adventures and serve as an important element of cohesion in the work. Thus, a little further on, when Gauvain and Lancelot's paths come together briefly, one of the first names by which Lancelot was known as a knight is used:

Et il esgarde sor destre, si voit venir hors de la forest les deus palefroiz qui portent lo Blanc Chevalier en la litiere, et la voie par ou il vienent assamble a la soe. (*PL* 226.23–5.)

A few lines further on Lancelot and Gauvain separate, and the narrative continues to follow Gauvain. The next formal switch picks up Lancelot's thread at this separation, again as the White Knight carried in the litter (*PL* 229.14–16). The tale follows him to the assembly which brings together Lancelot, Gauvain, and Arthur and his court, and the section ends with a doctor setting off with Lancelot (*PL* 233.24–6), here described as 'li chevaliers navrez', for he acquired a fresh wound at the assembly. This title and the moment of departure are picked up again when Lancelot's thread is resumed briefly, 'et retorne au chevalier de la litiere' (*PL* 236). The end of this section leaves him recovering from his injuries at the castle of the Lady of Nohaut, representing a period rather than a parti-cular moment (*PL* 237.9–11), and it is while he is lying in this castle that Gauvain's thread crosses his when the latter comes to the castle to try to see him. The end of a period of time rather than the picking up of a precise point of departure is marked by the beginning of a section recalling the opening of those dealing with the various stages of Lancelot's childhood in the Lake: 'Tant a esté li chevaliers an la garde a la dame de Nohaut que' (*PL* 241.12) recalls 'Or dit li contes que tant a esté Lanceloz en la garde a la Dame del Lac que' (*PL* 138.37–8). The section closes in a similar way, but now with a definite date for the end of the period of recovery from wounds:

Tant demora li chevaliers laianz que ses mires li dist qu'il estoit plus sains et plus haitiez del cors et des manbres qu'il n'avoit onques esté a nul jor; et bien avoit encores quinze jorz jusqu'a l'asemblee. Or relaisse li contes une piece a parler de lui et de sa compaignie, et retorne a parler de monseignor Gauvain. (*PL* 242.3–8.)

These periods of withdrawal—to the Lake, to recover from wounds, into captivity, to Sorelois—are characteristic of the patterns of Lancelot's interlace, and, after he has left the Lake, often coincide with Gauvain's periods of constant

motion in his untiring attempts to find the mysterious knight. Gauvain too has
his times of withdrawal from active life, while convalescing from wounds, but
these tend to coincide with the assemblies and their immediate aftermath; they
do not isolate him from court but keep him there, so that they have a different
function in the interlace.

This particular period of withdrawal ends, and Lancelot's adventures resume
the pattern characteristic of his times of activity when the tale returns to him
with the repeated description of his situation, as he waits in a hermitage for his
wounds to heal, but now the recovery is completed (*PL* 246.24–6). The resumption of his narrative is linked to a departure on a particular day on a journey
during which he achieves the second part of the adventure of the Dolorous
Guard, the ending of its enchantments. This is presented as the climax of this
particular phase of Lancelot's adventures through the placing of the announcement of the castle's change of name, of great significance in a romance in which
a name or lack of one is so important. All that intervenes between this achievement and the move back to Gauvain on Lancelot's arrival at the place of the
assembly is dismissed as unimportant, except for the making of a shield, a
recurrent theme since, for Arthur's knights, the hero is to be identified by a
succession of shields, not by a name:

Cele nuit demora en la Doloreuse Garde, et au matin s'an torna, que plus nel porent
retenir. Et des lors en avant fu apelez li chastiax la Joieuse Garde. Issi s'an part li chevaliers,
si oirre tant a petites jornees qu'a l'asemblee vient. Ne de chose qui entredeus li aveigne
ne parole li contes ci, fors tant que a la cité ou il avoit fait l'escu vermoil, fist un escu blanc
a une bande noire, et celui porta il a l'asenblee. Or retorne li contes a monseignor
Gauvain. (*PL* 250.30–7.)

Gauvain too journeys to the assembly which brings the paths of the two knights
together with Lancelot's appearance there, where he re-enters the story line (*PL*
253.35) in terms which recall the end of the previous section. The threads of
Gauvain and Lancelot separate again after Gauvain has discovered Lancelot's
name, and the formal switch is used at this point to give emphasis to Gauvain's
achievement of his quest (*PL* 256.16). This important stage in Lancelot's
establishment of his reputation as a knight is also emphasized by the description
used to identify him in the formula of transition: 'retorne au chevalier dont li
nons est aportez a cort. Qant li chevaliers fu queneüz de monseignor Gauvain'
(*PL* 257.8–9). The segment ends with the death of a knight at the hands of
Lancelot. This is the last but one in the series of fights forced upon him by the
oath to avenge the wounded knight he swore soon after his first arrival at
Arthur's court. The place where the change in direction is made, as Lancelot
mourns the death of his opponent, looks back therefore to his first visit to

Camelot, a theme which will be picked up again in his next series of adventures as he returns to Camelot for the first time since he first saw the Queen there and was knighted. Arthur's dreams of threatening disaster are placed between this battle and Lancelot's glimpse of the Queen by the river near Camelot. The sequence in which the trance of a lover is followed by the achievement of great deeds opens with a formal switch in which the terms used to identify the hero are associated with three recent episodes, each a link in a chain: the assembly, the establishment of Lancelot's name at court as the conqueror of the Dolorous Guard, and the series of fights arising from the oath, of which one is still to come:

Si se taist ores li contes atant de lui et de sa compaignie et retorne au chevalier dont messires Gauvains ot aporté lo non a cort, la ou il s'est partiz de la place ou il se combati a son oste.

Quant li chevaliers qui l'asemblee avoit vencue se parti de la o il se combatié a son oste, si erra tote jor sanz plus d'aventures trover. (*PL* 262.22–8.)

The episode in which a passing knight sees Lancelot lost in thought at the sight of the Queen and dares him to follow begins the trance sequence. This is then interrupted when the story switches to Arthur and the arrival of a knight bringing Galehot's challenge. This interlacing of threats to Arthur with Lancelot's trances prepares the way for Lancelot's rescue of Arthur and his kingdom under the inspiration of his love for the Queen, so that the technique of the rapid shift from one thread to another, involving a juxtaposition of contrasting episodes, is given a thematic significance. Once again the description of Lancelot used in the switching formula helps to weave the interrupted sequence together and to relate it to what has just gone before:

Au matin mut li rois, qant il ot messe oïe, et s'en ala en la forest. Ne de lui ne parole plus li contes ci endroit, ainz retorne a parler del chevalier qui l'asemblee avoit vaincue, la ou il se herberja chiés lo chevalier qu'il devoit sivre.

Quant li chevaliers qui l'asemblee ot vaincue ot geü chiés lo chevalier qui l'osta de son pensé . . . (*PL* 264.40–265.6.)

The story line follows Lancelot through his trance and rescue from drowning by Yvain, his capture by Daguenet, the meeting with the Queen and killing of the giants; but it then leaves him and follows Yvain back to court, so that the section concludes with the reactions of the court to the deeds of an unknown knight, not yet identified there as the winner of the assembly whose name has already been reported. This leads up to the formal switch back to Lancelot (here called the knight who killed the giants, *PL* 272.30) which recalls the familiar pattern to be found after he first left Nohaut.

These adventures are the last undertaken in the *PL* by Lancelot as the familiar knight errant. From now on, until he takes his seat at the Round Table, his story line alternates between periods of withdrawal, whether into prison with the Lady of Malohaut or into concealment with Galehot or into madness, and participation in great battles. The knight who killed the giants becomes the knight in the prison of the lady of Malohaut, and the segment ends with a detailed account of the prison and the dismissal of one of the Lady of the Lake's damsels from the story into a convent (*PL* 275). The next section concerns the first great battle against Galehot (the Third Assembly), which inevitably brings a number of threads together with the assembling of all the knights. In the romance great battles are not interrupted by formal changes in direction of the story line; nevertheless, the move from an account of the first day of battle, in which Gauvain plays the main role, to Lancelot in prison is given a certain emphasis. Geographic proximity is used to make the transition to Malohaut, which is near the battlefield, and information is then given about the lady of the land; a sentence beginning 'cele dame avoit *un* chevalier an prison' (*PL* 279.11) is followed by a description of the gaol, repeating details already given, but, and this is unusual in the romance, with no reference back.[22] It is as though this were to underline an important new stage in the story, especially in view of the omission of any allusion to Lancelot's previous designations, which have now all been brought together by Gauvain under the one identity of Lancelot do Lac. The narrative moves frequently between the combatants and, on Lancelot's temporary release from prison, follows him into battle until he withdraws again: 'Mais cil vainquié tot as armes vermoilles, et la nuit s'an parti, que l'an ne sot que il devint' (*PL* 282.30–1). It remains with Arthur and his knights until Galehot announces a truce, and the armies disperse with a formal switch to the Lady of Malohaut and her returning prisoner (*PL* 294.5–10). This section tells of the lady's vain attempts to discover who he is, ending with Lancelot still in Malohaut and the lady still mystified, a familiar note on which to transfer the narrative and one which is linked to the identity theme. This ending, in which the lady has the knight in her prison but does not know his name and suspects that he loves a great lady, is contrasted with the next segment, which begins with Arthur brooding at table (*PL* 296–7) because his knights have not found him the mysterious Red Knight who saved him from defeat and ends with Gauvain's departure on an unsuccessful quest for Lancelot. The formal switch back to Malohaut reinforces the contrast and parallel by picking up the details of the situation rather than an exact point in time:

Si se taist atant de monseignor Gauvain et de sa compaignie, que plus n'an parole, et retorne a la dame de Malohaut, qui mout est a malaise de savoir lo non au bon chevalier et son covine, come cele qui tant l'aimme con ele puet plus amer.

  Or dit li contes c'un jor lo fist fors traire de sa geole por parler a lui. (*PL* 299.19–25.)

This initiates a section which follows a similar pattern to the last one, with the story line following the Lady of Malohaut to and from court during the events which lead up to the next great assembly. More than one thread is taken up from the previous segment without any formal switches. The Lady of Malohaut helps to prepare Lancelot for this assembly as she had done for the previous one; Arthur follows the counsels of the *preudomme* (PL 304); Gauvain and his companions return from their quest, and their shame at their failure to keep their oaths (PL 304) picks up the end of the section in which this failure and the fact that they would be foresworn had already been foretold (PL 299); finally Galehot too returns, again with references back to the army which he brought on the first occasion. The story intertwines these threads, including the drawing together of many past events, during Lancelot's first private meeting with Guinevere when she questions him on his adventures. The threads separate at the end of this part of the text with the departure of Galehot and Lancelot for Sorelois, the beginning of another of Lancelot's withdrawals from the main action:

Au matin s'an torne li rois d'une part et Galehoz d'autre, et s'an va chascuns an sa terre. Mais atant se taist do roi et de sa compaignie, que plus n'an parole, ainz retorne a Galehot et a son compaignon, mais gaires n'an parole ici androit.

   Ce dit li contes que antre Galehot et son conpaignon errerent par lor jornees, que il vint en la terre dom il estoit sires. (PL 356.13–18.)

This is not so much a change of direction as a selection of which paths to follow, once the company disperses after the assembly and the making of peace that succeeds it. Lyonel reappears in the narrative for the first time since Lancelot became a knight, and this means there is one more thread to be interwoven, and one which will be important while Lancelot is hidden at such a distance from court, for Lyonel's journeys as a messenger serve to create some link between Lancelot and the outside world, not only through his visits to court but also by the crossing of his path with those of other knights. The significance of the reappearance of Lancelot's young cousin and squire in the narrative is underlined by the closing sentence before the next formal switch:

Mout fist Lanceloz grant joie de son coisin. Mais or se taist atant li contes de Galehot, que plus n'an parole ci androit, ainz s'an retorne au roi Artu qui est repairiez en sa terre. (PL 358.31–4.)

   The beginning of the next segment links the two sets of lovers through their shared suffering at separation:

Si moinent mout bone vie entre la reine et la dame de Malohaut, s'eles veïssent sovant les deus por cui fine amors les tenoit si cortes que assez i pansoient plus que a tot lo remenant. Et se li dui resont a malaaise en lointien païs, de rien ne se doivent plaindre, car eles ne sont pas an repos, ne a rien ne se delitent que a parler de lor amors qant aise les met ansanble et a panser qant l'une n'et avoc l'autre. (*PL* 359.1–7.)

This passage echoes the repeated references to the anguish of separation to be found in the passage leading up to the formal switch to Lancelot and Galehot leaving for Sorelois (*PL* 355.35–356.6) and in the description of their life in Sorelois after the journey there (*PL* 358.2–6). After this Lancelot plays no active part in the narrative for some considerable time, but the tale returns at intervals to describe briefly his unhappiness over his separation from the Queen. These sections dealing with the period of Lancelot's stay in Sorelois are linked by the same type of repetition as were the visits of the tale to the queens at Mostier Reial. Thus the first formal switch back to Lancelot in Sorelois (*PL* 472.20–6) echoes phrases concerning misery at separation used earlier (*PL* 355–6, 358, 359), and this part of the text repeats the general pattern of the first description of his stay there, except that it ends with a departure instead of beginning with one, and this time it is Lyonel who departs with a message for the Queen.

As Gauvain approaches Sorelois, a messenger brings news of his progress to Galehot, and he moves Lancelot to l'Isle Perdue. The last return of the tale of Lancelot in his hidden retreat picks up in the formal switch the same theme of his pining for Guinevere, then brings the paths of the two questing knights and Lancelot together, and all roads join for the war against the Saxons as Lancelot, Galehot, Hector, Gauvain, and the rest of the twenty companions journey to Scotland to help Arthur. They do not, however, come to court as Gauvain has not yet brought Lancelot to the King and thus completed his quest. Arthur and Lancelot do not meet when they are both captured by the Saxons. Although Lancelot is separated from Galehot and the other prisoners when he is released because of his madness, as has been seen, there is no clear formal change in direction at this point within the context of the two opposing armies. However, a certain emphasis is given to the beginning of this episode of his illness and healing through the use of the phrase 'Or si dit li contes' (*PL* 551.26). It marks a new phase in Lancelot's story which will end with him, for the third time saviour of Arthur, being received publicly in court and becoming a member of the Round Table. Once again a number of threads come together as all the knights return to court, and the passage establishing the relationship between the tales of all the knights and that of Lancelot leads up to the next important change of direction, or rather separation of threads, the second departure of Lancelot and Galehot for Sorelois (*PL* 572), marked, as has been seen, in a number of manuscripts with a formal switch.

Lancelot remains with Galehot throughout the last part of the romance until the final, fatal separation, caused by his decision to remain with Arthur as a member of his *maisnie*. The dreams which foretell Galehot's death through Lancelot precede the move from Galehot to Arthur at the beginning of the False Guinevere episode (*PL* 584). Messengers from Guinevere bring Lancelot and Galehot back from Sorelois to help the Queen (*PL* 596) without a formal switch, and Lancelot does not leave court again. With all the main characters remaining at court, Lyonel's knighting and his killing of the Crowned Lion of Lybia (*PL* 609-12) are not separated from the condemnation of the False Guinevere which precedes them by a formal change of direction or even by an 'Or dist li contes',[23] any more than was the installation of Lancelot as a Knight of the Round Table. It too is followed by the recording of the adventures by Arthur's clerks (*PL* 611-12) with a reference back to the earlier explanation of this practice. The formal switch after Lyonel's battle represents another separation of ways (*PL* 612.14): Lyonel has gone to the lady of the Lion, and once again Galehot returns to his country, but this time without Lancelot. Galehot's thread is followed briefly to his death, news of which brings the narrative back to Lancelot at Arthur's court, and the whole romance ends with the concluding formula, quoted earlier in this chapter, which makes it clear that the subject of the work is the tale of Lancelot and that it must be kept pure of all irrelevancies.

The distinguishing characteristic of the interlacing technique in relation to Lancelot is that the reader always knows where and who he is, even if many of Arthur's knights have no idea of his whereabouts or identity. There are therefore no breaks in his thread, but this does not mean that he has a continuous succession of adventures, as is evident in the pattern of formal switches. There are seventeen to or from Lancelot during a period in one place; ten at the beginning of a journey; seven during a journey; four times Lancelot's departure is not marked by a formal change in direction, but the narrative line stays at court after he has left and the first stages in his journey are picked up by a formal switch at the beginning of the next section. The considerable number of shifts made during a period in one place rather than at a precise point in time is linked to one of the main structural patterns of the work: a series of withdrawals of the hero from the main action interrupts the series of his adventures as an individual knight, withdrawals from which he emerges briefly and incognito in order to participate in general battles which bring all threads together. The placing of the formal transfers of the story line is used to give emphasis to the main stages in Lancelot's progress as a knight striving to establish a name in the world. So do the details given within the switching framework, in particular the terms used to identify the hero, whose name is not used in these linking passages, once he has left the Lake, until he has admitted his identity to Guinevere after the peace is made with Galehot. These designations of the hero for whom Arthur's best knights are searching without knowing his name help to articulate the narrative at each change of direction; the technique of interlace matches closely the nature of the theme personified in the hero, unknown to Arthur and his knights. From the first page the reader knows the identity of the hero of the tale, but is kept aware of the contrast between his knowledge and the ignorance of the characters in the romance through the form of the inter-lace, through the references to the tale, rather than through an omniscient author figure.

Gauvain, Hector, and the interlace

The pattern of interlace as it affects Gauvain, whose narrative thread is also followed without unexplained gaps after Lancelot's arrival at court, shares some characteristics with that of Lancelot, but also shows some interesting differ-ences. He plays no role in the part of the story dealing with Lancelot's child-hood, even when the tale moves to Arthur's court with the visits of Claudas or the *rendu*. He makes his first appearance during the brooding of Arthur after his conversation with Banyn, so that he has some association with the theme so important in the account of Lancelot's youth, that is the death of Ban and the disinheriting of Lancelot, but it is with Lancelot's arrival as a youth about to become a knight that his main role starts as the great established knight in contrast with the young unknown one. This role implies an illustrious past, about which no details are given, for it is made clear at the outset that the tale will narrate only those adventures of Gauvain which are relevant to Lancelot's story. Hence just before the Lady of the Lake and Lancelot ride into Camelot, Gauvain is listed as one of the knights accompanying Arthur to a day's hunting. The mysterious reference to a wound received in a battle against Gasoain d'Estrangot (*PL* 149.8–11)[24] suggests that he has a past, but it is never given the kind of historical explanation that we have for Ban's war with Claudas, because it has not the same relevance to the story.

Gauvain's adventures once Lancelot comes to Camelot are narrated because they have a direct link with Lancelot's life, for Gauvain spends nearly all his time either searching for Lancelot on his uncle's behalf or taking part in great assemblies and receiving serious wounds so that Lancelot has to take over the leadership of Arthur's armies. All his adventures on his first quest for the identity of the conqueror of the Dolorous Guard are followed through, as he eventually brings Lancelot's name back to court; but, as has been seen, the adventures on the quest with forty companions are not told because the quest was unsuccessful (*PL* 299), whereas on the quest with twenty companions only his adventures are told, because he alone succeeds (*PL* 365). In the same way, once Hector appears on the scene as young knight and lover, while Lancelot is hidden away in Sorelois, his adventures on his quest for Gauvain, who is seeking Lancelot, are followed through as part of the tale of Lancelot. His quest is linked to Lancelot through the nature of Gauvain's quest, and he succeeds in that quest and is ultimately made a companion of the Round Table at the same time as Lancelot.

Before Gauvain leaves the Dolorous Guard to look for the White Knight, he swears that he will not spend more than one night anywhere until he has achieved his quest (*PL* 220.4–6). This oath produces the characteristic pattern of interlace in relation to his adventures. The thread of such a quest starts from Arthur's court, and the switches take place not during a period in one place but usually as he sets off at the beginning of a quest (for example *PL* 220, picked up at 226; 299; 365–6), or in the morning after accepting a night's hospitality (*PL* 409), or as he rides along (*PL* 425). Apart from one imprisonment at the Doloreuse Chartre, his withdrawals from the action are the result of wounds received in great battles and keep him with Arthur and the Queen rather than separating him from them, and it is above all during his quests away from court that his individual thread is followed. The way that his strand is interwoven with others varies, but, as with Lancelot, there are a number of examples of switches being made to good effect, whether to increase suspense or to underline important stages in the thematic development.

An example of the interruption of Gauvain's story line at a dramatic point in the narrative is to be found at the end of the first section dealing with his adventures away from court. The section opens with a messenger travelling to Arthur's court with the news of the conquest of the Dolorous Guard; Gauvain goes with nine companions to see this wonder for himself, and the section ends with their visit to the enchanted cemetery, where false inscriptions say that the knight who conquered the castle is dead (*PL* 199.8). This news is confirmed by a damsel. This is the first of a series of events in which Arthur and his knights are misled and mystified by the inhabitants of the castle, and the section ends in the middle of one such mystification, with Gauvain still in the Dolorous Guard waiting to see what happens next:

> Et lors recommencent tuit lor duel, et dient que ja mais ne s'an iront tant qu'il sachent del covine de laianz aucune chose. Si se remainnent ensins et esgardent comment les choses se prendront. Mais or laisse li contes atant d'aus toz que plus n'en parole, ne del chastel ne de cels qi i sont, tant que leus resoit del parler.
>
> A l'ore que messires Gauvains ot fait lire les letres qui disoient que morz estoit li chevaliers as blanches armes, si renveia Ayglins des Vaux son frere au roi Artu por ces noveles dire. (*PL* 199.30–7.)

The suspense is increased by the timing of the next section which opens, like the previous one, with a switch to a messenger, again the brother of Aiglyn des

Vaus, carrying news to Arthur of strange events at the Dolorous Guard, this time the misleading inscriptions seen by Gauvain and his companions in the enchanted cemetery. Arthur, like Gauvain, travels to the Dolorous Guard to see for himself, but his arrival at the castle, where he fails to enter the first gate, is described before we learn of Gauvain's departure from the castle and subsequent imprisonment. The section ends again in suspense and mystification, with Arthur still outside the first door, sending a series of men to the gate at regular intervals for three whole days without being able to learn anything of what is going on within. The King at this point shares the ignorance of the reader as to what has happened to his nephew (*PL* 201.5-8). The tale then switches back to Gauvain grieving over the White Knight and follows the events which lead up to his imprisonment in the Chastelet:

Mais or se taist ci endroit li contes del roi et de la reine et de tote lor compaignie, et retorne a parler de monseignor Gauvain et de ses conpaignons et des avantures qui lor avindrent puis que il furent el chastel venu.

  Li contes dit que qant messires Gauvains et si compaignon orent aprise la mort au Blanc Chevalier et des autres compaignons lo roi, et par les letres des tombes et par la damoisele qui estoit as loges a cui il parlerent, si furent si dolant com li contes a devisé. Illuec demorerent jusqu'a l'avesprier. Et lors avalent jus do chastel por aler herbergier, si encontrerent un vavassor meslé de chienes qui mout sanbloit estre preudome. (*PL* 202.8-19.)

The section ends with Gauvain in prison, where he has found other knights of Arthur:

Et qant messires Gauvains et si compaignon les virent, si orent assez grant joie, car grant piece avoient esté perdu. Et cil refurent lié et dolant qant il les virent laianz amener: lié de ce que ja mais nes cuidoient veoir, et dolant de ce qu'il venoient en male prison. Mais ci endroit lait ores li contes a parler d'aus et retorne au chevalier qui lo chastel avoit conquise. (*PL* 204.19-25.)

The theme of the imprisonment rather than a precise correlation in time provides the lead into the next section. There has been a delay before Lancelot hears of the imprisonment (*PL* 204.26-8) as there has been for the reader and for Arthur, so that the order in which events are related in the interlacing pattern ties in closely with the order in which the characters and reader learn of them.

  The narrative line rejoins Gauvain and his companions briefly with their freeing by Lancelot (*PL* 214.20), in the middle of a section, but it is only with their return to Arthur (*PL* 219) that Gauvain resumes a major role as he prepares to set out in search of the conqueror of the Dolorous Guard. It is at the very moment when he has undertaken this important task that the tale leaves him:

Et lors s'en ist de la vile, et mesire Gauvain prist congié de lui, si entre en sa queste. Mais atant en taist ore li contes de lui et del roi Artu et retorne a parler del chevalier qui conquist la Dolerouse Garde. (*PL* 220.20–3.)

This is picked up with a formula which bridges the gap between the point of departure and the first important adventure:

Mais ci endroit laisse li contes un petit a parler de lui, si retorne a monseignor Gauvain qui lo quiert.

Messires Gauvains, ce dit li contes, puis qui'il fu antrez an la queste del chevalier qui la Dolereuse Garde avoit conquise, erra quinze jorz toz antiers, que onques novelles n'an aprist, tant que un jor avint que il ancontra une damoisele sor un palefroi. (*PL* 225.38–226.6.)

Gauvain's adventures on this first quest are linked to those of Lancelot through a series of crossings of threads as Gauvain in his search comes across Lancelot and fails either to recognize him as the object of his quest or to establish his identity (for example, *PL* 226.23–34, 233.4–11). The two damsels from the Lake also help to provide links between the two threads.

The interlacing of threads in Gauvain's later quest, resumed after the forty companions had failed to find the Red Knight (Lancelot), follows rather a different pattern, as the paths of the object of the quest and the quester cannot cross in the way they did when Lancelot was in Arthur's kingdom. Now Lancelot is at a distance in Sorelois, Gauvain is making his way there, and Hector follows in his footsteps, while Arthur and Guinevere remain in Logres. This first part of Gauvain's quest follows a straightforward chronological line. He sets out from Arthur's court with nineteen companions, five of them ride together for some time and then separate. The formal switch occurs here to indicate the concentration on a single thread (*PL* 366). Three days later, before any adventures worth recounting occur, the five knights meet again by chance. There follows the encounter with an unknown knight (Hector) who weeps and rejoices before a shield. He unhorses Gauvain's companions when they try to question him, but is beaten by a dwarf. Gauvain resolves to follow the knight and the dwarf to learn why the knight behaved so strangely, and again there is a formal switch where the threads separate:

Et maintenant les comande a Deu et lor dit que plus tost que il porront, lo sivent. Et il dient que si feront il. Ansi remanent tuit quatre, mais or se taist atant li contes d'aus et parole de monseignor Gauvain.

Or dit li contes que messires Gauvains s'en va et seust les esclox au chevalier et au nain. Si ot tote jor alé sanz avanture trover. (*PL* 371.32–8.)

Gauvain's adventures are then followed through up to his victory in his duel against Segurades. After the battle the story moves without formal switches between Gauvain, who is travelling to the castle of Helin des Taningues, and the Lady of Roestoc, until the time of her departure for Arthur's court where she hopes to get news of her vanished champion (the still unrecognized Gauvain). This beginning of her search for Gauvain is marked by the characteristic formula:

Et ele muet a l'endemain sanz plus atandre a grant compaignie de gent, et anquiert noveles do chevalier par toz les leus ou ele vient. Mais or se taist ci li contes de li et de sa conpaignie, que plus n'an parole ci androit, ainz retorne a monseignor Gauvain.

Or dit li contes que messires Gauvains et li vallez qui l'an moine sont a l'ostel venu. (*PL* 393.25–31.)

The story line moves back to Gauvain at the point when he reaches the castle of Helin. We are told that Gauvain knights Helin and passes on to his host's sister the tokens given him by the Lady of Roestoc. The section ends with Gauvain's separation from Helin at the river Severn and Helin's journey to Roestoc, only to find that the lady has already left for Arthur's court. The story then switches to the arrival of the Lady of Roestoc at Arthur's court (*PL* 396.22), and it is during this section of the narrative that chronological progression becomes less straightforward.

The author now uses the order in which he relates events to put the reader in the same state of mystification as the people at court, as a series of people, either sent by Gauvain or having met him, arrive to give messages concerning both past incidents of which we have already been given an account and those which have yet to be related. Thus the adventures are told in the inverse order to that in which they happened, and there is an interlacing of strands concerning past, present, and future. The reactions of those at court to these arrivals and messages are described at some length and serve to motivate Hector's quest for the as yet unidentified champion of the Lady of Roestoc, Gauvain. In one way, this recalls the excitement and curiosity aroused at court by the series of knights bringing news of the achievements of the Unknown Knight (Lancelot); then Arthur was inspired by a burning desire to learn more of this knight, and this led to Gauvain's quests for Lancelot. There is, however, the important difference that the reader had already been given the information concerning Lancelot and did not share Arthur's mystification, whereas here the reader shares some of the court's perplexity.

The unexpected arrivals at court (while Gauvain is away on the quest) are as follows: the arrival of a damsel with the strange divided shield is described at *PL* 401–2; Gauvain's meeting with the damsel bearing the shield on her way to Arthur's court is recounted at *PL* 424–5 with a reference back to the account already given of her arrival. The account is given at *PL* 401–4 of the arrival of the knight with a broken arm and the delivering of messages and gifts from the wounder of the knight to Guinevere, the Lady of Roestoc, her seneschal, and Hector. The messages link up with the past: the information which Guinevere gave to Gauvain before he left court (*PL* 364); the Lady of Roestoc's neglect of her champion (*PL* 390); the services given by Hector and the seneschal to the champion before his battle with Segurades (*PL* 383–6). The adventure which led to the wounding of the knight and the charging of him with the message, the handing over of the sword, and his journey to court in the company of the damsel with the shield are told at *PL* 423–5 with a reference back to the account already given at *PL* 420.13–30.

The departure of Hector is underlined by a formal switch (*PL* 407), without the narrative thread leaving the court:

Atant s'an part de la cort au mardi, antre none et vespres, et va au plus droit que il set an la terre de Norgales. Ci se taist ores un petitet de lui et de ses ovres et retorne a parler de la reine et de sa compaignie. (*PL* 407.7–10.)

This is followed by the arrival of a messenger from Helin des Taningues (*PL* 408), who repeats that the neglected champion of the Lady of Roestoc has given away her tokens. This message refers to events which have already been narrated (the battle between Gauvain and Segurades) and alludes to Gauvain's own message about the tokens. However, it also produces fresh information, as Gauvain revealed his identity to Helin, and his helmet is recognized, so that the identity of the knight sought is established after Hector's departure from court. The ending of this section with the message from Helin before he and the Lady of Roestoc are dismissed from the story with an allusion to future dissension between them, provides a link for the switch back to Gauvain, picking up his thread at the point when he separates from Helin:

La dolor que la dame a en son cuer ne vos porroie mies dire, si prant congié trop angois-sosement, et li vallez d'autre part. Et mout volentiers i feïst li rois et la reine tenir l'escu monseignor Gauvain. Mais li vallez dit que ses sires li avoit fait jurer qu'il lo raporteroit a son pooir, et se ce non, bien gardast que ja mais ne retornast vers lui, qu'il lo destruiroit. Por ce l'an laisa li rois porter, si s'an ala li vallez avoc la dame. Mais ele li fist l'escu tolir par force et dit que Helains meïsmes lo comparroit; qant il li avoit celé monseignor Gauvain, il nel deüst mies faire, car il estoit ses hom liges. Et por l'escu et por autres choses murent tel contanz dom il furent puis maint mau fait. Mais ci ne parole plus li contes d'aus, ainz retorne a monseignor Gauvain dou grant piece est taüz.

Ci androit dit li contes que qant messires Gauvains fu partiz de Helin cui il ot fait chevalier, si erra tote jor sanz avanture trover dom a parler face. (*PL* 409.7–22.)

We are then given an account of the adventures of Gauvain which includes the events that led up to the arrival of the messengers at court in the preceding sections. Each time there is emphasis on the fact that the delivery of the messages has already been told in the tale; the section ends with the departure of the knight with the broken arm and the damsel with the shield, whose arrival immediately precedes Hector's departure on his quest, so that again the point at which the switch is made (*PL* 425) provides a link between the two quests. In addition the opening formula of Hector's quest echoes that of the last section dealing with Gauvain: 'Hectors chevauche sanz aventure trover don a parler face' (*PL* 425.19–20.)

From now on the links between the two quests and the journeys of Lyonel are made in rather a different way. In the first place, there is the geographical connection in that Hector knows where Gauvain was last seen, so that he goes to the same places, and these geographical details may be given greater emphasis by being placed near the formal switch (*PL* 524); more details on Gauvain's whereabouts are given when Hector's thread is picked up at *PL* 529. The number of people who can give information increases as Hector gets nearer to Gauvain, as for example the *vallet* whom he meets and the hermit with whom Gauvain had stayed (*PL* 529). Another less obvious link is provided through the crossing of the paths of some of Gauvain's companions, first with Hector and then with Gauvain. Hector rescues Yvain and Sagremor from Marganor during the siege of the castle of l'Estroite Marche; they make a reference to the knight at the fountain who had unhorsed them, without realizing that the knight and their deliverer are one and the same person (*PL* 461). Hector tells them that he is searching for a knight whose name he does not know; he describes his shield, which the others identify as that of Gauvain (*PL* 462), so that at this point, through the meeting with these two knights, Hector learns that it is Gauvain he is seeking. Later the paths of Gauvain and Sagremor cross; from Sagremor Gauvain learns that Hector is searching for him, and he in turn is able to tell Sagremor that the knight who unhorsed him at the Fontaine do Pin was also the one who rescued him at Estroite Marche (*PL* 504). Another linking element between the two quests is that both Hector and Gauvain have some contact, whether directly or indirectly, with the war between the Duke of Cambenic and the King of Norgales.

Links with an individual quest can also give a form of coherence on the narrative level to the successive episodes. For example, much as in a folk-tale where the hero on his journey helps a number of creatures or objects, and earlier incidents are recalled when he in his turn receives help from those he has saved, so Hector rescues a number of people in the course of his journey, and these episodes are not abandoned without trace as his quest continues. Thus Synados, who has been rescued by Hector (*PL* 436–42), sends an offer of help when he hears that Hector is detained against his will at Estroite Marche (*PL* 462). When Hector is attacked by the men bearing the body of a knight he has killed in rescuing Synados, he is saved from death by the appearance of the dead man's brother whom he had delivered from another knight, Guinas de Blaqestan. This link with past events is given special prominence through the reference to the battle against Guinas at *PL* 472, in the passage leading up to the switch leaving Hector in prison (recalling the type characteristic of the Lancelot pattern of interlace). The transfer back to Hector gives further emphasis to these links both by the information given within the switching formula and by the events which begin the new section.

Et li vallez et messires Gauvains s'an vont vers Sorelois au plus droit que il li set mener. Mais or se taist li contes ci androit de monseignor Gauvain et de Sagremor, si retorne a Hestor, qui est an la prison au seignor des Marés, au pere Ladomas, celui cui Guinas de Blasquestam avoit navré o paveillon por s'anmie, et peres Matalez que Hestors avoit ocis qant il secorrut Signados de Vindesores,

Or dit li contes que qant il fu aresté au Chastel des Marés, si vinrent les novelles au Chastel de l'Estroite Marche. Et qant la fille au seignor l'oï, qui mout l'amoit, si vint a son pere et li dit que il lo secorre. Et il dit que si fera il a qanque il porra avoir de gent. Et la pucelle prant un message, si l'anvoie a Synados de Vindesores. Et li mande que cil est am prison qui lo gita des mains a ses anemis, et que il lo secorre, car ausi lo secorra ses sires de l'Estroite Marche a tant de gent comme il porra avoir. Et cil maintenant i vient a son pooir, si asanblent lor genz au chastel de l'Estroite Marche. Et Marganors meïsmes, qui estoit a l'Estroite Marche, manda totes ses genz que il i alassent por lui delivrer. Si furent bien, qant il partirent de l'Estroite Marche, deus mile, que chevalier, que serjant. Et Hestors est an prison, mais cil qui lo tienent n'ont mies talant de lui ocirre ne de faire morir, car mout l'aimme la dame, por ce que il l'avoit vangiee de Guinas de Blasqestant. Et li peres meïsmes dit que no porroit mies faire ocirre des or an avant, que que il li aüst forfait, 'car ge lo sauvai qant il antra çaianz.'

A ces consauz que il tenoient, vint une damoiselle qui mout estoit laianz amee, si estoit niece au seignor des Marés, cosine Ladomas, son fil. (*PL* 515.29–516.17.)

This is an example of a recurring pattern: the opening of a section with the linking of the present situation to incidents in the past and the appearance of a new character who starts off a fresh train of events. Thus once again the place where the switch is made is used to highlight those elements which give coherence to the work.

The two threads of Gauvain and Hector finally come together in the battle on the Pont Norgalois. Both their travels and an eyewitness to the capture of the bridge bring them into contact with Galehot, and, following a familar pattern of the interlace, another messenger brings the news to Arthur's court (*PL* 532). All threads converge with the war against the Saxons, the installation of Hector, Lancelot, and Galehot as Knights of the Round Table, and the recording of the knights' adventures by Arthur's clerks. Hector plays no further part in the romance, and Gauvain has no individual strand in the last part of the work, for he only acts within the context of the court and the company of the other knights and the Queen.

Conclusion on the pattern of interlace

There are therefore variations in the pattern of interlace which reflect the different roles of the characters or the different ways in which the threads can be interwoven. The characteristic pattern of Gauvain is one which emphasizes his constant journeying. People who seek his help comment on the fact that he is hardly ever at court and that he is difficult to find (*PL* 377.11–14, 394.17–19); he swears before he sets out that he will not stop for more than one night in one place; and his characteristic narrative switch leaves him setting out on or continuing a journey. His name is well known, his identity firmly established, but suspense is created by interruptions in the normal chronological order in which his adventures are told. His frequent journeys are part of the tale of Lancelot because it is Lancelot whom he is seeking, but even then only those travels which end in the completion of a quest are narrated. As he is, in contrast with Lancelot, an established knight, unexplained references to earlier adventures which are not told in this romance serve to give him a past, and his present (that is, his adventures contemporary with those of Lancelot, once the latter has left the Lake) is followed through without unexplained gaps. The achievement or failure of each quest is underlined by the positioning of the narrative switch. Its form is also used to bring out the thematic significance of these achievements, particularly in relation to the search for identity. The place of Gauvain's tale in the work as a whole is made clear in passages leading up to narrative switches.

Lancelot has no unexplained past or present as far as the reader is concerned,[25] but the other characters in the romance are in a very different position, and again the pattern of the interlace helps to bring this out by the juxtaposition of contrasting episodes through the shift from one narrative thread to another, and by the recurrent pattern of ending a section with comments and speculations by the court on the exploits and identity of the mysterious knight. The mystery of Lancelot as far as the court is concerned is prolonged by the series of withdrawals of the hero, characterized by a type of narrative switch in which there is an emphasis on duration rather than a link-up with a precise moment in time during a sequence of adventures. This contrasts with a kind of switch in the middle of dramatic events or in the course of Lancelot's wanderings, characteristic of other phases in his career and recalling that typically used for Gauvain. The pattern of Hector's interlace shares elements from those of Gauvain and Lancelot, just as his role as lover and young knight who has yet to establish his reputation has links in parallel and contrast with both these two knights. The threads of other characters are not followed through in the same way. Most of the characters who have an active part to play in the beginning of the story, while Lancelot is in the Lake, are dismissed from the tale before he leaves there. Arthur's thread is never followed through continuously, for as a ruler, however passive he may appear for much of the romance, he has a role to play outside the limits of the tale of Lancelot. Galehot too is in a similar position, and it is this which causes his death. His thread runs alongside that of Lancelot, from his first appearance in the romance until Lancelot decides to remain at court as a member of the King's *maisnie*. Once Galehot's thread is separated from Lancelot, it is soon cut off. The Lady of the Lake sometimes figures in the switch formulae in the first part of the work, but at no time is her thread followed with any continuity, and her sudden interventions in the action, whether in person or through her damsels, are in keeping with her role in the story. The references in the passages leading up to the switch formulae, and occasionally in other places, to adventures which are not told in this tale but are told elsewhere and recorded by Arthur's clerks help to present Lancelot's tale as part of a network of adventures in the wider Arthurian world.

The highly formalized narrative switches are used to mark changes in direction in the narrative, the shift to another thread or the separation of threads, never the coming together of threads. They can serve to emphasize the start of new phases in the action and thus to underline the beginning or the end of episodes, but they do not only separate, they can also link, rather like the *laisse* in the epic which, according to the handling of its opening or closing lines, could isolate one particular phase in the action or link it through repetition to what had gone before or was yet to come. In the epic the use of temporal adverbs or conjunctions is limited, in contrast to the normal pattern in romance, especially prose romance. In the Prose *Lancelot* the timing of events has been worked out with remarkable consistency, as F. Lot has shown,[26] and the relative chronology of events in the different strands of adventures is usually indicated in the switch formula, although variations in the order of the telling of the adventures may be used to achieve special effects, as has been seen in relation to Gauvain, and Ban's death. The switch mechanism serves both to link and to suspend. The changes in direction, the moves from one thread to another, are often prepared for and integrated into the general narrative structure through the use of repetition, contrast, and parallel, and it is this use of repetition outside the pattern of interlace in the narrower sense which it is proposed to examine in the next two chapters.

VIII

Repetition and other linking devices

Frequent repetition of familiar episodes and situations and the doubling of characters are features of Arthurian romance which may in some texts produce a monotonous effect. However, repetition, contrasts, and parallels can be used with subtlety and to good purpose, especially at a time when logical development of plot according to modern ideas of cause and effect often plays a restricted role in literary structure.[1] The non-cyclic Prose *Lancelot* provides a particularly good example of the skilful use of repetition both to give a firm texture and cohesion to the romance and to bring out the complex relationship between the individual work and a wider whole, existing beyond the text and encompassing it.

Types of linking devices

Types of repetition and linking motifs can be classified in terms either of motivation or of references forward and back. The repetition may consist of similar sequences, episodes, or smaller details, phrases, with no explicit links made between the repeated elements, although such repetitions are usually motivated in other terms through their integration into the thematic structure, an integration sometimes involving echoes of other Arthurian romances. For example, both Lancelot and Hector rescue knights falsely accused of misbehaviour with other knights' ladies (*PL* 221–3, 425–31). This echoes an episode in the *Conte del Graal* (3780–4085) and forms an element in the pairing of Lancelot and Hector as young knightly lovers who still have to make their name, a pairing which is related to the two main themes of identity and love and will be explored further below, pp. 231–5. Such repeated episodes or sequences, even if they contain no explicit cross-references by the tale or by one of the characters, do not appear gratuitous or unmotivated, because they may link up with the traditional behaviour of a particular character or type in Arthurian romance. An example of this is to be found in the lovers' trances of Lancelot and Hector which constitute an important element in the thematic structure and are also linked to the literary tradition concerning Lancelot and to the conventions of *fin' amor* existing outside the romance. Royal broodings could be placed in this category. These are linked both to the passive role assigned to Arthur in many Arthurian romances and to his function in this particular romance. There are two repeated sequences in which Lancelot's trances and Arthur's lapses into abstraction interlace (*PL* 206–8, 215–16). The series of episodes illustrating Kay's discourtesy and boastfulness, a recurring theme in Arthurian romance, provides another example (*PL* 175–6, 213–14, 368–70, 602).[2] Gauvain's repeated claim that he never hides his name (*PL* 476, 499) and the stopping of battles once his identity is known (*PL* 243, 245–6, 527–8, 537) pick up a common tradition,[3] but also form an important element in a series of contrasts between Gauvain and Lancelot which are closely related to the identity theme and will be examined further in the analysis of 'pairing' below.

We have seen in the previous chapter that the technique of interlace involves repetition. It may also arise from the basic narrative structure whose recurring elements are closely linked to the traditional framework of Arthurian romance.[4] These may often be bound up with the two main themes of the *PL* and in some cases also correspond to the emphasis on the feudal structure of the Arthurian kingdom, which, as we have seen in Chapter IV, is given special prominence in this particular work. The general narrative framework consists of an interlacing of the following elements (all references are to the *PL*):

A.   A series of withdrawals of Lancelot (echoed occasionally by a withdrawal of Lyonel or Hector who are sometimes paired with him).

1. Withdrawal into the Lake:

   (*a*) Lancelot is carried off by the Lady of the Lake (15).

   (*b*) Lyonel and Bohort are removed to the Lake by a damsel (69–70).

2. Retreats of Lancelot for the healing of wounds:

   (*a*) In a religious house (223–4) and in a curtained litter (225–6, 229–30), before the First Assembly.

   (*b*) With the Lady of Nohaut and elsewhere after the First Assembly (233, 236–42).

3. Imprisonments:

   (*a*) Lancelot imprisoned in Malohaut before the Third Assembly (275, 279–80); he is released to fight in the assembly (281–2), returns to prison (294), and is finally freed in time to fight in the Fourth Assembly (308–9).

   (*b*) Echoed by Hector's imprisonment for killing a knight (471–2) and release to fight for a lady (517).

4. Departures with Galehot for Sorelois:

   (*a*) After the Fourth Assembly (356–8).

   (*b*) After his installation as Knight of the Round Table (572).

B.   A series of quests for Lancelot by Gauvain and other knights, stemming from these withdrawals; these quests are undertaken to discover the identity of the Unknown Knight under his various guises in a succession of different-coloured arms.

1. Gauvain's first quest to find the identity of the White Knight, conqueror of the Dolorous Guard, and to release the damsel from her promise to stay in the tower until the White Knight returns (beginning 220, successful conclusion 256-7).

2. Gauvain's quest as one of forty companions seeking the Red Knight who had saved Arthur from defeat in the Third Assembly (beginning 297-9, abandonment 304).

3. (*a*) Gauvain's quest as one of twenty companions to make good the failure of the forty companions (beginning 361-5, successful conclusion 566).

   (*b*) Doubled with Hector's quest for Gauvain (beginning 406-7, Hector finds Gauvain 529-31, news reaches court 532).

The undertaking of these quests or of other knightly tasks follows a traditional pattern: the swearing of oaths neither to return until the task has been achieved (298, 363.5, 406) nor to stay more than one night in any one place (220.4-6, 361.39-362.1);[5] and to tell the truth on return (298, 406); the listing of the company of knights which is to undertake the quest (298-9, 364).[6]

C.   A series of great courts[7] bring Arthur and his knights together and attract visitors and messengers as well as providing a setting-off point for adventures and quests.

1. Visits to Arthur's great courts, linked with Arthur's failure to protect or avenge his vassals Ban and Bohort:

   (*a*) (i) Visit of *rendu* to Arthur's court (54-7); echoed later by the visit of the *preudomme* to Arthur after the Third Assembly (283-94).

   (ii) Doubled by visit of damsel from the Lake to court of Claudas (58-68).

2. (*a*) (i) The Feast of St John at which Lancelot is made a knight (except for the final girding of the sword) and undertakes his first knightly adventure (152-66).

   (ii) Doubled with the court (at Easter) at which Lyonel is made a knight and undertakes his first adventure and becomes a Knight of the Round Table (609-11).

   (*b*) Court (sixth day before the Feast of All Saints) at which Lancelot is installed as a companion of the Round Table (571).

   (*c*) Court (Christmas) at which Lancelot establishes Guinevere's identity and the integrity of the Round Table, brought as part of her dowry (594-608).

3. Messengers reaching court with news of Lancelot's achievements or of Gauvain's progress in establishing his identity (181-2, 196, 223, 401-9, 532).

4. Courts as a point of departure for quests:

   (*a*) Quest for the Red Knight (297-9).

   (*b*) Quest renewed (361-5).

D.   Battle assemblies[8] which bring Arthur and his knights and Lancelot together alternate with the quests for Lancelot and mark stages in the making of his name.

1. First Assembly, against the Roi d'Outre les Marches (230–4).
2. Second Assembly, against the Roi d'Outre les Marches (253–6).
3. Third Assembly, against Galehot, lord of the Roi d'Outre les Marches, with Gauvain seriously wounded on the first day of the battle (276–82).
4. Fourth Assembly, against Galehot, with Gauvain again wounded on the first day of the battle (304–27).
5. The war against the Saxons (539–68).

References back and the fulfilment of promises and predictions

Explicit connections between repeated elements may be made. A reference back may serve to provide a common element and motivate part of the repetition: for example, two sequences of dreams and interpretations which involve predictions and then their fulfilment, the first of which concerns Arthur (*PL* 260–2, 282–94, 327–8), the second, Galehot (*PL* 575–83, 612.28–9). Galehot sends for Arthur's wise men to interpret his dreams (*PL* 578.28–30), and in this they are more successful than they had been with Arthur's dreams, when the King needed the help of the *preudomme* to interpret the interpretation. There is also a link in the content of the dreams, once they have been interpreted: the war between Arthur and Galehot in which Arthur almost lost his land, as predicted by his clerks (*PL* 282.32–4, 322.14), also figures in Galehot's dream. These sequences, in addition, echo similar ones in earlier Arthurian tradition, in particular the version to be found in Robert de Boron's *Merlin*. Once again, the internal pairing is combined with an allusion to a wider Arthurian world lying outside the romance by means of variations on a theme already familiar to the author's thirteenth-century public.

   Repetition often takes the form of fulfilment of promises and predictions, with an explicit reference back to the making of the promise, the swearing of the oath, or the occasion on which the prediction was made. A series of almost identical single combats stems from Lancelot's injudicious promise, as a youth barely knighted, to avenge the wounded knight against anyone who loved the wounder (already dead) more than the wounded; *PL* 149.16–151.3, 160.7–20 describe the oath to be taken and the swearing of it; *PL* 224–5, 227.11–15, 258–60, 273–4 describe the combats arising from it. These battles are not directly linked to either of the main themes. Arthur had advised his knights not to

undertake such an open-ended commitment, and the destructive effects of
Lancelot's rash promise are underlined by his bitter regrets on each occasion
that he is compelled to kill a guiltless knight. There is a reference back in every
case to the oath he has sworn—an oath that leads to his imprisonment by the
Lady of Malohaut. A variation on the rash promise which has to be fulfilled to
the regret of the promiser is to be found in twinned form in the two episodes in
which first Gauvain and Hector (*PL* 532.37–533.3), and then Lancelot and
Galehot (*PL* 540.11–13), in return for information, promise to do what a damsel
asks them on a future occasion.[9] The fulfilment of these promises also leads to
imprisonment, this time by the Saxons (*PL* 548). A promise and its fulfilment
providing a thread of continuity intertwining with the identity theme is made
by the damsel from the Lake, who has promised not to leave the Dolorous
Guard until Lancelot returns or sends a message releasing her from her promise.
Gauvain in his turn promises to discover the identity of the conqueror of the
Dolorous Guard and to obtain the damsel's release, and so sets out on his first
quest for Lancelot. Another damsel from the Lake promises to tell Gauvain the
name of the Unknown Knight if he takes her to him. A prediction to be fulfilled interlaces with this set of promises and plays an important part in the
development of the identity theme. The first damsel prophesies that Gauvain
will see the Unknown Knight at the First, Second, and Third Assemblies: the
prediction is made *PL* 219.38–9, picked up 232.25–6, fulfilled 255–7, picked up
again 272.1–3, 272.9–18. As we have already seen in Chapter V, although the
marvellous can be used to suspend natural, logical connections, it can also,
through the framework of prediction and fulfilment, act as a form of cohesion.

Delay in the fulfilment of promises or the accomplishment of tasks can also
lead to a repeated pattern constituting a connecting thread through a succession
of adventures. Thus Arthur's brooding over the disappearance of the Red
Knight and the failure of the forty companions to keep their oath not to return
without news of the Unknown Knight leads to another of his broodings
followed by another swearing of oaths and by the quest undertaken by the
twenty companions. The delay in ending the enchantments at the Dolorous
Guard is linked with a repeated series of escapes of the lord of the castle,
Brandin des Illes: *PL* 194, 195, 200, 206, 214. This means that the enchantments
can only be ended either by Lancelot staying in the Dolorous Guard (hence
repeated attempts by the inhabitants to mystify Arthur into detaining Lancelot)
or by undertaking the adventure of the Perilous Cemetery. The luring back of
Lancelot to achieve this adventure leads to a reference back to the necessary
conditions for ending the enchantments, *PL* 248.27–9; this links up with *PL*
183.34–184.2 and with the final dispelling of the enchantments, 250.13–21, with
a change of name from Dolorous Guard to Joyous Guard, 250.31–2. This type of

repetition will usually involve intensification in the sense that the action is carried a degree further, through to the final accomplishment of the task.

The adventure of the Dolorous Guard (so important for the development of the identity theme) also provides an example of another characteristic form of repetition, the return to a place or a succession of visits by different people to the same place with a reference back to previous visits. Lancelot is the first to visit the cemetery in the Dolorous Guard on the occasion when, having conquered the castle, he raises the slab and discovers his own name (*PL* 194); then Gauvain visits the cemetery and is misled by false inscriptions (198-9); Arthur comes and is deceived in his turn (208); Gauvain returns with a damsel, and there is a reference back by the damsel to his earlier visit (240.14-15) and a link with Lancelot's first visit in that Gauvain tries and fails to lift the slab hiding Lancelot's name; the final visit is by Lancelot to end the enchantment (248-50). The inscriptions change each time, and on the final occasion the tombs disappear (250.19-21). There are also returns to the gates of the Dolorous Guard which link up with the love theme. Lancelot, in a lover's abstraction, twice leaves the Queen standing in front of the gates (*PL* 206-8, 215-16); he returns later with the Lady of Nohaut, refuses to enter, and addresses the gates which he had allowed to clang shut: 'Ha! porte, porte, por quoi ne fustes vos a tans overte?' There is then an explanatory reference back (*PL* 237.2-4). Lancelot's return to Camelot (*PL* 265-8), where he had been knighted and had seen the Queen for the first time (*PL* 151-66), picks up the first visit both through his own memories, reported in the narrative, and through another meeting with the Queen in which he is again struck dumb. In the Fourth Assembly, in a repetition linked to the identity theme, Lancelot stands on the same spot, in the same attitude, head bowed, deep in thought, as he had stood in the Third Assembly (the first battle against Galehot), but with black instead of red arms (*PL* 281, 309-11).

A characteristic linking motif, often including a reference back or prediction, is that of objects (usually with some magic qualities) presented as gifts. The three magic shields, sent to Lancelot by the Lady of the Lake (*PL* 187-8) when he has embarked on the conquest of the Dolorous Guard, not only help to enhance the supernatural quality of this adventure through which he learns his name, but also serve to identify the hero, who has not yet made his reputation at Arthur's court, during the adventures he undertakes between the capture of the castle and the First Assembly. During his battles against the defenders of the Dolorous Guard he progresses through the three shields, from the least powerful (that of one band, *PL* 191) to that of two bands (192), right up to the most powerful of all (with three bands, 193.4-9) for his final triumph. He follows the same progress upwards (*PL* 207, 215, 216) in his subsequent adventures, culminating with the rescue of Gauvain and his companions (219), and when Gauvain returns to Arthur he reports that he was freed by a knight bearing a shield with three bands (219.13–14). The shield depicting a knight and a lady divided by a crack, also a gift from the Lady of the Lake (*PL* 401–3) and concerning which a prediction is made (407.15–19), not only serves to pick up the love theme during one of Lancelot's periods of withdrawal but also gives continuity in more general terms. It does this by providing cross-references between Gauvain's progress on his quest and events at court (*PL* 424–5, 478.11–16), and by the fulfilment of the prediction and consequential reference back to the time when the prediction was made (547). During the period of Lancelot's madness it has a special effect on him (*PL* 553–4) and is used by the Lady of the Lake when she comes to heal him (555). It therefore plays an important part in an episode which not only includes another reference to the arrival of the shield (*PL* 556.14–16, 556.29–35) but also evokes the Lady of the Lake's first visit to court. The past is recalled through her dress, snow-white on both visits (*PL* 152, 554), and through her references to the earlier occasion (556.3–4) and to the childhood in the Lake (556.1–3, 556.21–3).[10] She tells Guinevere that Lancelot must wear the shield in battle, and it is presumably the same shield which enables him to open a door closed by enchantment (*PL* 564.15–18). Similarly, although on a lesser scale, the gift of the special sword to Hector provides an element of continuity (with an intriguing reversal of the usual chronological order of the narrative pattern) during the quest of Gauvain for Lancelot and of Hector for Gauvain, and ultimately provides the means for Gauvain's identification of Hector and the consequent interruption of the battle between the two knights.[11]

Another type of continuity is provided by recurring but interrupted background motifs of wars going on in the kingdom. These have already been discussed in Chapter IV in relation to Arthur's role. There are periodic references to the King's wars early in his reign (*PL* 2.8–11, 33.20–4, 53.36–9, 180.37–181.19). The war between Cambenic and Norgales crops up at intervals during the quests of Gauvain and Hector;[12] it gives rise to a large number of cross-references which help to knit together the narrative threads of the two knights. A similar function is served by wars in which Segurades plays a part, in which Gauvain becomes briefly involved and Girflet is taken prisoner.[13] Here the very gaps in our knowledge, what is not told in the tale, help to integrate the story of Lancelot into a wider Arthurian 'reality', just as the periodic references to encounters with Gauvain's companions on the quest for Lancelot, whose adventures are only told when they cross the paths of Hector or Gauvain, give a richer and more closely woven texture to the narrative.

Repeated descriptions of the same place are to be found; sometimes they include a reference back to the first description. For example, the description of the ways into Sorelois, the two *felons passages* and how they are guarded, is given more than once. On the first occasion the information is provided by the *conte* (*PL* 357). The detail of the guarding of the bridges is repeated when Lyonel tells Gauvain about it (*PL* 501). When Gauvain visits the hermit of the Roige Montaigne, he learns that Lyonel has also visited the hermitage and spoken of the difficulty of reaching Sorelois; this time the information is not repeated, but a reference back to the earlier point in the tale is given:

Lor li conte li hermites lo felon trespas de la chauciee qui est sor l'aive de Assurne, ensi comme li contes l'a autre foiz conté. (*PL* 526.13–14.)

When Gauvain arrives at one of the bridges, there is another reference back:

Li ponz de l'autre chauciee, don li contes vos avoit dit, avoit non li Ponz Irois. (*PL* 526.19–21.)

Then Gauvain is again told how the bridge is guarded by the knight who is charged with its defence (*PL* 526–7). The emphasis given, in the repeated references to the *felons passages*, to the inaccessibility of Sorelois, linked with the time of the adventures of the kingdom of Logres (*PL* 357.7–10), helps to give a special, mysterious quality to Lancelot's retreat and to Gauvain's achievement in reaching him there.[14]

On occasion, information will be reiterated in the narrative with no reference back (*PL* 275.16–22 and 279.11–15).[15] There is one example of a short account of an event which is later told in full: Lyonel's fight with the Crowned Lion of Lybia. The first brief reference is given during an explanation of Lyonel's name, with no reference forward to what *li contes* will tell in terms of the Lancelot tale, but only to what is to be found in Lyonel's story. Lyonel was born with a lion-shaped mark on his chest:

Et por ce fu apelez li anfes Lyoniaus, qui puis fist assez de hautes proeces si con li contes de sa vie lo tesmoigne; et mout dura la tache anmi son piz jusq'a un jor que il ocist le lion coroné de Libe en la cort lo roi Artu, qui estoit amenez au roi, por ce que en sa cort n'avoit onqes mes tel lion esté veüz. Et de celui lion porta messire Yvains la pel en son escu, car Lioneaus li dona quant l'ot mort, einsi comme l'estoire de ses fez le devise. (*PL* 358.24–31.)[16]

The full account of the adventure, related as part of the main narrative thread, is to be found near the end of the romance in an episode which presents a telescoped version of the 'making of a name' theme so important in the tale of Lyonel's cousin, Lancelot (*PL* 609–11). This full account also contains a reference to the giving of the skin to Yvain:

Et de celui lyeon porta messires Yvains, li filz au roi Urien, la pel en son escu, et por ce fu il apelez li Chevaliers au Lyeon. (*PL* 611.35–6.)

Lyonel leaves the court with the damsel who had brought the lion and is dismissed from the story with another reference to his own tale (*PL* 612.12–14).

In some cases, therefore, the reader has already been told of the perils to be surmounted before the knight learns from someone he meets what he has to confront; the difficulty of the adventure is emphasized through this double explanation and further reinforced in some cases by subsequent references back to the explanation given by the *conte*. A contrast to this pattern is to be found in the episode of the Estroite Marche where, at the outset, no explanation is given of the devastation round the castle or of the peculiar behaviour of the people (*PL* 442–4). This echoes the situation in the source of this adventure, the *Conte del Graal*, although eventually in the *PL* Hector is given a far more detailed account than is Perceval of the war in which the lord of the castle is involved.[17]

Explicit references to events or explanations to be found earlier in the romance can take two main forms: those by the tale, and those by the characters involved in or witness to the events. A good deal of reference back to earlier events is to be found at the narrative switches, when another thread is picked up with a brief recapitulation of the situation in which the person or persons concerned had been left. The extent of the recapitulation will vary considerably amongst the manuscripts, and in some it may be isolated from the ordinary narrative flow by the use of red ink. Repetition and references back within the pattern of the interlace have been studied in some detail in Chapter VII, but there are also a number of examples outside this pattern. I drew attention, in relation to the *felons passages* into Sorelois, to examples of allusions to explanations and descriptions given earlier. Another instance of references back to a place, the Forest of Brequehan (*PL* 409.35–6, 426.39–427.1), is to be found during Gauvain's quest for Lancelot and Hector's quest for Gauvain, which follows in the tracks of the King's nephew across Wales. The precise identification of the places through which Gauvain has passed and Hector has followed is linked to the particular structure of these two quests. As Hector passes through the forest and crosses the river, making enquiries as he goes, the tale's references to the topographical description given earlier helps to bind the two narrative threads together. In the same way, the information about the custom for the knights departing on a quest to swear to tell the truth on their return, given when Gauvain left on his quest, is reiterated with a reference back (*PL* 298.10–15) at the beginning of Hector's quest for Gauvain, so that at the very outset of the second quest a link is made. Another Arthurian custom, that of the recording of a knight's adventures on his return, receives a double emphasis.

The account of the procedure, given as the narrative mounts to a climax with Gauvain's completion of his quest and Lancelot's installation as a Companion of the Round Table (*PL* 571.20–30), is picked up again after Lyonel has defeated the Lion of Lybia (*PL* 611.38–612.1), thus underlining the pairing of Lancelot and Lyonel.

References back by the tale are also used when a knight or damsel who has been involved in an earlier adventure reappears at a later stage in the story. Banyn is reintroduced in the following terms:

Celui jor que li estrange bohordoient fu li jorz de la Pasque meesmes, si vanquié tot uns chevaliers dont li contes a parlé ça en arrieres, si estoit apelez Banyns et fillués fu au roi Ban de Benoyc. (*PL* 135.30–3.)

This picks up the information given when he first appears:

Et qant il fu dedanz, si ancontre un chevalier, filluel lo roi Ban, qui mout estoit de grant proesce. (*PL* 7.33–4.)

The explanation given at *PL* 135 is followed by a physical description of Banyn and a brief summary of his activities since his last appearance in the story, and then by Arthur's conversation with him which leads to the first of Arthur's broodings (on this occasion over his failure to avenge Ban). Thus, Banyn's reappearance at this point, and his identification in terms which link up with the first stages in that siege of Trebe which was to cause Ban's death and Lancelot's abduction to the Lake, help to round off the phase of the tale dealing with the period of the hero's childhood. The same type of formula is used to identify a knight whose arrival, wounded, at Arthur's court with a message from Gauvain is narrated (*PL* 404.9–24) before we are given the account of the battle in which he received the wound (*PL* 422–3).

Finally, references back by the tale, near the end of the romance, are used to highlight its concluding stages. First, the fulfilment of the prediction of Galehot's death:

Issi fu Galehoz morz por Lancelot, issi com li clercs lo distrent qui li expelerent son sonje si com li contez l'a autre foiz devisé. (*PL* 612.28–9.)

This links up with *PL* 582.26–583.2. Secondly, the concluding formula evokes the beginning of the romance:

Si tast atant li contes de lui, que plus n'en parole, car bien a a chief menees totes les avantures qi li avindrent puis qe la reine Helaine, qui sa mere fu, lo perdié par l'aventure que cist livres conta el comencement. (*PL* 613.4–7.)

These references back by the tale, placed at strategic points, both within and outside the pattern of the narrative switches, make it easier to follow the inter-weaving of the threads and mark the main stages in Lancelot's progress as knight and lover.

References back to past events by characters in the tale constitute an even more important cohesive element, as they are often linked to attempts to discover the identity of Lancelot under his different shields and arms, and hence to one of the main themes of the romance. Thus Gauvain, on more than one occasion, reminds the Queen of past events, opening with the phrase 'Membre vos'. For example, after hearing that a damsel had said 'C'est la tierce' (*PL* 272.2–18), he recalls the prediction of the maiden from the Lake that they would hear news of the knight whom they were seeking at the First, Second, and Third Assemblies (*PL* 219). When, in the Fourth Assembly, he sees the Black Knight standing on the edge of the battle at the same place and in the same attitude as the Red Knight, he reminds the Queen of the earlier occasion, using the phrase 'Menberroit vos', and expressing the wish that it were the same knight (*PL* 309).

The central example of the drawing together of strands through the evocation of past events by one of the characters comes in the meeting between Lancelot and Guinevere which leads to Lancelot's admission of his identity to the Queen and to their first kiss. Through a series of questions, Guinevere makes Lancelot go over all the events leading up to the Fourth Assembly: she compels him to admit to all his exploits, performed under the various arms he wore. Finally, when she presses him to reveal the source of this prowess, he repeats those words spoken by her as he took leave of her as the newly knighted youth, words which he invested with such a depth of meaning that they provided the inspiration for all his deeds: 'A Deu, biaus douz amis.' (*PL* 345, 165.23.) This, therefore, provides one of the key repetitions in the whole work.

Allusions by the characters to past events, on occasion reinforced by authorial explanations without references to *le conte,* provide some of the main cross-links between the quest of Gauvain and that of Hector as well as an element of continuity within each individual quest. They are also used to link up with the background motif of the war between the King of Norgales and the Duke of Cambenic, and to give periodic glimpses of the adventures of Gauvain's companions who encounter him or Hector on their travels. Thus, in Hector's quest, the lord of the Estroite Marche's account of the events leading to the capture of Yvain and Sagremor includes a reported reference by Yvain (*PL* 448.19–23) to a knight (Hector) who, after unhorsing four knights, is beaten by a dwarf at the Fontaine do Pin; this alludes to an episode which took place at the beginning of Gauvain's quest, before the paths of the five companions, having come together by chance, separated again (*PL* 367–71). Hector defeats the besiegers of the Estroite Marche and frees Yvain and Sagremor; when he names the land from which he comes, the two companions observe that it is the same region as that of the knight of the Fontaine do Pin, and they laugh (*PL* 461). When Sagremor later meets Gauvain and tells him about his release by a knight who is on a quest for Gauvain, this helps to link the two quests and enables Gauvain to tell Sagremor that Hector, the knight who is seeking him, is the knight of the Fontaine do Pin (*PL* 504.26–35). Another reference back to the incident at the Fontaine do Pin, this time in the form of an authorial explanation, without explicit reference to the *conte*, links up with an allusion to an adventure of which no account is given in the narrative (the capture of Girflet), with a conversation between Gauvain and a hermit about the war of Marez, son of a fellow hermit, Alier, (*PL* 475.37–477.8), and with a battle fought by Gauvain against the nephew of Segurades. The allusion serves to explain why Gauvain and Girflet do not recognize one another when they both become involved in the Duke of Cambenic's battle before Leverzep:

Et li chevaliers estoit Guiflez, li filz Do, mais il n'avoit mies ses armes, car messires Gauvains l'aüst bien coneü, ainz les avoit perdues a un poigneïz o il avoit esté pris, lo jor que messires Gauvains les laissa, la o Hestors les avoit abatuz toz quatre. Et ce fu de la guerre do li hermites avoit parlé a monseignor Gauvain, de Maret, lo fil Alier, et de Helahin d'Athingue, lo neveu Securades. Et ce fu cil Helains que messires Gauvains conquist a son hiaume meïsmes. (*PL* 481.6–13.)

Here the cross-reference involves some minor inconsistencies (not confined to any one group of manuscripts) concerning the name of the enemy of Marez. The imprisonment of Girflet is picked up again in the exchange of news between Gauvain and Sagremor (*PL* 503.35–504.6). Gauvain comments on the capture:

'Il ne fu onques, fait messires Gauvains, hom si sovant pris comme Guiflez. Et ce ne li vient mies de mauvaitié, car il est, si m'aïst Dex, et preuz et anprenanz et hardiz durement.' (*PL* 504.4–6.)

This echoes a theme to be found in the *First Continuation*, where Arthur weeps because no one has rescued Girflet, a prisoner for four years.[18] The King then sets out with a group of knights to rescue him.

During Gauvain's battle against the seneschal of Cambenic there is another example of an allusion which combines an accurate reference to past events with an inconsistency over a proper name. A veiled damsel asks Lyonel to tell her which knight he serves. He refuses, and she conjures him 'par la foi que vos devez a celi qui vos garanti qant vos aviez l'espee sor la teste' (*PL* 495.17–18). This reference and Lyonel's anguished reaction when he discovers that he has spoken harshly to 'la riens o monde que il onques plus avoit amee', is explained (again with no explicit reference to the *conte*):

Et ce estoit la damoiselle qui lo garanti qant l'espee li fu sor la teste por ocirre, si avoit non
Celice, et la dame avoit non Ninienne. Et icele Ninienne fu ce qui Lancelot norri au Lac.
(*PL* 496.18–21.)

This links up with *PL* 67–8 and 104–6 which tell of the wound of the damsel,
incurred when she was saying Lyonel from Claudas, and of the boy's love and
gratitude when he discovers what she has done for him. But the name given
earlier is Saraide (*PL* 57.27). It is a curious fact that in this romance which
attributes so much importance to establishing the right of the main characters
to their names, there should be several examples of confusion over the names of
the lesser characters or places, confusion which seems to be deep-seated within
the manuscript tradition.[19]

People met on journeys constitute an important source for the repetition of
information or the tying up of threads at strategic points. Hermits with whom
the knights errant spend the night play an important role in the exchange of
information which provides these cross-links.[20] Knights may get news from
those with whom they stay. Gauvain learns from his brother Agravain something of the war between Norgales and Cambenic, and from his *amie* that her
sister, daughter of the King of Norgales, has vowed to give her maidenhood to
Gauvain (*PL* 419–20). Messengers and prisoners make a significant contribution
when they bring news to court of the deeds of the knights errant and of what is
going on in the kingdom.[21] Lyonel has a special role to play as he travels
between Lancelot and Galehot in Sorelois and Guinevere at Arthur's court, and
meets Gauvain on his journeys.[22] Travelling damsels in general and damsels
from the Lake in particular also give (or extract) information (*PL* 205–6, 495–6),
sometimes in rather enigmatic form (*PL* 273), or remind knights of promises
not yet fulfilled (*PL* 226). As was seen in Chapter V, damsels from the Lake help
to interweave the strands of Lancelot and Gauvain during the period between
Lancelot's departure from the Dolorous Guard and the Third Assembly, and
they maintain links with the Lake and Lancelot's childhood there throughout
most of the romance.

These exchanges of information, references back to earlier events or outwards to those contemporaneous with the main tale, have the general effect of
tightening up the narrative process, of helping the reader as well as the
characters to keep track of what is happening, but they are not used indis-
criminately or mechanically. The technique is not just applied to the surface
structure of the work, but derives from the very nature of the theme—the
establishment of the reputation of a young knight in the Arthurian world—and
from the nature of the relationship between the individual tale and Arthurian
'reality'.

References forwards

It has been seen that predictions, whether made by damsels or wise men interpreting dreams or visions, are often picked up by references back, but they also look forwards, and this brings us to the allusions to future events which also play an important part in giving coherence to the work. The allusions to what the tale will tell are particularly interesting, although, compared with the references to what has already been told they are not very great in number.

There are two promises of what is to be told later which are in due course fulfilled in a straightforward manner. The first of these concerns Heliene sanz Per, one of the three most beautiful women listed in a description of Arthur, his Queen, and his court, given at the beginning of the visit of Claudas to Britain:

Et sachiez que onques a son tans el reiaume de Logres n'en ot une qui s'apareillast a li de grant biauté fors que deus seulement. Si fu l'une dame d'un chastel qui siet an la marche de Norgales et des Frans, si a non Gazevilté li chastiaus, et la dame ot non Heliene sanz Per, et cist contes an parlera ça avant. (*PL* 33.4–8.)

The tale does indeed later tell us more about Heliene, when it gives an account of an adventure undertaken by Hector. He rescues Heliene, who has been imprisoned by her husband until a knight can prove in battle that her beauty is greater than her husband's prowess. We have seen in Chapter III the significance both of this episode and of the earlier linking of Heliene sanz Per to Guinevere as one of the three supreme examples of feminine beauty. Thus, as with the picking up of past events in the narrative, the use of a reference forwards to a future episode is linked to the development of one of the main themes of the work.

Emphasis on the love theme is also to be found in the second of the allusions forwards in which the promise is picked up in full. The tale foretells the closing of the crack in the shield sent by the Lady of the Lake to Guinevere. It explains that the Queen always had the shield with her 'jusque a cele ore que il fu rejoinz par avanture que cist contes devisera ça avant' (*PL* 407.18–19). This occurs at the final physical consummation of Lancelot and Guinevere's love (*PL* 547), after which the reference back to the bringing of the shield is in the form of an explanation by Guinevere to Galehot.

The fulfilment of the next promise to be discussed is not quite so simple and straightforward. Right at the beginning of the romance there occurs the following passage:

et avoit non Lanceloz en sorenon, mais il avoit non an baptaisme Galaaz. Et ce par quoi il fu apelez Lanceloz ce devisera bien li contes ça avant, car li leus n'i est ores mies ne la raisons; ançois tient li contes sa droite voie et dit . . . (*PL* 1.7–11.)

We are told how Lancelot discovers his name in the Magic Cemetery by raising the slab beneath which is written: 'Ci gerra Lanceloz del Lac, li filz au roi Ban de Benoyc.' (*PL* 194.30–1.) In the *PL* we are not told why the *sorenon* Lancelot was inscribed there rather than the baptismal name Galaaz, but it is under the identity of Lancelot of the Lake, son of King Ban of Benoyc, that the hero finally makes his name, and the stages towards this are marked clearly within the work, as was seen in Chapter II, so that the reference forward follows the pattern of those already discussed in that it is linked to one of the main themes of the romance. The promise is therefore fulfilled in terms of the establishment of the hero's identity as Lancelot. The baptismal name Galaaz lapses without explanation; indeed, no promise of what the tale will tell has been made concerning it, and the achievement of the name Lancelot is presented as the winning of a glorious *sorenon*, not the loss of a baptismal name. However, as will be seen in the second part of this study, the change of name is given a different significance in the cyclic romance in relation to the development of the new theme of a Grailwinner who is to displace Lancelot as the greatest knight.

There is a promise which is not wholly fulfilled. This concerns the wounded knight who arrives at Camelot just before Lancelot's first visit there as a youthful squire:

Li chevaliers fu granz et genz et bien tailliez; mais son non ne nomme ores pas li contes ici endroit, et neporqant ça en avant sera bien seü comment il ot non, et comment il fu navrez, et por quoi il porta si longuement en ses plaies et les fers et les tronçons. (*PL* 149.26–30.)

Because no explanation is given immediately, the reader can participate in the astonished curiosity of Arthur and his knights when they see that the weapons have been left in the wounds. Shortly afterwards the promise of an explanation is partly fulfilled when the knight gives the reason for his arrival at court in this condition. He wishes the blades to be drawn out of his body, but an oath must be taken first:

'Sire, fait il, ja covendra que cil qui me desferrera me jurt sor sainz qu'il me vanchera a son pooir de toz cels qui diront qu'il ameront plus celui qui ce me fist que moi.' (*PL* 150.13–15.)

Such an oath would present the swearer with such an unending task that Arthur advises his knights not to undertake it. The short postponement of the explanation not only whets the curiosity but also gives additional emphasis to the nature of the oath and underlines the extreme rashness of Lancelot's insistence on swearing it and withdrawing the weapons. The consequences of his action, the series of battles which end in his imprisonment by the Lady of Malohaut, provide one of the cohesive elements in the adventures between the capture of the Dolorous Guard and the Third Assembly. However, one small part of the promise is not kept: the name of the knight is not given in the non-cyclic Prose *Lancelot*. Eventually the detail of the missing name is picked up in the cyclic romance, but only with the arrival of this wounded knight's brother in a similar condition.[23] This is an example of a backward linking within the cyclic romance through the doubling of an episode, a technique to be examined in Part II of this study.

There is an example of a reference forward which presents an interesting combination of what is told later and what is not picked up again. This occurs in a passage leading up to the account of Lyonel's discovery that he has been deprived of his land by Claudas:

Et ce fu li plus desfrenez cuers d'anfant qui onques fust que le Lyonel, ne nus ne retraist onques si naturelment a Lancelot com il faisoit. Et Galehoz li proz, li preuzdom, li sires des Estranges Illes, li filz a la Bele Jaiande, l'apela une foiz Cuer sanz Frain, por ce qu'il nel pooit vaintre por chastier, celui jor meïsmes que li rois Artus lo fist chevalier ensi com li contes devisera ça avant. (*PL* 60.33–9.)

An account is given of the knighting of Lyonel and of his insistence (like Lancelot) on undertaking the first adventure presenting itself at Arthur's court after he has become a knight (*PL* 609–11), but Galehot's remark is not repeated at that stage.

There is also a curse by Hector's *amie*, directed against the Queen who had tricked her into giving her lover permission to go on a quest for Gauvain:

Et cele li dit, si tost com ele la vit, que si liee poïst ele estre de la rien que ele plus ainme et tenoit chiere, ainz que ele morist de mort, comme ele est de celui que ele plus amoit que rien qui vive. (*PL* 407.22–5.)

This is followed by a prediction concerning the Queen, with no mention of the tale:

Et puis fu tel ore que ele no vousist avoir fait por nule rien, car ne demora mies granment que ele an fu autretant correciee o plus. (*PL* 407.25–7.)

There is no later reference back to make it clear when this is fulfilled, but it might be linked to the Queen's distress, first when Lancelot is captured by the Saxons (*PL* 549.14–15) and later when he goes mad (*PL* 553.20–5). There are also, as has already been seen, a number of examples of characters looking forward in terms of predictions and promises. Another way of giving a framework to events is to be found in the recounting of a person's intentions. The Lady of the Lake, during Lancelot's childhood, looks forward to the time when first he and then his cousins, each in his turn, will leave to become a knight:

Si se pense que tant les tandra entor li com ele les porra tenir; et qant Lanceloz sera chevaliers, si li remenra Lyoniaus et Bohorz en sa baillie; et qant Lyoniax revenra a chevalerie, au mains li remanra Bohorz en sa baillie. Ensin se bee a conforter de l'un por l'autre. (*PL* 111.30-4.)

The first stage is realized when the Lady of the Lake acknowledges that it is time for Lancelot to become a knight (*PL* 139.2-13). She takes him to Arthur's court and, before she leaves him, talks of his cousins, thus preparing us for the next stage:

'Et por ce que g'ei en vos mise tote l'amor qui puet venir de norreture, les retandrei ge o moi tant com ge les porrai retenir por remanbrance de vos. Et qant il covandra que Lyoniaus soit chevaliers, si me remandra Bohorz.' (*PL* 154.21-4.)

That is reached when she sends Lyonel out of the Lake to Lancelot (*PL* 358.7-9), and eventually Lyonel too becomes a knight (*PL* 609-11). Thus some of the main stages in the story are set out for us while Lancelot is still a child in the Lake, and these expectations are in due course fulfilled. This conforms to the general pattern of predictions or allusions forwards within the *PL*, which help to structure the narrative and to underline the main themes; such promises are fulfilled and intentions carried out within the limits of the non-cyclic romance.

Pairing of characters

A particularly characteristic way of using many of the types of repetition and linking analysed above is the pairing of characters, whether in contrast or parallel. This can operate in relation to characters within the *PL* or in other romances. In the account of Lancelot's upbringing, through a series of echoes and oppositions, as was seen in Chapter II, there is constant interplay between Lancelot, a fatherless child, brought up by a woman in isolation and in ignorance of his name but carefully prepared for knighthood, and the Perceval of Chrétien de Troyes, whose upbringing is similar to that of Lancelot, except for the desire to keep the youth wholly ignorant of chivalry. This is combined with a doubling of characters within the romance, based on a series of similarities and contrasts. The pairing does not necessarily remain stable; as in an old-fashioned court or country dance, the participants may at times change their partners within an overall pattern. Lancelot and Lyonel, for example, are coupled within a whole complex of family relationships and other pairings in a way designed both to bring out clearly Lancelot's special qualities, which set him apart from other youths destined for knighthood, and to establish clearly his identity in terms of heredity.

The romance opens with a reference to the two brothers, King Ban (father of

Lancelot) and King Bohort (father of Lyonel and Bohort), who married two sisters. Both these kings lose their lands to Claudas and die early in the romance (Bohort only two days after his brother) and they are both described as good, just kings and men of great worth, but Lancelot's father is given a little more space and a little more prestige than Bohort. Bohort is described in the following terms:

ce fu uns des homes do monde qui plus haute justise tint en sa vie que li rois Bohorz de Gaunes, fors li rois Bans de Benoyc, ses freres. (*PL* 18.31–3.)

He is also said to be the best *preudomme* and the most loyal baron, except for Ban, 'qui plus preuzdom estoit d'armes, ce set l'an bien' (*PL* 108.30–3). Both brothers are liege vassals of Arthur, but it is the King of Britain's shameful failure to avenge Ban which is stressed, and Bohort is scarcely mentioned in this context (*PL* 56–7, 137–8, 285). In the same way, while the two widowed sisters are both beautiful and virtuous queens, grieving for their dead husbands and vanished children, Queen Helene, mother of Lancelot, is given a slight edge over Queen Evaine, mother of Lyonel and Bohort. Helene's child vanishes through the intervention of a being with powers which have supernatural origins, even if they are to some extent rationalized in medieval terms.[24] Evaine is separated from her children through ordinary, human means (*PL* 19–20), although eventually they are taken to the land beneath the semblance of a lake. The sisters' illustrious ancestry is dwelt on more frequently in relation to Helene than to Evaine.[25] Both sisters are devout, share their griefs, and live saintly lives in the same convent; but it is Helene who founds the abbey Mostier Reial in memory of her husband and eventually becomes its abbess, and her piety exceeds that of her sister:

Et se ele [Evaine de Gaunes] estoit de boene vie et de grant religion, ce ne monta rien a la sainte vie que sa suers menoit, la reine Helaine de Benoyc. (*PL* 132.20–1.)

There follows a long description of all Helene's self-denying service to God and the privations which she gladly and triumphantly endured without loss of youth or beauty so that it was manifest that her religious life was pleasing to Him:

Et neporqant, si bele demostrance li fist Nostres Sires que ses servises li plaisoit que ele estoit grasse a mesure en son viaire, si estoit blanche et vermoille et coloree, et de si grant biauté que nus hom estranges ne cuidast que il poïst avoir la setiemme part de religion qui i estoit. (*PL* 133.4–8.)

Her sister's piety, although considerable, was not in the same heroic mould: 'Mais sa suer, la reine Evainne, estoit de foible complexion et malingeuse.' (*PL*

UNIVERSITY OF WINCHESTER
LIBRARY

133.9–10.) She struggled bravely with the rigours of the convent life until she was granted a vision of her children and of Lancelot, all well and happy, and then died peacefully. Thus the parents of Lancelot and his cousins are all noble and virtuous, but those of the hero, as is fitting, a little more so.

The family resemblances between the two boys are also given importance, but in a way which works always to the advantage of Lancelot. This is brought out clearly in a pair of episodes, each dealing with a difference of opinion between youth and tutor. The first of these, which concerns Lancelot, is preceded by a description of the young hero, praising his generosity, his judgement, and firmness of purpose. This prepares the way for an incident in which Lancelot's tutor wrongly condemns him for showing the generosity natural to him by giving away a horse and a deer; the boy explains his actions, but the tutor loses his temper and strikes Lancelot and his dogs, at which point the boy breaks his bow over his tutor's head and rides home angrily. The Lady of the Lake listens to his account of the affair and, after pressing him hard and playing upon the uncertainty over his origins in order to test him further, declares:

'Biax fiz, or ne seiez pas a malaise, car, si m'aïst Dex, ge voil que vos donoiz et roncins et autres choses, et vos avroiz assez quoi. Et se vos fussiez an l'aage de quarante anz, si feïssiez vos bien a loer del roncin et de la veneison que vos donates. Et des ores mais voil ge bien que vos soiez de vos sires et maistres, puis que vos savroiz bien par vos ce qui apartient a boene anfance. Et cui que vos fussiez filz, voirement n'avez vos pas failli a cuer de fil de roi, et si fustes vos filz a tel qui osast bien assaillir lo plus haut roi do monde par proesce de cors et de cuer.' (*PL* 47.33–48.3.)

The episode in which Pharien has great difficulty in restraining Lyonel from attempting to kill Claudas single-handed is preceded by a reference to Lyonel's close resemblance to Lancelot:

Et ce fu li plus desfrenez cuers d'anfant qui onques fust que le Lyonel, ne nus ne retraist onques si naturelment a Lancelot com il faisoit. (*PL* 60.33–5.)

This is followed by the reference to the occasion when Galehot called him 'Cuer sanz Frain', because 'il nel pooit vaintre por chastier'.[26] However, Lyonel's reluctance to listen to Pharien's advice is not presented as a sign of the boy's maturity of judgement at such an early age, as in the case of Lancelot, for Pharien, unlike Lancelot's tutor, has not been outgrown by his charge but is a good and wise knight, well qualified to set an example of loyal and chivalrous behaviour. There is indeed a contrast, throughout the account of Lancelot's upbringing right up to his arrival at Arthur's court, between the younger cousin's hotheaded immaturity and Lancelot's thoughtfulness and strength of purpose. The episode in which Lyonel is shocked to learn that he has been dispossessed of his land is followed by a number of incidents in which he is shown to be still dependent on Pharien; for example, he is childishly angry with his tutor when Pharien is unable to come to him because he is imprisoned.

The sequence which includes Lyonel's abortive rebellion against Pharien's tutelage should also be compared with a later one concerning Lancelot and the Lady of the Lake. The earlier sequence (*PL* 60–70) contains the following elements: Pharien weeps; Lyonel insists on knowing the cause; when he learns of his own disinheritance, he is deeply disturbed; when his desire to take independent action to achieve a personal revenge is restrained by Pharien, who, as a prisoner of Claudas, is unable to give practical assistance and can only counsel patience, he withdraws into angry brooding; he is finally helped to avenge himself on the son of Claudas by the magic wreaths of the Lady of the Lake's damsel, which give him magical protection, and is carried off, disguised as a greyhound, to the sanctuary of the Lake, leaving Claudas in possession of his land. Tears, insistence on knowing the cause, angry withdrawal, determination to take independent action, are also to be found in the later sequence (*PL* 139–48) but with a different outcome, underlining the different positions of Lancelot and Lyonel and the different powers of their protectors, the Lady of the Lake and Pharien. The Lady of the Lake, seeing that the time has come for Lancelot to leave the Lake and become a knight, is moved to tears; Lancelot tries to question her; he gets no satisfactory answer and withdraws angrily, determined to leave the Lake on his own in order to become a knight at Arthur's court; she persuades him not to leave, and promises to help him to achieve his desire. The sequence leads therefore to a positive result—not withdrawal from the outside world into the Lake, but departure from the Lake with the lady's full support, and a journey to the centre of chivalry, Arthur's court. Lyonel will make the same journey later, but he will serve a long apprenticeship as squire to Lancelot and as messenger between Galehot and Lancelot on the one hand and the Queen on the other. He will be helped by Gauvain when his horse is taken by a knight, another contrast with Lancelot who rescues Gauvain instead of receiving help from him. Ironically, it is Lyonel, the *Cuer sanz Frain*, who tries to restrain Lancelot when, moved by the power of love and his determination to help Guinevere, he wants to rout the Saxons single-handed (*PL* 563). Finally, in Lyonel's knighting and the undertaking of the fight with the Crowned Lion of Lybia, which proves his right to his own name, we have a telescoped version of Lancelot's own career, but with a major difference in the absence of the love theme.

The parallels and contrasts between Lancelot and Lyonel are particularly evident in the first part of the story which leads up to Lancelot's arrival at Camelot. As has been seen in Chapter II, the use of Lyonel as a foil for Lancelot enables the tutor to explore more deeply the theme of the youthful hero's uncertainty over his identity and his courageous reaction to this mystery over his origins. After Lancelot leaves the Lake, Lyonel is not mentioned until Lancelot retires into Sorelois, when he becomes an important link between the four separated lovers, the Queen and the Lady of Malohaut on the one hand, and Lancelot and Galehot on the other. He is, therefore, one of the few characters, apart from Lancelot, the Lady of the Lake, one of her damsels, and Arthur, who play a role in both the early part of the romance and the later stages of the story, and he helps to provide an element of continuity between the Lake childhood and Lancelot's adventures as a knight.

Other important pairings in the early part of the romance centre round the character of Claudas. I have already suggested in Chapter II that this character as it appears in the *PL* may derive from a splitting of an unpopular king, father of Lancelot (as is found in the *Lanzelet*), into two individuals: a just king, Ban, father of Lancelot, deprived of his land by a disloyal king, Claudas. There are, in fact, in the early part of the *PL* two sets of fathers and sons, opposed to one another but also linked by some parallels: the first is that of Ban and Lancelot, the second Claudas and Dorin. These oppositions are brought out in the five main examples of the rhetorical elaboration of traditional set themes to be found in the early part of the work: Ban's dying thoughts, first expressed in indirect speech and then in the prayer of the dying (*PL* 13-14); the formal portrait of Claudas (*PL* 30); the formal portrait of Lancelot (*PL* 39-41); the lament of Claudas for his dead son (*PL* 71-3); and the Lady of the Lake's discourse on chivalry (*PL* 142-6).

As Ban lies dying, he alludes to his wife's illustrious ancestry, a recurring theme in the romance in relation to Lancelot's great destiny. He prays to God that he may protect Helene and his infant son, whose future is now under threat, for Ban sees him doomed to be brought up in poverty and in the power of others. Ban loses his land and dies, leaving a dispossessed and fatherless son but one who, through both his inheritance of great qualities and his own personal efforts, is destined to achieve greatness as a knight.

Claudas, on the other hand, wins Ban's land but loses his son Dorin, who, as he declares in his lament, would have achieved greatness as a knight, had he lived, for he had the three qualities necessary to achieve great renown on this earth: 'C'est debonairetez et largece et fiertez.' He describes his *fierté* in the following terms:

'D'autre part, vos aviez fierté en vos si naturelment herbergiee que nus ne vos poïst faire amer home orgueilleus ne sorcuidié. Vos estiez de si grant felenie contre felon que vos nel poiez nes regarder, ainz diseiez que l'an ne devoit pas ses iauz aengier de mauvaise chose veoir, car parmi les ielz s'an sentoit li cuers el ventre de la puor.' (*PL* 72.11-16.)

The generosity of Dorin is contrasted with the reluctance to give which characterizes Claudas both in this lament (*PL* 72.26) and in the earlier portrait of the king, in which his niggardliness is emphasized:

Claudas fu li plus angoisseus princes et li plus avers do monde, ne ja rien ne donast se lors non qant il avoit si grant mestier de gent que consirrer ne s'en pooit. (*PL* 30.10–13.)

Ban and Dorin die, hence the topoi associated with death—the prayer of the dying and the deploration of the dead. Claudas and Lancelot both receive the full treatment in the other well-known topos, the portrait designed to praise or to blame, and the terms used in relation to moral qualities link up with the lament of Claudas and the opposition suggested there between father and son. First, on the physical side Claudas presents a mixture of good and bad features, reflecting the mixture of good and bad to be found in his character.[27] For example, his body is well made, but his face does not conform to the accepted ideal. His nose is 'cort et rechinié' (*PL* 30.16), while that of Lancelot is 'par messure lonc, un po hautet el mileu' (*PL* 39.32). His complexion is dark, 'noir', as compared with the ideal mixture of red and white to be found in Lancelot (*PL* 39.21–9). In his character it is the absence of generosity which is above all stressed, whereas the description of Lancelot seems to echo the words used by Claudas to praise the qualities of his dead son, his *debonaireté, fierté*, and *largece*. Of Lancelot it is said:

Ce fu li plus douz anfes et li plus debonaires de toz, la ou debonairetez se laissoit trover, mais contre felenie lo trovoit en passefelon. Ne de sa largece ne fu onques nus anfes veüz, car il departoit tot a ses conpaignons autresin volentiers com il lo prenoit. (*PL* 41.5–9.)

Dorin was killed at the very feast held by Claudas to celebrate his knighting. When the Lady of the Lake continues her preparation of Lancelot for his great destiny with her discourse on chivalry, delivered shortly before he leaves the Lake to become a knight, her description of those originally chosen to be knights links up again with the lament of Claudas for Dorin and the portrait of Lancelot:

'Au commencement, qant li ordres de chevalerie commança, fu devisé a celui qui voloit estre chevaliers et qui lo don en avoit par droiture d'eslection, qu'il fust cortois sanz vilenies, deboenneires sanz felenie, piteus vers les soffraiteus, et larges et appareilliez de secorre les besoigneus, prelz et apareilliez de confondre les robeors et les ocianz, droiz jugierres sanz amor et sanz haïne, et sanz amor d'aidier au tort por lo droit grever, et sanz haïne de nuire au droit por traire lo tort avant.' (*PL* 142.32–40.)

The phrase 'de si grant felenie contre les felons', used by Claudas and echoed in Lancelot's portrait, is picked up again in the Lady of the Lake's description of the two hearts which a knight should have:

'Chevaliers doit avoir deus cuers, un dur et sarré autresin com aimenz, et autre mol et ploiant autresi comme cire chaude. Cil qui est durs com aimanz doit estre encontre les desleiaus et les felons, car autresin com li àimanz ne sueffre nul polissement, autresin doit estre li chevaliers fel et cruieus vers les felons qui droiture depiecent et enpirent a lor pooirs. Et autresi com la cire mole et chaude puet estre flichie et menee la ou en velt, autresi doivent les boennes genz et les piteuses mener lo chevalier a toz les poinz qui apartienent a debonaireté et a dosor.' (*PL* 145.4–12.)

Thus Ban loses his land and dies, but leaves behind him the reputation of a good and well-loved lord,[28] and his son survives to bring honour to his father's memory. Claudas gains much land, but loses both the hearts of his people and his son. Ban regrets the loss of his land in a lament culminating in the swoon which precedes his death (*PL* 13.5–18). Claudas laments the price he has had to pay for the lands of Benoyc and Gaunes:

'Haï! regnes de Benoyc et celui de Gaunes, tant m'avroiz pené et travaillié. Tant fait grant folie, avocques lo grant pechié qui i est, cil qui autrui desherite et tost sa terre, car ja aseür une seule ore, ne par nuit ne par jor, n'i dormira. Et mout a petit seignorie sus son pueple cil qui les cuers n'an puet avoir. Voirement est nature dome et commenderesse sor toz establissemenz, car ele fait amer son droiturier seignor desor toz autres. Por c'est et fox et avugles qui, por coveitise de la terriene seignorie qui si po dure, se charge de pechié et de la puor de nul home deseriter, car nule granz dolors ne puet entrer ne paroir en cuer mortel que d'estre deseritez et essilliez, fors seulement de perdre son charnel ami leial, car a celi dolor ne se puet nule angoisse prandre, et ge m'en sui bien aparceüz.' (*PL* 81.25–37.)

Claudas is also opposed to Arthur as part of a wider series of parallels and contrasts between Claudas, Arthur, and Galehot. With Claudas and Arthur the opposition centres on *largece*, which, as we have seen, Claudas noticeably lacks. Arthur is first shown as failing in connection with Claudas because he is so beset with difficulties at the beginning of his reign that he cannot come to the aid of his vassal Ban; but he is soon presented in a more favourable light in the episode of the journey of Claudas to Britain. When Claudas is assessing his achievements as king, the point of comparison is Arthur. If even Arthur has not dared to attack him in spite of his conquest of the lands of two of the King of Britain's vassals, he must be feared by others:

'Si sai bien qe mout sui dotez d'autres genz, qant meesmes li rois Artus me crient et dote. Ne ge ne me tandrai pas por si preuz com ge doi estre, se ge ne faz tant qu'il taigne de moi tote sa terre.' (*PL* 31.24–7.)

He then wishes to crown his success by attacking Arthur himself and forcing him to pay homage for his land, but, because of the great reputation of the King of Britain, he wants to see first whether this fame is merited and then whether he has any chance of success against Arthur (*PL* 31.28–34). When he goes in disguise to Arthur's court, he is much impressed by the qualities he sees in the King:

Et esgarda lo contenement lo roi et sa largesce et sa debonaireté et son grant san et sa biauté et sa bonté et sa proesce, si lo vit de totes valors de cuer et de cors si entechié qu'il ne prisoit envers lui rien nul home dont il onqes eüst parole oïe. (*PL* 33.30-4.)

When, on the return journey, Claudas asks his squire's opinion of his plan to conquer Arthur, the latter has no hesitation in describing Arthur as the greatest of all kings and the pillar of the world's chivalry; he goes on to say that he would be prepared to renounce his allegiance to Claudas. The qualities in Arthur which he praises are those of *largece*, *proesce*, and *debonaireté*.

'Il est si biax chevaliers que plus bel ne covient a demander. Il est plains de si grant proesce et de si haute qu'il vaint de totes chevaleries et cels de son ostel et les estranges. Il est si larges et si abandonez que nus n'oseroit penser ce qu'il oseroit despendre. Il est si debonaires et plains de si grant compaignie qu'il ne remaint por les hauz homes qu'il ne face granz joies et granz honors as povres preuz, et done les riches dons et les plaisanz. Ensins fait gaaignier les cuers des riches et des povres, car il enhore les riches come ses compaignons, et les povres par lor proesces et por son pris et s'anor acroistre et vers Dieu et vers lo siegle, car bien gaaigne pris et honor vers le siegle et grace et amor de Deu cil qui fait el siegle ce qu'il doit de tel baillie come Dex li avra donee.' (*PL* 34.20-32.)

The description of Arthur given by the *serjant* makes it understandable that Lancelot's achievement of a seat at the Round Table and a permanent place in the King's *maisnie* should represent the climax in the tale of the making of his name. Nevertheless, it was Arthur's failure to protect Ban and Bohort which first gave Claudas the idea of attempting the conquest of Britain, and there are repeated sequences in the early part of the romance which prepare the way for more serious criticisms and humiliations of Arthur yet to come. The basic pattern in each sequence is as follows: the mourning of the widowed queen, reassurance concerning the safety of the children, public criticism of King Arthur for his failure to avenge his vassal. In the first of these sequences (*PL* 48-60) there is also a pairing of episodes in which Arthur and Claudas are in turn criticized in public for conduct unbecoming in a king. Sequence A contains these episodes: the grieving of the widowed queen near her abbey; her reassurance by a passing *rendu* who tells her that her son is alive and well; the *rendu*'s visit to Arthur's court, where he finds Arthur at high table with all his knights and makes public the King's failure to avenge Ban and his son, a sin of omission rather than commission; a visit by a damsel to the court of Claudas, where she criticizes him at table before all his knights for his treatment of the children of Bohort and accuses him of a lack of *san*, *debonaireté* and *cortesie*. Sequence B (*PL* 133-8) is composed of the following: the grief of the widowed queen Evaine over the disappearance of her sons; her reassurance by a vision that they are alive and well; Banyn's visit to court, which reminds Arthur of his failure to avenge the death of Ban and the disappearance of his son; Arthur's brooding at table, and, when forced to explain his behaviour, the public confession of his failure. The latter sequence, through the repetition of the brooding theme (presenting an essentially passive Arthur) later in the romance, helps to link the narrative of events before Lancelot leaves the Lake with the later part of the story.

There is therefore some ambiguity in the opposition between Arthur and Claudas, and this is confirmed by what might be called the reverse pairing between Arthur and Galehot, in which Arthur is the ruler who is accused of lack of *largece* and of having lost the hearts of his subjects, in comparison with Galehot who is so loved by his men that he is able to bring a vast array. Dreams foretelling the loss of Arthur's kingdom prepare the way for his indictment by a *preudomme* in an episode recalling in some ways the visit of the *rendu*. In both cases a man of God appears before Arthur and proceeds to rebuke him for his failure to perform his duties as king. The differences between the two incidents are as follows; (a) The *rendu* is eventually identified as a particular knight, Adragais li Bruns, who has served Uther and then withdrawn from the world into a religious order; the *preudomme* remains mysterious and is never identified.[29] (b) The *rendu*'s visit comes at a time of peace and festivity (rather like that of the loathly damsel in the *Conte del Graal*), that of the *preudomme* at a time of great anxiety at the end of a day of battle in which Arthur has only been saved from defeat at the hands of Galehot by a mysterious knight with a red shield who has just disappeared. (c) The *rendu* begins with *tu* to force attention, then switches to the usual and more respectful *vos*; the *preudomme* begins with a neutral *vos,* and then switches to the more fatherly *tu*, like that of a confessor.[30]

What is particularly interesting here is that many of the qualities which the *preudomme* finds lacking in Arthur are precisely those in which Claudas had been deficient and which had so impressed both Claudas and his squire on the occasion of their visit to Arthur's court. The *preudomme* accuses Arthur of not having properly fulfilled his duty as king:

'Si doiz savoir que nus hom mortex ne te baillast a garder la seignorie que tu tiens, mais Dex solement la te bailla por ce que tu l'an feïsses bone garde, et tu li as faite si mauvaisse que tu la destruiz qui garder la deüsses. Car li droiz do povre ne dou non puissant ne puet venir jusqu'a toi, ainz est li riches desleiaus oëz et henorez devant ta face por son avoir, et li povres droituriers n'i a loi por sa povreté. Li droit des veves et des orphelins est periz en ta seignorie.' (*PL* 283.21–8.)

He explains why Arthur's men are failing him:

'Ha! fait li preudom, ce n'est mie mervoille se ti home te faillent, car puis que li hon se faut, bien li doivent faillir li autre. Et tu ies failliz quant tu messerras contre ton Signor de tel signorie con tu devoies tenir de lui, non pas d'autrui. Pour ce convient que il te faillent, car ceste demostrance premiere t'a faite Dex, por ce que tu t'aparceüsses qu'il te voloit oster de ta seignorie, por ce qu'il te toloit cels par cui aide tu l'as longuement maintenue. Et neporqant, li un te faillent de lor gré, et li autre estre lor gré. Cil te faillent de lor gré cui tu deüsses faire les granz onors et porter les granz seignories et les granz compaignies: ce sont li bas gentil home de ta terre par cui tu doiz estre maintenuz, car li regnes ne puet estre tenuz se li comuns des genz ne s'i accorde. Cil te sont failli de lor gré. Li autre qui estre lor gré te faillent, ce sont cil de ta maison cui tu as donnees les granz richeces, cui tu as faiz seignors de ta maison. Cil te faillent estre lor gré, por ce que Dex lo velt.' (*PL* 285.28–286.4.)

The *preudomme* therefore condemns Arthur for not protecting the righteous poor against the rich and powerful, he reproaches him for still not having revenged the death of Ban, his loyal vassal, and the disinheritance of his widow, a failure which had first inspired Claudas with the idea of conquering Arthur. Arthur is told (*PL* 285–6) that he has lost the hearts of his knights because he has not shown generosity to the right people: he has not bestowed gifts on the lesser gentry but only on the great barons.[31] The *preudomme* says:

'Or te pran garde que puet valoir escuz ne auberz n'espee ne force de chevaus; sanz cuer d'ome nule rien ne puet valoir.' (*PL* 286.11–13.)

This should be compared with the bitter remarks of Claudas about the conquest of kingdoms being of no avail if one has not the hearts of the people:

'Et mout a petit seignorie sus son pueple cil qui les cuers n'an puet avoir.' (*PL* 81.28–9.)

The *preudomme* advises Arthur how to win back the hearts of his people by suitable gifts, adapted to the needs of the recipient. His remarks on the way that Arthur should improve his method of giving in order to show the quality of true *largece* (*PL* 287–8), especially the distinction made between the gifts for rich barons and for poor knights, should be compared with the praise of the *serjant* for Arthur (*PL* 34.23–32, quoted above) as a superbly generous king who knows how to win the hearts of his people through showing the particular form of graciousness appropriate to each rank, through making the right gifts and paying attention to both rich and poor men at his court. The *preudomme* says:

'Aprés donras as hauz omes, as rois, as dux, as contes, as hauz barons. Et coi? Les riches vaisselementes, les cointes joiaus, les biaus dras de soie, les boens chevaus, et si ne bee mie a els tant doner les riches dons come les biaus et les plaissanz, car l'an ne doit mie doner a riche home riches choses, mes plaisanz choses poi riches, car ce est uns anuiz de fondre l'une richece sor l'autre. Mais au povre home doit l'en doner tex choses qui soient plus boenes que beles, et plus porfitables que plaisanz, car povretez n'a mestier que d'amendement, et richece n'a mestier que de delit.' (*PL* 288.18–27.)

Galesguantins li Galois describes Galehot in very favourable terms which suggest that he has all the qualities the *preudomme* finds absent in Arthur:

'Sire, ge ai veü Galehot. Il est bien plus granz demi pié que chevalier que l'an saiche, si est
li hom del monde plus amez de sa gent et cil qui plus a conquis de son aage, car il est
juenes bachelers. Et dient cil qui l'ont a acointe que c'est li plus gentis chevaliers et li plus
deboenneres do monde et toz li plus larges.' (*PL* 264.30–4.)

But he adds hastily:

'Mais por ce, fait il, nel di ge mie que ge ja cuit ne il ne autres ait desus vos pooir, car se ge
lo cuidoie, ja ne m'aïst Dex se ge ne voloie miauz estre morz que vis.' (*PL* 264.34–7.)

This provides a significant variation on the remarks of the *serjant* to Claudas:

'Et se cist [Artus] estoit fox et mauvais et de grant coardise plains, ne voi ge mie encor, ne
ne sai l'ome qui au desouz lo poïst metre, tant com il voudra les prodomes croire qui con-
versent o lui; car il covandroit a celui qui lo cuideroit descrire qu'il fust plus riches hom
de lui, et eüst planté de meilleurs chevaliers en son pooir, ce que ge ne cuit ores mie que
nus ait, et qu'il fust miauz entechiez dou roi Artu, qui a painnes porroit avenir, car ge ne
cuidei onques en nul cors de haut home si hautes teches ne si beles come les soes me sam-
blent estre. Por ce ne m'est il pas avis qu'il poïst estre par nul hom descritez, ne Dex nel fist
onques tel por oblier enjusque la. Ne Dex ne fist onques home, tant soit mes charnex amis,
ne tant m'ait de granz biens faiz, s'il lo pooit descriter et ge l'an pooie garantir, que ge ne
l'an garantisse a mon pooir sanz moi mesfaire, et ençois me mesferoie gié que ge nel garantisse a mon pooir, et après an feroie ma penitance.' (*PL* 34.32–35.8.)

Galehot and Claudas share the same ambition—victory over Arthur—but
Claudas has not the superior qualities required to achieve this. Despite the loyal
reservation of Galesguantins, from the way that Arthur is presented at the
time of the war with Galehot it is clear that Galehot would have succeeded, had
it not been for Lancelot, where Claudas, seeing no prospect of success, had
drawn back.

If Arthur appears to Claudas and his *serjant* much as Galehot does to
Galesguantins with Arthur here providing the unfavourable point of comparison, there is also a different kind of link between Arthur and Galehot in two
series of dreams, both foretelling disaster. Arthur's efforts to respond to the advice
of the *preudomme* and the help of Lancelot save him from calamity; Galehot
cannot escape the doom which threatens him, and it is Lancelot who is to be the
unwilling cause of his death. Both Arthur and Galehot have alarming dreams.
Arthur's look forward and help to provide a framework for events in the central
part of the romance. Galehot's look both backwards to past events and forward
to the future, thus helping to relate the last section of the romance to its centre.
Arthur has three dreams at three-nightly intervals; in the first he dreams that he

loses his hair, in the second his fingers, and in the third his toes. Galehot has a dream more traditional to the epic, in that animals appear in it. He sees two lions, one of them crowned, fighting together; a leopard reconciles them, but in the end the leopard kills the uncrowned lion. He has only one dream, but it is preceded by the crumbling of his castles.

The two sets of dreams are explicitly linked in that Galehot decides to ask Arthur to send him the clerks who interpreted the King's dreams, and in that both would recall to the reader the interpretation of the falling of Vortigern's tower in the *Brut* of Wace and in the *Merlin* of Robert de Boron, although some of the details borrowed vary between the two dreams in the *PL*. In both episodes the clerks ask for more time,[32] but this is given greater emphasis in relation to Arthur's dreams, when the clerks make repeated requests for delay. In each case Arthur or Galehot is asked to swear that if the clerks interpret the dream, he will bear them no ill will:

'Et volons, comment qu'il aveigne, que vos nos creantoiz que maus ne nos en vendra.' (*PL* 262.3–4.)

'Mais vos nos creanteroiz leiaument que vos ne nos en savroiz mauvais gré.' (*PL* 582.15–16.)

As in the *Brut* and *Merlin*, Arthur's clerks cannot give the King a full and true interpretation of his dream, whereas in Galehot's case the leader of the clerks, Bademaguz, is wise enough to be able to reveal the whole truth, and there is no need for a mysterious outsider (Merlin in the *Brut* and *Merlin,* the unnamed *preudomme* in the *PL*).

It is only in Galehot's case that castles crumble and towers fall, as Vortigern's tower fell, and this crumbling of castles has indeed a *senefiance* for Galehot, as he himself guesses: 'C'est aucune senefiance.' (*PL* 575.10). This is confirmed by Bademaguz who tells Galehot that it is a warning to him against his overweening pride and a sign that his plan to conquer Arthur was against the will of God:

'Et ce que voz forterreces fondirent si tost com vos meïstes lo pié dedanz vostre terre, fu por ce que Dex voloit que vos aparceüssiez que force estoit et ancontre sa volenté, et qu'il avoit l'orgoil abatu par quoi vos aviez anpris a guerroier lo plus prodome do monde.' (*PL* 582.29–32.)

Thus the evocation of Vortigern, who allied himself with the pagan Saxons and was soon replaced by the true champion of Christianity, Uther, the father of Arthur, has a part to play in this intricate interlacing of changing oppositions. Near the beginning of the work we learn of the ambition of Claudas to conquer Arthur:

'Ge me pensai antan que g'estoie un des plus viguereus hom do monde, et que se ge pooie avoir lo reiaume de Logres, ge seroie li plus dotez rois qui onques fust et conquerroie tant

que ge seroie rois de tot lo monde; si pensoie a guerroier lou roi Artu tant que ge lou
poïsse metre au desouz.' (*PL* 34.4–8.)

Towards the end of the work Galehot reveals the proud and ambitious projects
which inspired the building of his castle, l'Orgueilleusse Angarde:

'Certes, dist Galehoz, voirement diriez vos qu'ele fu fermee de haut cuer, se vos saviez que
ge pensoie au jor que ge la fis faire, car j'avoie trente reiaumes conquis et mis en ma seignorie, si dis a moi meïsmes que g'estoie li plus viguerex hom del siegle et li plus redotez et
que ge n'oseroie nulle chose anprandre dont ge ne venisse bien a chief, por ce que toz avoie
mes anemis mis au desoz. Si me pansai que ge feroie tant que j'avroie lo reiaume de
Logres. Alors si seroie coronez et porteroie corone en cest chastel si richement c'onques
nuns rois si richement ne l'i porta, car ge avoie fait trente et une corone, si avoie enpensé
que tuit mi roi seroient a ceste feste et que por l'anor de mon coronement porteroit chascuns d'aus corone. Et sor chascune des torneles avroit un soztenal d'argent del grant a un
home, si avroit sor chascun un cierge. Et desus cele grant tor qui siet en mileu de cest
chastel seroit uns soztenaus d'or assez greignor qe nuns des autres, et desus reseroit uns
cierges, si seroient tuit li cierge si grant que il ardroient tote nuit, que ja por tens que il
poïst faire ne porroient estaindre. En ceste maniere, fait Galehoz, avoie an talant que ge
seroie coronez qant j'avroie lo roi Artus conquis' (*PL* 574.19–38.)

At this point, therefore, the words of Galehot recall those of Claudas, when he
revealed the plan to conquer Arthur which, in the end, he was too prudent to
undertake. Galehot has no such inhibitions; he had the qualities which made
such an enterprise feasible, but whatever may have been the weaknesses of
Arthur as ruler (compared with Galehot), it was not God's will that Galehot
should succeed. Thus Lancelot, by his intervention to save Arthur's kingdom, was
acting according to the will of God, although his conscious inspiration was his
love for Guinevere. Lancelot loses his father and his land through the war between
Claudas and Arthur's vassal, whom Arthur fails to protect or avenge. Arthur
keeps his land through the intervention of Lancelot and in accordance with
God's will; Galehot, a great knight and ruler, achieves a victory over Arthur with
Lancelot's help, only to surrender his greatest ambition, at the request of
Lancelot, and eventually to die, again because of Lancelot. Yet Galehot shows a
noble resignation before his fate which gives him a tragic grandeur unattained
by Arthur in this text, even if the latter is described as 'lo plus prodome do
monde' by Bademaguz. We have seen in Chapter III why it is important in
this romance, with Lancelot as its central figure, inspired to great deeds by his
love for the Queen, that Arthur should not be given heroic proportions
throughout the text. The shifting contrasts between the three figures, Claudas,
Arthur, and Galehot, whose relations with one another are to some extent
determined by their relationship to Lancelot, are brought out through a skilful

use of repetitions, oppositions, and parallels in such a way as to help to give cohesion to the whole work. It is interesting to note that both Galehot and Arthur are shown to be dependent in their great battles on the skill of the knightly hero Lancelot, a *povre chevalier* in so far as he holds no land. The *preu-domme* in his advice to Arthur emphasizes that a king relies for the defence of his land not only on his powerful barons, but also on the more humble gentry, without such great fiefs. The different pairings of the three rulers, Arthur, Galehot, and Claudas, indicate that even kings have to keep to their proper place, for they cannot maintain power alone.

There are other pairings both in contrast and in parallel in which an important element is the traditional opposition between the young knight who has yet to make his name and Gauvain, the established hero who has to prove his right to the name he already has. In these the echoing of other texts plays a significant role both in the interplay between the characters and in giving a coherent pattern to a string of adventures, apparently occurring by chance on a series of quests. These contrasts and echoes have been studied in Chapter II in relation to the development of the identity theme, and here I propose to concentrate on the technique of the interlacing of three pairs, Lancelot and Gauvain,[33] Lancelot and Hector, and Hector and Gauvain. All three are linked by quests: Hector sets out on a quest for Gauvain who is himself on a quest for Lancelot, hidden away in Sorelois; but these pursuits at one remove are interlinked by a series of pairings through doubling of episodes or motifs.

One of the main points of contrast between Lancelot and Gauvain is that Lancelot's identity is kept secret whereas Gauvain, by tradition, freely gives his name, and Hector follows his example.[34] However, as was seen in Chapter II, (pp. 22–4, 29–32), there are two balancing sequences, one concerning Lancelot's first adventures on becoming a knight (*PL* 162–78) and the second concerning Gauvain's first adventures on his renewed quest for Lancelot (*PL* 371–90). In both an unknown knight is unwillingly accepted as a champion for a judicial combat in defence of a lady's land by an emissary who has orders to get one of Arthur's greatest knights. The emissary doubts the prowess of his champion, and there are a series of testing battles on the journey. Lancelot is regarded as unsuitable for the task because he is young and unknown, and the emissary exploits his rather comic impetuosity in order to persuade him to test his strength against another would-be champion, a big knight with a damsel in a tent; the youth triumphs, defends the Lady of Nohaut successfully, and disappears, still unnamed. Gauvain is thought to be an unworthy champion not because he is young and inexperienced but because, as an unrecognized stranger who has appeared in a passive role, he is seen as a cowardly and inadequate substitute for Gauvain, a situation which also has comic overtones. He is measured against

Hector, considered by the emissary to be a far better prospect as champion, if only his *amie* (the damsel in a tent of this sequence) would allow him to take part. It is Hector who, unlike the big knight with the damsel in the tent of the first sequence, passes the tests on the journey with honour. Gauvain is forced to stand by, but in the end he wins his judicial battle and disappears before the Lady of Roestoc, whom he has defended, finds out who he is. Hector is then left with the task of finding Gauvain, who is himself seeking the unknown knight of the first sequence under the guise of the Red Knight (and the Black Knight).

Both sequences are variations on the theme of the Fair Unknown, with echoes for Lancelot from the *Conte del Graal* as well as *li Biaus Descouneüs,* for Gauvain from *Erec*.[35] The second sequence links Gauvain with Lancelot and with the identity theme at a time when the latter has been withdrawn from circulation into Sorelois, and it also contrasts Gauvain with Hector, who at this stage in the romance takes Lancelot's place in the main narrative as a young knight and lover in the process of establishing his reputation.

There are many parallels which pair Lancelot with Hector. They both fall into lovers' trances, when they are so deep in meditation that they are unaware of their surroundings and hear nothing that is said to them.[36] Hector falls into deep thought before the shield and, like Lancelot at the ford, unhorses the knights who disturb him. Both are mocked by Kay for their behaviour during their lovers' trances and both unhorse him, as did Perceval when disturbed during his meditation over the drops of blood in the snow.[37] Both rescue knights falsely accused of misconduct with regard to other knights' ladies (*PL* 221–3, 427–32), episodes which recall Perceval's fight with the Orgueilleus de la Lande.[38] There is also an interesting link with Hector's battle and that of Lancelot against the big knight who refused to let him see the damsel in the tent, one of the tests of his quality as a knight on the way to Nohaut; on both these occasions the knight refuses to arm himself with the identical phrase: 'Fi! fait il, por vos m'armerole gié!' (*PL* 173.11, 428.30). Thus, although Hector's name, unlike that of Lancelot, is known almost from the time of his first appearance in the narrative, he is also involved in the network of literary allusions with Lancelot and Perceval, a pattern of resonances which has been studied in Chapter II. Lancelot and Hector both have spells in prison for killing knights in fair combat (Lancelot in the glass gaol of the Lady of Malohaut, *PL* 275, 279; Hector at les Marés *PL* 471–2); both are released from prison to fight battles.

While Lancelot is in Sorelois, therefore, it is Hector who takes over the role of the young knight, paired with Gauvain in contrast and parallel, and again we will find reminiscences of the opposition between Perceval and Gauvain in the *Conte del Graal*. Both Gauvain (unrecognized) and Hector are taken to defend ladies in battle as substitute champions. The dwarf explains that the Lady of

Roestoc has asked him to fetch Gauvain, but, as he is impossible to find, being always away on adventure, he is bringing his lady the worst knight in the world (the unrecognized Gauvain). The sister of Heliene sanz Per obtains Hector's release from prison at les Marés to fight for Heliene as a substitute for Gauvain, whom she has been seeking for five years:

'Et ge ai esté an la maison lo roi Artu, puis cinc anz an ça, plus de vint foiz, ne onques monseignor Gauvain n'i poi trover, car ge li amenasse mout volentiers, se ge lo poïsse avoir.' (*PL* 520.2–5.)

This seems to echo the words of Grohadain the dwarf when he chooses the anonymous Gauvain as a poor substitute for himself (*PL* 377.11–14). It also recalls how Helin des Taningues, after vain efforts to find Gauvain at Arthur's court, decides to take the anonymous champion of the Lady of Roestoc as a worthy substitute to dub him knight (*PL* 394.17–19). There is a comic contrast between Hector's visit to the Castle of Estroite Marche, where he tries very hard not to become involved with the castellan's daughter, who comes to him as he lies in bed to ask him to become her husband (*PL* 463–4), and Gauvain's visit to the daughter of the King of Norgales (*PL* 506–14), where he is only too happy to be involved (on a less permanent basis) with the king's daughter, who has sent for him so that she may give her maidenhood to the most famous of knights. There is a subtle interplay here between these two episodes in the *PL* opposing Gauvain and Hector, two episodes in Chrétien's romance, opposing Gauvain and Perceval, and an adventure in the *First Continuation*.[39] In the *Perceval Continuation* the daughter of Norés de Lis makes a similar vow, but her surrender of virginity has tragic consequences in the death of her father and brother, although in the *Second Continuation* it produces a fine son, Guinglain, who will be paired with Perceval. Gauvain's night with the King of Norgales's daughter is, in contrast, followed by unsuccessful attempts by the knights of Norgales to storm the girl's bedchamber, which recall the burlesque encounter of Gauvain at the Castle of Escavalon. Gauvain uses Escalibor as well as other weapons and improvised missiles in both Chrétien and the Prose *Lancelot*. This contrasts with Perceval's inexperience in the scene with Blancheflor and with Hector's restrained behaviour towards the daughter of the lord of the Estroite Marche. Indeed, the whole episode of the Estroite Marche is closely modelled on Perceval's visit to Bel Repaire.[40] These resonances from Chrétien and the *Perceval Continuation* serve to underline the contrast between the famous and experienced knight, Gauvain, and the as yet unknown young knight and faithful lover, Hector. There are other parallels between the two knights. Hector and Gauvain both have their horses struck by dwarfs from whom they wish to obtain information (*PL* 372.25–9, 467.3–5). Gauvain has the strange attribute (to be found in the *First Continuation*)[41] that his strength wanes as noon approaches and then increases in a marvellous way:

Mais tex estoit sa costume que tozjorz ampiroit sa force a ore de midi, et si tost comme midis tornoit, si revenoit a doble et cuers et seürtez et force. Et lors i parut bien que si tost com midis torna, lo virent tuit cil qui l'esgardoient autresi frec et autresi viste com il avoit esté a l'ancommancement de la meslee. (*PL* 388.13–18.)[42]

In Hector's battle against Marganor it is said:

Ensin se contient tant que midis fu passez. Et lors ot Hestors si s'aleine reprise, si recovre et ot mout grant honte de ce que tant s'iere soferz sanz gaires grant proece faire. Si recort sus a Marganor mout vigucreusemcnt, si lo ficrt mout a bandon, si lo blecc mout ct ampire, tant que ja a mout grant paor. Si ne fait mais gaires Marganors que sosfrir, que mout a perdu de sanc. Et li sanble estre Hestors plus forz et plus vistes que il n'avoit esté au comancement. (*PL* 458.13–20.)

This seems to be a faint echo of Gauvain's increase in strength after noon, but without the suggestion of more than human power to be found in expressions such as *fantosme* (*PL* 388.24), used in relation to Gauvain.

Finally, all three pairings, Lancelot/Gauvain, Hector/Gauvain, Lancelot/ Hector, are interlinked in that both Hector and Lancelot have battles with Gauvain which are interrupted in the middle, when one or both combatants discover the identity of their opponent in episodes recalling the interrupted battle in *Yvain*:[43] Gauvain recognizes Hector's sword when they are fighting at the Pont Norgalois (*PL* 530.16–28); Lyonel stops the battle between Lancelot and Gauvain in the *Ille Perdue* (*PL* 537.1–5), a battle where in most manuscripts Gauvain appears to be struggling to hold his own.[44] Lancelot surpasses Hector in this matching against Gauvain, for his superiority over the King's nephew has already been established in the healing of Agravain, whose leg is cured by the blood of the second greatest knight (Gauvain, *PL* 417–19), and his arm by that of the greatest (Lancelot, *PL* 539.29–31). The superiority of Lancelot is also shown in the quality of the love which he can inspire and by which he is inspired: Guinevere, who has faith in Lancelot's prowess, is the inspiration behind his great deeds, whereas Hector's *amie* will not allow him to fight as champion for the Lady of Roestoc and does her utmost to stop him from going on the quest for Gauvain because she has not the same confidence in her *ami* and wants to isolate him from the outside world. It is only Guinevere's intervention that makes it possible for Hector to set out on the adventures which establish his reputation as a knight and win him a seat at the Round Table, in which he is installed on the same day as Lancelot (*PL* 571.19–20).

The three knights' respective rankings within the romance are made clear in a passage discussed in Chapter VI in relation to its Grail allusion (*PL* 571.24–31). The adventures of Gauvain and Hector are recorded by Arthur's clerks as branches of the tale of Lancelot in the great book in which all the deeds of the knights of the Round Table are inscribed and all the great Arthurian adventures, including those which lie outside the scope of this particular romance. These pairings of Lancelot, Hector, and Gauvain help, therefore, to establish their positions in the hierarchy of Arthurian knights. There are humorous overtones in some of the contrasts and parallels, but these are not presented in such a way as to constitute a serious criticism of traditional chivalric values in Arthurian romance. Even if all three knights may on occasion be made to appear as slightly comic figures, they are nevertheless given a positive role as defenders of the weak and upholders of justice for the lesser gentry, if not for the peasants, and there is not the same ambiguity over these pairings as has been seen in relation to Arthur, Claudas, and Galehot.

We have therefore in the *PL* a network of similar episodes, recurring narrative structures, and linking motifs, often playing an important role in the development of the two main themes and, through direct allusions to and resonances from other romances, in the integration of the Lancelot story into an Arthurian world which has an existence outside the individual tale. There are also many examples of the repetition of the same information or of allusions forwards and backwards to explanations already given or yet to be given, events already told in the tale or yet to be told. The distribution of these linking and interweaving techniques is of particular interest in any examination of both the structure of the non-cyclic *Lancelot* and its relationship with the *Lancelot-Grail* cycle, and I propose to make a survey in the next chapter of the use of these techniques in relation to the main phases in the tale of the making of Lancelot's name, as established in Chapters I and II.

IX

The Coherence of 'The Prose *Lancelot* Without the Grail'

Distribution of the linking devices within the thematic structure and the interlace

All references are to the PL (unless otherwise indicated) and to the phases in the development of the identity theme as set out in Chapter I.

Prologue and Phase I (pp. 1–166)

Lancelot's childhood in the lake, his journey to Camelot, and his knighting

A   *Internal links within phase I*

(*a*) Interweaving between three main locations: Lake, land of Claudas, court of Arthur.

Repeated descriptions of the widowed queens' holy life at Mostier Reial on the shores of the Lake, interlacing with repeated descriptions of Lancelot's development and education in the Lake (20–4, 38–48, 132–3, 138–9) so that the growth of the abbey and the growth of Lancelot run parallel.

Repeated sequences of the queens mourning the loss of their sons, their partial reassurance (through visitor or vision), a visitor to Arthur's court reminding him of his failure to avenge the death of Ban and the disappearance of his son (48–57, 133–8).

Journeys between the three locations:

Ban dies on a journey to Arthur (6, 12–14).

Claudas travels to and from Arthur's court in Britain (32–8).

A *rendu* goes between Mostier Reial and Arthur's court, but also has knowledge of what goes on in the Lake (50–1, 53–4, 57).

Damsels journey between the Lake and the land of Claudas (57–8, 69–70, 100–1, 103–4).

Lancelot's time in the Lake ends with his departure, accompanied by the Lady of the Lake, for Arthur's court (148); their meeting with Arthur (151); Lancelot's arrival at Camelot (155).

(*b*) Pairing of Lancelot and Lyonel (see Chaper VIII, pp. 218–22) and references to their lineage (13.12, 14.1–4, 49.39–50.2, 108.37–109.32, 153.39–154.3, 154.17–21).

(*c*) The Lady of the Lake recognizes that Lancelot should become a knight (111.16–34, 139.3–13, 147.8–34), fulfils her intention by bringing him to Arthur (151–4), and he is knighted, except for the girding of the sword (159–60).

(*d*) The description of Lancelot's white apparel and equipment is repeated (148, 151) and underlines the identity under which he first makes his name as White Knight, a designation used throughout phase II.

B *Preparation for events to come*

(*a*) The tale will tell why the hero was called Lancelot (1.9); in phase II (194) we learn how Lancelot discovered his name. (Identity theme)

The tale will tell more about Heliene sanz Per (33.7–8); picked up in phase V (519–24). (Love theme)

The tale will tell about the knighting of Lyonel by Arthur (60.36–9); picked up in phase VI (609–11). (Identity theme)

(*b*) The Lady of the Lake's intention that, after Lancelot leaves the Lake to become a knight, Lyonel will in due course follow him and be knighted (111.30–4, 154.21–4); fulfilled when Lyonel leaves the Lake to serve Lancelot in phase V (358) and is knighted in phase VI (609–11).

(*c*) People of Britain await the coming of someone of the lineage of the mother of Lyonel and Bohort to deliver them from the marvels which happen there (108–9); probably linked with Lancelot's achievements at the Dolorous Guard, especially the ending of the enchantments in phase III (248–50); it could also be linked to Lancelot's saving of Arthur and his kingdom from the defeat foretold in Arthur's dreams in phase IV (in the battles with Galehot).

(*d*) The arrival of the wounded knight (149); the explanation of the weapons being left in his wounds promised at 149.28–30, partly fulfilled at 150.12–15. Lancelot's first conversation with him (158–9) and the oath to avenge him (160.7–20) prepare the way for a series of battles in phase III (224–5, 227.11–15) and phase IV (258–60, 273–4), and his imprisonment by the Lady of Malohaut (274–5).

C *References outwards to past events in the wider Arthurian tradition (or the Bible), either by allusion to events not told in the romance or by incidents recounted in the romance but presented as coming from an Arthurian past in relation to the main thread*

(*a*) Arthur's wars at the beginning of his reign (2.8–11, 33.20–4, 53.36–9); these evoke in general terms the chronicle tradition and Robert de Boron.

(*b*) Birth of Merlin and the engendering of Arthur (21–3).

(*c*) Perceval/Perlesvaus (son of Pellés) who achieved the adventure of the Perilous Seat and saw the Grail marvels *apertement* (33): joint allusion to Chrétien and Robert de Boron.

(*d*) Great knights of the past: David, the Maccabees, Joseph of Arimathea, Galahaz King of Hosselice (called Gales in his honour) and son of Joseph, Perles de Listenois (no longer living) and his brother Helais li Gros (146): the Bible and Robert de Boron.

(*e*) Gauvain's wound received in battle with Gasoain d'Estrangot who had accused him of disloyalty (149.7–11).

Phase II (pp. 166–95)

Lancelot's first adventures as White Knight up to his conquest of Dolorous Guard and discovery of his own name

A   *Links with earlier events in the romance and internal links within phase II*

Many of the characters who played an active role during the period of Lancelot's childhood disappear from the narrative, but some links with the Lake continue through the damsels from the Lake.

(*a*) Instructions from the Lady of the Lake, sent through a damsel (188.3–23), continue the instructions she had given in person in phase I (142–7, 151, 154). Lancelot recognizes the damsel from his childhood (184.12, 187–8).

(*b*) Repetitions linked to the Dolorous Guard, an adventure important for the identity theme, in which Lancelot is assisted by a damsel from the Lake: explanations concerning the castle (183–4, 188–9) prepare for its conquest (189–93); Lancelot's discovery of his own name in the cemetery (194) follows up the indication given in phase I (1.9) without direct reference back, and the predictions of the Lady of the Lake, given directly (154.2–3), or through a damsel in phase II (188.4–7).

(*c*) The three magic shields sent by the Lady of the Lake (187–8) are used in turn, with one band (191.26), two bands (192.7), three bands (193.4–9); they will serve to identify the hero in the next phase.

B   *Preparation for events to come*

The adventure of the Dolorous Guard and the repeated explanations of the conditions necessary to end the enchantments (II, 183–4, 195, picked up in phase III, 248) look forward to the time when they are dispelled (III, 250.13–21).

C   *References outwards to past events in the wider Arthurian tradition, either by allusion to events not told in the romance or by incidents recounted in the romance but presented as coming from an Arthurian past in relation to the main thread*

(*a*) An incident in Arthur's wars against rebel kings which gave rise to the name of the ford, Gué la Reine (180.37–181.20).

(*b*) Tomb of Leucain and references to Joseph of Arimathea and the Grail (179.1–5); cf. *First Continuation*, III, *A* 7586–604.

Phase III (pp. 195–257)

Gauvain's first quest for Lancelot during which the First and Second Assemblies take place, the enchantments at Dolorous Guard are ended, and Lancelot's name is brought back to court

A *Links with earlier events in the romance and internal links within phase III*

(i) Promises and predictions made early in phase III, many linked to the Lady of the Lake, through her damsels bearing instructions, or through the magic objects she has sent, provide the framework for events (most of them linked to the identity theme):

(*a*) The oath of the damsel from the Lake to remain in a tower in the Dolorous Guard until released from her promise by Lancelot provides links throughout phase III (205, 208, 215, 218–20, 226, 235, 239) until she is released from her oath (239–40).

(*b*) Gauvain's promises to the damsel to seek her release and to the King that he will discover the identity of the knight who conquered Dolorous Guard (219–20) start a quest which continues throughout phase III (specific references to it 226.10–11, 233, 234, 235; completed 255, 256–7).

(*c*) The imprisoned damsel's prediction that Gauvain will get news of the knight he seeks at each of the three assemblies of Logres, made early in phase II (219.38–9), is fulfilled in relation to the First Assembly (232.25–6), and the Second Assembly (255), and continues into phase IV (270.35, 272). Two damsels from the Lake continue to provide connecting links with the childhood in the Lake and also within Gauvain's quest, often with references back: Lancelot meets a damsel from the Lake, who weeps over the imprisonment of Gauvain (204–5), and receives more instructions from the Lady of the Lake. Gauvain meets the same damsel (226) and again later (234) and she promises to help him to learn the name of the knight whom he seeks (235.23–4, 239.20–3); the damsel in the tower also takes up the task and makes the promise (240.28–9), and it is fulfilled (255).

(*d*) Ending of the enchantments at Dolorous Guard: the conditions for doing so were explained in phase II (183–4, 195), repeated in phase III (248), and fulfilled (248–50). This is linked to the repeated escapes of Brandin des Illes, the Lord of the Dolorous Guard, who could have ended the enchantments (194, 195, 200, 214).

(e) Repeated visits to Dolorous Guard continue, usually with references back, often linked to the identity theme and, in Gauvain's case, to his quest. Lancelot's return to the gates of the Dolorous Guard (236–7) is linked to his trances before them (207–8, 215) and to the love theme by his memories and the words he addresses to the gates. Repeated visits to the cemetery with its ever-changing inscriptions are an important linking element. Gauvain's return to it (240) is linked to phase II and the identity theme by his unsuccessful attempt to raise the slab beneath which is Lancelot's name, recalling Lancelot's first visit when he discovered who he was (194); Gauvain himself, through a reference back, recalls his own first visit (198–9); Lancelot's final visit to the cemetery (248–50) recalls the earlier descriptions of the cemetery with the reference to tombstones and helmets which have disappeared.

(*f*) The First Assembly (against the Roi d'Outre les Marches), which is linked to the quest for the White Knight's name by the damsel's prediction (*c*, above), is arranged (220); Lancelot is informed of it (221.1–21); it takes place (230–4). The renewal of battle (this time against the Roi des Cent Chevaliers) at the Second Assembly is arranged (234) and takes place (253–6). The reference to lo Blanc Chevalier picks up Lancelot's designation during his first adventures as a knight in phase II.

(*g*) The three magic shields sent by the Lady of the Lake and used by Lancelot during the conquest of the Dolorous Guard serve to identify the hero during his efforts to rescue Gauvain and are used in the same order as in phase II: one band 207.12, two bands 215.13, 215.27, three bands 216.30, 219.13–14, 224.23–6.

(*h*) Lancelot's promise to avenge the wounded knight (159–60) gives rise to a battle (224–5) and a reference back to this battle (227); the series of battles is continued in phase IV.

(ii) Lancelot's withdrawals from knightly activity: he is injured in a fall (223), by the first wound (225), by the second wound (231); he withdraws twice from the action to heal his injuries: before the First Assembly in a litter (225–9), before the Second Assembly, in a litter, to the castle of the Lady of Nohaut (236–9), and to the Hermit of Plaisseiz (241, with reference back to 214).

(iii) Repeated sequences of interlacing abstractions of Lancelot the lover and Arthur the king (206–8, 215–16) and reference back by a damsel from the Lake (219.1–2).

B   *Preparation for events to come*

The damsel's prediction concerning the Unknown Knight and the three assemblies (219.38–9) prepares the way for Lancelot's appearance at the Third Assembly. The series of battles stemming from Lancelot's promise (160) prepare the way for his imprisonment in phase IV.

C   *Reference outwards to past events in the wider Arthurian tradition*

An allusion to the engendering of Lohoz by Arthur in Lisanor before the marriage to Guinevere (204.15–18); Lohoz became mortally ill in the Doloreuse Chartre; there are references to Arthur's son in other Arthurian texts, the *Lanzelet* and the *Perlesvaus*, for example (see *PL* II, note to 204.15–18).

Phase IV (pp. 257–356)

Lancelot's adventures after the Second Assembly up to his imprisonment at Malohaut, Arthur's dreams, Galehot's invasion, the Third Assembly, the Forty Companions' unsuccessful quest for the Red Knight (Lancelot), the Fourth Assembly, Lancelot's meeting with Guinevere and her discovery of his name, the departure of Lancelot and Galehot for Sorelois.

A   *Links with earlier events in the romance and internal links within phase IV.*

(*a*) Repetitions in the basic structure echo III: a repeated pattern of a quest for an unknown knight who is withdrawn from knightly activity (here through imprisonment) and re-emerges to take part in two assemblies under different arms; he is sought by Gauvain who has sworn to Arthur that he will complete the quest, to the King's dismay on both occasions (suggested briefly in II, 220.7, developed a little further in IV, 297.25–35, 298.32–36).

The Third and Fourth Assemblies are linked to the First and Second through a similar pattern. News of invasion prepares the way for the future battle in III (220) and in IV (275–6); at the end of the battle the next assembly is arranged in III (234), in IV (283, 293). The Roi d'Outre les Marches, opponent of Arthur in the First and Second Assemblies, is a vassal of Galehot, Arthur's opponent in the Third and Fourth Assemblies, and takes part in the Fourth Assembly; his companion in the Second Assembly, the Roi des Cent Chevaliers, is Galehot's cousin and fights on his side in the Third and Fourth Assemblies. The damsel from the Lake's prediction in phase III (219.38–9) was that Gauvain should learn more of the knight whose name he seeks at the First, Second, and Third Assemblies; this is picked up in IV (270.35, 272, 273).

The Third and Fourth Assemblies are linked together by repeated sequences (276–82, 304–27) comprising the following elements: Galehot arrives with an army far larger than that of Arthur; Gauvain fights bravely on the first day, but is seriously wounded; Lancelot emerges from prison to fight for Arthur on the second day and pauses on the same spot in a similar attitude (there are references back in the narrative, 309.1–5, and by Gauvain, 309.23–31, to the earlier occasion).

Lancelot's withdrawal to prison is linked to his promise to avenge the wounded knight (phase I, 159–60, picked up in III, 224–5, 227.11–15), which gives rise to two more battles in phase IV (258–60, 273–4), connected by kinship as his two last victims were cousins; Lancelot is imprisoned in Malohaut because of this last battle, and the series, linking I, III, IV, ends in this prison. He emerges twice from prison to fight (cf. *Char.*), equipped with a different armour each time (cf. *Cligés* and *Char.*); there are two similar descriptions of his gaol without a cross-reference (275.16–23, 279.11–15).

(*b*) Lancelot's return to Camelot is linked through his memories (265.10–13) to his first visit as a youth and to his first sight of Guinevere (in phase I, 151–60). His dumb confusion when he meets the Queen (IV, 267–8) echoes that of his first meeting (I, 157–8); in both cases it is followed by a doubting of his prowess and his vindication in a battle (I, 163, II, 166–7, IV, 267–72; cf. the tale of the Fair Unknown). His trance by the water in IV (266–7) echoes that in II (179–81) and that in Chrétien's *Char*.

(*c*) Arthur's dreams, their interpretations, and fulfilment are linked with the threat to his land from Galehot and involve prediction and repetition. The dreams and their first interpretation (260–2) are partly fulfilled when Arthur fears that he will lose his land (282.32–4); he repeats part of the first interpretation (289.15–19), receives the second interpretation (289–92), picked up again (293); Gauvain says the prediction is fulfilled (322.14–16); Arthur's land is saved (327, with no reference back) when Galehot surrenders. The *preudomme*'s condemnation of Arthur for having failed to avenge Ban (285.11–13) echoes that of the *rendu* in phase I (56); see also Arthur's talk with Banyn which reminds him of his failure (138). The *preudomme*'s reproaches to Arthur for failing to show true generosity contrast with praise of Galehot (264.30–4) and of Arthur (34).

(*d*) Arthur's brooding at table, here linked to the identity theme, (296–7) echoes the brooding in phase I (137–8) and prepares for another (see B, below).

(*e*) Lancelot and Guinevere's conversation, leading up to the first kiss, alludes to nearly all his adventures in phase II, III, and IV; in particular the key words 'A Deu, biaus douz amis' (IV, 345.36) pick up phase I (165.23).

B   *Preparation for events to come*

(*a*) The sequence of brooding and departure on quest in phase IV (296–9) prepares for a similar sequence in V (359–64). The King broods over the Unknown Knight (296–7); Gauvain swears not to return until he has completed his quest, and associates his companions in his oath, the King is dismayed, the knights are listed and depart (297–9); we are told that they will fail to keep their promise (299.13–17), and they return without news of the knight (304.12–19). This prepares for another brooding by the King, this time over his knights' failure to keep their oath (359–61), followed by another oath by Gauvain, greater royal dismay, a second listing of knights, and departure on another quest (361–4; cf. also the *Perceval Continuations*).

(*b*) Galehot's fears (337) that he will be separated from Lancelot through Guinevere foreshadow his separation and death in phase VI.

C   *References outward to past events in the wider Arthurian tradition*

(*a*) The engendering of Arthur outside wedlock (283.19–21): cf. Geoffrey, Wace, and Robert de Boron.

(*b*) Allusion by Gauvain to the Grail Quest with the implication that it belongs to the past (297.21): cf. Chrétien, the *First* and *Second Perceval Continuations*, and Robert de Boron.

Phase V (pp. 356–572)

Lancelot's first withdrawal to Sorelois, Arthur's brooding, Gauvain's renewed quest for Lancelot with twenty companions, Hector's quest for Gauvain, the war against the Saxons, ending with Gauvain's achievement of his quest when he presents Lancelot to Arthur, Lancelot's installation as companion of the Round Table, and the recording of the deeds of Lancelot and the other knights by Arthur's clerks.

A   *Links with earlier events in the romance and internal links within phase V*

(*a*) Fulfilment of promises and intentions, memories.

Gauvain's failure to fulfil a promise leads to a repetition of the pattern at the beginning of phase IV: the withdrawal of the hero, the King brooding over the failure of his knights to find him, giving rise to a quest, the swearing of oaths, royal dismay, listing of companions, and departure (IV, 296–9, V, 359–64). The similar sequences are related through references back by the characters: Arthur, 361.23–31; Gauvain, 361.33–6, 363.1–4, 364.30–365.5. The quest with twenty knights stems from the earlier one, but differs from it in being successful; hence, while Gauvain's adventures during the uncompleted search were excluded as irrelevant (IV, 299.17–19), those he has during this completed one are recounted as part of the story of Lancelot (V, 365.35–6).

The episode of Hector's rescue of Heliene sanz Per (V, 519–24), fulfils the promise given by the tale in phase I (33.6–8), but without reference back.

The sending of Lyonel from the Lake to serve Lancelot as squire fulfils without reference back the intentions of the Lady of the Lake as expressed in phase I (111.30–4).

The description of the arrival of the Lady of the Lake, clad in white (554.30–2), recalls her arrival at Camelot in phase I (152.15–24), and she herself refers to the earlier visit to Arthur's court (V, 556.3–4).

Lyonel meets a damsel from the Lake (495–6) who saved him as a child; a reference back in the narrative (496.18–20) picks up, but with an inconsistency over the name, phase I, 67.35–68.6, 104.9–39.

References to peace with Galehot in V (418.18–19, 528.29) pick up phase IV (327–8).

(*b*) Echoes and pairings.

Battles with Gauvain, interrupted once his identity is known, in phase V (527–8, 537) echo phase III battle (243); cf. *Yvain*.

The doubting of Gauvain, an unknown champion for a judicial duel, tests on the way to the battle at Roestoc and victory (V, 371–89) echoes a sequence in phase II (162–78) where the unknown Lancelot is tested on the way to Nohaut (cf. *Erec* and *LBD*). Hector is paired with Lancelot as the young knight contrasted with Gauvain.

Hector's rescue of a knight falsely accused of dishonouring another knight's lady (V, 425.25–432.5) echoes one by Lancelot (III, 221.25–223.20).

A knight does not deign to put on armour and is defeated by Hector (V, 428.30), and by Lancelot (II, 173.11).

Hector's love trances (368–70, 425–6) recall those of Lancelot (II, 179–81, IV, 266–7; cf. *Char.* and *Perc.*).

Hector's imprisonment and release to fight a battle (V, 472, 516–17) echoes that of Lancelot (IV, 275, 279–81; cf. *Char.*).

Kay's discourteous behaviour and desire to be first (V, 368–70) echo II, 175.18–20, III, 213–14, and episodes in Chrétien.

Repeated descriptions of the ways into Sorelois (357.7–32, 501.3–8, 526.13 with reference back, 527, 529).

Repeated returns of the narrative to Sorelois to present Lancelot pining for Guinevere (358, 472, 531, 532).

Promises made to an unknown damsel in return for directions: made by Gauvain and Hector, 532.39–533.3, by Galehot and Lancelot, 540.1–15 (with reference back); fulfilled 548.3–25 (cf. *Char.*).

(*c*) Developing motif, linked to the love theme: the split shield sent by the Lady of the Lake with the prediction concerning its joining, followed by a promise from the tale to tell of it: 402–3, 407.18–19, 478.11–16, 547.3–25, 553.27, 554.24–7, 555.18–27, 556.14–21.

(*d*) Links between Gauvain's quest for Lancelot and Hector's quest for Gauvain:

Similar oaths sworn at outset: Gauvain, IV, 298.10–30, V, 361.37–362.4; Hector, V, 406.9–19.

Similar experience with dwarf: Gauvain, 372–80; Hector, 466–7.

Increase of strength after noon: Gauvain, 388.13–18, 530.9–13, 535.31–536.29;[1] Hector, 458.13–20.

Hector meets Gauvain and his companions near the beginning of their quest (368–71); there are references back to this meeting during Hector's quest (448.19–23, 461.31–8), during Gauvain's quest (481.6–10, 504.2–3, 504.27–35); Hector frees Yvain and Sagremor (461); Sagremor tells Gauvain about this (504.7–20); Gauvain learns from Sagremor that Hector is seeking him (504.24–38); he wants him to find him (528.24–5).

A sword is sent to Hector by Gauvain, the arrival of which is narrated before the sending (404.9–24, 420.13–30, 423.36–424.3 with reference back); Gauvain recognizes the sword (530.16); Hector thanks him (531.7–8).

Background theme common to both: Gauvain and Hector come into contact with the war between the King of Norgales and the Duke of Cambenic; Gauvain hears about it from Agravain (419.33–5), Hector hears of it at Estroite Marche (446.5–8), Gauvain hears more of it from a hermit (475.21–2, 477.10–19); the death of the Duke's son in the war leads to Gauvain's defence of a man against the seneschal of Cambenic (477.21–3, 483.24, 488.16–34); Gauvain takes part in the battle of Leverzep (479–83), reference back to incident in battle (489.36–490.2).

(*e*) Gauvain's quest, additional internal links:
The beginning of the quest, the oaths sworn and instructions given (363–5) prepare for the return of the twenty companions (540–1): 540.30–3 refers back to 363.1–7; 540.39–541.2, 541.13–14 refer back to 365.27–9.

Agravain's illness (413–19) and his healing, which establish the identity of the two best knights, are recalled through reference back (501.27–31), and completed (539).

The episode of the King of Norgales' daughter (484–515) is linked with Gauvain's visit to Agravain whose *amie* is also a daughter of the King of Norgales (419.39–420.6, 514.31–2, 515.9–16, 541.15–16).

Periodic indirect contact with Alier's war (374–90, 476.1–8, 481.10–13).

(*f*) Hector's quest, internal links between adventures: Hector is in danger and eventually imprisoned because in rescuing Synados he killed the latter's wife's cousin, as he learns from a character (467.32–3), who refers back to 441.30; but he is saved by the dead man's brother, whom he had saved from Guinas, as we learn from a narrative explanation and from a character (468.17–24).

B   *Preparation for events to come*
Galehot's intense love of Lancelot and his awareness that Lancelot's love for the Queen will end by separating him from his companion (IV, 337, V, 568–9, 570–1, 572–3) prepares for the prediction of the clerks in VI (582–3) and for the death of Galehot (612).

C   *References outwards to past events in the wider Arthurian tradition*
(*a*) How Galehot won Sorelois from Gloier (356.20–7).
(*b*) The building of the bridges into Sorelois by Lohoz, father of Gloier, at the time when 'Merlins prophecia les aventures qui devoient avenir', and which were the only means of entry while the adventures of Logres lasted (357.7–32).
(*c*) Gauvain and *la damoiselle chaitive* (362.26–30).
(*d*) 'Lo perron Merlin', where Merlin killed the enchanters (365.10–11).
(*e*) The Grail, the greatest of tales (571.30–1).

Phase VI (pp. 572–613)

Lancelot and Galehot's journey to Sorelois, the False Guinevere episode, casting doubt on the Queen's identity, the knighting of Lyonel and the fight with the Crowned Lion of Lybia, the death of Galehot.

A   *Links with earlier events in the romance and internal links within phase VI*

(*a*) The withdrawal of Lancelot by Galehot to his own land (572–3) echoes the earlier withdrawal at the beginning of phase V (356).

(*b*) Galehot's dreams and their interpretation (577–83) echo the similar sequence of Arthur's dreams and their interpretation (IV, 260–2, 283–94), with a specific reference back by Galehot, who sends for the clerks who interpreted Arthur's dreams (578.28–30); cf. Merlin and Vortigern in Robert de Boron. The dreams themselves, when interpreted (582), link up with past events, the war between Arthur and Galehot, and Lancelot's part in the making of peace in phase IV, and prepare for the death of Galehot (612).

(*c*) Galehot's ambitions, when he built his great castle (574, 582.29–32), link up with the war with Arthur (IV) and recall the ambitions of Claudas in phase I (31).

(*d*) Galehot's fear of being separated from Lancelot through Guinevere is realized (IV, 337, V, 568–9, 570–1, VI, 572–3, 582, 612).

(*e*) The fate of the Round Table, in danger from the False Guinevere (VI, 585–6), links up with the installation of Lancelot, once he has made his name, as companion of the Round Table (V, 571).

(*f*) The account given of Lyonel's knighting (VI, 609–11) fulfils the promise by the tale in phase I (60.39); it echoes Lancelot's knighting and his insistence on undertaking the first adventure which presents itself.

(*g*) Lyonel, like Lancelot at Dolorous Guard (II, 194), justifies his right to his name in an adventure, here the fight against the lion, undertaken as a young knight (611). The fight with the Lion of Lybia and the giving of the lion's skin to Yvain is mentioned in phase V (358.26–30) with no reference forward.

(*h*) There is a reference back at the end of the romance (613) to Queen Helene's loss of her son Lancelot at the beginning of the tale (I).

(*i*) Kay pushing himself forward is a recurrent motif in the romance (II, 175–6, V, 368–70, VI, 602–3, 605.35–6).

B   *Preparation for events to come*

None.

C   *References outwards to past events in the wider Arthurian tradition*

(*a*) Giving of the Round Table as part of the Queen's dowry (585–6); not the explanations given by Wace or Robert de Boron.

(*b*) The explanation of Yvain's name as Knight of the Lion (611, cf. 358); a different version from that in Chrétien's *Yvain*.

Conclusion to Part One

The successive phases or stages of this tale of Lancelot which ends with the death of Galehot have a firm thematic structure in which the love of Lancelot and Guinevere and the making of a name intertwine. This structure is reinforced, not only by the subtle use of a technique of interlace which, by the placing of the narrative switch, helps to underline the thematic development, but also by a number of recurring motifs and narrative devices, frequently involving the use of repetition, contrast, and parallel, which give a closely knit texture to the work. Repetition within the romance is used with extreme skill both to bring out its thematic structure and to integrate this particular tale into a wider Arthurian 'reality'.

This cohesion works in two directions. Firstly, there are explicit references, predictions, and promises, pointing forwards to what is to come. Thus, for example, already in phase I of the tale we are prepared for the knighting of Lyonel in VI and are promised further information on Heliene sanz Per, given in V. At the end of phase I the arrival of the wounded knight who wants to be avenged and Lancelot's rash oath to do so provide an open-ended motivation for a series of battles in III and IV, finally brought to a conclusion in V when Lancelot is imprisoned before the first battle against Galehot as a result of one of these revenges. In phase III the prediction of the damsel that more will be learnt of the Unknown Knight at the First, Second, and Third Assemblies links the end of the conquest of Dolorous Guard (in which Lancelot first learns his name) with the events in phase III, that is Gauvain's first quest and the two assemblies against the Roi d'Outre les Marches, and in IV with the first of the Galehot battles. Galehot's premonition, when he is arranging the first secret meeting between Lancelot and Guinevere, that the Queen will lose him the companionship of Lancelot, and so ultimately his own life, prepares the way for the tragic conclusion.

Secondly, cohesion is achieved by linking backwards. This can be done by explicit references by the tale or the characters to earlier events. Thus, the damsel who had been wounded when rescuing Lyonel from Claudas reminds Lancelot's young cousin on two separate occasions (in I and V) that he should love her because she saved his life, and the explanation in the narrative refers back to the earlier episode. It can also be achieved by repeated sequences or episodes without specific reference to the former occasion. These may principally involve the same characters: for example, the grieving queens of Benoyc and Gaunes, and visits to Arthur which remind him of his failure to avenge the death of his vassal Ban of Benoyc; or the interlacing on two occasions of Lancelot's trances before the Queen at the gate of the Dolorous Guard and the King's fits of abstraction at the fountain in III. Alternatively, the repeated series may involve different characters, with no direct causal link and no reference back. Thus, the doubting of the unknown knight presenting himself as champion in a judicial duel, followed by a series of tests leading up to a successful battle, occurs twice, first with Lancelot (II) and secondly with Gauvain (V), a repeated sequence linked closely with the identity theme. Sometimes the two possibilities may be combined, as, for example, in the two sets of dreams, those of Arthur (IV), and those of Galehot (VI), with a limited reference back in that Galehot sends for the wise clerks who had interpreted Arthur's dreams. The repeated sequence may be more closely linked through shared resonances with other well-known tales: the doubting of the champion sequence evokes *li Biaus Descouneus* and *Erec*; the dreams and their interpretation recall the story of Vortigern and Merlin, especially as told in the *Merlin* of Robert de Boron. Widely separated parts of the narrative may be linked through echoes provided in the series of contrasts and parallels characteristic of the technique of the pairing of characters. Thus, the changing contrasts and parallels between Arthur and Claudas, Arthur and Galehot, Galehot and Claudas, provide a series of echoes between I, IV, and VI.

Long quests producing a string of the apparently haphazard adventures which by tradition confront the questing knight could easily lead to a formless narrative, especially when two separate quests are involved, as is the case for Gauvain and Hector in phase V. However, the author, as we have seen, has taken care to provide adventures linked to the two main themes (the making of a name, and love as an inspiration for chivalry) and to the role of the knight as an upholder of justice in the lands of which Arthur is suserain. He has linked Hector, Gauvain, and Lancelot through a shifting system of pairs similar to that used with Arthur, Galehot, and Claudas, but here concentrated in one particular phase of the narrative. He has also provided a series of cross-references between the two quests, through meetings between Hector and some of Gauvain's companions on the quest, through information provided by hermits with whom knights and messengers such as Lyonel stay, through periodic contacts with the war between the King of Norgales and the Duke of Cambenic, which provides a common background to both quests, through messages sent back to Arthur's court, by motifs such as the sword, given to Gauvain and sent by him to Hector, which eventually allows them to recognize one another, and through repetition of certain phrases or items of information, often with references back, such as that concerning the ways into Sorelois.

Thus in the tale of Lancelot which ends with the death of Galehot each individual phase in the action is given an inner cohesion and is closely linked to other phases in terms of thematic structure and a whole series of interlocking devices. There are some small inconsistencies within the narrative which concern the names given to some of the minor characters or places,[2] but as a whole events are remarkably well-motivated within the romance's own terms and are given a strongly feudal setting in Arthur's kingdom.

This version of the tale is complete in itself in that there are no clear references in it which look beyond Lancelot's decision to become a member of the King's *maisnie* and its consequence in the death of Galehot. However, there are a few promises which, although partly fulfilled, leave certain obscurities. Two references provide a useful point of contrast here. 'Et ce par quoi il fu apelez Lanceloz ce devisera bien li contes ça avant' (1.9) is a promise fulfilled in that we are told how Lancelot learned his name and how his name was made at Arthur's coûrt; indeed the promise concerns one of the main themes of the romance. On the other hand, we hear why the wounded knight still had the weapons sticking in his body, but not, as promised, his name in this tale of Lancelot. There are indeed references to events which lie outside *le conte Lancelot* as told in this version of his story. For instance, there are a number of references to Joseph of Arimathea and to the Grail, but these allude to a Grail quest which has already taken place, with Perceval as Grailwinner and achiever of the adventure of the Perilous Seat. These form a whole series of allusions outwards, some of which seem to link up with extant works, Chrétien's *Conte del Graal*, the *First* and *Second Perceval Continuations*, Robert de Boron, and the chronicle tradition; others do not necessarily allude to any particular text but are there to provide a character with a past outside this romance.

Such references outwards also combine with resonances from the wider Arthurian tradition, achieved through the subtle variations on familiar narrative patterns and on the literary twelfth-century legacy of Lancelot, Yvain, Gauvain, and Perceval (although the last of these does not appear in person in the romance). This tale of Lancelot is therefore presented not as the first part of a vast cycle which will contain a Grail Quest, but as a noble tale which forms part of the record of the memorable deeds of Arthur's knights, kept by his clerks, of which the great tale of the Grail already forms a part.

PART TWO

Lancelot with the Grail

X

Lancelot with the Grail: first stage

The two versions of the Journey to Sorelois, the False Guinevere episode, and the Death of Galehot

There is another Prose *Lancelot* which, as great scholars such as Ferdinand Lot and Jean Frappier have shown, possesses a unity as a literary work, in spite of contrasts between the different branches. In that romance the tale of Lancelot's childhood and adventures up to his installation as a companion of the Round Table forms only the first part of a great cycle which includes a Grail Quest firmly integrated in Lancelot's own story through the person of his son Galahad, and a *Mort Artu* which recounts the tragic conclusion of Lancelot's love for Guinevere and the destruction of Arthur and the Round Table. The non-cyclic and the cyclic Prose Lancelot share the same text up to Lancelot's welcome into Arthur's court (at the end of Sommer III), although some scribes, seeing the obvious contradictions between the Grail allusions in this part of the tale and the Galahad Quest, have tried to remove them or alter them, as will be seen in the last part of Chapter XI. The cyclic and non-cyclic romances, therefore, only diverge at the end of Sommer III (at the end of phase V in the work studied in Part I of this book), when Galehot takes Lancelot away from court and journeys to his own lands. It is this divergence into two different versions of the journey to Sorelois, the False Guinevere episode, and the death of Galehot which I propose to study in this chapter.[1] I use the title 'version (*a*)' to designate the brief version ('special version' in the terminology of Micha) which corresponds to phase VI of the non-cyclic *Lancelot* and which brings the story to an end with the death of Galehot.[2] I use the title 'version (*b*)' to designate the cyclic version.[3] We have seen that version (*a*) (phase VI) is linked through references back and a variety of connecting devices to past events in the tale of Lancelot, and that there are no allusions forwards to events taking place after the death of Galehot. Version (*b*), while picking up elements from the earlier part of the story of Lancelot, above all looks forward to later events in the cycle, beyond the death of Galehot. I want first to examine the different kinds of unity which these two versions represent before discussing the theory of those critics who believe that (*a*) may represent an abridgement of (*b*) and that, in any case, from the beginning of the romance the author or 'architect' was preparing for a Galahad quest.[4]

I will first make a brief comparison between the narrative content in each of the two versions.

Summary of version (*a*)

Galehot and Lancelot set off for Sorelois, and Galehot falls from his horse (*PL* 572). Galehot expresses his fears over separation (*PL* 573). The two companions go on towards Sorelois, and a description of the Orgueilleusse Angarde follows (*PL* 574). The walls of the castle and all Galehot's fortresses fall (*PL* 575-7). He has an ominous dream and sends for Arthur's clerks to interpret it. The clerks do so and predict that Lancelot will cause Galehot's death within three years (*PL* 577-83).

Berthelais and a damsel bring a letter from the False Guinevere which alleges that the Queen is an impostor and claims the Round Table. A date for the trial is fixed (*PL* 584-6). Arthur is captured through the ruse of a boar-hunt, and the False Guinevere wins his love by means of a potion. The barons of Camelide[5] and Logres are summoned to the trial of the Queen; she is condemned to death by the barons of Camelide; her champion must fight three knights (*PL* 587-602). Lancelot insists on undertaking the battle; he defeats the three knights; Guinevere is vindicated as the true Queen and is reinstated; the False Guinevere dies (*PL* 602-8).

Lyonel is made a knight, insists on undertaking the first adventure presenting itself, and justifies his name by killing the Crowned Lion of Lybia (*PL* 609-11).

Galehot returns to his own country, hears a false report of Lancelot's death, and dies of grief; Lancelot's sole comfort in his sorrow is his love for the Queen (*PL* 612-13).

Summary of version (*b*)

Galehot and Lancelot journey to Sorelois: Galehot, deep in melancholy thoughts of his inevitable separation from Lancelot, falls from his horse; Lancelot faints. Galehot tells Lancelot of his dreams; a description of the Orgueilleuse Garde follows; the walls of all Galehot's castles crumble. Galehot sends for Arthur's clerks to interpret his dreams (*LM* I-II).

Berthelais and a damsel bring a letter from the False Guinevere accusing the Queen of being an impostor. The King decides that a judgement will be given at Candlemas (*LM* III).

Arthur's clerks interpret Galehot's dreams and predict that his death will be caused by Lancelot, who, because of his sinful love for Guinevere, will be surpassed by his own son, the virgin knight, yet to be born (*LM* IV).

Galehot entrusts his lands to Bademaguz of Gorre, and an explanation of the customs of Gorre is given. Lancelot and Galehot go to Arthur's court, where Meleagant wounds Lancelot in a tournament. The False Guinevere comes at Candlemas to accuse the Queen. Arthur is captured through the ruse of a boar-hunt. He falls in love with the False Guinevere (*LM* V–VI).

Arthur's barons and those of the False Guinevere assemble at the Feast of the Ascension, and she is presented as Queen (*LM* VII).

At Whitsun the King's judgement declares the False Guinevere to be Queen. Lancelot renounces his companionship of the Round Table and fights three knights to save the true Queen from punishment (*LM* VIII).

Guinevere withdraws with Lancelot and Galehot to Sorelois. Arthur's land lies under the papal interdict. The False Guinevere and Berthelais fall ill, confess their treachery, and die. Arthur is reconciled, first with the Queen, later with Lancelot (*LM* IX).

Gauvain is carried off by Caradoc to la Dolerose Tor, and Lancelot, Yvain and the Duke of Clarence set off secretly to rescue him, without taking leave of the King or the Queen; they undertake various adventures on their way, including that of the Val sans Retor (or Val as Faus Amans), are put under an enchantment by Morgain and freed from the spell by Lancelot (*LM* X–XXIV).

Lancelot is imprisoned by Morgain, then released temporarily to rescue Gauvain; he achieves this and returns to prison. Morgain sends a damsel to Arthur's court with a ring as proof of Lancelot's sinful love. Guinevere makes a spirited defence of Lancelot, but in secret is very angry with him. Lyonel and Galehot hear reports of his death which prove to be false. He is released from prison, but cannot return to court and goes to Sorelois. He flees from there and is thought to have killed himself (*LM* XXV–XXXIV).

Galehot dies of grief at the report of Lancelot's death (*LM* XXXV).[6]

Discussion of version (*a*)

We have already seen that version (*a*), corresponding to phase VI of the thematic structure of the non-cyclic romance (*PL* 572–613), is closely linked to the events in the tale of Lancelot which lead up to his installation as a companion of the Round Table and a member of the King's *maisnie*. It continues the development of the identity theme: Lancelot has proved his right to his own name; now, in the False Guinevere episode, when he defeats the three knights, he proves Guinevere's right to her identity as the true Queen, wife of Arthur. The episode of Lyonel's knighting (an account of which is promised early in the romance, *PL* 60.39) and his fight with the Crowned Lion of Lybia, fore-shadowed in a brief summary, given without a direct reference forward, when

Lyonel first leaves the Lake (*PL* 358), rounds off this theme, echoing as it does in a shortened form the pattern of Lancelot's progress towards the making of his name. The identity theme here once again intertwines with the love theme. The love is presented as a source of inspiration, a positive force as far as Lancelot and Guinevere are concerned; there is no mention of sin in relation to Guinevere's duty as wife and Queen, and all the emphasis is laid on the conflict between Lancelot's love for Guinevere and his companionship with Galehot. The latter's own premonitions, already expressed when he is arranging the first secret meeting between Lancelot and Guinevere (*PL* 337), and reinforced by the prediction that Lancelot will cause his death (*PL* 582-3), are shown to be justified when Lancelot, as a member of the King's *maisnie*, remains behind when Galehot has to return to his own land, and this separation causes the death of Galehot (*PL* 612). The shifting pattern of the pairing between the three powerful rulers who appear in the romance, Arthur, Galehot, and Claudas, is continued in version (*a*) through two sets of close parallels. The first of these is between the sequence of Arthur's dreams and interpretations, before his war with Galehot, and Galehot's dreams, interpreted by the same wise clerks, thus linking up with the past and predicting the dreamer's own death. The second set of parallels is between the ambitions of Claudas (*PL* 31) and those of Galehot (*PL* 574, 582). There is nothing in version (*a*) which looks beyond the death of Galehot, and nothing which is inconsistent with the earlier part of the story.

Discussion of version (*b*)

The most fundamental difference between version (*b*) and version (*a*) is that in (*b*) the False Guinevere episode and the events leading up to the death of Galehot are interlaced with elements preparing for later adventures in the cycle. Consequently, this version is not so tightly organized around the figure of Lancelot in terms of the two themes of the making of a name, and love as an inspiration for great chivalry. Indeed, the identity theme tends to slip into the background. Thus, whereas in (*a*), when Lancelot as Guinevere's champion defeats the three knights he establishes the identity of the true Guinevere and saves the Round Table, in (*b*) his victory protects her from punishment but does not prove her right to her name and to her position as Arthur's Queen. It is the illness of the impostor and Berthelais and their subsequent confessions which uncover the treachery. The knighting of Lyonel and the fight with the Crowned Lion of Lybia, which in version (*a*), as has been seen, establish his right to his own name and recall in miniature the first stage in Lancelot's career as a knight, are only mentioned briefly and in passing in the long version of (*b*) (*LM* XVIII.3) and not at all in the short version.

The love theme, on the other hand, is still given prominence, but, as we shall see, with a marked change in emphasis. The conflict between Galehot's love for Lancelot and Lancelot's love for Guinevere, which forms the climax of (*a*), is treated at even greater length in (*b*), and the development of this theme is closely linked to previous events by a number of references back, either by comment from tale (or narrator) or in the thoughts or words of the characters. For example, there are allusions to the sacrifice made by Galehot for Lancelot when, at the moment of victory, he surrendered to Arthur and made peace (*PL* 327), thus turning his great honour into shame: for example, *PL* 334.17–19, *LM* I, II.2, 17, IV.25. Lancelot does not press Galehot to reveal the cause of his grief: 'kar il li menbre de ce que Galehout l'avoit si debonairement soffert en sa dolor, sans rien demander, la ou il remeist ses compaignons' (*LM* II.3, picking up *PL* 330–2). After his first battle against Arthur, Galehot talks of his great desire to have the companionship of the Red Knight (Lancelot) who had saved the King from defeat (*LM* II.11, referring back to *PL* 281–2, 293.17–19).

However, the treatment of the relationships between the four principal characters directly involved in the love theme, Galehot, Arthur, Lancelot, and Guinevere, shows important differences in emphasis and, on occasion, a major change in direction which helps to prepare the way for the very different attitude towards the moral value of Lancelot and Guinevere's love to be found later in the cycle.

In the first place, Galehot is given greater prominence.[7] The account of the journey to Sorelois opens with a panegyric of him:

Mais de sa mort ne fet pas a parler ci endroit, kar mors a si preudome com Galehout estoit ne fet pas a ramentevoir devant le point. Et tuit li conte qui parolent de lui s'acordent a ce qu'il estoit en totes choses li plus vaillans de tos les haus princes enprés le roi Artu a cui l'en ne doit nului aparagier de cels qui vesquirent a cel termine. Et si retesmoigne li livres Tardamides de Vergials, qui plus parole des proesces Galehout que nus des autres, que neis li rois Artus ne fu mie de gaires plus vaillans, kar se Galehout puist vivre son droit aage al point et al corage qu'il avoit quant il comença a guerroier le roi Artu, il passast tos cels qui les autres avoient passés. (*LM* I.1–2.)

His ambition to conquer Arthur is presented as noble.[8] As in version (*a*) (*PL* 574) there are comments (here both by the tale, *LM* I.2, and by Galehot, *LM* II.14) on the proud spirit which inspired the building of the Orgueilleusse Angarde when he aimed to conquer the whole world. Galehot himself admits the element of rash presumption:

'Si vos i mosterai sempres une grant merveille dont je fas molt que fols del dire, kar nus grans bobans n'est si tost montés qu'altresi tost ne soit jus chaois; kar je baoie a fere trop grant desmesure et trop grant orgueil, dont il est remés molt grant partie.' (*LM* II.14.)

In version (*a*) he puts a brave face on the news of the crumbling of all his castles, but in (*b*) he is boldly defiant:

'C'est ore une chose, fet Galehout, que poi me grieve, kar je meismes vi fondre la forteresce que je plus amoie el monde n'onques mes cuers a mal aise n'en fu. Et si vos dirai ore le porquoi voiant mes gens qui si chevalchent. J'ai esté li plus merveillos hom qui onques fust et si ai eu si merveillos cuer que, s'il fust en un petit cors, je ne voi pas coment il peust durer, kar onques de nule grant emprise ne le trovai lache ne pereçeus, mais tos jors enprenant et volenteis assés plus que mes consels ne li osast doner. Et tels doit estre cuers qui bee a passer tos autres cuers de hautes oevres et doit savoir que autresi que tuit li autre cuer sont plus povres de lui, autresi sont il plus aver de conseil. Et ne vos merveilliés pas se les greignors merveilles dont vos aiés oï parler avienent en mon pooir, kar autresi com j'ai esté plus merveillos me doivent greignors merveilles avenir.' (*LM* II.27).

Whereas in (*a*) the crumbling of the castles is interpreted as a sign of God's displeasure at Galehot's arrogance in waging war on Arthur, 'lo plus prodome do monde' (*PL* 582), no such significance is given to their falling in (*b*). Galehot tells his men that the making of peace between him and Arthur was God's will, and he admits in general terms to Helie de Toulouse (the leader of Arthur's learned clerks) that he has killed many people and destroyed many towns during the course of the wars which he has waged. Helie replies:

'Ce sai je bien, fet li mestres, qu'il vos seroit grans mestiers que vos amendissiés vostre vie, kar nus hom qui tant ait conquis com vos avés ne porroit estre sans trop grant charge de pechiés: et ce n'est pas merveille.' (*LM* IV.49.)

The repeated use of the term *mescheance* with reference to Galehot's misfortunes (*LM* II.8, 9, 20, 25, V.3) is not here linked with the idea of sin.[9] The tale returns again and again to the sufferings of Galehot, doomed to lose his life through his great love of Lancelot. Unlike (*a*), in (*b*) Lancelot is not present when the interpretation of the dream is made, his torment at the thought that he will cause the death of his companion is not dwelt on in the same way as in (*a*), and the role of Guinevere in the destruction of Galehot is mentioned (*LM* IV.64). Galehot sacrifices himself once again when he supports Lancelot's advice to the Queen to return to Arthur, even though he knows that by so doing he will inevitably bring about his own separation from Lancelot and hence his own end (*LM* IX.34).

There is, however, a good deal of emphasis on the sins of Arthur, Lancelot, and Guinevere, linked from time to time with the potentially destructive effects of illicit love on essentially noble characters. These periodic hints at a new attitude towards a love such as that between Lancelot and Guinevere have particularly interesting consequences for the role of Arthur. On the one hand, his good qualities are emphasized, and Guinevere's love for Lancelot is condemned by Helie de Toulouse (*LM* IV.45) as a betrayal of 'le plus preudome del monde'; on the other, Arthur's great love of Lancelot is presented as of almost the same noble intensity as that of Galehot, but in terms which help to prepare us for the tragic conflict in the *Mort Artu*:

> Et quant li rois ot qu'il est si a certes corociés, si l'en vienent les lermes as iex d'anguoisse, si en est trop troblés en son corage, kar il amoit tos jors Lancelot de greignor amor que nus feist, fors Galehout. Et il le mostra puis bien par maintes fois la ou li losengier de sa maison li disoient malveises paroles et il disoit que por noient se peneroit nus de lui corocier vers Lancelot: 'kar il n'est, fet il, nus forfés en cest siecles, se il le me faisoit, por quoi je le haïsse mie. De sa vilenie me porroit il bien peser.' (*LM* IX.43, long version only.)

This foreshadows' Arthur's reluctance to allow himself to be convinced by the talebearer Agravain:

> 'Certes, fet li rois, s'il estoit voirs que Lancelos l'amast tres bien par amors, si nel porroie ge pas croire qu'il eüst cuer de fere si grant desloiauté comme de moi honir de ma fame; car en cuer ou il a si grant proesce ne se porroit enbatre traïsons, se ce n'estoit la greigneur deablie del monde.' (*Mort Artu*, 30.)

In version (*b*), unlike version (*a*), we are therefore allowed glimpses of Arthur as a great king, victim of adulterous love. Although there are references back to the loss of Lancelot's father and of his land in descriptions such as 'lo fil au roi mort de duel' (*LM* IV.25, 40), there is not the same emphasis on Arthur's failure to protect or avenge his vassal. Galehot talks to Lancelot about the loss of his land through Claudas and suggests a plan to win it back:

> Et l'endemain de nostre coronement si movrons a totes nos gens por conquerre le roialme de Benoÿc dont li rois Claudas de la Deserte vos a deserité: kar trop avés demoré a vengier la mort vostre pere et vostre deseritement et les grans dolors que vostre mere a eues. (*LM* V.6.)

This is a variation on the theme of criticism of Arthur for his delay in avenging Ban's death, a delay for which he is condemned by the *rendu* (*PL* 54–6) and the *preudomme* who visits him after the first battle against Galehot (*PL* 283–94). Arthur himself and his court are praised by Galehot in the following terms: 'li plus preudom qui soit, et en sa maison repaire la valors et la proesce de tot le monde' (*LM* V.12). This description recalls the favourable picture given of Arthur and his court on the occasion of the visit of Claudas to Britain to assess his chances of fulfilling his ambition to conquer Arthur (*PL* 33–5).

However, if Arthur is sinned against, he also sins, for he allows himself to be seduced by the False Guinevere when he accepts her without a trial as the true Queen and puts away his wife without the Church's permission. In version (*a*) the King is taken aback by the False Guinevere's accusations against the Queen, but suspends judgement and is only won over to blind support of the impostor's cause when he is given a special potion. By contrast, in version (*b*) Arthur seems to be very easily persuaded to take the claims of the False Guinevere seriously:

Quant la damoisele ot ensi parlé, si sont si mui c'onques n'i ot mot soné, et li rois fu molt esbahis; si regarde en haut et se seigne menu et sovent et tient a grant merveille ce qu'il a oï: si a tel duel et tel honte del blasme que la damoisele li met sus que par un poi qu'il ne desve, et bien pert al samblant de son vis que li cuers n'estoit mie a aise. 'Dame, fet il a la roine, venés avant, que bien est drois que l'en l'oie de vostre boche meismes; si vos delivrés de ceste chose, si m'aït Diex, se vos estes tele com ceste pucele vos met sus, vos avés mort deservie sor totes les pecheresces qui onques fuissent, et aprés ce avés le monde laidement deceu, kar l'en vos a tenue a la plus vaillant dame del monde et vos seriés la plus desloial et la plus fause, se c'estoit voirs.' (*LM* III.18.)

As in (*a*), Arthur remits the matter to a trial at a later date, and, on the orders of Berthelais, is captured before judgement is given. However, in the long version of (*b*) no potion is needed to make him fall in love with the False Guinevere (*LM* VI.36), although in the short version, as in (*a*), a potion is used,[10] much as the Saxon maiden used enchantments to entrap Arthur (*PL* 540.26, 541.36). A potion is mentioned later in the long version:

Et ele avoit si conreé le roi par poisons qu'il ne savoit riens contredire qui li pleust, si avoit ja tant fet que tuit le haoient li baron. (*LM* IX.5.)

But the delay in bringing in the potion in the long version of (*b*) means that there is less excuse for Arthur's surrender to the physical charms of the False Guinevere and his repudiation of the Queen. He declares the False Guinevere to be his real wife and queen and maintains that all his actions are guided by his desire to avoid the sin of remaining with a woman not his lawful wife (*LM* VII.22, 24); but Gauvain comments:

'Sire, bien sachiés que vos estes bien chargiés de cest mariage, kar l'en ne dist pas que vos l'aiés fet por issir de pechié, mais por entrer.' (*LM* VIII.55.)[11]

Arthur's sin receives public condemnation by the Church when the Pope puts the land under interdict (*LM* IX.4). God strikes first the False Guinevere and then Berthelais with illness (*LM* IX.5, 6, 22). The short version of (*b*) gives particular emphasis to the explanation that this illness is a divine punishment:

Cele nuit il avint une grande demonstrance de Nostre Segnor qui molt est soufrans, mes en la fin n'oublie il mie le mal del pechié ne la bonté del proudome. Cele nuit prist Nostre Sires de la fause Genievre si forte justice qu'ele perdi tout li pooir de ses piés et de ses mains et de tout son cors fors des ieus et de la langue. (*LM* IX.5, short version.)

Arthur too is given a sign of God's disapproval of his conduct with the False

Guinevere. While hunting, he comes upon a hermitage, asks for hospitality, suddenly falls ill, and seeks confession and absolution from a hermit who rebukes him in forthright terms as a vile sinner:

'tu es li plus viels foimentie del monde et li plus viels pechieres et foimentie et escommuniés et traïtres. La fus tu desloials ou tu guerpesis ta feme espose por une autre que tu tiens contre Dieu et contre raison, et de ce fus tu foimentie que tu li fausas la foi que tu li avoies creanté en Sainte Iglise, quant tu la feis jugier a destruire; et por ce que tu t'en partis desloialment sans le congié de Sainte Iglise es tu escommuniés, ne biens ne te porroit pas avenir tant com tu soies en tel point.' (*LM* IX.13.)

Arthur accepts the Church's condemnation, but still maintains that he was trying to avoid sin:

'Et je otroi molt bien que je sui de ma feme desevrés a tort et que je tieng ceste encontre Dieu, kar onques, puis que je la pris, biens ne me vint et ele meismes est chaoite en tel maladie dont je ne cuit pas qu'ele puisse garir: et si ne la pris je pas por ce que je cuidaisse fere pechié, kar tuit li baron del païs disoient qu'ele estoit ma loial espose et que je tenoie l'autre a tort.' (*LM* IX.14.)

The truth concerning the plot to deceive Arthur comes out when the False Guinevere, on being told by the hermit that she is in danger of death and damnation, confesses, as does Berthelais. To the last the King and the barons of Tarmelide maintain that they had only done what they thought was right, but again and again it is made clear in the text that Arthur is swayed by his passion for the False Guinevere (*LM* VI.36, 38, IX.4, 5). In the short version of (*b*) particular stress is laid on the disastrous effect that Arthur's concubine had upon him and his kingdom:

Et se il avoit amee l'autre, toute l'a mis en oubli por l'amor que il a mise en cesti. Et ele le tient si cort que toutes autres compaignies en a entrelaissies et mis arriere dos por la soie: si sont auques remeses les grans honors et les grans largeces que l'autre li faisoit avoir; si est tant enpierés que tous li siecles qui devant le soloit prisier le tenoit ore a honi outreement, car onques mes nus hom en si poi de tans de nul mariage tant n'empira. (*LM* IX.1–3, short version.)[12]

His lust makes him treat Guinevere very badly, and this is contrasted with her merciful behaviour towards the last and only surviving knight of the three who fight against Lancelot in the judicial battle (*LM* VIII. 44–5.) and towards the barons of Tarmelide who come to beg for forgiveness (*LM* IX.28–9).

Arthur's attitude towards Lancelot is not affected in the same way. He shows far greater hostility in version (*a*) than in (*b*), where he wants to protect Lancelot from the fight against three knights (*LM* VIII.17–19), and is deeply distressed when Lancelot renounces his companionship of the Round Table

(*LM* VIII.15, 56–60).[13] As we have seen, the strength of his love for Lancelot is emphasized, so that he is torn between conflicting emotions—his lust for the False Guinevere is contrasted with the more positive force of his love for Lancelot, based on his experience of Lancelot's great qualities as a knight. Arthur is therefore shown as a noble king, drawn by a false love into sin and conflict with the Church, so ready to doubt the identity of his own wife that he shocks his own barons, but still loyal to Lancelot.

If Arthur is presented as a rather bewildered sinner, Guinevere is far more clearly conscious of the nature of her own sin, and here there is a marked contrast between version (*b*) and both (*a*) and all that has gone before. For the first time the adulterous nature of the love of Lancelot and Guinevere and the wrong done to Arthur are brought out clearly in the narrative. The sinfulness of the love and its destructive quality provide a common element, linking Galehot's dreams and their interpretation with the False Guinevere episode, and this is underlined by the interlacing of the two episodes in version (*b*), where Galehot and Lancelot learn of the accusation against the Queen before Arthur's clerks interpret the dreams. This does not happen in version (*a*), where the dreams are interpreted before the False Guinevere's messengers go to Arthur's court.

The first outright condemnation of the love is to be found in Helie's interpretation of the leopard in Galehot's dream. He insists on talking to Galehot alone and then explains that the leopard is Lancelot, who will fail to achieve the greatest adventure of all, that of the Grail, because he is not virgin and chaste:

Cist ne porroit recovrer les taiches que cil avra qui l'aventure del Graal achevera, kar il covient tot premierement qu'il soit de sa nativité jusqu'a sa mort virges et chastes si entierement qu'il n'ait amor n'a dame n'a damoisele. Et cist nel puet ore avoir, kar je sai greignor partie de son conseil que vos ne cuidiés. (*LM* IV.37.)

Helie goes on to interpret a prophecy of Merlin in which a serpent (the Queen) robs the dragon (Galehot) of the leopard (Lancelot):

'En ceste maniere, fet Merlins, vendra li grans dragons et je sai de voir que c'estes vos, et li serpens qui le vos toldra, ce sera ma dame la roine qui aime le chevalier ou amera tant come dame porra plus amer chevalier.' (*LM* IV.44.)

Guinevere's love of Lancelot, which threatens Galehot's life, is also linked by Helie with the shameful accusation made against the Queen:

'Et sachiés que vos en verrés encore avenir une des grans merveilles qui onques avenissent en vostre tens, kar ma dame est apelee del plus lait blasme qui onques fust mis sor nule dame; si cuit miels qu'il li est avenu por cel pechié, qu'ele a enpris si grant desloialté come de honir le plus preudome del monde, que por nule autre cope.' (*LM* IV.45.)

Guinevere herself sees the same connection. She is being punished because she has wronged the King not as an impostor, but as an adulteress:

'je suis departie del roi mon seignor par mon meffet, je le conois bien: non pas por ce que je ne soie sa feme esposee et roine coronee et sacree ausi com il fu, et sui fille al roi Leodagan de Tarmelide, mais li pechiés m'a neü de ce que je me cochai o autre qu'a mon seignor.' (*LM* IX.1.)

This contrasts with the reference to an unspecified sin in version (*a*):

Mais se la reine en a duel, or enforce, car mout a grant paor que por aucun pechié que ele ait fait ça en arrieres voille Nostres Sires que soit honie et deshonoree en terre. (*PL* 595.21–3.)

However, in version (*b*) the Queen cannot commit herself wholly to the rejection of her love of Lancelot, for the *Charrette* episode, in which love is still shown to provide an inspiration for great deeds of benefit to others, is already being prepared for in the cyclic version. She goes on to say to Lancelot:

'Et neporquant il n'a si preude dame el monde qui ne deust fere un grant meschief por metre a aise un si preude chevalier com vos estes, mais Nostre Sire ne garde mie a la cortoisie del monde, kar cil qui est buens al monde est mals a Dieu.' (*LM* IX.2.)

This provides a significant variation on the words of the Lady of the Lake on her visit to heal Lancelot of his madness, discussed in Chapter III but so important that they are worth quoting here in full. She tells Guinevere to love above all others the man who loves her more than anyone or anything else, and then goes on to say:

Ne li pechié do siegle ne puent estre mené sanz folie, mais mout a grant raison de sa folie qui raison i trove et annor. Et se vos poez folie trover an voz amors, ceste folie est desor totes les autres annoree, car vos amez la seignorie et la flor de tot cest monde. Se vos poez de ce vanter que onques mais dame no pot faire, car vos iestes compaigne au plus preudome do monde et dame au meillor chevalier do monde. (*PL* 557.1–7.)

The Lady of the Lake saw honour as well as *folie* in the love of Lancelot and Guinevere, but in version (*b*) of the False Guinevere episode there are for the first time explicit references to the dishonour as well as to the benefits it may bring.

In version (*b*) Guinevere goes on to say that in her present situation she cannot go on enjoying her love to the full in the physical sense, but she does not commit herself finally to virtue:

'Mais des ore mes vos pri je que vos me doigneis un don que je vos demanderai, kar je sui ore el point ou il me convendroit miels garder que onques mes ne fis: si vos requier por la grant amor que vos avés a moi que vos des ore mes ne me querrois nule compaignie, ne

mes de baisier et d'acoler, se il vos plest, que vos ne le faciés por ma proiere. Mais ceste
compaignie vos rendrai tant com je serai en cest point; et quant j'en avrai lieu et tens et
vostre volentés sera, vos avrois volentiers le sorplus.' (*LM* IX.2.)

Thus in the cyclic version of the False Guinevere episode the writer skilfully
prepares the way both for the great adventure of the rescue of the Queen and
the prisoners of Gorre and for Lancelot's failure in the Quest; at the same time
he tries to avoid too abrupt a break with the treatment of the love theme in the
earlier part of the romance, where it is made quite clear that Lancelot's great
deeds which win him his seat at the Round Table were achieved through his
love for Guinevere. There is still a nice balance maintained between condemnation of the adulterous, sinful, and destructive aspect of the love and its more
sympathetic presentation as a source of joy and comfort for Guinevere,
honoured by the love of the greatest living knight, and of noble strength for
Lancelot. The wrong done against Arthur may be admitted here for the first
time in the romance, but the lovers still have a positive role to play in society.
The Queen insists on working through the law to defend herself and rejects
Galehot's offer to capture the False Guinevere and make sure that she never
comes to 'faire clamor':

'Certes, fet la roine, se Dieu plest, ensi ne le ferai je mie. Ja de cestui blasme ne quier estre
deffendue se par meismes le droit non, ne ja, se Dieu plest, autres pechiés ne m'i tendra,
ains atendrai le jugement le roi d'outre en outre. Et je vos pri por Dieu et por l'amor que
vos avés a moi que vos vos penés en cesti point de garder m'onor en totes choses et vos veés
bien que li besoins en est molt grans, n'entre vos .II. ne porrés pas a nos tant parler com vos
avés fet devant que ceste chose soit achievee, ains covendra que vos vos en soffrés et que
chascuns tiegne sa mesaise.' (*LM* VI.31.)

In one sense, Lancelot is held back from achieving his true rank by his love
for the Queen, for he has no ambition to regain his kingdom, lest the duties of
kingship should separate the lovers:

'J'ameroie miels a estre tos jors ansi com je sui hui que estre rois et avoir honor et la
richesce par coi je pedisse ma dame la roine ne ele moi, ne je ne vueil avoir plus de
seignorie que j'ai devant qu'i li plaise.' (*LM* V.10.)

It is of course true that he can and indeed already has played a glorious role in
society as a knight errant who has defended the cause of the weak and
unprotected throughout Arthur's lands.[14] However he is not willing to view
Guinevere's loss of her royal position as something that can be of benefit to him,
for he does not want her to be diminished through their love. Therefore, he
advises the Queen, as one who loves her, to go back to Arthur after the False
Guinevere's death, even if he would prefer her to stay in Sorelois:

'Dame, fet Lancelos, quant l'en vos avroit tote jor conseillie, si en ferois vos vostre volenté, mais ci ne covient il mie grant conseil, kar cil ne vos ameroit pas qui ceste honor vos loeroit a refuser, c'est la seignorie de Bretaigne et le roi Artu qui est vostre sires espos et li plus preudom del mond, et si en seriés trop blasmee. Tuit cil qui le vos diroient ne vos ameroient pas, et si vos amerions nos miels en ceste terre entre moi et mon seignor qui ci est. Mais nos volons miels soffrir paines et mesaises, kar autresi conois je son cuer comme le mien, ne l'en ne doit pas loer a chose que l'en l'aime ce que a mal li puet torner. Ensi le vos lo que vos le façois.' (*LM* IX.33.)

In both the Journey to Sorelois and the False Guinevere episode, therefore, the cyclic version looks forward to events in the cycle, but also tries to make links with the past, which often involve changing directions in the development of earlier themes. The adventures which occur between the Queen's reinstatement, after the death of the False Guinevere, and the death of Galehot continue to make the same connections backwards and forwards. The abduction of Gauvain by Caradoc has no organic connection with earlier themes or events, but references back are carefully introduced into the adventures of the knights who try to rescue him. For example, Yvain's first adventure on this quest, a meeting with a wounded knight in a chest, with the blades still in the wounds (*LM* XII.1-5), reminds the reader of the wounded knight whom Lancelot, soon after his arrival at Camelot, swore to avenge (*PL* 149-50, 160). A little later (*LM* XIII.1-14) we learn that this is in fact the brother of the first knight and are told the names of both. This is the one example of a promise of further information made on behalf of the tale in the *PL* (149.27-9), then partially fulfilled (*PL* 150), and completed only in the cyclic romance. The first knight refers back to the swearing of the oath by Lancelot (*PL* 160) and identifies himself (*LM* XIII.11-12).[15] Lancelot refers to the 'maintes paines et mains ennuis' which he has endured as a result of this oath; he had indeed been forced to kill a number of otherwise inoffensive knights (*PL* 224-5, 227, 258-60, 273-4) and had finally been imprisoned in Malohaut for one of these killings (*PL* 275). The adventure of the knight in the chest, through the contrast between Lancelot's success and Yvain's failure, serves to indicate the hero's place in the chivalric hierarchy, for only 'li mieldres chevaliers qui orendroit soit' (*LM* XII.3) is destined to achieve the adventure; but the episode, combining an echo and a reference back, has not otherwise the thematic significance usually associated with such repetitions in the *PL*.

In the same way, the main function of another adventure in which Yvain seeks to rescue a damsel and Sagremor, who has been tied to a stake, and is eventually joined in this rescue by Lancelot, is to provide a connection with the past. Sagremor was attempting to save a damsel who had taken Gauvain to the daughter of the King of Norgales. This is made clear in a passage which combines a reference back with a promise. The link back is made in the first place by an explanation in the narrative that one of the attacking party did not want to hurt Sagremor because he had been taken prisoner by Sagremor and Gauvain outside the portcullis of the King of Norgales and had promised 'qu'il seroit a tos jors mes en ses aides' (*LM* XVII.13, referring back to *PL* 513–14). Then the damsel is identified with an allusion back, but it is said that the time has not yet come for the revelation of the reasons for the attack:

Et la pucele qui au chaisne estoit pendue si estoit cele qui avoit amené mon seignor Gauvain a la fille al roi de Norgales, si comme li contes l'a devisé ça en arrieres, mais il n'esclaire mie comment et por quoi li chevalier avoient si hontosement mené la damoisele et Saigremor, kar bien vendra a tens a esclarier ça en avant. (*LM* XVII.14.)

This reference back is to *PL* 486–508, and the promise of more information is fulfilled at *LM* XIX.8–9, when the damsel explains why she was attacked by the knights. The rescue of Sagremor and the damsel is also used to link Yvain's adventures with those of Lancelot, since Lancelot comes to the rescue of Yvain and Sagremor during the battle (*LM* XIX.1–6).

There are, however, some references back and echoes which serve to underline the love theme. For example, when Lancelot is in Morgain's prison, he seeks to ransom himself, and Morgain refers back to an earlier episode (*PL* 302–3) when she replies:

'Il vos covient a dire ki vos amés par amors, si avrai trait de vos ce ke la dame de Maloaut n'em pot traire.' (*LM* XXVI.5.)

Lancelot is in the end released temporarily by Morgain to perform a task (the rescue of Gauvain), just as the Lady of Malohaut had released him temporarily to fight in a battle (the assembly against Galehot, *PL* 281–2). There is a reference back by Guinevere to her lover's imprisonment in the Roche as Saisnes which underlines the intensity of their love: she had never received news which grieved her as much as that of Lancelot's imprisonment by the Saxons (*LM* XXIX.13, picking up *PL* 549; see also *LM* VIII.45).

There are also some echoes or allusions which link up with that distinguishing feature of Lancelot as an Arthurian hero, his upbringing in the Lake by a fairy. In *LM* XXIV.17 there is a reference to a ring laying bare enchantments which recalls the ring given to Lancelot by the Lady of the Lake (*PL* 154.29–31), a gift which itself recalls Chrétien's *Chevalier de la Charrette*. In *LM* XXIV.28 Lancelot declares that he has an advantage in any adventure involving water: 'kar je i fui norris'. The water concerned eventually turns out to be only an enchantment, like the Lake in which he was brought up (*PL* 24.22–31).

There are also some passages picking up elements in the account of Lyonel's childhood which play a part in the pairing of the two cousins (see Chapter VIII). For example, Galehot calls Lyonel, who is to be knighted, 'cuers sans frain' and says that he is indeed like his cousin Lancelot (*LM* XV.4). This picks up one of his previous remarks, quoted in a passage comparing the two cousins and leading into the episode in which Lyonel, as a small boy, defies Claudas (*PL* 60.36–8). However, that passage promises an account of Lyonel's knighting, which is given in full in version (*a*) but to which there is only a brief reference in version (*b*). Similarly, the account of Lyonel's fight with the Crowned Lion of Lybia, recounted briefly by twenty manuscripts after the description of his first arrival in Sorelois (*PL* 358.26–31), is not picked up with a full account in version (*b*), as it is in version (*a*) (without an explicit reference back), but is given only a brief reference (*LM* XVIII.3). This is done with the phrase 'si com li contes qui de lui est le devise' in the base manuscript of the Micha edition (*A*, Corpus Christi College 45), but in Rawlinson Q.b.6 of Oxford the phrase used is 'si com li contes qui desus est le devise'.

In addition to references back, there is also an echo of one of Lancelot's major adventures, the ending of the enchantments at the Dolorous Guard, in the adventure at Escalon le Tenebros, where the knight who aims to achieve the adventure has to make his way through pitch darkness and stench, buffeted by blows from unseen forces, to open a door, and thereby end the enchantment and bring back light and peace to the castle. Here the fact that the Duke of Clarence (*LM* XVI.31–43) and Yvain (*LM* XX.10–15) fail, but Lancelot succeeds (*LM* XX.18–21), means that once again the adventure serves to establish Lancelot's position at the summit of the hierarchy of knights, but it does not play the same role in the thematic development as does the adventure at the Dolorous Guard in relation to the identity theme.

As well as episodes which, by echoing Lancelot's earlier adventures, help to make links with the part of the text common to both cyclic and non-cyclic manuscripts, the adventures arising from Gauvain's capture by Caradoc also prepare the way for events in later branches of the cycle. We have seen that in the treatment of the False Guinevere episode in version (*b*) there is a modification of the attitude towards the Lancelot–Guinevere love theme as it is to be found earlier in the text: the love is no longer presented wholly as an ennobling influence, a source of inspiration for great deeds, but also as potentially destructive, and its adulterous aspect is no longer to the same extent avoided. The development of the love theme during the adventures after the reconciliation of Guinevere and Arthur also presents, in addition to elements providing continuity, differences in emphasis which have a significance in relation to future events, and in particular to the adventure which follows Galehot's death, the *Conte de la Charrette*.

The continuity with the past is provided both by the references back studied above and by an episode like that of the Val sans Retor (also known as the Val as Faus Amans). Morgain has thrown a spell over the valley because she wants to keep her *ami* in her prison for ever. Only a knight who has always been true to his *amie* in everything can put an end to the enchantments, and all knights who have betrayed their *amies*, albeit only in thought, once they have entered the valley will have to remain there (*LM* XXII.1), whereas damsels, even if they have been false to their lovers, can enter and leave as they please. Both the Duke of Clarence and Yvain fail, and it is of course Lancelot who achieves the adventure. He is victorious over two fierce dragons, defeats three redoubtable adversaries, and breaks the spell (*LM* XXIV.35), to the misfortune of the damsels in the valley, as Morgain explains:

'Damoisele, fet Morgue, s'il est loials d'amors, c'est la grans honors et grant joie a s'amie; mais plus de damage i a d'autre part que li preus et la joie ne monte de s'amie, kar il a saiens de beles damoiseles et de bien amans ki grant piece ont eus lor amis a lor volontés, por ce k'il ne pooient de saiens issir. Et puis k'il seront hors, si changera molt lor aferes, kar jamais autresi sovent ne seront mes en lor compaignie.' (*LM* XXIV.36-7.)

However, if Lancelot frees the captive knights trapped in the valley, his achievement causes his own imprisonment, as Morgain is determined to deprive Guinevere of any joy from her love of Lancelot because she hates the Queen. She therefore sets out to destroy the trust between the lovers, and this is all the easier to do as Guinevere is already angry with Lancelot for having left court to rescue Gauvain without first taking leave of her. We have, therefore, the beginning of a contrast between Guinevere's readiness to suspect Lancelot's fidelity as lover and his unswerving loyalty—a contrast which evokes the situation typical of the lyric where the lover is constantly endeavouring to convince the lady of the authenticity of his love, while others try to undermine her trust in him. In the *PL* Guinevere may on one occasion have pretended to believe that Lancelot had thoughts for other women, but not because she had genuine doubts:

Et ce disoit ele bien por veoir coment ele lo porra metre a malaise, car ele cuide bien que il ne pansast d'amors s'a lui non, ja mar aüst il fait por li se la jornee non des noires armes. Mais ele se delitoit durement an sa messaise veoir et escouter. (*PL* 346.23-7.)

Lancelot, when he recovers from his madness, has fears that the Queen will love him less, but her love is in fact unquestioning and unreserved:

Et il an est mout estahis et avileniz de ce que or set il bien que or ont veü son mauvais contenement, si crient que la riens o monde que il plus aimme l'an ait moins chier. Mais il ne li estoit mies mestiers que il an aüst paor, car ele n'an avoit ne pooir ne volanté. (*PL* 558.2-6.)

Lancelot's heroic deeds, undertaken for her sake, have convinced her of the quality of his love.

In version (*b*) the Queen's anger at Lancelot's sudden departure (*LM* XVIII.6–7; short version XVIII.11) and Morgain's success in causing further doubts thus represent a new development in the love theme. In relation to this particular set of adventures, encountered on the way to the rescue of Gauvain, the change affects the presentation of Guinevere rather than Lancelot. The latter's position remains the same. His quality as lover has enabled him to achieve the adventure of the Val sans Retor and to resist all attempts to seduce him. He declares: 'Nus fins amans ne porroit de son cors fauser a la rien del monde que il plus aime ne plus que il feroit de son cuer.' (*LM* XXVI.27.) Even when forced to admit that he loves *par amors*, an admission which he had refused to make in the Lady of Malohaut's prison, he does so in terms which avoid all disloyalty:

'Damoisele, fet il, je vos dirai comme loials chevaliers que je sui amés de tant loial amie que je doi tant doter a fauser vers li plus que je ne feroie peril de mort ne honte ne nule desloialté.' (*LM* XXVI.28.)

Lancelot triumphantly surmounts all temptations, and Morgain's damsel is overcome by admiration at the *grant loialté* which she finds in him (*LM* XXVI.29). He alone is able to take from the water the dead knight and lady (*LM* XXVI.32–7) who died because of their love for one another, of which the lady's husband thought that it *tornast a vilenie*, although it was in fact *bone amor* (an incident with perhaps significantly ambiguous echoes of phrases used in a romance of *Tristan* such as that of Beroul).[16]

However, if Lancelot's love is still presented as a source of chivalric achievement and honour in relation to the adventures which he achieves on the quest for the captured Gauvain, not only are his earlier fears lest the Queen doubt the quality of his love, which were then groundless (in the *PL*), now more justified, but the adulterous aspect of the love also receives emphasis. Morgain stirs up trouble by stealing Lancelot's ring and by sending a damsel to court with a false account of a confession he had made, in peril of death, of vile sin with the Queen:

'Et por ce se fist confés tot en oiance de si vil pechié et si orible comme de son seignor, ki ci est, qu'il avoit longuement honi et de sa feme, et issi me commanda il que je le deisse en ceste cort, kar je estoie en la place ou il se fist confés.' (*LM* XXIX.10.)

The damsel goes on to say that Lancelot has sworn publicly that he will never again stay in a town for more than one night and will henceforth walk barefoot and never bear arms, and that he returns the ring to the Queen. Guinevere is therefore faced with threats both to the trust between the lovers and to their relationship with society. From the point of view of the doctrine of *fin' amor* Lancelot appears to have broken the secrecy of the love and to have sent back the ring in public. The confidence between them would therefore seem to have been endangered, and the love become a source of dishonour. The False Guinevere accusation was false, but the message from Lancelot, although un-authentic, draws public attention to a love of which the reader knows the existence, emphasizing its adulterous nature, a love which the Queen in the False Guinevere episode had already recognized in private as sinful. The Queen defends herself and Lancelot skilfully in public,[17] but the incident prepares the way for the duality in the treatment of the love theme in the *Charrette* episode. On the one hand, there are the rebuffs and the failures associated with Lancelot's love: Guinevere receives him coldly after he has crossed the Sword Bridge and defeated Meleagant; she is punishing him for the wrong she believes he has done her in relation to their love (*LM* XXXIX.20). He fails at one adventure in which he is destined to be surpassed by his own son, because his love for Guinevere disqualifies him from achieving it (*LM* XXXVII.36–41). On the other hand, the inspirational quality of Lancelot's love is still present in episodes in version (*b*) which both evoke memories of his earlier achievements in the *PL* and prepare the way for his exploits in his rescue of the Queen from Gorre, for which his love gives him strength. Version (*b*), therefore, in its treat-ment of the love theme skilfully combines some continuity with the *PL* and hints of what is to come in Guinevere's suspicions of Lancelot and in the admission both by her and by the tale of the potentially destructive nature of a love between a knight of the Round Table and Arthur's Queen.

These modifications to the love theme may represent significant changes in direction, but there are also a few examples of clear contradictions between version (*b*) and what has gone before, contradictions often linked to the new attitude towards the Lancelot–Guinevere love relationship. These arise in episodes preparing for a Grail Quest to come. As we have seen in Chapter VI, in *PL* 33.9–12 Perceval (in some manuscripts under the form Perlesvaus) is named as the knight who achieved the adventure of the Perilous Seat, and the Grail adventure is referred to in a number of passages as one which has already taken place. This is in flat contradiction of the prophecy, made by Merlin and reported by Helie de Toulouse, of the coming of the Grailwinner who will descend from Lancelot and will surpass him (*LM* IV.25). Helie goes on to give details:

'Je le sai bien, fet li mestres, que cil qui achevera les aventures de Bretaigne sera li mieldres chevaliers de tot le monde et aemplira le deerain siege de la Table Reonde, et cil a en escripture la senefiance de lion.' (*LM* IV.35.)

Merlin has prophesied that the Grailwinner will be pure and chaste, and will come from the chamber of the Maimed King:

'Et si nos dist Merlins qui encore ne nos a menti de rien que de la chambre al roi mehengnié de la Gaste Forest Aventureuse en la fin del roialme de Lisces vendra la merveilleuse beste qui sera esguardee a merveille es plains de la Grant Montaigne. Ceste beste sera diverse de totes autres bestes, kar ele avra viaire et teste de lion et cors d'olifant et autres menbres; si avra rains et nonbril de pucele virge enterrine, si avra cuer d'acier dur et serré qui n'avra garde de flechir ne d'amoloier; si avra parole de dame pensive et volenté de droit jugier.' (*LM* IV.38.)

The prophecy continues: 'Et lors remandront les aventures de la Grant Bretaigne et les merveilles perilloses.' (*LM* IV.39.) This recalls the phrase earlier applied to Perceval: 'et mena a fin les aventures del Reiaume Perilleus Aventureus, ce fu li regnes de Logres' (*PL* 33.11–12). But it now looks towards the future and towards a new and as yet unnamed hero.

Merlin plays a very different role here from the one which he had in the *PL*, where the diabolical side of his nature had not been neutralized by baptism, and he was imprisoned by the Lady of the Lake. In version (*b*), as the prophet of the Holy Grail cited by Helie de Toulouse, he recalls the Christianized Merlin of Robert de Boron who provides a link between the Grail and Arthur's kingdom through the setting up of the Round Table with its Perilous Seat.[18]

Conclusion on the relationship between versions (*a*) and (*b*)

The relationship between versions (*a*) and (*b*) might be explained in two different ways. Firstly, version (*a*) might derive from (*b*) and represent a lopping-off or rather a disentangling of one of the branches from the cyclic romance. Secondly, version (*b*) might be seen as an elaboration of (*a*), designed to lead into a *Lancelot-Grail* cycle.

The first of these possibilities was explored by A. Micha and has, of course, been accepted by those who believe that from the very opening words of the romance, 'En la marche de Gaule et de la Petite Bretaigne', the *Lancelot-Grail* cycle had been conceived as a unified whole, with a Grailwinner descended from Lancelot. However, as has been seen in Chapter VI of this book, the Grail allusions in the part of the text up to Lancelot's installation at the Round Table and his departure with Galehot do not look forward to a Grail Quest yet to come, with Galahad, son of Lancelot, as chief Grailwinner, destined to sit in the Perilous Seat; on the contrary, they look back to a Grail adventure belonging to the past in which Perceval achieves the Perilous Seat and sees *apertement* the Grail. The as yet unborn Grailwinner, descendant of Lancelot, is first introduced in version (*b*) of the False Guinevere episode in a passage which is in conflict with the earlier Grail allusions, but in harmony with later events in the cycle. This would seem to present a strong argument in favour of the theory that the writing of version (*b*) represents an important stage in the development of the cycle. As has been seen, it is here for the first time, in the interpretation of Galehot's dreams by Helie de Toulouse, that the very worldly values of the love story of Lancelot and Guinevere are within the same work confronted with the chaste, spiritual chivalry of the Galahad version of the Grail theme.[19]

The more likely interpretation of the relationship between versions (*a*) and (*b*) would therefore be the second possibility mentioned above, that (*b*) represents a skilful remoulding of (*a*). The last part of an existing non-cyclic *Lancelot* (phase VI of the *PL*) was rewritten in such a way that the prose tale of Lancelot's childhood, the establishment of his identity under the inspiration of his love for Guinevere, and his progress towards a seat at the Round Table, becomes a branch of a great cycle which will include themes already well known in the twelfth-century Arthurian tradition: the tale of the Cart, a Grail Quest, and a Death of Arthur. The author who rewrote the last part of this existing tale left untouched the earlier allusions to the Grail story. These represented the Quest as a tale from the past, told elsewhere, of which Perceval was the hero, therefore not belonging to the Lancelot story itself, but dominating the records of Arthurian adventures of which the tale of Lancelot also forms a part.

The opposing theory, according to which version (*a*) would present the reverse process, the disengaging of the first branch of the *Lancelot propre* from the cycle through the undoing of the interlace and the removal of all episodes or allusions preparing the way for later events, would seem much more unlikely. It would go against the usual trend in the development of prose romance in the thirteenth century, as I have suggested in my article in *Romania* which discusses in detail the theory put forward by Micha. As has been shown in Part I of this book, in version (*a*)'s account, the episodes of Galehot's journey with Lancelot, his dream, the False Guinevere episode, and Lyonel's fight with the Lion of Lybia form an integral part of the thematic structure of the non-cyclic Prose *Lancelot*, and the death of Galehot provides a natural conclusion to the tale of Lancelot as the only possible end to the conflict between Lancelot's love for Guinevere and his companionship with Galehot as presented earlier in the romance. There are no allusions or preparations for future events in the narrative, up to Lancelot's acceptance as a companion of the Round Table (the part of the story common to both cyclic and non-cyclic versions), which look beyond such an end to the story.

However, such an explanation of the relationship between versions (*a*) and (*b*) does not imply an attack on either the literary quality of version (*b*) or on the unity of the cycle as a whole, both so eloquently argued by scholars such as Lot,

Frappier, and Micha. The non-cyclic Prose *Lancelot* may have a thematic unity and cohesion of its own, but so, on a far grander scale, has the whole *Lancelot-Grail* cycle. Version (*b*), as we have seen, has most skilfully used both elements of continuity and changes of direction in the development of existing themes to prepare the way for the great and sometimes tragic events which are to follow and which will involve the Lancelot-Guinevere love story in the other two great Arthurian themes of the Grail and the end of the Kingdom of Logres with the death of Arthur. The elements of continuity and change in the later branches of the cycle, and the different significance given to earlier events through their incorporation within a new structure, will be the theme of the next chapter.

˙XI

Lancelot with the Grail: second stage

From the *Charrette* to the end of the *Agravain*

Throughout the part of the romance which follows the death of Galehot and leads up to the beginning of the *Queste*,[1] the love theme (Lancelot, the greatest knight alive, inspired by his love and absolute loyalty to Guinevere) is developed skilfully to preserve continuity. Links with the past are maintained while the advent of a new kind of chivalry is prepared, a chivalry for which Lancelot's love for Guinevere serves to disqualify rather than qualify him.

This is exemplified in the *Charrette* episode by the two tomb slabs in the same cemetery; each of these is linked to a different adventure and a different type of hero, but the heroes themselves are connected as father and son, a relationship which is to have an important thematic and structural significance. In the first of these tombs lies buried Galaad, the younger son of Joseph of Arimathea. The name and etymology of this Galaad, 'celui qui fu engendrez en Sorelice qui puis fu apelee Gales por lui' (*LM* XXXVII.28), picks up an earlier allusion in the list of great knights of the past given by the Lady of the Lake in her explanation of chivalry to the young Lancelot (*PL* 146.20). According to the inscription on the tomb, the slab will be raised by the knight who will free the prisoners of the Roialme sans Retor (*LM* XXXVII.29). This has a double resonance: it evokes both the scene in Chrétien's *Chevalier de la Charrette*, and the raising of the slab in the cemetery of the Dolorous Guard (*PL* 194), itself setting off echoes in the reader's memory of Chrétien's Lancelot, lover of Guinevere, and thus interlacing the theme of love with that of the making of a name.[2] In the prose-romance version of the *Charrette* story Lancelot, as the greatest living knight and lover of Guinevere, is destined to free the prisoners of Gorre, as is appropriate for the man who had achieved the rank of the best knight under the inspiration of love (see Part I, Chapter III). Lancelot himself recalls the Dolorous Guard when he sees the tombs in the cemetery:

Lors le mainent el cimentiere, et quant il voit les tombes, si li membre de la Dolerose Garde. (*LM* XXXVII.32.)

In the same cemetery, however, is the tomb of Symeu, of which the slab will only be raised by the knight 'qui abatroit les enchantemens del Roialme Aventureus et metroit fin as aventures et acompliroit le siege de la Table

274

Reonde' (*LM* XXXVII.29). Similar phrases are used early in the *PL*, but in relation to a different hero, Perceval (*PL* 33.9–12). We have therefore an important inconsistency here, combined with a picking up of an earlier passage, indicating a significant change in direction (and in Grail hero): a move from an allusion to a Grail Quest outside the tale of Lancelot to an allusion to a Grail Quest yet to come, which will form part of the *Lancelot-Grail* romance. Lancelot experiences fear at the sight of the flames coming from the tomb and fails to raise the slab. He is immediately plunged into gloom and laments: 'Ha, Diex, com grant damage!' He is deeply ashamed of his fear and what it implies for his position as the greatest knight. He explains his lament to a voice coming from the tomb:

'Certes, fet li chevaliers, jel dis por ce que je ai le siecle trop vilement traï et deceu, kar il me tienent al meillor des buens chevaliers: or sai je bien que je nel sui mie, kar il n'est pas buens chevaliers qui poor a.' (*LM* XXXVII.37.)

The voice (that of Symeu) tells Lancelot that he is still the greatest knight: 'kar cil qui sera buens chevaliers n'est pas encore avant venus et molt est sa venue pres.' He learns that he has all the prowess and worth which can be found 'en home corrompu', but will be surpassed in this adventure by someone who will be of his lineage and so full of virtue that as soon as he enters the chamber where the tomb is, the flames will be extinguished. The corruption and hence failure is here ascribed in the long version, on just this one occasion, to the sin of Lancelot's father rather than to his own sin:[3]

'Et se ce ne fust, ce sachiés vos bien, vos acomplissiés les merveilles que vostre parens acomplira et tot ce avés vos perdu par le pechié de vostre pere, kar il mesprist une sole fois vers ma cosine vostre mere. Et il estoit chastes et virges, quant il assambla a li et si avoit il .L. ans passés ou plus. Par cest pechié avés vos perdu ce que je vos ai dit, et neporquant les grans bontés qui en vos sont avés vos des grans vertus qui en vostre mere furent et sont encore.'[4] (*LM* XXXVII.40.)

In the short version this explanation is combined with a reference to Lancelot's own sin:

'Et saches que cil qui de chi me deliverra ert mes cousins et ert si prés tes carneus amis que plus ne porroit, et cil sera la flors de tous les vrais chevaliers. Et saches que tu meismes achievaisses les aventures qu'il metra a fin, mes tu les as perdues par les grans ardeurs de luxure qui sont en toi et por ce que tes cors n'est mie dignes de metre a fin les aventures del Saint Graal por les crueus pechiés et por les ors dont tes cors est envenimés: c'est la desloiaus luxure. Et d'autre part l'as tu perdu par .I. pechié que li rois Bans tes peres fist: car puis qu'il ot espousee ta mere qui encore vit jut il a une damoisele et de la vient une grant partie de ton meschief; ne tu n'as mie a non Lancelot en baptesme, mes Galaad: tes peres te fist ensi apeler por son pere qui ensi ot non.' (*LM* XXXVII.39–40, short version.)

The intertwining of the theme of the two tombs with Lancelot's names and with that of his descendant provides a new variation upon the identity theme and also serves to highlight the contrast between Lancelot's present status at the pinnacle of chivalry and his future displacement. Symeu tells Lancelot about his ancestor Galaad whom he has just taken from his tomb and explains that he shares his name:

'Et je te conois molt bien et tos cels qui de ton lignage sont, et saches que tu as non en baptesme le non al saint home de Iasus que tu as de la tombe geté, et je sui ses cosins germains, mais tes peres t'apela Lancelot por remenbrance de son aiel qui issi avoit non.' (*LM* XXXVII.39, long version.)

This picks up and reinterprets the reference at the beginning of the *PL*:

et avoit non Lanceloz en sorenon, mais il avoit non an baptaisme Galaaz. Et ce par quoi il fu apelez Lanceloz ce devisera bien li contes ça avant, car li leus n'i est ores mies ne la raisons. (*PL* 1.7–10.)

An account of how Lancelot gained his name is given in the *PL*, as promised, in the episode of the raising of the slab at the Dolorous Guard (*PL* 194). Here a new kind of explanation is given in order to prepare for what is to come. The use of Lancelot as a name rather than Galaaz[5] is explained later, in the account of the conception of Galahad (*LM* LXXVIII.58).

There are a number of important episodes or allusions, often with resonances of the identity theme, which concern adventures to be achieved or not to be achieved by Lancelot, lover of Guinevere. Those which emphasize the inspirational quality of that love link up with the past, with the love's role in the *PL* (as well as in Chrétien's poem); those which stress its destructive side foreshadow the future. Both achievement and condemnation are combined in the episode in which Gauvain and Hector find a burning tomb (*LM* LXV.25–33). According to an inscription on a red marble tomb the only knight who should enter the cemetery where the tomb is found is:

'li chaitis chevaliers qui par sa maleurose luxure a perdu a achever les merveilloses aventures del Graal, celes ou il ne porra jamés recovrer.' (*LM* LXV.25.)

This knight is identified in another inscription as the son of the *roine dolerose* (a name, in the form *Reine as Granz Dolors,* used to designate the mother of Lancelot in the *PL*, 16.21–3).

'Ja nus n'entrera en cest cimentire qui a honte ne s'en parte jusqu'atant que li fis a la roine dolerose i vendra.' (*LM* LXV.32.)

Passages such as these are balanced by many others which make clear Lancelot's present greatness. Arthur and his court still consider him the only knight capable of achieving the Grail adventure, and they weep when they hear a false rumour of his death:

Moult firent tuit grant duel et jone et viel, si ont laissié le rire et le jouer et dient que or ne sevent il plus par cui les aventures del Saint Graal soient menees a fin, quant cil est morz a cui il s'en atandoient. (*LM* LXXIII.2.)

A reference back to Lancelot's christening, when Ban was still alive (of which no account is given in the *PL*), once again links his present achievement with the past and his lineage. An old man prophesied the child's great chivalric achievements:

'De ceste petite creature vandra encore si grant chose que de sa prouesce et de sa valor sera tote terrienne chevalerie enluminee.' (*LM* LXXXI.17.)

Similarly, when Lancelot shows his quality as the greatest knight and lover by putting an end to the *carole* (a magic dance into which are drawn those who love or have loved),[6] there is a link with his father in the explanation given of its establishment by a young clerk, cousin of Ban, skilled in *nigremance* and *anchantement* (*LM* LXXXIII.4–8). The *carole* can only be ended with the arrival of 'li plus leaux chevaliers . . . et li mieldres et li plus biaux' (*LM* LXXXIII.8). King Ban had left his crown to be worn by this best and fairest knight, and it is his own son Lancelot who ends the *carole*, releases the dancers, and wins the crown. Another proof of Lancelot's quality is to be found in the chess set, linked to the *carole* in that it was created for the same damsel by the same clerk. The chess game is only to be won by a knight 'gracieuz et desirrez et amez sor touz autres' (*LM* LXXXIII.12)—a description which recalls the Lady of the Lake's parting words to Lancelot as she leaves him, an unknown youth, at Arthur's court:

'Mais or vos en alez, et bons et biax et gracieus et dessirrez de totes genz et amez sor toz chevaliers de totes dames; itex seroiz vos, car bien lo sai.' (*PL* 154.39–155.2.)

Lancelot's skill at chess is also mentioned in the description of him given in the account of his childhood in the Lake (*PL* 39.11–14).

These achievements of Lancelot, however, look backwards rather than for-wards, and as Lancelot's adventure at his grandfather's tomb approaches, there is increasing emphasis on the destructive side of his love: it is shown to bar his future progress and to threaten the kingdom of Logres with dissension. It even begins to throw a shadow over his past achievements, however strenuously Lancelot protests against this. Gauvain comes back to court and tells of the burning tomb and the inscription which says that the flames will not be quenched 'devant que li maleureux chevaliers vendroit, cil qui par sa chaitive laide luxure avoit perdu a achever les aventures del Saint Graal'. (*LM* LXXXIV.72.) He also reports that another inscription names the knight as 'le fil a la Roine Dolereuse'. The Queen identifies this knight as Lancelot and is deeply disturbed. She talks privately about it to Lancelot:

'Par mon chief, fait ele, ce estes vos dont les lestres parloient, car vos fustes filz a la Dolereuse Roine; si me poise moult, quant vos par eschaufement de char avez perdu a mener a chief ce por quoi toute terrienne prouesce sera travaillie: si poez or bien dire que chier avez achatee m'amor, quant vos par moi avez perdu ce que vos ne porrez recouvrer. Si sachiez que je n'an sui mie moins dolante que vos estes, mes plus par aventure, car c'est granz pechiez, quant vos avoit fait Diex le millor et le plus bel et le plus gracieux de touz et ancor vos avoit il donné tel eur que vos veissiez les merveilles del Saint Graal apertement: et or l'avez perdu par l'assemblee de nos .II.. Si me venist mielz, ce me samble, que onques ne fusse nee que par moi remainsissent tant de bien a faire come il remandront.'[7] (*LM* LXXXV.2.)

At this stage Lancelot rejects absolutely the suggestion that Guinevere's love has had a destructive effect upon him as a knight. He does so in a speech which is reminiscent of the scene in which his reluctant admission of his exploits under his various identities and his declaration that these feats were all inspired by the Queen's words 'biaus douz amis' led up to the lovers' first kiss:[8]

'Dame, fait Lanceloz, vos dites mal. Sachiez que je ja ne fusse venus a si grant hautesce com je sui, se vos ne fussiez, car je n'eusse mie cuer par moi au conmancement de ma chevalerie d'amprandre les choses que li autre laissoient par defaute de pooir. Mais ce que je baoie a vos et a vostre grant biauté mist mon cuer en l'orgueil ou j'estoie si que je ne poïsse trouver aventure que je ne menasse a chief; car je savoie bien, se je ne pooie les aventures passer par prouesce, que a vos ne vandroie je ja, et il m'i couvenoit avenir ou morir. Dont je vos di vraiement que ce fu la chose qui plus acroissoit mes vertuz.' (*LM* LXXXV.3.)

Guinevere is still uneasy that his love for her will make it impossible for him to achieve the greatest adventure of all, that of the Holy Grail:

'Donc ne me poise il mie, se vos m'amastes, quant en tel prouesce en estes venuz, mais il me poise quant vos en avez perdu a mener a chief les hautes aventures del Saint Graal por quoi la Table Reonde fu establie.' (*LM* LXXXV.3.)

But Lancelot stubbornly refuses to accept that without his love for her he could have achieved great prowess, and without prowess he could not have succeeded in the Grail adventure. His first arrival at Arthur's court, a young and naïve hero who at times reminds us of Perceval, is evoked by his words:

'Vos dites merveilles, fait Lanceloz, et si vos monsterrai coment. Je cuit que ja ne fusse venuz a la grant prouesce ou je sui se par vos ne fust, car je estoie jones anfes et nices et fors de mon païs et sanz grant prouesce ne poïsse je mie mener a fin ceste chose dont vos parlez, ne n'an feïsse riens, se je ne fusse de vos si bien come je sui.' (*LM* LXXXV.3.)

It is not until the middle of the *Queste* (p.66) that Lancelot is forced to accept that his love is having a destructive effect on his knightly quality.[9]

Lancelot's experiences during his first visit to Corbenic illustrate both his triumphs (linking with the past) and his future displacement as the greatest knight. He is able to save a damsel from a tub of hot water, an adventure which Gauvain (LXVI.4–8) was unable to achieve; he then raises the slab on a tomb of which the inscription reads as follows:

'Ja ceste tombe ne sera levee devant que li lieparz i mestra main, de qui li granz lions doit issir, et cil la levera legierement, et lors sera engendrez li granz lions en la bele fille au roi de la Terre Forainne.' (*LM* LXXVIII.46.)

When Lancelot achieves this adventure, he identifies himself as the leopard (to be found in Galehot's vision, *LM* II.10, IV.34–5) who is to engender the hero destined to surpass him. He achieves a glimpse of the Grail. His love for Guinevere here plays an ambiguous role. His sinful passion for her, because he is under the illusion that the daughter of Pellés is the Queen, prompts him to commit the carnal act which, through an involuntary betrayal of his love, is to engender Galahad, destined to be the pure and virgin knight. By this act the name Galahad, lost by Lancelot through *luxure,* is recovered in the chaste son, the fruit of this union:

Et tout ainsi com li nons de Galaad avoit esté perduz en Lancelot par eschaufement de luxure, tout ansi fu recouvrez en cestui par atenance de char: car il fu virges en volenté et en oevre jusqu'a la mort, si com l'estoire le devise. Einsinc fu recouvree flor pour flor, car en sa nessance fu flor de pucelage estainte et maumise; cil qui puis fu flor et mireor de chevalerie, il fu restorez par le conmun assamblement; et se virginitez fu empirie en ce qu'il fu conceuz, bien en fu li mesfaiz amandez en sa vie par sa virginité qu'il randi sainne et antiere a son Sauveor, quant il trespassa del siecle, et par les granz biens qu'il fist en sa vie[10] (*LM* LXXVIII.58.)

Lancelot's experiences at the tomb of his grandfather (Lancelot) also combine achievement, failure, and a link with the identity theme. Because he is still the best knight in the world, he is able to take his grandfather's head from the boiling fountain, raise the tomb slab, and lay the bodies of both his grandparents in the same grave. But he is not able to cool the boiling fountain or to restore light to the castle for he is *chauz et luxurieux,* as a hermit explains to him:

'Par mon chief, fait li prodom, or poez savoir que je vos di voir de ce que je vos dis que vos estiez chauz et luxurieux et que .I. chevaliers trop mielz antechiez de vos vendra et sera sa venue en vostre tans et el mien: ausi poez savoir que ce est voirs, car se vos fussiez tieux

que les aventures del Saint Graal fussent menees a chief par vos, la chalor de ceste fontainne fust remese en vostre venue. Mais puis que li feux de luxure n'est en vos estainz, ja
por bonne chevalierie qui soit en vos la chalor de ceste fontainne n'estaindra. Si vos en
poez aler de ci quant il vos plaira, car bien avez achevees les aventures que chevaliers anfer
puet achever; mais se vos fussiez si sains et si anterins com iert li prodom dont je vos cont,
as bonnes graces qui an vos sont je sai bien que ceste aventure et les autres qui par la Grant
Bretaingne sont espandues poïssiez vos bien mener a chief; mais vos i avez failli par les
granz pechiez dont vos estes sorpris.' (*LM* XCIII 22.)

It is after this adventure that Lancelot learns of the birth of the boy who is to
achieve the Grail Quest (*LM* XCIII.33) and guesses that this may be his son (*LM*
XCIII.34).

The motif of the raising of the tomb slab, therefore, runs right through this
part of the cycle. The love theme and that of the making of a name come
together as they had done when Lancelot's confession of his name to Guinevere
was a prelude to the lovers' first kiss, but in a way which transforms the earlier
episode and gives a new meaning to the two interlacing themes. Lancelot's discovery of his name through the raising of the slab after the conquest of the
Dolorous Guard and his establishment of a reputation under this name through
the inspiration of his love for Guinevere are now represented as a loss rather
than a gain.

Lancelot's painting of episodes in his past life,[11] while imprisoned by
Morgain, provides another example of the way in which events in the cyclic
romance place earlier adventures in a new context and hence give them a new
significance. In the non-cyclic romance the adulterous nature of the relationship of Lancelot and Guinevere was kept in the background as much as possible
(see Chapter III); but here, through the use that Morgain, from the moment that
she is aware of Lancelot's painting, intends to make of the pictures, the earlier
sequences are placed firmly in the framework of a conflict between the love and
Guinevere's marriage vows and the loyalty that Lancelot, Knight of the Round
Table, owes to Arthur. Tristan too made an image of his beloved and other
figures recalling scenes in his past life with Iseut in order to console himself
during his separation from her.[12] The account of the painting of the room,
through its recapitulation of earlier episodes in Lancelot's life, provides a focal
point, a gathering together of threads in the narrative, which plays a role similar
to that performed in the narrative structure by Lancelot's confession of his past
deeds, patiently extorted from him by the Queen in the *PL* (341–4; see Chapter
III). The earlier sequence led up to the first kiss, and this is evoked by Lancelot's
kissing of the picture of the Queen, which also recalls Tristan kissing the image
of Iseut in Thomas's *Tristan*.[13] This visual image of Guinevere gives him more
joy than he had experienced through any other woman except the original: 'Si

se delite assez plus qu'il ne feist en nule autre fame fors en sa dame.' (*LM* LXXXVI.23.) The force of Lancelot's love gives him the power to create the pictures as it had provided the inspiration for his deeds of chivalry:[14]

Lors dist Morgue a cele qui o lui estoit venue: 'Par foi, merveilles poez veoir de cest chevalier qui tant est soltis et an chevalerie et an toutes choses. Voirement feroit Amors del plus dur home soutif et angingneux: si le di por cest chevalier que ja jor de sa vie ne feist si bien ymages, se ne fust destroiz d'amors qui a ce l'out mené. Mes puis qu'il est si atorné, il n'est home el monde qui a son sens se preist.' (*LM* LXXXVI.22.)

The listing in the tale of the past events recorded by Lancelot reminds the reader of the important early stages in his progress towards both a seat at the Round Table and the winning of Guinevere's love. Thus we are told (*LM* LXXXVI.21) that he painted his arrival at Camelot (*PL* 151–5), his stupefaction before the Queen's beauty (*PL* 157–8), and his mission as champion of the Lady of Nohaut (*Pl* 162–77); he then painted (*LM* LXXXVI.23) the conquest of Dolorous Guard (*PL* 183–95), and the tournament where he had a red shield and was wounded by the King of a Hundred Knights (*PL* 230–1). In the end Lancelot depicts not only his own adventures but also those of the other knights, and thus provides in visual images the equivalent of the stories recorded by Arthur's clerks and related in the tale of Lancelot:

Aprés portrait de jor en jor toute l'estoire ne mie de lui seulement, mes des autres, si com li contes a devisé. (*LM* LXXXVI.23.)

But unlike the official records kept by the clerks, these paintings themselves are to play an actively destructive role in later events, for it is made clear at an early stage that Morgain is determined to use them to achieve her own sinister purpose. Lancelot is to be allowed to paint the whole room, and she interprets the pictures to one of her damsels in terms of the triangle so carefully avoided in the non-cyclic romance:

Lors monstre a cele les ymages qu'il avoit faites et li devise de chascunne la senefiance et li dist: 'Veez ci la roine et veez ci Lancelot et veez ci le roi Artus', tant qu'ele set bien que chascuns senefie. 'Or ne lairoie je, fait ele, en nule manniere que je le paintre ne tenisse tant que toute ceste chambre fust painte: car je sai bien qu'il i paindra touz ses fez et tous ses diz et toutes les ouvres de lui et de la roine; s'il l'avoit tout paint, je feroie tant que mes freres li rois Artus venroit ça et li feroie connoistre les faiz et la verité de Lancelot et de la roine.' (*LM* LXXXVI.22.)

The references back by means of the paintings therefore give a new slant to earlier events. The emphasis is no longer on Lancelot's service to the Arthurian kingdom under the inspiration of his love for Guinevere, but on the adulterous aspect: Morgain seizes upon the opportunities for presenting Lancelot's deeds in such a way that discord will spring from them. This looks forward to the *Mort Artu:* there Morgain makes malicious use of the paintings, and Arthur listens to her and to Agravain and Mordred. It is these two brothers who finally tear the kingdom apart, as is already forecast in *LM* C. 25, where it is said that the love of Arthur and Gauvain for Lancelot was so great that it would never have been shaken without the intervention of Agravain and Mordred:

Si an distrent tant que li grant parenté le roi torna a mort et a destruction, et il meismes entr'aux .II., et tuit li frere en furent puis occis, et li rois qui tant fu vaillanz an morut, dont ce fu domages et pechiez; car an celui tans n'estoit nus aussi puissanz hom conme li rois Artus, ne de sa richesce ne fu onques si debonnaires ne si cortois.

Once again references back are combined with preparations for and prophecies of what is to come. This is done in such a way as to present a shift in the value given to the love in the original account of Lancelot's exploits in the defence of both Guinevere and Arthur and his kingdom within the structure of the non-cyclic romance.

The love relationship is disruptive in other ways. Whereas in the *PL* Guinevere has complete trust in Lancelot and never doubts the quality of his love, here, as in the episodes leading up to the *Charrette* story, she is at times jealous and distrustful. Lancelot's involuntary night with the daughter of Pellés causes a rift between them. He is banished by the Queen from the court and laments in the following terms:

'Ha, Kamaalot, bonne cité et bele et bien garnie de toute chevalerie, beneuree de toute biauté de dames, en toi pris je conmancement de vie.' Et ce disoit il pour sa dame par cui il li ert avis qu'il vivoit. 'Et si ai pris en toi conmancement de mort et sanz faille je sui venuz au duel par quoi je morrai.' (*LM* CV.38.)

This lament evokes Lancelot's first meeting with Guinevere, which took place at Camelot on his first visit there as a youth (*PL* 157–65), and his lover's trance at the sight of the city (*PL* 265.11–15) when he returned there for the second time and thought of what had happened to him on the first visit. Now that meeting with Guinevere, which had then given him life, is threatening that very life. Once again the evocation of the past includes a reinterpretation of the value of the love to Lancelot. He goes mad again (*LM* CV.38, CVII.1–30),[15] as he had done earlier, when separated from Guinevere through imprisonment by the Saxons (*PL* 551–7), but with a significant difference. On the earlier occasion the Queen had not caused his madness; she tended him, he was calmed by the shield (its crack now joined) which symbolized their love, and was eventually healed by the Lady of the Lake, sender of the shield, who in conversation with the Queen praised the quality of the love and the honour which it bestowed on

Guinevere. Now it is Guinevere who has driven Lancelot to madness, and it is the Grail, in its pure spirituality totally opposed to earthly physical love, which heals him. The earlier shield is recalled when Lancelot has a new one made, depicting a knight kneeling before the Queen as if he were pleading for mercy, and weeps before it (*LM* CVII.46). This is also reminiscent of an episode in the *PL* (367–76) where Hector weeps before a shield because of his lady's refusal to let him undertake the adventure which could have proved his worth as her knight. Guinevere had been favourably contrasted with other ladies in the *PL* (see Chapter III), but now she too is playing a negative role.

Lancelot's own family are fully aware of the harm which the Queen is inflicting not only on him but also on the knights of the Round Table. Hector and Lyonel consider that 'moult doivent haïr l'eure que Lanceloz s'acointa de la reine' (*LM* CVI.5), a sentiment to be echoed later, in the *Mort Artu*. They and Bohort predict that many *preudomme* will die as a result of her banishment of Lancelot from the court (*LM* CVI.3–4, 40). We have, therefore, yet again elements of continuity combined with a fundamental change in direction which leads to a reappraisal of the love relationship of Lancelot and Guinevere.

There are also significant variations on the earlier system of pairing between Lancelot and his cousins (see Chapter VIII), variations closely linked with the replacement of Lancelot by his son Galahad as greatest knight. In the *PL* parallels between Lancelot and Lyonel are drawn to the advantage of the former; here the parallels are made between Bohort and Lancelot, sometimes in favour of Bohort, who is to be one of the three Grailwinners, chaste as the white bull with the one black spot in the *Queste* (149, 155–7). Bohort (*LM* XLV.21, 31, 36), as Lancelot had done before him (*PL* 188, 205), receives instructions from a damsel sent by the Lady of the Lake, the same one who had rescued him and his brother as children from Gaunes (*PL* 66–70) and who had revealed her identity to Lyonel in a similar way during Gauvain's battle against the seneschal of Cambenic (*PL* 495–6). This damsel says to Bohort:

'Si voi or bien que molt a bien ma dame sa norreture enploié en vos, et certes ele en serra molt liee, quant je li conterai que vos el peril de mort me donastes por l'amor de li ce dont vos vos deviés garantir; et si ne saviés qui g'estoie.' (*LM* XLV.37.)

The Lady of the Lake herself had said of Lancelot to the Queen:

'Et sachiez bien que, por la grant proece que an lui devoit estre, lo norri ge tant que il fust si granz et si biaus comme vos lo veïstes a cort.' (*PL* 556.21–3.)

This damsel from the Lake provides a link between the narrative threads of Lancelot and Bohort, for the former meets her (*LM* XLIX.12–13) not long after she has spoken to the latter. Another episode echoing one of Lancelot's

adventures as a young knight concerns a damsel encircled by metal bands. The
knight who takes off these bands must swear to avenge her against the man who
put them on and against anyone who was glad that she was bound in this way
(*LM* XLVII.8–18). Bohort swears the oath and removes the bands, just as
Lancelot, immediately after his knighting, had removed the weapons from a
wounded man after swearing to avenge him against all those who loved the
inflicter of the wounds more than the victim (*PL* 149, 159, 160 and a series of
subsequent battles). Bohort then demonstrates his loyalty to his cousin and firm
belief in his supremacy as a knight when he refuses to try to draw out of a
wounded knight a sword which can only be removed by the best knight. He
then fights Agravain to make him admit that Lancelot is a greater knight than
Gauvain (*LM* XLVII.28–31). In the *PL* it was the adventure in which Gauvain's
blood healed Agravain's leg, while that of Lancelot cured his arm, that
established the position of Gauvain as second only to Lancelot, at the top of the
hierarchy of great knights (*PL* 410–20 and 539). However, Lancelot's supremacy
is soon to be threatened, as is brought out in the most significant pairing of the
two knights. This is to be found in the two involuntary begettings: by Bohort on
King Brangoire's daughter (*LM* XLVII.34 to XLVIII.27) and by Lancelot on the
daughter of King Pellés (*LM* LXXVIII.56 to LXXIX.4, and XCIII.33–4). Bohort
himself recognizes the parallels between these two events when he says to
Lancelot, who is distressed by the momentous night spent with a woman other
than Guinevere, a night during which Galahad was conceived:

'Je sai bien, fait Boorz, que vos ne le feistes mie a vostre esciant, mais toutes voies fu il fait
par autel manniere com je fui deceuz de la fille le roi Brandegorre. Et se vos estes deceuz
par tel manniere, vos n'en devez mie estre courrouciez, mais liez et joianz, car je sai bien
que cil anfes achevera les aventures ou vos avez faillli: si vos en est grant honor avenue,
quant de vos est issue la flor de chevalerie.' (*LM* CI.13.)

The parallels between the two events are as follows. In each case the knight is
involved with a beautiful daughter of a king. The daughter of Brangoire is even
compared with the daughter of Pellés: 'onques mes ne fu nee si bele riens fors
solement la fille al Roi Pescheor' (*LM* XLVII.45). Both knights were unwilling
to become involved with a maiden, but for significantly different reasons:
Lancelot, because of his love for Guinevere; Bohort, because he wanted to
remain chaste. Both were deceived by supernatural means. The *maistresse* of
Brangoire's daughter uses a magic ring which makes Bohort temporarily forget
his own nature:

Et il prent l'anel, si le met en son doi; et si tost com il le ot mis, si li est tos li cuers muez
trop durement, kar s'il estoit ore de froide nature et virges en volenté et en oevre, or est de
tele dont ore ne li estoit a riens. (*LM* XLVIII.21.)

Brisane concocts a magic potion which persuades Lancelot that he is lying with Guinevere, when it is in fact the daughter of Pellés. Both physical unions are in the end presented as in accordance with the will of God, but for rather different reasons. In the case of Lancelot, his intentions are sinful, while those of the daughter of Pellés are pure:

Si se desirrent par diverses entancions, car ele ne le fait mie tant por la biauté de celui ne por luxure ne por eschaufement de char come ele fait por le fruit recevoir dont toz li païs doit venir a sa premiere biauté, qui par le dolereux cop de l'espee as estranges ranges avoit esté desertez et essilliez, si com il devise apertement en la Queste del Graal. Et cil la desirroit tout en autre manniere, car por sa biauté ne la couvoitoit il pas, mais il cuida que ce fust sa dame la roine et par ce fu il eschaufez qu'il la connut ausinc com Adam fist sa fame, mes non mie en tel maniere, car Adam connut sa fame leaument et par le conmandement Nostre Signor; et cil connut ceste em pechié et en avoutire et contre Deu et encontre Sainte Eglyse. (*LM* LXXVIII.57.)

But through God's will Lancelot's act is allowed to benefit mankind through its fruit, the child destined to be Grailwinner:

Et neporquant li Sires en qui tote pitié abite et qui ne juge mie selon les faiz as pecheors resgarda ceste assamblee selonc le preu a ceus del païs com cil qui ne voloit mie qu'il fussent touz dis en essil: si lor donna tel fruit engendrer et concevoir que por la flor de virginité qui iluec fust corrumpue et violee fu recouvree une autre flor de cui bien et de cui tandror mainte terre fu replenie et rasouagie; qu'ausinc com l'Estoire del saint Graal nos fait antandant, de ceste flor perdue fu restorez Galaad, li virges, li tres bons chevaliers, cil qui les aventures del saint Graal mist a fin et s'asist el perilleus siege de la Table Reonde ou onques chevaliers ne s'estoit assis qui ne fust morz. (*LM* LXXVIII.57.)

In the case of Bohort and his maiden, their innocence is emphasized: 'Ensi sont li virge mis ensemble, filz de roi et fille de roine et de roi.' (*LM* XLVIII.24.) Because of their innocence God had put in them a sweet fruit so that their virginity was not sacrificed for naught, for they had a noble son who was later Emperor of Constantinople.

Et por ce, se cist assamblemens fu fes par pechié et par ignorance des enfans, ne remest il pas que Diex n'en eust pitié, si ne soffri mie que lor virginités fust corrumpue por noient, ains i mist si haut fruit que de .II. si jovenes hantes ne descendi d'icel tens nul arbre plus puissant. (*LM* XLVIII.24.)

Bohort's firm intention to remain chaste is strongly stressed; indeed, the Lady of the Lake is surprised and shocked by this one lapse:

Et meesmement la Dame del Lac qui assés tost le sot par ses augures, si s'en merveille molt et dist c'or ne savoit ele cui croire, 'kar je cuidoie, fet ele, qu'il deust estre virges tot son aage.' Si en fu assés dolente quant ele le sot, et sans faille Boors avoit porposé a estre virges tos dis. (*LM* XLVIII.25.)

As this one breach was involuntary, Bohort is not disqualified from achieving, together with Perceval, a clearer vision of the Grail than any knight except for Galahad. Indeed, in a curious way, the whole episode of this one night of love in Bohort's life is used to bring out his superiority over Lancelot in this respect. After Bohort has seen the Grail, he is told that he has surpassed in purity and worth all the Arthurian knights who had come to Corbenic:

'Sire chevaliers, vos estes li plus nes et li plus prodom qui onques entrast ceanz de la meson le roi Artu. Or porrez dire, quant vos serez en vostre païs, que vos avez veu la lance vengerresce; si ne savez que ce est a dire ne ne savroiz devant que li perileux sieges de la Table Reonde avra trouvé son mestre, mais par celui qui s'i aserra savrez vos la verité de ceste lance et qui l'aporta en cest païs et dom ele vint. Et nonporquant se Lanceloz vostre cousin se fust ausi bien gardez, com vos avez porposé vos a garder, el conmancement de sa chevalerie, il meist tout ce a fin dont vos tuit estes ore en painne; car de chevalerie est il or si esmerez qu'il n'a son pareil el monde. Mais il est d'autre part si ampiriez que toutes les bonnes vertuz qui en lui deussent estre sont mortes et decheues par la foiblece de ses rains.' (*LM* XCVIII.42.)

Thus, whereas in the earlier Lancelot–Lyonel pairing, Lancelot was always given the edge over his cousin, here this new pairing, while maintaining links with the past, through the praise given to Bohort's chastity[16] in contrast with Lancelot's sensuality foreshadows events to come and prepares the way for a new kind of chivalry which demands different qualities.

There are other elements serving to bind these adventures which lead up to the Grail with those which culminated in Lancelot's achievement of a seat at the Round Table. The Lady of the Lake and her damsels provided an important cohesive element in the non-cyclic romance (see Chapter V) and they continue to play a role in the cyclic romance, although one less closely related to the main themes. There are a number of references to the childhood in the Lake when Lambegues meets Bohort (*LM* LI). There are allusions to the ring given by the Lady of the Lake to Lancelot when she took him to Arthur's court (*LM* LXXIV.10). It has the power to lay bare enchantments (*LM* XXXVII.3). This links up not only with events earlier in the romance (*PL* 154.29–31), but also with the one passage in Chrétien's *Chevalier de la Charrette* (2345–7) which refers to Lancelot's childhood in the Lake. This ring is now linked with the machinations of Morgain, who tries to get hold of it to destroy the trust between Lancelot and Guinevere and to remove Lancelot from its protection. We have therefore a new kind of opposition between representatives of different attitudes towards magic, replacing an earlier one between Merlin, unredeemed son of a devil, imprisoned before Lancelot is born, and the Lady of the Lake, who makes constructive use of the knowledge which she gains from him.[17] Now two types of fairy (that is, a lady with knowledge of magic) are opposed: the virtuous Lady of the Lake, who learned from Merlin but tries to work for the good of the Arthurian kingdom (in spite of her earlier role in encouraging the love between Lancelot and Guinevere, no longer viewed in the same favourable light); and the scheming Morgain, who also learned her magic from Merlin, but is the jealous rival of the Queen and always trying to cause trouble for Arthur. There is not the same emphasis as there had been in the *PL* on the Lady of the Lake's prediction of future events to other characters, but she uses auguries and casts her lot so that she can keep up with events happening at a distance from her (*LM* XLVIII.25, XLIX.15). She continues to send instructions, now not only to Lancelot (*LM* XLIX.13–14) and to Lyonel, but also to Bohort (*LM* XLV.31, 36). One of her damsels travels with Bohort and a figure from the past, Lambegues, to look for Lancelot at the Dolorous Guard. In the *PL* the Lady of the Lake had sent a damsel with a shield to Guinevere; now the Queen sends a damsel to the Lady of the Lake. Geographical indications (*LM* LXXIV.6) pick up details of the location of the Lake, already given in the account of Lancelot's childhood. The damsel is to go to Gaule (*PL* 1.1) to a castle called Trebe (*PL* 2–7). Near this castle is the Mostier Reial (*PL* 17–18), founded in memory of Ban who died near that spot. It is close to a lake, which is only a semblance of a lake (through enchantment) and full of fine houses (*PL* 24.26–8, 103–4); the lady is called Niniane (*PL* 23.10–11). The Queen sends a message:

'je li mant por Deu et par la foi qu'ele doit a celui qu'ele a norri qu'ele n'aimme mie mains de moi, qu'ele ne lest por riens qu'ele ne viengne a moi.' (*LM* LXXIV.6.)

This picks up the words of the Lady of the Lake on her visit to the Queen (*PL* 556.34–5) in a speech in which she urges Guinevere to give her love to Lancelot. Eventually the Lady of the Lake appears in person (*LM* CIV.52) seeking Lancelot—not as well informed, therefore, as she had been in the *PL*. On a second occasion (*LM* CV.27) she comes when Lancelot receives back his land, only to hand it over immediately to his brother Hector. Her arrival at this juncture is appropriate enough, for it was at the time of Ban's loss of his land and life that she had carried his son into the Lake. Lancelot's mother Helene, he learns (*LM* LXXIX.24), is still alive. He has a vision concerning her (*LM* XCI.30), just as Evaine, her sister, had a vision of Lyonel, Bohort, and Lancelot in the *PL* (133). Helene leaves her abbey and reappears in person in the story (*LM* CIV.51) for the first time since Lancelot left the Lake for Camelot, and she dies shortly after the land has been recovered from Claudas (*LM* CV.27).

The handling of the war with Claudas and the recovery of the lands which he took over is interesting as it reflects the change of emphasis in the presentation of Arthur, already noted in the previous chapter. In the non-cyclic romance, while Arthur, in an important passage, is contrasted favourably with

Claudas, the emphasis throughout is on his failure to fulfil his obligation to defend his vassal Ban or to avenge his dispossession and death. Thus Lancelot owed nothing to Arthur, but the King was three times saved by Lancelot; the hero's obligations are to Galehot rather than to Arthur, and he is not betraying his lord by loving Guinevere. Now, stress is not laid on Arthur's failure to fulfil his obligations, but rather on the various types of motivation of Lancelot and his cousins for winning back their lands. Lyonel is determined, as he was when still a small boy (*PL* 109), to avenge the loss of his father's land (*LM* LXXXV.53, XCIV.7). Lancelot is moved by a desire not so much to regain the land as to avenge an insult to the Queen:

'Et tout ce qu'il m'avoit mesfet et de moi et de mon pere et del roi Boorz qui mes oncles estoit et de mes cousins avoie je mis en soufrance dusques atant que je veisse mon point. Mais puis que la chose est ainsi montee que vos, qui riens n'em aviez forfet, l'avez comparé, je sui cil qui jamés ne sera granment a eise devant que vos an seroiz vengie si bien qu'il ne li remaindra plain pié de toute la terre qu'il tient. Et s'il est si hardiz qu'il m'atande, bien sache il que je nel lairai en mer ne en terre ne an leu ou li hom puist aler dusque a tant que je l'aie occis et vos anvoierai la teste, ja en si lontaingne terre ne sera aperceuz.' (*LM* C.49.)

When the land has been won back, and Arthur offers it to Lancelot, he refuses it, but suggests that Lyonel should have Gaule, Hector[18] Benoyc, and Bohort Gaunes. Bohort rejects the offer:

'Qu'est ce, sire, que vos volez fere? Certes se je volsisse recevoir l'anor del reaume, nel deussiez vos mie soufrir, car si tost come je avrai reaume, il me couvendra laissier toute chevalerie, ou je voille ou non, et ce seroit plus granz honor, se je estoie povres hom et bons chevaliers, que se je estoie riches rois recreanz.' (*LM* CV.28.)

For Bohort, the duties of kingship would interfere with his freedom to gain honour as a knight (and to achieve the Grail Quest); for Lancelot, they would separate him from his love, Guinevere. As the Lady of Malohaut had said earlier (*PL* 609, in the non-cyclic version of the False Guinevere episode), a lady is fortunate who has a landless knight like Lancelot as lover rather than a *riche home* such as Galehot.

In the course of the war there are many references to the past; for example, one of the battalions of Claudas is led by the brother of Ban's treacherous seneschal (killed by Banyn, *LM* CIII.6, *PL* 12); the grief of Claudas at the capture of Canart is compared with his grief at his son Dorin's death (*LM* CIV.42, *PL* 67-73). There are also parallels with earlier events. There are echoes of the secret visit of the rather tight-fisted Claudas to Britain (*PL* 31-8) in that of the emissaries of Claudas, sent to spy out the situation at Arthur's court. Like Claudas they are astonished at the richness and *largece* they find there:

car il n'avoient mie apris a veoir entor le roi Claudas si grant feste ne si grant largesce com il voient entor le roi Artu. (*LM* XCIV.17.)

One of them expresses similar views to those of the squire of Claudas who challenged his own lord when he heard that he was considering a war against Arthur (*PL* 31–8). Now one of these spies declares his intention of staying with Arthur because he is so impressed by what he has seen:

'Pour Dieu, fait li uns a son compaingnon, je ne sai que tu voudras faire, mais je sui cil qui jamés ne s'em partira, car ici est toute richesce terrienne et toute la bonté de chevalerie, et qui velt veoir le fil Largesce meesme, si voie le roi Artu, car si m'aïst Diex, il est si larges et si prodom qu'il n'a el monde si noiant ne si failli, s'il repairoit entor lui, qu'il n'en amendast. Et por la grant largesce que j'ai veue en lui n'en partirai jamais de son ostel tant conme je vivrai. Et tu t'en iras, se tu vels, ou tu remaindras, mais que que tu faces, je remaindrai ceanz.' (*LM* XCIV.17.)

This favourable view of Arthur is not now contrasted with his failure to avenge his vassal, for it is the personal victory of Arthur over Frolle which causes Claudas to flee. Arthur is determined, through his own effort in the war, to repay his debt to Lancelot for all that he has done for him in the past. He is distressed when Lancelot asks him not to take part personally in the fighting:

'De ceste chose sot li rois plus mal gré a Lancelot que de chose qu'il deïst onques mes, car Lanceloz l'avoit tant servi maintes foiz que il ne li quidast jamés avoir guerredonné la moitié de son servise, neis s'il li donnast le reaume de Logres.' (*LM* CV.4.)

When Arthur kills Frolle, Lancelot comes forward joyfully and says:

'Sire, si m'aïst Diex, bien le devez avoir le reaume, qui si bien l'avez conquis.' (*LM* CV.20.)

Thus Arthur has a far more glorious role here than he had in the non-cyclic romance (see Chapters IV and VIII).[19]

In addition to these events which link up explicitly with earlier episodes, there are also a number of incidents which provide analogues with previous adventures. Memories of the deep friendship between Lancelot and Galehot, which played so important a part in the non-cyclic romance, are indeed stirred by the introduction of the latter's nephew Galehodin, like his uncle (filz de la Jaiande) one of the biggest knights in the world (*LM* XCV.46), who asks Lancelot to accept his service 'por l'amor de mon oncle qu'il tant ama' (*LM* LXXVIII.34; see also XCV.30). However, we are also reminded of the powerful theme of Galehot's love for Lancelot by Bademaguz who, although his son has been killed by Lancelot, would be prepared to make great sacrifice to gain his companionship:

Mais samblant n'en ose fere por Lancelot que il aime plus que home del monde: si voldroit avoir fet tos les meschief qu'il porroit fere sans lui honir par covent qu'il eust Lancelot a compaignon tos les jors de sa vie; mais il n'ose pas cuidier que Lancelos le deignast estre et por ce ne l'en ose requerre. (*LM* L.44.)

This recalls the words of Galehot to Lancelot (*PL* 321, 324–5) and those in Arthur's court, when he explains what he would be prepared to do to have the Black Knight (Lancelot) with him for the rest of his life (*PL* 334.17–19). When Bademaguz gains the courage to speak, Lancelot replies in terms which are again reminiscent of his response to Galehot:

'Sire, fet Lancelos, vostre compaignie amaisse je molt, si m'aït Diex, par si que vos euissiés la moie, se je vos en peuisse fere otroi; mais bien sachiés que je sui plus a autrui qu'a moi: por ce ne la vos porroie je doner ne otroier par moi sol; si vos pri qu'il ne vos en poist. Mais bien sachiés qu'en tos les lieus ou vos me troverois me porrois prendre por vostre ami et vostre chevalier.' (*LM* L.46; cf. *PL* 573.31–5.)

The Queen gives Lancelot to Bademaguz as a companion as she had done for Galehot:

'Sire rois Bademaguz, je vos aim moult et por ce vos doing je cest home a compaingnon; si li pri qu'il vos otroit des ores mes sa compaingnie et vos tiengne a ami et a compaingnon plus que nul autre qui riens ne li soit.' (*LM* LXXXV.8.)

Some of the analogues do not simply recall events or motifs of the *PL* but also link up with Arthurian romance tradition in general. For example, there are the battles interrupted when the opponents recognize one another (*LM* LXXX.3–5, CVI.39, CVIII.6–8); these recall not only episodes in the *PL*, all concerning Gauvain (*PL* 243, 245–6, and above all 527–8, 537), but also the fight between Yvain and Gauvain in Chrétien's *Chevalier au Lion*. Kay's insistence on undertaking a task too great for him to perform (*LM* XXXVI) echoes not only *PL* 175–6, 213–14, 369–70, but also the beginning of Chrétien's *Charrette*. Arthur broods (*LM* XXXVI.5–6) as he had done on a number of earlier occasions in the *PL*, in Chrétien, and in the *Perceval Continuations*.[20] Quests led by Gauvain start from Arthur's court, knights are listed, oaths are taken (*LM* LX.11–15), as in the *PL* (296–9, 361–5) and the *Perceval Continuations*.[21]

These constant reappearances of familiar motifs should not be dismissed as mechanical repetitions which save medieval authors the effort of invention. In general, they serve to give some kind of unity to the Arthurian world and to enrich the individual episode with resonances from other tales. In the *Lancelot-Grail* cycle they are also used to special effect, eventually to reverse, in one sense, the binding process mentioned above. A traditional Arthurian world is carefully created with well-known landmarks and conventions, in which both the characters and the reader would feel at home, where even the mysterious could be expected to conform to a predictable pattern, even though doubt was already being thrown, from the cyclic version of the False Guinevere episode onwards, on one apparent certainty, that concerning the inspirational quality of *fin' amor*. The value of a love such as that of Lancelot for Guinevere in achieving knightly supremacy, so firmly established in the account of Lancelot's adventures up to his gaining of a seat at the Round Table, begins to be questioned, and, as a result, also the value of Lancelot's name. Apart from this, the kingdom of Logres seems, at first sight, to remain familiar, although there is a perceptible increase in violence. Even Lancelot and Gauvain, who had always grieved when forced to kill an opponent, no longer seem to experience quite the same reluctance and regret.[22] However, once the knights set out on the Quest for the Holy Grail, they and the reader discover that they have moved into a strange new world of which they no longer know the rules. On the surface there are still the marvels, knightly battles to be fought and damsels to be rescued, so characteristic of all the tales recorded by the clerks in the big book at Arthur's court, but these no longer function in the accustomed way. Indeed, the careful interweaving of well-known motifs to create the rich traditional Arthurian texture, with its suggestion of depth in time and space, is used to brilliant effect in the allegory of the *Queste* to undermine the whole foundation of the kingdom of Logres in the journey towards the realm of the purely spiritual reality and the heavenly chivalry.

The *Queste*

La Queste del Saint Graal or, more properly, *les Aventures del Saint Graal*[23] is an allegory depicting man's search for the vision of God. The significance of the allegory in all its complexities has been analysed in depth by a number of scholars.[24] What concerns us here is the way in which the *Queste* gives a new meaning to Lancelot's early adventures, obliges the reader to reinterpret them. The allegory owes much of its force to its firm integration into the tale of Lancelot. Although the narrative of Lancelot's education and exploits as a young knight, which forms the non-cyclic romance, never looks forward to a Grail Quest to be achieved by a descendant of the hero, the *Queste* itself constantly refers back to earlier events in Lancelot's life and picks up and transforms the two themes which characterize the *PL*.

The identity theme is given particular emphasis at the beginning of the *Queste*, in the first place by means of the relationship of father to son. Lancelot knights the youth without a name being used, but Bohort and Lyonel comment on the close resemblance between the two when Galahad first arrives at court (Q 3); Bohort thinks that he must be Lancelot's son.[25] This arrival of the young stranger both recalls and contrasts with Lancelot's coming to Camelot to be knighted and to undertake his first adventures. Like Lancelot, the establishment of Galahad's name is associated with the accomplishing of a certain task and with an inscription: in Lancelot's case, the inscription under the slab in the cemetery at Dolorous Guard (*PL* 194); in Galahad's, the inscription on the Perilous Seat.[26] Lancelot's displacement as the greatest knight, thus reversing all the signs of his destiny in the *PL*, has been carefully prepared for (in a series of episodes leading up to the *Queste*) as a future event, and is first shown to have happened with the appearance of the sword in the floating stone. This is a traditional piece of Arthurian marvellous, paralleled by Arthur's drawing of the sword from the stone in Robert de Boron's *Merlin*, but here it is a prelude to the reduction of the splendours of Camelot to empty shadows, mere illusions of reality. Lancelot has been told that he will be surpassed; the first warning comes in the cyclic version of the False Guinevere episode, but others occur with ever-increasing frequency as the *Queste* approaches. Now the prediction is to be fulfilled, and he acknowledges the fact by refusing to attempt to draw out the sword. A *preudomme* with clearly religious associations brings Galahad to court,[27] not a Lady of the Lake with magical attributes, however carefully these have been made respectable (see Chapter V). The lineage of the youth is announced straight away, whereas that of Lancelot was at this point in his career still wrapped in mystery as far as the court and Lancelot himself were concerned. The words used by the *preudomme* are particularly interesting as they pick up, but totally transform, phrases used earlier in relation to Lancelot:

'Rois Artus, je t'ameign le Chevalier Desirré, celui qui est estraiz dou haut lignage le Roi David et del parenté Joseph d'Arimacie, celui par cui les merveilles de cest païs et des estranges terres remaindront. Veez le ci.' (*Q* 7.25–9.)

The phrase 'le Chevalier Desirré' can be contrasted with the Lady of the Lake's farewell words to Lancelot:

'Mais or vos en alez, et bons et biax et gracieus et dessirrez de totes genz et amez sor toz chevaliers de totes dames; itex seroiz vos, car bien lo sai.' (*PL* 154.39–155.2.)

References to the lineage of David were made in the *PL* in relation to Lancelot and his cousins (*PL* 13.12, 108.37–109.2) but only to enhance the nobility of their ancestry: the emphasis is on King David as the first of the great knights (*PL* 146.14) rather than as ancestor of Christ. Joseph of Arimathea is mentioned too, but not as an ancestor of Lancelot (*PL* 146.17, 179.2, 292.5–6). Now, in the *Queste*, the descent from David has a new significance in relation to Galahad, who postfigures Christ and is to be the last in the lineage of Solomon (*Q* 221–8).[28] The prediction concerning Galahad made by the *preudomme*, that he would bring to an end the marvels of this and other lands, also recalls the words of the Lady of the Lake to Lancelot when she leaves him with Arthur:

'Qant plus avroiz achevees aventures felonesses et perilleusses, plus seürement anprenez les aventures a achever, car la ou vos lairoiz a achever les aventures par proesce que Dex ait mise en chevalier, il n'est pas encores nez qui maint a chief celes que vos avroiz laissiees.' (*PL* 154.33–8.)

In addition, they bring to mind her words on an earlier occasion, spoken to Leonces de Paerne who has been urging her to guard Lyonel and Bohort well:

'Ne nos ne savons a com grant chose il porroient encores monter, car ce savons nos bien que an la Grant Bretaine atandent tuit a estre delivré des mervoilles et des aventures qui i avienent par un qui sera del lignage a la mere a ces anfanz.' (*PL* 108.39–109.2.)

As has been seen in Chapter VI, when these passages were first written in the context of the non-cyclic romance, in both cases they referred to Lancelot's own great destiny, not to a hero, as yet unborn, who was to surpass him. 'Il n'est pas encores nez' is a standard emphatic negative, used several times in the romance. The reference to the delivering from the marvels and the adventures would be to Lancelot's ending of the enchantments at the Dolorous Guard (*PL* 247–50). However, once the tale of Lancelot was incorporated into a *Lancelot-Grail* cycle, it became possible, without changing a word in the text, to interpret the reference to the man who would be freeing the kingdom from *merveilles* and *aventures* as an allusion linking up with the words of the *preudomme* in the *Queste* and with all the predictions concerning the hero yet to come, from Galehot's dream onwards. However, the reference in *PL* 33.9–12 to Perceval as the accomplisher of the adventure of the Perilous Seat and the knight who brought to an end the adventures of the Reiaume Perilleus Aventureus, that is the kingdom of Logres, stubbornly refuses such a reinterpretation. When Galahad sits in the Perilous Seat, this is in clear contradiction to the earlier passage, hence the different attempts of various scribes to remove the flagrant inconsistency.[29]

The raising by the *preudomme* of the cloth over the inscription on the Perilous Seat to see the name (Galahad) parallels the look taken by the damsel from the Lake who sees the name under the slab at Dolorous Guard (*PL* 194.32–4). Both Lancelot and Galahad are asked who they are and fail to reply, but for different reasons. Galahad is presented as self-possessed and fully aware of his identity and destiny. He refuses to say who he is: 'ainz respondi tout pleinement qu'il ne lor diroit ore pas, car il le savroient bien a tens se il l'osoient demander' (Q 8.25–6). Lancelot, when asked, does not reply, firstly, because he does not know the answer, and secondly, because he is struck dumb by the Queen (*PL* 157–8). His quality as a knight is doubted in the Fair Unknown type of sequence leading up to his battle at Nohaut, and he only achieves fame at the Dolorous Guard (still not under his own name). In contrast, almost as soon as he arrives at court Galahad is identified as the chosen hero, the greatest knight, although it takes people some time to apprehend the new kind of greatness, one related to a new kind of chivalry, *la chevalerie celestiel*. Everyone present believes him to be:

cil par cui les merveilles dou Saint Graal doivent faillir, et bien lou conoissent par l'esprueve del Siege, ou onques hom ne s'estoit assiz a cui il n'en fust mescheu en aucune maniere, ne mes a cestui. (Q 9.6–9.)

On both occasions speculation concerning the name of the young hero is rife, but in the *Queste* it links the youth with the lineage of Ban and with Lancelot because of the strong family resemblance.[30]

News of the arrival at court of a remarkable youth (the son) soon reaches Guinevere in the *Queste* as it had done many years ago concerning another remarkable youth (the father), and she is again determined to see the young man, but this time above all because she suspects that it is Lancelot's son. Thus the love relationship intrudes here in a different form:

Et lors le desirre la roine a veoir assez plus qu'ele ne fesoit devant. Car par ce que ele a oï parler de la semblance pense ele bien que ce soit Galaad, que Lancelot avoit engendré en la fille au Riche Roi Pescheor, einsi com len li avoit ja conté par maintes fois et dit en quel maniere il avoit esté deceuz; et ce estoit la chose par coi ele fust plus courrouciee vers Lancelot, se la coulpe en fust soie. (Q 10.22–8.)

The speculation over the name of the new knight does not last long. Arthur raises the cloth over the Perilous Seat, finds the name Galahad, and tells Gauvain:

'Biax niez, or avons nos Galaad, le bon chevalier parfait que nos et cil de la Table Reonde avons tant desirré a veoir.' (Q 10.33–11.2.)

This is in contrast with the three quests (led by Gauvain) which were needed to identify the unknown hero (Lancelot) under his various disguises. Gauvain is as prepared to acknowledge the supremacy of Galahad as greatest knight as he had been that of Lancelot:

'Sire, fet messires Gauvain, et vos et nos le devons servir come celui que Diex nos a envoié por delivrer nostre païs des granz merveilles et des estranges aventures qui tant sovent i sont avenues par si lonc tens.' (Q 11.7–11.)

Arthur is equally ready to admit the Round Table's need of the new hero to succeed where others have failed (Q 11.18–21), as he had been to recognize his debt to Lancelot (*PL* 566.24–5). Galahad is quietly confident of his ability to achieve the adventure of the sword, 'car l'aventure estoit moie', as he says; so too was Lancelot when he insisted on undertaking his first knightly task as champion of the Lady of Nohaut (*PL* 162–3).

Once Galahad has withdrawn the sword, Lancelot's decline in status becomes manifest, and a damsel, witness to the event, presents this in terms of the loss of his name:

'Vos estiez hier matin li mieldres chevaliers dou monde; et qui lors vos apelast Lancelot le meillor chevalier de toz, il deist voir: car alors l'estiez vos. Mes qui ore le diroit, len le devroit tenir a mençongier: car meillor i a de vos, et bien est provee chose par l'aventure de ceste espee a quoi vos n'osastes metre la main. Et ce est li changemenz et li muemenz de vostre non, dont je vos ai fet remembrance por ce que des ore mes ne cuidiez que vos soiez li mieldres chevaliers dou monde.' (Q 12.31–13.6.)

The use of the phrase *li changemenz et li muemenz de vostre non* provides a variation on the theme of the making of a name, so important in the '*PL*. In the adventures preparing the way for the *Queste*, as has been seen, a new interpretation of the use of the *sorenon* Lancelot instead of the baptismal name Galaaz or Galaad is developed, in terms of the loss of the name Galaad through sin, as opposed to the gaining of the name Lancelot through a great exploit, as presented in the *PL*. Here, in the *Queste*, the reputation made under the name Lancelot is tarnished.

There is also an interesting variation on heredity, an important element in the identity theme. This is to be found in the Queen's comments on Galahad, once she has assured herself that he is Lancelot's son:

Et quant la roine l'ot bien avisé, si dist que voirement l'avoit Lancelot engendré, car onques mes ne se resemblerent dui home si merveilleusement come il dui fesoient. Et por ceu n'estoit ce pas merveille se il estoit de grant chevalerie garniz: car autrement forlignast il trop durement. (Q 14.26–30.)

She says to Galahad:

'Si m'ait Diex, ja de vostre pere nomer n'avroiz honte. Car il est li plus biax chevaliers dou monde et est estrez de toutes parz de rois et de reines et dou plus haut lignage que len sache, et a eu le los jusque ci d'estre li mieldres chevaliers dou monde: par quoi vos devriez par droit passer toz çax del siecle.' (Q 20.8–13.)

This should be compared with what the Lady of the Lake tells Lancelot before she agrees to take him to court:

'Et se vos saviez qui fu vostres peres, ne de qex genz vostres lignages est estraiz de par la mere, vos n'avriez pas paor, si com ge cuit, d'estre prozdom, car nus qui de tel lignage fust ne devroit pas avoir corage de mauveitié.' (*PL* 147.17–20.)

She expands this in her farewell words to him at Camelot (*PL* 153-4). In the *Queste* the Queen continues to emphasize the importance of heredity in the speech in which she pronounces for Galahad the name of his father, as she had once pronounced for Lancelot his own name in the scene leading up to their first kiss (*PL* 344.11–12):

'A non Dieu, fet ele, puis que vos nel volez dire, je le vos dirai. Cil qui vos engendra a non messires Lancelot del Lac, li plus biax chevaliers et li mieldres et li plus gracieus, et li plus desirrez a veoir de toutes genz et li mielz amez qui onques nasquist a nos tens. Por qoi il me semble que vos nel devez celer ne a moi ne a autre: car de plus preudome ne de meillor chevalier ne poïssiez vos estre engendrez.' (Q 20.21–8.)

There is a certain irony in this emphasis by Guinevere on the importance of heredity, an emphasis which reveals her lack of understanding of the new heavenly chivalry. Galahad has to redeem, to turn to good, the sinful inheritance from his father and the very act of his engendering, where Lancelot's intentions were sinful, although his mother's were not.[31]

The motif of the raising of a tomb slab is used twice in the *Queste*. On the first occasion (Q 35–40), Galahad is able to raise a slab in an abbey cemetery so that a body can be removed from it, and the diabolical marvels of the cemetery, the strange sights and sounds, are thus brought to an end. This recalls Lancelot's achievement in putting an end to the enchantments of the cemetery of the Dolorous Guard (*PL* 247-50). Both Lancelot as a young knight at Dolorous Guard and Galahad at the abbey succeed in bringing peace to troubled places through their courage and quality as the knights predestined to achieve these particular adventures. Lancelot was lured to the Dolorous Guard to end the enchantments by a false message that Guinevere was imprisoned there. Galahad achieved his adventure because he was a virgin and as pure of all sin as any man could be. *Deiables* were mentioned in relation to Lancelot's adventure, but the marvellous there was of a traditional Arthurian kind (see Chapter V), and no Christian explanation was given of it. In Galahad's adventure, however, although the strange sights and sounds are at first described in similar terms to those at Dolorous Guard, it is soon made clear that Galahad has to deal with the forces of Satan, and he hears a voice:

'Ha! Galaad, sainte chose, je te voi si avironné d'anges que mes pooirs ne puet durer encontre ta force: je te les le leu.' (Q 36.24–6.)

Galahad succeeds in expelling the unclean spirit, and then the significance of the adventure in terms of Christian allegory is given: Galahad's coming is compared with that of Christ, 'de semblance ne mie de hautece' (Q 38.21), and he is told that the body represents the Jews who rejected the Messiah: 'Einsi poez vos veoir en ceste aventure la senefiance de la Passion Jhesucrist et la semblance de son avenement.' (Q 39.19–21.)[32]

On the second occasion, the lifting of the stone over a grave and thereby the ending of the suffering of Symeu in the burning tomb, Galahad's achievement is contrasted with Lancelot's failure:

Il vint en l'abeie ou Lancelot avoit devant esté, la ou il avoit trovee la tombe Galaad le roi de Hoselice, le filz Joseph d'Arymacie, et la tombe Symeon ou il ot failli. (Q 264.4–7.)

This refers back to the *Charrette* episode (*LM* XXXVII.27–41), where Lancelot, as the knight destined to free the prisoners of Gorre, raised one slab but not this one, for only the knight destined to achieve the adventure of the Perilous Seat could do so. The raising of the slab, a traditional Arthurian motif, with its echoes of earlier episodes in the romance and in Chrétien and its link with the identity theme, is here given a new meaning within a clearly Christian allegory; it has resonances of the Harrowing of Hell and fits in with the pattern of Galahad postfiguring Christ.[33] Before Galahad arrives at Corbenic he has achieved all the adventures of Logres and thereby completed the transformation of the marvellous characteristic of the *PL* and the part of the cyclic romance leading up to the *Queste*:[34]

Et dedenz celui terme orent il si achevees les aventures dou roiaume de Logres, que poi en i veoit len mes avenir, se ce n'ert demostrance de Nostre Seignor merveilleuse. (Q 265.16–19.)

The destructive nature of Lancelot's love is explored further in a series of episodes in which he is only allowed glimpses of the Grail because of his *luxure*. The narrative passage which leads up to Lancelot's meeting with the hermit and the conversation they then have together also provides subtle variations on earlier themes. Skilful use is made of the description of nature in springtime, traditionally associated with the opening of a love lyric and often expressing a contrast between the joyful sights and sounds of nature and the melancholy mood of the lover. Lancelot, just deprived of his arms and horse, and reproached for his *luxure* by a mysterious voice, sees a contrast between the beautiful day, the song of birds,[35] which had often made him rejoice in the past, and his present humiliating situation:

Et quant li jorz parut biaus et clers et li oiselet comencerent a chanter parmi le bois et li soleux comença a luire par mi les arbres, et il voit le biau tens et il ot le chant des oisiaus dont il s'ert maintes foiz esjoiz, et lors se voit desgarni de toutes choses, et de ses armes et de son cheval, et bien set de voir que Nostre Sires s'est corrociez a lui; si ne cuide ja mes venir a cel point qu'il truist chose ou monde qui sa joie li poïst rendre. Car la ou il cuidoit joie trover et toutes honors terrianes a il failli, ce est as aventures dou Saint Graal; et ce est une chose qui mout le desconforte. (Q 62.9–19.)

Here there is play on the meanings of the term *joie*, the secular one, referring to the joyful experience of *fin' amor*, and the religious, referring to eternal bliss. We may compare the passage quoted above with the following words spoken by the Lady of the Lake to Guinevere:

'Mais an doit autresin bien garder de correcier ce que l'an aimme comme soi meïsmes, car il n'est mies amez veraiement qui sor totes riens terrienes n'est amez. Et qui aimme par amor, il ne puet mies avoir joie se de ce non que il aimme; don doit an amer la rien dont totes joies vienent.' (*PL* 557.15–20.)

In the conversation with the hermit Lancelot's reference to the gifts with which God had endowed him links up with the formal description of these gifts in *PL* 39–41 and the Lady of the Lake's comment that God has given him beauty (*PL* 154.4–7); but it is at the same time in contrast, through Lancelot's admission here that he has not made good use of these gifts because of his sin (identified as *luxure* by the voice).[36] This is in direct conflict with the message sent by the Lady of the Lake that he must make sure that he chooses the right kind of love (here love of a woman, rather than of God):

'Ce fu, fait ele, que vos ne metoiz ja vostre cuer en amor qui vos face aparecir mais amander, car cuers qui por amor devient pareceus ne puet a haute chose ataindre, car il n'osse. Mais cil qui tozjorz bee a amender puet ataindre a hautes choses, autresin com il les ose anprandre.' (*PL* 205.38–206.2.)

As he had done earlier, but to different effect, Lancelot tries to keep his love secret (*Q* 65). In response to the hermit's admonitions (to be compared with Galehot's efforts to get Lancelot to tell him about the love which is making him so unhappy, *PL* 331–2, 336), he sighs and falls silent, overcome by fear—another variation on the traditional theme of the lover afraid to confess to his love:

Si giete un sospir dou parfont dou cuer et est tel atornez qu'il ne puet issir parole de sa bouche. Et neporec il le diroit volentiers, mes il n'ose, come cil qui plus est coarz que hardiz. (*Q* 65.32–66.2.)

In the *PL* Galehot's questions are met with tears, silence, and sighs (*PL* 331–2, 336), and sighs lead up to Lancelot's confession of his love to Guinevere (*PL* 344–5). His confession to the hermit of his love for the Queen echoes in its rhythms and vocabulary his admission to her of the way he interpreted her words of farewell ('A Deu, biax douz amis', *PL* 165.23), when he set off as a youth for Nohaut. Lancelot says to the hermit:

'Sire, fet Lancelot, il est einsi que je sui morz de pechié d'une moie dame que je ai amee toute ma vie, et ce est la reine Guenievre, la fame le roi Artus. Ce est cele qui a plenté m'a doné l'or et l'argent et les riches dons que je ai aucune foiz donez as povres chevaliers. Ce est cele qui m'a mis ou grant boban et en la grant hautece ou je sui. Ce est cele por qui amor j'ai faites les granz proeces dont toz li mondes parole. Ce est cele qui m'a fet venir de povreté en richece et de mesaise a toutes les terriannes beneurtez. Mes je sai bien que par cest pechié de li s'est Nostre Sires si durement corociez a moi qu'il le m'a bien mostré puis ersoir.' (Q 66.8–21.)

He had said to Guinevere:

'Et vos deïstes que vostre chevaliers et vostre anmis voloiez vos que ge fusse. Et ge dis: 'A Deu, dame.' Et vos deïstes: 'A Deu, biaus douz amis.' Ne onques puis do cuer ne me pot issir. Ce fu li moz qui prodome me fera se gel suis. Ne onques puis ne vign an si grant meschief que de cest mot ne me manbrast. Cist moz m'an conforté an toz mes anuiz, cist moz m'a de toz mes maus garantiz et m'a gari de toz periz; cist moz m'a saolé an totes mes fains, cist moz m'a fait riche an totes mes granz povretez.' (PL 345.34–346.3.)

One notes the repetition of *ce est cele*, echoing the repetition of *cist moz*, and the traditional use of antithesis, *povreté/richece, mesaise/terriannes beneurtez*. Lancelot persists in maintaining, as he did in the confession to Guinevere, that his love for her has been the source of all his great knightly feats, but admits reluctantly that his sin with her is the cause of God's anger with him and of his inability to respond when he saw the Grail at the chapel.

The hermit extracts from Lancelot a promise that he will renounce his love (Q 67). Then the latter asks the meaning of the *trois paroles* which he had heard in the chapel:

'Lancelot, plus durs que pierre, plus amers que fuz, plus nuz et plus despris que figuiers.' (Q 61.16–17.)

It becomes clear that these words, as interpreted by the hermit (Q 67–70), are designed to counter the effect on Lancelot of the words of Guinevere (*Biaus douz amis*) as the young knight had understood them.

Lancelot's loss of the qualities given him by God through that first fateful meeting with Guinevere is explored further in his encounter with a *vallet* who contrasts his present humiliating situation with his past reputation:

'Si soliez estre la flor de terriane chevalerie! Chetis! bien estes enfantosmez par cele qui ne vos aime ne ne prise se petit non. Ele vos a si atorné que vos avez perdue la joie des ciex et la compaignie des anges et toutes honors terriannes, et estes venuz a toutes hontes recevoir.' (Q 118.10–15.)

This picks up and reverses the Lady of the Lake's words to Guinevere about her honourable role as the loved one of such a knight:

'Se vos poez de ce vanter que onques mais dame no pot faire, car vos iestes compaigne au plus preudome do monde et dame au meillor chevalier do monde. Et an la seignorie novelle que vos avez n'avez vos mies po gahaignié, car vos i avez gahaignié lui avant, qui est la flors de toz les chevaliers, et moi aprés, qanque ge porroie faire.' (*PL* 557.5-10.)

Another hermit lists the qualities which Lancelot had up to the time he became a knight: *virginité, humilité, soffrance, droiture, charité* (Q 123-5).[37] He declares: 'Einsi garniz de toutes bontés et de toutes vertuz terriennes entras tu ou haut ordre de chevalerie.' (Q 125.7-8.) He then goes on to present the first meeting with Guinevere as part of the devil's plot:

'Lors entra en la reine Guenievre, qui ne s'ert pas bien fete confesse puis que ele entra primes en mariage, et l'esmut a ce qu'ele te resgarda volentiers tant come tu demoras en son ostel, le jor que tu fus chevaliers. Quant tu veis qu'ele te resgarda, si i pensas; et maintenant te feri li anemis d'un de ses darz a descovert, si durement qu'il te fist chanceler. Chanceler te fist il, si qu'il te fist guenchir fors de droite voie et entrer en cele que tu n'avoies onques coneue: ce fu en la voie de luxure, ce fu en la voie qui gaste cors et ame si merveilleusement que nus nel puet tres bien savoir qui essaié ne l'a. Des lors te toli li anemis la veue. Car si tost come tu eus tes eulz eschaufez de l'ardor de luxure, maintenant enchaças humilité et atresis orgueil et vousis aler teste levee ausi fierement come un lyon, et deis en ton cuer que tu ne devoies riens prisier ne ne priseroies ja mes, se tu n'avoies ta volenté de cele que tu veoies si bele. Quant li anemis, qui ot toutes les paroles si tost come la langue les a dites, conut que tu pechoies mortelment en pensee et en volenté, si entra lors toz dedenz toi, et en fist aler celui que tu avoies si longuement ostelé.' (Q 125.26–126.11.)

Lancelot's confidence in the strength coming from his *joie* (*PL* 40.35–41.2.) and his conviction, expressed in the meeting leading to the kiss, that his achievements stem from that first sight of Guinevere and from her words of farewell are now shown to be sinful arrogance. This presents Lancelot's first meeting with the Queen in a completely new light. Once again there are precise allusions to the key points in the development of the love theme, leading up to a reinterpretation of Lancelot's great deeds, in terms not of the inspiration of love but of the remnants of the good qualities with which God had endowed him, traces of which have survived his contact with Guinevere:

'Et neporec Nostre Sires avoit mis tant de bien en toi qu'il ne pooit estre que de cele grant plenté n'i eust aucune chose de remanant. De cel remanant que Diex te lessa as tu fetes les granz proesces par les estranges terres, dont toz li monz parole.' (Q 126.23-7.)

What might he not have done if he had never seen Guinevere and had kept the virtues which God had given him? He would not have failed to achieve the Grail adventure and would not have been blind before the face of God, but would have seen *apertement.* The eyes often play a part in the imagery of love poetry; here the metaphor has a different significance, closely connected with the religious allegory of the *Queste.*

There is also, in the interpretation for Lancelot of a vision in which the elder of two knights is turned away, a completely new explanation of the death of Ban, one which denies that Ban died from grief as had previously been said (*PL* 14.13–18, 49.28):

'De celui issi li rois Bans tes peres, qui assez fu plus preudons et de sainte vie que mainte gent ne cuiderent, qui cuiderent que le duel de sa terre l'eust mort, mes non fist; ainz avoit toz les jorz de sa vie requis Nostre Seignor qu'Il le lessast partir de cest siecle quant il l'en requerroit. Si mostra bien Nostre Sires qu'Il avoit oïe sa proiere: car si tost come il demanda la mort dou cors, il l'ot et trova la vie de l'ame.' (Q 136.18–24.)

Lancelot's experiences when he intervenes in the tournament between the black and white knights also provide a reversal of the situation early in his career. There his intervention, first on Arthur's side (*PL* 281–2, 311–20) and then on that of Galehot (*PL* 326), turned a losing side into a winning one. Now he is taking part in an allegory, but has not yet comprehended what that means;[38] he follows the earlier pattern of knightly action, but with very different results. The white knights win in spite of the help he gives to the opposing side, and he himself is captured:

Et il se pense qu'il a hui esté menez la ou onques mes ne pot estre menez, ce est qu'il ne vint onques mes en tornoiement qu'il ne vainquist, ne ne pot estre pris en tornoiement; quant il se porpense de ce, si comence a fere trop grant duel et dit que or voit il bien qu'il est plus pechierres que nus autres. (Q 141.13–18.)

This failure leads once again to a contrast between past and present. A recluse says to him:

'Lancelot, Lancelot, tant come vos fustes chevaliers des chevaleries terrianes fustes vos li plus merveillex hons dou monde et li plus aventureus. Or premierement quant vos vos estes entremis de chevalerie celestiel, se aventures merveilleuses vos aviennent, ne vos en merveilliez mie.' (Q 143.7–11.)

This interplay between past and present which serves to invest past events with a new meaning is a key element in the Grail allegory[39] and gives the *Queste* itself a central role in the *Lancelot–Grail* cycle.

Gauvain too finds his position altered, and this change is also explored through a number of passages picking up and transforming characteristics and qualities ascribed to him in the *PL*. Then he was a successful achiever of quests in that he was the one knight who brought back to court the Unknown Knight's name and ultimately Lancelot himself, so that his adventures were worthy to be recorded as part of the tale of Lancelot (*PL* 571). Now, in the *Queste*, he is displaced as leader by Galahad, and he himself fails and has few adventures worthy to be recorded:

Messires Gauvain chevaucha des la Pentecoste jusqu'a la Magdaleine sanz aventure trover qui a conter face; si s'en merveilla, car en la Queste del Saint Graal cuidoit il que les aventures forz et merveilleuses fussent plus tost trovees que en autre leu. (Q 147.6–10.)

Earlier he had been the peacemaker, the courteous knight who always tried to avoid unnecessary violence and was very reluctant to kill any opponent (for example, *PL* 496.36–9). Here he is told that it is a sign of his sinfulness that he has killed seven brothers, rather than conquering them without killing as did Galahad (Q 54). In the end, he has killed more than ten knights (Q 147). He has no understanding of what the Grail Quest is about, hence his lack of significant adventures and the number of deaths which he causes, for he is working only on the physical, earthly level, not on the spiritual one. He is, however, still the much-loved knight. When other knights recognize him and discover that he is wounded, 'si en furent molt corrouciez li plusor: car sanz faille il estoit l'ome dou monde qui plus ert amez d'estrange gent' (Q 197.18–20; cf. *PL* 278–9, 307). Gauvain, the best of earthly knights after Lancelot in the *PL*, must fail in order to contrast the emptiness of earthly chivalry, of the values of this world, with the fullness of heavenly chivalry, of spiritual values, of the divine vision which can only be glimpsed in this life.

The beginning of the knights' quest for the Grail also follows the familiar pattern of similar scenes to be found in the *PL* and in other texts.[40] Oaths are sworn, with the leader (Galahad) taking the oath first and the others bound by the same bond (Q 23, *PL* 297–9, 361–5). The number who take the oath is stated—150 in the *Queste*, forty in Gauvain's first quest for the Red Knight, twenty in the second. The King shows his grief at the departure of Gauvain and so many knights (Q 21–2, *PL* 297–8, 362–4). Here, in the *Queste*, Arthur's grief has a more profound significance, for this departure from court marks the end of the old Arthurian way of life. Many of the knights will never return, including two of the three Grailwinners and those who are killed, and even for those who come back many of the old glories will have disappeared—those marvellous adventures of a particular kind which played such an important role in the life of the knights of the Round Table. Arthur has to arrange tournaments, for the adventures of Logres are at an end (*MA* 3.38–43; see also 70.23–4).

The adventures of the *Queste* therefore take Arthur's knights into unfamiliar territory, where resemblances to the kind of chivalric tests to which they are accustomed are completely illusory; but these adventures are nevertheless carefully woven into the fabric of the cycle as a whole.[41] This is done both through direct allusions to earlier events and through a series of contrasts and inversions which produce a kind of unity based on antithesis. Lancelot had used a succession of antitheses in his confession of love to Guinevere, part of the traditional language of the courtly love lyric. Here the antitheses are used to different effect. Lancelot's earthly chivalry, in which he saw his whole inspiration in his love for Guinevere, is opposed to Galahad's heavenly chivalry,[42] inspired by his love for God. This entails a reinterpretation of words and actions recorded in the *PL*. It is possible to give them a different meaning by placing them unaltered within a new structure, so that one can talk of unity or coherence in relation to the cycle as a whole, just as one could in relation to the non-cyclic *PL*. However, the one glaring inconsistency still remains—the naming early in the romance of Perceval as the knight who achieved the adventure of the Perilous Seat.

The *Mort Artu*

In the *Mort Artu* we return to Arthurian 'reality', and the emphasis on lineage and feudal relationships so characteristic of the *PL* reappears, but this time handled in such a way that the Tristan-Mark type of conflict, so carefully avoided in the non-cyclic romance, becomes a central theme and leads towards the final tragedy.[43] Lancelot, after the death of Galahad, regains the title of the greatest knight, but with a reversal of roles: he is no longer the saviour of the Arthurian kingdom but represents a threat to its harmony; his prowess causes Gauvain's death, although in the end it is not Lancelot's presence which brings about the death of Arthur, rather his absence.

The episode in which Morgain shows Arthur Lancelot's paintings (*MA* 51-4) provides the main source of references back, and Lancelot's love of Guinevere and the exploits inspired by it, which, when first narrated, appeared to be a means of saving Arthur's kingdom, now, as presented by Morgain to the King, become an instrument of destruction. The pictures are closely linked to Lancelot's confession of love to Guinevere (allusions to which play such an important role in the *Queste*), for they portray the deeds of chivalry which he reluctantly acknowledged to be his in the conversation with Guinevere leading up to his declaration of love. Morgain's retelling of these events is a biased one, as Frappier has pointed out.[44] She says to Arthur:

'Voirs est, fet soi Morgue, ge ne sei se vos le savez encore, que Lancelos ainme la reïne Guenievre des le premerain jor que il reçut l'ordre de chevalerie, et por l'amour de la reïne, quant il fu nouviaus chevaliers, fist il toutes les proesces qu'il fesoit.' (*MA* 52.33-8.)

This accords with what Lancelot himself says to Guinevere. However, when Morgain tells Arthur that Lancelot allowed Kay to enter the Dolorous Guard first because he was the Queen's knight, this seems to be a somewhat inaccurate version of the account in *PL* 215-16. Again, she presents Galehot's intervention to help the lovesick Lancelot in a very crude form compared with the original account:

Galehols li proia moult qu'il ne s'esmaiast ja de ceste chose, car il feroit tant qu'il avroit de la reïne ses volentez. (*MA* 53.15–17; to be contrasted with *PL* 336–9.)

The description of the kiss in the same vein:

'Il proia tant la reïne qu'ele s'otroia del tout a Lancelot et si le sesi de s'amor par un besier.' (*MA* 53.18–20.)

The version in *PL* 347–8 is much more restrained. It is no surprise, therefore, that the King sees Lancelot as Mark, under the influence of the dwarf and the barons, had seen Tristan—as a treacherous adulterer. Thus, guided by Morgain, he beholds in the paintings 'ma honte toute aparissant et la traïson Lancelot' (*MA* 53.21–2).

Bohort too reproaches Lancelot for the war that will come, once the King is certain that he has wronged him over his wife, a war which will constitute a reversal of the situation in the *PL*, where Lancelot saves Logres instead of threatening it. Bohort warns him:

'Or verroiz la guerre commencier qui jamés ne prendra fin a nos vivans. Car se li rois vos a jusques ci amé plus que nul home, de tant vos haïra il plus, des qu'il savra que vos li meffesiez tant com de lui vergonder de sa fame.' (*MA* 90.87–92.)

The term *fole amor* is used in relation to the love of Lancelot and Guinevere early in the *Mort Artu* (4), evoking resonances of the Tristan story, but without the existence of the love potion to justify a repudiation of the term by the lovers similar to that by Tristan and Iseut in Beroul's version.[45] It is used again later (*MA* 85), and a comparison between the following passages, parallel in other ways, illustrates the change in direction from a love which inspires great deeds in the *PL* to a love in which the adulterous element is emphasized. In the first passage, from the *PL*, Arthur and Gauvain are in a Saxon prison, while Lancelot, released as a madman by the Saxons, has just been cured and is shortly to rescue Arthur for the third time as well as Gauvain and one of his brothers. The Queen's feelings are described as follows:

Et la reine an ce sejor l'anama tant que ele ne voit mies comment ele se poïst consirrer de lui veoir. Et li poise de ce qu'ele lo set et lo voit a si volenteïf et a si corageus, car ele ne voit mies comment sa vie poïst durer sanz la soe, s'il s'an aloit ja mais de cort. Si voudroit bien que il aüst un po mains de hardement et de proece. (*PL* 558.16–21.)

The Queen does not allow her love to stand between Lancelot and chivalric achievement, and shortly after this, albeit reluctantly, gives him permission to go into battle and provides him with the arms which he uses to deliver Arthur.

We may contrast the following passage from the *Mort Artu*, which preludes the second denunciation by Agravain and the trap set for the lovers which is to lead to the death of Gauvain's brother Gaheriet and the war between the lineage of Lot and that of Ban:

Et se Lancelos avoit devant ce amee la reïne, il l'ama orendroit plus qu'il n'avoit onques mes fet a nul jor, et ele ausint lui; et se demenerent si folement que li pluseur de leanz le sorent veraiement, et messire Gauvains meïsmes le sot tout apertement, et ausi firent tuit si quatre frere.[46] (*MA* 85.33–9.)

In one respect the love between Lancelot and Guinevere in the *Mort Artu* differs from their relationship in the *PL* and from that of Tristan and Iseut, at least up to the time of Tristan's exile. Guinevere is jealous and suspicious in the *MA*, whereas in the *PL* she had complete confidence in Lancelot. This destructive aspect of the love had already been brought out in the cyclic romance, but is explored even more fully here. Whereas in the *PL* the love between Lancelot and Guinevere was contrasted with more negative relationships between various pairs (see Chapter III), here the disruptive power of the love is very evident to Lancelot's cousins and brother. Bohort says to the Queen:

'Dame, fet Boorz, ce est nostre granz domages et a tout nostre parenté; por ce si m'en poise durement que li aferes vet ensi, que tel i perdront qui deservi ne l'avoient pas, ne Fortune n'assembla onques l'amor de vos deus en tel maniere come ge la vi assemblee fors por nostre grant domage; car ge voi bien que messires mes cousins, qui est li plus preudom del monde et li plus biax, si ne crient orendroit que il ne puist venir au desus de tout le monde, se une chose ne li tolloit, ce est li corrouz de vos; mes sanz faille ice le puet trestorner de toutes bones aventures; car certes se il savoit les paroles que vos avez ici dites, je ne cuit pas que ge poïsse a lui venir a tens, que il ne se fust ainçois ocis. Si est, ce m'est avis, domages trop granz quant il, qui est li mieudres des bons, vos ainme si destroitement et vos le haez.' (*MA* 59.11–29.)

Through Guinevere's attitude, Lancelot's love is destroying his prowess, not enhancing it.[47] Bohort's comments suggest that the relationship is working in the reverse of the message sent by the Lady of the Lake to Lancelot: that he must aim for the kind of love which will enable him to achieve his potential as a knight (*PL* 205.38–206.2). Bohort goes on to emphasize the harm that Guinevere is doing to the knight greatest in prowess, noblest in lineage:

'Mes tout einsi comme il est ores vestuz et couverz de toutes bones vertuz, tout einsi le despoilleroiz vos et desnueroiz. Et si poez par ce dire veraiement que vos osteroiz d'entre les estoiles le soleill, ce est a dire la fleur des chevaliers del monde d'entre les chevaliers le roi Artu; et par ce poez vos veoir, dame, apertement que vos domageroiz moult plus cest roiaume et maint autre que onques dame ne fist par le cors d'un sol chevalier. Et ce est li granz biens que nos atendons de vostre amor.' (*MA* 59.73–84.)

Here Guinevere is accused of doing the opposite of what the Lady of the Lake had urged her to do, so that she could be proud of the fact that she loved the flower of chivalry:

'Et ge vos pri que vos lo retenez et gardez, et amez sor totes riens celui qui sor tote rien vos aimme, et metez jus tot orgoil anvers lui, que rien ne valt: nulle rien ne prise anvers vos.' (*PL* 556.37–557.1.)

For Bohort Guinevere's cruelty to Lancelot threatens the whole security of the kingdom. Thus in the *Mort Artu* the withdrawal of love is as disruptive as the unrestrained and indiscreet continuation of it, dangers which are both skilfully avoided in the *PL*. No wonder that Hector, Lyonel, and Bohort curse the hour in which Lancelot became acquainted with the Queen. However, the *Mort Artu* is so skilfully linked with the earlier events and Morgain plays her part so cunningly in the adventures before the *Queste* that it seems inevitable that the love which had brought so much benefit earlier should now prove such a threat both to Lancelot himself and to the whole Arthurian world. Indeed, in the non-cyclic romance it was only by stopping the story with the death of Galehot, and thus avoiding the triangle of knight, lady, and King, that the dangerous implications of the situation could be kept at arm's length.

One of the tragic consequences of the lovers' reckless passion in the *Mort Artu* is the enmity between the lineage of Lot and that of Ban.[48] This theme is all the more powerful in that it runs counter to the affectionate companionship developed between Lancelot and Gauvain during the *PL*, one which is evoked in a number of passages. There is an echo of his earlier quests for the name and person of Lancelot when Gauvain wants to find out who the mysterious knight is at a tournament (*MA* 20) and, accompanied by Gaheriet, tries to follow him (*MA* 23) and reports his identity (*MA* 30; cf. *PL* 256–7, 566). The King, who this time knows who the knight is, recalls past quests when he says to his nephew: 'Non est ce la premiere foiz que vos l'avez quis; non sera ce la derrienne, au mien escient.' (*MA* 24.)[49] Gauvain expresses his admiration for Lancelot (*MA* 27.23–8); Gaheriet, his beloved brother, refuses to accuse Lancelot, who is soon to kill him by accident, of betraying the King with his wife: 'Ja si preudom comme Lancelos est ne sera par moi encusez de ceste vilennie.' (*MA* 87.66–7.) Lancelot is reluctant to fight Gauvain and explains why: 'por ce qu'il est preudom et por la bone compaignie qu'il m'a puis tenue que je fui primes chevaliers' (*MA* 145.37–40). Gauvain had indeed been one of the first knights to welcome the young Lancelot to Arthur's court (*PL* 152, 163.21–4). In the *PL* (537) Lancelot gave up fighting Gauvain as soon as he found out who he was; in the *Mort Artu* (157) Lancelot gives up the battle against Gauvain without killing him, although the King's nephew never fully recovers from the wound which he received then and eventually dies from its after-effects. It is Gauvain's feelings that change: from the peacemaker of Wace and the *PL*, in the *Mort Artu*, after the death of Gaheriet, he becomes the inciter of war. The preparations for this role are to be found not in the *PL* but in the cyclic romance in the interpretation given to Gauvain's experiences at the Palais Aventureus (*LM* LXVI.36–8), and there are two allusions to this earlier episode in the *Mort Artu* (110.46–52, 131.12–15). However, there are other elements of continuity in the description of Gauvain's battle with Lancelot. He uses Escalibor (*MA* 151.19; *PL* 513.13, 530.14) and his strength increases at noon (*MA* 153–5; *PL* 388, 536).

There are other interesting links with the past. Two of these centre on the Dolorous Guard, now known as the Joyous Guard, and allude to the earlier conquest of it. Lancelot proposes to take the Queen to a castle:

'Il a non, fet Lancelos, li chastiax de la Joiouse Garde; mes quant je le conquis, a cel point que je fui noviax chevaliers, l'en l'apeloit la Dolereuse Garde.' (*MA* 96.31–4; *PL* 184–95, 250.)

Mador says of the Dolorous Guard:

'Ce chastel sei ge moult bien, car ge i fui une foiz en prison, et avoie doute de mort, quant Lancelos m'en gita et moi et mes autres compaignons.' (*MA* 104.42–5.)

He was in fact imprisoned by the lord of the Dolorous Guard in the Doloreuse Chartre (*PL* 203–5, 207.34, 214).[50] Camelot too was a very important place for the young Lancelot, as it was there that he was made a knight and first saw Guinevere (*PL* 155–60). His second sight of Camelot (*PL* 265) plunged him into a deep meditation on love as he remembered his first visit there. In the *Mort Artu* Lancelot sends his shield to the church of St Etienne at Camelot, to be displayed so that 'tuit cil qui des ore mes le verront aient en remembrance les merveilles que ge ai fetes en ceste terre'. He explains why he has chosen Camelot, mentioning only the knighting: 'Por ce que ge i reçui primes l'ordre de chevalerie; si en aing plus la cité que nule autre.' (*MA* 120.)

An evocation of the past with powerful resonances occurs when Arthur, at a stage when reconciliation is in his view no longer possible, is rescued by Lancelot, as he and his land had been twice from Galehot and once from the Saxons (*PL* 281–2, 327, 565) when Lancelot was still the Unknown Knight. The King's love and admiration for him revives when Lancelot stops Hector from killing him, and Arthur says:

'Avez veü que Lancelos a fet hui por moi, qui estoit au desuz de moi ocirre et ne volt pas metre main en moi? Par foi, ore a il passez de bonté et de cortoisie touz les chevaliers que ge onques veïsse; or voudroie ge que ceste guerre n'eüst onques esté commenciee, car plus a hui veincu mon cuer par debonereté que touz li monz n'eüst par force.' (*MA* 116.5–13.)

We have here an echo of Lancelot's earlier deeds which has not been distorted by Morgain, and Arthur wishes that the battle had never begun.

Finally, the theme which dominates the latter half of the *PL* and which makes it possible to present Lancelot, inspired by love for the Queen, as Arthur's benefactor, not his betrayer, is recalled at the end of the work. Lancelot asks to be buried in Galehot's tomb at the Joyous Guard. The inscription on the tomb reads:

CI GIST LI CORS GALEHOLT, LE SEGNOR DES LOINTAIGNES ILLES, ET AVEC LUI REPOSE LANCELOS DEL LAC QUI FU LI MIEUDRES CHEVALIERS QUI ONQUES ENTRAST EL ROIAUME DE LOGRES, FORS SEULEMENT GALAAD SON FILL. (*MA* 203.14–19.)

Thus the *Mort Artu* closes with a reminder of the death of Galehot, which had provided the conclusion to the non-cyclic romance, and of Galahad, the son who surpassed the father and whose coming was first prepared in the rewritten version of the episodes leading up to that death.[51]

The *Mort Artu* is therefore presented as the inevitable end to the tale of Lancelot and his love for Guinevere, although no shadow of such a tragic outcome falls over the account of Lancelot's progress towards the making of his name, a seat at the Round Table, and the Queen's love, as it is told in the *PL*. There are no predictions or references forward by the tale to the disastrous spiritual and social consequences of this love in relation to Lancelot's failure to achieve the Grail Quest and to the dissension which led to the end of the Round Table. It is through references back or suggestive parallels that the earlier events are presented in a new light. Thus the bulk of the *PL*, that is the non-cyclic romance (apart from the last part, concerning the False Guinevere episode and Galehot's death), is incorporated without change into the cycle and the work is given a unity, a coherence, of a very special and characteristically medieval kind: the later branches, which contain some significant changes in direction, indeed fundamental modifications of earlier themes, give a new meaning to the events in Lancelot's life as a young knight.

Epilogue: the continuing development of the cycle

The prose romance of Lancelot which begins 'En la marche de Gaule et de la Petite Bretagne' with the disinheriting of Lancelot's father and ends with the deaths of Arthur and of Lancelot already constitutes a *Lancelot-Grail* cycle, but further developments were to follow. The Quest for the Grail and the Death of Arthur, two of the important twelfth-century Arthurian themes, had been made part of the tale of Lancelot; now two others, the early history of the Grail and Robert de Boron's *Merlin*, are added, with a *Merlin Continuation* providing a bridge into the *Lancelot*. During three centuries scribes continue the process of knitting all these adventures more closely together by removing inconsistencies or introducing cross-references.[52] The integration of the Grail Quest (with a new Grail hero, Galahad) into the tale of Lancelot gave rise to the first important set of corrections and adaptations. The reference to Perceval or Perlesvaus as Grailwinner and achiever of the Adventure of the Perilous Seat (*PL* 33.8–15) was altered in various ways.[53] One group of manuscripts, of which BN fr. 110 is the oldest, also changes the allusion to Pellés de Listenois which presents him as already dead before Lancelot is knighted (*PL* 146.22–3). It also adjusts Gauvain's reference to the Grail Quest as an adventure which has already taken place (*PL* 297.21–2). The incorporation of Robert de Boron's *Merlin* into the cycle introduces another major inconsistency over the account of Merlin's birth (*PL* 21–3). Four manuscripts replace the account of the birth given in the *PL* by a brief reference to the tale of Merlin, differently worded in each case. Seven manuscripts repeat the Robert de Boron version either in full or in summaries of varying lengths, but, as I have pointed out elsewhere, they thereby raise the problem of how to fit the birth of a good Merlin into a context which demands an unredeemed Merlin; to deal with this a variety of modifications are made to the surrounding text.[54] Other less glaring inconsistencies are removed in some manuscripts. The appearance of Claudin, son of Claudas, in the cyclic romance conflicts with a statement in the *PL* (30.5–7) that Claudas had only one son, Dorin. A group of manuscripts, again including BN fr. 110, modifies the passage to read: 'n'avoit anfans que .ii. et cil estoient vallet mout bel, si avoit li ainsnés .xv. ans et avoit non Dorins, et li mainsnés n'avoit mie plus de .xvi. mois et si estoit apelés Claudins. Li ainsnés qui Dorins avoit a non . . .' The same group also omits an uncomplimentary remark made to Arthur by the *preudomme* who is interpreting his dreams (*PL* 290.28–36), perhaps in order to accord better with the rather more favourable role given to Arthur later in the cyclic romance (see Chapter X, pp. 258–9).[55]

More fundamental changes were also made to the *Lancelot–Grail* cycle; these created new romances which brought more Arthurian themes together, including the Tristan story. These later developments have been studied by F. Bogdanow and C. Pickford.[56] The general trend is towards the encompassing within one work of the main Arthurian themes.[57] This is in contrast with the earlier non-cyclic Prose *Lancelot*, which through allusions to tales outside the romance presented the individual story of Lancelot as a fragment of a wider Arthurian reality.

˙XII

General conclusion

For the non-cyclic Prose *Lancelot* two forms of coherence are equally important: internal coherence, within the individual text, and intertextual coherence, through which the individual text is shown to be part of a wider Arthurian 'reality'. These two forms are interrelated in that it is the placing of the tale of Lancelot within the literary tradition that helps to give it a meaningful shape, *conjointure* and *sens*.[1] The three principal means used to achieve this are as follows:

(*a*) Through allusions outwards to existing literary tradition belonging to the past in relation to the tale of Lancelot, whether to incidents to be found in other texts or to events to be found in no known text but fitting into the general framework provided by the literary tradition.

(*b*) Through allusions to events contemporary with the narrative, never told in full, which are concerned with particular wars going on in the Arthurian kingdom.

(*c*) Through resonances from earlier romances: familiar narrative patterns such as the tale of the *Bel Inconnu,* and episodes evoking adventures and motifs in earlier romances (especially those of Chrétien) are used with great power and subtlety to give a depth and richness to the work and to underline its main themes.

The individual tale of Lancelot has a clear structure and cohesion of its own. The technique of interlace is not used just to weave together a series of otherwise independent adventures. Analogy as a principle of coherence (as described by E. Vinaver in *The Rise of Romance*) is exploited to good effect.[2] The thematic structure is particularly clearly developed as the theme of identity intertwines with that of love; the relevance to the tale of almost all the adventures undertaken by various knights which are recounted in the story of Lancelot is shown, not simply through the fact that they are encountered by knights seeking the hero, but also by their very nature. They appear as variations on the themes of the making of a name or the winning of a love, echoing as they do the adventures of young unknown heroes or great lovers of earlier tradition. The tale of Lancelot is thus woven into the web of Arthurian literature.

The structure of the Arthurian kingdom too provides an important cohesive factor within the text and in relation to Arthurian tradition; it also creates a link with the world outside romance. Problems concerning kingship, feudal relationships, and the law are explored. The dependence of a king on the various ranks of nobility, not just the great lords but also the more humble gentry, is emphasized. While the King often has to remain passive, the Arthurian knight is given an important role in striving (painfully and often against considerable odds) to see that all men of gentle birth can get justice in Arthur's lands. The rising importance of the richer townspeople is not neglected, as the problems of Claudas with the inhabitants of Gaunes and the customs imposed on the lord of the Estroite Marche illustrate.[3] This more down-to-earth and topical element in the romance is combined with a restrained but imaginative use of the traditional Arthurian marvellous to give a special aura to the tale. The number of clearly marvellous features is limited to certain key episodes such as the conquest of Dolorous Guard, where Lancelot learns his name, but the occasional allusions to adventures from the great Arthurian past, to tales already told of events which happened before Lancelot came to Camelot, references to the Grail and to Merlin, give the hint of mystery and wonder appropriate to an Arthurian romance.

The transformation of the tale of Lancelot (without the Grail), with its own independent structure within a wider tradition, into a branch of a great cycle of which it forms an integral part sheds a particularly interesting light on a medieval creative process of reinterpretation through incorporation within a new whole.[4] There will be varying patterns of coherence within the various branches of the cycle. The series of adventures often known as the *Suites de la Charrette* will not, from some points of view, present such a firmly structured section of narrative as, for example, the first part of the *Lancelot propre* (up to 572.4 of the *PL*) or in a quite different way the *Queste* or the *Mort Artu*. Nevertheless, from the moment that the episodes of the Journey to Sorelois and the False Guinevere are rewritten with the first allusions to a chaste Grailwinner yet to come, a descendant of Lancelot who will surpass him, the Grail dominates the work. The episodes designed to prepare the way for a new hero are also skilfully devised so that they give a new meaning to what has already happened. Some of what had up till then seemed to be Lancelot's great achievements now appear, under the new light shed on them by the preparations for the Grail adventures, as signs of failure to come. The theme of identity, of discovery of one's name, ancestors, and destiny, as figured by the tomb slabs, acquires a different significance with this change in direction. Arthur's role within the work begins to alter subtly; the whole structure of the Arthurian kingdom no longer seems to be quite the same.[5]

The relationship of Lancelot's tale to other Arthurian tales has shifted too, for there is a greater emphasis on completeness. The romance is now to encompass the main events of the Arthurian world, the Grail Quest is no longer a tale already told elsewhere, but the great adventure yet to come and to be told in the romance. There are therefore fewer allusions outwards, and the adventures of many more knights are recounted, although some continuity with the past is kept through the use of similar episodes, echoing earlier events and often specifically linked with them through family relationships. Wider resonances are of course still important—for example, those of the Tristan story in the *Mort Artu*, where the echoes and a direct allusion serve to underline the theme of love as a destructive passion with dangerous social as well as spiritual consequences. But there are not the same opportunities for subtle indirect allusions to the Chrétien version of the Lancelot story in the later part of the cycle, now that the *Charrette* tale is incorporated in the romance.[6] The trend is towards inclusion, often with reinterpretation or partial if not total condemnation, rather than an interplay between the individual tale and other tales existing outside it. The Arthurian Bible ('Old and New Testament') is now contained in one volume, and the 'New Testament' gives clear indications as to how we should under-stand the earlier events before the coming of the Grail. This is done not by rewriting the earlier story but by placing events in a new context, by retelling them in a way which gives them a different emphasis or function within the whole. An example of this is to be found in the key episode of Lancelot and Guinevere's first kiss. The original account of this in *PL* 347–8 should be compared with Lancelot's painting of these events of his life (*LM* LXXXVI.21–3), through which, unwittingly, he gives a dangerous weapon to Morgain so that she can destroy Guinevere and Arthur; she gives a cunningly slanted version to Arthur in the *Mort Artu*, where, from the beginning, the love is presented as a relapse into sin and a destructive passion threatening society. We may also compare Lancelot's confession of love to Guinevere in *PL* 345–6 with his reluctant renunciation of this love in the *Queste* (66). Another important example of the process is the transformation of the gaining of a glorious name in the cemetery of the Dolorous Guard into the shameful loss of a baptismal name in the light of the later tomb-raising episodes.

The study of the *Conte Lancelot* and of the way that it developed into a great cycle reminds us of the complex nature of 'unity' or coherence in medieval literature. The non-cyclic Prose *Lancelot* had an inner coherence, based on thematic structure, interlacing of narrative threads, interplay of contrasts and parallels, feudal relationships and kinship, the linking of key locations by journeys and messengers, repeated sequences and echoes. In this romance, through the interplay between these various elements, the relationships between the individual knight and society and between the knight and the lady are explored as well as some of the possible conflicts within that society. In this interplay intertextuality plays a very important part: the medieval audience was clearly expected to recognize subtle variations on familiar themes, to be aware of literary resonances. The individual tale of Lancelot only achieves its full meaning in relation to theme and form when set within a wider tradition. It forms a whole, but is nevertheless presented in one sense as a fragment of a wider 'reality', that to be found in the tales of all Arthur's knights as recorded in the great book by the King's clerks. Once the tale of Lancelot is extended to form part of a Grail cycle, we have a new set of contrasts and parallels, so that the original patterns have a new function within the different, wider structure which now embraces the main themes of twelfth-century Arthurian tradition and develops them in a new way.

To acknowledge the existence of a coherent structure within the non-cyclic Prose *Lancelot* is not to question whether the cyclic romance is so organized. Conversely, to recognize and admire the organic structure, the 'unity', in the terms of Lot and of Frappier, of the *Lancelot-Grail* cycle does not mean that the coherence of the non-cyclic Prose *Lancelot* is denied. Each element in a medieval text can only be properly interpreted according to the function which it has within the work as a whole. The episode of Lancelot learning his name at the Dolorous Guard and the scene in which Lancelot and Guinevere first kiss, although identical from the textual point of view in the non-cyclic and cyclic versions, do not have the same meaning within the overall structure of each work. We are no longer trying to explain continuity and contrast (with the change in Grailwinner) between Sommer III (*PL* 1–572.4) and the rest of the cycle in terms of relics of vanished cycles, or a series of interpolations for which there is no manuscript evidence, or an overall plan directed by an 'architect', but not worked out in detail, but in terms of two successive stages, both of which have survived. We have an independent Prose *Lancelot* which does not include the Grail and has its own coherent structure, and a *Lancelot-Grail* cycle with its 'unity and diversity'. A tale which had presented Lancelot's love for Guinevere in purely positive terms as the source of Lancelot's prowess, an inspiration for deeds which defend the cause of the weak and innocent and save Logres, but a love described in terms which stir the passions of Paolo and Francesca, becomes only part of a cycle in which the potentially destructive aspects of such a love are made manifest; a different kind of chivalry is explored through the incorporation of the themes of the Grail and the Death of Arthur. Apart from the allusion to Perceval and the Perilous Seat, awkward in the *Lancelot-Grail* but part of a consistent pattern of allusion in the non-cyclic romance, the combination of continuity and contrast between the account of Lancelot's early years as a knight and the later branches of the cycle becomes a meaningful element within the *Lancelot-Grail* romance, so that the 'diversity' becomes an integral part of the 'unity'.

APPENDIX I

The *Perlesvaus* and the non–cyclic prose *Lancelot*

The *Perlesvaus* and the *PL* have certain elements in common which suggest some direct form of relationship between them. The most important of these are: (*a*) The decline in Arthur's power through lack of the kingly and knightly quality of *largece*, and the advice given to him by a *preudomme*. (*b*) A conflict with Claudas, who has taken the land of Ban de Benoyc, vassal of Arthur and father of Lancelot: an account of the disinheriting of Lancelot is given in the *PL*, and a reference back to this occurs in the *Perlesvaus*, where Claudas now rebels once more against Arthur. (*c*) The love theme of Lancelot and Guinevere (common also to Chrétien's *Charrette*).[1]

Thomas E. Kelly agrees with Jessie Weston 'that the *Perlesvaus* stands in close connection with the Lancelot story in a form intermediate between the earliest version (that represented by the *Lanzelet*) and the fully developed romance, which we know today'.[2] He believes that the *Perlesvaus* precedes not only the *Queste* but also the *Lancelot propre*, for the following reasons. (*a*) In the *Perlesvaus* Lancelot retains the position given him in Chrétien's *Charrette* as Guinevere's lover and leading knight at Arthur's court, but he has not yet reached the position of superiority allotted him in the Vulgate *Queste*; he is superior to Gauvain, but subordinate to Perlesvaus. (*b*) There is no mention of the Lady of the Lake, so important in the *PL*, nor of Galehot nor of Galahad. I think that the question should be re-examined in terms both of the relationship with the non-cyclic prose romance, which might represent Weston's 'intermediate form' of the Lancelot story, and of a more subtle interplay between texts than was envisaged by earlier scholars. These tended to be above all concerned to establish the existence of vanished cycles and to postulate a somewhat rigid framework for each individual text. Kelly himself points out that the *Perlesvaus* has neither a real beginning nor end and that 'from the outset the author assumes that his readers are familiar with an earlier adventure of the central hero'. He goes on to say: 'The opening and closing lines of the romance indicate, therefore, that the *Perlesvaus* is both a continuation of an earlier work and the prelude to an announced sequel of its own.'[3] He then underlines the freedom with which the writer treated inherited tradition: for example, the resurrection of Perceval's mother, who dies at the moment of his departure from home in Chrétien, but plays a major role throughout most of the *Perlesvaus*. He concludes: 'Thus, while the *Perlesvaus* completes the Grail story begun by Chrétien, being in that sense a sequel to the earlier work, it is also an independent composition which freely interprets and adapts the source materials on which it is based.'[4] This illuminating comment does somewhat undermine some of his own arguments for the dependence of the Prose *Lancelot* on the *Perlesvaus*—those which suggest that the *Perlesvaus* does not base itself sufficiently closely on the Prose *Lancelot* to be using it as a source. I propose to compare the way in which the two romances use allusions to events recounted in other Arthurian texts, to stories known to their audience, in order to see whether this sheds light on the relationship between the two texts and to study further the way in which a medieval text's own individual structure can be thrown into relief by the very techniques which emphasize that it is also part of a wider tradition, one tale amongst the many linked to Arthur's court.

There is interplay with Chrétien's *Conte del Graal* in both works. As has already been seen, in the *PL* there is considerable emphasis on parallels and contrasts between Lancelot and Perceval, both young heroes brought up in isolation from society and in ignorance of their names; this interaction between the verse and prose romances, as was shown in Chapter II, has an important role within the thematic structure of the *PL*, especially in relation to the identity theme. There are also references in the *PL* which place the tale of Lancelot in general terms in relation to the greatest tale of all, that of the Holy Grail; they are used to define the material relevant to Lancelot's story and to establish its position within a network of tales, as well as to enhance its importance through resonances of the most marvellous and most honoured tale of all. These references do not correspond with the version of the Grail story to be found in the *Perlesvaus*, but combine elements from Chrétien and Robert de Boron. They allude to the successful accomplishment of the adventure in terms of the achievement of the Perilous Seat, not to the asking of questions; they do not present the *Lancelot* as an integral part of a cycle including a Grail Quest yet to come, and they form part of a network of allusions to existing Arthurian tradition (see Chapter VI above). The *Perlevaus* also has a close relationship with Chrétien's *Conte del Graal*. It too appears to assume a knowledge of Chrétien on the part of its public; but in one important respect the association between this prose romance and the *Conte del Graal* is different: the *Perlesvaus* is presented as a continuation of Chrétien's poem, although it also contains elements from the Robert de Boron Grail tradition, such as the ancestry of the Grail Guardians, as well as material from the *Perceval Continuations*. The allusions to the failure of Perceval to ask the questions at the Grail Castle and the repercussions of this failure constitute the starting-point for a Grail story which is to involve not just Perceval, but Arthur, Gauvain, Lancelot, and the whole of the Arthurian kingdom, in the struggle between the Old Law and the New. Perlesvaus, the hero, is a transformed Perceval, a perfect knight whose fault lies in the past, before the beginning of the romance, but who now has to right the wrong through different means, for it is too late for him to ask the questions.

In both the *Perlesvaus* and the *PL* the decline of Arthur's power and the decrease in the support he receives from his knights have a function within the structure of the individual work. In the *PL* there are a series of oppositions in which Arthur is contrasted, first favourably (for his *largece* and the splendour of his court and ability to attract great knights) with Claudas (reluctant to show *largece* and imprisoner of children), and then unfavourably (as lacking in *largece*, and failing to avenge Ban's death and Lancelot's disappearance) with Galehot (praised for the very qualities which had distinguished Arthur from Claudas). These oppositions have an important part to play in relation to Lancelot's position as lover of Guinevere, saviour of Arthur, and future Knight of the Round Table (see Chapters III, IV, and VIII). Arthur's response to the counsels of the *preudomme*, combined with Lancelot's help, leads to a renewed flowering of his court and kingdom. In the *Perlesvaus* there is a strong emphasis on Arthur's present lethargy and failure to show kingly qualities, compared with his past glory (*Perl.*, lines 58–89, 332–9, 517–29), and his decline and that of his kingdom are linked with Perceval's failure to ask the questions and provide a parallel with the fate of the land of the Fisher King, laid waste by Perceval's silence at the Grail Castle; Arthur's recovery through his pilgrimage to St Augustine's Chapel and his response to the counsels given him by the hermit *preudomme* lead to the restoration of the New Law and the return of his former glory (*Perl.*, lines 569–81, 933–6; cf. *PL* 304.4–12). If the *Perlesvaus* were written after the *PL*, the allusions to the contrast with Arthur's former reputation would, for a reader familiar with the *PL*, have further resonances in keeping with the function of this particular branch within the work as a whole; the episode serves to emphasize from the beginning that the theme of the work, the upholding of the New Law, embraces the affairs of earthly feudal society as well as the spiritual allegory of the eucharistic vision and adventures such as the conquest of the Chastel Mortel which remind us of the Harrowing of Hell. It might be considered that resonances from the *Perlesvaus* would not serve to enhance the role of the episode of Arthur's counselling by the *preudomme* in the *PL* in quite the same way, especially as the Grail references in the work do not accord with the *Perlesvaus* version.

One of the most obvious links between the *PL* and the *Perlesvaus* concerns the character of Claudas. As I have suggested in Chapter II, the role of Claudas (mentioned as an opponent of Arthur in the *Second Continuation*) seems to arise directly from the importance ascribed to heredity in the work and from the need to avoid any suggestion of disloyalty by vassal to feudal lord on the part of Lancelot. In the *Lanzelet* the hero's father lost his land through his tyranny, which caused his barons to rebel against him. In the *PL* we have two different characters to cover the two aspects, the loss of land and the rebellion; firstly, Ban, a good king and faithful vassal, who loses his land because of his loyalty to his lord Arthur, when the latter is heavily involved in the wars occurring after the death of Uther; secondly, Claudas, a violent usurper, whose treatment of the dispossessed sons of Bohort of Gaunes causes the barons of that land to rebel. Lancelot's loss of his land brings the loss of his name and is, therefore, linked to one of the two main themes of the work. The establishment of his identity, largely through the inspiration of his love for Guinevere, is the subject of the romance, but this does not involve the recovery of his land from Claudas, as the responsibilities of governing a kingdom would interfere with his role as knight, spurred on by his love for the Queen to perform a useful function in society through the undertaking of adventures in defence of justice and stability within Arthur's realm. Thus the role of Claudas grows directly from the development of the Lancelot tradition within the romance, although care has been taken to fit him into the general 'historical' background to the work. In the *Perlesvaus*, on the contrary, the importance of Claudas stems precisely from the fact that he provides a link with events recounted elsewhere, so that the romance is presented as part of a wider tradition, much as allusions to events not recounted in the *PL* are used to suggest that the tale of Lancelot is part of a network of adventures recorded in the great book at Arthur's court. In the *Perlesvaus*, no account is given of the loss of Ban's land to Claudas, but there are a number of references to the dead Ban and one to the conquest of his land by Claudas (*Perl.*, lines 8556–60). Equally, the troubles between Claudas and Arthur which are recounted in the romance are given no final conclusion, although a sequel is promised in the colophon of the Brussels manuscript:

Apres iceste estoire conmence li contes si conme brians des illes guerpi li rois artus por lanc(elot) que il namoit mie et conme il laseura li rois claudas qui le roi ban de benoic toli sa terre. Si parole cist contes conment il le conquist et par quel maniere et si com galobrus de la uermeille lande uint a la cort le rois artus por aidier lanc(elot). Quar il estoit de son lignage. Cist contes est mout lons et mout auentureus et poisanz. Mes li liures sen tera ore atant trusqua vne autre foiz. (*Perl.* I, p. 409.)

No sequel has come down to us, the importance of the colophon has been much discussed, and some scholars have dismissed the reference to a continuation to the story as a promise and nothing more.[5] Kelly regards the promise itself, whether or not it was ever intended to be fulfilled, as significant:

Of much greater relevance is the very promise of such a continuation, as contained in the colophon of the Brussels manuscript. For here we have convincing proof that the work is, as far as its narrative structure is concerned, a cyclical composition which must first be placed into a larger context if we hope to describe it adequately. On the one hand, the narrative contained in *P* is a continuation of an earlier story, succeeding where the first two *Continuations* of Chrétien's *Conte du Graal* had failed, by bringing the Perceval–Grail story to a satisfactory conclusion; and at the same time it carefully prepares for and points towards a Lancelot-sequel of its own. In the broad sense of the term, therefore, the *Perlesvaus* does not by itself constitute a 'work'; it is but one part or branch of a larger whole, which alone, properly speaking, can be described as the 'work'.[6]

Some critics have dismissed the account of the conflict with Brian des Illes and Claudas in branches IX, X, and XI as an irrelevant intrusion, but I think that Kelly is right to deny that it is extraneous. He suggests that it depicts man's vocation to co-operate in the transmission of the New Law and its defence from its enemies, internal as well as external, thereby sharing in his own redemption.[7] The dissension fomented by Brian and Claudas links up with existing Arthurian tradition, and, in my view, these episodes would be much more effective in relation to the central themes of the work if they were designed to evoke memories of events in the *PL*. Once again, the author of the *Perlesvaus* has shown great skill in bringing out his main theme through interplay with existing texts.[8] The fact that the beginning of the conflict between Claudas and Lancelot's family is only alluded to and that its end is also not given is in accord with the idea of the never-ending struggle to uphold the New Law.

The references in the *Perlesvaus* to Lancelot's love for Guinevere depend for their full effect on the public's knowledge of earlier romances in which the relationship between the two is explored in depth. Lancelot achieves greatness through his love for the Queen in Chrétien's *Charrette*, but it is in the *PL*, where he emphasizes that all his chivalric achievements have their source in his love for Guinevere, and where the Lady of the Lake describes love for a great knight such as Lancelot as the *folie* to be honoured above all others, that the closest similarities are to be found (*Perl.*, pp. 167–8, 302; *PL* 345–6, 556–7). The episode in which Lancelot refuses to renounce his love for Guinevere (*Perl.*, pp. 167–8) would have greater depth and power for a reader with memories of his confession of love to her, which forms the central point in the *PL* (345–6). On the other hand, an evocation in the *PL* of the *Perlesvaus*, where Lancelot accepts that he must renounce the greatest adventure of all if he continues to love the Queen, would undermine one of the main themes of the *PL*, in which the value of his love as an inspiration for prowess, for the achievement of the greatest adventures, is never questioned. In the *PL*, as has been seen in Chapter III, the conflict in loyalty between love for the lady and duty to one's lord is carefully avoided. In the *Perlesvaus* this opposition is again played down: through Guinevere's death, associated with a rebellion against Arthur and the death of his son Lohoz, the sinful relationship between the two is brought to an end without Lancelot's renunciation of his love. He continues to remain faithful to the Queen's memory[9] and is inspired to perform great deeds in defence of Arthur and the New Law. If he is never pure enough to see the Grail, he nevertheless is permitted to play an active role as champion of the New Law and, as in the *PL*, saves Arthur and his kingdom. Once again, the interplay between the *PL* and the *Perlesvaus* would serve to underline the main theme in the latter. I do not consider that Lancelot's displacement from the position of the greatest of Arthur's knights by Perlesvaus is (as Kelly suggests) an argument against the *Perlesvaus* looking back to the *PL* rather than the reverse. The hero of an Arthurian romance is normally placed at the top of the hierarchy, or at least presented as the equal of Gauvain, the traditional leader of Arthur's knights, as is illustrated by the romances of Chrétien. Lancelot's demotion from the supreme position familiar to readers of the *PL* would reinforce the emphasis given to spiritual values in the *Perlesvaus*, particularly when combined with passages evoking his great love for Guinevere as it has been expressed in the *PL*.

The network of allusions does not end there. Gauvain and, to a lesser degree, Lancelot are constantly in search of Perlesvaus, who keeps on changing his shield and thereby concealing his identity (*Perl.*, pp. 193, 194, 195, 198, 199, 207–8); this recalls a recurring pattern in the *PL*. Gauvain laments in both romances over his repeated failure to recognize the knight whom he is seeking (*Perl.*, lines 4490–4; *PL* 226–7, 233, 255). The change of name of the Biau Couart to the Bel Hardi (*Perl.*, pp. 241, 243) parallels changes of name in the *PL* and the Chrétien romances; memories of the *Bel Inconnu* are also present. Gauvain's reputation is tested in the *Perlesvaus* (pp. 93–6, 291–5) while he is incognito, as it is in the *PL* (372–90). The Round Table appears to have been part of the Queen's dowry in the *Perlesvaus* (lines 7843–8) as it is in the *PL* (585.39–586.7), and Arthur is threatened with its removal in both romances. The play on identity is not so central to the *Perlesvaus* as it is to the *Conte del Graal* or the *PL*, but it helps to link the romance to an Arthurian world which would be familiar to an early thirteenth-century audience.[10]

Similar techniques are therefore used in the *PL* and the *Perlesvaus* to relate the individual work to existing literary tradition and to highlight some of the main themes in the text through the evocation of memories of earlier works or through variations on or transformations of familiar narrative patterns or motifs. The *PL* refers to adventures which are deemed irrelevant to the particular tale being told but which are recorded elsewhere.[11] The Brussels colophon promises a sequel to the account of the conflict with Claudas. A study of the interplay between the two romances would seem to suggest that the *PL* may well represent the 'intermediate form' of the Lancelot story which Kelly is prepared to accept as having a close association with the *Perlesvaus*. We are not here concerned with a highly developed and strictly defined formal relationship, as, for example, between the various branches of the *Lancelot-Grail* cycle (the Vulgate), but with an enriching association between two romances through a subtle interplay of echoes and contrasts. The *Perlesvaus* will have greater power, its theme of man's redemption, of the Quest for the Grail and struggle to maintain the New Law, in terms of eucharistic vision and political and military endeavour, will come across more effectively when read by a public aware of allusions to and interlinking with other texts. These would seem to include the *PL*, the '*Lancelot* without the Grail', which defines its own relationship with the Grail story through a series of allusions which combine elements from Chrétien and Robert de Boron, but do not accord with the version in the *Perlesvaus*.

A list of references to the text with cross-references to other editions

References to the non-cyclic romance

PL	LM	Sommer III	*Lancelot and the Grail*
1	Ia 1	3	5, 80, 287
1.7–11	Ia 1	3.8–11	21, 148, 215, 237–8, 249, 276
1.20–5	Ia 2	3.19–24	81
2.8–19	Ia 4–5	4.13–22	12, 208, 237
2–7	Ia 5–18	4–8	287
3.17–18	Ia 8	5.12–13	81
3.34–6	Ia 10	5.26–9	18
4.1–2	Ia 10	5.32–3	19
6	Ia 15–18	7–8	236
7.1–6	Ia 18	8.7–12	111–12
7.10–12	Ia 18	8.15–17	167
7.33–4	IIa 2	8.33–4	211
9.14–16	IIa 6	9.39–41	167
12	IIa 15	12	288
12.32–13.4	IIa 15–IIIa 1	12.26–38	167–8
12–14	IIIa 1–5	12–14	236
13.5–18	IIIa 2	12.39–13.9	222, 224
13.12	IIIa 2	13.3–4	143, 237, 292, 362, 366
13.26–14.9	IIIa 3–4	13.17–36	143, 222, 236–7, 358, 362, 366
14.13–18	IIIa 5	13	301
15.28–30	IIIa 8	14.40–1	179, 203
16.21–3	IIIa 10	15.22–4	276, 366
17.34–8	IIIa 13	16.20–3	115, 170, 287
18.1–9	IIIa 13–IV a 1	16.25–33	161, 172, 287
18.28–33	IVa 3	17.9–14	158, 219
18.39–40	IVa 4	17.20–1	158
19–20	IVa 2–7	17–18	219
20.8–11	IVa 7	18.22–5	172
20–1	Va 1–3	18–19	236
20.39–21.10	Va 3	19.6–17	5, 170, 178–9
21–3	VIa 1–7	19–21	237, 309

PL	LM	Sommer III	*Lancelot and the Grail*
21.11–12	VIa 1	19.18–19	178
21.12–13	VIa 1	19.19–20	112
21.19–21	VIa 1	19.24–7	112
21.21–3	VIa 2	19.27–9	178
21.24–34	VIa 2–3	19.29–20.2	112, 179, 360
21.35–7	VIa 3	20.2–4	113, 179, 360
22.20–1	VIa 5	20.24–5	359
22.27–32	VIa 6	20.29–34	113
22.40–23.2	VIa 7	21.1–2	114
23.3–9	VIa 7	21.2–8	114
23.10–11	VIa 8	21.10	287
23.29–30 (variants)			372
24.4–7 (variants)			372
24.7–11	VIa 11	22.1–4	179–80, 287, 356
24.14–18	VIa 11	22.7–10	21, 180
24.19–20	VIa 12	22.11	179–80
24.22–31	VIa 12	22.14–22	116, 180, 266, 287
24.32–5	VIa 12	22.22–5	170, 180, 236
24.36	VIIa 1	22.26–7	161
25.4–5	VIIa 1	22.32–3	179
30.1	VIIa 14	26.22–3	161
30.3–5	VIIIa 1	26.25	160, 172
30.5–7	VIIIa 1	26.27–9	309
30.10–31.17	VIIIa 1–3	26.32–27.28	222–3
30.32–31.9	VIIIa 2	27.9–21	49, 362
31.18–19	VIIIa 4	27.29	160, 173, 179, 246
31.24–7	VIIIa 4	27.34–6	224, 246, 256
31.28–34	VIIIa 4	27.37–43	224, 246, 288–9
32.38–33.2	VIIIa 8	28.37–40	82, 173, 236, 259, 288–9
33.4–15	VIIIa 8	28.41–29.11	70, 150–1, 215, 237, 239, 243, 270–1, 275, 293, 309, 369
33.20–3	VIIIa 9	29.15–17	82–3, 208, 237
33.23–8	VIIIa 9	29.17–22	109
33.30–4	VIIIa 10	29.24–7	225, 259, 370
34.4–8	VIIIa 11	29.35–30.3	229
34.19–20	VIIIa 11	30.12	73, 110, 242, 259
34.20–32	VIIIa 12	30.12–23	225, 227, 242, 259, 288–9, 370
34.32–35.8	VIIIa 13	30.23–36	228, 259
35.19–23	VIIIa 14	31.4–7	73, 259, 288–9
38.25	VIIIa 22	33.20	173, 236, 259, 288

PL	LM	Sommer III	*Lancelot and the Grail*
38.28–30	IXa 1	33.23–6	179, 181, 236
38–9	IXa 1–3	33–4	15, 119, 236, 277
38.34–7	IXa 1	33.29–32	180
39.15–18	IXa 3	34.6–9	160, 180
39–41	IXa 3–7	34–5	222–3, 236, 277, 298
40.14–24	IXa 5	34.38–35.4	50–1, 362
40.34–41.2	IXa 6	35.14–20	51, 300, 351, 362, 367
41.4–10	IXa 7	35.22–7	94, 223, 370
41.15–19	IXa 7	35.31–5	180
41.20	IXa 8	35.36	180
43.9–10	IXa 11	37.11	116
44.3–25	IXa 13–14	37–8	21, 116
44.7–8	IXa 13	38.39–40	363
45.16–26	IXa 16–17	38.33–41	15
47.1–3	IXa 20	40.1–3	356
47.29–32	IXa 22	40.23–5	356
47.33–48.3	IXa 22	40.25–33	220, 236
48.4–20	IXa 22–Xa 1	40.33–41.6	160, 170–1, 180, 236
48–60	Xa 1–XIa 10	40–50	225, 236
48.20–1	Xa 1	41.6	171
49.28	Xa 4	42.3	301
49.39–50.2	Xa 5	42.13–15	143, 237, 362, 366
50–51	Xa 7	42–3	236
53.25–9	Xa 14	45.1–4	83, 105
53–4	Xa 15	45	236
53.34–54.2	Xa 15	45.9–15	83, 159, 173, 208, 237
54.3–7	Xa 15	45.15–19	110, 159, 173
54–7	Xa 16–23	45–7	83, 84, 204, 219, 242, 259
57.4	Xa 24	47.33	173, 236
57.9–16	Xa 24–XIa 1	47.38–43	162, 171
57.27	XIa 2	48.10	214
57–8	XIa 3–5	48–9	236
58–68	XIa 4–XIIIa 1	48–56	204
58.14	XIa 4	48.33	173
58.20–31	XIa 4–5	48.37–49.4	159
60–70	XIa 11–XIIIa 6	50–8	221
60.33–9	XIa 11	50.30–6	217, 220, 237, 246, 255, 267
60.29–61.5	XIa 11–XIIIa 1	50.26–39	158–9
63.36–7	XIIa 6	52.41	159
64.1–4	XIIa 6–7	53.3–6	159
66	XIIa 11	54	283
67	XIIa 14	55	288

PL	LM	Sommer III	*Lancelot and the Grail*
67	XIIa 15	55	214, 243, 283
67.32–5	XIIa 15	55.40–56.1	117, 214, 283
68.7–11	XIIa 16	56.10–13	118
68.21–35	XIIa 17–XIIIa 1	56.21–35	168, 172
69.2–4	XIIIa 1	57.1–2	118
69.12–13	XIIIa 3	57.9–11	118, 127
69.19–20	XIII 3	57.14–15	118
69–70	XIII 3–5	57	203, 236, 283
70.3–16	XIIIa 6	57.33–58.2	181
70.17–20	XIIIa 6–XIVa 1	58.2–5	161, 168, 172
70–1	XIVa 1–2	58	372
71–3	XIVa 3–7	59–60	15, 94, 222–3, 288, 370
73–8	XIVa 8–21	60–4	372
78	XIVa 22	64	353
80.15–21	XIVa 27	65.41–66.5	118, 177
81.25–37	XIVa 30	66.40–67.9	224, 227
82.28–30	XIVa 32	67.35–7	362
82–9	XIVa 31–49	67–73	372
83–6	XIVa 33–41	68–71	353
90	XIVa 50–1	73–4	353
92	XIVa 55–6	75	353
99.33–5	XVa 4	81.16–17	122
100–1	XVa 6–10	81–2	236
103–4	XVa 14–15	84	117, 236, 287
104–6	XVa 16–20	84–6	122, 214, 243
106.25–9	XVa 21	86.18–22	356
106.39–107.2	XVa 22	86.31–2	118
107.5–6	XVa 22	86.35–6	119
107.22–3	XVa 24	87.7–8	21
108.3–5	XVa 25	87.25–6	14
108.30–3	XVa 27	88.1–2	219
108.37–109.2	XVa 27	88.6–12	143–4, 237, 292–3, 362
109	XVa 29	88	13, 288
110.34–111.3	XVa 32	89.26–32	13, 351
111.4–6	XVa 33	89.33–4	13
111.14–15	XVa 33	89.40	13
111.16–34	XVa 34–5	89.41–90.14	15, 237, 356
111.28–37	XVa 35	90.8–16	181, 218, 237, 243
112.21–3	XVIa 2	90.34–5	21
113.34	XVIa 5	91.38	361
115–17	XVIIa 4–10	92–4	353
128–30	XVIIa 38–40	103–4	353

PL	LM	Sommer III	*Lancelot and the Grail*
130.14–17	XVIIa 41	104.17–21	173
130.18	XVIIIa 1	104.22–4	161
131.29–132.5	XVIIIa 3–4	105.24–37	181
132.5–14	XVIIIa 4–XIXa 1	105.37–106.5	171, 181
132–3	XIXa 1–4	106	236, 287
132.20–1	XIXa 2	106.11–12	171, 219
133.4–8	XIXa 4	106.30–4	171, 219
133.9–10	XIXa 4	106.34–5	219–20
133–8	XIXa 4–XXa 12	106–10	225, 236
133.23–30	XIXa 5	107.4–10	115–16, 287
134.17–22	XIXa 6–XXa 1	107.31–6	158, 162, 173–4
134.23–31	XXa 1	107.36–108.2	107, 158
135.16	XXa 3	108.22	158
135.30–3	XXa 4	108.34–6	211
135.40–136.4	XXa 4	109.2–5	110
137–8	XXa 8–11	109–10	33, 219, 242, 349, 374
138.10–13	XXa 11	110.26–9	20, 242
138.16–17	XXa 11	110.31–2	95
138.31–6	XXa 12	111.2–7	152, 162, 174, 360
138.37–8	XXIa 1	111.8–9	181, 185
138–9	XXIa 1	111	236
139–40	XXIa 1–5	111–12	15, 218, 221, 237, 356
141–7	XXIa 7–23	112–17	15, 222–4, 238, 356, 370
141.23–142.4	XXIa 8–9	113.5–22	351
142.16–30	XXIa 10–11	113.31–114–2	12
142.37–40	XXIa 11	114.8–10	109
143.3	XXIa 11	114.13–14	356
144.15–16	XXIa 14	115.17–18	357
144.36–7	XXIa 16	115.35–6	357
145.25–37	XXIa 18	116.18–29	357
146.10–14	XXIa 19	116.39–117.2	144, 238, 292
146.17–19	XXIa 19	117.4–6	145, 238, 292
146.19–21	XXIa 19	117.6–7	149, 238, 274, 366
146.22–4	XXIa 19	117.8–10	149, 238, 309, 358
147.8–34	XXIa 21–2	117–18	221, 237, 356
147.17–20	XXIa 21	117.37–40	13, 295, 362, 366
147.24–33	XXIa 22	118.2–11	358
148.1–15	XXIa 23	118.16–29	237
148.16–19	XXIa 24	118.30–2	236
148.23	XXIa 24	118.36	15, 367

PL	LM	Sommer III	*Lancelot and the Grail*
148.28–34	XXIa 25	118.40–119.3	120, 236
148.34–149.5	XXIa 25–XXIIa 1	119.3–14	161, 174, 177, 181–2
149.7–11	XXIIa 1	119.15–19	88, 192, 238
149.16–151.3	XXIIa 2–5	119.23–120.36	205, 237, 265
149.26–30	XXIIa 2	119.32–6	216, 237, 265
150.13–15	XXIIa 4	120.11–13	216, 237, 265
150.17–20	XXIIa 4	120.14–17	22
150.25–6	XXIIa 4	120.20–2	365
151–2	XXIIa 6–8	121	136, 177, 182, 204, 207–8, 236–8, 242–3, 281, 306
153.36–7	XXIIa 12	123.1–2	120
153.39–154.3	XXIIa 12	123.4–8	144, 237–8, 296, 366
154.4–7	XXIIa 12	123.8–11	298
154.8–12	XXIIa 12	123.12–16	237–8, 261
154.17–21	XXIIa 13	123	237
154.21–4	XXIIa 13	123.24–7	218, 237
154.29–31	XXIIa 14	123.31–3	120, 127, 266, 286
154.33–155.2	XXIIa 14	123.35–42	120–1, 145, 238, 277, 292–3, 366
155	XXIIa 16	124	56, 236, 242, 281, 307
157–8	XXIIa 22–3	125–6	58, 207, 241, 281, 293, 307
157.21–2	XXIIa 21	125.26–7	62
157.27–31	XXIIa 22	125.31–5	71
157.37–9	XXIIa 23	125.39–41	50
158.3–10	XXIIa 23	126.3–9	17, 58, 62
158–9	XXIIa 24–6	126–7	237
159–60	XXIIa 28	127	237, 240–1, 282, 307
160.7–20	XXIIa 28–9	127.23–33	205, 237, 240–1, 265
161.36–8	XXIIa 33	128.32–5	51
162.20–1	XXIIa 35	129.9–10	102
162.25–9	XXIIa 36	129.12–16	102
162–78	XXIIa 37–XXIIIa 27	129–40	231, 244, 281
162.35–7	XXIIa 37	129.20–1	22, 295, 363
162.38–163.1	XXIIa 37	129.22–3	23
163.13–20	XXIIa 38	129.34–41	23, 40, 204, 242, 295
163.21–4	XXIIa 39	129.41–130.1	306
163.34–6	XXIIa 40	130.9–11	23, 40, 242
164.23	XXIIa 42	130.28	183
165.19–20	XXIIa 43	131.12–14	51
165.23	XXIIa 43	131.15	51, 59, 212, 242, 282, 298
165.25	XXIIa 43	131.16	51
166.3	XXIIa 45	131.28	176
166.3–5	XXIIa 45	131.29–30	51

PL	LM	Sommer III	*Lancelot and the Grail*
166.19–21	XXIIa 45	131.40–1	161, 174
166.20–3	XXIIa 45–XXIIIa 1	131.42–132.1	174, 176, 182–3
166–74	XXIIIa 1–17	132–7	40, 242
171.6–7	XXIIIa 10	134.41–2	23
172.34–5	XXIIIa 13	136.4–5	52
173.11	XXIIIa 14	136.15	232, 244
174.11	XXIIIa 17	137.3–4	23
174.14–24	XXIIIa 17	137.5–14	183, 371
174.32–3	XXIIIa 18	137.22–4	23, 52
175.15–22	XXIIIa 20	137.39–138.1	24, 183, 244
175.26–176.13	XXIIIa 20–1	138.3–23	203, 244, 246, 290
177.30–2	XXIIIa 25	139.28–30	183
178.3–23	XXIIIa 26–7	139.38–140.14	23
178.33–4	XXIIIa 28	140.21–2	350, 361
179.1–5	XXIIIa 28	140.26–9	145, 238, 292
179	XXIIIa 29	140–1	52, 242, 244, 363
180.24	XXIIIa 31	141.34	53
180.33–4	XXIIIa 31	141.40–1	24
180.37–181.19	XXIIIa 33–4	142.1–21	183, 208, 238
181.20	XXIIIa 33–4	142.20–1	158, 183, 359
181.35–182.26	XXIIIa 35–6	142.32–143.9	175–6, 183, 204
182.27	XXIVa 1	143.10	175–6
182.28	XXIVa 1	143.10–11	350, 361
182–95	XXIVa 1–33	143–53	281, 307
183.34–184.2	XXIVa 4	144.8–14	122, 206, 238, 239
184.11–12	XXIVa 5	144.20–1	123, 238
187–8	XXIVa 14–15	147	207, 238
187.37–188.2	XXIV 14	147.17–21	123, 238
188.3–7	XXIVa 15	147.21–5	123, 237–8, 283
188.20–3	XXIVa 15	147.38–40	124, 237, 283
188–9	XXIVa 17	148	238, 283
189–93	XXIVa 19–30	148–52	238
191.26	XXIVa 24	150.16–17	124, 207, 238
191.36	XXIVa 25	150.26	124, 207
192.7	XXIVa 25	150.33–4	207, 238
192.14–20	XXIVa 26	151.1–6	124
193.4–9	XXIVa 28	151.26–8	124, 207, 238
194.1–3	XXIVa 30	152.12–14	125, 206, 239
194–5	XXIVa 31	152.15–16	126
194.30–1	XXIVa 32	152.38	25, 144, 207, 216, 237–9, 246, 274, 276, 292
194.32–4	XXIVa 32	152.39–40	126, 238–9, 276, 293

PL	LM	Sommer III	*Lancelot and the Grail*
195.10–17	XXIVa 33	153.9–15	126–7, 183, 206, 238–9
195.18–26	XXIVa 33–XXVa 1	153.16–23	6, 163, 175
195–6	XXVa 1–3	153–4	6, 27, 175, 204, 362
197.35	XXVa 6	155.2	349, 363
198.11	XXVa 7	155.9	349, 363
198.18–22	XXVa 7	155.15–18	127
198–9	XXVa 8–10	155–6	207, 240
198.32–8	XXVa 8	155.26–32	127
199.6–8	XXVa 9	155.36–8	127, 193
199.20–9	XXVa 10	156.6–13	27, 132
199.30–7	XXVa 10–XXVIa 1	156.13–20	163, 169, 175, 193
200	XXVIa 2–3	156–7	125, 206, 239
201.5–8	XXVIa 4	157.17	194
202.8–19	XXVIa 6–XXVIIa 1	158.3–13	194
202–4	XXVIIa 1–6	158–60	125, 307
204.12–23	XXVIIa 6	159.31–160.1	87
204.15–18	XXVIIa 6	159.34–6	87, 240
204.19–29	XXVIIa 6–XXVIIIa 1	159.37–160.7	183–4, 194
204.29–33	XXVIIIa 1	160.7–10	184, 239
205.15–19	XXVIIIa 3	160.26–9	130, 239–40
205–6	XXVIIIa 3–4	160–1	132, 214, 239, 283, 371
205.38–206.2	XXVIIIa 4	161.2–6	53, 66, 77, 132, 239, 283, 298, 305
206	XXVIIIa 5–6	161	206
206.15–16	XXVIIIa 5	161.14	125, 207
206–8	XXVIIIa 6–10	161–2	54, 203, 207, 239–40, 349, 363
207.12	XXVIIIa 8	162.3	125, 207, 240
207.34	XXVIIIa 9	162.20	307
208.16–20	XXVIIIa 11	162.35–7	184, 239
208	XXVIIIa 11–12	162–3	127, 207
209.1–5	XXVIIIa 12–XXIXa 1	163.9–15	163, 184
209.5–11	XXIXa 1	163.14–20	54, 184
209–14	XXIXa 1–15	163–7	125, 194, 240, 307
209.31–2	XXIXa 2	163.36–7	87, 240
213–14	XXIXa 12–13	166	203, 240, 244, 290
214.33–5	XXIXa 15	167.22–4	125, 206, 239
215.9	XXIXa 16	167.33–4	130, 239
215.12	XXIXa 16	167.35–6	130
215.13	XXIXa 16	167.36–7	240
215.27	XXIXa 16	168.6	125, 207, 240
215–16	XXIXa 17–18	168	54, 203, 207, 239–40, 303, 349, 363

PL	LM	Sommer III	*Lancelot and the Grail*
216.30	XXIXa 20	168.37–8	125, 207, 240
218.3–7	XXIXa 23	169.32–6	169, 175, 361
218.13–14	XXXa 1	169.42–170.1	54
218.18–28	XXXa 1–XXXIa 1	170.5–12	6, 165, 169, 175–6, 184, 239
218.37–219.2	XXXIa 1	170.17–21	62
219.3–5	XXXIa 2	170.21–3	194, 208
219.13–14	XXXIa 2	170.29–30	208, 240
219.23	XXXIa 3	170.35–6	130, 239
219.38–9	XXXIa 3	171.3–4	28, 30, 91, 130, 206, 212, 239–41
220.4–6	XXXIa 3	171.6–8	193, 204, 239, 361
220.7	XXXIa 4	171.8–9	241
220.8–15	XXXIa 4	171.8–13	90, 130, 239–41
220.20–1	XXXIa 4	171.17	204
220.21–5	XXXIa 4–XXXIIa 1	171.17–21	161, 165, 184, 194–5
220.31	XXXIIa 1	171.26–7	350, 361
221.2–11	XXXIIa 2	171.33–41	55, 62, 130, 240
221–3	XXXIIa 4–8	172–3	54, 202, 232, 244
223.21–3	XXXIIa 8	173.25–7	204, 329
223.24–6	XXXIIa 9	173.28	360
223–4	XXXIIa 10–11	173–4	203, 240
224.23–6	XXXIIa 12	174.16–19	28, 240
224–5	XXXIIa 12–14	174–5	205, 237, 240–1, 265
225.38–226.6	XXXIIa 15–XXXIIIa 1	175.15–21	161, 169, 193, 195, 203, 240
226.10–11	XXXIIIa 1	175.23–4	130, 214, 239
226.18–21	XXXIIIa 1	175.28–31	132, 239
226.23–34	XXXIIIa 2–3	175.33–41	28, 185, 195, 240, 319
227.11–15	XXXIIIa 4	176.12–15	205, 237, 240–1, 265, 319
228–9	XXXIIIa 7–8	177	90, 240
229.14–16	XXXIIIa 8–XXXIVa 1	177.29–31	185
229–30	XXXIVa 1–3	177–8	203
230.3–5	XXXIVa 3	178.9–10	28, 123, 329
230–4	XXXIVa 4–XXXVa 2	178–81	205, 239–40, 281
232.25–6	XXXIVa 10	180.9–10	206, 239
233	XXXIVa 11	180	6, 185, 195, 203, 239, 319
233.27	XXXVa 1	180.39	6
234.1–17	XXXVa 2	181	90, 240–1
234.18–39	XXXVa 3	181	239
235.1	XXXVa 4	181.34	349
235.12–13	XXXVa 5	181.41–2	130, 132, 239
235.23–4	XXXVa 5	182	239

PL	LM	Sommer III	*Lancelot and the Grail*
236.8–13	XXXVa 6–XXXVIa 1	182.21–6	185
236–7	XXXVIa 1–3	182–3	128, 185, 203, 207, 239–40
237–8	XXXVIIa 1–2	183–4	350
237.39	XXXVIIa 2	183.30	349, 363
239.4–8	XXXVIIa 5	184.21–4	29, 130, 239
239.20–3	XXXVIIa 6	184	239
239.34–240.5	XXXVIIa 7–8	184–5	239
240.13–33	XXXVIIa 9–10	185	128, 207, 239–40
241.9–12	XXXVIIa 10–		
	XXXVIIIa 1	185.34–7	169, 185, 203, 240
241–2	XXXVIIIa 1–2	186	240
242.3–8	XXXVIIIa 2	186.16–20	185, 203, 240
242.9	XXXIXa 1	186.21	161
242.17	XXXIXa 1	186.27	130
242–6	XXXIXa 1–9	186–9	131, 350
243.23–36	XXXIXa 4	187.19–27	203, 243, 290, 349, 351, 363
245.6–15	XXXIXa 7	188.22–9	203, 290, 351
246.6	XXXIXa 9	189.6	349, 363
246.24–6	XLa 1	189.18–20	186
248.27–9	XLa 5	190.37–8	206, 238–9
248–50	XLa 6–10	190–2	25, 129, 183, 206–7, 237–40, 293, 296
250.26–7	XLa 10	192.20–1	55
250.31–2	XLa 10	192.24	206, 307
250.30–9	XLa 10–XLIa 1	192.22–31	28, 157, 162, 186
250–2	XLIa 1–5	192–4	130, 350
253–6	XLIa 6–XLIIa 1	194–6	186, 205, 240
255.1–2	XLIa 10	195.27–8	34
255.32–3	XLIa 11	196.8–9	30, 130, 206, 239
256.9–18	XLIa 12	196.20–9	166, 186
256.20	XLIIa 1	196.30–1	157
256–7	XLIIa 2	196–7	30, 36, 166, 204, 206, 239, 306
257.8–9	XLIIa 1–XLIIIa 1	197.9–10	6, 186
258–60	XLIIIa 4–7	198–9	205, 237, 241, 265
260.15–17	XLIIIa 7	199.17–20	168–9
260.18–31	XLIVa 1	199.21–8	108, 261
260–2	XLIVa 1–4	199–200	91, 205, 228–9, 242, 246, 354, 363
262.19–28	XLIVa 4–XLVa 1	200.35–201.3	169, 176, 187, 350, 361
263.19–20	XLVa 2	201.23–4	56
263.32	XLVIa 1	201.33	176
264.30–4	XLVIa 3	202.19–23	87, 228, 242

PL	LM	Sommer III	*Lancelot and the Grail*
264.34–7	XLVIa 3	202.23–5	228
264.38–265.6	XLVIa 4–XLVIIa 1	202.25–33	161, 176, 187
265.11–15	XLVIIa 1	202.37–41	56, 207, 242, 282, 307
266–7	XLVIIa 4–6	203–4	242, 244, 363
267.16	XLVIIa 6	204.20–1	56, 242
267.18–268.23	XLVIIa 6–9	204.22–205.15	56, 207, 242, 351
270.35	XLVIIa 15	206.35	30, 130, 239, 241
270.38–9	XLVIIa 15	206.37	30, 242
271.10	XLVIIa 16	207.4	176
272.1–18	XLVIIa 17–18	207.26–39	31, 206, 212, 239, 241–2
272.20–32	XLVIIa 18–XLVIIIa 1	207.39–208.8	31, 161, 176, 187
273.3	XLVIIIa 1	208.16	214, 241
273–4	XLVIIIa 2–5	208–9	205, 237, 241, 265
275	XLVIIIa 7–8	209–10	188, 203, 209, 232, 241, 244, 265, 361
275–6	XLIXa 1	210	241
276	XLIXa 2	210–11	91–2, 205, 241
277	XLIXa 4	211	92, 205, 241
278–9	XLIXa 7	212	205, 241, 302
279–80	XLIXa 8–11	212–13	188, 203, 209, 232, 241, 244
281–2	XLIXa 13–16	214–15	188, 203, 205, 207, 241, 244, 257, 266, 301, 307, 363
282.32–283.4	XLIXa 17	215.21–30	92, 204–5, 241–2
283.5–10	XLIXa 17	215.31–5	204, 259, 354
283.19–21	XLIXa 18	216.1–3	242
283.21–33	XLIXa 18	216.3–14	94, 226
285.11–14	XLIXa 21	217.12–15	20, 32, 72, 219, 242, 259
285.28–286.4	XLIXa 22	217.26–36	94, 226–7
286.11–13	XLIXa 23	217.42–218.2	227
286.32–8	XLIXa 24	218.19–24	109
287–9	XLIXa 25–30	218–20	227, 370
289–92	XLIXa 31–40	220–3	93, 204–5, 242, 246
290.28–36	XLIXa 35	221.25–32	309
292.1–8	XLIXa 38	222.25–32	147–8, 292
293.1–15	XLIXa 41–2	223	241
293.17–19	XLIXa 42	223.31–4	95, 98, 257
293.27–9	XLIXa 43	223.39–40	204–5, 242
294.1	XLIXa 43 (different reading)	224.2	98, 205
294.3–10	XLIXa 43–La 1	224.4–12	161, 175, 188
294–6	La 1–8	224–6	203
296.1–2	La 6	225.28–9	67

PL	LM	Sommer III	*Lancelot and the Grail*
296.20–5	La 8	226.1–6	57, 67
296.28–35	La 8–LIa 1	226.8–15	175
296–7	LIa 1–2	226	33, 95, 188, 242–3, 290, 349
297–9	LIa 3–9	226–8	38, 204, 242–3, 290, 302, 349
297.20–4	LIa 3	226.35–9	33, 151, 243, 309, 359
297.25–35	LIa 3–4	226–7	241, 302
298.10–15	LIa 6	227.16–20	154, 156, 204, 210, 244
298.27–30	LIa 7	227.28–31	95–6, 156, 204, 210, 244
298.32–7	LIa 7	227.32–5	96, 241
298.39–299.12	LIa 8	227–8	204, 243
299.12–17	LIa 9	228.7–10	96, 189, 242
299.17–25	LIa 9–LIIa 1	228.9–16	34, 157, 188, 192–3, 204, 243
300.6–10	LIIa 2	228.31–5	96–7
301.4	LIIa 4	299.18	97
301.34	LIIa 7	229.41–2	92, 97
302.9–10	LIIa 7	230.8–10	97
302.26–303.24	LIIa 9–10	230–1	266
304.4–12	LIIa 12	231.26–33	97, 189, 317
304.12–19	LIIa 12	231.33–9	34, 97, 189, 204, 242
304–27	LIIa 13–70	231–49	205, 241
306.28–9	LIIa 19	233.28–9	83
307.21–39	LIIa 21	234	302
308.17–309.1	LIIa 23–5	234–5	203
309.1–33	LIIa 25–7	235	34, 207, 212, 241, 363
309.33–310.18	LIIa 27–8	235–6	92, 177
310.19–20	LIIa 29	236.22	207, 241, 363
311.5–10	LIIa 30	236.40–237.3	57, 207, 241, 363
311–20	LIIa 32–53	237–44	301
312.13–14	LIIa 33	237.39–40	57
312.22–8	LIIa 34	238.4–8	57–8
320.17–321.32	LIIa 53–6	244.5–245.2	290, 350
322.14–20	LIIa 57	245.21–6	98, 205, 242
324.33–325.24	LIIa 64–5	247	75, 98, 290, 350
326	LIIa 66–8	248	301
327.4–11	LIIa 68	248.42–249.7	99, 257
327.11–16	LIIa 69	249.7–11	99, 257
327–8	LIIa 69–71	249	99–100, 205, 242, 354, 243, 307
330–2	LIIa 77–81	251–2	257, 298
333.36–8	LIIa 84	253.33–5	74.
334.5–7	LIIa 85	253.38–41	74

PL	LM	Sommer III	*Lancelot and the Grail*
334.17–19	LIIa 85	254.5–7	74–5, 257, 290
334.22–4	LIIa 86	254.9–11	100
334.32–335.21	LIIa 86–7	254.17–38	62–3
336.1–30	LIIa 90–1	255	298, 304
336.31–2	LIIa 91	255.29–30	35
337.3–18	LIIa 91	255–6	63, 242, 245–6, 256
337.37–9	LIIa 93	256.22–4	75
338.36–8	LIIa 96	257.10–12	35
339.18–22	LIIa 97	257.24–6	35
339.33–6	LIIa 98	257.35–7	63
341–4	LIIa 102–7	259–60	125, 280
341.1–2	LIIa 101	258.30–1	58
341.4–5	LIIa 101	258.32–3	58
341.30–342.7	LIIa 102	259	51, 58
342.39–40	LIIa 104	259.36–7	125
343.5	LIIa 104	259.41	125
343.15–28	LIIa 105	260.6–18	131
344.11–12	LIIa 106	260.30–1	35, 296
344.17–18	LIIa 107	260.33–4	131
344.27–346.3	LIIa 107–9	261	51, 58–9, 212, 242, 298–9, 312, 318, 367
346.7–9	LIIa 110	261.40–1	63
346.9–11	LIIa 110	261.41–262.2	63
346.23–7	LIIa 111	262.11–14	63, 268
347–8	LIIa 113–15	263	63, 304, 312, 351–2
349.7–8	LIIa 115	264.2–3	100
349.13–15	LIIa 116	264.6–8	36
349.16–21	LIIa 116	264.8–12	36
349.21–5	LIIa 117	264.13–16	36
352.20–4	LIIa 123	266.17–21	67
355.35–356.6	LIIa 131–2	268.35–269.3	74, 190
356.13–18	LIIa 132–LIIIa 1	269.8–13	189, 203, 246, 361
356.20–7	LIIIa 1	269.14–21	245
357.7–14	LIIIa 3	269.35–270.2	86, 133, 209, 244–5
357.25–32	LIIIa 4	270.12–19	133, 244–5
358.2–6	LIIIa 5	270.26–9	190, 203, 244
358.7–18	LIIIa 6	270.29–39	14, 218, 237, 362
358.24–31	LIIIa 7	271	47, 153, 209, 246, 256, 267, 360
358.31–5	LIIIa 7–LIVa 1	271.5–8	6, 7, 189, 361
359.1–7	LIVa 1	271.12–18	189–90
359–61	LIVa 3–7	271–3	38–9, 242–3, 349

PL	LM	Sommer III	*Lancelot and the Grail*
361.23–31	LIVa 7	273.8–16	243
361.33–6	LIVa 7	273.16–19	243
361.37–362.4	LIVa 7	273.19–24	204, 242–4, 290, 302, 349
362.12–15	LIVa 8	273.31–4	243, 302
362.26–30	LIVa 9	273.41–274.3	88, 245
363.1–4	LIVa 10	274.11–13	243, 245
363.5	LIVa 10	274.14–15	204
363.14–34	LIVa 11–12	274.21–39	243, 302
364.6–9	LIVa 12–13	275.4–6	243, 302
364.14–19	LIVa 13	275.11–13	197
364.24–30	LIVa 14	275.17–22	204, 242, 290
364.30–365.5	LIVa 15	275	242–3, 245
365.9–11	LIVa 16	275.37–8	133, 245
365.27–9	LIVa 16	276.11–13	245
365.35–366.3	LIVa 17	276.18–22	38–9, 152, 154, 157, 162, 166, 193, 195, 243, 360
366.4–13	LVa 1	276.23–31	106, 159–60, 350, 361
367.1–2	LVa 3	277.13–14	106, 212
368–71	LVa 6–12	278–80	203, 212, 231, 244, 246, 283, 290, 363
371.32–8	LVa 13–LVIa 1	280.41–6	166–7, 195
372.25–9	LVIa 3	281.27–31	233, 244, 319
373.38	LVIa 6	282.31	50
374–5	LVIa 6–9	282–3	69, 231, 244–5, 362
375.9	LVIa 9	283.35	50
375.20–3	LVIa 10	284.4–6	68
375.32	LVIa 10	284.14–15	145
377–80	LVIa 14–22	285–7	23, 40, 231, 244–5, 319, 350, 363
377.11–14	LVIa 14	285.23–6	40, 200, 233
377.15–16	LVIa 14	285.26–8	40
383–6	LVIa 28–37	289–92	197, 231, 244, 319, 363
388.13–18	LVIa 41	293.39–294.1	234, 244, 307
388.24	LVIa 41	294.7	234, 307
389	LVIa 44–5	294–5	231, 244, 319, 363
390	LVIa 46–7	295.14–23	197
392.36–7	LVIa 51	297.14–16	69
393.25–31	LVIa 53–LVIIa 1	297.41–298.5	196
394.6	LVIIa 1	298.16	103
394.17–19	LVIIa 2	298.25–8	200, 233
396.22	LVIIIa 1	300.12	196

PL	LM	Sommer III	*Lancelot and the Grail*
401.13–14	LVIIIa 11	303.31–2	68–9
401–3	LVIIIa 13–16	304–5	39, 60, 134–5, 196, 204, 208, 244
404	LVIIIa 19	305–6	43, 139, 204, 211, 245, 362
405.23–5	LVIIIa 22	306.41–307.1	68
406–7	LVIIIa 24–6	307–8	154, 156, 158, 165, 176, 204, 244
407.8–12	LVIIIa 26–LIXa 1	308.10–14	165, 176, 197, 204
407.15–19	LIXa 1	308.17–19	135, 208, 215, 244
407.22–5	LIXa 1	308.21–3	217
407.25–7	LIXa 1	308.24–5	217
408–9	LIXa 3–5	309	110, 197, 204, 362
409.7–22	LIXa 6–LXa 1	309.27–40	103, 157, 193, 197, 350, 361
409.35–6	LXa 1	310.10–11	210
410–19	LXa 2–22	310–17	139, 234, 245, 284
418.18–19	LXa 20	316.18–19	100, 243, 354
418.24–6	LXa 20	316.24–6	103, 355
419.25–31	LXa 24	317.17–22	43
419.33–5	LXa 24	317.24–5	103, 105, 245, 362
419.39–420.6	LXa 25	317.27–31	106, 214, 245
420.9–13	LXa 25	317.35–7	42
420.13–30	LXa 25–6	317.37–318.9	43, 139, 197, 245, 362
420.37–8	LXa 26	318.15–16	42
421	LXa 28–9	318–19	139
422–3	LXa 30–3	319–20	211
423.36–424.3	LXa 34	320.25–31	245
424.12	LXa 35	320.38	67
424.15–17	LXa 35	320.41–321.1	67–8
424.35–425.15	LXa 37	321.15–29	196, 208
425.15–19	LXa 37–LXIa 1	321.29–32	165, 193, 198
425.19–20	LXIa 1	321.32–3	157, 198, 350, 361
425.22–426.14	LXIa 1–3	321–2	244, 363
426.15–432.35	LXIa 4–18	322–7	55, 202, 232, 244
426.39–427.1	LXIa 5	322.38–9	210
427.18–20	LXIa 6	323.10–12	103–4
428.30	LXIa 9	324.6	232, 244
433.16–19	LXIa 20	327.19–23	104
435.18	LXIa 24	328.40–1	157, 359
436–42	LXIa 27–41	329–34	67, 198, 245
442–4	LXIa 42–7	334–6	210, 355
445.17–18	LXIa 48	336.26	104
445–7	LXIa 49–52	336–8	104, 245, 355, 362, 373

UNIVERSITY OF WINCHESTER
LIBRARY

PL	LM	Sommer III	Lancelot and the Grail
447.30–3	LXIa 54	338.19–21	39
448.19–23	LXIa 55	339.1–4	212, 244
458.13–20	LXIa 79	346.28–34	234, 244
461.30–462.1	LXIa 86–7	349.17–25	198, 213, 244
462.5–7	LXIa 87	349.30–1	198
462.18–35	LXIa 88–9	349.42–350.20	198
463–4	LXIa 91–3	350–1	233, 355
465.32–466.5	LXIa 95	352.18–24	107
466–7	LXIa 96–9	352–3	233, 245
467.32–3	LXIa 99	353.26–8	245
468.1–2	LXIa 100	353.33–4	374
468.17–24	LXIa 101	354.6–11	245
471–2	LXIa 109–LXIIa 1	356–7	190, 199, 203, 232, 244
473	LXIIa 1–3	357–8	14, 362
474.34–8	LXIIIa 3	358.32–5	105, 362
475	LXIIIa 4	359	213
475.21–8	LXIIIa 4	359.10–15	245, 362
475–6	LXIIIa 5–6	359–60	24, 105, 213, 245, 362
476.29–31	LXIIIa 7	360.5–7	203, 349, 363
477.10–19	LXIIIa 7–8	360.21–6	103, 105, 245, 362
477.21–6	LXIIIa 8	360.27–32	105, 245, 362
478.11–16	LXIIIa 10	361.6–11	208, 244
478.31	LXIIIa 11	361.23	362
479	LXIIIa 12–13	362	245, 362
481.6–13	LXIIIa 15	363.4–10	24, 105, 213, 244–5, 362
482.36	LXIIIa 19	364.18	349, 363
483.24	LXIIIa 20	364.37–8	245
486–508	LXIIIa 22–LXIVa 36	365–82	140, 245, 266
488	LXIIIa 32	368	245, 362
493	LXIVa 1	372	14, 168, 361–2
495–6	LXIVa 6–8	373–4	122, 138, 213–14, 243, 283, 362
496.36–9	LXIVa 9	374	302
499.35–7	LXIVa 15	376.30–2	203, 349, 363
501	LXIVa 18–19	377	138, 209, 244
501.27–31	LXIVa 20	378.2–7	106, 245
502.7	LXIVa 21	378.18–19	350, 361
503.26	LXIVa 25	379.20	349, 363
503.35–504.6	LXIVa 25–6	379.26–33	87, 213, 244, 362
504.16–38	LXIVa 26–7	379.39–380.13	198, 213, 244
506.11–15	LXIVa 30	381.8–13	101, 353
506–14	LXIVa 32–51	381–7	233

PL	LM	Sommer III	*Lancelot and the Grail*
513.13	LXIVa 48	386.12	307
513–14	LXIVa 50	386	266
514.31–2	LXIVa 51	387.12–13	245
515.9–16	LXIVa 52	387.27–30	245
515.29–516.17	LXIVa 53–LXVa 2	387.35–388.19	199
516–17	LXVa 3–5	388–9	203, 244
519.10–15	LXVa 8	390.14–19	69, 237, 243
519.17–20	LXVa 9	390.20–3	69
519.22–4	LXVa 9	390.24–6	69
519.26–31	LXVa 9	390.28–32	70
519.35–7	LXVa 10	390.36–8	70
520.2–5	LXVa 10	390.41–391.2	233
521.14–17	LXVa 13	391.38–40	70
521.34–7	LXVa 14	392.13–15	70
522.26	LXVa 16	392.37	145
524.30–525.2	LXVa 20–1	394.12–22	198
525	LXVIa 1–3	394–5	14, 362
526.4–5	LXVIIa 1	395.15–16	157, 350, 561
526–7	LXVIIa 1–4	395	209, 244, 362
527–8	LXVIIa 6	396	203, 243, 290, 351
528.24–5	LXVIIa 7	397.11–12	244
528.29	LXVIIa 8	397.15–16	100, 243, 354
529.4–27	LXVIIIa 1–2	397.27–398.13	198, 362
529.30–1	LXVIIIa 3	398.15–17	244
530.9–13	LXVIIIa 4	398	244
530.14	LXVIIIa 4	398.33	307
530.15–28	LXVIIIa 4	398.34–399.1	140, 204, 234, 245
531.5–13	LXVIIIa 6–LXIXa 1	399.12–19	163, 245, 361
531.21–3	LXIXa 1	399.24–6	37, 244
532.13–23	LXIXa 3–LXXa 1	400.8–17	163, 175, 199, 204, 244, 362
532.28–533.4	LXXa 1–2	400.21–32	140, 206, 244
535–6	LXXa 9–10	402–3	244, 307, 363
537	LXXa 12	403	14, 43, 203, 234, 243, 290, 306, 362
538.31–3	LXXa 16	405.3–4	44, 46
539.6–7	LXXa 17	405.13	44
539	LXXa 18	405	7, 205
539.29–31	LXXa 18	405.30–2	234, 245, 284
540.1–15	LXXa 19	405.39–406.4	140, 206, 244
540.22–3	LXXa 20	406.10–11	101
540.26–9	LXXa 20	406.13–16	72, 140, 260, 357
540–1	LXXa 21–2	406	245

PL	LM	Sommer III	*Lancelot and the Grail*
541.15–16	LXXa 22	406.33–4	245
541.35–7	LXXa 23	407.8–10	72, 140, 260
542–3	LXXa 26–8	407–8	14, 362
543	LXXa 28	408	64
545–6	LXXa 31–4	409–10	14, 362
547.3–25	LXXa 35–6	411.4–20	64, 70, 136, 208, 215, 244
547.25–8	LXXa 36	411.20–2	64
548–9	LXXa 37–41	411–12	140, 206, 244, 362
549.14–15	LXXa 41	412.32–3	217, 266
551–7	LXXIa 1–17	414–19	164, 190, 282, 352
552.4–9	LXXIa 2	414.34–8	140
553–4	LXXIa 6–7	415–16	136, 208, 217, 244, 282
554	LXXIa 8	416–17	208, 243
555.18–27	LXXIa 9	417	208, 244, 282
555.28–30	LXXIa 9	417.28–31	61, 352
556.3–4	LXXIa 10	418.3–4	137, 208, 243
556.14–16	LXXIa 11	418.10–12	137, 208, 244
556.17–21	LXXIa 12	418.12–16	137, 244
556.21–3	LXXIa 12	418.16–18	137, 208, 283
556.23–8	LXXIa 12	418.18–22	137, 367
556.28–9	LXXIa 12	418.22–3	137
556.29–36	LXXIa 12–13	418.23–9	134, 137, 208, 287
556.37–557.20	LXXIa 13–14	418.30–419.9	50, 66, 77, 137, 263, 298, 300, 306, 318, 367
558.2–6	LXXIa 16	419.27–31	64, 268
558.8–11	LXXIa 16	419.31–5	64
558.16–21	LXXIa 17	419.39–420.1	64–5, 304
563	LXXIa 28–9	423	221
564.15–18	LXXIa 31	424.14–16	136, 140, 208
565	LXXIa 35	425	307
566.17–21	LXXIa 36	425.39–42	44–5, 204, 306
566.24–5	LXXIa 36	426.1–2	44, 294
567.32	LXXIa 39	426.37	357
568.1–3	LXXIa 40	427.1–2	140
568.6	LXXIa 40	427.5	357
568–9	LXXIa 42	427	75, 245–6
569.11–15	LXXIa 43	427.38–428.1	44–5
569.16–17	LXXIa 43	428.1–2	45
569.29–30	LXXIa 44	428.9–10	45
570–1	LXXIa 46–7	428–9	65, 75, 245–6

PL	LM	Sommer III	*Lancelot and the Grail*
571	LXXIa 48–9	429	152–4, 156–7, 204, 211, 234–5, 245–6, 301, 360
572.2–4	LXXIa 49	430.4–6	5, 7, 8, 164, 190

PL	*LM* vol. III	Sommer IV	*Lancelot and the Grail*
572.4–5	I 1	3.1–3	164–5, 190, 203, 246
572.19–24	I 2	3.16–21	76
572.28–30	I 2	3.24–6	76, 100, 245–6
572.31–4	I 3	3.27–4.2	254
573.1–35	I 3–4	4	76, 245, 254, 290
574	I 6	365–6	73, 230, 246, 254, 256–7
575–7	I 7–10	366–7	205, 229, 254, 355
577–8	I 12	368	100, 246, 254
578.28–30	I 13	368.29–32	205, 246, 254
579–80	I 14–17	368–9	362
580–3	I 18–22	370–2	76, 93–4, 100, 205, 211, 229, 245–6, 254, 256, 258, 354, 363
584.1–4	I 22–II 1	372.22–5	191
584–6	II 1–6	372–4	46, 246, 254, 319
587–90	II 7–14	374–7	46, 254
591–2	II 15–16	377–8	71
592.28–38	II 17	378.37–379.3	71
594	II 20	380	204
595.21–3	II 22	381.2–3	78, 263
596.9–12	II 23	381.23–6	65, 191
596.21	II 23	381.33	50
596.34–8	III 1	382.2–4	108–9
598.10–13	III 3	383.4–7	365
599.36–7	III 7	384.15–16	45
602.15–29	III 13	386.6–17	46, 254
602–3	III 14	386	203–4, 246, 254
603.2–4	III 14	386.27–9	61
604.1–3	IV 2	387.17–18	50, 61
605.18	IV 4	388.17	5
605.35–6	IV 5	388.28–30	246
606.16–18	IV 7	389.12–14	65, 204, 254
608.16	IV 13	390.34	65
608.25	IV 14	390.41	46, 204, 254

PL	LM	Sommer IV	Lancelot and the Grail
609.14–19	IV 16	391.18–21	65–6
609.25–7	IV 17	391.26–8	75, 288
609.29–611	IV 18–22	391–3	47, 138–9, 159, 191, 204, 209, 217–18, 237, 246, 254, 256
611.35–6	IV 21	393.5–7	48, 153, 161, 210, 246, 352
611.38–612.3	IV 23	393.9–13	47, 153, 156, 191, 210–11
612.12–15	IV 22–3	393	5, 153, 164, 191, 210, 360
612.18–613.3	IV 23–4	393	77, 205, 211, 245–6, 254, 256
613.4–11	IV 24	—	160, 211, 246, 254, 352

References to the cyclic romance

LM Long Version	LM Short Version	Sommer IV	Lancelot and the Grail
I 1–3	—	—	257
II 2	—	—	257
II 3	—	—	257
II 8	—	—	258
II 9	—	—	258
II 10	—	—	279
II 11	—	—	257
II 14		6	257, 365
II 17		6–7	257
II 20		7	258
II 25		9	258
II 27		9	258
III 18		14–15	260
IV 25		23	257, 259, 270
IV 34–5		26	270, 279, 368
IV 37		26	262, 368
IV 38		27	368
IV 39		27	271, 368
IV 40–2		27	259, 368
IV 44		28	262
IV 45		28	259, 262
IV 49		29–30	258
IV 64		34	258
V 3		35	258
V 6		36	259
V 10		36	264
V 12		37	259
VI 31		48	264

LM Long Version	*LM* Short Version	Sommer IV	*Lancelot and the Grail*
VI 36	VI 36 n.d	50.8–10	260–1, 365
VI 38		50	261
VII 22		55	260
VII 24		55	260
VIII 15		59–60	262
VIII 17–19		60–1	261
VIII 44–5		66	261, 266
VIII 55	VIII 55	69–70	260, 365
VIII 56–60		70–1	262
IX 1	IX 1–3	72 n.1	261, 263
IX 2	—	72 n.1	263–4
IX 4		73	260–1
IX 5		—	260–1, 365
IX 5–6	IX 5	73	260
IX 13		76	260–1
IX 14	—	—	261
IX 22		79	260
IX 28–9		81	261
IX 33	—	—	265
IX 34	—	—	258
IX 43	—	—	259
XII 1–5		92–3	265
XIII 1–14		93–6	265, 362, 365
XV 4		102	267
XVI 31–43		107–8	267
XVII 13	—	—	266
XVII 14	—	—	266
XVIII 3	—	—	256, 267
XVIII 6–7	XVIII 11	104	269
XIX 1–6		100	266
XIX 8–9		101	266
XX 10–15		110	267
XX 18–21		111	267
XXII 1		117	268
XXIV 17		120	266
XXIV 28	—	—	266
XXIV 35		123	268
XXIV 36–7		123	268
XXVI 5		127	266
XXVI 27	—	—	269
XXVI 28	—	—	269
XXVI 29	—	—	269

LM Long Version	*LM* Short Version	Sommer IV	*Lancelot and the Grail*
XXVI 32–7		128–9	269, 365
XXIX 10	10–11	140–1	269
XXIX 13	—	—	266
XXXVI 5–6		156–7	290
XXXVI 10–11		158	290
XXXVII 3	—	—	286
XXXVII 27		175	297
XXXVII 28	XXXVII 32	175	274, 297
XXXVII 29	—	—	274–5, 297
XXXVII 32	—	—	274
XXXVII 36		175	270, 297
XXXVII 37		176	270, 275, 297
XXXVII 38–41	XXXVII 39–40	176–7	270, 275–6, 297, 368
XXXIX 20	—	—	270
XLV 21		248	283
XLV 31		250	283, 287
XLV 36–7		251	283, 287
XLVII 8–18		256–8	284
XLVII 28–31		260–2	284
XLVII 45	—	—	284
XLVIII 21		269	284
XLVIII 24		269–70	285
XLVIII 25		270	285, 287
XLIX 12–13		277	283
XLIX 13–14		277–8	287
L 22		288	368
L 26–9		289	360
L 44		292–3	289–90
L 46		293	290
LI		297–300	286
LX 11–15		320–1	290
LXV 25		339	276
LXV 32		341	276
LXVI 4–8		342	279
LXVI 36–8		348–9	307

LM Long Version	*LM* Short Version	Sommer V	*Lancelot and the Grail*
LXXIII 2		59	277
LXXIV 6		65	287
LXXIV 10		66	286
LXXVI 34		82–3	367

LM Long Version	*LM Short Version*	*Sommer V*	*Lancelot and the Grail*
LXXVIII 34		102	289
LXXVIII 46		106	279
LXXVIII 49–			
LXXIX 4		109–12	276, 279, 284–5, 370
LXXIX 17–19		117–18	368
LXXIX 24		120	287, 360
LXXX 3–5		125–6	290
LXXXI 17		143	277
LXXXI 22		145	360
LXXXIII 4–8		149–50	277
LXXXIII 12		151	277
LXXXIV 72		191–2	278
LXXXV 2		193	278
LXXXV 3		193	278–9
LXXXV 4		194	368
LXXXV 8		195	290
LXXXV 53		210	288
LXXXVI 21		217–18	281, 312
LXXXVI 22		218	281, 312
LXXXVI 23		218	281, 312
XCI 30	—	—	287
XCIII 22		248	279–80
XCIII 33–4		251	280, 284
XCIV 7		257–8	288
XCIV 17		260	288–9
XCV 7–9		265	369
XCV 30		272	289
XCV 33		272	289
XCV 38		274	369
XCV 46		276	289
XCVII 6		291	368
XCVIII 42		301	286
XCIX 25–6		309–10	368
C 25	—	—	282
C 49		325	288
CI 8		332	368
CI 13		334	284
CII 18		340	360
CIII 6		343	288
CIV 42		353	288
CIV 51		355–6	287, 360
CIV 52		356	287

LM Long Version	LM Short Version	Sommer V	*Lancelot and the Grail*
CV 4		370	289
CV 20		374	289
CV 27		377	287, 360
CV 28		377	288
CV 38		380–1	282
CVI 3–4	—	—	283
CVI 5	cf. CVI 5	382	283
CVI 39		390–1	290
CVI 40		391	283
CVII 1–30		393–400	282
CVII 46		403	283
CVIII 6–8		406–7	290

Queste	*Lancelot and the Grail*
3.6–11	371
3.25–32	291
7.25–8	292
8.25–6	293
9.6–9	294
10.22–8	294
10.33–11.2	294
11.7–11	294
11.18–21	294
12.31–13.6	295
14.26–30	295
19.19–26	370
20.8–13	295
20.21–8	296
21–2	302
23	302
35–40	296
36.24–6	296
38.21	296
39.19–21	296–7
54	302
61.16–17	299
62.9–19	297
65–6	298
66	279, 298–9, 312
67.5–9	299
67.18–70.25	299, 302, 370

Queste	*Lancelot and the Grail*
78.19–21	369
118.10–15	299
123–5	300, 370
125.26–126.11	300
126.23–7	300
136.18–24	301
138	370
141.13–18	301
143.7–11	301
147.6–10	301–2
147.22	302
149	283
155–7	283
197.18–20	302
221–8	292
228.20–4	371
251–2	370
264.4–7	297
265.16–19	297

Mort Artu	*Lancelot and the Grail*
3.38–43	302
4	304
20	306
23	306
24	306
27.23–8	306
30	259, 306
51–3	303–4
59	305, 371
70.23–4	302
85.33–9	304–5
87.66–7	306
90.87–92	304
96.31–4	307
104.42–5	307
110.46–52	307
116.5–13	307
120	307
131.12–15	307
145.37–40	306

Mort Artu	*Lancelot and the Grail*
151.19	307
153–5	307
157	306
178.35–8	365
203.14–19	308

Notes

Only abbreviated bibliographical details are given of works that are listed in full in the Bibliography.

Introduction

1. E. Brugger, 'L'Enserrement Merlin'.
2. J. D. Bruce, 'The Composition of the Old French Prose *Lancelot*'; *Evolution of Arthurian Romance.*
3. A. Pauphilet, *Le Legs du Moyen Âge*, pp. 212–17.
4. F. Lot, *Étude sur le Lancelot en prose.* The term *Lancelot propre* is used to describe volumes III, IV, and V of Sommer's edition.
5. J. Frappier, *Étude sur la Mort le roi Artu*, in particular the appendix to the 2nd edition, 'Genése et unité de structure du Lancelot en prose (*essai de mise au point*)'. See also 'Plaidoyer pour l'"Architecte", contre une opinion d'Albert Pauphilet sur le *Lancelot en prose*'. J. Neale Carman presents a complicated, ingenious, but unconvincing variation on Frappier's theory according to which a 'powerful and resourceful chairman' guided 'an ideologically diversified group in the making of a complex plan' (*A Study of the Pseudo-Map cycle*, p. 97). He considers that Robert de Boron's *Joseph* and the *Perlesvaus* represent false starts by members of the group.
6. A. Micha, 'L'esprit du *Lancelot-Graal*', and 'Sur la composition du *Lancelot en prose*'.

Chapter I

1. For details see E. Kennedy, *Lancelot do Lac*, II, pp. 29–31, 378–80.
2.
> Issi, vos en feré le conte
> Non pas rimé, qui an droit conte
> Si com li livres Lancelot
> Ou il n'a de rime un seul mot
> Por mielz dire la verité
> Et por tretier sanz fauseté.

This reference to a book in prose about Lancelot occurs in a rhymed preface in a British Library MS (Add. 21212) which P. Meyer considered was probably written shortly after 1226. See P. Meyer, 'Mélanges de poésie française', p. 498.
3. Robert de Boron's work is usually assigned to the end of the twelfth or the early thirteenth century: see P. Le Gentil in *ALMA*, p. 253, and A. Micha, *Étude sur le 'Merlin' de Robert de Boron*, p. 9 n. 16, for brief analyses of the various theories. The short version of the *First Perceval Continuation* is usually given a date early in the thirteenth century; according

to its editor, W. Roach, it was probably influenced by Robert de Boron; see *Les Romans du Graal*, pp. 117–18.

4. For a detailed analysis of the various theories on the date of the *Perlesvaus*, see T. E. Kelly, *Le Haut Livre du Graal*, pp. 9–15.

Chapter II

1. 'L'aventure, c'est la quête de l'identité', J. Le Goff, Introduction to E. Köhler, *L'Aventure chevaleresque*, p. xvi. See also F. Wolfzettel, 'Zur Stellung und Bedeutung der Enfances in der altfranzösischen Epik', *Zeitschrift für neufranzösische Sprache und Litteratur*, 84 (1974), pp. 1–32. U. Ruberg explores the role of the search for the hero's name in the structure of the Prose *Lancelot* in both French and German versions, 'Die Suche im *Prosa Lancelot*'. H. Schwake, 'Zur Frage der Namenssymbolik im höfischen Roman', *Germanisch-Romanische Monatschrift*, 51, Neue Folge 20 (1970), p. 352, suggests that the late naming of the hero in Arthurian romance should be interpreted as the winning of a name, to which is opposed the losing of one, especially in terms of temporary loss of name and regaining of it. Jacques Roubaud, 'Enfances de la prose', pp. 355–60, emphasizes the part played by the naming theme in giving coherence to the branch of the Prose *Lancelot* corresponding to *S* III. He presents the enigma of Lancelot's name in terms of 'cette fatalité du nom, à la fois malédiction, tabou, secret, possession dangereuse et constamment égarée, incertaine, impossible' (p. 360). I do not think that the theme has these dark and sinister overtones in the non-cyclic romance; but, as will be seen in Part II of this study, once the *Lancelot-Grail* cycle has been created, these early adventures can be reinterpreted and the mystery of Lancelot's name linked to a loss of name rather than a winning one. E. Soudek, 'Die Funktion der Namensuche und der Zweikämpfe in Ulrich von Zatzikhovens *Lanzelet*', *Amsterdamer Beiträge zur älteren Germanistik*, 2 (1972), pp. 173–85, discusses the importance of the quest for a name in the *Lanzelet*.

2. P. Märtens, 'Zur Lanzelotsage', lists resemblances between the *Lanzelet* and the prose *Lancelot*. See also W. Richter, *Der Lanzelet des Ulrich von Zatzikhoven* and, for a comparison of the narrative structures in Chrétien's *Chevalier de la Charrette*, the *Lanzelet*, and the Prose *Lancelot*, see W. Haug, *Das Land, von welchem niemand wiederkehrt*.

3. J. Weston, *The Legend of Sir Lancelot du Lac*, pp. 94–6, discusses possible cross-influences between the Lancelot and Perceval stories. *Erec, Yvain, Char., Perc., Lanz., LBD,* and the *PL* all provide variations on the theme of the making or remaking of a name and the testing of a champion. On the theme of the Fair Unknown, see E. Brugger, ' "Der Schöne Feigling" in der arthurischen Literatur'; C. Luttrell, *The Creation of the First Arthurian Romance*; W. H. Schofield, *Studies on the Libeaus Desconnus*.

4. See W. H. Jackson, 'Ulrich von Zatzikhoven's *Lanzelet* and the theme of resistance to royal power', *German Life and Letters*, 28 (1975), pp. 285–97, for an interesting examination of the theme of the tyrannical king and possible parallels with both the experiences of the Morville family, one of whom gave Ulrich the French version of his tale, and the German literary tradition of the twelfth and thirteenth centuries.

5. *Lanz.* 4706–10.

6. *Perc.* 466–7.

7. *Perc.* 435–54.

8. Benoyc/Genewis has been identified by Lot, *Étude*, pp. 147–8, n. 8, with Gwynedd (North Wales). Brugger, *Festschrift Heinrich Morf*, pp. 53–96, identifies Genewis/Benoyc/Gomeret with Old Breton Guenet (Vannes) and regards Gaunes as a variant of Guenet. See also Carman, *A Study of the Pseudo-Map Cycle*, pp. 1–16.

9. Claudas de la Deserte had already made a brief appearance in the *2nd Cont.*, 29652, 31304–403. See Chapter IV, p. 81, and Appendix I.

10. For a different view see M. P. Cosman, *The Education of the Hero in Arthurian Romance*, p. 115, who would suggest that the father's warlike character in *Lanz.* derives from Wolfram's *Parzival*.

11. J. Frappier, 'L' "Institution" de Lancelot dans le *Lancelot en prose*'.

12. See Chapter V and E. Kennedy, 'The role of the supernatural in the First Part of the Prose *Lancelot*'.

13. Cf. G. Duby, *The Chivalrous Society* (London, 1977), p. 184: 'What was it that set the knight apart from the upstart? The latter was careful over money, but the former was noble because he spent all he had, light-heartedly, and because he was deeply in debt.' See also Raoul de Hodenc, *Le Roman des Eles*, ed. K. Busby, Utrecht Publications in General and Comparative Literature, vol. 17 (Amsterdam and Philadelphia, 1983), lines 150–266, for a discussion of *largece* as a knightly quality.

14. See Chapter IV and E. Kennedy, 'Social and political ideas in the French Prose *Lancelot*'.

15. See also Chapters VIII and IX. The pattern continues in the cyclic romance; see A. Micha, 'Sur la composition du *Lancelot en prose*'.

16. There are three major royal broodings: *PL* 137–8, 296–7, 359–61; and two minor ones (at Dolorous Guard): *PL* 206, 215. Cf. *Perc.* 907–11, 9216–23, *1st Cont.* III, *A* 3362–699. See E. Kennedy, 'Royal broodings and lovers' trances in the First Part of the Prose *Lancelot*'.

17. See also Chapter VIII for an analysis of the technique of repetition with variation and Chapter IV for the role of Arthur and his court.

18. Cf. *Char.* 3660–1, where we learn Lancelot's name from the Queen.

19. *LBD* and the *PL* have the following elements in common: a messenger arrives at Arthur's court to fetch a champion for his lady; the unknown youth proposes himself; the messenger doubts his quality as champion; he undergoes a series of tests on the way to the battle; the mission is successfully accomplished.

20. Cf. a rather similar episode in *1st Cont.* III, *A* 8412–600. There is also a kind of parallel in the *Vengeance Raguidel* (of uncertain date in relation to the *PL*) 125–9, 187–94, 221–6.

21. Note once again the interplay with Chrétien's work through variation on a known theme. In *Char.* 2211–43, those who see Lancelot fight are astonished at his success because they know him only as the knight who mounted the degrading cart.

22. See for example *Erec*, 3963–4132, and *Perc.* 4294–500, where Kay fails to bring back a knight by force to Arthur, and Gauvain succeeds by courtesy.

23. See *PL* 297–8, 361–5.

24. Gauvain gives his name: *PL* 197.35, 198.11, 235.1, 237.39, 243.32, 246.6, 482.36, 503.26; he gives his name, declaring that it has never been concealed: *PL* 476.29–32, 499.35–7. Cf. *Lanz.* 2492–4; *Perc.* 5621–5; *1st Cont.* III, *A* 1664–8; *2nd Cont.* 29320–5, 30681–5. In some

texts, *LBD* for example, to complete the contrast the Unknown Knight is Gauvain's own son.

25. See *PL* 236–8, 242–6, 250–2; *Perc.* 7061–144, 7285–311.

26. The contrast between Gauvain and Perceval has been interpreted in a number of different ways. See, for example, W. Kellerman, *Aufbaustil und Weltbild Chrestiens von Troyes im Percevalroman* (Halle, 1936); J. Frappier, *Chrétien de Troyes et le mythe du Graal* (Paris, 1972); P. Haidu, *Aesthetic Distance in Chrétien de Troyes: Irony and Comedy in Cligès and Perceval* (Geneva, 1968); K. Busby, *Gauvain in Old French Literature* (Amsterdam, 1980). I think that critics tend to overemphasize a contrast between a spiritual Perceval and a worldly Gauvain; I would see rather an opposition between a young and inexperienced unknown knight and an experienced well-known one in which both are shown at times in comic situations.

27. See, for example, Gauvain's problems with the dwarf on the way to Roestoc, *PL* 377–81.

28. See *LBD* 593–828.

29. The contrast between the public humiliation of the knight and the admiration then evoked by his historic exploit would arouse memories of the situation in Chrétien, where Lancelot is received with scorn as the knight of the shameful cart, but also celebrated as the knight whose exploits show him to be the awaited deliverer.

30. *Lanz.* 2760–3405; *Cligés*, 4552–860. See J. Delcourt-Angélique, 'Le motif du tournoi de trois jours avec changement de couleur destiné à préserver l'incognito'. *An Arthurian Tapestry: essays in memory of Lewis Thorpe*, ed. K. Varty (Glasgow, 1981), pp. 160–86. She studies the use of the theme in *Cligés*, *Lanzelet*, and *Ipomedon* and gives a full bibliography.

31. For the royal broodings see note 16 above. For the narrative sequence after the brooding, cf. *2nd Cont.* 29024–208. The closest parallel for the passage leading up to the listing of companions on the quest is with *1st Cont.* III, *A* 3362–699, but the names correspond more closely with the list in *Erec*, 1672–710 (see also W. Foerster's edition of the text (Halle, 1934), 1692–750, which has more names in common with the *PL* and with that in the *2nd Cont.* 29024–66.

32. There are episodes in *Lanz.* 3072–431 and *1st Cont.* III, *A* 6290–406, 6536–9, which have features in common with this incident. See note to *PL* 320.17–328.9.

33. *1st Cont.* III, *A* 3362–699.

34. K. Busby would seem to see a parallel between Gauvain's 'inability to adhere single-mindedly to a particular course of action', which he considers to be one of his character-istics in other texts, and the interruption to his quest for Lancelot when he 'commits himself to a subsidiary quest for the identity of a knight who meekly allows himself to be belaboured by a dwarf' (*Gauvain in Old French Literature*, pp. 322–3). I think that the sequence of adventures presenting themselves to Gauvain during his quest for Lancelot should be interpreted in a different way, in accordance with the principle of analogy underlying the system of medieval interlace, as is shown in Chapters II and III of this study. The types of adventure undertaken are significant in relation to the development of the main themes of identity and love rather than to the characterization of Gauvain. The 'constant references to lack of adventure' (see VII, n. 21 for a list) are linked in the non-cyclic romance not to a 'lack of grace' (Busby, p. 32), but to the criteria of relevance to the tale of Lancelot (see Chapters VI and VII); in the *Queste* the irrelevance of most of the

knights' activities in relation to the search for the Grail is explicitly associated with lack of grace, but that connection is not made here.

35.   *Z. f. rom. Phil.* 63 (1943), p. 323 n.2; C. Luttrell, *The Creation of the First Arthurian Romance*, pp. 87–92, 264–8.

36.   *PL* 243.23–36, 245.6–15, 527–8, 536–7. See also Chapter VIII, p. 234 and n. 43.

37.   Cf. *Trist.* 889–94 and 1165–72. For further discussion of parallels with the Tristan story see Chapter III, pp. 65, 71–2 and n. 8.

38.   The *Merlin* continuations of the Vulgate cycle, *S* II, p. 92, and of the *Huth Merlin,* ed. G. Paris and J. Ulrich, SATF (Paris, 1886), vol. II, pp. 61–8, endeavour to reconcile the Robert de Boron version and that given here.

Chapter III

1.   Voss writes of the description of the young Lancelot, with his very large chest, and of Guinevere's comment that its apparently disproportionate size was necessary to contain his extra-large heart:

> In die Sprache der wissenschaftlichen Analyse übersetzt, kann dies nur bedeuten: Lancelot erfüllt das Ideal, das er repräsentiert, vollkommen, doch enthält dieses Ideal selbst eine Aporie, die es als absolutum bereits von innen her erschüttert, ehe es noch im direkten Vergleich mit dem sich allmählich zur 'Queste' hin enthüllenden Ideal geistlichen Rittertums von höherer Warte aus verworfen wird. (*Der Prosa-Lancelot*, p. 65)

Such an interpretation of the description as itself casting doubt from within on the ideal it represents could be *read back* into the passage only when it has been placed in a *Lancelot-Grail* framework, as will be seen in Part Two of this study. Within the context of the non-cyclic romance the size of Lancelot's heart, and hence chest, accords with the emphasis given by the young Lancelot to the virtues of the heart as opposed to those of the body (see Chapter II above and *PL* 110.34–111.3, 141.23–142.4). The appropriateness to the heroic proportions of the heart of what in another would be a disproportionately large chest also corresponds to the appropriateness of a certain lack of *mesure* in a great lover.

2.   M. P. Cosman, *The Education of the Hero in Arthurian Romance*, p. 121, n. 49, connects the *joie* in *PL* 40.35–9 only with exultation expressed through music, but she does not attempt to explain the phrase 'ainz lo disoit de la grant seürté qu'il avoit en ce dont tote sa joie venoit'. She does not appear to realize that this description of Lancelot does not relate only to the young boy in the Lake, but also to the knight and lover which he is to become.

3.   See E. Kennedy, 'Social and political ideas in the French Prose *Lancelot*'.

4.   See E. Kennedy, 'Royal broodings and lovers' trances in the First Part of the Prose *Lancelot*'.

5.   See also the meeting of Lancelot and Guinevere, when Daguenet brings him back as prisoner and he is so overcome when he hears the Queen speak that he lets his lance fall (*PL* 267–8).

6.   This would appear to be the reading central to the manuscript tradition, although some manuscripts read *il la besa,* instead of *ele lo baisoit.* In all manuscripts the sentences

leading up to this point present Guinevere as taking the initiative. See notes and variants to *PL* 348.30.

7.   Cf. W. Foerster's edition of the *Chevalier de la Charrette*, 208–21. In the *PL* Bademaguz of Gorre fights on the side of Galehot against Arthur, and another Bademaguz, learned clerk of King Arthur, appears in the part of the romance known as the Journey to Sorelois, immediately preceding the False Guinevere episode. The use of the name Bademaguz at this point would remind the reader of Lancelot's rescue of the Queen from danger in Chrétien's poem, where Bademaguz is father of Meleagant; it is also appropriate (with its *-magus* element) for an interpreter of visions who takes over part of the role of Merlin in Geoffrey of Monmouth, Wace, and Robert de Boron. For the origin of the name in Chrétien see E. Kennedy, 'King Arthur in the First Part of the Prose *Lancelot*', p. 194, n. 4.

8.   The False Guinevere alleges that there has been a substitution in the bridal bed. This would recall the episode in the Tristan story in which Brengain is substituted for Iseut in the bridal bed. See also Carman, in *A Study of the Pseudo-Map Cycle*, pp. 55–9, who regards the episode as a modification of the folk theme of the substitute wife in terms of reminiscences of recent historical events.

9.   See *1st Cont.* III, *A* 1648–733; see also Gauvain and the sister of Guingambresil in *Perc.* 5837–6027.

10.   This episode provides another parallel between a young knight in the *PL* (here Hector, not Lancelot) and the young Perceval; it would evoke memories of Perceval at the Chastel de Bel Repaire, *Perc.* 1706–2937, and of Blancheflor's visit to his room.

11.   In the *PL* the reference to Perceval's sister represents an allusion outwards and back into the past to an already existing Grail text: see Chapter VI. Once this passage forms part of a *Lancelot-Grail* cycle an opposition between Guinevere and the pure sister of Perceval assumes a new significance so that the allusion can be reinterpreted in the light of later events, although the reference to Perceval himself cannot be so easily 'reread'.

12.   See E. Kennedy, 'King Arthur in the First Part of the Prose *Lancelot*'.

13.   J. Frappier analyses Galehot as a great tragic figure in 'Le personnage de Galehaut dans le *Lancelot* en prose'. It should be remembered that for the journey to Sorelois and the death of Galehot he bases his study on the cyclic version.

14.   See also E. Kennedy, 'Le rôle d'Yvain et Gauvain dans le *Lancelot* en prose (version non-cyclique)'. Lancelot's madness recalls that of Yvain: see notes to *PL* 551.26–555.37; there is an allusion to Yvain in the last pages of the romance, *PL* 611.35–6, and a similar closing formula, *PL* 613.4–11.

Chapter IV

1.   P. Zumthor, writing of early medieval romance in general, underlines the importance of the Arthurian setting with regard both to the individual romance's coherence and to its integration within an existing and continuing tradition:

Le type-cadre arthurien remplit ainsi, outre la fonction d'historicisation mentionée plus haut, deux fonctions proprement narratives: il crée l'unité du récit, puisqu'il désigne de façon indubitable le lieu stable d'où tout provient et où tout, périodiquement, retournera; il constitue le cadre, non seulement de tel roman, mais virtuellement d'un nombre infini de romans passés et à venir. (*Le roman jusqu'à la fin du XIIIe siècle*, pp. 66–7).

For the presentation of Arthur within the existing tradition see E. Kennedy, 'King Arthur in the First Part of the Prose *Lancelot*'. Although Arthur is a passive figure in most of Chrétien's romances, it seems likely that his public would have been familiar with his more active role in Wace and that implicit in the romance is the idea of Arthur as a great king, focus of chivalry, head of the Round Table. This is made more explicit in *Cligés*, where he leads his army into battle in a subsidiary episode, and it is emphasized by Alexandre's determination to visit Britain because of what he has heard of King Arthur: *Cligés*, 62–5, 142–64; cf. *Brut*, 9029–32. For V. M. Lagorio, 'The Apocalyptic Mode in the Vulgate Cycle of Arthurian Romances', Arthur personifies the father figure, the *rex justus* who effects a terrestrial Golden Age; but it is his failure to achieve this ideal which tends to be emphasized in the *PL*.

2. Arthur and Lancelot make war against Claudas in *Perlesvaus*. See Appendix I.

3. Carman, *A Study of the Pseudo-Map Cycle*, pp. 6–7, points out that Aramont's holdings outside Brittany are those which in the twelfth century belonged to the Plantagenets; with them are contrasted Capetian lands. He also draws parallels between Mostier Reial and Fontevrault.

4. See Mary Williams, '"Kerrins, li viauz rois de Riel" *Erec*, 1985', *Studies in French Language and Medieval Literature presented to M. K. Pope* (Manchester, 1939), pp. 405–12. The readings in the edition of M. Roques (1922–40) are 'Bans de Ganieret' (1923) and 'Quirions, li rois vialz d'Orcel' (1933).

5. See Chapter VIII, 'Pairing'.

6. See *PL* 78, 83–6, 90, 92, 115–7, 128–30 and E. Kennedy, 'Social and political ideas in the French Prose *Lancelot*'.

7. The theme of Arthur's wars against the rebel kings is developed further in the Vulgate *Merlin* Continuation in *S* II. For another allusion of the same type, introduced to explain a name, see *PL* 506.11–15, where the name Sagremors li Desreez is explained within the context of one of Arthur's wars against the Saxons. Cf. *Brut*, 9033–407 and 9455–526 for his struggle against the Irish and the Scots.

8. A number of critics have explored the expression of social tensions in medieval romance in relation to the *Lancelot-Grail* cycle in general or to later branches in particular. See, for example, R. H. Bloch, *Medieval French Literature and Law*, pp. 13–62, 202–10; D. Boutet, A. Strubel, *Littérature, politique et société*, p. 89; J. Frappier, 'Le Graal et la chevalerie', pp. 92–3; E. Kennedy, 'Social and political ideas in the French Prose *Lancelot*', 'King Arthur in the First Part of the Prose *Lancelot*'; E. Köhler, *L'Aventure chevaleresque*'; E. Peters, *The Shadow King*, pp. 196–209; Y. Robreau, *L'Honneur et la honte*.

9. See Chapter III, p. 73, and Chapter VIII, 'Pairing'.

10. Cf. the Passage des Pierres in *Char.* 2169–238.

11. Lot, *Étude*, p. 168 n. 1, links Galehot with Eseâlt, a character in *Lanzelet* (7544), described as a good knight and the tallest giant that ever was known in the whole world. He suggests that Eseâlt stems from a misreading of [G]alehalt or [G]alehot.

12. See Foerster's edition of *Erec*, 1692–750, for a fuller list of names and more correspondences with the *PL*. The list in the edition of M. Roques, 1672–710, is shorter,

13.   daß nie kein kindischer man
                                 kürlobes mê gewan,
                                 unz daß er in ein lant gereit,
                                 als uns diu âventiure seit,
                                 mit Artûs sînem vater hêr,
                                 dâ ir noch beider immer mêr
                                 die Britûne bîtent,
                                 wan si dar umbe strîtent,
                                 daß si noch süln wider komen.
                                               (*Lanz.* 6903–11)

In *Perlesvaus*, lines 4004–12, 6344–54, *S* II, p. 316, and *Livre d'Artus*, *S* VII, p. 52, the death of Lohoz is ascribed to Kay. In *S* II, p. 124, the circumstances of the engendering of Lohoz in Lisanor are given. See also R. Bromwich, *Trioedd Ynys Prydein: the Welsh Triads*, 2nd ed. (Cardiff, 1978), pp. 416–18, and K. Busby, 'The enigma of Loholt', *An Arthurian Tapestry: essays in memory of Lewis Thorpe* (Glasgow, 1981), pp. 28–36.

14.   See also *Vengeance Raguidel*, 5738–809, where Gauvain fights Guengasouain in order to avenge Raguidel, but the date of this text in relation to the *PL* is uncertain.

15.   Cf. in *Lanz.* 3130–5, Count Ritschart of Tumane to whom a hundred picked knights had sworn allegiance and to ride under his banner. See also Webster, *Lanz*, n. 60 and n. 105, and *PL II*, note to 320.17.

16.   See M. Vale, *War and Chivalry* (London, 1981), p. 68, and G. Duby, *Le dimanche de Bouvines, 27 juillet 1214* (Paris, 1973). Duby comments, in relation to the accounts by the chroniclers of the battle of Bouvines, on the similarities and differences between a tournament and a real battle between the opposing armies of two kings. In the eyes of the Anonyme de Béthune, he writes: 'la mêlée se résume en ces voltes éblouissantes sans mise à mort; en un jeu de passes et d'estocades auquel se livrent, isolés un moment dans l'arène, quelques héros étincelants. Une compétition, dont chacun rêve de remporter le premier prix, parce qu'il aura mieux galopé que les autres, transperçant les "echelles" adverses, renversant leurs cavaliers dans sa course, ceci dans les règles du jeu, et sans aide.' (pp. 164–5.) But Duby also brings out the more serious confrontation between the two kings (pp. 168–77); the victory of Philippe Auguste can be seen as a kind of *Jugement de Dieu*. A battle such as Bouvines or the battles between Arthur and Galehot can be regarded as a 'procédure de paix', a real *ordalie* (pp. 145–54). The battle between Arthur and Galehot leads to a peace, referred to more than once in the text (*PL* 327–8, 418.19, 528.29, 582.23). Although the means by which Galehot is brought to make peace is not the usual one of defeat inflicted upon him through force of arms, which would show his opponent's cause to be just in the eyes of God (Duby, p. 154), it is made clear that it was the will of God that Galehot should not have carried through this battle against Arthur to a defeat of that king (*PL* 582.29–32).

17.   See Chapter II, p. 20 and n. 16 and Kennedy, 'Royal broodings and lovers' trances in the First Part of the Prose *Lancelot*'.

18.   See also *PL II*, note to 283.5–10. For the scribes' repeated requests for more time (*PL* 261.16–21) cf. *Merlin*, para. 20 and *PL* 581. This is a detail not in Geoffrey of Monmouth or Wace. Clerks make a similar stipulation to both Arthur (*PL* 262.1–4) and Galehot (*PL* 582.14–16) before they are willing to interpret the dreams. The account of Galehot's dreams

is closer than that of Arthur's to the version in *Merlin*, para. 19, in that the visions are preceded by the crumbling of castles (*PL* 575–7), but further away in that Arthur's clerks are more successful and do not need the help of an outsider such as the *preudomme* or Merlin. The *preudomme* who counsels Arthur in the *PL* and completes the interpretation is never identified nor is his timely arrival explained. For Merlin's appearances under various disguises, when Arthur most needs him, see Zumthor, *Merlin le Prophète*, p. 196, Ménard, *Le rire et le sourire*, pp. 354–6, J. Marx, 'Le sort de l'âme de Merlin mise en cause par l'évolution de son caractère', *Mélanges R. Crozet* (Poitiers, 1966), II, pp. 981–3.

19. See Chapter III, n. 7.

20. See E. Kennedy, 'Social and political ideas in the French Prose *Lancelot*', pp. 96–100.

21. See E. Kennedy, art. cit., p. 102 and Philippe de Beaumanoir, *Coutumes de Beauvaisis*, ed. Am. Salmon (Paris, 1899), vol. II, xlv. 1453. Beaumanoir refers in another work to Lancelot: 'Grant reparlance est de l'enfance Lancelot', (*Œuvres poétiques de Beaumanoir*, SATF, Paris, 1885, II, p. 279). Köhler in *L'Aventure chevaleresque*, p. 33, writes: 'Le parfait miroir des princes que constitue le *Lancelot propre* dans le cycle de la Vulgate est vu entièrement dans la perspective de la petite noblesse.'

22. There is an interesting parallel between Lambegues, riding up proudly to place himself in the power of a victorious Claudas in order to save the city of Gaunes, and a victorious Galehot, kneeling to pay allegiance to a defeated Arthur. This is part of a series of contrasts and parallels between Arthur, Claudas, and Galehot: see Chapter VIII, 'Pairing'.

23. See Perceval's visit to the Chastel de Bel Repaire, *Perc.* 1706–2397. For detailed references to the similarities see *PL* II, notes to 442.38–465.

24. See *PL* II, notes to 418.25, 446.1–12, for comments on the names of the barons involved in the siege in Chrétien and the *PL*.

25. Medieval kings held their great courts and wore their crowns at the great religious festivals, as is recorded, for example, in the *Anglo-Saxon Chronicle*.

26. Meleagant at the opening of the *Chevalier de la Charrette*, the red knight and the loathly damsel in the *Conte del Graal* are all examples of disturbing visitors to court.

27. For example, Hector defends the Castle of Estroite Marche, whose lord is a vassal of Arthur. Gauvain fights a judicial duel before the Duke of Cambenic, also a vassal of Arthur.

Chapter V

1. See E. Kennedy, 'The role of the supernatural in the First Part of the Old French Prose *Lancelot*'. I use the term 'marvellous' in this chapter to designate what excites wonder because it 'appears to defy the ordinary laws of Nature' (J. Stevens, *Medieval Romance*, London, 1973, p. 100) or, in the terms of D. Poirion, 'la manifestation d'un écart culturel entre les valeurs de référence, servant à établir la communication entre l'auteur et son public, et les qualités d'un monde *autre*' in medieval literature (*Le Merveilleux dans la littérature française du moyen âge*, pp. 3–4). I will not attempt to observe the distinction made by Todorov between *le merveilleux*, *le fantastique*, and *l'étrange* because it does not seem appropriate to the *PL*. He defines *le merveilleux pur* as that which is immediately accepted as supernatural, where 'les éléments surnaturels ne provoquent aucune réaction particulière

ni chez les personnages ni chez le lecteur implicite. Ce n'est pas une attitude envers les évènements rapportés qui caractérise le merveilleux, mais la nature même de ces évènements' (*Introduction à la littérature fantastique*, Paris, 1970, p. 59). He regards ambiguity and uncertainty as a necessary element in *le fantastique*, that is 'l'hésitation éprouvée par un être qui ne connaît pas les lois naturelles, face à un évenement en apparence surnaturel' (ibid., p. 29). He uses the term *l'étrange* to denote the strange events which are shown to have a natural explanation. The *PL* uses the terms *merveille, merveilleus* to describe: (*a*) strange events which are clearly presented as not in conformity with the ordinary laws of nature, but which may receive the type of explanation which attempts to place them in relation to the Christian supernatural system; (*b*) strange events over which there is uncertainty as to whether they are supernatural or natural; (*c*) extraordinary events which excite wonder, but are either immediately or in due course shown to be neither supernatural nor mysterious. The way that a *merveille* is perceived is important in the romance, as will be seen during the course of this chapter in relation to the use of terms such as *veoir apertement* and *descovrir*.

2. E. Brugger, *Z. f. fr. Spr. u. Lit.* 30, p. 209 and 31, p. 273. For Merlin's link with North Britain and Scotland see A. O. H. Jarman in ALMA, pp. 20–30 and Basil Clarke, *Life of Merlin: Geoffrey of Monmouth, Vita Merlini* (Cardiff, 1973), pp. 1–5.

3. Cf. *Brut,* 7421–56, in particular 7423–8. In Wace and in Geoffrey of Monmouth the devil only seems like a man to the senses of touch and hearing, and he never shows himself. This is developed further in the *PL*.

4. See *Merlin,* para. 23, 52–75. Zumthor, *Merlin le Prophète,* pp. 240–2, considers the episodes of the birth of Merlin and Merlin's imprisonment by the Lady of the Lake to be an interpolation. He expresses the same view in 'Merlin dans le *Lancelot-Graal*', *Romans du Graal,* pp. 149–64, but modifies it in the light of J. Frappier's objection (pp. 165–6) that an analysis of the structure of the work and of the manuscript tradition makes it clear that the episodes form an integral part of the text. See Kennedy, *PL* I, pp. 12–20 for a discussion of the manuscript tradition and variant readings.

5. See Part Two, Chapter XI for a study of the adaptations made by later scribes to remove inconsistencies between this version of the birth of Merlin and that to be found in Robert de Boron, once a version of his *Merlin* has been incorporated in the cycle (*S* II).

6. Cf. Yonec, the bird lover, who reassures his *amie* by taking communion, Marie de France, *Lais,* 'Yonec', 137–88; see also *le Lai de Desiré,* 387–416, *Les Lais anonymes des XIIᵉ et XIIIᵉ siècles,* ed. P. M. O. Tobin (Genève, 1976).

7. *Char.* 2045–55, 2088–115.

8. *Perc.* 3028–64, 3466–79.

9. Her love and pride in him, just as great as a mother for her own child, is often stressed: *PL* 24.7–11, 47.1–3, 47.29–32, 106.25–9, 111.16–34, 139–40, 147.9–14. See Chapter XI, n. 9 for a discussion of E. Baumgartner's comment on the Lady of the Lake's *désir de maternité*, combined with her strong resistance to Merlin's love.

10. See Chapter II, p. 13 and J. Frappier, 'L'"Institution" de Lancelot dans le *Lancelot en prose*'.

11. See *PL* 142–7 and Chapter VI, n. 3. The Lady of the Lake explains that 'chevaliers fu establiz outreement por Sainte Eglise garantir' (*PL* 143.3). Duby in Chapter 22 of *Les trois ordres ou l'imaginaire du féodalisme* (Paris, 1978) analyses the Lady of the Lake's account of the

origin of chivalry and suggests that it gives greater importance to the knight than to the clergy and thus represents a desacralization of knighthood. However, if all men have to obey the knight (*PL* 144.15-16) and the Church must sustain him spiritually (*PL* 144.36-7), it is also stressed that he must serve the Church; when he receives the order of knighthood, he has to make a solemn promise to God that he will perform faithfully the duties of a knight (*PL* 145.25-37), and if he fails to do so, he will have sinned in the sight of God.

12.   See E. Kennedy, 'The role of the supernatural in the First Part of the Old French Prose *Lancelot*', p. 174.

13.   For a discussion of the phrase *n'est pas encores nez qui*, a strong negative in the text, see Chapter VI, p. 145.

14.   Cf. *Char.* 1856-70.

15.   See Chapter VIII, where the linking function of returns to places is discussed.

16.   See E. Faral, *Recherches sur les sources latines des contes et romans courtois du moyen âge* (Paris 1913), pp. 307-88; F. Schürr, *Das altfranzösische Epos* (Munich, 1926), pp. 312-15. See also E. Köhler, 'Le rôle de la *coutume* dans les romans de Chrétien de Troyes', *Rom.* 81 (1960), pp. 386-97, who interprets the Arthurian 'coutume' as a poetical representation of economic and political realities of the twelfth century, and L. Carasso-Bulow, *The Merveilleux in Chrétien de Troyes' Romances* (Genève, 1976), who sees in these customs 'a gradual socialization and rationalization of fairy material' and believes that they are 'transpositions of mythical laws and prohibitions' (p. 127). For later developments in the verse romances see B. Schmolke-Hasselmann, *Der arthurische Versroman von Chrestien bis Froissart* (Tübingen, 1980), pp. 73-5.

17.   See, for example, Perceval's cousin in *Perc.* 3582-92, and two texts perhaps later than the *PL*: *1st Cont.* (long version), II, E 2642-65, and *Meraugis de Portlesguez*, 5096-116.

18.   See, for example, the damsel from the Lake in *Lanz.* 4674-737, who tells the hero who he is; the damsel in *Perc.* 3428-690, whom Perceval finds by chance and who turns out to be his cousin; the damsel in *Char.* 606-709, who gives news of Guinevere to Lancelot and Gauvain.

19.   Cf. *Erec*, 6631, where 'des le tans Merlin' is used to indicate a distant past.

20.   D. Poirion writes of the split shield: 'Bel exemple de transformation d'un talisman en symbole par renversement de l'effet et de la cause (la soudure semble l'effet de l'union amoureuse)' (*Le Merveilleux dans la littérature française du moyen âge*, p. 94). It might also be said that the split dividing the two lovers could symbolize the lover's fear, a fear which also inspires Lancelot to achieve the exploits which gain him Guinevere's love and therefore the closing of the crack.

21.   Cf. *Char.* 2348-50.

22.   Cf. in *Char.* 622-34 the promise given by Gauvain and Lancelot to a damsel in return for directions.

23.   This Saxon damsel is given the name Canile (variants: camille, gamile, canize) in a later passage (*PL* 568.6), but the confusion over the name is to be found in most manuscripts. See *PL* II, notes and variants to 540.26, 567.32, 568.6. F. Lot suggests that the name Canile/Camille and some of the characteristics of the maiden are borrowed from the *Roman d'Eneas*, where Camille, the virgin warrior, is a woman of *grant poeir* and knowledge (*Étude*, p. 182 n.3).

Chapter VI

1.   A considerable number of manuscripts read 'a veoir voz granz repostailles'. See *PL* II, notes and variants to 14.1–5.

2.   G. Duby gives a number of examples of particular importance being given in genealogical literature of the twelfth century to the mother's lineage when its illustriousness equals or surpasses that of the father. ('Structure de parenté et noblesse, France du nord, XIᶜ–XIIᶜ siècles', *Miscellanea mediaevalia in memoriam Jan Frederik Niermeyer*, Groningen, 1967; also published in a translation by C. Postan in *The Chivalrous Society*, London, 1977, pp. 134–48,)

3.   See *PL* II, note to 146.10–24 and M. Andrieu, *Le Pontifical romain au Moyen Âge* (*Studi e testi* 86–9) (Città del Vaticano, 1938–41), I, p. 302, II, pp. 579–81, III, pp. 448, 549. P. Matarasso (*The Redemption of Chivalry*, p. 115) writes that the date chosen for Lancelot's knighting, the feast of St John the Baptist (*PL* 147.24–33) 'suggests that he was conceived from the outset as a forerunner'. F. Lot (*Étude*, p. 467) has pointed out that youths were often knighted on St John's day in the thirteenth century, but he suggests that fiction may have influenced reality. This may well be so, but I would not give the choice of St John's day the very specialized allegorical significance attributed to it by Matarasso. The connection between knighthood and St John lies in his advice to serving soldiers (Luke 3:14). The way in which it was understood is clearly explained by Peter of Blois, *Patrologia Latina* ccvii, ep. xciv, col. 294. John of Salisbury also draws on this in the *Policraticus*, VI, 10.

4.   See also 2 reg. 6 (2 Sam. 6) and I Par. 13–16 (I Chron. 13–16), where David brings the Ark of the Covenant to the City of David.

5.   Lot, *Étude*, p. 118; A. Micha, 'La tradition manuscrite du *Lancelot en prose*', *Rom.* 85, p. 304.

6.   See TL VI, columns 489–90 for other examples of this usage.

7.   The long version of the *First Continuation* is generally accepted as later than the short version and the *Second Continuation* (*Romans du Graal*, pp. 115, 117–18). It may be later than the *PL*.

8.   The name Leucain is mysterious. In *Jos.* Alain is son of Bron and nephew of Joseph, and there is no mention there of Leucain. It is possible that it is a corruption of Alain or Helain, who is mentioned elsewhere in the text (see p. 149 below), but there is no evidence for this in the variant readings.

9.   See Lot, *Étude*, p. 120 n. 1. In the Authorized Version (Num 26: 28–9 and Chron. 7: 14) the form is Gilead.

10.   See Chapter XI, n. 5. The baptismal name Galaaz may perhaps be designed to provide yet another link between Perceval le Galois and Lancelot do Lac.

11.   Robert de Boron, *Le Roman du Graal*, ed. B. Cerquiglini (Paris, 1981), p. 63; *Li Chevaliers as deus espees*, ed. W. Foerster (Halle, 1877), 2604; see *Perl.* II, pp. 195–6 for a discussion of the name.

12.   For a discussion of the date of the *Perlesvaus* relative to the *PL* see Chapter I and Appendix I. *Le Chevaliers as deus espees* is generally considered to have been written after 1225.

13.   See *PL* II, variants to 146.22.

14.   BN 110, 111, 113–16, and Bonn, University Library 526 give this reading. This group of

manuscripts makes a habit of removing inconsistencies and of introducing readings which emphasize links between the various branches of the cycle. See below, p. 309, and *PL* II, p. 38 n. 1.

15.   For a different view see A. Micha, *Rom.* 85 (1964), pp. 297–8, which I discuss in *PL* II, pp. 89–90. J. Frappier (*Étude*, p. 454) suggests that originally the allusion was to Galahad, but that there was a scribal correction in the archetype of all extant manuscripts. However, this would not fit in with the types of interpolation or correction to be found in the manuscript tradition: see E. Kennedy, 'The scribe as editor'. F. Lot (*Étude*, p. 120 n. 15) suggests that at this stage the author had not worked out his plan in all its details.

16.   For example, several substitute *Galaad* or *Galaaz* for *Perlesvaus* or *Perceval* and adapt the surrounding text in different ways. For full details see *PL* II, variations and notes to 33.9–14.

17.   Twelve manuscripts give *Perceval* instead of the *Perlesvaus* reading to be found in ten manuscripts.

18.   In the *Didot Perceval*, ed. W. Roach (Philadelphia, 1941), p. 149, Perceval sits in the Perilous Seat which cracks beneath him. The crack is closed and the adventure achieved on p. 242. However, it is not certain whether the romance is a *remaniement* of a work by Robert de Boron or the work of a continuator. For a summary of the discussion see P. Le Gentil in *ALMA*, pp. 257–62, and for the most recent analysis of the problem see A. Micha, *Étude sur le 'Merlin' de Robert de Boron*, pp. 5–29.

19.   I would not, therefore, accept J. Frappier's contention that such a literary allusion would be 'sans aucune importance structurale pour l'œuvre où elle est insérée' (*Étude*, p. 453).

20.   For details see *PL* II, notes and variants to 297.20–1.

21.   J. L. Weston, 'The relation of the *Perlesvaus* to the cyclic romances', p. 351.

22.   Frappier, *Étude*, p. 58, writes of the use of allusions to material in other Arthurian texts: 'les grandes œuvres du cycle arthurien étaient supposées connues du lecteur, et il s'est établi entre elles un véritable réseau de correspondances'. The Prose *Tristan* uses similar methods to integrate the individual romance into the existing tradition. See E. Ruhe, 'Repetition und Integration; Strukturprobleme des *Roman de Tristan en prose*', in *Der altfranzösischen Prosaroman* (München, 1978), pp. 131–59, in particular pp. 142–3. E. Baumgartner suggests that the links between the Prose *Tristan* and the *Lancelot-Grail* cycle through the use of characters or situations from the earlier romance without explicit allusions to their literary past in another text also has an effect: 'Le lecteur ne finit-il pas par croire à l'existence de ce monde imaginaire?' (*Le Tristan en prose: essai d'interprétation d'un roman médiéval*, Genève, 1975, p. 232.)

Chapter VII

1.   Set phrases such as 'Q'en vos deviseroie gié totes les choses' (*PL* 435.18), 'de tel maniere com ge vos ai dit' (*PL* 22.20–1) do sometimes occur. The first person plural is also occasionally used: for example, 'mais or dirons des deus chevaliers qui se combatent' (*PL* 181.20–1).

2.   Allusions to *le conte* in the text at times refer to a written source, based on the oral reports of the knights returning from their adventures; at other times they refer to the tale being told or to the narrative process (here in relation to Lancelot's story) with an emphasis on the selection of the relevant material. The distinction between these meanings is not always made clear in the text. For an interesting analysis of the relationship between the text and the authority for what is told in the various branches of the *Lancelot-Grail* cycle, see A. Leupin, 'Narrateurs et scripteurs dans la Vulgate arthurienne'. He does not study in detail the part of the cycle which corresponds to the *PL*. See also M. Perret, 'De l'espace romanesque à la matérialité du livre' for a study of the 'procédés d'effacement de la voix du narrateur' in medieval romance with special reference to the *Queste*. Cf. B. Cerquiglini, *La Parole médiévale* (Paris, 1981), p. 123, who writes, in relation to the prose versions of the *Joseph*: 'Au début du XIIIe siècle apparaît un nouveau traitement, autoritaire, dogmatique, de la parole: le discours, localisé et identifié, est rapporté au récit et à la voix qui énonce ce dernier; toute voix interférente (dont celle de l'auteur) est éliminée. Nouvelle situation du discours au sein du texte littéraire, situation que l'on nommera: prose.'

3.   R. Howard Bloch places similar passages from the later branches of the *Lancelot-Grail* cycle in the wider context of contemporary law, of a move towards the use of sworn depositions in legal procedures; he draws parallels between the judicial and literary inquest in *Medieval French Literature and Law*, pp. 202–10. See also 'From Grail Quest to Inquest', and L. R. Muir and R. H. Bloch, 'Further thoughts on the *Mort Artu*'.

4.   The main passages referring to the tales of other knights are *PL* 138.33–5, 358.30, 365.35–366.3, 571.24–31, 612.13–14.

5.   The adventures of Gauvain and Hector are also linked with those of Lancelot on other levels: see Chapters II, III, and VIII. 'Pairing of characters'.

6.   See E. Baumgartner, *L'Arbre et le Pain*, pp. 83–95, for an analysis of the role of explanations introduced by 'voirs fu' in the *Queste*.

7.   See also *PL* 21.24, 21.35.

8.   Cf. *PL* 223.24–6 where, after the journey to court of the knight rescued by Lancelot, the return to Lancelot's narrative thread is marked by a reference to time, followed by 'ce dist li contes'.

9.   For a general study of interlace, see E. Vinaver, *The Rise of Romance*, pp. 68–122, and *A la recherche d'une poétique médiévale*, pp. 129–61. W. W. Ryding, *Structure in Medieval Narrative*, studies the beginnings of interlace in twelfth-century romance (pp. 139–46), but although he then cites the thirteenth-century *Lancelot-Grail* as the finest example of the technique, he in fact only analyses in any detail the interlace of the *Queste*, which is of a rather special kind (pp. 146–52): see Pauphilet, *Études*, pp. 162–9. C. J. Chase in a forthcoming article, 'Multiple quests and the art of interlacing in the thirteenth-century *Lancelot*', examines the technique in the *PL* and the long version of the cyclic romance.

10.   Banyn plays a small part in the later branches of the cyclic romance: *LM* L.26–9, LXXXI.22, CII.18.

11.   There are some brief references to Lancelot's mother in the later branches of the cyclic romance: for example, *LM* LXXIX.24; she appears briefly during the war against Claudas, *LM* CIV.51, and sees her son Lancelot when Gaunes has been recaptured, *LM* CV.27. See also below, Chapter XI.

12. For other examples see *PL* 113.34, 218.5.

13. See also *PL* 493.25.

14. See above, pp. 159–60.

15. BN 110, 111, 112, 113–16, BL Add. 10293, Grenoble 378, Bonn 526, Bodmer (Geneva) 105.

16. See Gauvain's oath, *PL* 220.4–6, and the Lady of the Lake's parting instructions to Lancelot, *PL* 154.8–12.

17. See U. Mölk, 'Du nouveau sur la technique de l'entrelacement', where he discusses the 'contact inattendu' between the two narrative threads which, he suggests, destroys the 'attente-réalisation' of Ban's arrival at Arthur's court.

18. See, for example, *PL* 260 and 275.

19. See also *PL* 356 and 358.

20. A similar pattern is used in relation to a messenger bearing news to Galehot, *PL* 531.9.

21. *PL* 178.33–4, 182.28, 220.31, 262.27, 366.5, 409.21, 425.19, 502.7, 526.5; cf. *2nd Cont.* 30512–13.

22. This is in contrast with the repeated description of the ways into Sorelois where references back are given (see below, p. 209). For a discussion of the use of cross-reference within the text see Chapter VIII, pp. 205–18.

23. The move of the court to Camelot, where the fight takes place, is marked by a small decorated initial in BN 768. Rouen 1055 (06), which uses many small decorated initials, does not place one there but a few lines earlier: 'En tel maniere remainent entre Gal' et lanc' des le noel'.

24. See above, Chapter IV, p. 88.

25. Lancelot has, of course, a literary past to which a different type of allusion is made.

26. Lot, *Étude*, Chapter III. See also U. Ruberg, *Raum und Zeit im Prosa-Lancelot*, pp. 105–83, for an analysis of the handling of time and of the interlace in both the German *Prosa-Lancelot* and its French source. P. Imbs, 'La Journée dans la *Queste del Saint Graal* et la *Mort le roi Artu*', concentrates on the later branches of the cycle.

Chapter VIII

1. See, for example, W. Brand's study of repetition, *Chrétien de Troyes* (München, 1972); Ryding, *Structure in Medieval Narrative*; E. Vinaver, *A la recherche d'une poétique médiévale*, pp. 130–6; N. J. Lacy, 'Spatial form in Medieval Romance'; E. Baumgartner, *Le 'Tristan en prose'*, pp. 273–83; E. Ruhe, 'Repetition und Integration'.

2. See P. Ménard, *Le Rire et le sourire*, p. 328 n. 159, for a list of episodes in which Kay is unhorsed in a humiliating way, usually after he has behaved discourteously, and pp. 455–8 for further examples of his unpleasant, mocking character.

3. *Perc.* 5621–5, *1st Cont.* III, *A* 1664–8, *2nd Cont.* 29320–5, 30681–5, 31062–5, *Yvain*, 6221–313, and *Meraugis*, 5445–83.

4. Cf. A. Micha, 'Sur la composition du *Lancelot en prose*', pp. 239–40.

5. Cf. *1st Cont.* III, *A* 3681–6, *2nd Cont.* 29024–37.

6. Cf. *1st Cont.* III, *A* 3769–800, *2nd Cont.* 29037–69.

7. See Chapter IV, pp. 107–10.

8. See Chapter IV, pp. 89–102.

9. Cf. *Char.* 622–34, 703–9, where Lancelot and Gauvain make a similar promise to a damsel for news of Guinevere's whereabouts. See also Chapter V, n. 18.

10. The appearance of the Lady of the Lake when needed and her reference to the childhood in the Lake recall the allusion in Chrétien, *Char.* 2345–50.

11. The arrival of a wounded knight with the sword which he presents to Hector as a gift from Gauvain is related first, *PL* 404.17–27; the episode in which Gauvain acquires the sword is recounted later, *PL* 420.13–30; the charging of the wounded knight with the message is narrated at *PL* 423.36–424.3 with a reference back to the earlier telling by the tale.

12. The references to the war between Cambenic and Norgales are as follows: *PL* 419.33–5, 446.5–8, 474.34–7, 475.21–8, 477.10–19, 477.21–3, 479–83, 488.21–501.39.

13. See *PL* 373–9, 476.1–25, 481.10–13, 504.4–5.

14. The reference to *les aventures* and *dui passage . . . assez felon et orgoillos* would evoke memories of the land of Gorre in *Char.* which is associated with mysterious adventures and is difficult of access, for it can only be entered by two *felons passages* (*Char.* 653–5). However, the bridges into Gorre offer stranger perils, although the Passage des Pierres is defended in a similar way. See Chapter IV, n. 10.

15. See also Chapter VII, p. 188.

16. Twenty manuscripts give this reading; twenty omit the part of the text which occurs between *anmi son piz* and *enmi le piz*, probably through a jump from like to like. For details see *PL* II, p. 243.

17. Cf. *PL* 445–7 and *Perc.* 2002–25.

18. *1st Cont.* III, *A* 3673–7.

19. See *PL* II, variants to 496.18–21. For the confusion over the name of the Saxon maiden see Chapter V, n. 23. For other inconsistencies over proper names see *PL* II, notes and variants to 481.10–13, 478.31.

20. See, for example, *PL* 475–9, 526, 529.

21. For example, *PL* 195–6, 223, 408–9, 532.

22. For Lyonel's journeys to and from Sorelois and between Lancelot and the Queen, see *PL* 358, 473, 493–501, 525, 536–7, 542–3, 545–6, 548–9, 579–80.

23. See *LM* XIII.7–13.

24. See Chapter V, pp. 111–15.

25. References to Helene's ancestry are as follows: *PL* 13.12, 14.1–5, 49.38–50.2, 147.17–18; to that of Evaine: 108.37–109.2.

26. See also Pharien's lament for Lyonel when he thinks that he is dead: 'Car tels estoit li vostres cuers que nus nel poïst afrener par enseignier. Se vos iestes aparceüz avant et nos après quex maus puet venir de refuser et de despire consoil leial' (*PL* 82.28–30).

27. The portrait may follow the traditional pattern, but it also reflects very accurately the character of the man as seen in his actions in the romance. The refusal of Claudas to be involved in 'amer par amors' (*PL* 30.32–31.9) also contrasts with the dominant role played by love in Lancelot's life, already hinted at in his portrait as a youth (*PL* 40.18–24, 40.35–41.2).

28. The vavasour whom Lancelot meets near the Lake describes Ban as 'uns des plus preudomes do monde' (*PL* 44.7-8).

29. For parallels with Merlin see Chapter IV, pp. 92-4.

30. See E. Kennedy, 'The use of *Tu* and *Vous* in the First Part of the Old French Prose *Lancelot*', pp. 143-4, 146-7.

31. Cf. the decline of Arthur's kingdom through his failure to show *largece* as a king should in *Perl.*, lines 58-91, 329-61. Note that the qualities demanded of a king, *largece*, *debonaireté*, are the same as those demanded of a knight (with the addition of *fierté*) according to Claudas and the Lady of the Lake. For this emphasis on royal *largece* see also D. Boutet, A. Strubel, *Littérature, politique et société*, p. 89; Le Goff in the introduction to E. Köhler, *L'Aventure chevaleresque*, p. xv, and Köhler, op. cit., p. 44.

32. *PL* 261.14-21, 581.14-15; cf. *Merlin*, para. 20.

33. See also E. Kennedy, 'Le rôle d'Yvain et Gauvain dans le *Lancelot* en prose (version non-cyclique)'.

34. See Chapter II, n. 24.

35. See Chapter II, pp. 39-42, and *PL* II, notes to 162.35-163.39, 371-89.

36. Lancelot's trances: by the river, *PL* 179-81, 266-9; before the gate of Dolorous Guard, *PL* 207, 215; before battle, *PL* 281, 309-11. Hector's trances: *PL* 368-71, 425-6. See also E. Kennedy, 'Royal broodings and lovers' trances in the First Part of the Prose *Lancelot*'.

37. *Perc.* 4164-431.

38. *Perc.* 3780-4085.

39. The episodes at Bel Repaire (*Perc.* 1706-2937), and at the Castle of the King of Escavalon (*Perc.* 5748-6209); Gauvain's adventure with the daughter of Norès de Lis (*1st Cont.* III, *A* 1648-733).

40. The knight's approach to a strong castle, surrounded by devastation, his violent battering on the door to gain admittance, the worn appearance of the garrison, the two single combats, the damsel's nocturnal visit to the knight's bedchamber are all common features in the two works.

41. *1st Cont.* III, *A* 6247-54.

42. There are also references to Gauvain's increase in strength after noon in *PL* 536.17-29 which only occur in a small group of manuscripts; for details see the variants to these lines in *PL* II.

43. *Yvain*, 6221-313. See *Cligés*, 4861-919 and n. 3 to this chapter, and Chapter II, n. 36 for other examples of interrupted battles.

44. The small group of manuscripts which add extra references to Gauvain's increase in strength also contain a series of passages, not to be found elsewhere, which emphasize Gauvain's prowess, so that Lancelot's supremacy as the greatest knight is not so evident; see *PL* II, pp. 36, 351.

Chapter IX

1. See Chapter VIII, n. 42.

2. See Chapter VIII, n. 19.

Chapter X

1. See also my article in *Romania*, 'The two versions of the False Guinevere Episode in the Old French Prose *Lancelot*'.

2. For the details of the manuscripts giving version (*a*) in whole or in part, see Chapter I, p. 5 and n.1.

3. The references for the cyclic version are to Micha's edition and are to the long cyclic version, unless there is indication to the contrary. For this part of the text (vol. I of his edition), Micha uses MS Corpus Christi (Cambridge) 45 for the long cyclic version. For the short cyclic version (which is only clearly distinct from the long one after VIII.31, the departure of Guinevere for Sorelois, and is to be found in vol. III of his edition) he uses Grenoble 865. This manuscript gives the beginning of the non-cyclic version (*a*) and switches to the cyclic version, *PL* 574.6, *LM* II.8.

4. See Micha's articles in *Romania*, 'Les épisodes du Voyage en Sorelois et de la Fausse Guenièvre', and 'L'esprit du *Lancelot-Graal*'. He discusses the question further in 'La tradition manuscrite du *Lancelot en prose*' (*Rom.* 85), pp. 479–82. He examines the literary quality of the two versions in 'Le départ en Sorelois. Réflexions sur deux versions'. Frappier argued at first that the two versions represented 'un temps d'arrêt' between volumes I and II of the *Lancelot propre*, and that volume I might have circulated separately (*Étude*, pp. 129–33). In the Appendix which he added to the second edition he does not pursue this suggestion further, but writes: 'Mais, malgré leurs divergences, ces deux versions se ressemblent assez pour qu'elles soient l'une et l'autre le développement d'un canevas commun, et si la version longue, comme il est probable, n'a pas été rédigée la première, elle ne saurait passer pour un remaniement tardif, car la *Charrette* suppose nécessairement son existence.' (*Étude*, pp. 451–2). He then goes on to maintain his view that a Grail Quest with Galahad as hero was envisaged from the beginning of *S* III and that 'l'unité de structure n'est pas sérieusement compromise par les incertitudes du tome III et du début du tome IV' (*Étude*, p. 455). He does not explain further the existence or relationship of the two versions. F. Lot, *Étude*, pp. 115, 359–77, suggests that the short version—which he calls version (*b*), representing in my terminology the non-cyclic version (*a*)—is a clumsy first draft, followed by a pause, during which the author clarified his ideas. However, he does not dismiss totally the idea that the shorter version might represent an abridgement of the longer one. J. Neale Carman discusses the False Guinevere episode in his *Study of the Pseudo-Map Cycle*, pp. 55–9, but mainly in terms of the modification of the folk theme of the substitute wife in terms of reminiscences of recent historical events.

5. *Camelide* is the reading of BN 768; Rouen 06 and the Laurenziana manuscript give *carmelide*; the Pierpont Morgan manuscript reads *tarmelide*.

6. Micha bases his chapter numbering on the order to be found in the long version of (*b*). For the differences in order between the long and short versions of (*b*) see vol. III of the Micha edition, p. x.

7. Frappier has studied the role of Galehot in the Prose Lancelot, using the text common to both cyclic and non-cyclic romances, and then the cyclic version (*b*) of the journey to Sorelois and the False Guinevere episode: 'Le personnage de Galehaut dans le *Lancelot* en prose'.

8.   There are some parallels between Galehot's ambitions as they are recalled in version (*b*) (*LM* II.14–16) and those of Claudas, but there are not the same similarities in phrasing as in (*a*), where the presumption of Galehot in aspiring to conquer Arthur is clearly condemned. See Chapter VIII, 'Pairing'.

9.   In the *Mort Artu*, the terms *mescheance, mescheoir* are used to express the idea of fate, sometimes combined with a suggestion of merited misfortune (for example, *MA* 178.35–8). See also Frappier, *Étude*, pp. 254–88, for the role of fate in the *Mort Artu*. For the use of the term *mescheance* in the *Post-Vulgate* Cycle, see F. Bogdanow, *The Romance of the Grail*, pp. 149–55.

10.   'Car ele fist poisons qu'ele li dona a boire par quoi li rois l'ama tant et fist tant qu'il le mist en son lit et en fist son bon et l'ama sor toutes femes del monde' (Grenoble 865, London, BL Add. 10293).

11.   The short version of (*b*) makes the same point: 'car on ne quide pas que vous l'aiés fet por vous oster de pechié, mes por vostre voloir acomplir en pechié'.

12.   In the long version the deterioration of Arthur as king under the influence of the False Guinevere is expressed in different terms and very briefly (*LM* IX.5, quoted above, p. 260).

13.   In version (*a*) Lancelot is so angry with Arthur for his treatment of the Queen that he wants to renounce his homage immediately, but refrains lest his action should be mis-interpreted: 'Mais Lanceloz ne l'acole mies de bon cuer, car il lo het orandroit plus que nul home et volantiers li eüst son homage randu sanz plus atandre. Mais il crient que a vilenie li fust tenu, si çoille ensin son pensé, por ce qu'il ne velt que nus son covine aparçoive' (*PL* 598.10–13).

14.   See Chapter IV. It has also been seen that in the *PL* a more glorious role tends to be given to knights than to rulers; see Chapter IV, pp. 94–5, and n. 20, and Chapter VIII, p. 231.

15.   Another detail of the earlier occasion is evoked in *LM* XIII.15, when Meliant says that he killed the knight who wounded him, thus echoing a similar statement in *PL* 150.25–6.

16.   See, for example, in Beroul's *Tristan*, 380, 2327.

17.   Note the parallel between Guinevere's successful defence of her reputation and Lancelot's knightly achievement in relation to the dead knight's lady, similarly accused (*LM* XXVI.32–7).

18.   For a discussion of Merlin's role in the later branches of the cycle, see Chapter XI, n. 17.

19.   In the *Perlesvaus*, which, as I have suggested in Chapter I, I consider to have been written later than the *PL* (although possibly earlier than the cyclic romance and hence the Vulgate *Queste*), Lancelot's love is condemned as adulterous and proves an obstacle to his success in the Grail adventure. He refuses to repent of it (lines 3652–95) and, as a result, he fails to see the Grail (lines 3746–53). See also Appendix I.

Chapter XI

1.   From the beginning of the *Charrette* to the beginning of the Agravain (*S* IV; *LM*, vol. II) Micha continues to use Corpus Christi 45 for the long version; for the short version (*LM*, vol. III) he uses BN fr. 110. For the Agravain (*S* V; *LM*, vols. IV–VI) he uses an Oxford

manuscript, Bodleian Rawlinson 899; for the short version (at foot of page in vol. IV, in appendices in vols. V and VI), BL Add. 10293.

2. The incorporation of Chrétien's *Charrette* story in the *Lancelot-Grail* cycle does not, therefore, exclude a continuing interplay with the verse romance tradition. Dornbush, pp. 172–243, gives an interesting analysis of this process in somewhat different terms, without reference to the well-known narrative pattern of the Fair Unknown. But this would seem to be an essential element in the network of resonances, linked as it is with one of the central themes of both Chrétien's romances and the Prose *Lancelot* in non-cyclic and cyclic forms. Frappier writes of these two borrowings from Chrétien (in the Dolorous Guard adventure and the Prose *Charrette*): 'Cette discrimination adroite des éléments d'une même aventure utilisés dans des parties assez éloignées l'une de l'autre, tend bien à prouver qu'elle soit d'un seul auteur' (*Étude*, p. 88). I am not convinced that the evidence for one author is overwhelming, but would argue that the second borrowing is designed to give the first one a new meaning within a wider structure. See also H. Fromm, 'Zur Karrenritter-Episode im *Prosa-Lancelot*. Struktur und Geschichte', who underlines the importance of the identity theme.

3. Frappier considers this to be in flagrant contradiction with the *Queste* (*Étude*, p. 47) and writes in the Appendix: 'L'unité de conception . . . ne saurait s'accommoder d'une divergence de doctrine comme celle qui apparaît par exemple entre la *Queste*, d'après laquelle chaque homme n'est coupable que de ses propres fautes, et l'épisode de la tombe de Siméon dans la *Charrette en prose* où il est dit que le fils porte le poids du péché commis par le père' (*Étude*, p. 449).

4. I have emended the Micha reading 'I ans' in accordance with the correction in vol. IX of his edition. The reference to the qualities which Lancelot inherited from his mother links up with the allusions in the account of his childhood to his noble inheritance from his mother Helene: *PL* 13.10–12, 14.1–4, 49.39–50.2, 147.17–20, 154.1–2.

5. The name Galaaz, after the incorporation of the Grail theme within the romance, acquires a new depth of meaning with mystic associations which it did not possess in the *PL*. The name Galahaz, given to the brother of Joseph of Arimathea, is linked to Gales in the list of great knights in *PL* 146.20; as was pointed out in Chapter VI, p. 149, it has a kind of biblical link in that in the Old Testament Galaad is named as the grandson of Joseph, son of Jacob. But the Galahaz in the list of knights is no Christ-figure, and there is no hint in the *PL* that we have here an evocation of the Mount Galaad (Gilead in the *AV*) of Genesis, 'heap of testimony', traditionally interpreted as a mystical equivalent to Christ. See Lot, *Étude*, p. 120, nn. 1 and 3; Pauphilet, *Études*, pp. 136–8; and in particular P. Matarasso, *The Redemption of Chivalry*, pp. 38–9, who quotes *The Song of Songs, a twelfth-century French version*, ed. C. E. Pickford (Oxford, 1974), lines 1747–68. See also E. Anitchkof, 'Le Galaad du *Lancelot-Graal* et les Galaads de la Bible'.

6. See A. Micha, 'L'esprit du *Lancelot-Graal*', p. 367: 'La carole magique où Lancelot chante l'éloge de la reine et dont il ne peut plus sortir a un sens clairement symbolique.'

7. This speech evokes two earlier passages. The reference to *la Dolereuse Roine* links up with the name which Lancelot's mother used to designate herself after she had lost her husband by death and her child by abduction (*PL* 16.21–3); the description of Lancelot recalls the words of the Lady of the Lake quoted above (*PL* 154.39–155.2).

8.   See *PL* 344–6; see also in the formal portrait of Lancelot the acknowledgement of the strength which he draws from his love (*PL* 40.35–9, quoted above, in Chapter III, p. 50). Lancelot's speech to a damsel who cured him of poisoning (*LM* LXXVI.34) provides an even clearer echo of his first confession of love to Guinevere.

9.   Cf. *Perlesvaus*, where Lancelot cannot bring himself to renounce his love from the depths of his heart: 'Sire, fait Lanceloz, icel pechié vos jehirai je hors de la boche dont je ne puis estre repentanz el cuer. Je aim bien ma dame, qui roïne est, plus que nulle rien qui vive, et si l'a .i. des meillors rois del mont a feme. La volenté me senble si bone et si haute que je ne la puis lessier, et si m'est enracinee el cuer qu'ele ne s'em puet partir. La gregnor valor qui est en moi si me vient par la volenté' (*Perl.*, lines 3655–61).

10.   This passage underlines the Christian significance given in the cyclic romance to the winning back by the son of the baptismal name 'Galahad', lost by the father. It prepares the way for the development of the theme in terms of the Fall and the Redemption; this is explored further in the *Queste*. See P. Matarasso, *The Redemption of Chivalry*, p. 90: 'In Galahad we have the man in whom the divine likeness has been perfectly restored, that likeness which in Lancelot had been defaced and rendered well-nigh unrecognizable'; see also p. 94: 'Lancelot, who is also a figure of Adam and of Everyman, is indeed loosed from sin as a result of Galahad's coming.' Note also E. Baumgartner's comment (*L'Arbre et le Pain*, p. 105 n. 18) on the use of the term *aombré* in relation to the engendering of Galahad. *Aombrement* often designates the incarnation of Christ in the Virgin, but is ambiguous: 'L'ombre et le mal ont partie liée, mais l'*aombrement* est signe de la fécondation, et ce n'est qu'à ce prix qu'est possible la Rédemption, et dans le cas de Galaad, l'achèvement des aventures du Graal.' She also makes an interesting suggestion concerning a parallel between the conception of Galahad and the Lady of the Lake's abduction of Lancelot when discussing the theme of the child conceived without sin, without pleasure: 'Cette subtile variante qu'est la Dame du Lac dans le *Lancelot*. Se refusant à tout rapport sexuel, la Dame du Lac satisfait en effet son désir de maternité en enlevant Lancelot à sa mère et en simulant même une scène de naissance lorsqu'elle plonge dans le lac tenant sur son sein l'enfant qu'elle a préalablement et rituellement mis à nu' (ibid., p. 105 n. 17). It is quite true that in the *PL* the author takes great care to preserve the Lady of the Lake's purity and virtue and to ensure both that her relationship with Lancelot should have no sexual connotations and that her knowledge of magic should have no sinister associations (see above, pp. 15 and 114–15), but she has an *ami*, a knight, *biax et proz* (*PL* 148, 556–7 and p. 137 above).

11.   For an analysis of Lancelot's painting in terms of 'the clerk–knight configuration', see Dornbush, pp. 82–106.

12.   Thomas, *Le Roman de Tristan*, ed. J. Bédier, SATF (Paris, 1892), I, pp. 299–332.

13.   Thomas, *Le Roman de Tristan*, ed. Bédier, line 945; *Les Fragments du Tristan de Thomas*, ed. B. H. Wind (Leiden, 1950), p. 98.

14.   To be compared with the courtly love lyric, where the song itself is an expression of the quality of the love.

15.   The motif of a lover's madness would not only evoke that of Yvain but also that of Tristan whose madness may be feigned but whose grief at his separation from Iseut is real.

16.   See also Lot (*Étude*, p. 76 n.3) who shows that Bohort's future greatness is prepared

well in advance; he lists a number of episodes, including that of the *Charrette*, and comments: 'Et quant Bohort apparaît sur la charrette c'est pour mettre fin à la "coutume". L'intention est évidente; seule la pureté de Bohort peut faire disparaître l'infamie qui s'attache à la "charrette": tout est pur aux purs.'

17.   See Chapter V. A second ring which uncovers enchantments, given by the Lady of the Lake to Guinevere and by her to Lancelot to protect him against Morgain (*LM* LXXXV.4), helps to underline the opposition between the Lady of the Lake and Morgain. The allusions to Merlin in the cyclic romance have also changed in character and are more in accordance with his role in the work of Robert de Boron. For example, Helie, when he interprets Galehot's dreams, cites a prophecy by Merlin which prepares the way for a Grail Quest to be achieved by a virgin knight descended from Lancelot (*LM* IV.35–42). See also Zumthor, *Merlin le Prophète*, pp. 181–4. In the later branches of the cycle most of the references to him concentrate on his role in establishing the Round Table and as prophet of both the Grail and of historical events such as Arthur's last battle. However, there are a few allusions with the associations of magic and marvels characteristic of the *PL*: the *lit Merlin* for example, 'ou nus ne se couche qui ne perde le sens et le memoire, car li leus est enchantez' (*LM* CI.8). There is also the *Tor Merlin*, which is full of marvels (*LM* L.22).

18.   Lot (*Étude*, p. 73 n.6) suggests that the function of the episode at the Chastel des Marés, in which Lancelot and the reader learn for the first time (*LM* LXXIX. 17–19) that Hector is Lancelot's half-brother, is to provide a relative to whom Lancelot can hand over his land, won back from Claudas. This news is prepared during the *Charrette* episode (*LM* XXXVII.40) where Ban's adultery is first mentioned. In the *PL* there is no hint of such a kinship, but, as was seen in Chapters II, III, and VIII, there is another kind of connection between them: Hector plays the role of young knight and lover making a name for himself while Lancelot is withdrawn from the action and hidden in Sorelois.

19.   However, Arthur is allowed no role in the Grail adventures. E. Baumgartner (*L'Arbre et le Pain*, pp. 151–3) has pointed out that the Grail vision is refused to kings and is the privilege of chivalry. Galahad comes from a line of kings, but is designated as knight, not king, until he is finally crowned at Sarras: 'Dans cette perspective, on peut se demander si les liens que tissent l'auteur entre Josephé l'évêque et Galaad le chevalier ne signifient pas la transmission de la connaissance des mystères, des *repostailles* de Dieu, de la classe des prêtres, détenteurs d'ordinaire du sacré à la classe chevaleresque en la lacune des rois.' She adds, however, that the knights receive revelations but do not serve in the Grail rituals. See also Frappier, 'Le Graal et la chevalerie', especially pp. 92–4; D. Boutet and A. Strubel, *Littérature, politique et société*, p. 96.

20.   For details of the parallels see Chapter II, nn. 16 and 31 and E. Kennedy, 'Royal broodings and lovers' trances'.

21.   *1st Cont. A* 3362–699; *2nd Cont.* 29024–208. There is a variation in the cyclic romance on the theme of the quest for a great, unknown, and elusive knight, now that Lancelot's identity is known at court and he is sought under his own name. The emphasis is now on failure to recognize under various arms the famous knight who has made a great name for himself, and the following comment by Gauvain is revealing: 'Par Dieu, nos somes les plus foles genz del monde, qui toute jor veismes Lancelot et si nel conneumes mie' (*LM* XCVII. 6.). See also *LM* XCIX. 25–6.

22. See for example *LM* XCV. 7–9, 38.

23. See Pauphilet, *Études*, p. 26, Baumgartner, *L'Arbre et le Pain*, pp. 49–53.

24. I am particularly indebted to the studies of the following: A. Pauphilet, E. Gilson, M. Lot-Borodine, F. W. Locke, R. Tuve, P. Matarasso, E. Baumgartner. For full details see the Bibliography.

25. P. Matarasso (*The Redemption of Chivalry*, p. 39) suggests that it is somewhat startling to discover in the first pages of the *Queste* that neither father nor cousins recognize the stripling youth when the nuns present him to Lancelot with the request that he should knight him. She points out, however, that the deliberate incognito and simple non-recognition would be familiar to the reader as they abound in the cycle as a whole, and also that non-recognition can have a symbolic significance: 'It can either imply lack of discernment on the part of the active participant in an encounter, akin to the spiritual blindness which becomes so important a theme in the *Queste,* or it may indicate that the "unrecognized" is in some way changed or "not himself". This is perfectly true, but I think that it is also important to emphasize that in Lancelot's childhood and early adventures the incognito and non-recognition do not just represent a mechanical use of Arthurian convention, but are closely linked to the identity theme, and that there are resonances of that here. G. A. Savage writes of the development of the motif of the Bel Inconnu at the beginning of the *Queste* ('Father and son in the *Queste del Saint Graal*').

26. Baumgartner points out that for Galahad the feast of Pentecost telescopes into one day the ordinary trajectory of the Arthurian hero, from *l'épreuve qualifiante*, the sword in the stone, to *l'épreuve glorifiante*, the Perilous Seat (*L'Arbre et le Pain*, p. 71). In the last part of the *PL* (not common to the cyclic romance) the account of Lyonel's progress at Easter from knighting to a seat at the Round Table via the fight against the Crowned Lion which proves his right to his own name, also provides a telescoped version of Lancelot's career, but without the religious overtones; see Chapter II. Todorov distinguishes between two types of test: *épreuve narrative* and *épreuve rituelle*. Those of Galahad, who succeeds in passing the tests because he is *élu*, are *rituelles* ('La Quête du Récit', p. 139). Lancelot's tests as a youth on the way to Nohaut are 'narrative', that at the Dolorous Guard 'ritual'.

27. For the scriptural sources for Galahad's arrival at Camelot and the theological implications, see Gilson, *Les Idées et les lettres*, pp. 69–72, and P. Matarasso, op. cit., pp. 43–51, who point out that the role of the *preudomme* recalls that of John the Baptist.

28. There are a number of parallels between Galahad and David, who is both a type of Christ and his ancestor. See Matarasso, op. cit., pp. 41–3. The association with chivalry is still an important aspect of this descent from David and Solomon through biblical time up to Arthurian time. See Baumgartner, *L'Arbre et le Pain*, p. 95: 'Ainsi, ce qui se dit sur la Nef, ce qui s'y déchiffre plutôt, non seulement sature le temps jusqu'à son origine absolue et institue Galaad comme unique et ultime héritier du rameau de l'Arbre, de l'Epée de David, mais déroule également une chronologie parallèle à la chronologie sacrée, imaginée à la *semblance* du modèle scripturaire du temps successif du Père et du Fils, mais dont le dernier temps s'ouvre et s'achève par la venue au monde et l'assomption du *Chevalier Desirré*, du maître et du pasteur de toute chevalerie.' See also Q 78.19–21, and Frappier, *Le roman jusqu'à la fin du XIIIe siècle*, p. 511.

29. See Chapter VI, n. 15 and *PL* II, variants to *PL* 33.8–15.

30. Matarasso, op cit., p. 40 suggests that there is a symbolic truth in Lancelot's reluctance to accept Galahad's identity: 'It is only when he is well advanced along the path of penitence and self-awareness that he can face up to the knowledge of Galahad's identity, which involved for him the acceptance also of his own failure to fulfil his predestined role.' It is only at *Q* 138 that he is obliged to face the truth.

31. See above, p. 285, and *LM* LXXVIII. 57.

32. For a discussion of the biblical parallels and the allegorical interpretation see Matarasso, op. cit., pp. 53–5.

33. See Matarasso, op. cit., pp. 77–8, for a discussion of the way that the passage reflects the contemporary attitudes to eschatology.

34. See Matarasso, op cit., pp. 79–80, for the replacement of *pesmes aventures* by the occasional miraculous intervention of Divine Providence.

35. Pauphilet, (*Études,* p. 109) points out that birds were the symbol of Christ. He also draws attention to a similar description (*Q* 251–2): 'Et c'est pourquoi lorsque l'auteur veut dépeindre la joie du "temps novel", après Pâques, il ne manque pas de noter que les oiseaux chantent dans les bois, gracieuse image de la présence de Dieu dans le monde délivré par la Passion de l'Eucharistie.'

36. Lancelot's sin is to choose the wrong kind of love, to adore a woman, not God. Matarasso (op cit., pp. 146–7) points out that the *Queste*'s presentation of this love as 'perverted', and the antithesis between *virginité* and *luxure* mean that it is not merely adulterous, but idolatrous. See also R. Tuve, *Allegorical Imagery*, p. 424.

37. Compare the qualities of heavenly chivalry here with those listed in the Lady of the Lake's discourse on chivalry (*PL* 141–6) and with the qualities attributed to the young Lancelot in his formal portrait (*PL* 41) and to the young Dorin in the lament of Claudas for his son (*PL* 71–3). The hermit's phrase, 'hebergiees en toi si naturelment' (*Q* 124.25), echoes that used by Claudas (*PL* 72.11). For a discussion of the virtues listed and the order in which they appear in the speeches of this hermit and the one whom Lancelot met earlier (*Q* 68), see Pauphilet, *Études*, pp. 40–4, and P. Matarasso, op. cit., pp. 121–7, 149–53. The latter interprets *charité* (*Q* 125) in this list of virtues as almsgiving. This would link up with the emphasis in the *PL* on *largece*, generosity, as a quality to be possessed by a true knight or king (*PL* 33–4, 41, 71–2, 287–9), but once again the meaning is transformed.

38. The knights departing on the Quest were warned that surface appearances were misleading and that the reality lay elsewhere, for the adventures taking place were on a spiritual plane (*Q* 19.19–26).

39. See Baumgartner, *L'Arbre et le Pain*, pp. 83–95, for an analysis of the significance of time, of the ages of the Old Testament, of Christ, and of Galahad, in the allegory.

40. See Chapter II, nn. 16 and 31.

41. Baumgartner uses the term *récriture* when writing of the role of adventure and chance in the *Queste* and the use of traditional Arthurian material and conventions: 'Récriture dont la caractéristique principale, me semble-t-il, est l'obstination avec laquelle l'auteur surimpose un sens nouveau à un motif traditionnel sans chercher pourtant à en oblitérer le sens originel' (*L'Arbre et le Pain,* p. 68). I think that on a non-allegorical level this process starts with the rewriting of the Journey to Sorelois and False Guinevere episode, a

rewriting which gives a new meaning to Lancelot's early adventures. See also Baumgartner, 'Les aventures du Graal', p. 26.

42. Note the parallels between the scene in which the knighting of Lancelot is finally completed, not by Arthur but by the Queen, when he receives his sword sent by Guinevere (*PL* 174), and that in which Perceval's sister girds the sword of David on Galahad and makes him truly a knight (Q 228.20–24). Lancelot's knighting of Galahad with another sword (Q 3) had not made him fully a knight in terms of heavenly chivalry: see Matarasso, op. cit., p. 71, and Baumgartner, *L'Arbre et le Pain*, p. 94 n. 20.

43. For a study of the influence of the Tristan story on the *Mort Artu* see J. Frappier, *Étude*, pp. 188–95.

44. Frappier, *Mort Artu*, p. 283, *Étude*, p. 29. H. Blake, 'Étude sur les structures narratives dans *La Mort Artu* (XIIIe siècle)', writes of the episode in Morgain's castle: 'Cette scène est à la fois la représentation métonymique du fonctionnement de l'écriture du *Lancelot en prose*, mettant l'accent sur un acte de communication, et la mise en "abyme" de la réduplication constante qui s'opère à l'intérieur de ce cycle et qui constitue la base même des structures narratives de la *Mort Artu*' (p. 733).

45. See, for example, Beroul's *Tristan*, 496–502, in a speech by Iseut to Mark, where she rejects the terms *fole amor* and *amor vilaine* , and 1381–3, where Tristan, in explaining to the hermit that their love comes only from the potion, uses the phrase 'ele m'aime en bone foi'.

46. Cf. *Trist.* 571–80, where the lovers' indiscretion leads up to the second trap set by the barons.

47. This too links up with the *Tristan* in a version such as that of Beroul (for example, 2160–78). Bohort's allusion outwards to Tristan, who, he says, only five years ago died because of his love for Iseut (*MA* 59.55–7) parallels the allusions outwards from the *PL* discussed in Chapters IV, V, and VI. At this stage the Grail story has been incorporated in the romance, but the *Tristan* is still a tale told elsewhere.

48. Boutet and Strubel point out that Arthur, in his determination to wage war against Lancelot, is moved not by a desire for power, conquest, or political calculation but by a desire for vengeance. Lancelot has killed Gauvain's brother. Arthur feels bound to support his nephew, who relies on him, as uncle and suserain, to assuage his hatred: 'Ainsi le lien féodal se retourne-t-il contre le monde arthurien' (*Littérature, politique et société*, p. 98).

49. A. J. Kennedy, 'Lancelot incognito at Winchester in the *Mort Artu*', p. 171, interprets Lancelot's decision to fight incognito in the following terms: 'To have Lancelot participate *incognito* at Winchester, then, may have been for the author of the *Mort Artu* an economical and expressive way of drawing attention to the sudden reassertion of Lancelot's old self (in particular, his pride), now that he has returned to Guinevere and the secular environment of the Court.'

50. This is evident from the fact that it is the Lord of the Dolorous Guard, Brandin des Illes, who is forced by Lancelot to order the prisoners' release, and it is spelt out in a number of manuscripts: see *PL* II, variants to 205.23–6.

51. Blake, art. cit., p. 742, points out that the *Estoire Lancelot* begins and ends with a marvellous lake; Micha, 'Deux sources de la "Mort Artu"', has drawn attention to the inverse symmetry of the two hands in the concluding episodes of the last two branches: in the

Queste a hand reaches down from heaven, in the *Mort Artu* a hand reaches up from the lake. Blake comments on the opening and closing with the Lake: 'C'est encore un exemple du fonctionnement d'un roman qui reproduit certains signes littéraires désignant le monde romanesque du *Lancelot* pour l'amener à la mort.'

52.   See my article, 'The scribe as editor', where I analyse the types of corrections and additions made by scribes. Detailed variants for the passages discussed below are to be found in *PL* II. E. Ruhe, 'Repetition und Integration', p. 138, recalls 'Barthes's distinction in *Critique et vérité* (Paris, 1966), pp. 76–7, between the four functions in relation to a medieval text (*scriptor, compilator, commentator, auctor*), but the medieval scribes concerned with the *Lancelot-Grail* manuscripts do not always seem to have confined their activities to the function of *scriptor*.

53.   Full variants for this passage are given in *PL* II.

54.   See *PL* II, pp. 12–20, 38, Kennedy, 'The scribe as editor', pp. 525–7. Allusions to incidents concerning Merlin related in other texts are added by some manuscripts. See art. cit. and notes and variants to *PL* 23.29–30, 24.4–7.

55.   G. Hutchings, *P. Char.,* pp. 122–31, gives examples of additions to a later branch of the cycle which give Gauvain more adventures.

56.   F. Bogdanow, *The Romance of the Grail*; C. E. Pickford, *L'Évolution du roman arthurien en prose*.

57.   See J. Frappier, 'Le roman en prose en France au XIIIe siècle', p. 506: 'La tendance à parfaire la somme des aventures, à vouloir, pour ainsi dire, épuiser la *matière de Bretaigne*, ne s'est pas limitée au cycle du *Lancelot-Graal*. . . . Cet effort de totalisation s'est exercé de plusieurs façons: tantôt l'extensible univers arthurien s'annexe des sujets nouveaux, tantôt l'histoire des principaux héros est prolongée par celle de leurs ancêtres ou celle de leurs descendants.'

Chapter XII

1.   The same is true of individual branches of the *Lancelot-Grail* cycle. Cf. H. Blake, 'Étude sur les structures narratives dans *La Mort Artu* (XIIIe siècle)', p. 733: 'L'interrogation de *La Mort Artu* que nous proposons ici tient compte du double fonctionnement de ce récit: le rapport intertextuel que *La Mort Artu* entretient avec le reste du *Lancelot en prose* influe directement sur les structures narratives qui fonctionnent à l'intérieur de l'œuvre.'

2.   N. J. Lacy, 'Spatial Form in Medieval Romance', p. 168, points out that what we take to be an ordinary resemblance represents much more to a medieval mind, for which similarity is evidence of relationship. 'To us, an episode may recall a similar one and provide a cohesiveness in the work. The medieval reader would more likely see instead a definite and essential relationship between similar episodes, and such a work would possess not only cohesiveness but *coherence* as well.'

3.   In Gaunes the 'borjois de la vile' and the knights of the region rise together against Claudas to protest against his treatment of the children of Bohort of Gaunes (*PL* 70–1, 73–8, 82–9). The 'borjois de la vile' put pressure on the lord of the Estroite Marche by threatening to leave the town unless he finds a husband for his daughter and institutes a custom

that all knights who come to the castle are obliged to spend a night there and fight in defence of the city the next day (*PL* 446–7).

4.   T. Todorov, 'La quête du Récit', p. 143, writes of the technique used within the *Queste*: 'Le récit consistera en un apprentissage du passé. Même les aventures qui nous semblaient obéir à la logique narrative se trouvent être des signes d'autre chose, des parties d'un immense rite.' In the *Queste,* the branch of the cycle to which Todorov confines himself, the adventures in the text are designed from the beginning to be reinterpreted as 'part of a rite' through the 'reading backwards' process. In the 'rewriting' and hence 're-reading' of the *PL* two stages are involved: in the non-cyclic romance the adventures were originally designed to be interpreted within a structure in which narrative 'logic' is already less significant than another form of 'logic'; once these adventures are incorporated into a *Lancelot-Grail* cycle the reader is led to reinterpret them in the light of his reading of the Grail adventures—in the terms of Todorov, to see them as signs of something else.

5.   R. Voss, *Der Prosa-Lancelot,* p. 96, explains the unresolved oppositions, the dualism, which for him form an integral part of the structure of the *Lancelot-Grail* cycle, as arising from the conflicting ideals to be found in contemporary experience. I would agree that conflicting ideals may play their part, as indeed they do in the literature of most ages, but what is here of particular interest is the complex literary process, the developing structure which embraces, gives coherence and artistic form to a series of oppositions and congruences.

6.   There is indeed interplay between Chrétien's poem and the prose *Charrette* episode itself: see Chapter XI, n. 2. Chrétien would not, to the same extent, have formed part of a common literary background for readers during the later stages of the evolution of the cyclic romance, in the fifteenth-century versions, for example.

Appendix I

1.   J. Neale Carman, 'The Conquests of the Grail Castle and Dolorous Guard', compares Lancelot's conquest of the Dolorous Guard and the capture of the Grail Castle in the *Perlesvaus.* He suggests that the two episodes are closely related and that the *PL* is probably the borrower, as he considers that its version is less well motivated. However, he has not taken into account either the role of the adventure at the Dolorous Guard in the development of the identity theme in the *PL* (see Chapter II above) or the pattern of motivation in the romance as a whole. C. Lloyd-Morgan, 'The relationship between the *Perlesvaus* and the Prose *Lancelot',* analyses the elements common to the two romances and concludes that the *PL* was an important source for the *Perlesvaus.*

2.   J. L. Weston, 'The relation of the *Perlesvaus* to the cyclic romances', p. 349; T. E. Kelly, *Le Haut Livre du Graal: Perlesvaus,* p. 28.

3.   T. E. Kelly, op. cit., p. 24. The colophon in the Brussels MS which promises a sequel is discussed below. See p. 318 and n. 5.

4.   Kelly, op. cit., p. 25.

5.   See Nitze in his edition of the *Perlesvaus,* vol. II, p. 342. J.-C. Payen interprets the failure to finish the Claudas episode as evidence that the author 'a de la peine à conclure, et le roman n'en finit plus' ('L'art du récit dans le *Merlin* de Robert de Boron, le *Didot Perceval* et

le *Perlesvaus*', *R. Phil.* 17, 1964, pp. 570–85). For a discussion of the various views see Kelly, op. cit., pp. 24–5.

6.   Kelly, op. cit., p. 29.

7.   Kelly, op. cit., pp. 173–80.

8.   Cf. Kelly, op. cit., pp. 115–23, for a discussion of the importance of the allusions to Alexander's Celestial Journey in *Perl*.

9.   See *Perl.*, lines 7530–1, 7549–50, 7536–40, 8214–21; he spends a whole night at Guinevere's tomb, pp. 317–19.

10.   Amongst the parallels with the *PL* and/or with Chrétien, the following are particularly interesting: Arthur's brooding (*Perl.*, pp. 326–7, 384, 385; cf. note to *PL* 137–8); the wounds of a dead knight bleed when Lancelot comes near and a dwarf reproaches him (*Perl.*, p. 134; cf. *PL* 468, where this happens to Hector); Lancelot enters a perilous cemetery, (*Perl.*, pp. 342–4; cf. the marvellous cemetry in Chrétien's *Charrette* and at the Dolorous Guard in the *PL*.

11.   See pp. 152–4 above.

BIBLIOGRAPHY

This bibliography includes the more important books and articles dealing with the tale of Lancelot to be found in the non-cyclic version (*PL*) and with the evolution of the *Lancelot-Grail* cycle. For manuscripts and editions of the text see B. Woledge, *Bibliographie des romans et nouvelles en prose française antérieurs à 1500* (Genève, 1954), and *Supplément 1954-1973* (Genève, 1975), the articles by A. Micha cited below, and *PL*, vol. II. For a full bibliography of all the branches of the *Lancelot-Grail* cycle, see the annual *BBSIA*, and the *Arthurian Bibliography*, ed C. E. Pickford and R. W. Last (Ipswich, 1981-3).

Modern Editions

The Vulgate Version of the Arthurian Romances, ed. H. O. Sommer (Washington, 1909–16), 7 vols. Abbreviated to *S*.

Lancelot do Lac: the non-cyclic Old French Prose Romance , ed. E. Kennedy (Oxford, 1980). Abbreviated to *PL*.

Lancelot: roman en prose du XIIIe siècle, ed. A. Micha (Paris–Genève, 1978–83), 9 vols. Abbreviated to *LM*.

Le Roman en prose de Lancelot du Lac: le Conte de la Charrette, ed. G. Hutchings (Paris, 1938). Abbreviated to *P. Char.*

La Queste del Saint Graal, ed. A. Pauphilet, CFMA (Paris, 1923). Abbreviated to *Q* or *Queste*.

La Mort le roi Artu, ed. J. Frappier, 3rd edn., TLF (Genève–Paris, 1964). Abbreviated to *MA*.

Critical Works

Adler, A., 'The education of Lancelot: "Grammar"–"Gramarye"', *BBSIA* 9 (1957), pp. 101–7.

Anitchkof, E., 'Le Galaad du *Lancelot-Graal* et les Galaads de la Bible', *Rom.* 53 (1927), pp. 388–91.

Barron, W. R. J., 'A propos de quelques cas d'écorchement dans les romans anglais et français du moyen âge', *Mélanges Jeanne Lods* (Paris, 1978), pp. 49–68.

Baumgartner, E., *Le 'Tristan en prose': Essai d'interprétation d'un roman médiéval* (Genève, 1975).

——, 'Les aventures du Graal', *Mélanges Charles Foulon* (Rennes, 1980), vol. I, pp. 23–8.

——, *L'Arbre et le Pain: Essai sur la Queste del Saint Graal* (Paris, 1981).

Blaess, M., 'Arthur's sisters', *BBSIA* 8 (1956), pp. 69–77.

Blake, H., 'Étude sur les structures narratives dans *La Mort Artu* (XIIIe siècle)', *Revue Belge de Philologie et d'Histoire*, 50 (1972), pp. 733–43.

Bloch, R. H., 'From Grail Quest to Inquest: the Death of King Arthur and the Birth of France', *MLR* 69 (1974), pp. 40–55.

——, *Medieval French Literature and Law* (Berkeley, 1977).

Bogdanow, F., *The Romance of the Grail* (New York, 1966).

——, 'Morgain's role in the thirteenth-century French romances of the Arthurian cycle', *Medium Aevum*, 38 (1969), pp. 123–33.

——, 'The treatment of the Lancelot-Guinevere theme in the Prose *Lancelot*', *Medium Aevum*, 41 (1972), pp. 110–20.

Boutet, D. and Strubel, A. *Littérature, politique et société dans la France du moyen âge* (Paris, 1979).

Brault, G. J., *Early Blazon* (Oxford, 1972).

Bruce, J. D., 'The composition of the Old French Prose *Lancelot*', *RR* 9 (1918), pp. 241–68, 353–95; 10 (1919), pp. 48–66, 97–122.

——, *The evolution of Arthurian Romance*, 2nd edn., 2 vols. (Göttingen–Baltimore, 1928).

Brugger, E., 'Ein Beitrag zur arthurischen Namenforschung: Alain de Gomeret', *Aus Romanischen Sprachen und Literaturen: Festschrift Heinrich Morf* (Halle, 1905).

——, 'L'Enserrement Merlin: Studien zur Merlinsage', *Z.f.fr.Spr.u. Lit.* 29 (1906), pp. 56–

140; 30 (1906), pp. 169–239; 31 (1907), pp. 239–81; 33 (1908), pp. 145–94; 34 (1909), pp. 99–150; 35 (1910), pp. 1–55.

——, 'Der Schöne Feigling" in der arthurischen Literatur', *Z.f.rom.Phil.* 61. (1941), pp. 1–44; 63 (1943), pp. 123–73, 275–328; 65 (1949), pp. 121–92, 289–433; 67 (1951), pp. 289–98.

Brummer, R., *Die erzählende Prosadichtung in den romanischen Literaturen des XIII. Jahrhunderts* (Berlin, 1948).

Busby, K., *Gauvain in Old French Literature* (Amsterdam, 1980).

Caples, C. B., 'Feudal Chivalry in the Prose *Lancelot*', *DA* 32 (1971–2), 1505A (Harvard University).

Carman, J. Neale, 'The Relationship of the *Perlesvaus* and the *Queste del Saint Graal*', *Bulletin of the University of Kansas, Humanistic Studies*, vol. 5, No. 4 (1936).

——, 'Prose *Lancelot,* III, 29', *R.Ph.* 6 (1952–3), pp. 179–86.

——, 'The Conquests of the Grail Castle and Dolorous Guard', *PMLA* 85 (1970), pp. 433–43.

——, *A Study of the Pseudo-Map Cycle of Arthurian Romance* (Kansas, 1973).

Chace, C. J., 'Multiple quests and the art of interlacing in the thirteenth-century *Lancelot*', *Kentucky Romance Quarterly* (forthcoming): an expanded version of a paper presented at the Thirteenth International Arthurian Congress, Glasgow, 1981.

Cosman, M. P., *The Education of the Hero in Arthurian Romance* (Chapel Hill, 1965).

Darrall, C. M., 'A Comparison of two Episodes in the Prose *Lancelot*', *Medium Aevum,* 41 (1972), pp. 121–3.

Dornbush, J. M., 'Conjointure and Continuation in the Old French Prose *Lancelot*: Essays on Form and Craft in Thirteenth-century Romance', *DA* 37 (1976–7), 5809A (Princeton University).

Duby, G., *Les Trois Ordres ou l'imaginaire du féodalisme* (Paris, 1978).

Frappier, J., 'L'"Institution" de Lancelot dans le *Lancelot en prose*', *Mélanges Hoepffner* (Paris, 1949), pp. 269–78. Reprinted in *Amour Courtois et Table Ronde* (Genève, 1973), pp. 169–79.

——, 'Le Cortège du Graal', *Lumière du Graal* (Paris, 1951), pp. 175–224. Reprinted in *Autour du Graal* (Genève, 1977), pp. 17–61.

——, 'Le Graal et la chevalerie', *Rom.* 75 (1954), pp. 165–210. Reprinted in *Autour du Graal*, pp. 89–128.

——, 'Plaidoyer pour L'"Architecte" contre une opinion d'Albert Pauphilet sur le *Lancelot en prose*', *R. Ph.* 8 (1954–5), pp. 27–33.

——, 'The Vulgate Cycle', *ALMA*, pp. 295–318.

——, 'La bataille de Salesbieres', *Mélanges Rita Lejeune* (Gembloux, 1969), pp. 1007–23. Reprinted in *Amour Courtois et Table Ronde*, pp. 209–23.

——, *Étude sur la Mort le roi Artu*, 3rd edn. (Genève, 1972).

——, 'Le personnage de Galehaut dans le *Lancelot* en prose', *Amour Courtois et Table Ronde*, pp. 181–208; this is a fuller version of an article originally published in *R. Ph.* 17 (1964), pp. 535–54.

——, 'La mort Galehaut', *Histoire, mythes et symboles. Études de littérature française* (Genève, 1976), pp. 137–47.

——, 'Le roman en prose en France au XIIIᵉ siècle', *Le roman jusqu'à la fin du XIIIᵉ siècle*, pp. 503–12.

——, 'Le cycle de la Vulgate (*Lancelot* en prose et *Lancelot-Graal*)', *Le roman jusqu'à la fin du XIIIe siècle*, pp. 536–89.

Fromm, H., 'Zur Karrenritter-Episode im *Prosa-Lancelot*. Struktur und Geschichte', *Medium Aevum deutsch. Beiträge zur deutschen Literatur des hohen und späten Mittelalters. Festschrift für Kurt Ruh zum 65. Geburtstag* (Tübingen, 1979), pp. 69–97.

Gallais, P., 'L'hexagone logique et le roman médiéval', *CCM* 18 (1975), pp. 1–15, 133–48.

Gerritsen, W. P., and van Oostrom, F. P., 'Le *Lancelot en prose* et ses traductions moyen-néerlandaises', *Arturistiek in artikelen*, ed. F. P. van Oostrom (Utrecht, 1978), pp. 137–47.

—— and ——, 'Les adaptateurs néerlandais du *Lancelot-Graal* aux prises avec le procédé narratif des romans arthuriens en prose', *Mélanges Charles Foulon*, vol. II, pp. 105–14.

Gilson, E., 'La mystique de la grâce dans la *Queste del Saint Graal*', *Rom.* 51 (1925), pp. 321–47. Reprinted in *Les Idées et les lettres* (Paris, 1932), pp. 59–91.

Hatcher, A. and M., 'The Kiss: *Inferno* V and the Old French Prose *Lancelot*', *Comparative Literature*, 20 (1968), pp. 97–109.

Haug, W., '*Das Land, von welchem niemand wiederkehrt*' (Tübingen, 1978).

Imbs, P., 'La Journée dans la *Queste del Saint Graal* et la *Mort le roi Artu*', *Mélanges Hoepffner* (Paris, 1949), pp. 279–93.

Kelly, D., '*Translatio studii*: Translation, Adaptation, and Allegory in Medieval French Literature', *PQ* 57 (1978), pp. 287–310.

Kelly, T. E., *Le Haut Livre du Graal: Perlesvaus, a structural study* (Genève, 1974).

——, 'Love in the *Perlesvaus*: Sinful Passion or Redemptive Force?', *RR* 66 (1975), pp. 1–12.

Kennedy, A. J., 'Lancelot incognito at Winchester in the *Mort Artu*', *BBSIA* 27 (1975), pp. 170–1.

Kennedy, E., 'The two versions of the False Guinevere Episode in the Old French Prose *Lancelot*', *Rom.* 77 (1956), pp. 94–104.

——, 'Social and political ideas in the French Prose *Lancelot*', *Medium Aevum*, 26 (1957), pp. 90–106.

——, 'King Arthur in the First Part of the Prose *Lancelot*', *Medieval Miscellany presented to E. Vinaver* (Manchester, 1965), pp. 186–95.

——, 'The scribe as editor', *Mélanges Jean Frappier* (Genève, 1970), vol. I, pp. 523–31.

——, 'The use of *Tu* and *Vous* in the First Part of the Old French Prose *Lancelot*', *The History and Structure of French. Essays in Honour of T. B. W. Reid* (Oxford, 1972), pp. 135–49.

——, 'The role of the supernatural in the First Part of the Old French Prose *Lancelot*', *Studies in Medieval Literature and Language in Memory of Frederick Whitehead* (Manchester, 1973), pp. 173–84.

——, 'Royal broodings and lovers' trances in the First Part of the Prose *Lancelot*', *Mélanges J. Wathelet-Willem, Marche Romane* (Liège, 1978), pp. 301–14.

——, Le rôle d'Yvain et Gauvain dans le *Lancelot* en prose (version non-cyclique)', *Lancelot-Yvain-Gauvain*, (Paris, 1984), pp. 19–27.

Köhler, E., 'Zur Entstehung des altfranzösichen Prosaromans', *Trobadorlyrik und höfischer Roman* (Berlin, 1962), pp. 213–22.

——, *L'aventure chevaleresque, idéal et réalité dans le roman courtois* (Paris, 1974).

Lacy, N. J., 'Spatial Form in Medieval Romance', *Yale French Studies*, 51 (1974), pp. 160–9.

Lagorio, V. M., 'The Apocalyptic Mode in the Vulgate Cycle of Arthurian Romances', *PQ* 57 (1978), pp. 1–22.

Leupin, A., 'Narrateurs et scripteurs dans la Vulgate arthurienne', *Digraphe*, 20 (1979), pp. 83–109.

Lloyd-Morgan, C., 'The relationship between the *Perlesvaus* and the *Prose Lancelot*', *Medium Aevum*, 53 (1984), pp. 239–53.

Locke, F. W., *The Quest for the Holy Grail: A Literary Study of a Thirteenth-century Romance* (Stanford, 1960).

Lot, F., *Étude sur le Lancelot en prose* (Paris, 1918). The reprint in 1954 contains some additional material, including articles by M. Lot-Borodine.

——, 'Sur la date du *Lancelot en prose*', *Rom.* 57 (1931), pp. 137–46.

Lot-Borodine, M., *Trois essais sur le roman de Lancelot du Lac et la Quête du Saint Graal* (Paris, 1919).

——, 'Le double esprit et l'unité du *Lancelot* en prose', Mélanges Ferdinand Lot (Paris, 1925), pp. 477–90. Reprinted in F. Lot, *Étude sur le Lancelot en prose*, 1954 reprint.

——, 'Les apparitions du Christ aux messes de l'*Estoire* et de la *Queste del Saint Graal*',' *Rom.* 72 (1951). pp. 203–23.

——, 'Les grands secrets du Saint Graal dans la *Queste* du Pseudo-Map', *Lumière du Graal* (Paris, 1951), pp. 151–74.

——, *De l'amour profane à l'amour sacré, études de psychologie sentimentale au moyen âge* (Paris, 1961).

Luttrell, C., *The Creation of the First Arthurian Romance: a Quest* (London, 1974).

Lyons, F., 'La Mort le Roi Artu: an interpretation', *The Legend of Arthur in the Middle Ages: Studies presented to A. H. Diverres* (Cambridge, 1983), pp. 138–47.

Märtens, P., 'Zur Lanzelotsage', *Romanische Studien* (ed. Boehmer), V (1880), pp. 557–700.

Marx, J., *La Légende arthurienne et le Graal* (Paris, 1952).

——, *Nouvelles recherches sur la littérature arthurienne* (Paris, 1965).

Matarasso, P., *The Redemption of Chivalry: a Study of the Queste del Saint Graal* (Genève, 1979).

Mela, C., 'Le motif des enfances, le mystère de l'origine et le roman en prose', *Perspectives médiévales*, No. 3 (1977), pp. 65–9.

Ménard, P., *Le Rire et le sourire dans le roman courtois en France au moyen âge (1150–1250)* (Genève, 1969).

Mendozza, S., 'Il problema dell'unità del corpus *Lancelot-Graal*' (Rendiconti dell'Istituto Lombardo di Scienze e Lettere), *Classe Lettere*, 99 (1965), pp. 409–34.

Meyer, P., 'Mélanges de poésie française', III, *Rom.* 6 (1877), pp. 494–8.

Micha, A., 'Deux sources de la "Mort Artu"', *Z.f.rom.Phil.* 66 (1950), pp. 369–72. Reprinted in *De la chanson de geste au roman* (Genève, 1976), pp. 313–16.

——, 'Les épisodes du Voyage en Sorelois et de la Fausse Guenièvre', *Rom.* 76 (1955), pp. 334–41. Reprinted in *De la chanson de geste au roman*, pp. 243–50.

——, 'La Table Ronde chez Robert de Boron et dans la *Queste del Saint Graal*', *Romans du Graal*, pp. 119–36. Reprinted in *De la chanson de geste au roman*, pp. 183–205.

——, 'Les manuscrits du *Lancelot en prose*', *Rom.* 81 (1960), pp. 145–87; *Rom.* 84 (1963), pp. 28–60 and 478–99.

——, 'L'esprit du *Lancelot-Graal*', *Rom.* 82 (1961), pp. 357–78. Reprinted in *De la chanson de geste au roman*, pp. 251–72.

——, 'Tradition manuscrite et versions du Lancelot en prose', *BBSIA* (1962), pp. 99–106.

——, 'Lancelot au verger de Corbenic', *Le Moyen Age* (Livre Jubilaire, 1963), pp. 381–90.

——, 'La tradition manuscrite du *Lancelot en prose*', *Rom.* 85 (1964), pp. 293–318, and 478–517; *Rom.* 86 (1965), pp. 330–59.

——, 'La tradition manuscrite du *Lancelot en prose*. Les deux versions du *Lancelot en prose*', *Rom.* 87 (1966), pp. 194–233. Reprinted in *De la chanson de geste au roman*, pp. 273–312.

——, 'Le départ en Sorelois, Réflexions sur deux versions', *Mélanges Delbouille* (1964), vol. II, pp. 495–507.

——, 'Sur la composition du *Lancelot en prose*', *Mélanges Lecoy* (Paris, 1973), pp. 417–25. Reprinted in *De la chanson de geste au roman*, pp. 233–41.

——, 'L'épreuve de l'épee dans la littérature française du moyen âge', *De la chanson de geste au roman*, pp. 183–200. Reprinted from *Rom.* 70 (1948), pp. 37–50.

——, *Étude sur le 'Merlin' de Robert de Boron* (Genève, 1980).

Mölk, U., 'Du nouveau sur la technique de l'entrelacement: à propos des *Enfances Lancelot*', *BBSIA* 24 (1972), pp. 212–13.

Morris, R., *The Character of King Arthur in medieval literature* (Ipswich, 1982).

Muir, L. R., and Bloch, R. H., 'Further thoughts on the *Mort Artu*', *MLR* 71 (1976), pp. 26–30.

Oostrom, F. P. van, *Lantsloot vander Haghedochte. Onderzoekingen over een Middelnederlandse bewerking van de Lancelot en prose* (Amsterdam, 1981).

Pastoureau, M., *Armorial des chevaliers de la Table Ronde* (Paris, 1983).

Paton, L. A., *Studies in the Fairy Mythology of Arthurian Romance,* 2nd ed. (New York, 1960).

Pauphilet, A., *Études sur la Queste del Saint Graal attribuée à Gautier Map* (Paris, 1921).

——, 'Sur la composition du *Lancelot-Graal*', *Le Legs du Moyen Âge* (Melun, 1950), pp. 212–17.

Payen, J.-C., 'La culpabilité de Guenièvre dans le *Lancelot-Graal*', *Lettres Romanes*, 20 (1966), pp. 103–14.

Perret, M., 'De l'espace romanesque à la matérialité du livre: l'espace énonciatif des premiers romans en prose', *Poétique*, 50 (1982), pp. 174–82.

Peters, E., *The Shadow King: Rex Inutilis in Medieval Law and Literature 751-1327* (New Haven-London, 1970).

Pickford, C. E., *L'Évolution du roman arthurien en prose vers la fin du moyen âge d'après le manuscrit 112 du fonds français de la Bibliothèque Nationale* (Paris, 1960).

Poirion, D., *Le Merveilleux dans la littérature française du moyen âge* (Paris, 1982).

Richter, W., *Der Lanzelet des Ulrich von Zatzikhoven* (Frankfurt-am-Main, 1934).

Robreau, Y., *L'Honneur et la honte: leur expression dans les romans en prose du Lancelot-Graal (XIIᵉ-XIIIᵉ siècles)* (Genève, 1981).

Roubaud, J., 'Généalogie morale des Rois-Pêcheurs et Enfances de la prose', *Change,* 16-17 (1973), pp. 228–47 and 348–65.

Ruberg, U., 'Die Suche im *Prosa-Lancelot*', *Z.f.d.A.* 92 (1963), pp. 122–57.

——, *Raum und Zeit im Prosa-Lancelot* (München, 1965).

Ruhe, E., 'Repetition und Integration; Strukturprobleme des *Roman de Tristan en prose*', in *Der Altfranzösiche Prosaroman: Funktion, Funktionswandel und Ideologie am Beispiel des Roman de Tristan en prose*, ed. E. Ruhe and R. Schwaderer (München, 1979), pp. 131–59.

Rutledge, A. A., 'Narrative structures in the Old French Prose *Lancelot*', DA 35 (1974–5), 2954A (Yale University).

Rychner, J., *L'Articulation des phrases narratives dans la Mort Artu* (Neuchatel-Genève, 1970).

Ryding, W. W., *Structure in Medieval Narrative* (The Hague-Paris, 1971).

Savage, G. A., 'Father and son in the *Queste del Saint Graal*', *R.Ph.* 31 (1977–8), pp. 1–16.

Schmolke-Hasselman, B., 'The Round Table: Ideal, Fiction, Reality', *Arthurian Literature* II (Woodbridge and Totowa, 1982). pp. 41–75.

Schofield, W. H., *Studies on the Libeaus Desconnus* (Studies and Notes in Philology and Literature, Harvard University, 4: Boston, 1895).

Thorpe, L., *The 'Lancelot' in the Arthurian Prose Vulgate*, Monograph Series No. 1, published by the Dept. of English, Wheaton College (Illinois, 1980).

Tiemann, H., 'Zur Geschichte des altfranzösischen Prosaromans, Bemerkungen zu einigen neueren Werken', *RF* 63 (1951), pp. 306–28.

Todorov, T., 'La Quête du Récit', *Poétique de la Prose* (Paris, 1971), pp. 129–50.

Tuve, R., *Allegorical Imagery: Some Medieval Books and Their Posterity* (Princeton, 1966).

Vinaver, E., 'King Arthur's Sword, or the Making of a Medieval Romance', *Bulletin of the John Rylands Library*, 40 (1958), pp. 513–26.

——, 'The Historical Method in the Study of Literature', *The Future of the Modern Humanities*, ed. J. C. Laidlaw (Cambridge, 1969), pp. 86–105.

——, *A la recherche d'une poétique médiévale* (Paris, 1970).

——, *The Rise of Romance* (Oxford, 1971).

——'Landmarks in Arthurian Romance', *The Expansion and Transformations of Courtly Literature*, ed. N. B. Smith and J. T. Snow (Athens, USA, 1980).

Voss, R., *Der Prosa-Lancelot. Eine strukturanalytische und strukturvergleichende Studie auf der Grundlage des deutchen Textes* (Meisenheim-am-Glan, 1970).

Webster, K. G., trans., Ulrich von Zatzikhoven, *Lanzelet*, with additional notes and introduction by R. L. Loomis (New York, 1951).

Welz, E., 'Poetry and Truth: On two episodes of the Medieval *Prose-Lancelot*', *Euph.* 73 (1979), pp. 121–31.

West, G. D., *An Index of Proper Names in French Arthurian Prose Romances* (Toronto, 1978).

Weston, J. L., 'The relation of the *Perlesvaus* to the cyclic romances', *Rom.* 51 (1925), pp. 348–62.

——, *The Legend of Sir Lancelot du Lac* (London, 1901).

Whitehead, F., 'Lancelot's Redemption', *Mélanges Delbouille*, vol. II, pp. 729–39.

Wolfgang, L. D., 'Perceval's Father: Problems in Medieval Narrative Art', *R.Ph.* 34 (1980–81), pp. 28–47.

York, E. C., 'The Concept of Treason in the Prose *Lancelot*', *Kentucky Foreign Languages Quarterly*, 12 (1965), pp. 117–23.

Zumthor, P., *Merlin le Prophète* (Lausanne, 1943).

——, 'Merlin dans le Lancelot-Graal: étude thématique', *Romans du Graal*, pp. 149–66.

——, *Essai de poétique médiévale* (Paris, 1972).

——, 'Genèse et évolution du genre', *Le roman jusqu'à la fin du XIIIe siècle*, pp. 60–73.

Supplementary bibliography

Studies which appeared 1984–5, too late for use in *Lancelot and the Grail*:

Bar, F., 'Faits de style parlé dans le *Lancelot*', *Approches du Lancelot en prose*, ed. J. Dufournet (Paris, 1984), pp. 49–57.

Baumgartner, E., 'La couronne et le cercle: Arthur et la Table Ronde dans les manuscrits du *Lancelot-Graal*', *Texte et image dans l'Antiquité classique et au Moyen Âge: actes du colloque international de Chantilly* (Paris, 1984), pp. 191–200.

——, 'Joseph d'Arimathie dans le *Lancelot* en prose', *Lancelot: actes du colloque d'Amiens des 14 et 15 janvier, 1984*, ed. D. Buschinger (Göppingen, 1984), pp. 7–15.

Burns, E. Jane, *Arthurian Fictions: Rereading the Vulgate Cycle* (Colombus, Ohio, 1985).

Chênerie, M.-L., 'L'aventure du chevalier enferré, ses suites et le thème des géants dans le *Lancelot*', *Approches du Lancelot en prose*, pp. 59–100.

Combarieu, M. de, 'Le *Lancelot* comme roman d'apprentissage. Enfance, démesure et chevalerie', *Approches du Lancelot en prose*, pp. 101–36.

Dufournet, J., 'Un personnage exemplaire et complexe du *Lancelot*: Pharien', *Approches du Lancelot en prose*, pp. 137–56.

Gouttebroze, J.-G., 'Le don de l'épée dans le *Lancelot*', *Lancelot: colloque*, pp. 51–61.

Harf-Lancner, L., 'Les deux Guenièvre dans le *Lancelot* en prose', *Lancelot: colloque*, pp. 63–97.

——, *Les Fées au Moyen Âge* (Paris, 1984).

Keen, M., *Chivalry* (New Haven and London, 1984).

Kennedy, E., 'Le personnage de Lancelot dans le *Lancelot* en prose', *Lancelot: Colloque*, pp. 99–106.

Méla, C., 'La Reine et le Graal: la conjointure dans les romans du Graal, de Chrétien de Troyes au Livre de Lancelot* (Paris, 1984).

Micha, A., 'Sur un procédé de composition de *Lancelot*: les récits rétrospectifs', *Approches du Lancelot en prose*, pp. 7–23.

——, 'L'inspiration religieuse dans le *Lancelot* en prose', *Lancelot: colloque*, pp. 107–16.

Paradis, F., 'La triple mise au monde d'un héros, ou trois images d'une féminité maîtrisée dans le début du *Lancelot* en prose, *Approches du Lancelot en prose*, pp. 157–76.

Poirion, D., 'La Douloureuse Garde', *Approches du Lancelot en prose*, pp. 25–48.

Speckenbach, K., 'L'attente de la fin du monde dans le cycle du *Lancelot-Graal*. Traité sur l'influence de Joachim de Fiore sur le roman en prose', *Lancelot: colloque*, pp. 213–24.

Suard, F., 'Lancelot et le chevalier enferré', *Approches du Lancelot en prose*, pp. 177–96.

Index

UNIVERSITY OF WINCHESTER
LIBRARY